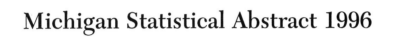

Michigan Statistical Abstract 1996

Michigan Statistical Abstract 1996

MICHIGAN EMPLOYMENT SECURITY COMMISSION

ANN ARBOR

THE UNIVERSITY OF MICHIGAN PRESS

Copyright © by the University of Michigan 1996
All rights reserved
Published in the United States of America by
The University of Michigan Press
Manufactured in the United States of America
⊖ Printed on acid-free paper

1999   1998   1997   4   3   2

A CIP catalogue record of this book is available from the British Library.

ISBN 0-472-08370-8
ISSN 0076-8308

Editor and Compiler: **Jeffrey H. Aula**, Economic Analyst
Research and Statistics, Michigan Employment Security Commission

ACKNOWLEDGMENTS

Research and Statistics staff, Michigan Employment Security Commission, assisted in Abstract content, development, information acquisition, and data compilation.

David I. Verway, Ph.D. Professor Verway created and edited earlier editions of the Abstract and provided invaluable input on table selection for this volume. Professor Verway's other contributions include preparation of the chapter notes and coordinating the librarian focus group.

Mary Erwin , Assistant Director, University of Michigan Press, supported publication of this volume through its many phases of development. Ms. Erwin also provided invaluable advice on content, style, and other editorial considerations.

The contributions to this volume by the many government agencies and private organizations that provided reports, data, and special tabulations are gratefully acknowledged. The source note below each table provide specific information on contributors.

Special contributions were made by the following individuals: **Carolyn Lauer**, of the Michigan Information Center, provided a significant portion of the census data. **Cheryl Parish** , of the Michigan Department of Transportation, assembled all of the transportation related data in Chapter 15. **Chin-li Wang**, State Demographer, provided population figures and population forecast. Significant help was also provided by **Douglas Drake**, of the Michigan Department of Management and Budget, who developed a comprehensive trend series on Michigan education expenditures and **Robert Kleine**, of Public Sector Consultants, who advised on the government chapter.

Suggested Citation:
Michigan Employment Security Commission, <u>Michigan Statistical Abstract - 1996 Edition</u> (Detroit, Michigan: 1996). Published by the University of Michigan Press (Ann Arbor, Michigan)

Preface

After nearly a decade without a standard Michigan statistical data book, the Michigan Employment Security Commission (M.E.S.C.) has produced a new edition of the <u>Michigan Statistical Abstract</u>. The 1996 edition of the <u>Michigan Statistical Abstract</u> is an encyclopedic reference work covering Michigan's social, demographic, and economic statistics. The data was compiled from a broad range of statistical publications, reports, and special studies prepared by both government and non-government sources.

This edition of the Michigan Statistical Abstract contains more than 350 tables relating to Michigan and the state's counties, cities, townships, and school districts. The primary focus is on presenting the latest information available for this printing, but many tables contain extensive historical series, as well, and national data where appropriate. The subjects covered include Michigan's labor market, industry structure, population and housing, health and vital statistics, education, income and social welfare, law enforcement and the courts, government, and the environment. A special section contains population forecasts and employment projections for Michigan.

The <u>Michigan Statistical Abstract</u> was first published in 1955 and continued in print for the next three decades, ending with the twentieth edition in 1986/1987. Many of the tables in the previous editions have been retained and updated. A large number of new data sources were researched for the current edition and the range of reference topics has been greatly expanded and diversified. Also, considerable effort was devoted to presenting the tables in an attractive, accessible format. To promote the quality and usability of this publication, staff of the M.E.S.C. consulted with numerous information specialists to help define the book's contents. In summary, this volume incorporates all the strengths of previous editions as well as a wealth of information on current issues and topics.

More information on the subjects covered in this volume may be obtained from the source indicated at the end of each table. Publications cited as sources usually contain additional statistical detail and more extended discussions of definitions and concepts than can be presented here. Additionally, a list of source contacts is provided in the appendix to assist users in contacting data providers. Users seeking further information about specific topics should consult the source documents and data providers listed for each specific topic. These sources can most directly respond to any requests for additional information. The Michigan Employment Security Commission should be contacted if it is cited as the source agency for the data.

The data presented in this book have been extensively reviewed. Users should let MESC staff know if any errors were overlooked. More generally, comments or observations that would improve the content and presentation of the Abstract are welcome.

CONTENTS

I: Population and Housing 1

II: Health and Vital Statistics 53

III: Education 93

IV: Labor Market 140

V: Employment Projections 207

VI: Income / Output / Prices 233

VII: Social Insurance and Human Services 250

VIII: Law Enforcement and the Courts 304

IX: Government 348

X: Tourism and the Environment 366

XI: Agriculture / Forestry / Fishing / Mining 419

XII: Construction 434

XIII: Manufacturing 443

XIV: The Automotive Economy 459

XV: Transportation / Communication / Energy 479

XVI: Trade 504

XVII: Finance / Insurance / Real Estate 531

XVIII: Services 545

XIX: Other Enterprise and Science Statistics 566

Appendix A: MSAs and Other Geographic Areas 612

Appendix B: Data Source Contact List 633

Index 638

User Guide to Tables

Sample Table:

Table IV-1. Employment Status of the Civilian Non-Institutional Population 16 Years and Older, Michigan and United States: 1956-1995 Continued

(Data in Thousands)

Year	Michigan**					United States				
	Labor Force	Labor Force Particip ation Rate(%)	Employ ment	Unemployment		Labor Force	Labor Force Particip ation Rate(%)	Employ ment	Unemployment	
				Number	Rate(%)				Number	Rate(%)
1969	3,594	N.A.	3,449	145	4.0	80,734	60.1	77,902	2,832	3.5
The years 1970 through 1989 were intentionally omitted from this sample for space reasons.										
1990	4,583	65.4	4,238	345	7.5	124,787	66.4	117,914	6,874	5.5
1991	4,565	64.7	4,145	420	9.2	125,303	66.0	116,877	8,426	6.7
1992	4,644	65.5	4,236	408	8.8	126,982	66.3	117,598	9,384	7.4
1993	4,690	65.9	4,363	327	7.0	128,040	66.2	119,306	8,734	6.8
1994	4,753	66.6	4,473	280	5.9	131,056	66.6	123,060	7,996	6.1
1995	4,719	65.8	4,467	252	5.3	132,304	66.6	124,900	7,404	5.6

** Beginning in 1970, data for Michigan based on new methodology and not directly comparable to prior years. N.A. data not available.
Source: U.S. Bureau of Labor Statistics, Current Population Survey (Washington, D.C.: monthly/annually), and Michigan Employment Security Commission, Research and Statistics (Detroit, Michigan; monthly/annually)

Because of the tremendous range and variety of data presented in this book, it was necessary to develop the tables in a range of formats. Despite this diversity it is possible to make some generalizations about table appearance and layout that can be helpful to the user.

First many of the tables are organized either by year or by area. The sample table in this section provides a good example of a Michigan "time series" table in which statewide data is presented across a lengthy span of years. For a sample of a table organized by area, the user can refer to Table 16 in chapter XVI which shows the number of establishments, employment, and the average weekly wage for Michigan's retail industry, by county, in a particular year.

The tables that do not fit these patterns are typically "subject/detail" tables. These tables will usually show state data for various aspects of a particular subject for one year or several years. For example, Table II-16, on page 72, in the Health and Vital Statistics Chapter shows life expectancy at birth by sex and race in Michigan for the period 1950-1992. Another example is Table IV-23, on page 172, in the Labor Market chapter which shows wage rates for different occupations in Michigan.

Second, the basic building blocks that make up the tables are very consistent throughout the book:

(1)   At the top of each table is the table title. The title displays the chapter number, the number of the table within the chapter and an overview of table content. In the sample above, the title indicates that the table is the first table in Chapter IV and that it provides data on the employment status of the Michigan and U.S. populations.

(2)   Depending on the table, there may appear a set of additional headnotes following the title. In the sample table, line 2 indicates that the table is continued from the previous page. Line 3 tells the reader that the data has been rounded to the nearest thousand. (The issue of data rounding and unit indicators is discussed in some detail in the "Data Presentation Conventions" section of this guide.)

(3)   The material following each table is known as the table footnote. The last line (or two lines) of this material, typically provides the reader with the source of the data and the source's location. In the sample table, the U.S. Bureau of Labor Statistics in Washington, D.C. and the Michigan Employment Security Commission's Research and Statistics office, located in Detroit, Michigan are cited as the sources.

(4)   In some cases more detailed information is needed by the user to correctly interpret or evaluate the data in a table. This information is usually found in the table footnote. In the sample table, the footnote indicates that the pre-1970 employment status data for Michigan is not strictly comparable with the data for later years. Also, the footnote indicates that labor force participation rate data for Michigan is not available for certain years.

More information on data concepts and sources is available in the chapter notes that introduce each chapter. The table notes and chapter introductions should provide sufficient information to resolve most questions users may have about the data. Readers who have very specialized or technical questions should refer to appendix B (beginning on p. 633) for a listing of data source contacts.

Data Presentation Conventions: Statistical publications often present data in rounded or converted form rather than in absolute terms. For example, data may be presented in thousands, millions, or billions, depending on the subject. There are two primary reasons for this convention. Sometimes data are not available in absolute form from the source. In other cases, the numbers are rounded in order to save space to show more data. In these cases, Unit Indicators are included with the table to show the specified quantities in which data items are presented.

When all the data is presented using the same Unit Indicator, the indicator will generally appear under the title in the upper left hand corner, as in the sample table. Sometimes, for space reasons, it may be located within the table itself. An example of this presentation can be found in Chapter IV Labor Market, Table IV-18. on page 165.

When data in a table are shown in absolute form (other than percentages), Unit Indicators are unnecessary. When a table presents information that requires more than one Unit Indicator, the appropriate unit reference is found in the respective column headings. An example of this format can be found in Chapter XIII, Manufacturing, Table XIII-1, page 445.

Some common Unit Indicators found in this Abstract are:

Data in Thousands or just *Thousands*: This is used to indicate data that have been rounded to the nearest thousandth. In this case, to determine the absolute number it is necessary to multiply a data point by 1,000. The sample table shows Michigan's labor force as 4,719 in 1995. The absolute level of Michigan's 1995 labor force is 4,719,000 (4,719 x 1,000).

Data in Millions or just *Millions*: This is used to indicate data that have been rounded to the nearest millionth. In this case, to determine the absolute number it is necessary to multiply a data point by 1,000,000. An example of data presented in millions can be found in Chapter VI (Income / Output / Prices), Table VI-1 on page 236. The value of Michigan's Total Personal Income in 1994 is stated as $212,080. The absolute level of Michigan's Total Personal Income in 1994 is $212,080,000,000 ($212,080 x 1,000,000).

Data in Billions or just *Billions*: This is used to indicate data that have been rounded to the nearest billionth. In this case, to determine the absolute figure it is necessary to multiply the data point by 1,000,000,000. An example of data presented in billions can be found in Chapter XIV (The Automotive Economy), Table XIV-13, on page 473. The value of Expenditures on Motor Vehicle & Parts Manufacture for 1993 appears as $11.63. The absolute level is $11,630,000,000 ($11.63 x 1,000,000,000).

Percent Sign, (%): The percent sign is used to indicate the percentage share one data element represents of another. In the sample table, the Unemployment Rate (%) indicates what percent of the labor force is unemployed. It is calculated as: number unemployed ÷ labor force. The resulting value is then multiplied by 100 to obtain the unemployment rate. Specifically, in 1995, Michigan's unemployment rate is calculated as follows: 252 ÷ 4,719 = .053. Multiplying .053 by 100 yields an unemployment rate of 5.3%. All other data items stated as percentages are calculated in the same manner.

Index Numbers: Index numbers are a technique used by statisticians to weight multiple data points and combine them into a single number. One of the most common applications of this technique are indexes measuring inflation and the cost of living. In fact, the construction of the Consumer Price Index by the U.S. Bureau of Labor Statistics provides a good example of how index number work. Periodically, households are surveyed to determine their "market basket," that is, the kind of goods and services they typically purchase. These items are then weighted according to their size and importance. Merchants and service providers are surveyed in succeeding years and the weights from the "market basket" are applied to compute the price index number for each year.

Indexes track price or other developments over time using a base period concept. In the case of the current Consumer Price Index series, the base period is 1982-1984. The index numbers for these years average 100. The Detroit area index number for 1994 equals 144. This means that prices in the Detroit area have increased by 44 percent compared to their average in the 1982-1984 period.

Index numbers appear in only two chapters of the book. The Consumer Price Indexes for the U.S. and the Detroit area appear in Chapter VI: Income/Output/Prices. A Michigan tourism activity index appears in Chapter X: Tourism and the Environment.

Chapter I
Population and Housing

The Bureau of the Census enumerates the population of the United States at the beginning of each decade. Since 1930, census day has been set as of 1 April. The decennial census is the official tally of residents upon which apportionment of the U.S. House of Representatives is based.

To develop the 1990 Census of Population and Housing, the Census Bureau sent a short questionnaire to every dwelling unit that could be identified. Residents were asked to list their names along with their relationship to the member in whose name the residence was owned, being purchased, or rented. Other population items on the short form were gender, race, year of birth, marital status, and whether the member was of Spanish/Hispanic origin. The short form also asked respondents to complete a few questions regarding the nature of the home itself: number of rooms, value of owner-occupied housing, monthly rent for rented homes, whether a mobile home, single house, apartment, and so forth. Data on vacant units also were collected.

Persons living in nursing homes, military quarters, college dormitories, and so forth are classified as living in group quarters. Census takers also were sent into areas popular with the homeless so as to count this segment of the population. The homeless also are classified as living in group quarters.

Despite these efforts at a complete count, people were missed for one reason or another, and there are unofficial estimates of their number. The census data reported in the Michigan Statistical Abstract are the official figures, not adjusted for the undercount.

Long-form questionnaires were sent to a sample of households so as to develop statistics on income, education, and other population and housing data considered vital to the national interest. Data on income and poverty rate (Tables I-4 and I-5) were developed by the Census Bureau from these samples. Poverty rate represents the percentage of people who are classified as living below the poverty threshold. Users of this Abstract will find other kinds of income data in Chapter VI. Data on the labor force are found in Chapter IV; and on education in Chapter III.

Intercensal estimates of the populations of counties are prepared by the Office of Demographic Research and Statistics in Michigan's Department of Management and Budget in Lansing. There, demographers coordinate with the Bureau of the Census in developing these data, which are based on driver licenses and other administrative records. Part of this program is the estimation of components of population change for the state and its counties. The Michigan Department of Public Health is the repository of data on births and deaths used by the Office of Demographic Research and Statistics. More detailed death and birth data can be found in Chapter II. Net migration, the other component of population change, is a residual, after allowing for births and deaths.

Population projections for states have been prepared by the Bureau of the Census. The Office of Demographic Research in Michigan's Department of Management and Budget has county projections underway.

Michigan Statistical Abstract users who need more detailed population and housing data or who wish to learn about data limitations or definitions should contact their local public or school library regarding the availability of printed documents or machine readable documents published by the Bureau of the Census. This state's U.S. Bureau of Census liaison is the **Michigan Information Center [(517) 373-7910]**. Other contacts are the Michigan Metropolitan Information Center [(313) 577-8359], and the Census Bureau's Regional Office [(313) 259-0056].

LIST OF TABLES

Table   **Page**

I-1A.   Population of Michigan and the United States, and Components of Change by
        Decade: 1810-1990 3

I-1B.   Population of Michigan and the United States, and Components of Change by
        Year: 1970-1995 4

I-2.   Population of Michigan, by County: 1940, 1950, 1960, 1970, 1980,1990, and
        1994 5

I-3.   Components of Population Change in Michigan, by County: 1980-1990 and
        1990-1994 7

I-4.   Selected Age, Ethnic, and Economic Characteristics of Michigan's Population,
        by County: As of the 1990 Census 10

I-5.   Selected Age, Ethnic, and Economic Characteristics of Michigan's Population,
        by City and Village: As of the 1990 Census 13

I-6.   Residence in 1985 of Michigan's Population 5 Years Old and Older, by County:
        1990 36

I-7.   Reported Ancestry in Michigan, by County: 1990 38

I-8.   Percentage of Year-Round Housing Units Built in Michigan Since 1980 or Before
        1940, by County: As of the 1990 Census 47

I-9.   Housing Units and Occupancy Status in Michigan, by County: 1990 Census 48

I-10.   Population Estimates and Projections for Michigan, by County: 1990, 1995,
        Estimates 2000 - 2020 Projections 50

I-11.   Population Estimates and Projections for Michigan, by Age and Sex: 1990, 1995,
        Estimates 2000 - 2020 Projections 52

Table I-1A. Population of Michigan and the United States, and Components of Change by Decade: 1810 - 1990

| Year | Michigan | | | | | | U.S. Population | U.S. Percent(%) Change |
| | Population | Change | | Births | Deaths | Net Migration | | |
		Level	Percent(%)					
1810	4,762	--	--	--	--	--	7,239,881	--
1820	8,896	4,134	86.8	--	--	--	9,638,453	33.1
1830	31,639	22,743	255.7	--	--	--	12,866,020	33.5
1840	212,267	180,629	570.9	--	--	--	17,069,453	32.7
1850	397,654	185,387	87.3	--	--	--	23,191,876	35.9
1860	749,113	351,459	88.4	--	--	--	31,443,321	35.6
1870	1,184,059	434,946	58.1	--	--	--	38,558,371	22.6
1880	1,636,937	452,878	38.2	--	--	--	50,189,209	30.2
1890	2,093,890	456,953	27.9	--	--	--	62,979,766	25.5
1900	2,420,982	327,092	15.6	--	--	--	76,212,168	21.0
1910	2,810,173	389,191	16.1	524,796	347,781	212,176	92,228,496	21.0
1920	3,668,412	858,239	30.5	789,159	434,451	503,531	106,021,537	15.0
1930	4,842,325	1,173,913	32.0	964,493	501,486	710,906	123,202,624	16.2
1940	5,256,106	413,781	8.5	897,985	511,269	27,065	132,164,569	7.3
1950	6,371,766	1,115,660	21.2	160,055	57,567	1,013,172	151,325,798	14.5
1960	7,823,194	56,200	0.9	195,056	67,912	-41,300	179,323,175	18.5
1970	8,881,826	61,800	0.8	171,667	76,321	-6,500	203,302,031	13.4
1980	9,262,044	-4,000	0.0	145,563	75,102	-57,100	226,545,805	0.9
1990	9,295,297	42,000	0.5	153,080	78,501	-11,400	248,709,873	0.8

Table I-IB. Population of Michigan and the United States, and Components of Change by Year: 1970 - 1995

Year	Michigan						U.S. Population	U.S. Percent(%) Change
	Population	Change		Births	Deaths	Net Migration		
		Level	Percent(%)					
1970	8,881,826	61,800	0.8	171,667	76,321	-6,500	203,302,031	13.4
1971	8,974,000	92,200	1.0	162,244	77,395	-21,800	206,827,000	1.7
1972	9,029,000	55,000	0.6	146,854	79,210	-21,200	209,284,000	1.2
1973	9,078,000	49,000	0.5	141,550	78,522	-16,300	211,357,000	1.0
1974	9,118,000	40,000	0.4	137,414	76,143	-22,100	213,342,000	0.9
1975	9,118,000	0	0.0	133,931	74,522	-60,300	215,465,000	1.0
1976	9,129,000	11,000	0.1	131,378	75,801	-46,500	217,563,000	1.0
1977	9,171,000	42,000	0.5	138,416	74,144	-17,900	219,760,000	1.0
1978	9,218,000	47,000	0.5	138,802	74,773	-17,200	222,095,000	1.1
1979	9,266,000	48,000	0.5	144,452	73,480	-19,500	224,567,000	1.1
1980	9,262,044	-4,000	0.0	145,563	75,102	-57,100	226,545,805	0.9
1981	9,209,000	-53,000	-0.6	140,579	75,818	-138,000	229,466,000	1.3
1982	9,115,000	-94,000	-1.0	137,950	75,536	-157,700	231,664,000	1.0
1983	9,048,000	-67,000	-0.7	133,026	76,639	-126,800	233,792,000	0.9
1984	9,049,000	2,000	0.0	135,782	76,401	-56,200	235,825,000	0.9
1985	9,076,000	27,000	0.3	138,052	78,635	-32,600	237,924,000	0.9
1986	9,128,000	51,000	0.6	137,626	80,177	-6,900	240,133,000	0.9
1987	9,187,000	60,000	0.7	140,130	80,100	1,000	242,289,000	0.9
1988	9,218,000	31,000	0.3	139,635	81,207	-28,700	244,499,000	0.9
1989	9,253,000	35,000	0.4	148,164	78,566	-28,700	246,819,000	0.9
1990	9,295,297	42,000	0.5	153,080	78,501	-11,400	248,709,873	0.8
1991	9,368,000	72,000	0.8	149,478	79,738	-18,500	252,177,000	1.4
1992	9,437,000	69,000	0.7	150,000	79,800	-1,000	255,082,000	1.2
1993	9,457,000	20,000	0.2	139,560	82,286	-24,700	257,783,000	1.1
1994	9,492,000	35,000	0.4	138,741	83,543	-18,700	260,341,000	1.0
1995	9,549,000	57,000	0.6	N.A.	N.A.	N.A.	262,755,000	0.9

Source: Michigan Department of Management and Budget, Office of the State Demographer (Lansing, Michigan). N.A. data not available.

Table I-2. Population of Michigan, by County: 1940, 1950, 1960, 1970, 1980, 1990, and 1994

County	1940	1950	1960	1970	1980	1990	1994
Alcona	5,463	5,856	6,352	7,113	9,740	10,145	10,389
Alger	10,167	10,007	9,250	8,568	9,225	8,972	9,819
Allegan	41,839	47,493	57,729	66,575	81,555	90,509	96,085
Alpena	20,766	22,189	28,556	30,708	32,315	30,605	30,814
Antrim	10,964	10,721	10,373	12,612	16,194	18,185	19,528
Arenac	9,233	9,644	9,860	11,149	14,706	14,931	15,953
Baraga	9,356	8,037	7,151	7,789	8,484	7,954	8,061
Barry	22,613	26,183	31,738	38,166	45,781	50,057	52,231
Bay	74,981	88,461	107,042	117,339	119,881	111,723	111,772
Benzie	7,800	8,306	7,834	8,593	11,205	12,200	13,264
Berrien	89,117	115,702	149,865	163,940	171,276	161,378	161,734
Branch	25,845	30,202	34,903	37,906	40,188	41,502	41,990
Calhoun	94,206	120,813	138,858	141,963	141,557	135,982	139,991
Cass	21,910	28,185	36,932	43,312	49,499	49,477	48,920
Charlevoix	13,031	13,475	13,421	16,541	19,907	21,468	22,833
Cheboygan	13,644	13,731	14,550	16,573	20,649	21,398	22,471
Chippewa	27,807	29,206	32,655	32,412	29,029	34,604	36,591
Clare	9,163	10,253	11,647	16,695	23,822	24,952	27,589
Clinton	26,671	31,195	37,969	48,492	55,893	57,883	60,897
Crawford	3,765	4,151	4,971	6,482	9,465	12,260	13,387
Delta	34,037	32,913	34,298	35,924	38,947	37,780	38,605
Dickinson	28,731	24,844	23,917	23,753	25,341	26,831	27,058
Eaton	34,124	40,023	49,684	68,892	88,337	92,879	96,805
Emmet	15,791	16,534	15,904	18,331	22,992	25,040	27,034
Genesee	227,944	270,963	374,313	445,589	450,449	430,459	433,300
Gladwin	9,385	9,451	10,769	13,471	19,957	21,896	23,937
Gogebic	31,797	27,053	24,370	20,676	19,686	18,052	18,016
Grand Traverse	23,390	28,598	33,490	39,175	54,899	64,273	69,582
Gratiot	32,205	33,429	37,012	39,246	40,448	38,982	39,785
Hillsdale	29,092	31,916	34,742	37,171	42,071	43,431	44,829
Houghton	47,631	39,771	35,654	34,652	37,872	35,446	36,375
Huron	32,584	33,149	34,006	34,083	36,459	34,951	35,214
Ingham	130,616	172,941	211,296	261,039	275,520	281,912	278,423
Ionia	35,710	38,158	43,132	45,848	51,815	57,024	59,193
Iosco	8,560	10,906	16,505	24,905	28,349	30,209	24,034
Iron	20,243	17,692	17,184	13,813	13,635	13,175	13,131
Isabella	25,982	28,964	35,348	44,594	54,110	54,624	57,053
Jackson	93,108	107,925	131,994	143,274	151,495	149,756	153,287
Kalamazoo	100,085	126,707	169,712	201,550	212,378	223,411	228,796
Kalkaska	5,159	4,597	4,382	5,372	10,952	13,497	14,536
Kent	246,338	288,292	363,187	411,044	444,506	500,631	520,123
Keweenaw	4,004	2,918	2,417	2,264	1,963	1,701	1,880

Table I-2. Population of Michigan, by County: 1940, 1950, 1960, 1970, 1980, 1990, and 1994 Continued

County	1940	1950	1960	1970	1980	1990	1994
Lake	4,798	5,257	5,338	5,661	7,711	8,583	9,631
Lapeer	32,116	35,794	41,926	52,361	70,038	74,768	81,240
Leelanau	8,436	8,647	9,321	10,872	14,007	16,527	18,122
Lenawee	53,110	64,629	77,789	81,951	89,948	91,476	95,667
Livingston	20,863	26,725	38,233	58,967	100,289	115,645	129,080
Luce	7,423	8,147	7,827	6,789	6,659	5,763	5,571
Mackinac	9,438	9,287	10,853	9,660	10,178	10,674	10,910
Macomb	107,638	184,961	405,804	625,309	694,600	717,400	728,563
Manistee	18,450	18,524	19,042	20,393	23,019	21,265	22,633
Marquette	47,144	47,654	56,154	64,686	74,101	70,887	70,683
Mason	19,378	20,474	21,929	22,612	26,365	25,537	27,200
Mecosta	16,902	18,968	21,051	27,992	36,961	37,308	38,620
Menominee	24,883	25,299	24,685	24,587	26,201	24,920	24,532
Midland	27,094	35,662	51,450	63,769	73,578	75,651	79,245
Missaukee	8,034	7,458	6,784	7,126	10,009	12,147	13,347
Monroe	58,620	75,666	101,120	119,215	134,659	133,600	137,716
Montcalm	28,581	31,013	35,795	39,660	47,555	53,059	56,886
Montmorency	3,840	4,125	4,424	5,247	7,492	8,936	9,513
Muskegon	94,501	121,545	149,943	157,426	157,589	158,983	163,436
Newaygo	19,286	21,567	24,160	27,992	34,917	38,202	42,738
Oakland	254,068	396,001	690,259	907,871	1,011,793	1,083,592	1,441,997
Oceana	14,812	16,105	16,547	17,984	22,002	22,454	23,493
Ogemaw	8,720	9,345	9,680	11,903	16,436	18,681	20,250
Ontonagon	11,359	10,282	10,584	10,548	9,861	8,854	8,673
Osceola	13,309	13,797	13,595	14,838	18,929	20,146	21,375
Oscoda	2,543	3,134	3,447	4,726	6,858	7,842	8,494
Otsego	5,827	6,435	7,545	10,422	14,993	17,957	20,101
Ottawa	59,660	73,751	98,719	128,181	157,174	187,768	205,333
Presque Isle	12,250	11,996	13,117	12,836	14,267	13,743	14,028
Roscommon	3,668	5,916	7,200	9,892	16,374	19,776	21,881
Saginaw	130,468	153,515	190,752	219,743	228,059	211,946	211,287
St. Clair	76,222	91,599	107,201	120,175	138,802	145,607	152,351
St. Joseph	31,749	35,071	42,332	47,392	56,083	58,913	59,999
Sanilac	30,114	30,837	32,314	35,181	40,789	39,928	41,567
Schoolcraft	9,524	9,148	8,953	8,226	8,575	8,302	8,596
Shiawassee	41,207	45,967	53,446	63,075	71,140	69,770	71,644
Tuscola	35,694	38,258	43,305	48,603	56,961	55,498	57,017
Van Buren	35,111	39,184	48,395	56,173	66,814	70,060	73,848
Washtenaw	80,810	134,606	172,440	234,103	264,748	282,937	290,542
Wayne	2,015,623	2,435,235	2,666,297	2,670,368	2,337,891	2,111,687	2,064,908
Wexford	17,976	18,628	18,466	19,717	25,102	26,360	28,115
Michigan	**5,256,106**	**6,371,766**	**7,823,194**	**8,881,826**	**9,262,044**	**9,295,297**	**9,496,147**

Source: U.S. Bureau of the Census, Michigan Information Center (Lansing, Michigan).

Table I-3. Components of Population Change in Michigan, by County: 1980 - 1990 and 1990 - 1994

County	1980 to 1990				1990 to 1994			
	Population Change	Births	Deaths	Net Migration	Population Change	Births	Deaths	Net Migration
Alcona	405	1,093	1,356	668	244	410	676	511
Alger	-253	1,183	1,054	-382	847	403	493	938
Allegan	8,954	13,763	6,404	1,595	5,576	6,005	3,009	2,580
Alpena	-1,710	4,234	2,887	-3,056	209	1,503	1,265	-28
Antrim	1,991	2,400	1,917	1,508	1,343	1,053	909	1,199
Arenac	225	2,147	1,606	-316	1,047	840	763	970
Baraga	-530	1,114	1,033	-612	107	464	457	100
Barry	4,276	6,870	3,679	1,084	2,174	3,025	1,640	788
Bay	-8,158	16,849	9,661	-15,346	49	6,654	4,309	-2,295
Benzie	995	1,667	1,291	619	1,064	726	569	908
Berrien	-9,898	25,729	15,354	-20,274	356	10,255	6,694	-3,204
Branch	1,314	6,375	3,793	-1,268	488	2,398	1,648	-262
Calhoun	-5,597	20,490	12,970	-13,117	4,009	8,887	5,833	955
Cass	-22	6,502	4,211	-2,313	-557	2,179	1,847	-890
Charlevoix	1,561	3,267	1,996	290	1,365	1,291	842	917
Cheboygan	749	3,061	2,233	-79	1,073	1,192	1,028	909
Chippewa	5,575	3,846	2,828	4,557	1,987	1,704	1,169	1,452
Clare	1,130	3,559	2,829	400	2,637	1,625	1,378	2,390
Clinton	1,990	8,351	3,316	-3,044	3,014	3,474	1,590	1,130
Crawford	2,795	1,767	1,096	2124	1,127	775	534	886
Delta	-1,167	5,404	3,642	-2,929	825	1,901	1,609	533
Dickinson	1,490	3,537	2,950	904	227	1,416	1,347	158
Eaton	4,542	12,224	5,810	-1,872	3,926	4,977	2,726	1,675
Emmet	2,048	3,620	2,295	724	1,994	1,575	1,047	1,466
Genesee	-19,990	69,624	34,151	-55,463	2,841	30,990	15,632	-12,517
Gladwin	1,939	2,928	2,158	1,169	2,041	1,220	1,084	1,905
Gogebic	-1,634	2,058	2,699	-993	-36	733	1,136	367
Grand Traverse	9,374	9,340	4,620	4,654	5,309	3,929	2,154	3,534

Table I-3. Components of Population Change in Michigan, by County: 1980 - 1990 and 1990 - 1994 Continued

County	1980 to 1990				1990 to 1994			
	Population Change	Births	Deaths	Net Migration	Population Change	Births	Deaths	Net Migration
Gratiot	-1,466	5,759	4,004	-3,221	803	2,423	1,673	53
Hillsdale	1,360	6,317	3,768	-1,189	1,398	2,460	1,618	557
Houghton	-2,426	4,727	4,208	-2,945	929	1,806	1,744	867
Huron	-1,508	5,322	3,883	-2,946	263	1,781	1,739	221
Ingham	6,392	44,390	17,026	-20,972	-3,489	18,498	7,606	-14,382
Ionia	5,209	8,800	4,131	541	2,169	3,440	1,742	471
Iosco	1,860	5,711	2,940	-911	-6,175	2,095	1,369	-6,901
Iron	-460	1,536	2,045	49	-44	509	920	367
Isabella	514	6,955	3,123	-3,317	2,429	2,973	1,423	879
Jackson	-1,739	21,391	12,797	-10,333	3,531	9,372	5,723	-118
Kalamazoo	11,033	32,669	15,504	-6,132	5,385	14,131	7,120	-1,627
Kalkaska	2,545	2,084	1,044	1,505	1,039	850	496	684
Kent	56,125	87,259	35,606	4,472	19,492	39,107	15,771	-3,845
Keweenaw	-262	195	360	-97	179	77	140	242
Lake	872	1,135	1,238	975	1,048	459	589	1,179
Lapeer	4,730	10,558	4,721	-1,107	6,472	4,560	2,205	4,117
Leelanau	2,520	2,161	1,349	1,708	1,595	910	654	1,339
Lenawee	1,528	13,089	7,369	-4,193	4,191	5,468	3,305	2,028
Livingston	15,356	14,598	6,285	7,044	13,435	6,852	3,003	9,586
Luce	-896	836	733	-999	-192	296	291	-198
Mackinac	496	1,454	1,225	268	236	544	514	206
Macomb	22,800	95,023	52,509	-19,714	11,163	42,187	25,406	-5,618
Manistee	-1,754	2,697	2,607	-1,844	1,368	962	1,168	1,573
Marquette	-3,214	11,567	5,039	-9,743	-204	4,001	2,304	-1,901
Mason	-828	3,709	2,871	-1,666	1,663	1,448	1,175	1,391
Mecosta	347	4,484	2,566	-1,571	1,312	1,855	1,309	766
Menominee	-1,281	3,498	2,698	-2,082	-388	1,173	1,163	-398
Midland	2,073	11,035	4,502	-4,461	3,594	4,891	2,049	752

Table I-3. Components of Population Change in Michigan, by County: 1980 - 1990 and 1990 - 1994 Continued

County	1980 to 1990				1990 to 1994			
	Population Change	Births	Deaths	Net Migration	Population Change	Births	Deaths	Net Migration
Missaukee	2,138	1,855	1,012	1,295	1,200	741	497	956
Monroe	-1,059	18,845	9,576	-10,328	4,116	7,503	4,230	843
Montcalm	5,504	8,002	4,498	2,000	3,827	3,509	1,999	2,317
Montmorency	1,444	964	1,118	1,598	577	339	544	782
Muskegon	1,394	25,703	13,916	-10,393	4,453	10,878	6,140	-285
Newaygo	3,285	5,975	3,340	650	4,532	2,813	1,536	3,255
Oakland	71,799	146,327	76,158	1,630	58,405	69,222	34,143	23,326
Oceana	452	3,693	2,059	-1,182	1,038	1,479	908	467
Ogemaw	2,245	2,600	2,104	1,749	1,569	1,140	1,129	1,558
Ontonagon	-1,007	1,070	1,123	-955	-181	379	520	-39
Osceola	1,218	3,067	1,856	7	1,229	1,287	873	815
Oscoda	984	1,107	979	856	652	402	449	699
Otsego	2,964	2,563	1,463	1,864	2,144	1,225	715	1,635
Ottawa	30,594	28,624	10,305	12,275	17,565	13,554	4,950	8,961
Presque Isle	-524	1,804	1,545	-784	285	587	663	362
Roscommon	3,402	2,184	2,456	3,674	2,105	989	1,237	2,353
Saginaw	-16,113	34,717	17,655	-33,175	-659	14,995	7,914	-7,740
St. Clair	6,805	20,697	12,542	-1,350	6,744	8,837	5,499	3,406
St. Joseph	2,830	9,257	5,180	-1,247	1,086	3,589	2,415	-88
Sanilac	-861	5,927	4,188	-2,600	1,639	2,243	1,802	1,198
Schoolcraft	-273	1,093	1,001	-365	294	423	440	311
Shiawassee	-1,370	10,390	5,218	-6,542	1,874	4,257	2,376	-8
Tuscola	-1,463	8,042	4,452	-5,053	1,519	3,267	2,024	276
Van Buren	3,246	10,729	6,311	-1,173	3,788	4,785	2,760	1,763
Washtenaw	18,197	39,016	14,540	-6,279	7,605	17,383	6,652	-3,126
Wayne	-226,156	348,427	224,472	-350,110	-46,779	162,365	91,127	-118,017
Wexford	1,258	4,090	2,545	-287	1,755	1,719	1,076	1,113
Michigan	33,253	1,398,722	777,594	-587,876	200,870	616,636	342,216	-73,550

Source: Michigan Department of Management and Budget, Office of the State Demographer (Lansing, Michigan).

Table I-4. Selected Age, Ethnic, and Economic Characteristics of Michigan's Population, by County: As of the 1990 Census

County	Total Population	Age of Population			Ethnic Heritage			Number of Households	Median Household Income($)	Poverty Rate(%)
		Under 17 Years	65 & Older	85 & Older	Black	Hispanic	Native American			
Alcona	10,145	2,009	2,443	188	27	55	56	4,261	$18,013	17.25
Alger	8,972	2,102	1,549	151	213	43	302	3,337	21,569	14.48
Allegan	90,509	25,517	10,425	1,048	1,448	2,895	541	31,709	30,596	9.50
Alpena	30,605	7,606	4,593	450	35	145	93	11,838	22,598	13.48
Antrim	18,185	4,404	3,162	302	23	96	210	6,980	22,636	13.21
Arenac	14,931	3,751	2,419	206	10	167	138	5,642	19,489	20.65
Baraga	7,954	1,973	1,554	145	49	34	918	3,065	19,424	16.82
Barry	50,057	13,219	5,849	574	104	521	188	17,763	30,516	9.07
Bay	111,723	27,685	14,980	1,284	1,242	3,494	717	42,188	27,940	12.53
Benzie	12,200	2,799	2,098	206	30	129	237	4,772	21,577	12.86
Berrien	161,378	41,113	22,145	2,119	24,872	2,683	676	61,025	27,245	14.71
Branch	41,502	10,948	5,511	504	705	468	219	14,921	25,332	14.08
Calhoun	135,982	34,133	18,160	1,808	14,383	2,583	687	51,812	27,476	14.29
Cass	49,477	12,627	6,477	552	3,725	651	468	18,239	28,002	11.88
Charlevoix	21,468	5,491	3,085	288	17	112	377	8,243	24,738	10.40
Cheboygan	21,398	5,284	3,716	330	15	80	476	8,201	21,006	15.56
Chippewa	34,604	7,649	4,339	393	2,184	278	3,818	11,541	21,449	17.08
Clare	24,952	6,203	4,403	333	40	132	156	9,698	17,163	23.71
Clinton	57,883	15,698	5,390	542	218	1,286	274	20,212	36,180	6.02
Crawford	12,260	3,039	1,827	183	264	79	145	4,441	21,497	14.59
Delta	37,780	9,582	5,802	602	16	136	806	14,531	22,791	14.61
Dickinson	26,831	6,592	4,908	587	23	116	130	10,633	24,809	9.90
Eaton	92,879	24,196	9,217	985	3,310	2,199	435	34,027	35,734	6.81
Emmet	25,040	6,342	3,531	418	133	118	683	9,516	26,015	8.51
Genesee	430,459	113,682	43,829	4,156	84,257	8,877	3,109	161,296	31,030	16.46
Gladwin	21,896	5,446	3,813	305	19	136	114	8,357	18,587	22.32
Gogebic	18,052	3,786	4,323	464	243	67	283	7,449	17,343	14.88
Grand Traverse	64,273	16,513	7,890	840	259	503	548	23,965	29,034	8.55

Table I-4. Selected Age, Ethnic, and Economic Characteristics of Michigan's Population, by County: As of the 1990 Census Continued

County	Total Population	Age of Population			Ethnic Heritage			Number of Households	Median Household Income($)	Poverty Rate(%)
		Under 17 Years	65 & Older	85 & Older	Black	Hispanic	Native American			
Gratiot	38,982	9,988	5,348	781	328	1,467	143	13,659	$24,530	14.08
Hillsdale	43,431	11,590	5,711	596	113	395	138	15,637	26,019	12.80
Houghton	35,446	7,543	6,336	610	158	164	148	13,172	17,650	21.04
Huron	34,951	8,840	6,418	623	22	372	88	13,268	21,852	15.01
Ingham	281,912	64,927	24,376	2,741	27,837	13,478	1,913	102,648	30,162	16.62
Ionia	57,024	15,132	5,743	642	3,003	1,176	220	18,447	29,430	11.33
Iosco	30,209	7,604	4,544	406	632	357	221	11,588	20,091	14.16
Iron	13,175	2,761	3,566	309	4	67	102	5,655	16,307	17.12
Isabella	54,624	11,884	4,576	474	635	714	1,011	17,591	22,659	24.85
Jackson	149,756	36,513	18,557	1,878	11,983	2,303	646	53,660	29,156	12.01
Kalamazoo	223,411	51,638	23,724	2,621	19,879	3,950	1,007	83,702	31,060	13.47
Kalkaska	13,497	3,763	1,797	127	10	87	111	4,934	22,078	14.23
Kent	500,631	134,944	54,007	6,062	40,314	14,684	2,744	181,740	32,358	9.15
Keweenaw	1,701	317	500	28	1	6	4	777	13,821	20.58
Lake	8,583	2,036	1,835	173	1,146	60	81	3,536	14,562	26.41
Lapeer	74,768	20,845	6,471	574	483	1,493	318	24,659	35,874	8.19
Leelanau	16,527	4,090	2,466	220	16	188	450	6,274	28,589	9.01
Lenawee	91,476	24,227	11,059	1,144	1,431	5,515	295	31,635	31,012	10.40
Livingston	115,645	31,165	9,474	851	673	974	701	38,887	45,439	4.13
Luce	5,763	1,479	994	91	2	27	330	2,154	20,370	17.68
Mackinac	10,674	2,602	1,816	164	5	33	1,689	4,240	19,397	16.40
Macomb	717,400	161,988	88,457	7,203	10,400	7,978	2,600	264,991	38,931	5.19
Manistee	21,265	4,815	3,897	370	54	323	189	8,580	19,977	17.62
Marquette	70,887	17,426	7,978	722	1,170	566	939	25,435	25,137	12.61
Mason	25,537	6,351	4,372	476	155	399	187	9,984	21,701	14.06
Mecosta	37,308	7,752	4,190	384	978	389	251	12,260	20,784	25.07
Menominee	24,920	6,243	4,295	455	7	59	382	9,766	21,586	12.75
Midland	75,651	19,603	7,540	711	719	1,035	333	27,791	33,948	11.09

Table I-4. Selected Age, Ethnic, and Economic Characteristics of Michigan's Population, by County: As of the 1990 Census Continued

County	Total Population	Age of Population			Ethnic Heritage			Number of Households	Median Household Income($)	Poverty Rate(%)
		Under 17 Years	65 & Older	85 & Older	Black	Hispanic	Native American			
Missaukee	12,147	3,416	1,812	162	3	67	74	4,389	$20,932	17.29
Monroe	133,600	36,017	13,827	1,304	2,339	2,077	476	46,508	35,462	8.64
Montcalm	53,059	14,285	6,580	579	960	888	384	18,563	23,880	15.32
Montmorency	8,936	1,971	2,044	203	1	60	48	3,600	17,819	17.52
Muskegon	158,983	42,393	20,798	1,970	21,617	3,623	1,331	57,798	25,617	15.26
Newaygo	38,202	10,727	5,204	469	468	968	244	13,776	23,468	15.88
Oakland	1,083,592	253,384	117,888	11,520	77,488	19,630	3,888	410,488	43,407	6.04
Oceana	22,454	6,287	3,075	281	58	1,390	233	8,071	22,383	17.89
Ogemaw	18,681	4,656	3,390	248	18	104	140	7,190	17,665	21.75
Ontonagon	8,854	1,961	1,720	126	4	35	108	3,641	21,147	13.19
Osceola	20,146	5,646	2,814	246	57	143	117	7,347	20,880	18.55
Oscoda	7,842	1,790	1,616	145	2	50	41	3,160	17,772	17.80
Otsego	17,957	4,849	2,433	231	18	67	102	6,522	26,356	9.47
Ottawa	187,768	52,471	18,474	1,975	997	7,947	629	62,664	36,507	5.99
Presque Isle	13,743	3,297	2,716	224	11	37	43	5,376	20,941	14.70
Roscommon	19,776	3,952	4,933	279	37	94	100	8,516	17,047	18.05
Saginaw	211,946	55,989	25,603	2,565	36,849	13,186	898	78,256	27,980	17.25
St. Clair	145,607	38,144	17,919	1,696	2,987	2,558	743	52,882	30,692	10.93
St. Joseph	58,913	16,084	7,694	808	1,600	546	221	21,579	27,510	11.49
Sanilac	39,928	10,645	6,223	580	39	905	194	14,658	23,107	14.30
Schoolcraft	8,302	1,977	1,536	164	7	32	517	3,294	20,112	16.61
Shiawassee	69,770	18,685	7,768	794	93	1,053	394	24,864	30,283	10.59
Tuscola	55,498	14,916	6,696	582	478	1,150	336	19,469	27,374	12.86
Van Buren	70,060	19,329	8,854	954	4,690	2,254	644	25,402	25,491	15.13
Washtenaw	282,937	57,918	21,226	2,344	31,720	5,731	1,051	104,528	36,307	12.16
Wayne	2,111,687	537,389	264,502	24,702	849,109	50,506	7,954	780,535	27,997	20.07
Wexford	26,360	7,181	3,631	357	34	153	176	9,923	22,915	14.64
Michigan	9,295,297	2,322,814	1,108,461	106,907	1,291,706	201,596	55,131	3,424,122	$31,020	13.10

Source: U.S. Bureau of the Census, Michigan Information Center (Lansing, Michigan).

Table I-5. Selected Age, Ethnic, and Economic Characteristics of Michigan's Population, by City and Village: As of the 1990 Census

City/Village	Total Population	Age of Population			Ethnic Heritage			Number of Households	Median Household Income($)	Poverty Rate(%)
		Under 17 Years	65 & Older	85 & Older	Black	Hispanic	Native American			
Addison village	632	184	75	7	1	13	2	245	$21,333	18.18
Adrian city	22,097	5,587	3,242	544	723	2,958	88	7,479	24,788	20.65
Ahmeek village	148	16	61	3	0	0	1	81	7,942	31.51
Akron village	421	100	65	7	0	27	0	159	22,500	16.83
Alanson village	677	212	70	6	7	3	20	264	17,250	26.70
Albion city	10,066	2,389	1,237	142	3,096	473	27	3,399	20,078	25.36
Algonac city	4,551	1,266	608	56	6	44	44	1,664	26,237	11.51
Allegan city	4,547	1,192	619	64	186	85	18	1,730	26,121	14.17
Allen village	201	45	40	4	0	0	0	83	21,250	23.00
Allendale CDP	6,950	1,486	400	57	234	83	22	1,738	29,167	14.09
Allen Park city	31,092	6,106	6,305	471	144	986	66	12,030	39,925	3.26
Alma city	9,034	2,068	1,386	361	42	567	32	3,099	22,017	17.20
Almont village	2,354	684	230	11	1	59	12	828	32,243	6.39
Alpena city	11,354	2,674	2,191	275	27	53	49	4,714	20,472	13.45
Alpha village	219	46	59	3	0	0	0	98	15,795	19.46
Anchorville CDP	3,202	804	326	25	5	48	16	1,293	30,271	4.10
Ann Arbor city	109,592	17,937	7,881	990	9,905	2,827	370	41,657	33,344	16.08
Applegate village	297	90	40	3	0	13	0	100	21,875	23.57
Argentine CDP	1,907	484	163	21	2	19	14	683	38,194	4.74
Armada village	1,548	482	173	39	1	47	6	503	42,083	5.09
Ashley village	518	131	112	27	0	11	2	174	26,250	9.32
Athens village	990	267	139	11	5	6	4	366	26,940	6.61
Auburn city	1,855	435	227	19	1	29	3	727	31,492	8.39
Auburn Hills city	17,076	3,462	1,014	56	1,641	496	109	6,453	34,825	7.38
Au Gres city	838	152	176	18	0	12	12	377	19,737	21.30
Augusta village	927	208	100	7	0	3	9	380	26,343	11.00
Au Sable CDP	1,542	390	199	7	16	19	13	603	22,054	10.55
Bad Axe city	3,484	889	663	108	9	50	8	1,356	19,827	20.06

Table I-5. Selected Age, Ethnic, and Economic Characteristics of Michigan's Population, by City and Village: As of the 1990 Census Continued

City/Village	Total Population	Age of Population			Ethnic Heritage				Number of Households	Median Household Income($)	Poverty Rate(%)
		Under 17 Years	65 & Older	85 & Older	Black	Hispanic	Native American				
Baldwin village	821	202	250	60	274	5	9		330	$9,437	35.60
Bancroft village	599	187	52	5	0	13	5		197	27,857	10.94
Bangor city	1,922	568	282	39	246	101	22		739	16,441	29.24
Baraga village	1,231	355	197	19	0	9	281		507	13,450	27.49
Barnes Lake-Millers Lake CDP	1,304	354	111	8	0	12	4		443	31,429	12.74
Baroda village	657	151	100	10	1	11	1		275	25,385	6.26
Barryton village	393	97	89	5	0	2	2		171	17,946	20.77
Barton Hills village	320	53	52	6	4	0	0		123	140,880	0.00
Battle Creek city	53,540	14,046	7,717	886	8,854	978	337		21,457	25,306	18.26
Bay City	38,936	9,686	5,988	519	953	2,189	308		15,570	21,380	18.06
Beal City CDP	345	70	46	6	0	0	0		114	29,688	3.57
Bear Lake village	339	90	47	7	0	11	4		131	20,938	13.11
Beaverton city	1,150	327	216	19	0	16	2		491	13,398	34.00
Beecher CDP	14,465	4,861	975	58	8,390	638	163		4,832	17,305	38.40
Beechwood CDP	2,676	738	276	21	7	175	7		956	35,712	4.59
Belding city	5,969	1,704	846	132	24	138	10		2,218	22,987	13.33
Bellaire village	1,104	284	140	19	1	1	11		446	22,396	10.58
Belleville city	3,270	624	538	36	59	42	7		1,536	31,843	5.08
Bellevue village	1,401	400	184	19	6	27	0		508	22,308	12.27
Benton Harbor city	12,818	5,068	1,011	79	11,817	122	18		4,334	8,866	58.00
Benton Heights CDP	5,465	1,766	748	94	3,123	25	34		1,887	13,929	35.94
Benzonia village	449	78	96	17	5	10	14		192	19,402	13.78
Berkley city	16,960	4,027	2,380	200	27	187	80		6,611	36,693	3.72
Berrien Springs village	1,927	490	266	27	141	87	17		760	23,828	12.75
Bessemer city	2,272	465	591	58	1	7	20		1,014	15,472	14.88
Beulah village	421	63	93	12	0	7	22		167	21,719	12.47
Beverly Hills village	10,610	2,156	1,894	174	125	126	8		4,075	61,941	1.15
Big Rapids city	12,603	1,287	1,080	181	634	197	69		3,257	14,990	44.45

Table I-5. Selected Age, Ethnic, and Economic Characteristics of Michigan's Population, by City and Village: As of the 1990 Census Continued

City/Village	Total Population	Age of Population			Ethnic Heritage			Number of Households	Median Household Income($)	Poverty Rate(%)
		Under 17 Years	65 & Older	85 & Older	Black	Hispanic	Native American			
Bingham Farms village	1,001	150	172	7	14	3	0	410	$107,506	1.50
Birch Run village	992	214	121	6	2	28	1	416	24,722	12.00
Birmingham city	19,997	3,647	2,893	329	87	155	33	9,120	57,573	2.30
Blissfield village	3,172	856	515	59	15	179	13	1,230	25,646	5.43
Bloomfield Hills city	4,288	767	755	133	57	71	1	1,517	150,001	4.31
Bloomfield Township CDP	42,137	8,638	5,641	375	1,011	527	40	15,618	84,494	1.43
Bloomingdale village	503	140	82	8	1	9	0	191	20,441	18.15
Boyne City	3,478	910	571	51	2	20	48	1,422	20,497	14.58
Boyne Falls village	369	106	47	4	0	0	4	140	18,281	17.52
Breckenridge village	1,301	317	215	21	0	54	2	527	19,375	15.01
Breedsville village	213	70	20	2	0	33	2	70	21,250	27.04
Bridgeport CDP	8,569	2,253	873	101	1,433	793	61	3,104	30,486	15.80
Bridgman city	2,140	472	410	101	2	17	7	841	29,293	9.31
Brighton city	5,686	1,404	627	100	10	52	28	2,374	35,551	5.15
Britton village	694	201	67	2	1	26	0	242	32,734	5.04
Bronson city	2,342	699	372	46	8	62	3	902	19,867	20.58
Brooklyn village	1,027	239	154	14	0	6	3	422	24,375	10.05
Brown City	1,244	348	148	16	0	13	5	459	20,125	16.17
Brownlee Park CDP	2,536	641	324	21	25	71	36	1,031	17,210	32.39
Buchanan city	4,992	1,339	723	56	561	54	26	1,990	24,084	13.49
Buckley village	402	139	41	3	0	1	6	136	20,625	27.43
Buena Vista CDP	8,196	2,302	953	68	5,040	875	59	3,036	20,043	28.87
Burlington village	294	98	24	1	0	1	1	97	21,458	20.18
Burr Oak village	882	247	97	8	0	8	5	321	23,889	12.61
Burt CDP	1,169	338	70	3	18	62	11	376	34,375	1.67
Burton city	27,617	7,002	3,042	192	710	578	274	10,447	29,961	14.28
Byron village	573	161	71	2	0	7	3	206	23,594	10.10
Cadillac city	10,104	2,706	1,648	233	21	72	79	4,001	21,170	15.52

Table I-5. Selected Age, Ethnic, and Economic Characteristics of Michigan's Population, by City and Village: As of the 1990 Census Continued

City/Village	Total Population	Age of Population			Ethnic Heritage			Number of Households	Median Household Income(%)	Poverty Rate(%)
		Under 17 Years	65 & Older	85 & Older	Black	Hispanic	Native American			
Caledonia village	885	243	106	9	0	0	0	342	$31,161	3.95
Calumet village	818	158	244	26	7	6	7	437	7,992	36.59
Camden village	482	137	62	4	0	4	1	181	20,000	18.76
Canton CDP	57,047	16,831	2,759	159	1,167	792	154	19,544	47,009	4.77
Capac village	1,583	485	217	18	6	115	10	579	24,632	15.61
Carleton village	2,770	846	185	9	7	29	18	981	32,045	14.09
Carney village	197	56	26	1	0	0	0	71	17,273	13.59
Caro village	4,054	1,005	709	83	9	168	41	1,698	20,576	18.79
Carrollton CDP	6,521	1,575	765	54	390	621	25	2,404	27,213	13.53
Carson City	1,158	291	197	26	4	36	3	471	20,313	21.40
Carsonville village	583	175	71	8	0	6	1	206	21,786	22.97
Caseville village	857	168	255	17	0	6	5	397	16,731	13.06
Casnovia village	376	120	52	5	0	1	0	121	30,500	3.11
Caspian city	1,031	228	274	18	0	7	8	469	12,011	20.29
Cass City village	2,276	524	462	70	5	29	20	890	25,363	12.02
Cassopolis village	1,822	482	224	22	729	30	13	705	18,967	25.37
Cedar Springs city	2,600	766	331	64	4	40	20	908	23,200	18.44
Cement City village	493	136	63	2	1	5	2	172	19,038	12.88
Center Line city	9,026	1,683	2,323	267	71	92	36	3,906	22,758	8.52
Central Lake village	954	209	193	18	7	0	20	363	19,457	14.98
Centreville village	1,516	389	168	43	39	13	5	477	23,315	14.89
Charlevoix city	3,116	663	590	56	5	19	98	1,401	21,710	8.94
Charlotte city	8,083	2,224	1,073	176	15	249	44	3,050	27,123	9.78
Chatham village	268	70	43	0	0	1	12	102	30,000	12.62
Cheboygan city	4,999	1,289	900	140	3	22	126	1,939	19,120	19.08
Chelsea village	3,772	884	738	220	32	20	13	1,390	37,478	2.79
Chesaning village	2,567	624	442	48	0	77	4	1,004	22,788	15.17
Clare city	3,021	736	678	116	7	12	24	1,229	17,861	23.47

Table I-5. Selected Age, Ethnic, and Economic Characteristics of Michigan's Population, by City and Village: As of the 1990 Census Continued

City/Village	Total Population	Age of Population			Ethnic Heritage			Number of Households	Median Household Income(%)	Poverty Rate(%)
		Under 17 Years	65 & Older	85 & Older	Black	Hispanic	Native American			
Clarkston village	1,005	169	161	24	0	5	1	431	$43,333	3.48
Clarksville village	360	95	82	9	2	2	3	142	23,214	12.97
Clawson city	13,874	2,878	1,851	228	30	128	36	5,544	36,532	3.73
Clayton village	384	134	26	0	8	32	1	117	24,063	25.40
Clifford village	354	86	56	7	0	1	0	123	24,583	19.01
Climax village	677	222	49	6	0	8	3	224	35,227	5.04
Clinton village	2,475	659	318	20	2	20	1	929	31,569	5.79
Clinton CDP	85,866	19,904	9,289	780	2,586	1,001	245	32,459	39,215	5.65
Clio city	2,629	659	279	25	11	39	22	1,096	25,431	13.18
Coldwater city	9,607	2,529	1,556	214	33	121	56	3,728	22,562	17.48
Coleman city	1,237	362	178	19	5	1	5	494	19,271	21.79
Coloma city	1,679	429	188	10	3	22	11	630	28,636	8.34
Colon village	1,224	301	245	19	0	5	2	503	21,121	9.92
Columbiaville village	934	287	104	11	0	13	2	325	24,688	16.79
Comstock Northwest CDP	3,402	906	357	12	170	59	24	1,226	36,679	7.56
Comstock Park CDP	6,530	1,522	473	32	54	90	31	2,586	33,103	5.42
Concord village	944	269	121	9	0	8	0	350	27,443	7.94
Constantine village	2,032	589	233	13	8	26	19	749	24,046	14.08
Coopersville city	3,421	1,057	326	38	9	54	7	1,175	32,684	8.99
Copemish village	222	56	39	1	3	2	1	85	11,250	39.82
Copper City village	198	42	48	2	0	0	0	84	18,333	8.74
Corunna city	3,091	768	444	81	18	58	21	1,115	24,784	16.03
Croswell city	2,174	646	293	41	9	256	7	810	18,768	22.93
Crystal Falls city	1,922	402	591	65	3	14	12	816	17,885	12.52
Custer village	312	94	59	5	0	4	3	111	20,662	15.41
Cutlerville CDP	11,228	3,064	957	46	159	172	80	4,290	29,172	7.11
Daggett village	260	65	56	2	0	0	1	110	15,938	22.34
Dansville village	437	146	35	4	2	6	4	137	36,250	10.14

Table I-5. Selected Age, Ethnic, and Economic Characteristics of Michigan's Population, by City and Village: As of the 1990 Census Continued

City/Village	Total Population	Age of Population			Ethnic Heritage			Number of Households	Median Household Income($)	Poverty Rate(%)
		Under 17 Years	65 & Older	85 & Older	Black	Hispanic	Native American			
Davison city	5,693	1,282	889	114	8	85	33	2,503	$30,393	8.46
Dearborn city	89,286	19,593	16,056	1,336	494	2,483	286	35,442	34,909	10.78
Dearborn Heights city	60,838	11,795	10,225	738	277	1,398	251	23,432	36,771	5.50
Decatur village	1,760	480	273	30	121	69	32	705	19,129	20.87
Deckerville village	1,015	242	220	59	2	79	3	364	18,750	23.92
Deerfield village	922	266	94	8	3	27	4	332	33,750	5.66
De Tour Village	407	66	94	7	0	1	70	175	19,773	12.35
Detroit city	1,027,974	283,961	124,933	12,506	777,916	28,473	3,587	374,057	18,742	32.41
Detroit Beach CDP	2,113	696	116	8	0	12	7	668	30,417	17.10
De Witt city	3,964	1,274	184	19	25	112	9	1,307	44,004	3.63
Dexter village	1,497	333	216	19	1	11	12	633	32,411	4.74
Dimondale village	1,247	380	80	3	0	16	5	422	41,371	3.70
Douglas village	1,040	168	279	55	1	34	9	476	24,022	13.06
Dowagiac city	6,409	1,774	1,058	154	994	130	141	2,478	20,628	15.50
Dryden village	628	172	58	9	0	3	2	195	33,750	8.07
Dundee village	2,664	648	365	34	2	23	4	1,088	30,899	9.19
Durand city	4,283	1,219	581	144	2	69	20	1,488	26,868	16.15
Eagle village	120	31	11	1	0	3	0	41	34,688	8.28
East Detroit city	35,283	7,606	6,636	466	87	290	132	13,443	34,069	4.95
East Grand Rapids city	10,807	3,138	1,191	87	98	71	15	3,784	60,355	2.56
East Jordan city	2,240	602	335	35	3	15	63	875	20,696	14.84
Eastlake village	473	116	62	1	3	9	1	184	16,324	13.64
East Lansing city	50,677	5,018	2,277	286	3,513	1,268	163	13,500	24,716	33.77
East Tawas city	2,887	611	740	84	3	9	18	1,274	19,146	15.32
Eastwood CDP	6,340	1,481	955	137	947	168	24	2,563	26,153	11.02
Eaton Rapids city	4,695	1,273	628	74	4	108	23	1,798	29,706	8.43
Eau Claire village	494	142	56	7	9	6	4	184	24,083	12.25
Ecorse city	12,180	3,209	1,484	100	4,787	820	111	4,570	18,956	26.86

Table I-5. Selected Age, Ethnic, and Economic Characteristics of Michigan's Population, by City and Village: As of the 1990 Census Continued

City/Village	Total Population	Age of Population			Ethnic Heritage				Number of Households	Median Household Income($)	Poverty Rate(%)
		Under 17 Years	65 & Older	85 & Older	Black	Hispanic	Native American				
Edgemont Park CDP	2,532	530	463	31	108	58	7		1,079	$35,054	5.80
Edmore village	1,126	286	217	18	1	47	5		456	17,768	24.71
Edwardsburg village	1,142	300	157	14	2	8	3		460	22,460	12.54
Elberta village	478	131	67	9	0	4	18		185	15,769	18.32
Elk Rapids village	1,626	375	308	32	3	22	26		699	22,226	10.10
Elkton village	958	258	149	8	0	25	4		368	22,687	14.39
Ellsworth village	418	131	67	12	2	1	1		149	18,603	6.91
Elsie village	957	233	169	24	0	16	8		374	24,444	12.82
Emmett village	297	80	31	3	0	1	0		95	32,083	9.69
Empire village	355	69	61	5	0	1	1		163	18,750	12.19
Escanaba city	13,659	3,145	2,621	356	7	75	314		5,728	19,982	19.56
Essexville city	4,088	1,043	578	33	20	93	25		1,513	33,267	7.58
Estral Beach village	430	125	66	8	0	10	11		145	35,125	7.36
Evart city	1,744	499	270	33	8	25	13		689	14,417	26.53
Fairgrove village	592	146	88	8	0	21	1		224	21,389	20.83
Fair Haven CDP	1,505	366	181	10	3	7	4		564	31,417	3.65
Fair Plain CDP	8,051	1,821	1,270	81	2,632	117	46		3,285	25,940	12.10
Farmington city	10,132	1,621	2,410	286	82	78	12		4,673	41,040	3.64
Farmington Hills city	74,652	16,009	8,774	889	1,429	887	124		29,234	51,986	2.98
Farwell village	851	240	128	13	3	14	2		331	15,288	21.94
Fennville city	1,023	311	114	14	2	250	5		357	28,088	15.05
Fenton city	8,444	2,037	1,192	211	35	98	40		3,214	33,998	9.17
Ferndale city	25,084	6,175	3,044	333	348	426	211		9,858	28,964	10.66
Ferrysburg city	2,919	721	261	17	7	27	21		1,151	35,643	8.43
Fife Lake village	394	107	45	7	0	1	1		153	20,781	15.04
Flat Rock city	7,290	2,062	716	48	52	139	33		2,670	35,000	13.18
Flint city	140,761	40,422	15,100	1,619	67,485	4,014	1,038		53,894	20,176	30.58
Flushing city	8,542	1,939	1,353	168	16	96	19		3,302	37,816	4.47

19

Table I-5. Selected Age, Ethnic, and Economic Characteristics of Michigan's Population, by City and Village: As of the 1990 Census Continued

City/Village	Total Population	Age of Population			Ethnic Heritage			Number of Households	Median Household Income($)	Poverty Rate(%)
		Under 17 Years	65 & Older	85 & Older	Black	Hispanic	Native American			
Forest Hills CDP	16,690	4,741	1,199	65	106	96	33	5,502	$59,346	1.93
Forestville village	153	41	41	0	0	4	0	71	18,333	21.90
Fountain village	165	45	33	1	0	0	2	67	13,929	15.00
Fowler village	912	258	152	19	0	6	1	334	32,750	4.82
Fowlerville village	2,648	775	272	35	0	30	44	968	29,234	11.61
Frankenmuth city	4,408	819	1,178	307	1	36	3	1,838	36,151	3.28
Frankfort city	1,546	300	385	81	3	13	41	646	19,911	12.71
Franklin village	2,626	537	391	21	45	27	8	975	91,423	0.61
Fraser city	13,899	3,184	1,860	227	23	149	68	5,180	36,644	5.38
Freeland CDP	1,421	367	140	12	0	39	4	529	33,125	7.82
Freeport village	458	134	46	6	0	12	0	152	27,708	9.25
Free Soil village	148	23	33	4	3	0	2	62	20,250	9.72
Fremont city	3,875	946	762	73	11	25	7	1,645	25,392	11.14
Fruitport village	1,090	258	178	18	3	13	4	406	29,083	3.69
Gaastra city	376	83	100	11	0	2	2	157	16,625	14.71
Gagetown village	337	71	64	4	2	23	0	127	18,750	25.98
Gaines village	427	127	39	5	0	9	14	150	22,143	19.86
Galesburg city	1,863	520	263	49	12	20	15	707	22,580	15.66
Galien village	596	194	66	5	4	0	1	214	22,440	8.24
Garden village	268	65	51	3	0	2	11	109	11,776	21.00
Garden City	31,846	7,576	3,153	194	76	483	133	11,213	38,717	4.27
Gaylord city	3,256	778	687	127	0	13	19	1,290	20,200	14.12
Gibraltar city	4,297	1,052	288	16	7	41	18	1,579	41,291	3.43
Gladstone city	4,565	1,096	884	87	3	21	95	1,853	22,134	13.44
Gladwin city	2,682	697	616	104	4	23	10	1,071	14,788	27.99
Gobles city	769	229	97	11	2	6	9	280	24,318	12.09
Goodrich village	916	280	70	6	1	13	5	310	38,000	7.01
Grand Beach village	146	16	52	5	0	0	0	69	50,000	2.67

Table I-5. Selected Age, Ethnic, and Economic Characteristics of Michigan's Population, by City and Village: As of the 1990 Census Continued

City/Village	Total Population	Age of Population			Ethnic Heritage			Number of Households	Median Household Income($)	Poverty Rate(%)
		Under 17 Years	65 & Older	85 & Older	Black	Hispanic	Native American			
Grand Blanc city	7,760	1,736	950	161	219	90	16	3,176	$38,132	3.87
Grand Haven city	11,951	2,687	2,233	306	59	145	92	4,772	28,989	9.61
Grand Ledge city	7,579	1,981	855	86	21	118	27	3,057	31,563	8.27
Grand Rapids city	189,126	49,718	24,711	3,508	35,073	9,394	1,568	69,029	26,809	16.12
Grandville city	15,624	4,203	1,593	155	112	215	35	5,643	36,906	3.67
Grant city	764	227	130	10	0	51	3	289	17,895	13.34
Grass Lake village	903	241	110	11	0	2	4	333	33,448	3.32
Grayling city	1,944	490	406	92	1	16	29	730	15,481	26.20
Greater Galesburg CDP	1,260	287	145	11	2	12	17	484	31,759	8.08
Greenville city	8,101	2,196	1,314	177	14	197	37	3,183	21,916	14.29
Greilickville CDP	1,165	246	166	17	2	7	5	455	40,278	2.38
Grosse Ile CDP	9,781	2,267	938	54	8	134	35	3,506	62,619	2.30
Grosse Pointe city	5,681	1,188	929	116	23	63	8	2,387	62,947	1.85
Grosse Pointe Farms city	10,092	2,247	1,785	194	23	72	7	3,837	66,844	1.33
Grosse Pointe Park city	12,857	3,001	1,525	199	112	185	36	4,853	54,586	4.56
Grosse Pointe Shores village	2,955	544	567	50	11	42	4	1,055	115,310	0.58
Grosse Pointe Woods city	17,715	3,922	3,178	255	13	124	9	6,560	55,657	1.74
Gwinn CDP	2,370	595	236	18	35	21	34	939	23,341	12.88
Hamtramck city	18,372	4,068	3,732	300	2,578	292	93	7,908	16,751	28.50
Hancock city	4,547	870	1,079	176	62	31	26	1,802	19,245	15.23
Hanover village	481	147	61	4	0	0	3	166	25,083	19.54
Harbor Beach city	2,089	519	504	71	0	19	13	863	15,438	23.40
Harbor Springs city	1,540	331	363	76	5	2	77	612	23,387	8.03
Harper Woods city	14,903	2,592	4,098	427	132	152	27	6,572	33,098	4.42
Harrietta village	157	41	33	2	0	0	1	59	14,844	31.25
Harrison city	1,835	429	318	20	3	15	18	748	16,875	24.23
Harrison CDP	24,685	5,343	2,135	131	498	355	98	9,947	39,210	5.06
Harrisville city	470	77	135	15	5	0	6	207	19,853	17.29

Table I-5. Selected Age, Ethnic, and Economic Characteristics of Michigan's Population, by City and Village: As of the 1990 Census Continued

City/Village	Total Population	Age of Population			Ethnic Heritage			Number of Households	Median Household Income($)	Poverty Rate(%)
		Under 17 Years	65 & Older	85 & Older	Black	Hispanic	Native American			
Hart city	1,942	442	403	95	19	165	20	734	$16,735	19.59
Hartford city	2,341	661	277	23	15	147	61	872	19,458	22.51
Harvey CDP	1,377	386	114	9	2	6	44	510	24,295	8.33
Haslett CDP	10,230	2,296	1,032	102	192	184	53	4,572	35,125	7.71
Hastings city	6,549	1,740	1,099	164	8	83	31	2,515	25,085	12.37
Hazel Park city	20,051	5,376	2,258	162	72	278	274	7,284	26,615	14.22
Hemlock CDP	1,601	411	162	25	0	27	1	600	25,536	12.14
Hersey village	354	102	39	4	0	4	1	126	24,107	22.11
Hesperia village	846	252	163	13	2	14	9	336	20,288	20.14
Highland Park city	20,121	5,325	2,841	302	18,673	137	40	8,033	9,805	42.36
Hillman village	643	117	230	72	0	2	2	263	10,733	22.94
Hillsdale city	8,170	1,932	1,312	243	45	72	26	2,957	21,688	16.33
Holland city	30,745	7,869	4,236	589	324	4,347	103	10,572	30,689	11.77
Holly village	5,595	1,558	567	80	53	133	35	2,056	28,995	11.58
Holt CDP	11,744	3,325	868	109	126	286	48	4,342	34,060	8.57
Homer village	1,758	510	223	24	2	32	4	649	22,625	17.94
Honor village	292	70	48	4	1	3	13	117	16,985	16.03
Hopkins village	546	147	76	6	1	1	15	198	26,339	8.81
Houghton city	7,498	875	584	56	64	70	27	2,010	16,059	40.62
Houghton Lake CDP	3,353	700	843	83	2	5	11	1,443	16,635	19.27
Howard City village	1,351	446	162	14	2	19	64	469	20,435	22.55
Howell city	8,184	1,953	1,157	173	12	85	84	3,266	31,674	9.16
Hubbardston village	404	91	54	6	0	4	2	138	22,411	12.20
Hubbell CDP	1,174	291	251	45	0	4	6	421	17,083	15.34
Hudson city	2,580	767	338	45	5	50	3	912	25,152	17.08
Hudsonville city	6,170	1,680	960	98	11	48	18	2,177	32,114	3.70
Huntington Woods city	6,419	1,602	939	76	30	59	1	2,376	61,057	2.09
Imlay City	2,921	753	507	72	23	287	14	1,119	25,313	12.06

Table I-5. Selected Age, Ethnic, and Economic Characteristics of Michigan's Population, by City and Village: As of the 1990 Census Continued

City/Village	Total Population	Age of Population			Ethnic Heritage			Number of Households	Median Household Income($)	Poverty Rate(%)
		Under 17 Years	65 & Older	85 & Older	Black	Hispanic	Native American			
Inkster city	30,772	8,337	3,486	268	19,199	332	131	11,201	$25,198	23.20
Ionia city	5,935	1,627	838	160	52	210	35	2,263	23,614	16.30
Iron Mountain city	8,525	1,962	1,817	225	13	66	56	3,562	23,004	12.12
Iron River city	2,095	390	678	81	0	7	30	949	12,290	27.37
Ironwood city	6,849	1,431	1,827	244	6	34	31	2,992	16,857	16.22
Ishpeming city	7,200	1,638	1,425	144	3	19	58	2,990	21,199	15.55
Ithaca city	3,009	784	402	45	1	122	19	1,143	26,570	9.72
Jackson city	37,446	10,086	5,290	607	6,615	954	217	14,723	20,830	24.71
Jenison CDP	17,882	5,416	1,769	204	57	200	19	5,482	42,626	1.56
Jonesville village	2,283	618	350	19	16	19	6	895	24,618	11.44
Kalamazoo city	80,277	16,847	8,712	1,264	15,053	2,153	440	29,409	23,207	26.23
Kaleva village	484	118	119	11	0	5	2	209	15,400	20.00
Kalkaska village	1,952	592	315	51	4	6	29	715	19,647	15.98
Keego Harbor city	2,932	636	243	27	9	82	28	1,235	30,417	12.76
Kent City village	899	283	74	11	0	5	0	319	24,659	14.13
Kentwood city	37,826	9,452	3,635	266	2,113	761	159	15,247	34,324	4.98
Kinde village	473	106	103	9	3	1	5	198	18,125	20.87
Kingsford city	5,480	1,382	1,022	160	8	22	31	2,160	25,581	9.14
Kingsley village	738	247	92	9	0	10	4	253	23,750	12.19
Kingston village	439	120	71	4	2	5	6	165	21,932	19.91
K. I. Sawyer AFB CDP	6,577	2,394	2	0	398	255	45	1,711	19,889	9.43
Laingsburg city	1,148	319	111	18	0	6	1	415	26,161	8.84
Lake Angelus city	328	61	44	5	4	4	0	122	80,930	0.65
Lake Ann village	217	46	35	2	1	2	3	91	27,500	11.98
Lake City	858	201	190	22	0	9	4	357	20,050	17.58
Lake Fenton CDP	4,091	923	377	19	9	39	16	1,499	48,202	2.48
Lake Linden village	1,203	280	295	30	1	5	1	534	14,243	18.95
Lake Michigan Beach CDP	1,694	449	192	13	13	20	11	658	25,417	10.26

Table I-5. Selected Age, Ethnic, and Economic Characteristics of Michigan's Population, by City and Village: As of the 1990 Census Continued

City/Village	Total Population	Age of Population			Ethnic Heritage			Number of Households	Median Household Income($)	Poverty Rate(%)
		Under 17 Years	65 & Older	85 & Older	Black	Hispanic	Native American			
Lake Odessa village	2,256	622	355	52	3	141	8	902	$23,973	13.08
Lake Orion village	3,057	640	454	89	11	32	13	1,240	38,750	4.83
Lakeview village	1,108	287	209	25	7	48	2	410	20,560	20.94
Lakewood Club village	659	211	52	4	18	21	2	218	25,536	14.31
Lambertville CDP	7,860	2,177	627	37	6	92	12	2,609	44,366	2.58
L'Anse village	2,151	491	508	85	0	11	123	882	18,365	14.19
Lansing city	127,321	33,308	12,171	1,205	23,626	10,112	1,281	50,635	26,398	19.43
Lapeer city	7,759	1,868	951	104	368	143	62	2,844	22,833	20.13
Lathrup Village city	4,329	956	623	46	991	51	6	1,577	59,072	2.75
Laurium village	2,268	586	506	46	3	11	12	936	17,437	18.23
Lawrence village	915	248	154	20	12	80	12	358	16,776	27.74
Lawton village	1,685	483	330	117	22	125	7	538	23,472	13.71
Lennon village	534	135	39	3	0	1	9	190	34,500	9.31
Leonard village	357	90	42	5	0	2	1	121	37,045	4.74
Le Roy village	251	74	41	5	0	0	0	90	20,500	13.73
Leslie city	1,872	511	195	26	1	17	4	658	29,698	9.76
Level Park-Oak Park CDP	3,502	884	425	34	160	30	10	1,308	32,123	8.76
Lexington village	779	118	261	25	0	9	7	403	19,397	15.56
Lincoln village	337	58	113	5	1	4	1	167	16,250	12.28
Lincoln Park city	41,832	9,634	6,024	383	386	1,588	219	16,257	30,638	8.53
Linden city	2,415	647	231	17	0	32	6	891	38,125	7.52
Litchfield city	1,317	329	241	41	3	32	12	508	21,122	14.10
Livonia city	100,850	22,033	13,180	1,395	265	1,355	182	35,916	48,645	2.59
Lowell city	3,983	1,060	567	90	10	56	16	1,456	28,542	4.51
Ludington city	8,507	2,049	1,782	271	41	176	77	3,589	18,611	15.63
Luna Pier city	1,507	466	143	17	2	27	20	526	24,886	17.11
Luther village	343	101	58	2	0	2	7	127	13,750	29.47
Lyons village	824	245	73	5	0	8	3	286	28,594	13.14

Table 1-5. Selected Age, Ethnic, and Economic Characteristics of Michigan's Population, by City and Village: As of the 1990 Census Continued

City/Village	Total Population	Age of Population			Ethnic Heritage			Number of Households	Median Household Income($)	Poverty Rate(%)
		Under 17 Years	65 & Older	85 & Older	Black	Hispanic	Native American			
McBain city	692	167	233	57	1	1	0	245	$22,212	13.14
McBride village	236	54	43	4	0	2	0	91	16,786	24.48
Mackinac Island city	469	104	36	4	0	2	135	208	22,361	7.55
Mackinaw City village	875	196	155	14	0	4	58	372	22,031	8.90
Madison Heights city	32,196	6,952	3,727	340	292	399	159	12,850	31,757	8.38
Mancelona village	1,370	386	189	24	0	1	32	514	18,271	21.74
Manchester village	1,753	475	212	18	10	18	4	651	34,479	3.71
Manistee city	6,734	1,545	1,402	155	34	129	67	2,896	18,010	21.63
Manistique city	3,456	784	762	112	0	12	197	1,468	17,581	19.57
Manitou Beach-Devils Lake CDP	2,061	476	268	10	0	32	4	853	29,250	7.31
Manton city	1,161	322	195	16	0	2	11	468	16,042	23.16
Maple Rapids village	680	189	73	8	0	4	8	244	24,000	20.93
Marcellus village	1,193	348	151	11	16	14	3	432	23,333	16.62
Marine City	4,556	1,213	693	65	2	24	20	1,693	27,088	11.15
Marion village	807	200	129	13	0	4	17	331	14,107	28.21
Marlette city	1,924	513	341	64	7	42	1	713	21,656	16.81
Marquette city	21,977	4,019	2,616	311	621	129	384	7,942	24,365	16.57
Marshall city	6,891	1,645	1,107	120	96	229	20	2,754	30,000	8.47
Martin village	462	127	59	7	0	7	0	170	29,875	12.24
Marysville city	8,515	1,908	1,425	80	4	74	26	3,359	34,075	3.97
Mason city	6,768	1,714	705	71	246	174	46	2,381	33,607	5.71
Mattawan village	2,456	705	259	8	39	53	16	896	30,962	8.01
Maybee village	500	178	49	5	0	8	0	154	35,536	6.37
Mayville village	1,010	284	164	35	0	3	10	352	25,350	17.75
Mecosta village	393	120	53	6	16	0	10	144	14,861	33.25
Melvin village	148	34	18	3	0	0	0	56	27,500	2.05
Melvindale city	11,216	2,424	1,581	89	324	627	114	4,670	26,179	12.12
Memphis city	1,221	353	162	10	9	23	2	448	29,479	9.15

25

Table I-5. Selected Age, Ethnic, and Economic Characteristics of Michigan's Population, by City and Village: As of the 1990 Census Continued

City/Village	Total Population	Age of Population			Ethnic Heritage			Number of Households	Median Household Income($)	Poverty Rate(%)
		Under 17 Years	65 & Older	85 & Older	Black	Hispanic	Native American			
Mendon village	920	277	98	9	17	7	3	333	$25,682	12.28
Menominee city	9,398	2,228	1,773	165	4	29	70	4,018	20,829	10.72
Merrill village	755	202	118	13	0	42	6	275	26,518	15.88
Mesick village	406	131	46	5	0	7	3	153	13,462	26.74
Metamora village	447	126	28	1	0	0	2	153	29,792	7.33
Michiana village	164	12	54	10	5	4	0	82	33,438	4.88
Michigan Center CDP	4,863	1,115	713	48	7	47	29	1,894	27,078	9.18
Middletown CDP	1,010	244	122	9	0	20	3	378	25,174	17.47
Middleville village	1,966	629	182	17	7	22	13	683	30,346	6.96
Midland city	38,053	9,047	4,524	520	654	638	135	14,812	38,747	9.49
Milan city	4,040	1,019	463	45	49	92	16	1,543	32,580	5.57
Milford village	5,511	1,526	572	74	9	70	18	1,999	37,323	6.37
Millersburg village	250	73	44	5	0	0	0	88	14,632	21.16
Millington village	1,114	298	169	20	2	16	7	425	22,772	15.75
Minden City village	233	68	46	0	0	0	0	84	18,750	7.26
Mineral Hills village	200	53	27	1	0	0	7	84	18,036	19.42
Mio CDP	1,886	480	356	35	1	12	12	765	14,917	28.25
Monroe city	22,902	6,053	3,412	445	1,057	415	92	8,430	29,088	15.39
Montague city	2,276	607	291	20	1	45	13	884	28,170	9.06
Montgomery village	388	109	58	5	0	0	0	132	21,042	12.78
Montrose city	1,811	506	202	10	1	21	15	675	25,250	13.63
Morenci city	2,342	660	341	45	3	77	2	867	24,954	15.54
Morley village	528	142	75	7	3	2	8	203	18,657	22.20
Morrice village	630	175	56	6	0	6	10	221	28,977	10.02
Mount Clemens city	18,405	3,873	2,648	261	3,274	334	125	7,287	25,716	11.85
Mount Morris city	3,292	885	379	32	59	53	44	1,331	21,755	18.41
Mount Pleasant city	23,285	2,955	1,657	245	539	376	216	6,661	19,185	38.74
Muir village	667	182	76	6	0	5	0	248	30,329	13.15

Table I-5. Selected Age, Ethnic, and Economic Characteristics of Michigan's Population, by City and Village: As of the 1990 Census Continued

City/Village	Total Population	Age of Population			Ethnic Heritage			Number of Households	Median Household Income($)	Poverty Rate(%)
		Under 17 Years	65 & Older	85 & Older	Black	Hispanic	Native American			
Mulliken village	590	199	45	4	0	22	6	187	$31,429	6.53
Munising city	2,783	622	635	104	2	4	95	1,121	21,010	13.05
Muskegon city	40,283	10,182	5,905	764	10,916	1,416	389	14,770	18,748	26.51
Muskegon Heights city	13,176	4,193	1,719	139	9,215	342	75	4,920	13,778	35.13
Napoleon CDP	1,332	339	174	16	0	13	4	496	19,485	14.89
Nashville village	1,654	468	196	24	0	19	11	610	20,956	21.82
Negaunee city	4,741	1,107	898	70	1	16	48	1,931	23,345	13.61
Newaygo city	1,336	427	179	27	0	49	7	475	21,393	18.86
New Baltimore city	5,798	1,323	680	51	27	48	21	2,261	35,219	7.99
Newberry village	1,873	501	353	47	0	10	127	732	19,542	23.54
New Buffalo city	2,317	533	351	23	18	27	14	950	30,065	8.03
New Era village	520	163	67	9	0	1	4	175	30,341	4.26
New Haven village	2,331	758	141	5	670	51	31	772	26,087	17.46
New Lothrop village	596	171	52	3	0	11	9	205	32,639	5.00
Niles city	12,458	3,045	2,166	310	1,542	285	64	5,178	23,700	13.67
North Adams village	512	120	77	13	0	8	0	195	22,969	10.10
North Branch village	1,023	293	122	9	0	23	0	381	20,833	14.99
North Muskegon city	3,919	841	880	142	19	32	14	1,552	37,281	3.77
Northport village	605	106	191	41	0	17	4	248	22,031	6.29
Northview CDP	13,712	3,687	1,120	86	208	189	19	5,024	37,454	4.11
Northville city	6,226	1,354	751	84	9	48	15	2,481	49,282	2.97
Norton Shores city	21,755	5,102	3,217	168	298	375	145	8,306	33,646	7.23
Norway city	2,910	659	631	56	1	3	11	1,221	21,875	9.95
Novi city	32,998	8,015	2,630	282	259	372	104	12,699	47,518	3.26
Oakley village	362	106	45	2	0	16	0	135	17,656	20.21
Oak Park city	30,462	8,174	3,894	304	10,449	444	33	10,885	36,090	10.85
Okemos CDP	20,216	5,090	1,561	235	786	352	74	7,472	47,799	9.91
Olivet city	1,604	339	107	7	68	26	10	445	23,646	16.46

Table I-5. Selected Age, Ethnic, and Economic Characteristics of Michigan's Population, by City and Village: As of the 1990 Census Continued

City/Village	Total Population	Age of Population			Ethnic Heritage			Number of Households	Median Household Income($)	Poverty Rate(%)
		Under 17 Years	65 & Older	85 & Older	Black	Hispanic	Native American			
Omer city	385	84	68	5	0	1	1	137	$20,694	25.59
Onaway city	1,039	258	236	30	2	6	6	472	11,958	32.10
Onekama village	515	100	118	11	0	14	5	222	18,438	15.37
Onsted village	801	241	88	3	3	23	2	287	25,469	12.36
Ontonagon village	2,040	434	485	69	0	5	13	845	21,048	11.85
Orchard Lake Village city	2,286	529	156	13	56	23	2	696	106,234	3.87
Ortonville village	1,252	352	133	8	0	17	5	452	33,229	7.07
Oscoda CDP	1,061	211	163	13	16	23	7	476	23,937	12.96
Ossineke CDP	1,091	309	130	8	2	3	0	415	21,437	12.95
Otisville village	724	191	89	3	0	5	7	277	23,214	17.82
Otsego city	3,937	1,129	480	46	14	36	18	1,500	26,184	9.49
Otter Lake village	474	134	40	1	0	0	0	157	26,544	15.46
Ovid village	1,442	353	231	54	0	56	1	530	25,302	13.02
Owendale village	285	79	33	1	0	4	2	112	14,792	34.67
Owosso city	16,322	4,302	2,282	234	23	392	109	6,477	23,220	15.71
Oxford village	2,929	700	317	39	8	41	9	1,151	37,639	5.08
Parchment city	1,958	435	286	25	87	29	12	827	30,742	6.00
Parma village	809	246	75	8	0	4	0	291	27,917	12.97
Paw village	3,169	725	559	76	66	63	22	1,313	19,298	14.26
Paw Lake CDP	3,782	892	556	26	8	50	11	1,494	29,148	9.90
Pearl Beach CDP	3,394	639	540	39	1	31	24	1,341	48,646	8.10
Peck village	558	136	98	7	2	9	7	214	20,833	18.97
Pellston village	583	150	72	4	2	9	27	212	18,393	18.94
Pentwater village	1,050	208	281	32	1	10	7	461	23,636	9.86
Perrinton village	393	99	44	9	1	12	0	153	26,023	18.77
Perry city	2,163	685	172	15	1	23	15	725	30,750	12.07
Petersburg city	1,201	360	124	11	0	13	7	422	31,029	9.94
Petoskey city	6,056	1,364	1,154	192	22	32	159	2,585	26,055	6.82

28

Table I-5. Selected Age, Ethnic, and Economic Characteristics of Michigan's Population, by City and Village: As of the 1990 Census Continued

City/Village	Total Population	Age of Population			Ethnic Heritage			Number of Households	Median Household Income($)	Poverty Rate(%)
		Under 17 Years	65 & Older	85 & Older	Black	Hispanic	Native American			
Pewamo village	520	144	87	12	0	1	0	188	$30,000	7.90
Pierson village	207	69	15	3	0	0	1	68	23,125	12.29
Pigeon village	1,207	298	255	46	3	41	1	482	21,523	13.97
Pinckney village	1,603	513	128	10	0	16	7	518	37,813	6.93
Pinconning city	1,291	329	217	19	0	52	19	542	18,269	22.96
Plainwell city	4,057	1,028	641	118	5	31	26	1,488	27,330	9.40
Pleasant Ridge city	2,775	621	328	34	22	35	2	1,064	54,658	4.14
Plymouth city	9,560	1,755	1,566	268	29	105	35	4,267	38,326	4.57
Plymouth Township CDP	23,646	5,077	2,335	146	286	271	58	8,813	53,806	1.44
Pontiac city	71,166	20,514	6,190	627	30,033	5,701	592	24,777	21,962	26.67
Portage city	41,042	10,471	3,484	240	1,139	593	147	15,467	39,045	4.21
Port Austin village	815	164	192	17	1	0	4	361	17,266	17.30
Port Hope village	313	58	79	8	0	1	2	133	20,000	21.14
Port Huron city	33,694	9,072	4,692	587	2,296	1,175	285	13,158	21,522	22.12
Portland city	3,889	1,052	471	53	1	43	20	1,448	28,304	9.96
Port Sanilac village	656	137	174	12	3	8	4	290	23,661	10.85
Posen village	263	60	68	8	0	0	1	110	19,432	21.86
Potterville city	1,523	451	91	6	7	29	17	580	27,469	11.46
Powers village	271	46	71	12	0	1	2	134	12,159	9.70
Prescott village	314	84	40	6	0	2	0	119	10,987	35.48
Prudenville CDP	1,513	279	416	24	0	4	5	685	16,039	19.25
Quincy village	1,680	524	171	18	3	8	7	637	22,542	17.40
Quinnesec CDP	1,254	416	102	9	1	6	3	403	29,300	7.98
Ravenna village	919	243	133	4	0	16	2	337	27,721	6.35
Reading city	1,127	362	126	14	2	23	10	400	20,500	17.23
Redford CDP	54,387	12,648	8,972	975	379	829	194	20,123	37,162	4.10
Reed City	2,379	645	439	68	20	26	7	944	18,333	21.18
Reese village	1,414	342	170	11	0	17	1	564	31,250	5.25

29

Table I-5. Selected Age, Ethnic, and Economic Characteristics of Michigan's Population, by City and Village: As of the 1990 Census Continued

City/Village	Total Population	Age of Population			Ethnic Heritage				Number of Households	Median Household Income($)	Poverty Rate(%)
		Under 17 Years	65 & Older	85 & Older	Black	Hispanic	Native American				
Richland village	465	110	47	2	0	2	2		175	$40,833	1.72
Richmond city	4,141	1,058	570	117	0	34	12		1,540	34,437	4.19
River Rouge city	11,314	3,163	1,358	107	3,977	378	75		4,268	17,500	28.51
Riverview city	13,894	2,970	2,005	362	163	219	34		5,066	39,735	6.68
Robin Glen-Indiantown CDP	1,395	468	70	1	16	58	4		514	22,564	18.75
Rochester city	7,130	1,227	832	71	88	75	15		3,451	35,926	4.67
Rochester Hills city	61,766	15,445	5,347	670	844	875	131		22,353	54,996	2.60
Rockford city	3,750	1,163	410	32	6	52	14		1,378	31,487	6.30
Rockwood city	3,141	810	269	24	2	41	20		1,095	37,609	8.59
Rogers City	3,642	855	750	77	2	8	8		1,490	21,430	13.06
Romeo village	3,520	926	484	58	215	47	13		1,320	30,337	13.67
Romulus city	22,897	6,426	1,660	92	4,999	434	150		7,844	31,723	12.94
Roosevelt Park city	3,885	754	944	116	67	29	7		1,691	28,955	2.73
Roscommon village	858	224	194	15	2	1	17		361	16,053	21.81
Rosebush village	333	88	46	7	2	6	9		128	23,295	14.14
Rose City	686	177	192	43	1	1	3		216	12,283	32.44
Roseville city	51,412	11,658	7,028	536	513	627	234		19,537	32,337	6.19
Rothbury village	407	114	33	0	1	18	7		144	23,875	12.22
Royal Oak city	65,410	12,880	10,280	979	332	695	163		28,344	36,835	4.56
Saginaw city	69,512	20,989	8,306	858	28,046	7,304	371		26,179	17,736	31.72
Saginaw Township North CDP	23,018	4,976	3,517	405	763	733	38		9,198	35,625	5.97
Saginaw Township South CDP	13,987	2,980	2,404	180	293	528	37		5,862	37,012	5.13
St. Charles village	2,144	549	294	12	2	73	20		818	22,321	18.94
St. Clair city	5,116	1,247	802	87	5	38	11		2,015	32,676	5.89
St. Clair Shores city	68,107	12,640	12,638	1,139	141	646	228		27,218	36,929	3.64
St. Helen CDP	2,390	449	644	38	3	16	24		1,069	12,778	31.24
St. Ignace city	2,568	658	449	66	4	4	545		1,020	20,024	13.54
St. Johns city	7,284	2,022	888	95	9	221	16		2,777	27,451	9.49

Table I-5. Selected Age, Ethnic, and Economic Characteristics of Michigan's Population, by City and Village: As of the 1990 Census Continued

City/Village	Total Population	Age of Population			Ethnic Heritage			Number of Households	Median Household Income($)	Poverty Rate(%)
		Under 17 Years	65 & Older	85 & Older	Black	Hispanic	Native American			
St. Joseph city	9,214	1,544	1,985	292	283	113	20	4,200	$28,566	7.25
St. Louis city	3,828	937	757	123	20	201	10	1,449	19,552	21.06
Saline city	6,660	1,637	716	184	33	67	25	2,495	43,706	3.09
Sand Lake village	456	119	74	14	0	0	3	180	21,154	7.87
Sandusky city	2,403	587	469	77	9	76	4	958	22,171	14.50
Sanford village	889	212	88	1	0	15	6	350	29,375	10.12
Saranac village	1,461	411	235	27	5	15	6	587	21,685	15.52
Saugatuck city	954	136	200	20	3	14	2	499	23,792	10.91
Sault Ste. Marie city	14,689	3,372	2,187	271	70	81	2,112	5,623	21,166	18.94
Schoolcraft village	1,517	414	177	15	5	10	9	574	31,687	6.40
Scottville city	1,287	338	262	34	11	30	6	547	18,869	18.88
Sebewaing village	1,923	428	375	34	0	52	4	801	23,786	11.15
Shelby CDP	48,655	11,440	3,601	193	141	465	149	16,836	47,930	2.81
Shelby village	1,871	559	278	25	7	284	16	662	18,333	24.15
Shepherd village	1,413	412	184	28	2	27	10	531	25,625	15.78
Sheridan village	730	204	100	3	3	9	6	261	23,375	8.39
Sherwood village	320	100	29	1	0	0	4	111	27,500	18.24
Shields CDP	6,634	1,627	679	95	36	170	16	2,295	39,221	4.41
Shoreham village	737	130	161	13	5	5	1	337	37,083	6.52
Shorewood-Tower Hills-Harbert CDP	1,636	333	401	32	5	13	1	686	29,679	1.90
Skidway Lake CDP	2,569	650	548	20	1	20	31	1,060	13,479	34.96
Southfield city	75,728	14,324	12,850	1,632	22,053	1,300	183	32,112	40,579	5.83
Southgate city	30,771	6,355	4,139	274	362	856	153	12,128	36,526	4.62
South Gull Lake CDP	1,453	298	225	20	3	6	3	597	46,908	5.98
South Haven city	5,563	1,429	1,024	194	841	55	44	2,186	25,967	16.88
South Lyon city	5,857	1,333	1,067	113	3	31	11	2,338	33,095	6.54
South Monroe CDP	5,266	1,373	850	126	80	87	20	2,033	27,851	15.14
South Range village	745	134	201	13	0	3	2	349	16,190	11.61

31

Table I-5. Selected Age, Ethnic, and Economic Characteristics of Michigan's Population, by City and Village: As of the 1990 Census Continued

City/Village	Total Population	Age of Population			Ethnic Heritage			Number of Households	Median Household Income($)	Poverty Rate(%)
		Under 17 Years	65 & Older	85 & Older	Black	Hispanic	Native American			
South Rockwood village	1,221	330	108	4	0	4	0	409	$40,812	3.69
Spartlingville CDP	1,974	590	154	6	2	32	23	671	28,299	9.58
Sparta village	3,968	1,162	480	60	2	68	17	1,487	28,283	7.79
Spring Arbor CDP	2,010	361	436	125	17	16	6	630	23,806	12.13
Springfield city	5,582	1,293	687	110	329	95	48	2,268	25,470	14.53
Spring Lake village	2,537	517	485	36	3	10	8	1,082	29,811	5.47
Springport village	707	210	70	9	1	8	1	255	24,821	14.69
Stambaugh city	1,281	278	364	31	0	8	13	587	14,025	20.22
Standish city	1,377	381	244	25	1	23	17	583	16,148	27.48
Stanton city	1,504	425	215	17	4	38	12	555	18,370	25.40
Stanwood village	174	53	19	2	4	0	0	61	25,250	9.78
Stephenson city	904	179	321	65	1	1	0	369	15,757	16.33
Sterling village	520	103	178	54	0	3	2	172	21,875	12.78
Sterling Heights city	117,810	28,638	10,872	856	475	1,314	274	40,835	46,470	3.55
Stevensville village	1,230	245	245	18	3	7	3	541	26,207	3.91
Stockbridge village	1,202	337	168	17	0	14	10	449	29,808	10.85
Stony Point CDP	1,598	476	106	4	11	35	18	518	34,926	11.25
Sturgis city	10,130	2,729	1,686	254	76	135	29	3,962	23,642	11.86
Sunfield village	610	215	54	5	0	15	1	196	24,427	13.39
Suttons Bay village	561	115	90	13	2	2	2	234	29,688	5.54
Swartz Creek city	4,851	1,098	601	39	48	91	50	1,914	38,180	7.61
Sylvan Lake city	1,884	340	290	27	11	16	5	829	44,464	3.11
Tawas City	2,009	453	451	87	13	14	8	749	23,113	10.87
Taylor city	70,811	18,603	5,632	441	2,980	1,991	404	24,861	32,659	11.92
Tecumseh city	7,462	1,938	1,025	112	11	310	30	2,903	33,545	5.75
Tekonsha village	722	195	72	7	0	1	7	273	25,588	9.90
Temperance CDP	6,542	1,712	691	55	22	76	8	2,277	41,213	4.46
Thompsonville village	416	119	58	4	1	12	2	155	14,531	27.11

Table I-5. Selected Age, Ethnic, and Economic Characteristics of Michigan's Population, by City and Village: As of the 1990 Census Continued

City/Village	Total Population	Age of Population			Ethnic Heritage				Number of Households	Median Household Income($)	Poverty Rate(%)
		Under 17 Years	65 & Older	85 & Older	Black	Hispanic	Native American				
Three Oaks village	1,786	492	244	20	0	9	3		689	$22,813	12.56
Three Rivers city	7,413	2,073	1,101	155	807	81	21		2,927	21,477	21.12
Traverse City	15,155	3,024	2,547	361	35	105	139		6,202	27,396	8.67
Trenton city	20,586	4,354	2,958	274	32	283	67		7,855	41,129	4.21
Trowbridge Park CDP	1,831	529	149	6	0	11	56		618	29,549	11.42
Troy city	72,884	18,239	6,134	526	983	927	110		26,167	55,407	2.83
Turner village	158	52	16	4	0	0	2		54	12,125	38.46
Tustin village	236	73	32	1	0	0	0		79	18,750	26.52
Twining village	169	42	32	4	0	6	0		70	15,278	26.88
Twin Lake CDP	1,328	369	145	7	0	15	15		467	30,192	11.76
Ubly village	821	167	166	13	0	0	1		355	24,954	8.28
Union City village	1,767	487	215	15	0	14	24		678	21,750	18.13
Unionville village	590	169	100	9	0	49	0		221	22,292	16.32
Utica city	5,081	1,273	497	44	20	75	28		1,888	33,214	6.77
Vandalia village	357	132	53	7	283	18	1		120	11,196	50.44
Vanderbilt village	605	183	62	6	2	0	7		226	20,333	16.38
Vandercook Lake CDP	4,642	1,132	612	31	36	66	26		1,724	28,539	8.47
Vassar city	2,559	725	341	31	107	48	6		960	21,974	18.44
Vermontville village	776	229	74	11	2	12	4		271	25,855	18.37
Vernon village	913	254	73	6	2	7	6		303	38,021	8.12
Vicksburg village	2,216	627	312	30	2	37	4		854	26,919	12.96
Wakefield city	2,318	502	630	93	1	1	20		920	16,393	15.94
Waldron village	581	177	73	7	0	10	1		224	20,887	18.47
Walker city	17,279	4,144	1,915	229	182	260	76		6,669	32,827	4.27
Walkerville village	262	93	25	2	0	7	18		87	18,750	32.53
Walled Lake city	6,278	1,312	715	51	7	25	34		2,794	35,433	8.37
Warren city	144,864	28,594	21,555	1,677	1,047	1,583	657		54,602	35,980	6.50
Waterford CDP	66,692	15,048	6,493	524	701	1,538	390		25,476	39,463	5.33

Table I-5. Selected Age, Ethnic, and Economic Characteristics of Michigan's Population, by City and Village: As of the 1990 Census Continued

City/Village	Total Population	Age of Population			Ethnic Heritage			Number of Households	Median Household Income($)	Poverty Rate(%)
		Under 17 Years	65 & Older	85 & Older	Black	Hispanic	Native American			
Watervliet city	1,867	496	258	19	6	12	15	703	$23,750	13.16
Waverly CDP	15,614	3,639	1,636	147	1,066	448	49	6,248	39,876	3.94
Wayland city	2,751	745	442	104	6	31	24	1,006	30,448	8.32
Wayne city	19,899	5,074	2,423	270	1,494	433	146	7,138	31,250	9.58
Webberville village	1,698	526	121	13	0	23	3	579	33,164	9.49
Weidman CDP	696	194	67	2	0	2	21	253	21,905	21.74
West Bloomfield Township CDP	54,843	12,902	5,390	522	1,077	668	64	19,337	68,661	1.80
West Branch city	1,914	462	410	78	0	16	11	763	16,150	21.23
Westland city	84,724	18,866	9,122	967	2,829	1,594	466	33,110	34,995	7.11
West Monroe CDP	3,919	1,089	342	21	9	69	15	1,475	27,527	11.38
Westphalia village	780	180	118	15	0	4	0	290	36,413	2.05
Westwood CDP	8,957	1,411	1,429	106	567	77	11	3,932	31,487	13.86
White Cloud city	1,147	301	180	15	40	21	26	420	19,583	19.55
Whitehall city	3,027	707	566	96	17	58	31	1,173	26,359	8.35
White Pigeon village	1,458	406	158	11	1	15	4	536	27,455	9.77
Whitmore Lake CDP	3,251	696	240	15	11	30	12	1,318	39,128	4.28
Whittemore city	463	122	96	8	0	5	1	199	10,750	34.13
Williamston city	2,922	780	344	41	12	69	15	1,212	28,581	7.84
Wixom city	8,550	1,693	521	47	27	103	36	4,114	31,755	3.53
Wolf Lake CDP	4,110	1,102	453	21	30	119	61	1,466	27,632	10.56
Wolverine village	283	90	52	4	0	0	1	105	17,125	24.08
Wolverine Lake village	4,727	1,189	288	17	4	31	10	1,658	42,167	4.84
Woodhaven city	11,631	3,138	641	88	76	303	45	3,963	47,513	3.61
Woodland village	466	151	47	4	0	4	0	152	32,727	5.25
Woodland Beach CDP	2,309	680	181	9	7	27	6	774	32,937	5.99
Wurtsmith AFB CDP	5,080	1,835	3	1	425	173	34	1,298	20,328	8.53
Wyandotte city	30,938	7,120	5,010	341	73	653	184	12,319	28,312	9.73
Wyoming city	63,891	17,006	6,221	444	1,736	2,234	349	24,168	31,103	7.07

Table I-5. Selected Age, Ethnic, and Economic Characteristics of Michigan's Population, by City and Village: As of the 1990 Census Continued

City/Village	Total Population	Age of Population			Ethnic Heritage				Number of Households	Median Household Income($)	Poverty Rate(%)
		Under 17 Years	65 & Older	85 & Older	Black	Hispanic	Native American				
Yale city	1,977	544	416	67	1	18	1		742	$20,767	14.46
Ypsilanti city	24,846	3,867	1,707	181	6,243	476	117		8,551	21,219	29.47
Zeeland city	5,417	1,499	995	175	23	174	8		1,968	32,861	6.68
Zilwaukee city	1,850	390	245	19	4	68	1		682	31,343	8.89
Michigan	**9,295,297**	**2,322,814**	**1,108,461**	**106,907**	**1,291,706**	**201,596**	**55,131**		**3,424,122**	**31,020**	**13.10**

Note: CDP refers to Census Designated Places. CDPs are statistical counterparts of incorporated places but are not legally incorporated places. Their boundaries, which usually coincide with visible features or the boundary of an adjacent incorporated place, have no legal status or officials elected to serve traditional municipal functions.
Source: U.S. Bureau of the Census - Michigan Information Center (Lansing, Michigan).

Table I-6. Residence in 1985 of Michigan's Population 5 Years Old and Older, by County: 1990

County	Persons 5 Years and Older	Lived in a Different House in 1985:				
		Total Different	Percent(%) Different	Same County	Different County	Different State
Alcona	9,630	4,035	41.9	1,522	2,414	629
Alger	8,423	3,347	39.7	1,584	1,730	615
Allegan	83,073	34,082	41.0	16,573	17,201	3,930
Alpena	28,600	10,490	36.7	6,196	4,214	1,535
Antrim	16,931	7,206	42.6	2,973	4,177	992
Arenac	13,931	5,021	36.0	2,406	2,560	415
Baraga	7,421	2,700	36.4	1,569	1,093	398
Barry	46,363	18,263	39.4	7,676	10,521	2,083
Bay	103,806	34,108	32.9	22,361	11,443	2,974
Benzie	11,352	4,753	41.9	1,991	2,750	707
Berrien	149,502	65,912	44.1	42,468	21,935	15,096
Branch	38,298	16,136	42.1	9,187	6,862	2,711
Calhoun	125,982	54,879	43.6	34,693	19,381	8,321
Cass	46,036	17,633	38.3	8,498	8,996	5,083
Charlevoix	19,848	8,944	45.1	4,700	4,200	1,121
Cheboygan	19,954	7,938	39.8	3,859	3,915	1,001
Chippewa	32,536	17,020	52.3	6,884	9,753	2,448
Clare	23,132	10,408	45.0	4,657	5,723	1,101
Clinton	53,558	20,037	37.4	8,559	11,386	1,959
Crawford	11,350	5,347	47.1	1,876	3,461	739
Delta	35,267	12,270	34.8	8,484	3,705	1,784
Dickinson	25,010	9,800	39.2	5,961	3,805	2,532
Eaton	86,257	38,739	44.9	15,422	23,028	4,705
Emmet	23,151	10,244	44.2	5,279	4,926	1,369
Genesee	397,363	163,698	41.2	122,992	39,293	16,813
Gladwin	20,329	8,274	40.7	3,600	4,631	710
Gogebic	17,026	5,521	32.4	3,167	2,329	1,504
Grand Traverse	59,416	30,550	51.4	15,627	14,682	4,587
Gratiot	36,280	13,994	38.6	7,627	6,295	1,439
Hillsdale	40,097	16,808	41.9	8,951	7,800	3,106
Houghton	33,324	14,294	42.9	5,440	8,323	2,836
Huron	32,512	10,018	30.8	6,364	3,610	866
Ingham	261,303	146,846	56.2	72,300	68,950	19,244
Ionia	52,576	22,031	41.9	10,819	11,040	1,952
Iosco	27,660	14,963	54.1	5,525	8,525	4,231
Iron	12,466	4,078	32.7	2,364	1,702	1,054
Isabella	51,126	28,557	55.9	9,145	19,018	2,772
Jackson	138,690	60,818	43.9	35,926	24,286	8,062
Kalamazoo	207,118	106,960	51.6	60,522	43,999	14,512
Kalkaska	12,463	5,947	47.7	2,397	3,516	697
Kent	457,039	218,454	47.8	144,949	69,364	27,072
Keweenaw	1,617	396	24.5	137	256	93

Table I-6. Residence in 1985 of Michigan's Population 5 Years Old and Older, by County: 1990 Continued

County	Persons 5 Years and Older	Lived in a Different House in 1985:				
		Total Different	Percent(%) Different	Same County	Different County	Different State
Lake	8,006	3,674	45.9	1,109	2,557	673
Lapeer	69,298	28,520	41.2	1,311	15,185	2,398
Leelanau	15,280	6,727	44.0	2,511	4,145	896
Lenawee	84,798	36,284	42.8	21,676	14,257	5,481
Livingston	106,957	50,107	46.8	17,940	31,743	6,212
Luce	5,387	2,217	41.2	1,271	903	307
Mackinac	9,944	3,892	39.1	1,866	1,993	597
Macomb	668,523	264,808	39.6	159,983	100,540	22,636
Manistee	19,948	6,810	34.1	3,588	3,139	827
Marquette	65,846	30,102	45.7	13,979	14,731	7,671
Mason	23,752	9,673	40.7	5,714	3,889	1,418
Mecosta	35,029	18,656	53.3	5,024	13,231	1,845
Menominee	23,341	7,927	34.0	5,317	2,557	1,818
Midland	69,980	30,480	43.6	14,896	14,976	6,343
Missaukee	11,210	4,283	38.2	2,010	2,238	306
Monroe	123,400	46,743	37.9	27,706	18,512	10,100
Montcalm	48,949	21,172	43.3	11,238	9,799	1,802
Montmorency	8,416	3,220	38.3	1,060	2,153	338
Muskegon	146,192	61,179	41.8	43,051	17,719	7,236
Newaygo	34,998	14,611	41.7	7,275	7,181	1,537
Oakland	1,005,695	470,004	46.7	259,850	196,177	65,958
Oceana	20,687	8,672	41.9	4,694	3,889	1,266
Ogemaw	17,422	7,476	42.9	3,190	4,245	620
Ontonagon	8,318	2,615	31.4	1,386	1,195	601
Osceola	18,621	7,415	39.8	3,230	4,134	767
Oscoda	7,308	3,344	45.8	1,203	2,116	288
Otsego	16,570	8,134	49.1	3,988	4,096	911
Ottawa	171,792	79,413	46.2	39,368	38,862	9,878
Presque Isle	12,889	4,008	31.1	2,025	1,935	362
Roscommon	18,706	8,502	45.5	2,917	5,565	942
Saginaw	195,660	72,200	36.9	50,512	20,660	7,948
St.Claire	134,538	55,613	41.3	32,214	22,839	4,934
St. Joseph	54,282	22,141	40.8	13,182	8,813	4,556
Sanilac	36,967	13,615	36.8	7,094	6,332	1,335
Schoolcraft	7,808	2,615	33.5	1,492	1,112	429
Shiawassee	64,627	23,713	36.7	13,634	9,812	2,580
Tuscola	51,526	17,789	34.5	9,875	7,753	1,553
Van Buren	64,695	26,397	40.8	13,310	12,895	4,761
Washtenaw	263,994	153,228	58.0	64,000	81,177	33,468
Wayne	1,941,269	764,161	39.4	598,488	148,302	72,800
Wexford	24,293	10,563	43.5	5,129	5,324	1,277
Michigan	**8,594,737**	**3,704,222**	**43.1**	**2,234,436**	**1,395,479**	**473,473**

Source: U.S. Bureau of the Census, Michigan Information Center; census tape STF-3 (Lansing, Michigan).

Table I-7. Reported Ancestry in Michigan, by County: 1990

ANCESTRY	Alcona	Alger	Allegan	Alpena	Antrim	Arenac	Baraga	Barry	Bay	Benzie
Ancestry Reported	**12,663**	**11,508**	**115,898**	**39,422**	**22,627**	**18,976**	**10,371**	**63,909**	**158,292**	**16,486**
Arab	19	12	60	76	14	5	5	79	171	7
Belgian	43	113	153	61	44	26	18	215	1,040	52
Canadian	79	24	182	45	94	39	2	159	381	62
Czech	61	48	559	49	256	61	29	184	344	149
Danish	47	26	651	87	118	37	17	254	264	102
Dutch	395	228	25,713	524	1,460	363	126	6,606	4,405	754
English	2,160	1,162	14,255	4,586	3,873	2,055	653	11,999	14,340	2,827
Finnish	47	1,478	175	162	121	70	2,752	326	296	110
French (ex Basque)	1,578	1,654	4,660	5,406	1,498	3,160	1,583	3,158	20,843	1,164
French Canadian	176	301	1,109	855	339	259	96	913	4,876	240
German/Austrian	3,112	1,949	27,061	11,035	5,552	4,972	1,427	17,618	45,369	4,126
Greek	6	14	193	39	22	20	5	126	130	16
Hungarian	130	30	480	144	78	224	24	126	1,337	85
Irish	1,368	1,006	13,521	3,424	2,740	2,018	558	7,822	15,849	2,068
Italian	214	219	1,777	428	308	281	117	957	1,933	239
Lithuanian	28	41	337	47	48	36	6	149	233	42
Norwegian	179	157	604	804	202	68	409	405	538	527
Polish	842	735	4,525	6,797	1,080	2,217	244	1,840	25,993	731
Russian	68	15	163	142	79	101	8	136	517	47
Scotch-Irish	311	120	1,306	548	439	215	72	903	1,738	295
Scottish	473	209	1,958	897	706	476	88	1,308	2,939	555
Slovak	29	37	464	103	126	171	14	230	609	61
Swedish	166	679	2,036	458	489	145	592	1,164	1,578	433
Ukrainian	11	17	118	41	21	88	25	52	346	16
United States or American	229	371	3,817	1,307	1,536	633	148	2,800	2,033	455
Welsh	83	27	504	91	75	51	12	333	522	125
Other Ancestry	669	836	9,517	1,266	1,309	1,182	1,341	4,047	9,668	1,198

Table I-7. Reported Ancestry in Michigan, by County: 1990 Continued

ANCESTRY	Berrien	Branch	Calhoun	Cass	Charlevoix	Cheboygan	Chippewa	Clare	Clinton	Crawford
Ancestry Reported	201,358	50,739	167,317	62,839	27,164	26,580	44,637	28,630	76,363	15,861
Arab	291	57	169	102	34	12	137	27	194	28
Belgian	368	78	365	289	80	85	86	132	206	76
Canadian	429	117	539	56	93	103	241	212	215	78
Czech	1,675	87	323	196	491	101	118	125	985	81
Danish	977	113	713	244	155	39	175	114	425	253
Dutch	7,875	2,874	8,830	3,705	1,349	770	1,448	1,330	3,324	544
English	20,041	7,277	27,455	7,663	4,418	3,617	6,276	5,051	13,135	2,330
Finnish	543	113	432	137	183	161	1,485	109	350	146
French (ex Basque)	6,739	2,138	6,788	2,057	2,071	4,429	4,175	2,321	3,428	1,326
French Canadian	1,301	444	1,770	440	425	352	713	478	923	237
German/Austrian	63,160	16,883	43,168	18,743	6,456	6,437	7,296	7,375	27,987	3,872
Greek	519	59	459	65	19	63	127	56	141	9
Hungarian	1,527	198	605	677	120	137	150	193	474	109
Irish	23,888	6,900	21,292	8,462	3,401	2,936	5,130	3,662	8,631	1,643
Italian	5,539	1,051	3,312	1,118	319	313	1,432	408	1,290	264
Lithuanian	836	96	289	152	40	43	53	47	111	31
Norwegian	1,466	147	1,009	245	304	191	395	105	405	50
Polish	7,748	2,948	4,683	3,086	1,672	2,134	2,100	1,153	2,360	785
Russian	1,141	81	517	116	75	45	78	48	284	79
Scotch-Irish	2,635	549	2,438	894	426	367	1,423	385	998	273
Scottish	3,077	844	3,476	970	890	698	1,779	733	1,575	460
Slovak	905	123	629	253	70	80	241	87	1,173	45
Swedish	4,158	478	2,154	1,274	480	788	1,195	312	1,021	282
Ukrainian	250	31	345	109	63	19	101	58	93	18
United States or American	6,096	2,568	7,258	2,797	1,939	932	1,340	1,842	2,049	1,372
Welsh	852	235	998	353	149	93	119	107	264	75
Other Ancestry	37,322	4,250	27,301	8,636	1,442	1,635	6,824	2,160	4,322	1,395

Table I-7. Reported Ancestry in Michigan, by County: 1990 Continued

ANCESTRY	Delta	Dickinson	Eaton	Emmet	Genesee	Gladwin	Gogebic	Grand Traverse	Gratiot	Hillsdale
Ancestry Reported	54,222	40,214	124,353	32,477	537,591	26,775	24,550	82,404	48,913	54,358
Arab	91	35	580	10	2,876	20	15	134	65	88
Belgian	1,865	900	409	112	1,015	47	104	226	129	98
Canadian	66	61	444	170	2,833	138	19	279	207	153
Czech	304	199	483	239	3,284	108	192	1,605	555	90
Danish	423	203	738	216	1,460	92	112	650	373	171
Dutch	909	640	6,002	1,292	13,659	883	179	3,703	2,247	2,511
English	3,366	3,498	21,974	4,776	67,755	4,103	1,542	12,050	7,590	8,497
Finnish	2,038	1,719	477	190	1,903	127	5,155	665	89	67
French (ex Basque)	11,213	4,549	5,951	2,450	31,822	2,367	1,178	5,905	2,654	2,490
French Canadian	2,572	1,118	1,696	471	12,168	411	260	1,373	853	455
German/Austrian	9,736	7,858	36,308	8,514	109,782	8,129	3,387	22,609	15,514	18,508
Greek	113	31	313	58	1,464	20	20	134	91	52
Hungarian	65	52	585	212	7,006	293	31	532	376	300
Irish	4,840	2,975	15,379	4,064	66,368	3,350	1,575	9,340	5,507	7,621
Italian	748	4,807	2,567	529	9,453	399	2,574	1,667	421	831
Lithuanian	97	12	108	78	600	43	29	137	39	45
Norwegian	1,301	907	972	278	2,969	77	552	1,138	221	191
Polish	2,174	2,299	4,244	2,470	24,488	1,445	1,925	5,022	1,591	1,475
Russian	94	77	381	123	1,918	91	19	272	112	53
Scotch-Irish	375	230	1,788	530	7,492	492	137	1,179	634	685
Scottish	586	448	2,732	924	12,611	676	109	2,621	1,479	1,171
Slovak	88	175	834	215	5,239	135	704	432	858	130
Swedish	6,618	4,911	2,399	776	6,126	253	2,134	2,298	631	464
Ukrainian	49	46	192	22	1,148	25	*	205	48	95
United States or American	649	658	4,035	1,194	22,622	1,122	876	3,187	2,215	3,413
Welsh	87	32	701	187	2,582	122	13	383	221	388
Other Ancestry	3,755	1,774	12,061	2,377	116,948	1,807	1,709	4,658	4,193	4,317

Table I-7. Reported Ancestry in Michigan, by County: 1990 Continued

ANCESTRY	Houghton	Huron	Ingham	Ionia	Iosco	Iron	Isabella	Jackson	Kalamazoo	Kalkaska
Ancestry Reported	**47,482**	**44,477**	**363,714**	**66,977**	**34,329**	**17,299**	**66,971**	**184,146**	**294,941**	**16,637**
Arab	79	63	2,462	21	34	16	200	198	828	35
Belgian	83	126	1,119	154	162	70	283	708	587	111
Canadian	78	185	1,279	145	155	9	237	816	530	73
Czech	230	170	1,621	165	130	174	452	328	1,413	60
Danish	133	58	1,956	840	130	175	373	552	1,670	65
Dutch	637	611	12,453	4,814	1,040	190	2,645	7,808	35,701	875
English	4,332	4,571	51,591	10,687	4,822	1,493	8,964	29,831	41,236	2,320
Finnish	13,199	91	2,325	280	216	2,091	318	675	853	130
French (ex Basque)	4,686	2,821	16,284	3,186	2,912	1,494	3,857	8,539	11,717	1,268
French Canadian	557	315	5,067	1,139	488	185	1,148	2,045	2,652	283
German/Austrian	7,612	18,510	90,655	21,578	9,667	2,828	20,036	50,643	69,241	3,937
Greek	71	36	1,587	45	75	5	176	376	897	18
Hungarian	159	383	2,029	181	279	74	454	897	2,309	83
Irish	2,537	3,800	42,972	9,446	4,072	1,040	8,644	26,159	35,966	1,987
Italian	2,237	465	8,681	811	639	1,927	1,569	2,831	6,305	299
Lithuanian	44	62	989	101	45	59	137	383	655	16
Norwegian	880	190	2,723	316	173	294	498	962	2,091	125
Polish	1,613	7,278	15,074	1,633	2,332	1,631	3,243	11,747	10,933	772
Russian	124	162	2,309	60	162	74	255	587	1,007	58
Scotch-Irish	433	608	5,187	1,009	559	125	951	2,643	4,539	261
Scottish	453	1,210	9,254	1,421	1,004	200	1,647	3,849	6,650	473
Slovak	274	59	2,214	148	245	98	380	572	1,489	36
Swedish	2,153	288	6,319	824	614	2,059	1,051	2,259	5,375	264
Ukrainian	16	77	958	13	100	2	156	260	578	15
United States or American	1,445	581	8,866	2,972	1,405	252	3,380	8,250	7,973	1,844
Welsh	107	114	2,527	329	145	46	283	987	1,630	107
Other Ancestry	3,310	1,643	65,213	4,659	2,724	668	5,634	19,241	40,116	1,122

Table 1-7. Reported Ancestry in Michigan, by County: 1990 Continued

ANCESTRY	Kent	Keweenaw	Lake	Lapeer	Leelanau	Lenawee	Livingston	Luce	Mackinac	Macomb
Ancestry Reported	**658,126**	**2,233**	**9,980**	**100,702**	**21,765**	**117,858**	**163,619**	**7,696**	**14,270**	**1,003,361**
Arab	1,969	*	8	202	15	179	577	4	12	12,627
Belgian	867	9	7	729	90	688	584	20	65	19,548
Canadian	850	14	31	581	49	362	1,144	54	44	4,887
Czech	2,097	*	70	343	694	725	671	25	51	3,515
Danish	5,027	2	53	246	137	217	919	18	113	2,021
Dutch	125,304	5	575	3,517	880	4,127	3,922	382	419	13,089
English	71,821	222	1,400	13,753	2,938	16,875	23,919	944	1,894	81,478
Finnish	2,274	848	7	349	90	417	2,279	416	294	5,200
French (ex Basque)	26,484	158	564	6,370	1,769	6,215	9,432	1,017	1,610	58,725
French Canadian	6,162	7	144	2,607	231	1,301	3,131	53	199	18,422
German/Austrian	141,241	225	2,336	28,283	5,763	39,227	42,803	1,682	3,075	235,443
Greek	1,457	2	2	205	39	195	498	5	11	7,091
Hungarian	2,510	11	70	1,091	94	1,076	2,121	32	51	8,502
Irish	72,019	83	1,137	12,791	2,253	15,824	22,108	870	1,473	112,000
Italian	13,770	159	159	2,630	300	2,092	5,733	104	245	102,119
Lithuanian	4,683	12	145	176	75	230	552	*	15	3,446
Norwegian	3,996	65	83	459	501	590	1,137	83	91	3,662
Polish	45,040	48	424	5,833	2,150	3,548	13,303	218	649	154,187
Russian	1,828	16	16	291	64	215	871	18	76	5,496
Scotch-Irish	7,131	8	184	2,050	353	1,514	2,856	149	343	12,739
Scottish	10,263	32	217	3,029	613	2,308	4,988	159	388	19,188
Slovak	1,965	23	7	745	87	595	1,476	34	46	12,742
Swedish	14,904	81	298	1,044	557	934	2,509	429	514	7,908
Ukrainian	1,175	*	9	322	20	174	865	10	20	7,912
United States or American	13,852	12	398	4,641	177	3,765	3,687	263	264	15,301
Welsh	2,512	*	38	527	142	911	1,233	27	27	3,935
Other Ancestry	76,925	191	1,598	7,888	1,684	13,554	10,301	680	2,281	72,218

Table I-7. Reported Ancestry in Michigan, by County: 1990 Continued

ANCESTRY	Manistee	Marquette	Mason	Mecosta	Menominee	Midland	Missaukee	Monroe	Montcalm	Montmorency
Ancestry Reported	28,071	96,985	34,207	47,491	35,385	102,551	15,361	182,157	62,315	11,827
Arab	2	94	10	87	4	210	14	258	78	9
Belgian	18	518	172	137	1,271	291	23	1,468	79	64
Canadian	99	133	89	168	25	418	39	498	118	65
Czech	318	482	269	291	863	637	67	1,065	310	51
Danish	368	408	1,259	443	397	569	107	186	3,898	29
Dutch	856	1,297	1,563	2,489	456	3,394	3,509	4,088	4,412	382
English	2,998	11,519	3,998	7,015	1,690	15,501	2,243	18,037	9,999	1,902
Finnish	585	15,663	126	288	539	564	196	390	193	106
French (ex Basque)	1,741	11,649	1,885	2,734	5,122	6,700	828	20,382	3,710	1,122
French Canadian	320	1,764	531	627	926	2,036	247	2,972	792	167
German/Austrian	7,624	15,469	9,310	13,268	11,065	31,595	3,661	58,701	17,725	3,334
Greek	42	311	104	85	43	272	14	359	70	8
Hungarian	148	306	67	178	340	791	32	2,846	244	64
Irish	2,639	7,481	3,814	5,734	2,490	12,166	1,502	23,565	8,253	1,176
Italian	280	5,443	468	953	513	1,896	107	6,892	621	197
Lithuanian	132	192	515	89	77	130	31	237	94	9
Norwegian	387	1,926	443	462	885	965	61	401	307	46
Polish	4,744	3,615	2,870	2,192	2,602	5,640	422	12,005	1,666	733
Russian	86	208	64	91	77	376	36	369	100	31
Scotch-Irish	277	752	484	557	209	1,481	222	1,907	894	210
Scottish	521	1,127	773	1,196	319	2,607	306	2,492	1,416	471
Slovak	146	516	121	209	144	1,077	19	1,409	124	24
Swedish	1,519	6,894	2,120	1,533	3,260	1,713	521	1,344	1,129	172
Ukrainian	33	116	43	48	35	274	12	528	18	8
United States or American	480	2,899	730	2,522	389	2,828	199	5,455	1,398	780
Welsh	130	314	213	226	71	671	95	782	231	44
Other Ancestry	1,578	5,889	2,166	3,869	1,573	7,749	848	13,521	4,436	623

Table I-7. Reported Ancestry in Michigan, by County: 1990 Continued

ANCESTRY	Muskegon	Newaygo	Oakland	Oceana	Ogemaw	Ontonagon	Osceola	Oscoda	Otsego	Ottawa
Ancestry Reported	**208,619**	**46,697**	**1,464,508**	**27,373**	**22,236**	**11,299**	**25,587**	**8,824**	**22,602**	**242,349**
Arab	200	19	15,495	26	12	8	9	12	72	318
Belgian	625	80	6,308	284	89	13	68	53	77	500
Canadian	268	78	10,064	43	111	5	86	18	111	463
Czech	1,041	185	6,566	227	102	57	58	37	65	954
Danish	2,030	424	6,041	265	91	34	126	26	117	1,378
Dutch	21,829	7,160	26,436	2,509	926	150	2,116	283	699	84,980
English	22,519	6,403	179,322	3,479	2,705	868	4,150	1,157	2,754	21,081
Finnish	1,121	184	13,452	100	50	3,282	135	24	239	704
French (ex Basque)	12,212	2,517	71,193	1,378	2,305	1,140	1,642	652	1,797	7,759
French Canadian	3,572	446	23,409	307	313	93	341	130	336	1,763
German/Austrian	47,344	10,644	306,280	7,136	6,172	1,825	7,468	2,669	5,924	49,532
Greek	650	96	7,335	34	24	20	29	14	31	255
Hungarian	1,495	124	16,438	114	216	4	82	80	192	1,232
Irish	21,629	4,784	177,573	2,797	2,540	656	3,083	863	2,795	18,951
Italian	3,312	606	62,707	325	386	205	258	134	371	3,754
Lithuanian	693	136	6,992	75	45	34	36	25	26	813
Norwegian	2,987	245	9,415	329	95	286	153	15	113	1,429
Polish	10,894	1,674	119,945	893	1,177	486	792	381	3,375	9,618
Russian	254	120	34,259	33	62	17	62	27	106	422
Scotch-Irish	2,411	610	24,141	511	346	80	403	161	348	2,027
Scottish	2,431	740	43,688	497	553	141	649	177	609	3,433
Slovak	1,642	125	11,209	42	61	42	40	24	62	1,237
Swedish	10,485	1,492	2,166	905	298	726	1,035	84	398	5,469
Ukrainian	463	65	8,140	18	27	9	45	20	67	295
United States or American	4,579	3,821	37,697	1,836	2,185	489	878	984	835	5,253
Welsh	609	153	9,224	110	92	27	146	55	104	903
Other Ancestry	31,324	3,766	211,013	3,100	1,253	602	1,697	719	979	17,826

Table I-7. Reported Ancestry in Michigan, by County: 1990 Continued

ANCESTRY	Presque Isle	Roscommon	Saginaw	St. Clair	St. Joseph	Sanilac	Schoolcraft	Shiawassee	Tuscola	Van Buren
Ancestry Reported	**17,022**	**23,613**	**273,298**	**199,318**	**0**	**0**	**11,885**	**91,102**	**75,536**	**90,283**
Arab	2	90	341	632	66	96	*	103	58	34
Belgian	32	66	656	3,102	84	312	72	142	378	120
Canadian	27	96	594	1,545	151	517	35	457	611	161
Czech	52	129	2,024	584	311	224	106	2,075	202	504
Danish	30	102	544	399	250	253	92	334	237	451
Dutch	304	895	4,122	3,476	4,776	1,107	369	3,395	1,782	7,286
English	1,749	3,778	23,900	24,859	9,308	8,050	1,200	15,251	10,323	11,752
Finnish	28	186	677	591	157	147	255	262	218	100
French (ex Basque)	1,304	2,053	18,718	15,455	2,887	2,624	1,871	5,244	5,786	3,297
French Canadian	163	453	4,846	4,831	621	588	329	1,569	1,774	876
German/Austrian	5,409	6,084	84,888	58,288	25,312	14,847	2,394	26,378	25,394	22,463
Greek	12	30	675	316	186	51	18	117	56	158
Hungarian	74	189	1,955	1,678	350	614	41	714	1,382	487
Irish	1,325	2,930	25,160	25,815	8,707	5,537	1,119	11,410	8,558	11,724
Italian	199	432	5,163	6,145	1,250	957	144	1,603	891	2,107
Lithuanian	15	36	661	384	167	62	8	73	71	310
Norwegian	141	108	999	930	417	157	279	514	274	692
Polish	4,402	1,314	19,944	15,765	2,508	4,023	309	3,001	4,752	4,579
Russian	86	67	1,277	692	107	82	27	199	265	254
Scotch-Irish	242	409	3,007	3,614	1,015	709	220	1,127	1,295	1,160
Scottish	384	668	5,049	5,833	1,189	1,899	267	2,034	1,974	1,531
Slovak	53	84	3,141	1,103	297	125	95	2,061	513	757
Swedish	138	354	2,138	1,664	1,050	381	1,104	1,312	549	2,193
Ukrainian	17	30	512	686	124	159	6	153	221	139
United States or American	228	1,439	5,181	6,480	3,517	2,034	279	4,813	2,444	3,828
Welsh	17	139	1,063	865	334	175	22	415	241	335
Other Ancestry	589	1,452	56,063	13,586	7,926	2,730	1,224	6,346	5,287	12,985

Table I-7. Reported Ancestry in Michigan, by County: 1990 Continued

ANCESTRY	Washtenaw	Wayne	Wexford	Michigan
Ancestry Reported	**369,908**	**2,459,221**	**34,116**	**11,897,353**
Arab	2,397	31,274	98	77,070
Belgian	913	7,751	55	60,266
Canadian	1,535	9,839	106	47,616
Czech	1,879	6,996	195	54,841
Danish	1,628	4,366	348	51,184
Dutch	9,290	28,417	2,397	560,792
English	47,323	168,455	5,033	1,315,736
Finnish	2,473	12,064	280	109,357
French (ex Basque)	14,230	98,766	2,241	652,807
French Canadian	4,152	30,399	639	176,092
German/Austrian	90,242	347,060	8,367	2,692,600
Greek	2,230	11,823	35	42,678
Hungarian	3,901	33,933	161	109,178
Irish	42,010	234,050	3,965	1,321,320
Italian	11,021	93,825	454	412,209
Lithuanian	1,527	8,935	76	38,384
Norwegian	3,060	7,701	344	72,261
Polish	19,287	220,025	1,432	889,527
Russian	5,246	10,313	109	76,093
Scotch-Irish	5,553	27,047	535	157,483
Scottish	9,865	41,804	648	252,104
Slovak	2,100	18,619	148	84,864
Swedish	5,902	16,696	2,443	194,063
Ukrainian	1,742	13,498	29	43,914
United States or American	9,096	54,568	1,502	322,467
Welsh	2,714	9,432	225	55,588
Other Ancestry	68,592	911,565	2,251	2,016,859

Note: The Bureau of the Census collects ancestry information based on the self identification of the respondent. Ancestry and race are different concepts. Ancestry is a country of origin concept. Data on Hispanics are collected from a separate question. For data on race and hispanic origin see table I-4. * No data. Source: U.S. Bureau of the Census - Michigan Information Center, census STF-3 (Lansing, Michigan).

Table I-8. Percentage of Year-Round Housing Units Built in Michigan Since 1980 or Before 1940, by County: As of the 1990 Census

County	Percentage(%) Built by Time Period		County	Percentage(%) Built by Time Period	
	1980 to March 1990	1939 or Earlier		1980 to March 1990	1939 or Earlier
Alcona	17.5	15.2	Lake	19.5	13.0
Alger	16.2	25.7	Lapeer	19.4	21.6
Allegan	20.0	26.0	Leelanau	24.9	22.7
Alpena	11.4	24.2	Lenawee	10.5	34.8
Antrim	21.1	22.2	Livingston	22.1	13.6
Arenac	19.6	16.0	Luce	11.9	26.8
Baraga	15.6	35.1	Mackinac	17.6	20.9
Barry	15.9	29.7	Macomb	17.0	6.2
Bay	7.5	29.2	Manistee	14.5	32.6
Benzie	19.1	25.9	Marquette	10.5	29.7
Berrien	10.0	24.2	Mason	15.2	32.0
Branch	12.9	31.4	Mecosta	19.2	20.9
Calhoun	8.4	29.7	Menominee	15.5	33.8
Cass	11.4	24.7	Midland	17.1	11.1
Charlevoix	21.2	24.8	Missaukee	20.3	18.8
Cheboygan	17.9	21.8	Monroe	12.8	23.3
Chippewa	14.2	21.9	Montcalm	17.2	28.1
Clare	16.0	10.7	Montmorency	18.3	9.9
Clinton	17.3	27.6	Muskegon	11.5	20.1
Crawford	20.6	9.9	Newaygo	19.5	18.9
Delta	13.7	33.8	Oakland	18.0	10.1
Dickinson	16.4	37.3	Oceana	18.3	27.7
Eaton	18.3	22.3	Ogemaw	20.1	14.8
Emmet	21.5	26.8	Ontonagon	12.1	34.2
Genesee	10.1	15.9	Osceola	19.5	24.0
Gladwin	19.3	10.5	Oscoda	16.1	8.3
Gogebic	11.4	49.0	Otsego	22.8	9.5
Grand Traverse	26.7	17.7	Ottawa	25.7	17.8
Gratiot	12.3	35.9	Presque Isle	14.5	23.6
Hillsdale	13.5	36.1	Roscommon	17.3	9.0
Houghton	9.7	57.3	Saginaw	7.7	23.8
Huron	15.7	29.1	St. Clair	16.0	25.8
Ingham	13.8	20.6	St. Joseph	12.4	30.0
Ionia	13.5	37.8	Sanilac	13.1	31.9
Iosco	16.3	11.5	Schoolcraft	15.1	28.8
Iron	12.4	39.3	Shiawassee	9.9	32.8
Isabella	19.5	18.7	Tuscola	12.1	28.0
Jackson	11.1	29.4	Van Buren	16.4	26.5
Kalamazoo	16.4	20.9	Washtenaw	15.8	16.8
Kalkaska	21.0	10.0	Wayne	5.5	24.5
Kent	20.4	22.7	Wexford	17.5	25.4
Keweenaw	12.6	56.8	**Michigan**	**13.6**	**20.8**

Source: U.S. Bureau of the Census, Michigan Information Center (Lansing, Michigan).

Table I-9. Housing Units and Occupancy Status in Michigan, by County: 1990 Census

County	Total Housing Units	Occupancy Status			County	Total Housing Units	Occupancy Status		
		Percent(%) Owner	Percent(%) Renter	Percent(%) Not Occupied			Percent(%) Owner	Percent(%) Renter	Percent(%) Not Occupied
Alcona	10,414	35.4	5.6	59.1	Gratiot	14,699	70.8	22.1	7.1
Alger	5,775	46.3	11.5	42.2	Hillsdale	18,547	65.1	19.2	15.7
Allegan	36,395	70.3	16.8	12.9	Houghton	17,296	52.9	23.2	23.8
Alpena	14,431	64.1	17.9	18.0	Huron	19,755	53.3	13.8	32.8
Antrim	13,145	43.0	10.1	46.9	Ingham	108,542	55.2	39.4	5.4
Arenac	8,891	51.7	11.8	36.5	Ionia	19,674	72.4	21.3	6.2
Baraga	4,684	48.4	17.1	34.6	Iosco	19,517	40.6	18.8	40.6
Barry	20,887	71.5	13.6	15.0	Iron	9,039	50.1	12.4	37.4
Bay	44,234	73.3	22.1	4.6	Isabella	19,950	57.3	30.9	11.8
Benzie	8,557	45.6	10.1	44.2	Jackson	57,979	68.2	24.4	7.4
Berrien	69,532	61.1	26.7	12.2	Kalamazoo	88,955	60.6	33.5	5.9
Branch	18,449	61.5	19.4	19.1	Kalkaska	9,151	43.4	10.5	46.1
Calhoun	55,619	66.2	27.0	6.8	Kent	192,698	65.7	28.6	5.7
Cass	22,644	63.6	17.0	19.5	Keweenaw	2,257	29.8	4.7	65.6
Charlevoix	13,119	48.4	14.4	37.2	Lake	12,114	23.6	5.6	70.8
Cheboygan	14,090	46.3	11.9	41.8	Lapeer	26,445	75.5	17.7	6.8
Chippewa	18,023	47.0	17.0	36.0	Leelanau	11,171	45.8	10.4	43.8
Clare	19,135	39.7	10.9	49.3	Lenawee	35,104	68.4	21.8	9.9
Clinton	20,959	80.1	16.4	3.6	Livingston	41,863	78.5	14.4	7.1
Crawford	8,727	40.9	10.0	49.1	Luce	3,594	47.4	12.5	40.1
Delta	17,928	61.7	19.3	18.9	Mackinac	9,254	34.8	11.0	54.2
Dickinson	12,902	65.5	17.0	17.6	Macomb	274,843	74.4	22.0	3.6
Eaton	35,517	69.9	25.9	4.2	Manistee	13,330	50.3	14.1	35.6
Emmet	14,731	47.9	16.7	35.4	Marquette	31,049	52.6	29.3	18.1
Genesee	170,808	66.5	27.9	5.6	Mason	14,119	53.7	17.1	29.3
Gladwin	14,885	45.8	10.4	43.9	Mecosta	17,274	49.6	21.4	29.0
Gogebic	10,997	52.9	14.8	32.3	Menominee	12,509	61.6	16.4	21.9
Grand Traverse	28,740	62.4	21.0	16.6	Midland	29,343	72.9	21.8	5.3

Table I-9. Housing Units and Occupancy Status in Michigan, by County: 1990 Census Continued

County	Total Housing Units	Occupancy Status		
		Percent(%) Owner	Percent(%) Renter	Percent(%) Not Occupied
Missaukee	7,112	51.2	10.5	38.3
Monroe	48,312	74.9	21.4	3.7
Montcalm	22,817	64.6	16.7	18.6
Montmorency	8,791	33.4	7.6	59.0
Muskegon	61,962	69.4	23.9	6.7
Newaygo	20,105	56.4	12.2	31.5
Oakland	432,684	68.9	25.9	5.1
Oceana	12,857	50.4	12.4	37.2
Ogemaw	13,977	41.9	9.6	48.6
Ontonagon	5,332	55.3	13.0	31.7
Osceola	11,444	51.3	12.9	35.8
Oscoda	8,112	31.9	7.1	61.0
Otsego	10,669	48.3	12.8	38.9
Ottawa	66,624	75.9	18.1	5.9
Presque Isle	8,917	50.4	9.8	39.7
Roscommon	19,881	35.1	7.7	57.2
Saginaw	81,931	67.5	28.0	4.5
St. Clair	57,494	69.6	22.4	8.0
St. Joseph	24,242	66.6	22.4	11.0
Sanilac	19,465	59.8	15.5	24.7
Schoolcraft	5,487	46.2	13.8	40.0
Shiawassee	25,833	74.8	21.5	3.8
Tuscola	21,231	74.5	17.2	8.3
Van Buren	31,530	61.8	18.8	19.4
Washtenaw	111,256	51.9	42.0	6.0
Wayne	832,710	59.9	33.9	6.3
Wexford	12,862	57.6	19.5	22.9
Michigan	**3,847,92**	**63.1**	**25.8**	**11.1**

Source: U.S. Bureau of the Census, Michigan Information Center (Lansing, Michigan).

Table I-10. Population Estimates and Projections for Michigan, by County: 1990, 1995, Estimates 2000 - 2020 Projections

County	1990	1995	2000	2005	2010	2015	2020
Alcona	10,145	10,600	10,600	10,800	10,900	11,000	11,000
Alger	8,972	9,800	9,900	10,000	10,100	10,200	10,200
Allegan	90,509	97,700	102,600	107,100	111,900	116,900	121,800
Alpena	30,605	30,500	30,600	30,400	30,100	29,600	29,000
Antrim	18,185	20,200	21,700	23,200	24,600	26,200	27,700
Arenac	14,906	16,100	16,800	17,500	18,200	18,800	19,400
Baraga	7,954	8,500	8,400	8,200	8,100	8,000	7,900
Barry	50,057	52,600	54,600	56,300	57,900	59,300	60,400
Bay	111,723	111,500	111,500	110,700	109,400	107,700	105,800
Benzie	12,200	13,700	14,500	15,300	16,200	16,900	17,700
Berrien	161,378	162,600	162,300	161,800	160,800	159,700	158,900
Branch	41,502	42,700	43,800	44,900	46,100	47,200	48,200
Calhoun	135,982	140,900	142,900	144,400	145,500	146,400	147,200
Cass	49,477	49,500	49,800	50,200	50,400	50,400	50,200
Charlevoix	21,468	23,000	24,700	26,200	27,900	29,600	31,300
Cheboygan	21,398	23,000	23,700	24,400	25,100	25,700	26,100
Chippewa	34,604	36,900	39,300	41,900	44,600	47,700	51,000
Clare	24,952	28,000	29,700	31,400	33,100	35,000	36,900
Clinton	57,883	61,600	63,400	64,700	65,600	66,100	66,300
Crawford	12,260	13,500	14,900	16,300	17,700	19,300	20,900
Delta	37,780	38,600	38,800	38,900	39,100	39,200	39,400
Dickinson	26,831	27,200	27,400	27,500	27,700	27,900	28,100
Eaton	92,879	98,000	102,100	105,900	109,600	113,500	117,400
Emmet	25,040	27,300	28,800	30,100	31,400	32,800	34,300
Genesee	430,459	436,700	437,700	435,500	431,100	425,300	419,000
Gladwin	21,896	24,300	25,700	27,100	28,500	29,900	31,100
Gogebic	18,052	17,900	16,900	15,900	14,900	14,100	13,300
Grand Traverse	64,273	70,800	76,500	81,800	87,400	93,500	99,600
Gratiot	38,982	39,900	40,100	40,100	40,100	39,900	39,500
Hillsdale	43,431	45,200	46,600	47,900	49,200	50,400	51,600
Houghton	35,446	36,100	36,500	36,900	37,500	38,100	38,600
Huron	34,951	35,200	35,100	34,800	34,500	34,200	33,900
Ingham	281,912	278,200	280,100	280,500	280,200	280,100	280,000
Ionia	57,024	59,800	61,300	62,500	63,800	64,800	65,500
Iosco	30,209	24,500	24,900	25,100	25,300	25,500	25,800
Iron	13,175	13,100	12,700	12,300	11,900	11,600	11,200
Isabella	54,624	56,200	57,700	59,000	60,500	62,100	63,400
Jackson	149,756	154,100	156,700	158,700	160,400	162,000	163,400
Kalamazoo	223,411	228,100	233,800	237,900	241,300	244,500	247,500
Kalkaska	13,497	14,700	15,900	17,100	18,500	19,900	21,200
Kent	500,631	525,400	553,500	579,800	607,300	636,900	667,400
Keweenaw	1,701	2,000	1,900	1,800	1,800	1,700	1,700

Table I-10. Population Estimates and Projections for Michigan, by County: 1990, 1995, Estimates 2000 - 2020 Projections Continued

County	1990	1995	2000	2005	2010	2015	2020
Lake	8,583	9,600	10,200	10,700	11,300	12,000	12,700
Lapeer	74,768	83,800	89,600	95,400	101,100	106,500	111,500
Leelanau	16,527	18,500	19,400	20,000	20,600	21,400	22,200
Lenawee	91,476	96,700	99,600	102,300	104,600	106,700	108,500
Livingston	115,645	133,500	148,800	163,700	178,800	195,000	212,500
Luce	5,763	5,600	5,600	5,600	5,600	5,500	5,400
Mackinac	10,674	10,900	11,300	11,900	12,700	13,800	15,300
Macomb	717,400	733,400	755,500	768,500	774,200	776,400	777,400
Manistee	21,265	22,900	22,900	23,000	23,100	23,100	22,900
Marquette	70,887	65,400	69,100	68,900	68,400	67,600	66,700
Mason	25,537	27,400	27,300	27,500	27,800	28,100	28,200
Mecosta	37,308	37,700	38,400	39,100	40,000	40,700	41,400
Menominee	24,920	24,500	23,600	22,500	21,500	20,600	19,600
Midland	75,651	79,700	83,000	85,700	87,900	89,800	91,300
Missaukee	12,147	13,500	14,400	15,400	16,400	17,600	18,600
Monroe	133,600	139,500	143,000	145,700	147,700	149,100	150,000
Montcalm	53,059	57,800	60,400	62,900	65,500	68,000	70,400
Montmorency	8,936	9,700	10,800	11,900	13,200	14,700	16,200
Muskegon	158,983	164,500	166,400	167,600	168,800	169,900	170,800
Newaygo	38,206	43,600	46,600	49,700	53,200	57,100	61,000
Oakland	1,083,592	1,153,600	1,218,900	1,276,000	1,329,500	1,385,100	1,444,100
Oceana	22,455	23,800	24,300	24,700	25,100	25,500	25,700
Ogemaw	18,681	20,600	22,400	24,400	26,400	28,600	30,800
Ontonagon	8,854	8,600	8,300	8,000	7,700	7,400	7,000
Osceola	20,146	21,800	22,400	23,000	23,600	24,200	24,700
Oscoda	7,842	8,700	9,500	10,300	11,200	12,100	13,100
Otsego	17,957	20,700	23,200	25,800	28,500	31,600	34,800
Ottawa	187,768	210,300	229,800	249,000	269,300	291,600	315,600
Presque Isle	13,743	14,400	14,400	14,600	14,800	15,000	15,200
Roscommon	19,776	22,600	24,600	26,500	28,600	30,800	33,200
Saginaw	211,946	212,500	213,800	213,700	212,600	211,100	209,300
St. Clair	145,607	154,100	161,600	168,400	174,900	181,300	187,400
St. Joseph	58,913	60,600	61,700	62,500	63,300	63,900	64,300
Sanilac	39,928	42,200	42,800	43,500	44,300	45,000	45,500
Schoolcraft	8,302	8,700	8,800	8,900	8,900	9,000	8,900
Shiawassee	69,770	72,000	72,800	73,300	73,300	72,900	72,200
Tuscola	55,498	57,400	58,500	59,300	59,900	60,300	60,300
Van Buren	70,060	74,600	78,700	82,800	87,100	91,500	95,800
Washtenaw	282,937	292,900	306,300	318,400	329,600	340,400	351,200
Wayne	2,111,687	2,062,600	2,022,600	1,970,300	1,914,500	1,864,500	1,821,800
Wexford	26,360	28,600	29,100	29,500	29,800	30,200	30,500
Michigan	**9,295,277**	**9,556,100**	**9,786,700**	**9,963,800**	**10,121,300**	**10,285,000**	**10,454,700**

Source: Michigan Department of Management and Budget, Office of the State Demographer, January 1996 (Lansing, Michigan).

Table I-11. Population Estimates and Projections for Michigan, by Age and Sex: 1990, 1995, Estimates 2000 - 2020 Projections

Age Group	1990	1995	2000	2005	2010	2015	2020
Total, Both Sexes	**9,295,297**	**9,556,063**	**9,786,685**	**9,963,788**	**10,121,298**	**10,284,960**	**10,454,737**
0-4	713,578	734,330	689,816	656,616	654,717	675,239	693,517
5-9	690,138	719,108	742,400	697,989	665,098	663,858	685,321
10-14	665,572	689,664	721,686	744,743	700,692	668,138	667,315
15-19	700,201	691,339	717,091	748,620	770,930	728,609	697,455
20-24	706,575	671,133	664,889	690,174	721,063	742,308	702,248
25-29	764,264	672,467	639,280	633,600	659,808	691,288	711,886
30-34	810,420	762,727	673,043	640,130	635,114	662,424	694,952
35-39	744,802	795,301	750,147	661,990	629,957	625,531	653,297
40-44	657,391	728,556	779,952	735,799	649,258	617,791	613,824
45-49	520,093	639,497	711,280	761,943	719,111	634,460	603,667
50-54	424,090	502,987	621,586	691,869	741,920	700,827	618,681
55-59	391,190	404,516	481,486	595,832	664,202	713,422	675,043
60-64	402,882	364,388	380,280	453,466	562,331	628,257	676,568
65-69	367,805	363,642	331,831	347,376	415,401	516,682	579,004
70-74	286,418	316,252	316,277	290,192	305,188	366,272	457,320
75-79	211,919	230,958	258,327	260,049	240,729	254,817	307,247
80-84	132,789	153,007	171,187	194,771	199,716	188,714	203,466
85 Plus	105,170	116,191	136,127	158,629	186,063	206,323	213,926
Median Age, Both Sexes	32.5	33.9	35.3	36.3	37.0	37.5	37.9
Total, Female	**4,782,567**	**4,909,563**	**5,022,887**	**5,109,375**	**5,186,350**	**5,267,110**	**5,351,292**
0-4	348,854	358,869	337,114	320,898	319,978	330,042	339,013
5-9	336,748	351,702	362,913	341,208	325,146	324,561	335,104
10-14	324,994	336,501	352,937	364,051	342,506	326,591	326,196
15-19	344,231	338,074	350,397	366,627	377,437	356,671	341,372
20-24	356,064	328,774	323,992	336,097	352,229	362,668	342,752
25-29	387,600	342,942	316,996	312,431	324,993	341,653	351,840
30-34	413,590	387,514	344,171	318,423	314,151	327,134	344,342
35-39	378,963	408,276	383,897	341,025	315,732	311,703	324,816
40-44	334,269	372,862	403,126	379,086	336,782	311,849	308,005
45-49	264,326	327,532	366,777	396,626	373,138	331,571	307,098
50-54	217,542	257,468	320,432	358,952	388,455	365,784	325,274
55-59	203,953	209,182	247,624	308,395	345,763	374,573	353,153
60-64	212,242	192,971	199,868	236,793	295,143	331,198	359,261
65-69	202,105	196,804	179,973	186,683	221,475	276,404	310,526
70-74	165,363	180,425	177,070	162,436	168,865	200,535	250,460
75-79	129,200	139,562	153,417	151,237	139,595	145,606	173,008
80-84	86,919	99,042	109,308	121,992	122,333	114,981	121,876
85 Plus	75,604	81,063	92,875	106,415	122,629	133,586	137,196
Median Age, Females	33.5	35.1	36.6	37.9	38.7	39.2	39.5
Total, Male	**4,512,730**	**4,646,500**	**4,763,798**	**4,854,413**	**4,934,948**	**5,017,850**	**5,103,445**
Median Age, Males	31.4	32.7	33.8	34.6	35.3	35.7	36.2

Source: Michigan Department of Management and Budget, Office of the State Demographer, January 1996 (Lansing, Michigan).

CHAPTER II
HEALTH AND VITAL STATISTICS

Vital statistics and data on diseases are reported to county health departments by courts, attending physicians, ministers, rabbis, priests, and so forth. Then they are sent to the Michigan Department of Public Health. Michigan Health Statistics is published annually by the Michigan Department of Public Health. This document offers statewide data on natality, mortality, marriages, divorces, and communicable diseases. Other reports from the Michigan Department of Public Health include Cancer Incidence and Mortality, Infant Death Report, and Michigan Maternal and Infant Health Surveillance Report.

County data on births, deaths, marriages, and divorces are available separately. Under a data sharing arrangement, the Michigan Department of Management and Budget prepares county data on births and deaths for its components of population change series (Table I-3).

Statistics on motor vehicle accidents, injuries, and deaths also are collected and tabulated by the Michigan Department of State Police. Some of them are reproduced in Chapter VIII of this Abstract. For data on mental health, users should look to the Michigan Department of Mental Health, also in Lansing.

The Michigan Department of Public Health also oversees health care facilities, and compiles data in this regard. The Michigan Hospital Association, collects statistics and publishes them in Hospital Trends.

At the national level, Vital Statistics of the United States is published by the National Center for Health Statistics. The Centers for Disease Control and Prevention in Atlanta, Georgia, tabulates national data on diseases.

Birth and death rates are given as the number of live births or deaths per 1,000 population. Fertility rates represent the number of live births per 1,000 women aged 15-44.

LIST OF TABLES

Table		Page
II-1.	Live Births, Live Birth Rates, Deaths, and Death Rates in Michigan and the United States: 1966-1993	57
II-2.	Fertility Rates, Michigan and the United States, Selected Years: 1940-1993	58
II-3.	Live Birth Rates in Michigan, by Age of Mother: 1970-1992	59
II-4.	Number of Deaths by Six Leading Causes Among Michigan Residents: 1955-1992	60
II-5.	Number of Deaths Among Michigan Residents from 13 Leading Causes, by Race and Age: 1992	61

LIST OF TABLES

Table   **Page**

II-6.   Number of Deaths Among Michigan Residents, by Age and Sex: 1991-1992 62

II-7.   Injury Deaths per 100,000 Population in Michigan, by Cause: 1991 62

II-8.   Number of Michigan Deaths Caused by Firearm Injury, by Sex and Age:
         1991 63

II-9.   Infant, Neonatal, Postneonatal, Perinatal, Fetal, and Maternal Deaths, Michigan
         Residents: 1955-1992 64

II-10.   Infant Deaths and Infant Death Rates in Michigan, by Race: 1970-1993 65

II-11.   Selected Vital Statistics for Michigan, by County: 1992 66

II-12.   Infant Deaths, Live Births, and Infant Death Rates in Michigan, by County:
         1991-1992 68

II-13.   Reported Abortions in Michigan, Selected Years: 1980-1993 70

II-14.   Reported Abortions in Michigan, by County of Residence: 1993 71

II-15.   Life Expectancy at Birth in Michigan and the United States by Sex, Selected
         Years: 1901-1992 72

II-16.   Life Expectancy at Birth by Sex and Race in Michigan, Selected Years:
         1950-1992 72

II-17.   Expected Remaining Years of Life by Sex, Race, Age: Michigan 1992 73

II-18.   Numbers of Invasive Cancers Among Michigan Residents by Age, Race, and
         Sex: 1992 74

II-19.   Incidence Rates of Invasive Cancers Among Michigan Residents by Age, Race,
         and Sex: 1992 75

II-20.   Numbers of Deaths Due to Invasive Cancers Among Michigan Residents by Age,
         Race, and Sex: 1992 76

II-21.   Death Rates Due to Invasive Cancers Among Michigan Residents by Age, Race,
         and Sex: 1992 77

LIST OF TABLES

Table   **Page**

II-22. Numbers and Percentages of Invasive Cancers by Primary Site, Sex, and Race: 1992 78

II-23. Numbers and Percentages of Cancer Deaths by Primary Site, Sex, and Race: 1992 80

II-24. Leading Primary Sites of Invasive Cancer and Age-Specific/Age-Adjusted Incidence Rates in Michigan, by Age, Race, and Sex: 1992 82

II-25. Numbers of Reported Cancer Cases, Deaths, Preliminary Age-Adjusted Incidence, and Final Death Rates in Michigan, by County: 1990-1992 Time Period 83

II-26. Five Year Cancer Relative Survival Rates in Michigan, by Selected Sites and Stage: Year Range 1983-1989 85

II-27. Number and Fatality Rate of Fatal Occupational Injuries in Michigan, by Major Industry: 1992 86

II-28. Reported Cases of Certain Communicable Diseases in Michigan, Selected Years: 1950-1993 87

II-29. Marriages in Michigan, by Order of Marriage and Age of Bride and Groom: 1992 87

II-30. Number of Divorces and Annulments, and Divorce and Annulment Rates in Michigan: Selected Years: 1900-1993 88

II-31. Estimated Number of Children Involved in Divorces and Annulments, Average Number of Children per Decree, and Rate per 1,000 Children Under 18 Years of Age in Michigan: Selected Years: 1960-1993 88

II-32. Occupational Injury and Illness Incidence Rates in Michigan, by Industry Division: 1991 89

II-33. Occupational Injury, Illness Incidence Rates, and Average Lost Workdays in Michigan, by Establishment Size: 1991 89

II-34. Number and Percent Distribution of Fatal Occupational Injuries in Michigan, by Event or Exposure: 1992 90

CHAPTER II
HEALTH AND VITAL STATISTICS

LIST OF TABLES

Table   **Page**

II-35.   Total Number of Hospital Discharges for Deliveries, Number, and Percent of Primary and Repeated C-Sections in Michigan: 1985-1990 91

II-36.   Selected Hospital Admission Statistics for Michigan: 1982-1992 91

II-37.   Selected Hospital Patient Statistics for Michigan: 1982-1992 92

II-38.   Hospital Inpatient and Outpatient Surgeries in Michigan: 1982-1992 92

II-39.   Tobacco Abstinence by Women in Michigan: 1988-1991 92

II-40.   Percent of Mothers Breast-Feeding in Michigan: 1988-1991 92

Table II-1. Live Births, Live Birth Rates, Deaths, and Death Rates in Michigan and the United States: 1966-1993

Year	Michigan Live Births		Michigan Deaths		United States Live Births		United States Deaths	
	Number	Rate	Number	Rate	Number	Rate	Number	Rate
1966	165,794	19.9	74,596	9.0	3,606,274	18.4	1,863,149	9.5
1967	162,756	18.9	75,360	8.7	3,520,959	17.8	1,851,323	9.4
1968	159,058	18.3	76,855	8.9	3,501,564	17.5	1,930,082	9.7
1969	165,760	19.0	76,693	8.8	3,600,206	17.8	1,921,990	9.5
1970	171,667	19.3	76,321	8.6	3,731,386	18.4	1,921,031	9.5
1971	162,244	18.1	77,395	8.6	3,555,970	17.2	1,927,542	9.3
1972	146,854	16.3	79,210	8.8	3,258,411	15.6	1,963,944	9.4
1973	141,550	15.6	78,522	8.7	3,136,965	14.9	1,973,003	9.4
1974	137,414	15.1	76,143	8.4	3,159,958	14.9	1,934,388	9.2
1975	133,931	14.7	74,522	8.2	3,144,198	14.8	1,892,879	8.9
1976	131,378	14.4	75,801	8.3	3,167,788	14.8	1,909,440	8.8
1977	138,416	15.1	74,144	8.1	3,326,632	15.4	1,899,597	8.6
1978	138,802	15.1	74,773	8.1	3,333,279	15.3	1,927,788	8.7
1979	144,452	15.6	73,480	7.9	3,494,398	15.9	1,913,841	8.5
1980	145,162	15.7	74,991	8.1	3,612,258	15.9	1,989,841	8.8
1981	140,579	15.2	75,818	8.2	3,629,238	15.8	1,977,981	8.6
1982	137,950	15.0	75,536	8.2	3,680,537	15.9	1,974,797	8.5
1983	133,026	14.5	76,639	8.4	3,638,933	15.5	2,019,201	8.6
1984	135,782	15.0	76,401	8.4	3,669,141	15.5	2,039,369	8.6
1985	138,052	15.2	78,635	8.7	3,760,561	15.8	2,086,440	8.7
1986	137,626	15.1	80,177	8.8	3,756,547	15.6	2,105,361	8.7
1987	140,466	15.3	79,795	8.7	3,809,394	15.7	2,123,323	8.7
1988	139,635	15.1	80,075	8.7	3,909,510	15.9	2,167,999	8.8
1989	148,164	16.0	78,566	8.5	4,040,958	16.4	2,150,466	8.7
1990	153,080	16.5	78,501	8.4	4,158,212	16.7	2,148,463	8.6
1991	149,478	16.1	79,738	8.6	4,110,907	16.3	2,169,518	8.6
1992	143,827	15.5	78,916	8.5	4,065,014	15.9	2,175,613	8.5
1993	139,560	14.8	82,286	8.7	4,039,000	15.7	2,268,000	8.8

Source: Michigan Department of Public Health, Michigan Health Statistics 1992 (Lansing, Michigan: 1993).

Table II-2. Fertility Rates, Michigan and the United States, Selected Years: 1940-1993

Year	Michigan			United States		
	Total Rate	White Rate	Black Rate	Total Rate	White Rate	Black Rate
1940	78.9	N.A.	N.A.	79.9	77.1	N.A.
1950	110.5	N.A.	N.A.	106.2	102.3	N.A.
1960	123.1	N.A.	N.A.	118.0	113.2	153.5
1970	91.7	87.9	123.5	87.9	84.1	115.4
1971	84.5	80.8	119.5	81.8	77.3	109.7
1972	75.1	71.2	111.0	73.4	68.9	99.9
1973	71.2	67.2	105.8	69.2	64.9	93.6
1974	68.0	54.7	92.8	68.4	64.2	89.7
1975	65.5	62.6	89.5	66.7	62.5	87.9
1976	63.5	60.8	83.4	65.8	61.5	85.8
1977	65.9	63.3	83.8	67.8	63.2	88.1
1978	65.0	62.5	80.4	66.6	61.7	86.7
1979	66.6	64.1	81.1	68.5	63.4	88.3
1980	66.3	64.2	78.3	68.4	64.7	88.1
1981	63.2	61.8	71.3	67.4	63.9	85.3
1982	61.7	60.5	68.6	67.3	63.9	84.3
1983	59.3	58.0	66.7	65.8	62.5	82.0
1984	63.1	61.7	71.6	65.4	62.3	81.5
1985	63.8	62.8	69.6	66.2	63.1	82.4
1986	63.2	61.4	73.5	65.4	62.1	82.6
1987	64.3	61.8	78.2	65.7	62.3	84.1
1988	63.9	61.1	79.2	67.2	63.4	87.0
1989	67.9	62.9	93.8	69.2	65.1	90.8
1990	69.1	65.3	93.5	70.9	66.9	91.9
1991	62.7	59.2	81.2	69.6	N.A.	N.A.
1992	65.1	61.5	84.6	68.9	N.A.	N.A.
1993	68.3	59.8	80.6	68.3	N.A.	N.A.

N.A. denotes data not available.
Source: Michigan Department of Public Health, Michigan Health Statistics 1992 (Lansing, Michigan: 1993).

Table II-3. Live Birth Rates in Michigan, by Age of Mother: 1970-1992

Year	Age Range of Mother							
	10 - 14	15 - 19	20 - 24	25 - 29	30 - 34	35 - 39	40 - 44	45 and Older
1970	1.0	68.2	176.2	154.2	76.2	32.4	8.3	0.4
1971	1.0	64.7	161.7	138.6	69.1	27.9	7.2	0.4
1972	1.1	63.7	137.6	124.1	58.6	22.8	5.9	0.4
1973	1.2	62.8	127.5	118.3	54.2	19.9	4.9	0.2
1974	1.1	58.5	121.9	115.7	51.5	16.3	4.1	0.2
1975	1.1	55.3	117.0	112.3	48.4	16.0	3.9	0.2
1976	0.9	51.1	111.6	113.0	46.9	15.0	3.2	0.2
1977	1.0	50.9	115.5	114.9	52.6	15.2	3.1	0.2
1978	0.8	48.3	112.7	112.6	54.0	16.3	3.0	0.2
1979	0.9	47.6	114.6	115.2	56.7	16.6	3.0	0.2
1980	0.8	44.8	113.1	115.6	58.4	16.4	3.1	0.1
1981	0.9	51.4	122.9	112.6	58.9	14.0	2.6	0.2
1982	1.0	51.0	121.4	111.1	59.5	15.6	2.6	0.1
1983	1.0	51.4	115.9	108.5	58.8	15.9	2.8	0.2
1984	1.0	43.8	103.8	111.4	65.2	19.3	3.0	0.1
1985	1.0	43.9	104.1	115.1	67.1	20.5	3.1	0.2
1986	1.0	45.2	101.6	114.4	68.3	21.8	2.9	0.1
1987	1.0	46.9	102.3	117.1	71.5	22.9	3.3	0.2
1988	1.1	47.8	99.2	115.8	73.0	23.9	3.6	0.2
1989	1.2	54.6	105.7	122.3	78.2	26.4	3.8	0.2
1990	1.3	58.8	112.3	125.0	77.5	27.5	4.1	0.2
1991	1.3	56.4	111.1	118.7	77.4	28.0	4.4	0.0
1992	1.1	53.3	105.2	111.6	76.2	29.6	4.8	0.2

Source: Michigan Department of Public Health, Michigan Health Statistics 1992 (Lansing, Michigan: 1993).

Table II-4. Number of Deaths by Six Leading Causes Among Michigan Residents: 1955-1992

Year	Heart Disease	Cancer (All Forms)	Cerebro-vascular Disease	Accidents		Diabetes	Pneumonia
				Motor Vehicle	All Forms		
1955	23,440	10,297	7,362	2,129	4,213	1,415	1,538
1956	24,661	10,489	7,114	1,826	3,925	1,443	1,723
1957	25,369	10,810	7,632	1,680	3,643	1,510	2,045
1958	25,215	10,946	7,547	1,466	3,306	1,595	2,076
1959	25,323	11,113	7,700	1,587	3,666	1,715	1,810
1960	25,728	11,331	7,682	1,710	3,688	1,784	2,002
1961	25,519	11,476	7,745	1,656	3,692	1,778	1,692
1962	27,226	11,752	7,783	1,668	3,758	1,908	1,824
1963	27,483	12,078	8,168	2,005	4,033	2,049	1,995
1964	27,496	12,087	7,940	2,286	4,416	2,055	1,714
1965	28,134	12,419	7,769	2,271	4,494	2,153	1,987
1966	28,277	12,506	7,732	2,407	4,737	2,243	2,026
1967	28,757	13,030	7,846	2,265	4,519	2,182	1,973
1968	29,680	13,292	7,913	2,466	4,603	2,298	2,341
1969	29,396	13,328	7,706	2,579	4,766	2,188	2,229
1970	29,204	13,551	7,691	2,309	4,428	2,180	2,004
1971	30,095	13,594	7,826	2,274	4,426	2,103	1,981
1972	30,865	14,045	7,999	2,450	4,566	2,222	2,009
1973	29,944	14,220	7,987	2,389	4,630	2,074	1,958
1974	29,220	14,241	7,645	1,929	4,211	1,940	1,637
1975	28,298	14,445	7,262	1,841	4,002	1,819	1,690
1976	29,233	14,880	7,354	1,993	3,912	1,719	1,812
1977	28,895	15,125	6,818	1,993	3,945	1,615	1,639
1978	29,406	15,249	6,520	2,138	3,970	1,551	1,828
1979	29,296	15,409	6,067	1,967	3,839	1,449	1,454
1980	29,790	15,828	6,164	1,880	3,627	1,467	1,712
1981	30,172	16,142	6,121	1,727	3,390	1,487	1,644
1982	30,099	16,566	5,839	1,555	3,113	1,347	1,665
1983	30,412	16,785	5,721	1,419	2,947	1,470	2,007
1984	30,100	16,907	5,631	1,630	3,049	1,476	2,018
1985	30,618	17,281	5,528	1,676	3,228	1,387	2,193
1986	31,270	17,321	5,421	1,736	3,202	1,494	2,513
1987	30,521	17,669	5,481	1,725	3,143	1,479	2,377
1988	30,218	17,890	5,237	1,806	3,237	1,522	2,626
1989	28,031	18,264	5,173	1,750	3,228	2,052	2,633
1990	27,527	18,413	5,090	1,669	3,137	2,009	2,863
1991	27,517	19,204	5,165	1,494	3,011	2,113	2,773
1992	26,863	19,217	5,087	1,426	2,844	2,114	2,697

Source: Michigan Department of Public Health, Michigan Health Statistics 1992 (Lansing, Michigan: 1993).

Table II-5: Number of Deaths Among Michigan Residents from 13 Leading Causes, by Race and Age: 1992

Cause	Race			Age Group					
	Total	White	Black	Under 1	1-14 Years	15-24 Years	25-44 Years	45-64 Years	65 & over
All Causes	78,916	66,377	11,868	1,460	612	1,298	4,993	13,490	57,059
Heart Disease	26,863	23,194	3,473	15	21	32	609	2,996	22,187
Malignant Neoplasms	19,217	16,452	2,615	3	72	84	819	4,983	13,256
Cerebrovascular Disease	5,087	4,442	607	8	2	8	139	518	4,412
Accidents	2,844	2,370	424	29	262	441	721	441	949
Chronic Obst. Pulmon. Disease	3,076	2,798	257	2	5	10	23	458	2,578
Pneumonia/Influenza	2,697	2,367	316	20	13	12	73	203	2,376
Diabetes Mellitus	2,114	1,702	389	0	1	7	92	422	1,592
Chronic Liver Disease/Cirrhosis	947	710	220	2	2	2	224	372	345
Homicide	1,047	320	718	13	38	357	481	117	41
Suicide	1,063	945	105	0	6	179	456	231	191
Atherosclerosis	774	710	60	0	0	0	1	33	740
AIDS	573	298	272	0	3	13	428	116	11

Source: Michigan Department of Public Health, Michigan Health Statistics 1992 (Lansing, Michigan: 1993).

Table II-6: Number of Deaths Among Michigan Residents, by Age and Sex: 1991-1992

Age	1991			1992		
	Total	Male	Female	Total	Male	Female
Less Than 1	1,554	903	646	1,460	840	618
1-4	299	157	142	256	162	93
5-9	143	77	66	167	102	65
10-14	176	132	44	189	130	59
15-19	648	483	165	537	388	149
20-24	736	581	155	761	581	179
25-29	816	584	232	807	578	224
30-39	2,506	1,653	851	2,454	1,676	776
40-49	3,657	2,310	1,344	3,740	2,398	1,341
50-59	6,253	3,732	2,517	5,965	3,556	2,404
60-69	14,161	8,331	5,824	13,709	8,063	5,642
70 Plus	48,785	21,963	26,796	48,867	22,012	26,827
Unknown	4	2	2	4	1	3

Source: Michigan Department of Public Health, Michigan Health Statistics 1992 (Lansing, Michigan: 1993).

Table II-7. Injury Deaths per 100,000 Population in Michigan, by Cause: 1991

Category	Number of Deaths*	Age-Adjusted Rate(%)**
Total Injury Deaths	**5,452**	**53.5**
Homicide	1,150	12.9
Suicide	1,142	11.4
Other	123	1.2
Unintentional	3,037	28.0
Fire/Burn	209	2.0
Drowning	140	1.5
Motor Vehicle	1,513	15.7
Falls	476	2.8
Firearms	28	0.3

*Total number includes unknown age. ** Data is adjusted for comparability across populations with varying age distributions. Age-Adjusted Rate excludes unknown age. Source: National Center for Health Statistics, Mortality Data Tapes and Demographic Detail.

Table II-8. Number of Michigan Deaths Caused by Firearm Injury, by Sex and Age: 1991

Age/Gender	Cause			
	Unintentional	Homicide	Suicide	Other
Total, Age/Gender	**28**	**800**	**659**	**11**
0-4	0	8	0	0
5-9	1	4	0	0
10-14	6	16	6	0
15-24	12	333	103	6
25-34	4	229	121	0
35-49	1	160	185	2
50-64	2	33	97	2
65-84	2	16	130	1
85 Plus	0	0	16	0
Unknown Age	0	1	1	0
Total Male	**27**	**669**	**598**	**9**
0-4	0	4	0	0
5-9	1	2	0	0
10-14	5	15	6	0
15-24	12	302	93	6
25-34	4	192	109	0
35-49	1	119	162	1
50-64	2	25	87	1
65-84	2	9	125	1
85 Plus	0	0	16	0
Unknown Age	0	1	0	0
Total Female	**1**	**131**	**61**	**2**
0-4	0	4	0	0
5-9	0	2	0	0
10-14	1	1	0	0
15-24	0	31	10	0
25-34	0	37	12	0
35-49	0	41	23	1
50-64	0	8	10	1
65-84	0	7	5	0
85 Plus	0	0	0	0
Unknown Age	0	0	1	0

Source: National Center for Health Statistics, Mortality Data Tapes and Demographic Detail (Hyattsville, MD).

Table II-9. Infant, Neonatal, Postneonatal, Perinatal, Fetal, and Maternal Deaths, Michigan Residents: 1955-1992

Year	Under 1 Year	Under 28 Days	28-364 Days	Perinatal	Fetal	Maternal
1955	4,873	3,707	1,166	6,381	3,029	61
1956	5,047	3,796	1,251	6,655	3,245	84
1957	5,093	3,884	1,209	6,668	3,154	79
1958	4,980	3,789	1,191	6,516	3,101	69
1959	4,846	3,674	1,172	6,250	2,928	72
1960	4,702	3,580	1,122	6,247	3,008	75
1961	4,604	3,475	1,129	5,875	2,735	78
1962	4,367	3,251	1,116	5,669	2,703	56
1963	4,150	3,109	1,041	5,407	2,540	71
1964	4,043	3,071	972	5,293	2,466	62
1965	3,936	2,909	1,027	5,139	2,475	54
1966	3,751	2,830	921	4,909	2,295	54
1967	3,595	2,714	881	4,693	2,195	52
1968	3,438	2,617	821	4,476	2,064	44
1969	3,356	2,550	806	4,488	2,175	27
1970	3,492	2,671	821	4,522	2,060	29
1971	3,157	2,412	745	4,139	1,923	32
1972	2,801	2,115	686	3,700	1,765	35
1973	2,561	1,902	659	3,392	1,682	26
1974	2,387	1,734	653	2,947	1,438	19
1975	2,205	1,563	642	2,673	1,356	16
1976	1,978	1,424	554	2,495	1,264	14
1977	1,945	1,367	578	2,452	1,284	11
1978	1,931	1,281	650	2,302	1,201	15
1979	1,921	1,295	626	2,285	1,175	11
1980	1,851	1,284	567	2,235	1,135	16
1981	1,851	1,281	570	2,151	1,040	7
1982	1,672	1,202	470	1,989	954	11
1983	1,573	1,067	506	1,843	933	6
1984	1,595	1,100	495	1,884	929	4
1985	1,575	1,071	504	1,867	953	9
1986	1,565	1,079	486	1,782	865	11
1987	1,538	1,029	509	1,701	824	8
1988	1,542	1,068	474	1,659	761	11
1989	1,645	1,070	575	1,792	881	13
1990	1,638	1,073	565	1,722	830	10
1991	1,554	1,003	551	1,620	775	16
1992	1,460	962	498	1,576	755	15

Source: Michigan Department of Public Health, Michigan Health Statistics 1992 (Lansing, Michigan: 1993).

Table II-10. Infant Deaths and Infant Death Rates in Michigan, by Race: 1970-1993

Year	Total	Rate	White	Rate	Black	Rate	Other	Rate
1970	3,492	20.3	2,661	18.5	811	30.6	14	16.1
1971	3,157	19.5	2,293	17.1	843	31.5	17	19.1
1972	2,801	19.1	1,957	16.3	835	32.4	8	8.5
1973	2,561	18.1	1,749	15.2	796	31.5	11	11.9
1974	2,387	17.4	1,673	14.8	705	30.9	7	7.4
1975	2,205	16.5	1,574	14.3	616	27.1	8	8.4
1976	1,978	15.1	1,383	12.8	575	26.4	16	14.5
1977	1,945	14.1	1,373	12.0	559	24.7	8	7.6
1978	1,931	13.9	1,344	11.7	566	25.2	13	8.6
1979	1,921	13.3	1,352	11.3	550	23.6	12	7.4
1980	1,851	12.8	1,246	10.4	582	24.8	15	8.2
1981	1,851	13.2	1,261	10.8	564	25.6	18	9.7
1982	1,672	12.1	1,110	9.7	548	25.4	13	7.2
1983	1,573	11.8	1,048	9.5	506	23.8	15	8.7
1984	1,595	11.7	1,034	9.3	541	24.2	15	8.4
1985	1,575	11.4	1,053	9.2	510	23.3	11	6.0
1986	1,565	11.4	999	8.9	553	23.7	13	6.7
1987	1,538	10.9	953	8.4	567	22.7	17	8.5
1988	1,542	11.0	952	8.5	570	22.6	19	9.1
1989	1,645	11.1	946	8.2	672	22.5	23	9.1
1990	1,638	10.7	930	7.9	689	21.6	18	6.9
1991	1,554	10.4	857	7.5	683	21.7	13	5.2
1992	1,460	10.2	781	7.0	656	22.1	23	10.3
1993	1,319	9.5	770	7.1	530	18.8	19	6.4

Source: Michigan Department of Public Health, Michigan Health Statistics 1992 (Lansing, Michigan: 1993).

Table II-11. Selected Vital Statistics for Michigan, by County: 1992

County	Live Births	Birth Rate	Deaths	Death Rate	Marriages	Marriage Rate	Divorces	Divorce Rate
Alcona	97	9.6	159	15.7	87	17.2	54	10.6
Alger	94	10.5	118	13.2	71	15.8	33	7.4
Allegan	1,435	15.9	669	7.4	713	15.8	426	9.4
Alpena	382	12.5	298	9.7	253	16.5	156	10.2
Antrim	262	14.4	223	12.3	176	19.4	95	10.4
Arenac	183	12.3	176	11.8	118	15.8	54	7.2
Baraga	129	16.2	95	11.9	57	14.3	34	8.5
Barry	706	14.1	381	7.6	402	16.1	257	10.3
Bay	1,576	14.1	1,012	9.1	903	16.2	464	8.3
Benzie	178	14.6	114	9.3	135	22.1	51	8.4
Berrien	2,477	15.3	1,449	9.0	1,389	17.2	747	9.3
Branch	539	13.0	385	9.3	329	15.9	228	11.0
Calhoun	2,075	15.3	1,377	10.1	1,250	18.4	677	10.0
Cass	541	10.9	453	9.2	367	14.8	265	10.7
Charlevoix	284	13.2	212	9.9	234	21.8	110	10.2
Cheboygan	293	13.7	244	11.4	180	16.8	116	10.8
Chippewa	402	11.6	283	8.2	290	16.8	117	6.8
Clare	376	15.1	316	12.7	214	17.2	137	11.0
Clinton	832	14.4	373	6.4	443	15.3	245	8.5
Crawford	164	13.4	134	10.9	96	15.7	77	12.6
Delta	411	10.9	368	9.7	308	16.3	138	7.3
Dickinson	322	12.0	307	11.4	228	17.0	132	9.8
Eaton	1,192	12.8	620	6.7	775	16.7	528	11.4
Emmet	359	14.3	255	10.2	292	23.3	154	12.3
Genesee	7,261	16.9	3,642	8.5	3,396	15.8	1,730	8.0
Gladwin	299	13.7	267	12.2	187	17.1	129	11.8
Gogebic	178	9.9	264	14.6	144	16.0	42	4.7
Grand Traverse	921	14.3	501	7.8	671	20.9	355	11.0
Gratiot	547	14.0	398	10.2	292	15.0	153	7.8
Hillsdale	553	12.7	389	9.0	325	15.0	278	12.8
Houghton	411	11.6	409	11.5	267	15.1	119	6.7
Huron	416	11.9	417	11.9	263	15.0	122	7.0
Ingham	4,297	15.2	1,837	6.5	2,478	17.6	1,203	8.5
Ionia	813	14.3	388	6.8	485	17.0	248	8.7
Iosco	474	15.7	306	10.1	288	19.1	184	12.2
Iron	111	8.4	222	16.9	85	12.9	64	9.7
Isabella	709	13.0	344	6.3	400	14.6	180	6.6
Jackson	2,188	14.6	1,292	8.6	1,284	17.1	908	12.1
Kalamazoo	3,307	14.8	1,671	7.5	1,821	16.3	1,088	9.7
Kalkaska	199	14.7	104	7.7	117	17.3	63	9.3
Kent	9,081	18.1	3,496	7.0	4,703	18.8	2,357	9.4
Keweenaw	20	11.8	30	17.6	17	20.0	8	9.4
Lake	107	12.5	129	15.0	81	18.9	42	9.8

66

Table II-11. Selected Vital Statistics for Michigan, by County: 1992 Continued

County	Live Births	Birth Rate	Deaths	Death Rate	Marriages	Marriage Rate	Divorces	Divorce Rate
Lapeer	1,016	13.6	504	6.7	641	17.1	381	10.2
Leelanau	216	13.1	132	8.0	95	11.5	57	6.9
Lenawee	1,247	13.6	783	8.6	631	13.8	466	10.2
Livingston	1,596	13.8	726	6.3	934	16.2	602	10.4
Luce	74	12.8	73	12.7	39	13.5	36	12.5
Mackinac	135	12.6	120	11.2	204	38.2	39	7.3
Macomb	9,828	13.7	5,873	8.2	6,217	17.3	2,913	8.1
Manistee	243	11.4	280	13.2	176	16.6	96	9.0
Marquette	921	13.0	529	7.5	655	18.5	324	9.1
Mason	322	12.6	250	9.8	227	17.8	146	11.4
Mecosta	412	11.0	268	7.2	295	15.8	147	7.9
Menominee	268	10.8	255	10.2	223	17.9	90	7.2
Midland	1,137	15.0	469	6.2	696	18.4	375	9.9
Missaukee	190	15.6	121	10.0	88	14.5	41	6.8
Monroe	1,845	13.8	960	7.2	884	13.2	616	9.2
Montcalm	824	15.5	445	8.4	502	18.9	303	11.4
Montmorency	81	9.1	121	13.5	63	14.1	30	6.7
Muskegon	2,541	16.0	1,433	9.0	1,376	17.3	866	10.9
Newaygo	674	17.6	349	9.1	375	19.6	235	12.3
Oakland	16,343	15.1	7,956	7.3	8,843	16.3	4,986	9.2
Oceana	344	15.3	224	10.0	203	18.1	137	12.2
Ogemaw	264	14.1	261	14.0	173	18.5	81	8.7
Ontonagon	88	9.9	123	13.9	59	13.3	27	6.1
Osceola	313	15.5	205	10.2	173	17.2	67	6.7
Oscoda	103	13.1	98	12.5	75	19.1	34	8.7
Otsego	288	16.0	148	8.2	186	20.7	98	10.9
Ottawa	3,193	17.0	1,152	6.1	946	10.1	361	3.8
Presque Isle	145	10.6	163	11.9	84	12.2	41	6.0
Roscommon	237	12.0	280	14.2	150	15.2	92	9.3
Saginaw	3,534	16.7	1,778	8.4	1,621	15.3	930	8.8
St. Clair	2,110	14.5	1,277	8.8	1,134	15.6	741	10.2
St. Joseph	811	13.8	562	9.5	536	18.2	362	12.3
Sanilac	501	12.5	450	11.3	317	15.9	174	8.7
Schoolcraft	90	10.8	96	11.6	88	21.2	37	8.9
Shiawassee	980	14.0	558	8.0	599	17.2	298	8.5
Tuscola	811	14.6	447	8.1	409	14.7	272	9.8
Van Buren	1,109	15.8	627	8.9	598	17.1	333	9.5
Washtenaw	4,093	14.5	1,593	5.6	2,229	15.8	1,216	8.6
Wayne	37,264	17.6	20,857	9.9	11,701	11.1	7,639	7.2
Wexford	408	15.5	242	9.2	263	20.0	168	12.7
County Not Stated	27	---	1	---	---	---	---	---
Michigan	**143,827**	**15.5**	**78,916**	**8.5**	**71,322**	**14.9**	**40,425**	**8.7**

Source: Michigan Department of Public Health, Michigan Health Statistics 1992 (Lansing, Michigan: 1993). --- No data.

Table II-12. Infant Deaths, Live Births, and Infant Death Rates in Michigan, by County: 1991-1992

County	1991			1992		
	Infant Deaths	Live Births	Death Rate	Infant Deaths	Live Births	Death Rate
Alcona	0	99	0.0	0	97	0.0
Alger	0	93	0.0	0	94	0.0
Allegan	6	1,406	4.3	7	1,435	4.9
Alpena	2	360	---	1	382	---
Antrim	1	241	---	3	262	---
Arenac	3	224	---	0	183	0.0
Baraga	0	108	0.0	1	129	---
Barry	3	728	---	6	706	8.5
Bay	19	1,597	11.9	18	1,576	11.4
Benzie	2	164	---	2	178	---
Berrien	33	2,337	14.1	26	2,477	10.5
Branch	6	549	10.9	5	539	---
Calhoun	19	2,142	8.9	19	2,075	9.2
Cass	4	434	---	6	541	11.1
Charlevoix	2	305	---	2	284	---
Cheboygan	3	269	---	3	293	---
Chippewa	1	393	---	2	402	---
Clare	2	383	---	2	376	---
Clinton	4	832	---	6	832	7.2
Crawford	2	203	---	2	164	---
Delta	6	468	12.8	4	411	---
Dickinson	4	359	---	2	322	---
Eaton	7	1,172	6.0	4	1,192	---
Emmet	4	395	---	6	359	16.7
Genesee	90	7,513	12.0	73	7,261	10.1
Gladwin	2	284	---	2	299	---
Gogebic	1	176	---	0	178	0.0
Grand Traverse	9	953	9.4	10	921	10.9
Gratiot	5	612	---	4	547	---
Hillsdale	6	596	10.1	3	553	---
Houghton	2	438	---	0	411	0.0
Huron	5	414	---	5	416	---
Ingham	32	4,517	7.1	30	4,297	7.0
Ionia	14	850	16.5	7	813	8.6
Iosco	2	543	---	0	474	0.0
Iron	2	125	---	1	111	---
Isabella	5	702	---	8	709	11.3
Jackson	16	2,262	7.1	20	2,188	9.1
Kalamazoo	39	3,409	11.4	33	3,307	10.0
Kalkaska	1	213	---	1	199	---
Kent	98	9,432	10.4	74	9,081	8.1
Keweenaw	0	16	0.0	0	20	0.0
Lake	3	109	---	2	107	---

Table II-12. Infant Deaths, Live Births, and Infant Death Rates in Michigan, by County: 1991-1992 Continued

County	1991			1992		
	Infant Deaths	Live Births	Death Rate	Infant Deaths	Live Births	Death Rates
Lapeer	16	1,124	14.2	11	1,016	10.8
Leelanau	4	209	---	2	216	---
Lenawee	8	1,362	5.9	6	1,247	4.8
Livingston	8	1,636	4.9	7	1,596	4.4
Luce	0	58	0.0	2	74	---
Mackinac	0	123	0.0	0	135	0.0
Macomb	69	10,288	6.7	53	9,828	5.4
Manistee	0	230	0.0	5	243	---
Marquette	6	955	6.3	12	921	13.0
Mason	1	355	---	1	322	---
Mecosta	10	455	22.0	4	412	---
Menominee	4	290	---	2	268	---
Midland	6	1,180	5.1	7	1,137	6.2
Missaukee	4	158	---	2	190	---
Monroe	9	1,880	4.8	10	1,845	5.4
Montcalm	5	842	---	5	824	---
Montmorency	1	86	---	0	81	0.0
Muskegon	38	2,644	14.4	23	2,541	9.1
Newaygo	4	682	---	7	674	10.4
Oakland	128	16,555	7.7	132	16,343	8.1
Oceana	4	332	---	3	344	---
Ogemaw	0	280	0.0	3	264	---
Ontonagon	1	94	---	2	88	---
Osceola	1	314	---	4	313	---
Oscoda	2	90	---	0	103	0.0
Otsego	1	280	---	0	288	0.0
Ottawa	21	3,306	6.4	17	3,193	5.3
Presque Isle	0	129	0.0	2	145	---
Roscommon	4	239	---	1	237	---
Saginaw	42	3,664	11.5	51	3,534	14.4
St. Clair	17	2,077	8.2	16	2,110	7.6
St. Joseph	8	868	9.2	11	811	13.6
Sanilac	4	557	---	9	501	18.0
Schoolcraft	2	107	---	0	90	0.0
Shiawassee	9	1,009	8.9	4	980	---
Tuscola	8	791	10.1	3	811	---
Van Buren	11	1,156	9.5	10	1,109	9.0
Washtenaw	36	4,221	8.5	39	4,093	9.5
Wayne	595	40,001	14.9	590	37,264	15.8
Wexford	2	413	---	3	408	---
Unknown	0	13	0.0	1	27	---
Michigan	**1,554**	**149,478**	**10.4**	**1,460**	**143,827**	**10.2**

Source: Michigan Department of Public Health, Michigan Health Statistics 1992 (Lansing, Michigan: 1993). --- No data.

Table II-13. Reported Abortions in Michigan, Selected Years: 1980-1993

Characteristics	1980	1985	1990	1991	1992	1993
Number of Abortions Reported	**45,455**	**42,678**	**36,183**	**34,555**	**34,496**	**35,737**
Number for Residents	43,964	41,400	34,655	33,119	33,160	34,329
Percent(%) for Residents	96.7	97.0	95.8	95.8	96.1	96.1
Number of Abortions to Women Under 18 Years	**N.A.**	**N.A.**	**3,820**	**3,146**	**3,081**	**3,102**
Percent of All Women	N.A.	N.A.	10.6	9.1	8.9	8.7
Number of Abortions per 1,000 Live Births (Residents)	**302.9**	**302.6**	**224.5**	**220.8**	**233.5**	**250.6**
AGE						
Under 20 Years	31.4	30.6	25.3	23.4	22.5	21.0
20-24 Years	35.9	34.0	33.0	34.9	35.5	35.9
25-29 Years	19.0	19.4	20.9	20.4	20.5	20.7
30 or More Years	13.0	15.7	20.8	21.2	21.4	22.2
Not Married	**78.4**	**82.4**	**81.1**	**81.8**	**82.8**	**83.5**
Had Previous Term Pregnancy	**45.6**	**47.7**	**51.5**	**53.8**	**52.6**	**56.3**
Previous Induced Abortions	**66.2**	**59.5**	**55.3**	**53.4**	**55.4**	**51.4**
None	9.5	14.6	16.6	17.7	17.3	19.5
Two or More	19.5	17.3	17.7	16.6	14.6	9.5
Gestation(%) 12 Weeks or Less	**83.5**	**83.5**	**87.7**	**87.2**	**87.7**	**87.3**
Procedure Used: Suction	**94.5**	**96.0**	**99.3**	**99.1**	**99.3**	**97.9**
Type of Facility	**56.7**	**32.4**	**42.7**	**43.8**	**42.8**	**39.1**
Clinic	15.1	48.6	55.4	54.7	55.9	59.7
Physician's Office	0.55	0.26	0.09	0.10	0.07	0.08
With Complications Mentioned	**0.08**	**0.07**	**0.10**	**0.09**	**0.26**	**0.55**

N.A. data not available.
Source: Michigan Department of Public Health, Abortions In Michigan, January through December 1993 (Lansing, Michigan: 1994).

Table II-14. Reported Abortions in Michigan, by County of Residence: 1993

County	Number of Abortions	County	Number of Abortions	County	Number of Abortions
Alcona	10	Hillsdale	61	Montcalm	58
Alger	8	Houghton	15	Montmorency	14
Allegan	129	Huron	44	Muskegon	444
Alpena	35	Ingham	1,477	Newaygo	38
Antrim	13	Ionia	83	Oakland	3,683
Arenac	26	Iosco	48	Oceana	27
Baraga	3	Iron	2	Ogemaw	35
Barry	81	Isabella	161	Ontonagon	2
Bay	269	Jackson	395	Osceola	19
Benzie	22	Kalamazoo	1,098	Oscoda	7
Berrien	502	Kalkaska	20	Otsego	34
Branch	60	Kent	924	Ottawa	217
Calhoun	444	Keweenaw	0	Presque Isle	10
Cass	107	Lake	9	Roscommon	36
Charlevoix	29	Lapeer	153	Saginaw	725
Cheboygan	25	Leelanau	21	St. Clair	502
Chippewa	64	Lenawee	111	St. Joseph	134
Clare	51	Livingston	288	Sanilac	65
Clinton	107	Luce	13	Schoolcraft	1
Crawford	22	Mackinac	18	Shiawassee	150
Delta	8	Macomb	2,981	Tuscola	98
Dickinson	5	Manistee	22	Van Buren	207
Eaton	226	Marquette	57	Washtenaw	1,407
Emmet	51	Mason	30	Wayne	13,542
Genesee	1,808	Mecosta	82	Wexford	51
Gladwin	32	Menominee	1	County Not Reported	11
Gogebic	0	Midland	138	**Michigan**	**34,329**
Grand Traverse	116	Missaukee	17		
Gratiot	74	Monroe	216		

Source: Michigan Department of Public Health, <u>Abortions In Michigan, January through December 1993</u> (Lansing, Michigan: 1994).

Table II-15. Life Expectancy at Birth in Michigan and the United States by Sex, Selected Years: 1901-1992

Year	Mich. - Life Expectancy		U. S. - Life Expectancy		Year	Mich. - Life Expectancy		U.S. - Life Expectancy	
	Male	Female	Male	Female		Male	Female	Male	Female
1901	53.4	55.1	47.6	50.6	1982	70.6	77.4	70.9	78.1
1910	53.9	56.2	48.4	51.8	1983	70.7	77.4	71.0	78.1
1920	55.1	56.0	53.6	54.6	1984	70.8	77.2	71.2	78.2
1930	59.8	62.8	58.1	61.6	1985	70.6	77.4	71.2	78.2
1940	63.4	64.4	60.8	65.2	1986	70.7	77.4	71.3	78.3
1950	65.7	71.2	65.6	71.1	1987	71.1	77.4	71.5	78.4
1960	67.1	73.3	66.6	73.1	1988	71.3	77.6	71.5	78.3
1970	67.2	74.6	67.1	74.7	1989	71.6	77.7	72.2	79.1
1975	68.5	75.7	68.8	76.6	1990	71.7	78.1	71.8	78.8
1980	70.0	76.9	70.0	77.4	1991	71.7	78.0	72.2	79.1
1981	70.3	77.1	70.4	77.8	1992	71.9	78.2	N.A.	N.A.

N.A. Data not available.
Source: Michigan Department of Public Health, Michigan Health Statistics 1992 (Lansing, Michigan: 1993).

Table II-16. Life Expectancy at Birth by Sex and Race in Michigan, Selected Years: 1950-1992

Group	1950	1960	1970	1980	1985	1990	1992
Total Sex/Race							
Male	65.7	67.1	67.5	70.0	70.6	71.7	71.9
Female	71.2	73.3	74.6	76.9	77.4	78..1	78.2
White							
Male	66.2	67.5	68.2	71.0	71.7	73.1	73.1
Female	71.9	74.0	75.3	77.6	78.1	79.0	73.1
Black							
Male	60.4	63.6	59.9	63.5	62.9	63.8	64.0
Female	63.4	67.7	68.3	72.2	72.5	73.2	72.7

Source: Michigan Department of Public Health, Michigan Health Statistics 1992 (Lansing, Michigan: 1993).

Table II-17. Expected Remaining Years of Life by Sex, Race, Age: Michigan 1992

Age in Years	Total, Both Sexes and Races	Total Male	Total Female	Total Whites	White Male	White Female	Total Black	Black Male	Black Female
0 - 1	75.1	71.9	78.2	76.3	73.3	79.2	68.4	64.0	72.7
1 - 5	74.9	71.7	77.9	75.8	72.8	78.7	68.9	64.6	73.1
5 - 10	71.0	67.9	74.0	71.9	69.0	74.8	65.2	60.8	69.3
10 - 15	66.1	63.0	69.1	67.0	64.1	69.8	60.3	56.0	64.4
15 - 20	61.2	58.1	64.1	62.1	59.2	64.9	55.4	51.1	59.5
20 - 25	56.4	53.4	59.3	57.3	54.4	60.0	50.8	46.6	54.7
25 - 30	51.7	48.8	54.4	52.5	49.7	55.1	46.4	42.6	50.0
30 - 35	46.9	44.2	49.6	47.7	45.0	50.2	42.0	38.5	45.3
35 - 40	42.2	39.5	44.8	42.9	40.3	45.4	37.6	34.2	40.7
40 - 45	37.6	35.0	40.0	38.2	35.7	40.6	33.4	30.3	36.2
45 - 50	33.1	30.6	35.3	33.6	31.2	35.8	29.4	26.5	32.0
50 - 55	28.7	26.3	30.9	29.1	26.7	31.2	25.6	23.0	27.8
55 - 60	24.5	22.2	26.5	24.8	22.5	26.9	21.9	19.6	23.9
60 - 65	20.4	18.3	22.3	20.7	18.5	22.6	18.4	16.4	20.2
65 - 70	16.7	14.7	18.3	16.9	14.9	18.5	15.2	13.3	16.8
70 - 75	13.4	11.6	14.7	13.5	11.9	14.9	12.4	10.6	13.7
75 - 80	10.4	9.0	11.5	10.5	9.0	11.5	9.9	8.5	10.9
80 - 85	7.8	6.6	8.5	7.8	6.7	8.5	7.4	6.4	8.1
85 Plus	5.5	4.7	5.9	5.5	4.7	5.9	5.5	4.7	5.9

Source: Michigan Department of Public Health, Michigan Health Statistics 1992 (Lansing, Michigan: 1993).

Table II-18. Numbers of Invasive Cancers Among Michigan Residents by Age, Race, and Sex: 1992

Age in Years	All Races			White			Black			Other		
	Total	Male	Female	Total	Male	Female	Total	Male	Female	Total	Male	Female
Less than 5	157	79	78	130	63	67	25	15	10	2	1	1
5-9	48	24	24	38	19	19	8	5	3	2	0	2
10-14	80	43	37	67	37	30	10	3	7	3	3	0
15-19	123	46	77	104	36	68	17	9	8	2	1	1
20-24	240	98	142	207	86	121	31	12	19	2	0	2
25-29	356	164	191	305	139	165	46	22	24	5	3	2
30-34	585	235	348	498	195	302	79	37	41	8	3	5
35-39	933	343	589	781	289	491	138	48	90	14	6	8
40-44	1,387	482	903	1,135	395	738	232	79	153	20	8	12
45-49	1,864	680	1,184	1,585	574	1,011	267	98	169	12	8	4
50-54	2,389	1,063	1,326	2,054	896	1,158	319	160	159	16	7	9
55-59	3,294	1,738	1,556	2,811	1,455	1,356	463	270	193	20	13	7
60-64	5,199	3,046	2,149	4,519	2,615	1,900	655	411	244	25	20	5
65-69	7,157	4,328	2,828	6,236	3,709	2,526	891	597	294	30	22	8
70-74	7,330	4,468	2,862	6,499	3,931	2,568	809	525	284	22	12	10
75-79	5,930	3,575	2,353	5,324	3,180	2,142	591	387	204	15	8	7
80-84	3,672	2,018	1,649	3,321	1,808	1,508	338	201	137	13	9	4
85+	2,561	1,222	1,338	2,291	1,075	1,215	263	141	122	7	6	1
Age Not Stated	20	5	14	20	5	14	0	0	0	0	0	0
All Ages	43,325	23,657	19,648	37,925	20,507	17,399	5,182	3,020	2,161	218	130	88

Source: Michigan Department of Public Health, Cancer Incidence & Mortality - Michigan 1992 (Lansing, Michigan: 1994).

Table II-19. Incidence Rates of Invasive Cancers Among Michigan Residents by Age, Race, and Sex: 1992

Age in Years	All Races			White			Black		
	Total	Male	Female	Total	Male	Female	Total	Male	Female
Less than 5	22.0	21.7	22.4	22.8	21.6	24.1	19.5	23.1	15.8
5-9	7.0	6.8	7.1	6.7	6.6	6.9	7.2	0.0	0.0
10-14	12.0	12.6	11.4	12.4	13.4	11.5	8.9	0.0	12.5
15-19	17.6	12.9	22.4	18.6	12.6	24.8	13.6	14.5	12.8
20-24	34.0	28.0	39.9	35.5	29.5	41.6	28.5	23.5	32.9
25-29	46.6	43.5	49.3	47.7	43.3	51.2	43.7	46.1	41.6
30-34	72.2	59.2	84.1	72.8	57.4	87.6	71.3	74.7	67.0
35-39	125.3	93.8	155.4	124.0	92.0	155.6	136.1	106.0	160.3
40-44	211.0	149.2	270.1	202.7	141.7	262.5	272.6	204.2	329.7
45-49	358.4	265.9	447.9	352.3	257.2	445.9	436.0	347.4	511.7
50-54	563.3	514.7	609.5	554.8	492.3	615.3	672.8	753.8	607.1
55-59	842.0	928.2	762.9	823.6	882.2	768.8	1,018.9	1,338.4	763.9
60-64	1,290.5	1,597.8	1,012.5	1,275.4	1,546.8	1,025.5	1,456.0	2,052.4	977.5
65-69	1,945.9	2,611.9	1,399.3	1,921.0	2,528.4	1,419.7	2,198.0	3,345.5	1,295.6
70-74	2,559.2	3,690.9	1,730.7	2,540.5	3,627.9	1,741.5	2,800.7	4,370.6	1,683.1
75-79	2,798.2	4,321.9	1,821.2	2,802.3	4,280.4	1,851.4	2,843.5	4,856.9	1,591.8
80-84	2,765.3	4,399.4	1,897.2	2,755.4	4,371.7	1,904.7	2,906.8	4,759.6	1,850.1
85+	2,435.1	4,133.1	1,769.7	2,408.1	4,089.2	1,764.7	2,727.4	4,512.0	1,871.7
Age-Adjusted Rate	420.3	535.2	345.2	416.2	522.5	348.3	469.0	657.2	338.8

Source: Michigan Department of Public Health, Cancer Incidence & Mortality - Michigan 1992 (Lansing, Michigan: 1994).

75

Table II-20. Numbers of Deaths Due to Invasive Cancers Among Michigan Residents by Age, Race, and Sex: 1992

Age in Years	All Races			White			Black			Other		
	Total	Male	Female	Total	Male	Female	Total	Male	Female	Total	Male	Female
Less than 5	25	14	11	17	10	7	6	4	2	2	0	2
5-9	24	12	12	19	10	9	4	1	3	1	1	0
10-14	26	18	8	25	18	7	1	0	1	0	0	0
15-19	29	20	9	20	15	5	7	4	3	2	1	1
20-24	55	28	27	48	25	23	7	3	4	0	0	0
25-29	78	36	42	57	29	28	19	5	14	2	2	0
30-34	118	47	71	97	38	59	19	8	11	2	1	1
35-39	225	97	128	172	76	96	48	18	30	5	3	2
40-44	398	198	200	306	151	155	90	47	43	2	0	2
45-49	586	287	299	456	220	236	120	62	58	10	5	5
50-54	967	492	475	792	390	402	165	97	68	10	5	5
55-59	1,296	704	592	1,046	574	472	231	117	114	19	13	6
60-64	2,134	1,204	930	1,782	1,007	775	328	185	143	24	12	12
65-69	2,962	1,689	1,273	2,490	1,415	1,075	447	258	189	24	15	9
70-74	3,208	1,800	1,408	2,783	1,544	1,239	409	249	160	14	6	8
75-79	2,887	1,578	1,309	2,569	1,396	1,173	308	175	133	10	7	3
80-84	2,195	1,134	1,061	1,960	1,001	959	219	125	94	16	8	8
85+	2,004	880	1,124	1,813	772	1,041	187	106	81	4	2	2
Age Not Stated	0	0	0	0	0	0	0	0	0	0	0	0
All Ages	19,217	10,238	8,979	16,452	8,691	7,761	2,615	1,464	1,151	147	81	66
Median Age at Last Birth	70.5	70.0	71.0	71.0	70.5	71.5	67.5	68.0	67.0	64.0	64.0	64.0

Source: Michigan Department of Public Health, Cancer Incidence & Mortality - Michigan 1992 (Lansing, Michigan: 1994).

76

Table II-21. Death Rates Due to Invasive Cancers Among Michigan Residents by Age, Race, and Sex: 1992

Age in Years	All Races			White			Black		
	Total	Male	Female	Total	Male	Female	Total	Male	Female
Less than 5	3.5	3.8	3.2	3.0	3.4	2.5	4.7	0.0	0.0
5-9	3.5	3.4	3.6	3.4	3.5	3.3	0.0	0.0	0.0
10-14	3.9	5.3	2.5	4.6	6.5	2.7	0.0	0.0	0.0
15-19	4.1	5.6	2.6	3.6	5.2	0.0	5.6	0.0	0.0
20-24	7.8	8.0	7.6	8.2	8.6	7.9	6.4	0.0	0.0
25-29	10.2	9.6	10.8	8.9	9.0	8.7	18.0	0.0	24.3
30-34	14.6	11.8	17.2	14.2	11.2	17.1	17.2	16.1	18.0
35-39	30.2	26.5	33.8	27.3	24.2	30.4	47.3	39.8	53.4
40-44	60.5	61.3	59.8	54.6	54.2	55.1	105.8	121.5	92.7
45-49	112.7	112.2	113.1	101.4	98.6	104.1	196.0	219.8	175.6
50-54	228.0	238.2	218.3	213.9	214.3	213.6	348.0	457.0	259.6
55-59	331.3	376.0	290.3	306.5	348.0	267.6	508.4	580.0	451.2
60-64	529.7	631.6	438.2	502.9	595.7	418.3	729.1	923.8	572.9
65-69	805.3	1,019.3	629.9	767.4	965.3	604.2	1,102.7	1,445.8	832.9
70-74	1,120.0	1,486.9	851.5	1,088.7	1,425.9	840.9	1,415.9	2,072.9	948.2
75-79	1,362.3	1,907.7	1,013.2	1,352.2	1,879.1	1,013.9	1,481.9	2,196.3	1,037.8
80-84	1,653.0	2,472.2	1,220.7	1,626.2	2,420.4	1,211.3	1,883.4	2,960.0	1,269.4
85+	1,905.5	2,976.4	1,486.7	1,905.7	2,936.6	1,512.0	1,939.2	3,392.0	1,242.7
Age-Adjusted Rate	182.8	234.5	148.7	175.8	224.1	144.1	238.9	323.6	181.2

Source: Michigan Department of Public Health, Cancer Incidence & Mortality - Michigan 1992 (Lansing, Michigan: 1994).

Table II-22. Numbers and Percentages of Invasive Cancers by Primary Site, Sex, and Race: 1992

Primary Site	Total Number	Total (%)	White Male Number	White Male (%)	White Female Number	White Female (%)	Black Male Number	Black Male (%)	Black Female Number	Black Female (%)	Other Male Number	Other Male (%)	Other Female Number	Other Female (%)
Gastrointestinal Tract and Digestive System	8,551		3,896		3,394		679		523		41		18	
Lip/Oral Cavity/Pharynx	913	2.1	503	2.5	266	1.5	101	3.3	36	1.7	6	4.6	1	1.1
Stomach	672	1.6	316	1.5	214	1.2	76	2.5	54	2.5	9	6.9	3	3.4
Colon	3,630	8.4	1,515	7.4	1,652	9.5	226	7.5	219	10.1	13	10.0	5	5.7
Rectum	1,411	3.3	710	3.5	552	3.2	73	2.4	70	3.2	4	3.1	2	2.3
Pancreas	816	1.9	335	1.6	337	1.9	71	2.4	66	3.1	2	1.5	5	5.7
Other Gastrointestinal	1,109	2.6	517	2.5	373	2.1	132	4.4	78	3.6	7	5.4	2	2.3
Respiratory System and Pleura	6,820		3,611		2,253		634		298		19		5	
Larynx	516	1.2	345	1.7	79	0.5	71	2.4	19	0.9	2	1.5	0	0.0
Lung and Bronchus	6,158	14.2	3,175	15.5	2,130	12.2	556	18.4	275	12.7	17	13.1	5	5.7
Other Respirator	146	0.3	91	0.4	44	0.3	7	0.2	4	0.2	0	0.0	0	0.0
Bones and Soft Tissue	279	0.6	138	0.7	107	0.6	16	0.5	14	0.6	3	2.3	1	1.1
Melanoma of Skin	985	2.3	564	2.8	402	2.3	3	0.1	5	0.2	0	0.0	4	4.5
Breast	6,135	14.2	37	0.2	5,395	31.0	8	0.3	673	31.1	0	0.0	22	25.0
Genitourinary Organs	14,969		9,795		3,402		1,362		343		42		25	
Cervix Uteri	508	1.2	0	0.0	418	2.4	0	0.0	86	4.0	0	0.0	4	4.5
Corpus Uteri	1,298	3.0	0	0.0	1,192	6.9	0	0.0	99	4.6	0	0.0	7	8.0
Ovary	781	1.8	0	0.0	718	4.1	0	0.0	56	2.6	0	0.0	7	8.0
Prostate Gland	8,857	20.4	7,640	37.3	0	0.0	1,185	39.2	0	0.0	32	24.6	0	0.0
Other Genital	511	1.2	268	1.3	209	1.2	7	0.2	24	1.1	1	0.8	2	2.3

Table II-22. Numbers and Percentages of Invasive Cancers by Primary Site, Sex, and Race: 1992 Continued

Primary Site	Total		White Male		White Female		Black Male		Black Female		Other Male		Other Female	
	Number	(%)	Number	(%)	Number	(%)	Number	(%)	Number	(%)	Number	(%)	Number	(%)
Genitourinary Organs-Continued														
Urinary Bladder	1,898	4.4	1,274	6.2	497	2.9	87	2.9	35	1.6	4	3.1	1	1.1
Kidney and Renal Pelvis	1,004	2.3	547	2.7	340	2.0	72	2.4	38	1.8	5	3.8	2	2.3
Other Urinary	112	0.3	66	0.3	28	0.2	11	0.4	5	0.2	0	0.0	2	2.3
Brain/Central Nervous System	624	1.4	334	1.6	243	1.4	23	0.8	21	1.0	1	0.8	2	2.3
Lymphomas	**1,697**		**750**		**763**		**100**		**66**		**7**		**3**	
Hodgkin's Disease	279	0.6	123	0.6	117	0.7	21	0.7	17	0.8	1	0.8	0	0.0
Non-Hodgkin's Lymphomas	1,418	3.3	627	3.1	646	3.7	79	2.6	49	2.3	6	4.6	3	3.4
Multiple Myelomas	425	1.0	168	0.8	175	1.0	38	1.3	43	2.0	1	0.8	0	0.0
Leukemias	944	2.2	467	2.3	375	2.2	46	1.5	47	2.2	5	3.8	4	4.5
All Other	1,896	4.4	747	3.6	890	5.1	111	3.7	128	5.9	11	8.5	4	4.5
Total	**43,325**	**100.0**	**20,507**	**100.0**	**17,399**	**100.0**	**3,020**	**100.0**	**2,161**	**100.0**	**130**	**100.0**	**88**	**100.0**

Source: Michigan Department of Public Health, Cancer Incidence & Mortality - Michigan 1992 (Lansing, Michigan:1994).

Table II-23. Numbers and Percentages of Cancer Deaths by Primary Site, Sex, and Race: 1992

Primary Site	Total		White Male		White Female		Black Male		Black Female	
	Number	(%)	Number	(%)	Number	(%)	Number	(%)	Number	(%)
Gastrointestinal Tract and Digestive System	**4,732**		**2,167**		**1,820**		**410**		**298**	
Lip/Oral Cavity/Pharynx	280	1.5	141	1.6	90	1.2	41	2.8	7	0.6
Stomach	490	2.5	209	2.4	177	2.3	56	3.8	39	3.4
Colon	1,746	9.1	789	9.1	735	9.5	106	7.2	106	9.2
Rectum	295	1.5	131	1.5	119	1.5	23	1.6	19	1.7
Pancreas	944	4.9	409	4.7	392	5.1	72	4.9	63	5.5
Other Gastrointestinal	977	5.1	488	5.6	307	4.0	112	7.7	64	5.6
Respiratory System and Pleura	**5,718**		**3,028**		**1,843**		**540**		**266**	
Larynx	165	0.9	100	1.2	27	0.3	28	1.9	10	0.9
Lung and Bronchus	5,503	28.6	2,903	33.4	1,798	23.2	508	34.7	253	22.0
Other Respirator	50	0.3	25	0.3	18	0.2	4	0.3	3	0.3
Bones and Soft Tissue	**140**	**0.7**	**62**	**0.7**	**61**	**0.8**	**7**	**0.5**	**7**	**0.6**
Melanoma of Skin	**165**	**0.9**	**101**	**1.2**	**62**	**0.8**	**1**	**0.1**	**0**	**0.0**
Breast	**1,597**	**8.3**	**9**	**0.1**	**1,357**	**17.5**	**5**	**0.3**	**212**	**18.4**
Genitourinary Organs	**3,110**		**1,570**		**1,065**		**275**		**174**	
Cervix Uteri	169	0.9	0	0.0	119	1.5	0	0.0	47	4.1
Corpus Uteri	136	0.7	0	0.0	116	1.5	0	0.0	19	1.7
Ovary	475	2.5	0	0.0	420	5.4	0	0.0	52	4.5
Prostate Gland	1,299	6.8	1,060	12.2	0	0.0	231	15.8	0	0.0
Other Genital	190	1.0	24	0.3	136	1.8	2	0.1	25	2.2

Table II-23. Numbers and Percentages of Cancer Deaths by Primary Site, Sex, and Race: 1992 Continued

Primary Site	Total		White Male		White Female		Black Male		Black Female	
	Number	(%)	Number	(%)	Number	(%)	Number	(%)	Number	(%)
Urinary Bladder	421	2.2	253	2.9	128	1.6	20	1.4	17	1.5
Kidney and Renal Pelvis	404	2.1	227	2.6	139	1.8	22	1.5	11	1.0
Other Urinary	16	0.1	6	0.1	7	0.1	0	0.0	3	0.3
Brain/Central Nervous System	485	2.5	256	2.9	189	2.4	24	1.6	13	1.1
Lymphomas	**809**		**376**		**354**		**45**		**32**	
Hodgkin's Disease	68	0.4	36	0.4	24	0.3	3	0.2	5	0.4
Non-Hodgkin's Lymphomas	741	3.9	340	3.9	330	4.3	42	2.9	27	2.3
Multiple Myelomas	366	1.9	152	1.7	144	1.9	30	2.0	35	3.0
Leukemias	718	3.7	377	4.3	267	3.4	39	2.7	31	2.7
All Other	1,377	7.2	593	6.8	599	7.7	88	6.0	83	7.2
Total	**19,217**	**100.0**	**8,691**	**100.0**	**7,761**	**100.0**	**1,464**	**100.0**	**1,151**	**100.0**

Source: Michigan Department of Public Health, Cancer Incidence & Mortality - Michigan 1992 (Lansing, Michigan: 1994).

81

Table II-24. Leading Primary Sites of Invasive Cancer and Age-Specific/Age-Adjusted Incidence Rates in Michigan by Age, Race, and Sex: 1992

Age Group	Total Population		
	Rank and Site	Number	Rate
All Ages	1. Prostate Gland	8,857	83.8
	2. Lung and Bronchus	6,158	60.9
	3. Breast	6,135	60.7
	4. Colon	3,630	34.1
	All Sites	43,325	420.3
0 - 14 Years	1. Leukemias	71	3.4
	2. Brain and Other Central Nervous System	68	3.3
	3. Bones and Soft Tissue	24	1.2
	4. Kidney and Renal Pelvis	18	0.9
	All Sites	285	13.8
15 - 24 Years	1. Hodgkin's Disease	56	4.0
	2. Leukemias	38	2.7
	3. Brain and Other Central Nervous System	36	2.6
	4. Non-Hodgkin's Lymphomas	27	1.9
	All Sites	363	25.8
25 - 34 Years	1. Breast	122	7.7
	2. Melanoma of Skin	86	5.5
	3. Cervix Uteri	76	4.8
	4. Hodgkin's Disease	666	4.2
	All Sites	941	59.8
35 - 44 Years	1. Breast	658	46.9
	2. Melanoma of Skin	177	12.6
	3. Lung and Bronchus	135	9.6
	4. Cervix Uteri	129	9.2
	All Sites	2,320	165.5
45 - 54 Years	1. Breast	1,066	112.9
	2. Lung and Bronchus	574	60.8
	3. Colon	258	27.3
	4. Prostate Gland	233	24.7
	All Sites	4,253	450.4
55 - 64	1. Prostate Gland	1,638	112.9
	2. Lung and Bronchus	1,520	60.8
	3. Breast	1,218	27.3
	4. Colon	602	24.7
	All Sites	8,493	450.4
65 and Over	1. Prostate Gland	6,962	630.6
	2. Lung and Bronchus	3,904	353.6
	3. Breast	3,059	277.1
	4. Colon	2,645	239.6
	All Sites	26,650	2,413.7

Source: Michigan Department of Public Health, Cancer Incidence & Mortality - Michigan 1992 (Lansing, Michigan: 1994).

Table II-25. Numbers of Reported Cancer Cases, Deaths, Preliminary Age-Adjusted Incidence, and Final Death Rates in Michigan, by County: 1990-1992 Time Period

County	Incidence		Mortality	
	Number	Age-Adjusted Rate	Number	Age-Adjusted Rate
Alcona	277	472.8	111	178.3
Alger	164	413.1	85	204.8
Allegan	951	331.7	488	163.4
Alpena	537	433.5	249	193.7
Antrim	345	415.2	151	178.0
Arenac	294	464.4	137	201.8
Baraga	144	418.8	69	176.1
Barry	492	292.6	260	150.9
Bay	1,648	403.5	752	179.9
Benzie	244	439.5	108	190.4
Berrien	1,978	334.9	1,145	188.2
Branch	601	405.5	263	175.1
Calhoun	2,048	413.4	932	183.5
Cass	313	174.8	311	171.8
Charlevoix	355	425.6	155	182.5
Cheboygan	398	426.4	194	202.8
Chippewa	521	443.1	203	164.4
Clare	463	409.0	230	199.7
Clinton	578	346.3	262	154.8
Crawford	184	378.6	81	158.0
Delta	578	380.1	296	183.6
Dickinson	333	289.7	212	165.4
Eaton	1,018	369.6	468	168.5
Emmet	422	454.3	184	187.3
Genesee	5,867	446.6	2,504	190.2
Gladwin	403	407.6	199	198.2
Gogebic	284	281.3	204	178.4
Grand Traverse	1,069	498.0	362	162.5
Gratiot	521	375.5	216	152.4
Hillsdale	522	334.2	260	162.0
Houghton	524	355.2	287	179.9
Huron	584	371.3	272	161.8
Ingham	2,931	408.6	1,255	175.0
Ionia	607	370.0	291	176.0
Iosco	548	457.0	261	207.7
Iron	249	329.6	167	194.4
Isabella	466	347.8	232	173.7
Jackson	1,897	369.3	1,002	189.1
Kalamazoo	2,743	404.5	1,174	170.6
Kalkaska	196	398.3	86	177.6
Kent	5,890	389.4	2,587	166.3
Keweenaw	40	---	18	---

83

Table II-25. Numbers of Reported Cancer Cases, Deaths, Preliminary Age-Adjusted Incidence, and Final Death Rates in Michigan, by County: 1990-1992 Time Period Continued

County	Incidence		Mortality	
	Number	Age-Adjusted Rate	Number	Age-Adjusted Rate
Lake	214	444.1	127	262.0
Lapeer	783	382.0	349	172.8
Leelanau	229	341.9	113	167.9
Lenawee	1,015	333.3	567	179.4
Livingston	1,114	361.6	562	188.7
Luce	97	375.3	49	---
Mackinac	212	444.5	96	183.9
Macomb	11,251	449.4	4,606	182.2
Manistee	431	432.6	209	203.3
Marquette	898	413.6	365	163.7
Mason	486	424.8	200	167.4
Mecosta	345	307.0	210	179.8
Menominee	353	338.4	177	156.1
Midland	829	357.7	333	143.8
Missaukee	154	331.6	64	133.2
Monroe	915	220.2	743	180.5
Montcalm	710	400.9	322	177.9
Montmorency	242	497.8	97	183.3
Muskegon	2,206	395.2	988	172.2
Newaygo	626	445.2	276	190.1
Oakland	15,201	437.6	5,974	171.2
Oceana	323	395.4	139	161.5
Ogemaw	326	380.4	200	224.6
Ontonagon	133	326.1	73	158.8
Osceola	333	443.0	138	174.4
Oscoda	168	422.7	78	186.7
Otsego	269	415.4	115	167.0
Ottawa	2,035	375.2	799	145.7
Presque Isle	289	437.5	121	174.6
Roscommon	537	454.4	206	167.1
Saginaw	2,809	393.9	1,305	179.4
St. Clair	2,134	430.5	940	184.8
St. Joseph	786	377.2	381	177.1
Sanilac	603	374.6	300	177.1
Schoolcraft	92	232.8	63	152.7
Shiawassee	849	382.6	406	179.8
Tuscola	721	390.3	333	176.4
Van Buren	916	381.4	493	199.7
Washtenaw	2,732	408.3	1,135	173.2
Wayne	32,045	447.4	14,283	197.5
Wexford	412	420.7	174	176.0
Michigan	**127,403**	**412.3**	**56,834**	**180.8**

Source: Michigan Department of Public Health, Cancer Incidence & Mortality - Michigan 1992 (Lansing, Michigan: 1994). --- No data.

Table II-26. Five Year Cancer Relative Survival Rates in Michigan, by Selected Sites and Stage: Year Range 1983-1989

Primary Site	Stage	
	Total*	Localized**
Gastrointestinal Tract and Digestive System		
Lip/Oral Cavity/Pharynx	52.1	77.7
Stomach	18.0	56.2
Colon	59.1	91.8
Rectum	56.6	84.8
Pancreas	3.3	8.2
Other Gastrointestinal	---	---
Respirator System and Pleura		
Larynx	66.0	84.4
Lung and Bronchus	13.2	46.1
Other Respirator	---	---
Bones and Joints	56.2	---
Connective and Soft Tissue	61.0	---
Melanoma of Skin	84.0	92.1
Breast	79.3	93.2
Genitourinary Organs		
Cervix Uteri	66.8	89.6
Corpus Uteri	82.9	94.0
Ovary	40.6	88.4
Prostate Gland	77.6	91.9
Other Genital	---	---
Urinary Bladder	79.1	90.6
Kidney and Renal Pelvis	55.1	85.5
Other Urinary	---	---
Brain/Central Nervous System	26.7	26.4
Lymphomas		
Hodgkin's Disease	78.1	---
Non-Hodgkin's Lymphomas	51.7	---
Multiple Myelomas	27.2	---
Leukemias	37.6	---
All Other	---	---
Total	**53.0**	---

*Survival rates by site are based on cases diagnosed between 1983 and 1989. **Survival rates by site are based on cases diagnosed between 1983 and 1987. --- No data. Source: National Cancer Institute, SEER Cancer Statistics Review, 1973-1990, (Washington, D.C. 1993).

Table II-27. Number and Fatality Rate of Fatal Occupational Injuries in Michigan, by Major Industry: 1992

Industry	Number of Fatalities	Fatality Rate
Total	**143**	**3**
Private Industry	134	---
Agriculture	15	17
Agriculture Production, Crops	9	---
General Farms, Primary Crop	8	---
Agricultural Production Livestock	4	---
Mining	3	---
Construction	23	13
General Building Contractors	4	---
Heavy Construction, Except Building	4	---
Special Trades Contractors	15	---
Electrical Work	3	---
Masonry, Stonework, Tile Setting and Plastering	4	---
Manufacturing	21	2
Fabricated Metal Products	6	---
Industrial Machinery and Equipment	4	---
Transportation and Public Utilities	16	10
Trucking and Warehousing	3	---
Trucking and Courier Services, Except Air	3	---
Transportation by Air	3	---
Electric Gas, and Sanitary Services	8	---
Wholesale and Retail Trade	30	3
Wholesale Trade	5	---
Durable Goods	4	---
Retail Trade	25	---
Food Stores	3	---
Grocery Stores	3	---
Automotive Dealers and Service Stations	8	---
Eating and Drinking Places	5	---
Miscellaneous Retail	4	---
Finance, Insurance and Real Estate	6	1
Real Estate	3	---
Services	20	2
Business Services	7	---
Amusement and Recreation Services	3	---
Engineering and Management Services	3	---
Government	9	1

--- Fatality rate only calculated for broad industry groups. The fatality rate represents the number of fatal occupational injuries per 100,000 employed.
Source: Michigan Department of Labor, MIOSHA Information Division, Census of Fatal Occupational Injuries in Michigan, 1992 (Lansing, Michigan: 1994).

Table II-28: Reported Cases of Certain Communicable Diseases in Michigan, Selected Years: 1950-1993

Disease	1950	1960	1970	1980	1985	1990	1992	1993
Diphtheria	84	9	---	1	---	---	---	---
Smallpox	---	---	---	---	---	---	---	---
Typhoid Fever	43	14	14	12	8	8	4	8
Whooping Cough	9,184	1,129	195	38	54	88	16	110
Measles	38,245	36,161	1,834	250	113	545	15	9
Hepatitis	48	2,113	4,594	1,799	1,490	1,111	1,238	10,414
Tuberculosis	5,538	4,127	1,992	1,185	535	504	496	463
Meningococcal Infect.	133	169	69	77	107	69	87	63
Poliomyelitis	2,029	88	2	1	---	---	---	---
Syphilis	8,830	3,647	3,920	1,110	673	2,625	1,022	551
Gonorrhea	8,678	8,372	20,359	35,125	33,516	30,779	21,470	17,870
AIDS	---	---	---	---	64	576	706	1,735

--- No Data.
Source: Michigan Department of Public Health, Michigan Health Statistics 1992 (Lansing, Michigan: 1993).

Table II-29: Marriages in Michigan, by Order of Marriage and Age of Bride and Groom: 1992

Age	Bride - Number of Times Married						Groom - Number of Times Married					
	1st	2nd	3rd	4 or More	Not Stated	Total	1st	2nd	3rd	4 or More	Not Stated	Total
16	22	0	0	0	0	22	23	0	0	0	0	23
17	105	2	0	0	0	107	107	0	0	0	0	107
18	573	17	1	1	0	592	591	1	0	0	0	592
19	1,165	43	6	3	0	1,217	1,217	0	0	0	0	1,217
20-24	16,137	1,206	164	23	6	17,536	16,965	561	7	0	3	17,536
25-29	15,832	3,248	471	80	4	19,635	16,886	2,600	136	9	4	19,635
30-34	7,123	3,945	772	164	0	12,004	7,183	4,190	587	44	0	12,004
35-39	3,047	3,173	856	229	2	7,307	2,515	3,715	923	153	1	7,307
40-44	1,312	2,481	814	185	0	4,792	743	2,705	1,035	309	0	4,792
45-49	605	1,711	640	195	1	3,152	223	1,765	877	287	0	3,152
50-54	251	981	409	154	3	1,798	88	1,002	497	210	0	1,798
55-59	105	565	255	86	0	1,011	38	567	294	112	0	1,011
60-64	86	464	198	63	0	811	33	517	191	70	0	811
65-69	41	362	133	49	0	585	13	371	144	57	0	585
70-74	25	234	78	21	0	358	10	259	71	18	0	358
75 & Over	16	263	94	19	0	392	5	279	76	32	0	392
No Age	1	1	0	0	0	2	1	1	0	0	0	2
Total	46,446	18,696	4,891	1,272	17	71,322	46,641	18,533	4,838	1,301	9	71,322

Source: Michigan Department of Public Health, Michigan Health Statistics 1992 (Lansing, Michigan: 1993).

Table II-30. Number of Divorces and Annulments, and Divorce and Annulment Rates in Michigan: Selected Years 1900-1993

Year	Number	Rate	Year	Number	Rate
1900	2,435	2.0	1985	38,775	8.5
1910	3,716	2.6	1986	39,553	8.7
1920	8,679	4.7	1987	39,857	8.7
1930	10,639	4.4	1988	40,103	8.7
1940	12,054	4.6	1989	40,276	8.7
1950	15,979	5.0	1990	40,568	8.7
1960	16,656	4.3	1991	40,103	8.6
1970	29,934	6.7	1992	40,425	8.6
1980	45,047	9.7	1993	40,470	8.6

Source: Michigan Department of Public Health, Michigan Health Statistics 1992 (Lansing, Michigan: 1993).

II-31. Estimated Number of Children Involved in Divorces and Annulments, Average Number of Children per Decree, and Rate per 1,000 Children Under 18 Years of Age in Michigan: Selected Years 1960-1993

Year	Estimated Number of Children Involved in Divorces and Annulments	Average Number of Children Per Decree	Rate per 1,000 Under 18 Years of Age
1960	19,209	1.15	6.5
1970	40,596	1.36	12.5
1980	46,603	1.04	16.9
1981	45,461	1.05	18.2
1982	41,156	1.04	16.9
1983	38,712	1.02	16.2
1984	37,629	1.00	14.8
1985	38,673	1.00	15.3
1986	39,378	1.00	15.7
1987	39,321	1.00	14.8
1988	39,635	0.99	15.0
1989	39,897	0.99	15.2
1990	39,792	0.98	16.0
1991	39,000	0.97	15.6
1992	39,579	0.98	15.8
1993	39,372	0.97	15.7

Source: Michigan Department of Public Health, Michigan Health Statistics 1992 (Lansing, Michigan: 1993).

Table II-32. Occupational Injury and Illness Incidence Rates in Michigan, by Industry Division: 1991

Industry Division	Incidence Rates per 100 Full-Time Workers			
	Total Cases	Lost Workday Cases	Non-Fatal Cases Without Lost Workdays	Lost Workdays
Total, All Industries	**10.2**	**4.6**	**5.6**	**102.5**
Private Sector Total	**10.4**	**4.6**	**5.9**	**104.7**
Agriculture/Forestry/Fishing	10.2	5.0	5.2	86.4
Mining	10.8	7.2	3.5	187.7
Construction	11.0	5.3	5.7	152.0
Manufacturing	17.8	7.0	10.8	165.2
Transportation/Public Utilities	9.4	5.3	4.1	121.6
Wholesale Trade	8.6	4.0	4.6	92.2
Retail Trade	7.7	3.7	4.0	72.4
Finance/Insurance/Real Estate	2.6	1.3	1.2	21.7
Services	5.6	2.7	2.8	63.3
Public Sector Total	**8.8**	**5.0**	**3.7**	**87.6**
State Government	6.0	3.2	2.8	82.2
Local Government	10.1	5.9	4.2	90.2

Source: Bureau of Labor Statistics and Michigan Department of Labor, MIOSHA Information Division, <u>Occupational Injuries and Illnesses, Michigan Survey 1991</u> (Lansing, Michigan: December 1993).

Table II-33. Occupational Injury, Illness Incidence Rates, and Average Lost Workdays in Michigan, by Establishment Size: 1991

Establishment Size By Number of Employees	Total Case Incidence Rate			
	Total	Lost Workdays	Without Lost Workdays	Average Lost Workdays
1 to 3 Employees	0.9	0.7	0.2	14.0
4 to 10 Employees	2.9	1.3	1.6	42.0
11 to 19 Employees	5.1	2.7	2.4	34.0
20 to 49 Employees	7.5	3.4	4.1	23.0
50 to 99 Employees	10.8	5.2	5.6	20.0
100 to 249 Employees	13.0	6.3	6.6	21.0
250 to 499 Employees	11.4	5.5	5.9	20.0
500 to 999 Employees	10.9	5.5	5.5	20.0
1,000 to 2,499 Employees	11.7	5.1	6.5	22.0
2,500 Plus Employees	14.0	5.2	8.8	22.0
Total	**10.2**	**4.6**	**5.6**	**22.0**

Source: Bureau of Labor Statistics and Michigan Department of Labor, MIOSHA Information Division, <u>Occupational Injuries and Illnesses, Michigan Survey 1991</u> (Lansing, Michigan: December 1993).

Table II-34. Number and Percent Distribution of Fatal Occupational Injuries in Michigan, by Event or Exposure: 1992

Event or Exposure	Number of Fatalities	Percent(%) of Total
Total	143	100
Transportation Accidents	44	31
Highway Accident	20	14
Collision Between Vehicles, Mobile Equipment	14	10
Nonhighway Accident, (Farm, Industrial Premises)	8	6
Noncollision Accident	7	5
Worker Struck By Vehicle	11	8
Assaults and Violent Acts	35	24
Homicides	26	18
Shooting	23	16
Stabbing	3	2
Self-Inflicted Injury	8	6
Contact With Objects and Equipment	18	13
Struck By Object	9	6
Struck by Falling Object	5	3
Caught In or Compressed By Equipment or Objects	8	6
Falls	20	14
Fall To Lower Level	14	10
Fall On Same Level	3	2
Exposure To Harmful Substances or Environments	22	15
Contact With Electric Current	16	11
Exposure To Caustic, Noxious, or Allergenic Substances	4	3
Fires and Explosions	4	3

Source: Bureau of Labor Statistics and Michigan Department of Labor, MIOSHA Information Division, Census of Fatal Occupational Injuries in Michigan, 1992 (Lansing, Mich: 1994).

Table II-35. Total Number of Hospital Discharges for Deliveries, Number, and Percent of Primary and Repeated C-Sections in Michigan: 1985-1990

Hospital Discharge Year	All Deliveries			No Previous C-Section Deliveries			Deliveries With Previous C-Section		
	Total Deliveries	Cesarean Deliveries		Total Deliveries	Cesarean Deliveries		Total Deliveries	Cesarean Deliveries	
		Number	Percent(%)		Number	Percent(%)		Number	Percent(%)
1985	134,222	31,129	23.2	121,239	18,958	15.6	12,983	12,171	93.7
1986	132,700	33,210	25.0	119,420	20,784	17.4	13,280	12,426	93.6
1987	136,544	34,681	25.4	121,831	21,146	17.4	14,713	13,535	92.0
1988	137,557	34,395	25.0	122,156	20,801	17.0	15,401	13,594	88.3
1989	144,877	34,729	24.0	128,047	20,921	16.3	16,830	13,808	82.0
1990	148,035	34,465	23.3	130,809	21,018	16.1	17,226	13,447	78.1

Source: Michigan Department of Public Health, Division for Health Statistics, Michigan Inpatient Data Base (Lansing, Michigan).

Table II-36. Selected Hospital Admission Statistics for Michigan: 1982-1992

Year	Total Admissions	Admissions per 1,000 Population	Set Up and Staffed Beds	Inpatient Days	Average Length of Stay	Occupancy Rate
1982	1,402,663	154	39,773	11,203,014	8.0	77.2
1983	1,382,861	153	39,430	11,044,238	8.0	76.7
1984	1,329,929	147	38,803	10,153,448	7.6	71.5
1985	1,254,105	138	37,546	9,153,117	7.3	66.8
1986	1,188,329	130	36,409	8,546,414	7.2	64.3
1987	1,147,764	125	35,498	8,399,232	7.3	64.8
1988	1,121,243	121	34,590	8,332,575	7.4	65.8
1989	1,099,540	119	34,036	8,218,826	7.5	66.2
1990	1,069,361	115	33,951	8,116,557	7.6	65.5
1991	1,071,264	114	32,976	7,864,792	7.3	65.4
1992	1,061,850	113	31,686	7,482,593	7.0	64.6

Source: Michigan Hospital Association, Hospital Trends (Lansing, Michigan: 1994).

Table II-37. Selected Hospital Patient Statistics for Michigan: 1982-1992

Year	Outpatient Visits	Outpatient Visits per 1,000 Population	Outpatient Revenue as a Percent(%) of Total Gross Revenue	Uncompensated Care
1982	13,246,503	1,453	15.3	$143,599,373
1983	10,954,480	1,210	15.6	177,353,216
1984	10,684,872	1,179	17.2	214,936,113
1985	10,415,712	1,146	19.0	221,576,886
1986	11,781,865	1,289	21.8	239,279,699
1987	12,349,038	1,342	24.0	301,939,424
1988	13,828,471	1,497	26.2	352,694,428
1989	14,876,780	1,604	26.8	368,041,814
1990	15,319,550	1,648	28.7	398,870,641
1991	16,441,728	1,755	30.7	448,461,230
1992	17,117,753	1,814	32.3	539,799,759

Source: Michigan Hospital Association, Hospital Trends (Lansing, Michigan: 1994).

Table II-38. Hospital Inpatient and Outpatient Surgeries in Michigan: 1982-1992

Year	Total Surgeries	Inpatient Surgeries	Outpatient Surgeries
1982	851,490	620,791	230,699
1983	864,881	586,592	278,289
1984	847,266	526,141	321,125
1985	848,684	465,455	383,229
1986	845,457	419,366	426,091
1987	849,772	398,741	451,031
1988	857,584	374,237	483,347
1989	872,062	377,113	494,949
1990	889,408	356,925	532,483
1991	903,019	356,842	546,177
1992	900,797	346,646	554,151

Source: Michigan Hospital Association, Hospital Trends (Lansing, Michigan: 1994).

Table II-39. Tobacco Abstinence by Women in Michigan: 1988-1991

Year	Percent(%) of Women Abstaining From Tobacco Use During Last Three Months of Pregnancy
1988	69.1
1989	68.2
1990	70.8
1991	75.2

Source: Michigan Department of Public Health, Division of Health Statistics, PRAMS Survey.

Table II-40. Percent of Mothers Breast-Feeding in Michigan: 1988-1991

Year	Percent(%) Breast - Feeding Mothers		
	All	Low Income	Black
1988	43.9	26.3	17.2
1989	47.5	24.5	16.3
1990	49.7	26.6	21.7
1991	49.7	31.7	27.0

Source: Michigan Department of Public Health, Division of Health Statistics, PRAMS Survey.

CHAPTER III
EDUCATION

Data on educational attainment of the population are developed from a sample of households in the decennial <u>Census of Population</u> (see page 1). Data on the performance of the public school system are collected by the Michigan Department of Education. These statistics include data such as enrollment, number of teachers and teacher's salaries, number of districts, revenues, expenditures, dropout rates, performance on standardized tests such as the SAT (Scholarship Aptitude Test), ACT (American College Testing), and MEAP (Michigan Educational Assessment Program).

Many of the statewide data series on the public elementary and secondary schools were published by the Michigan Department of Education in <u>Condition of Michigan Education 1992</u>. Public universities and colleges also are required to report to the Michigan Department of Education. Most private institutions of higher education also report selected items, such as enrollment, tuition costs, and degrees granted. Private and parochial schools are not legally required to report to the Michigan Department of Education. Consequently data about this important component of the education system are of limited availability.

In the nation's capital, the National Center for Educational Statistics is a repository of both state and national data on education. It publishes the annual <u>Digest of Educational Statistics</u> and a companion report, <u>The Condition of Education.</u>

In Table III-14, the *DROPOUT RATE* refers to the percentage of students who have left a school district over a twelve-month period. In calculating the dropout rate, adjustment is made for those students who transfer in, transfer out, and graduate. The *GRADUATION RATE* refers to the probability that an individual entering the ninth grade will graduate from the 12th grade. The probability is estimated based on the grade to grade dropout/retention pattern for a particular year.

List of Tables

Table		Page
III-1.	Educational Attainment of the Population 25 Years Old and Over in Michigan, by County: 1990	95
III-2.	Selected K-12 Public School Statistics in Michigan: 1963-1964 through 1993-1994	96
III-3.	Public School Summary Revenue and Enrollment Statistics in Michigan: School Fiscal Year 1979-1993	97
III-4.	Summary of K-12 and ISD Revenues in Michigan, by Source: Fiscal Year 1992-1993	97
III-5.	Summary of K-12 and ISD Revenues by Fund in Michigan: Fiscal Year 1992-1993	98

List of Tables

Table   Page

III-6.   Summary of K-12 and ISD Expenditures in Michigan: Fiscal Year 1992-1993 . . . 99

III-7.   Performance Summary of Michigan Public School Students in Mathematics and
         Reading: 1991-1994 100

III-8.   Performance Summary of Michigan Public School Students in Science, by
         Achievement Category: Selected Years 1989-1994 100

III-9.   Average SAT and ACT Scores of Michigan and United States Students:
         1985-1994 100

III-10. Earned Degrees Conferred by Higher Education Institutions in Michigan, by Sex
         and Degree: 1980-1993 101

III-11. Earned Degrees Conferred in Michigan, by Field of Study and Degree Level:
         1993-1994 102

III-12. Estimate of Michigan Resident Student Expenses at Michigan Degree-Granting
         Institutions: 1994-1995 106

III-13. Michigan Community College Tuition and Fees: 1994-1995 Academic Year . . . 107

III-14. Public School Dropout and Graduation Rates(%) in Michigan, by District:
         1992-1993 School Year 108

III-15. Michigan Educational Assessment Program (MEAP) Scores, by School District:
         1993-1994 School Year 117

III-16. Community College Addresses and Telephone Numbers in Michigan: 1994 137

III-17. Public University Addresses and Telephone Numbers in Michigan: 1994 138

III-18. Private College and University Addresses and Telephone Numbers in Michigan:
         1994 138

Table III-1. Educational Attainment of the Population 25 Years Old and Over in Michigan, by County: 1990

County	Percent(%)			County	Percent(%)			County	Percent(%)		
	Less Than High School	High School Graduate	College Graduate		Less Than High School	High School Graduate	College Graduate		Less Than High School	High School Graduate	College Graduate
Alcona	31.45	68.55	9.01	Gratiot	22.93	77.07	10.87	Missaukee	30.61	69.39	8.04
Alger	26.98	73.02	11.50	Hillsdale	24.79	75.21	11.33	Monroe	25.91	74.09	10.52
Allegan	25.56	74.44	11.98	Houghton	26.06	73.94	18.02	Montcalm	26.61	73.39	8.17
Alpena	26.40	73.60	11.42	Huron	32.01	67.99	8.87	Montmorency	32.41	67.59	8.74
Antrim	23.62	76.38	13.70	Ingham	16.13	83.87	29.17	Muskegon	25.75	74.25	11.15
Arenac	34.60	65.40	7.13	Ionia	22.78	77.22	8.86	Newaygo	28.93	71.07	10.53
Baraga	29.52	70.48	8.28	Iosco	23.68	76.32	10.36	Oakland	15.37	84.63	30.15
Barry	21.74	78.26	10.80	Iron	27.03	72.97	10.02	Oceana	26.68	73.32	10.41
Bay	26.01	73.99	11.02	Isabella	20.26	79.74	21.52	Ogemaw	36.97	63.03	7.22
Benzie	23.35	76.65	15.10	Jackson	22.31	77.69	12.92	Ontonagon	25.43	74.57	9.21
Berrien	25.27	74.73	16.74	Kalamazoo	16.58	83.42	27.13	Osceola	27.94	72.06	8.66
Branch	26.21	73.79	10.35	Kalkaska	30.38	69.62	7.14	Oscoda	33.43	66.57	7.91
Calhoun	23.16	76.84	13.82	Kent	19.71	80.29	20.71	Otsego	20.55	79.45	13.73
Cass	27.72	72.28	9.24	Keweenaw	35.66	64.34	11.11	Ottawa	20.23	79.77	18.72
Charlevoix	20.30	79.70	16.04	Lake	38.71	61.29	6.58	Presque Isle	34.32	65.68	8.75
Cheboygan	26.46	73.54	9.95	Lapeer	22.40	77.60	9.35	Roscommon	30.61	69.39	7.93
Chippewa	26.41	73.59	10.80	Leelanau	14.90	85.10	24.14	Saginaw	25.19	74.81	12.97
Clare	33.09	66.91	6.79	Lenawee	23.67	76.33	12.85	St. Clair	25.20	74.80	10.65
Clinton	16.32	83.68	14.58	Livingston	14.43	85.57	19.56	St. Joseph	26.24	73.76	10.90
Crawford	26.80	73.20	12.56	Luce	30.41	69.59	9.55	Sanilac	27.85	72.15	8.42
Delta	23.11	76.89	11.27	Mackinac	28.62	71.38	10.41	Schoolcraft	28.41	71.59	8.86
Dickinson	21.48	78.52	13.02	Macomb	23.07	76.93	13.47	Shiawassee	21.25	78.75	10.31
Eaton	14.47	85.53	18.53	Manistee	26.70	73.30	10.48	Tuscola	27.05	72.95	8.12
Emmet	18.46	81.54	19.22	Marquette	18.23	81.77	20.26	Van Buren	28.16	71.84	12.11
Genesee	23.23	76.77	12.77	Mason	23.87	76.13	11.84	Washtenaw	12.79	87.21	41.87
Gladwin	35.20	64.80	6.48	Mecosta	22.26	77.74	17.92	Wayne	30.05	69.95	13.65
Gogebic	23.73	76.27	11.42	Menominee	25.72	74.28	9.27	Wexford	25.38	74.62	12.63
Grand Traverse	15.14	84.86	22.05	Midland	16.76	83.24	27.42	**Michigan**	**23.22**	**76.78**	**17.36**

Source: Bureau of the Census, Michigan Information Center (Lansing, Michigan).

Table III-2. Selected K-12 Public School Statistics in Michigan: 1963-1964 through 1993-1994

School Year	Enrollment	Number of Teachers*	Student/Teacher Ratio	Average Teacher Salary ($)	Number of Districts
1963-1964	1,856,895	69,376	26.8	$6,474	1,515
1964-1965	1,917,890	72,935	26.3	6,745	1,227
1965-1966	1,968,403	76,047	25.9	6,896	993
1966-1967	2,033,982	80,637	25.2	7,535	866
1968-1969	2,079,704	85,346	24.4	8,238	712
1969-1970	2,122,915	87,487	24.3	9,134	648
1970-1971	2,164,386	89,049	24.3	10,045	638
1971-1972	2,178,745	90,672	24.0	11,034	624
1972-1973	2,212,505	91,190	24.8	11,671	608
1973-1974	2,193,270	93,852	23.4	12,070	602
1974-1975	2,159,966	94,221	22.9	12,852	597
1975-1976	2,139,720	93,580	22.9	14,059	590
1976-1977	2,127,917	92,677	23.0	15,064	587
1977-1978	2,081,936	90,780	22.9	15,426	581
1978-1979	1,869,811	81,926	22.8	16,445	576
1979-1980	1,804,658	80,411	22.4	18,016	575
1980-1981	1,743,677	76,850	22.7	21,779	574
1981-1982	1,668,330	72,338	23.1	24,304	574
1982-1983	1,609,964	68,752	23.4	25,712	573
1983-1984	1,569,441	67,877	23.1	27,104	570
1984-1985	1,542,257	68,591	22.5	28,440	567
1985-1986	1,529,626	68,977	22.2	30,067	566
1986-1987	1,522,930	69,510	21.9	31,412	564
1987-1988	1,519,742	69,724	21.8	33,151	563
1988-1989	1,505,108	69,629	21.6	34,685	562
1989-1990	1,495,976	69,803	21.4	37,072	562
1990-1991	1,502,577	70,555	21.3	39,421	559
1991-1992	1,514,094	71,599	21.1	41,467	524
1992-1993	1,523,766	71,765	21.2	43,870	524
1993-1994	1,531,663	69,433	22.1	44,839	524

* Refers to Full Time Equivalent
Source: Michigan Department of Education (Lansing, Michigan).

Table III-3. Public School Summary Revenue and Enrollment Statistics in Michigan*: School Fiscal Year 1979-1993

School Fiscal Year July 1 to June 30	Total Kindergarten-12 Grade (K-12) and Intermediate School District (ISD)	Kindergarten through 12 Grade	Intermediate School District	4th Friday Enrollment	Revenue per Pupil
1979-1980	$5,346,340,305	$4,975,432,284	$370,908,021	1,804,658	$2,963
1980-1981	5,485,330,020	5,198,015,671	287,314,349	1,743,677	3,146
1981-1982	5,795,306,636	5,387,091,006	408,215,630	1,668,330	3,474
1982-1983	5,937,857,677	5,510,128,562	427,729,115	1,609,964	3,688
1983-1984	6,238,104,037	5,787,584,631	450,519,406	1,569,441	3,975
1984-1985	6,710,805,556	6,235,466,344	475,339,212	1,542,257	4,351
1985-1986	7,157,990,621	6,635,878,206	522,112,415	1,529,626	4,680
1986-1987	7,652,581,875	7,098,234,047	554,347,828	1,522,930	5,025
1987-1988	8,122,633,842	7,525,521,973	597,111,869	1,519,742	5,345
1988-1989	8,696,328,321	8,017,918,158	678,410,163	1,505,108	5,778
1989-1990	9,511,708,027	8,761,722,698	749,985,329	1,495,976	6,358
1990-1991	10,375,706,490	9,586,497,666	789,208,824	1,502,577	6,905
1991-1992	11,110,647,875	10,252,634,950	858,012,916	1,572,958	7,064
1992-1993	11,399,562,492	10,525,871,780	873,690,712	1,580,784	7,211

* Data excludes transfers and other.
Source: Michigan Department of Education, Bulletin 1011 (Lansing, Michigan; annually), and Michigan Department of Management and Budget.

Table III-4. Summary of K-12 and ISD Revenues in Michigan, by Source: Fiscal Year 1992-1993

Source	Total Kindergarten-12 Grade (K-12) and Intermediate School District (ISD)	Kindergarten through 12 Grade	Intermediate School District
Total Local	$6,955,195,399	$6,458,689,859	$496,505,540
Total Intermediate	6,771,888	6,563,975	207,913
Total State	3,301,543,636	3,071,149,129	230,394,507
Total Federal	535,050,831	389,693,079	145,357,752
Total	$10,798,561,754	$9,926,096,042	$872,465,712
Transfers From Others In State	258,962,970	224,225,618	34,737,352
Transfers From Others Outside State	780,353	114,619	665,734
Transfers From Other Funds	181,884,996	161,127,650	20,757,346
Proceeds From Sales of Bonds	601,000,738	599,775,738	1,225,000
Other	639,831,918	618,519,738	21,312,180
Total Transfers and Other	$1,682,460,975	$1,603,763,363	$78,697,612
Grand Total, All Revenues	$12,481,022,729	$11,529,859,405	$951,163,324
Grand Total, Excluding Transfers & Other (Including Bonds)	$11,399,562,492	$10,525,871,780	$873,690,712

Source: Michigan Department of Education, Bulletin 1011, and Michigan Department of Management and Budget (Lansing, Michigan).

Table III-5. Summary of K-12 and ISD Revenues by Fund* in Michigan: Fiscal Year 1992-1993

Revenue Fund	Revenue($)
K-12	
General Fund Direct	$8,230,869,248
Plus Indirect State FICA/RET	706,460,342
Debt Retirement Direct	520,772,512
Building & Site Direct (Cap Projects)	82,701,171
School Services Direct	358,590,377
Trust & Agency Direct	26,702,392
Subtotal K-12 Direct	9,926,096,042
Bond Proceeds Available for Expenditure	599,775,738
Subtotal K-12 Available Not Including Transfers & Other	**$10,525,871,780**
ISD	
General Fund Direct	$130,229,402
Plus Indirect State FICA/RET	34,698,366
Debt Retirement Direct	2,505,883
Building & Site Direct (Cap Projects)	1,132,244
School Services Direct	495,470
Trust & Agency Direct	958,537
Special Education	571,781,671
Vocational Education	118,329,289
Cooperative Education	12,334,850
Subtotal ISD Direct	872,465,712
Bond Proceeds Available for Expenditure	1,225,000
Subtotal ISD Available Not Including Transfers & Other	**$873,690,712**
TOTAL K-12 and ISD DIRECT	**$10,798,561,754**
TOTAL K-12 and ISD AVAILABLE NOT INCLUDING TRANSFER	**$11,399,562,492**
ENROLLMENT ("4th Friday") 94= 1,587,612	**$1,580,784**
REVENUE per PUPIL	**$7,211**

* Fund data is Direct Only, Excludes Transfers and Other.
Source: Michigan Department of Education, Bulletin 1011, and Michigan Department of Management and Budget (Lansing, Michigan).

Table III-6. Summary of K-12 and ISD Expenditures in Michigan: Fiscal Year 1992-1993

Expenditures	Total, All Funds: K-12 and ISD	K-12 General Fund	Fund Category				
				Intermediate School District (ISD)			
			Total, All ISD Funds	General Fund	Special Education	Vocational Education	Cooperative Education
Instruction	$5,146,251,992	$4,967,032,233	$179,219,759	$14,645,561	$116,923,974	$43,508,552	$4,141,672
Support Services	3,421,517,613	3,094,486,205	327,031,408	100,093,813	174,567,402	36,219,615	16,150,578
Community Services	76,322,414	64,646,533	11,675,881	8,991,355	597,474	1,406,795	680,257
Capital Outlay	161,049,240	146,038,018	15,011,222	4,712,880	4,981,393	4,698,026	618,923
Subtotal Direct Expenditures	8,805,141,259	8,272,202,989	532,938,270	128,443,609	--	--	--
State Paid FICA & Retirement	699,143,807	666,399,135	32,744,672	32,744,672	*	*	*
Fund Total plus State Fringes	9,504,285,066	8,938,602,124	565,682,942	161,188,281	297,070,243	85,832,988	21,591,430
Debt Retirement Fund	614,947,521	611,710,930	3,236,591	3,236,591	--	--	--
Building and Site Fund	765,022,161	757,730,332	7,291,829	7,291,829	--	--	--
School Services Fund	448,964,436	447,838,937	1,125,499	1,125,499	--	--	--
Trust and Agency Fund	26,688,003	25,188,420	1,499,583	1,499,583	--	--	--
Total, All Funds plus State Fringes	$11,359,907,187	$10,781,070,743	$578,836,444	$174,341,783	$297,070,243	$85,832,988	$21,591,430

* Fund data is included in ISD general fund figures.   -- Category does not apply to specific fund.
Source: Michigan Department of Education, Bulletin 1011, and Michigan Department of Management and Budget (Lansing, Michigan).

Table III-7. Performance Summary of Michigan Public School Students in Mathematics and Reading: 1991-1994

Grade	School Year	Mathematics				Reading			
		Total Students	Achievement Category - Percent(%)			Total Students	Achievement Category - Percent(%)		
			Low	Moderate	High		Low	Moderate	High
Fourth Grade	1991-1992	115,482	35.5	28.2	36.3	115,218	26.2	39.0	34.7
	1992-1993	114,226	29.9	27.8	42.3	114,066	32.1	31.2	36.7
	1993-1994	114,874	24.6	26.4	48.9	114,741	27.4	29.0	43.6
Seventh Grade	1991-1992	112,608	37.8	30.2	32.0	112,319	38.6	31.5	29.9
	1992-1993	114,171	28.5	36.0	35.4	113,975	34.0	33.2	32.8
	1993-1994	114,566	25.9	32.9	41.3	114,374	29.5	31.8	38.7
Tenth Grade	1991-1992	97,970	56.5	24.8	18.7	97,273	27.2	34.1	38.7
	1992-1993	103,291	47.7	29.2	23.1	102,619	29.2	32.5	38.3
	1993-1994	101,328	42.2	30.9	26.9	101,369	29.9	27.7	42.5

Source: Michigan Department of Education, Michigan Educational Assessment Program (Lansing, Michigan).

Table III-8. Performance Summary of Michigan Public School Students in Science, by Achievement Category: Selected Years 1989-1994

Grade	Year	Total Students	Category 4 (High)	Category 3	Category 2	Category 1 (Low)
Fifth Grade	1989	111,143	69.1	25.4	5.1	0.4
	1992	115,470	71.0	23.8	4.8	0.4
	1993	114,431	73.9	21.8	4.0	0.4
	1994	114,812	75.6	20.4	3.6	0.3
Eighth Grade	1989	102,607	52.1	32.0	14.1	1.9
	1992	110,430	57.1	30.3	11.1	1.5
	1993	112,674	59.4	29.1	10.0	1.4
	1994	112,749	61.7	27.6	9.4	1.3
Eleventh Grade	1989	95,024	39.8	35.1	19.8	5.3
	1992	91,919	46.5	36.1	14.6	2.8
	1993	90,250	51.3	35.3	11.4	2.0
	1994	92,271	51.9	34.8	11.2	2.0

Source: Michigan Department of Education, Michigan Educational Assessment Program (Lansing, Michigan).

Table: III-9. Average SAT and ACT Scores of Michigan and United States Students: 1985-1994

Year	SAT				ACT	
	Mathematics		Verbal		Michigan	United States
	Michigan	United States	Michigan	United States		
1985	514	475	462	431	18.9	18.8
1986	513	476	459	430	18.8	18.7
1987	513	476	457	428	18.8	18.8
1988	514	476	458	427	18.6	18.6
1989	514	476	454	424	20.6	20.6
1990	519	474	461	422	20.6	20.6
1991	523	476	464	423	20.6	20.6
1992	528	478	469	424	20.8	20.7
1993	537	479	472	423	20.8	20.7
1994	N.A.	N.A.	N.A.	N.A.	21.0	20.8

Source: Michigan Department of Education, Michigan Educational Assessment Program (Lansing, Michigan) and College Entrance Examination Board, Annual College Bound Senior Report (New York, New York: annually). N.A. data not available.

Table III-10. Earned Degrees Conferred by Higher Education Institutions in Michigan, by Sex and Degree: 1980-1993

Institution/Year	Bachelor's Degree		Master's Degree		Doctorate Degree	
	Male	Female	Male	Female	Male	Female
Public Institution						
1980 - 1981	16,252	14,842	7,223	6,740	924	372
1981 - 1982	16,391	15,230	7,081	6,724	882	387
1982 - 1983	16,278	15,767	6,803	6,485	963	429
1983 - 1984	15,902	15,314	6,286	5,880	902	432
1984 - 1985	15,898	15,228	6,139	5,236	827	410
1985 - 1986	15,132	14,588	5,587	5,151	814	358
1986 - 1987	14,820	14,499	5,401	5,007	809	451
1987 - 1988	14,456	15,243	5,212	5,198	821	448
1988 - 1989	14,722	15,960	5,246	5,636	811	415
1989 - 1990	15,092	16,767	5,539	6,013	843	387
1990 - 1991	15,986	18,678	5,907	6,692	920	525
1991 - 1992	16,383	18,978	6,050	6,770	989	499
1992 - 1993	16,786	19,341	6,237	6,940	921	527
Private Institution						
1980 - 1981	3,768	2,995	665	424	31	7
1981 - 1982	4,100	3,474	693	426	27	14
1982 - 1983	3,920	3,616	705	360	41	5
1983 - 1984	3,556	3,293	633	402	43	9
1984 - 1985	3,209	2,857	440	226	11	3
1985 - 1986	3,469	3,595	601	384	24	12
1986 - 1987	3,239	3,201	552	326	24	5
1987 - 1988	4,069	4,379	598	458	35	11
1988 - 1989	3,966	4,505	656	503	44	5
1989 - 1990	4,199	4,976	653	534	69	39
1990 - 1991	4,285	5,339	878	698	31	11
1991 - 1992	4,275	5,264	839	721	42	21
1992 - 1993	4,258	5,326	980	793	44	21
Total Institutions						
1980 - 1981	20,020	17,837	7,888	7,164	955	379
1981 - 1982	20,491	18,704	7,774	7,150	909	401
1982 - 1983	20,198	19,383	7,508	6,845	1,004	434
1983 - 1984	19,458	18,607	6,919	6,282	945	441
1984 - 1985	19,107	18,085	6,579	5,462	838	413
1985 - 1986	18,601	18,183	6,188	5,535	838	370
1986 - 1987	18,059	17,700	5,953	5,333	833	456
1987 - 1988	18,525	19,622	5,810	5,656	856	459
1988 - 1989	18,688	20,465	5,902	6,139	855	420
1989 - 1990	19,291	21,743	6,192	6,547	912	426
1990 - 1991	20,271	24,017	6,785	7,390	951	536
1991 - 1992	20,658	24,242	6,889	7,491	1,031	520
1992 - 1993	21,044	24,667	7,217	7,733	965	548

Source: Michigan Department of Education, Postsecondary Education (Lansing, Michigan: annually).

Table III-11. Earned Degrees Conferred in Michigan, by Field of Study and Degree Level: 1993-1994

Level and Field of Study	Total	Community Colleges	Public Universities	Independent Colleges & Universities
Associate's Degree - Total	**27,568**	**22,331**	**1,341**	**3,896**
Agri Business & Agri Production	39	24	15	0
Agricultural Sciences	0	0	0	0
Renewable Natural Resources	56	17	37	2
Architecture and Environmental Design	6	6		
Area and Ethnic Studies	3	3	0	0
Marketing and Distribution	272	148	14	110
Communications	94	38	8	48
Communication Technologies	114	111	3	0
Computer and Information Sciences	579	381	0	198
Consumer, Personal, and Misc. Services	228	221	1	6
Education	809	779	8	22
Engineering	131	128	0	3
Engineering & Related Technologies	1,849	1,370	293	186
Foreign Languages	7	7	0	0
Allied Health	0	0	0	0
Home Economics	2	0	0	2
Vocational Home Economics	519	394	88	37
Law	456	326	40	90
Letters	27	24	0	3
Liberal/General Studies	6,688	6,477	47	164
Library and Archival Sciences	23	23		
Life Sciences	39	39	0	0
Mathematics	7	7	0	0
Multi/Interdisciplinary Studies	46	39	7	0
Parks and Recreation	17	17	0	0
Philosophy and Religion	1	1	0	0
Theology	20	0	0	20
Physical Sciences	280	279	0	1
Science Technologies	69	49	15	5
Psychology	88	83	0	5
Protective Services	1,180	1,088	78	14
Public Affairs	110	61	2	47
Social Sciences	39	27	0	12
Construction Trades	98	95	3	0
Mechanics and Repairers	629	525	100	4
Precision Production	1,204	1,030	132	42
Transportation and Material Moving	77	70	0	7
Visual and Performing Arts	384	309	22	53
Health & Professionally Related Fields	5,409	4,517	307	585
Business & Administration Management	5,969	3,618	121	2,230

Table III-11. Earned Degrees Conferred in Michigan, by Field of Study and Degree Level: 1993-1994 Continued

Level and Field of Study	Total	Public Universities	Independent Colleges & Universities	Percent Female(%)
Bachelor's Degrees-Total	**44,925**	**35,339**	**9,586**	**54.1**
Agri Business & Agri Production	354	354	0	35.0
Agricultural Sciences	135	134	1	52.6
Renewable Natural Resources	369	369	0	40.9
Architecture and Environmental Design	414	225	189	43.7
Area and Ethnic Studies	123	121	2	66.7
Marketing and Distribution	380	330	50	50.0
Communications	2,041	1,842	199	60.3
Communication Technologies	128	124	4	41.4
Computer and Information Sciences	755	590	165	28.3
Consumer, Personal, and Misc. Services	23	22	1	39.1
Education	3,604	3,170	434	79.4
Engineering	4,038	3,166	872	18.9
Engineering & Related Technologies	734	655	79	11.4
Foreign Languages	514	396	118	74.1
Allied Health	1	1	0	100.0
Home Economics	518	439	79	92.1
Vocational Home Economics	58	57	1	96.6
Industrial Arts	3	3	0	0.0
Law	100	49	51	85.0
Letters	1,833	1,431	402	67.6
Liberal/General Studies	941	846	95	61.4
Life Sciences	1,741	1,396	345	50.1
Mathematics	504	382	122	46.0
Multi/Interdisciplinary Studies	406	352	54	53.9
Parks and Recreation	533	501	32	52.3
Philosophy and Religion	186	112	74	33.9
Theology	85	0	85	25.9
Physical Sciences	621	469	152	32.0
Science Technologies	14	0	14	14.3
Psychology	2,432	2,112	320	72.3
Protective Services	1,160	1,079	81	35.6
Public Affairs	983	814	169	81.5
Social Sciences	4,018	3,318	700	46.7
Construction Trades	2	0	2	0.0
Mechanics and Repairers	10	7	3	0.0
Precision Production	39	36	3	28.2
Transportation and Material Moving	92	85	7	17.4
Visual and Performing Arts	1,617	1,177	440	60.1
Health & Professionally Related Fields	3,223	2,602	621	82.6
Business & Administration Management	10,193	6,573	3,620	49.9

Table III-11. Earned Degrees Conferred in Michigan, by Field of Study and Degree Level: 1993-1994 Continued

Level and Field of Study	Total	Public Universities	Independent Colleges & Universities	Percent Female(%)
Master's Degrees-Total	**15,481**	**13,664**	**1,817**	**51.9**
Agri Business & Agri Production	43	43	0	37.2
Agricultural Sciences	42	42	0	42.9
Renewable Natural Resources	95	95	0	47.4
Architecture and Environmental Design	143	137	6	32.2
Area and Ethnic Studies	55	55	0	50.9
Communications	272	268	4	65.1
Computer and Information Sciences	259	245	14	27.0
Education	3,358	3,153	205	76.4
Engineering	1,484	1,379	105	15.4
Engineering & Related Technologies	27	27	0	11.1
Foreign Languages	80	80	0	67.5
Home Economics	76	70	6	77.6
Law	50	50	0	38.0
Letters	266	252	14	66.5
Liberal/General Studies	31	28	3	64.5
Library and Archival Sciences	283	283	0	84.1
Life Sciences	215	209	6	47.0
Mathematics	176	175	1	42.0
Multi/Interdisciplinary Studies	72	71	1	48.6
Parks and Recreation	53	53	0	41.5
Philosophy and Religion	33	26	7	30.3
Theology	90	0	90	30.0
Physical Sciences	230	220	10	26.5
Psychology	250	165	85	66.4
Protective Services	35	23	12	20.0
Public Affairs	980	978	2	73.2
Social Sciences	381	363	18	42.8
Visual and Performing Arts	325	259	66	60.9
Health & Professionally Related Fields	992	827	165	75.3
Business & Administration Management	5,085	4,088	997	38.3
Doctoral Degrees-Total	**1,483**	**1,441**	**42**	**37.2**
Agri Business & Agri Production	15	15	0	13.3
Agricultural Sciences	38	38	0	34.2
Renewable Natural Resources	26	26	0	23.1
Architecture and Environmental Design	17	17	0	23.5
Area and Ethnic Studies	2	2	0	0.0

Table III-11. Earned Degrees Conferred in Michigan, by Field of Study and Degree Level: 1993-1994 Continued

Level and Field of Study	Total	Public Universities	Independent Colleges & Universities	Percent Female(%)
Doctoral Degrees - Continued				
Communications	21	21	0	57.1
Computer and Information Sciences	19	19	0	5.3
Education	228	218	10	64.0
Engineering	233	232	1	9.4
Foreign Languages	36	36	0	63.9
Home Economics	2	2	0	50.0
Letters	44	44	0	59.1
Liberal/General Studies	1	1	0	0.0
Library and Archival Sciences	2	2	0	50.0
Life Sciences	164	164	0	36.6
Mathematics	37	37	0	16.2
Multi/Interdisciplinary Studies	19	19	0	26.3
Parks and Recreation	3	3	0	33.3
Philosophy and Religion	18	13	5	22.2
Theology	14	0	14	0.0
Physical Sciences	166	166	0	24.1
Psychology	104	92	12	63.5
Public Affairs	11	11	0	45.5
Social Sciences	119	119	0	30.3
Visual and Performing Arts	54	54	0	44.4
Health & Professionally Related Fields	55	55	0	60.0
Business & Administration Management	35	35	0	42.9
First Professional Degrees-Total	**2,756**	**1,578**	**1,178**	**39.5**
Law	1,511	577	934	39.4
Theology	165	0	165	6.1
Health & Professionally Related Fields	1,080	1,001	79	44.8

Source: Michigan Department of Education, Postsecondary Education (Lansing, Michigan).

Table III-12. Estimate of Michigan Resident Student Expenses at Michigan Degree-Granting Institutions: 1994-1995

Institution	Total Enrollment	Undergraduate Tuition		Room and Board	Books and Personal	Travel
		In-State	Out-State			
Public Colleges and Universities						
Central Michigan University	14,430	$2,725	$6,660	$3,836	$1,200	$500
Eastern Michigan University	19,563	2,965	6,972	4,100	1,050	515
Ferris State University	12,250	3,430	6,950	4,170	1,260	412
Grand Valley State University	10,631	3,020	6,680	4,060	1,200	600
Lake Superior State University	3,154	3,312	6,450	4,230	1,225	300
Michigan State University	34,634	4,660	11,058	3,764	1,668	---
Michigan Technological University	6,355	3,640	8,245	3,976	1,500	450
Northern Michigan University	7,649	2,682	5,013	3,965	1,065	500
Oakland University	10,016	2,856	8,238	4,008	1,050	515
Saginaw Valley State University	6,474	3,100	6,323	3,800	1,380	420
University of Michigan	23,201	4,894	15,222	4,659	2,173	---
University of Michigan - Dearborn	6,603	3,160	10,057	1,500	1,346	911
University of Michigan - Flint	8,073	2,916	9,534	1,718	1,416	1,050
Wayne State University	20,811	3,194	6,929	5,445	1,482	1,210
Western Michigan University	27,901	3,060	7,140	4,100	1,760	500
Non-Public Colleges and Universities						
Adrian College	1,194	11,350	11,350	3,750	1,050	515
Albion College	1,634	14,920	14,920	4,826	1,050	515
Alma College	1,186	12,694	12,694	4,552	1,050	515
Andrews University	2,069	10,131	10,131	3,090	1,605	615
Aquinas College	2,138	11,208	11,208	4,124	1,050	515
Baker College - Auburn Hills	176	5,580	5,580	2,250	2,750	1,600
Baker College - Flint	3,680	5,580	5,580	2,250	2,750	1,600
Baker College - Muskegon	1,607	5,580	5,580	2,250	2,750	1,600
Baker College - Owosso	1,075	5,580	5,580	2,650	1,750	1,600
Calvin College	3,842	10,230	10,230	3,710	1,080	400
Center for Creative Studies	895	11,760	11,760	4,100	2,410	1,129
Cleary College	1,150	6,690	6,690	---	600	---
Concordia College	510	10,250	10,250	4,560	1,050	515
Davenport College - Grand Rapids	4,077	7,380	7,380	3,782	1,518	982
Davenport College - Kalamazoo	1,701	7,380	7,380	3,782	1,518	982
Davenport - Lansing	1,461	7,380	7,380	3,782	1,518	982
Detroit College of Business	4,608	7,644	7,644	3,782	1,518	982
Detroit College of Law	---	12,000	12,000	7,785	2,265	3,450
General Motors Institute	2,382	11,730	11,730	3,462	3,730	2,320
Grace Bible College	96	4,700	4,700	3,240	1,100	200
Hillsdale College	1,140	11,300	11,300	4,700	1,000	500
Hope College	2,437	12,359	12,359	4,341	1,315	250
Jordan College	2,028	5,760	5,760	2,575	1,050	915
Kalamazoo College	1,271	16,249	16,249	5,094	1,110	180

Table III-12. Estimate of Michigan Resident Student Expenses at Michigan Degree-Granting Institutions: 1994-1995 Continued

Institution	Total Enrollment	Undergraduate Tuition		Room and Board	Books and Personal	Travel
		In-State	Out-State			
Non-Public Colleges and Universities - Cont						
Kendall College of Art & Design	652	$9,990	$9,990	$3,790	$2,190	$935
Lawrence Institute of Technology	4,964	7,640	7,640	3,216	700	---
Madonna College	4,030	5,288	5,288	3,896	1,050	515
Michigan Christian College	257	5,420	5,420	3,300	1,050	515
Northwood University	1,680	9,665	9,665	4,385	1,100	500
Olivet College	726	11,030	11,030	3,680	1,050	515
Reformed Bible College	176	6,290	6,290	3,200	1,050	515
Sacred Heart Seminary	203	4,155	4,155	4,100	1,050	515
Sienna Heights College	1,150	9,240	9,240	3,880	1,050	515
Spring Arbor College	878	9,556	9,556	3,750	1,050	515
St. Mary's College	389	5,704	5,704	3,300	600	600
University of Detroit - Mercy	4,788	11,230	11,230	4,330	2,766	562
Walsh College	2,059	4,894	4,894	2,575	1,050	915
William Tyndale College	399	5,517	5,517	2,575	1,050	915

Notes: --- denotes information that is not applicable.
Source: Michigan Department of Education (Lansing, Michigan).

Table III-13. Michigan Community College Tuition and Fees: 1994-1995 Academic Year

Institution	Total Enrollment	Tuition		Institution	Total Enrollment	Tuition	
		In-State	Out-State			In-State	Out-State
Alpena	2,441	$1,519	$2,201	Macomb	27,578	$1,584	$2,359
Bay de Noc	2,316	1,778	2,416	Mid-Michigan	2,329	1,429	2,282
Bay Mills	410	2,000	2,000	Monroe County	3,668	873	1,293
Delta	10,650	1,800	2,390	Montcalm	2,024	1,260	1,936
Glen Oaks	1,416	1,364	2,015	Muskegon	5,112	1,250	1,800
Gogebic	1,729	1,102	1,505	North Central Michigan	2,032	1,348	1,767
Grand Rapids	13,059	1,468	2,140	Northwestern Michigan	4,428	1,700	2,732
Henry Ford	15,509	1,462	2,268	Oakland	54,094	1,531	2,523
Jackson	5,656	1,434	1,812	Schoolcraft	9,551	1,300	1,950
Kalamazoo Valley	8,902	1,116	2,077	Southwestern Michigan	2,779	1,260	1,596
Kellogg	7,389	1,333	2,170	St. Clair County	4,590	1,630	2,368
Kirtland	869	1,496	1,946	Washtenaw	10,814	1,594	2,245
Lake Michigan	3,636	1,350	1,650	Wayne County	10,049	1,775	2,270
Lansing	21,781	1,316	1,383	West Shore	1,326	1,333	2,077

Source: Michigan Department of Education (Lansing, Michigan: annually).

Table III-14. Public School Dropout and Graduation Rates(%) in Michigan, by District: 1992-1993 School Year

School District	Dropout Rate(%)	Graduation Rate(%)	School District	Dropout Rate(%)	Graduation Rate(%)
State Totals	**5.21**	**81.60**	Bangor Township Schools	14.76	53.11
Adams Twp School District	0.78	96.55	Baraga Area School District	0.00	100.00
Addison Community Schools	0.29	98.94	Bark River Harris School District	0.00	100.00
Adrian City School District	8.27	71.92	Bath Community Schools	4.03	83.89
Airport Community School District	1.00	97.98	Battle Creek Public Schools	7.51	72.55
Alba Public Schools	0.00	103.13	Bay City School District	7.02	75.38
Albion Public Schools	7.18	72.52	Beal City Schools	4.68	81.77
Alcona Community Schools	10.12	64.66	Bear Lake School District	0.00	100.00
Algonac Community School District	2.36	90.78	Beaver Island Community School	0.00	100.00
Allegan Public Schools	7.40	73.61	Beaverton Rural Schools	1.28	94.80
Allen Park Public Schools	4.01	84.86	Bedford Public Schools	4.89	80.94
Allendale Public School District	1.83	92.27	Beitung Twp School District	1.06	95.52
Alma Schools	4.11	84.52	Belding Area School District	7.96	71.32
Almont Schools	1.56	94.13	Bellaire Public Schools	0.53	97.30
Alpena Public Schools	8.70	70.46	Bellevue Comm School District	7.26	72.95
Anchor Bay School District	6.11	80.07	Bendle Public Schools	1.64	92.21
Ann Arbor Public Schools	10.94	62.79	Bentley Community School District	3.80	88.18
Arenac Eastern School District	4.14	83.07	Benton Harbor Area Schools	21.96	40.57
Armada Schools	3.04	89.17	Benzie County Central School	2.24	92.17
Ashley Community Schools	2.31	93.02	Berrien Springs Public Schools	4.00	84.73
Athens Area Schools	5.06	82.35	Bessemer Schools	1.03	96.12
Atherton Comm School District	2.39	91.20	Big Bay De Noc School District	2.78	88.58
Atlanta Community Schools	1.33	92.54	Big Rapids Public Schools	2.40	91.58
Au Gres Sims School District	4.43	79.63	Birch Run Area School District	1.93	92.30
Avondale School District	1.30	95.43	Birmingham City School District	2.97	88.27
Bad Axe Public Schools	1.30	94.98	Bissfield Community Schools	3.52	86.95
Baldwin Community Schools	2.11	91.90	Bloomfield Hills Schools	1.95	92.16
Bangor Public Schools	35.67	42.20	Bloomingdale Public School District	13.19	59.25

Table III-14. Public School Dropout and Graduation Rates(%) in Michigan, by District: 1992-1993 School Year Continued

School District	Dropout Rate(%)	Graduation Rate(%)	School District	Dropout Rate(%)	Graduation Rate(%)
Boyne City Public School District	2.22	91.33	Caseville Public Schools	1.09	95.45
Boyne Falls Public School District	6.10	75.09	Cass City Public Schools	2.95	89.98
Brandon School District	5.45	79.70	Cassopolis Public Schools	13.43	57.53
Brandywine Public School District	6.16	77.94	Cedar Springs	1.45	94.54
Breckenridge Comm Schools	2.66	91.37	Cen Off Holland Cty School District	6.53	76.84
Bridgeport Spaulding C S D	7.52	72.77	Center Line Public School	5.62	79.96
Bridgman Public Schools	3.45	87.49	Central Lake Public Schools	3.52	86.28
Brighton Schools	0.86	96.41	Central Montcalm Public School	2.63	87.77
Brimley Area Schools	10.53	63.37	Centreville Public Schools	6.50	73.56
Britton Macon Area School District	2.46	89.42	Charlevoix Public Schools	3.99	84.65
Bronson Community School District	7.23	73.87	Charlevoix-Emmet	5.49	80.26
Brown City Comm Schools	0.00	100.00	Chassell Twp School District	4.72	81.05
Buchanan Community School District	14.52	54.13	Cheboygan Area Schools	3.88	85.26
Buckley Comm School District	1.98	101.84	Chelsea School District	2.74	89.25
Buena Vista School District	14.85	61.98	Chesaning Union Schools	1.62	93.93
Bullock Creek School District	1.06	95.83	Chippewa Hills School District	3.74	85.76
Burr Oak Comm School District	4.95	91.99	Chippewa Valley Schools	1.76	93.28
Byron Area Schools	2.56	89.80	City of Harper Woods Schools	5.60	79.29
Cadillac Area Public Schools	6.30	76.12	Clare Public Schools	1.08	95.76
Caledonia Community Schools	0.15	98.85	Clarenceville School District	5.49	80.75
Camden Frontier Schools	14.56	54.78	Clawson City School District	2.68	89.55
Capac Community School District	3.69	86.80	Climax Scotts Comm Schools	2.86	88.68
Carman-Ainsworth Schools	8.01	73.24	Clinton Community Schools	3.59	86.58
Carney Nadeau Public Schools	0.00	100.00	Clio Area School District	1.61	92.51
Caro Schools	1.32	94.39	Coldwater Community Schools	7.89	72.56
Carrollton School District	3.74	85.19	Coloma Community Schools	9.19	66.27
Carson City Crystal Area SD	2.78	89.39	Colon Community School District	4.06	86.43
Carsonville-Port Sanilac S/D	0.00	96.96	Columbia School District	2.66	90.46

Table III-14. Public School Dropout and Graduation Rates(%) in Michigan, by District: 1992-1993 School Year Continued

School District	Dropout Rate(%)	Graduation Rate(%)	School District	Dropout Rate(%)	Graduation Rate(%)
Comstock Park Public Schools	1.50	102.81	East Jordan Public Schools	9.87	66.48
Comstock Public Schools	5.19	82.21	East Lansing School District	3.63	86.42
Concord Community Schools	1.12	94.34	Eaton Rapids Public Schools	6.68	76.91
Constantine Public Schools	7.52	73.26	Eau Claire Public Schools	17.96	43.96
Coopersville Public School District	1.30	95.08	Ecorse Public School District	35.76	23.48
Corunna Public School District	1.87	92.50	Edwardsburg Public Schools	3.07	96.41
Crawford Ausable Schools	13.99	53.84	Elk Rapids Schools	0.82	96.53
Crestwood School District	1.94	92.69	Elkton-Pigeon-Bay Port Schools	2.07	90.99
Croswell Lexington Comm School Dist	0.32	98.73	Ellsworth Community Schools	4.44	84.00
Dansville Ag School	2.82	88.47	Engadine Consolidated Schools	4.55	78.55
Davison Comm Schools	1.21	95.28	Escanaba Area Public Schools	1.37	94.79
Dearborn City School District	3.24	87.26	Essexville Hampton School District	0.73	97.41
Dearborn Hgts School District No. 7	3.78	86.43	Evart Public Schools	0.92	96.34
Decatur	5.46	80.01	Fairview Area School District	4.51	84.45
Deckerville Comm School District	3.79	86.26	Farmington Public School District	2.64	89.84
Deerfield Public Schools	5.66	76.66	Farwell Area Schools	8.55	70.48
Delta-Schoolcraft	1.60	93.74	Fennville Public Schools	6.71	76.05
Delton Kellogg School District	5.20	80.69	Fenton Area Public Schools	7.10	74.56
Detour Area Schools	2.04	92.56	Ferndale City School District	4.32	81.58
Detroit Public Schools	12.79	71.57	Fitzgerald Public Schools	2.39	92.07
Dewitt Public Schools	3.09	87.24	Flat Rock Community Schools	0.47	97.73
Dexter Community School District	2.24	91.29	Flint City School District	11.64	62.90
Dowagiac Union Schools	14.59	51.34	Flushing Community Schools	0.64	97.23
Dryden Community Schools	1.06	95.74	Forest Area Community S/D	1.29	95.29
Dundee Community Schools	4.55	83.24	Forest Hills Public Schools	0.35	98.58
Durand Area Schools	2.29	91.22	Forest Park School District	1.61	92.73
East China School District	6.24	76.91	Fowler Public Schools	0.52	97.67
East Detroit Public School	3.99	85.06	Fowlerville Community Schools	1.92	92.79

Table III-14. Public School Dropout and Graduation Rates(%) in Michigan, by District: 1992-1993 School Year Continued

School District	Dropout Rate(%)	Graduation Rate(%)	School District	Dropout Rate(%)	Graduation Rate(%)
Frankenmuth School District	0.60	97.50	Grosse Ile Township Schools	2.86	89.18
Frankport Area Schools	6.02	77.59	Grosse Pointe Public Schools	2.25	91.42
Fraser Public Schools	4.45	83.51	Gull Lake Community Schools	0.39	98.24
Free Soil Community School District	0.00	100.00	Gwinn Area Community Schools	2.74	87.90
Freeland Comm School District	1.46	94.55	Hale Area Schools	8.57	70.11
Fremont Public School District	4.30	83.49	Hamilton Community Schools	3.99	86.33
Fruitport Community Schools	6.81	74.84	Hamtramck Public Schools	8.40	83.30
Fulton Schools	0.71	97.26	Hancock Public Schools	6.38	77.52
Galesburg Augusta Comm Schools	7.64	71.68	Harbor Beach Comm Schools	0.61	97.56
Galien Township School District	7.98	71.99	Harbor Springs School District	4.14	84.68
Garden City School District	3.45	86.80	Harper Creek Comm Schools	5.28	80.55
Gaylord Community Schools	4.00	85.32	Harrison Community Schools	10.55	65.62
Gerrish Higgins School District	19.96	43.55	Hart Public School District	3.22	87.73
Gibraltar School District	4.88	81.90	Hartland Consolidated Schools	1.17	95.13
Gladstone Area Schools	0.33	98.76	Haslett Public Schools	1.28	94.73
Gladwin Community Schools	1.81	93.75	Hastings Area School District	2.94	88.94
Glen Lake Comm Schools	1.53	93.27	Hazel Park City School District	4.20	85.63
Gobles Public School District	1.19	94.20	Hemlock Public School District	3.14	89.27
Godfrey Lee Schools	3.28	110.29	Hesperia Community Schools	5.59	78.99
Godwin Heights Public Schools	5.26	79.75	Highland Park City Schools	6.46	75.35
Goodrich Area School District	0.23	98.81	Hillman Community Schools	0.20	109.03
Grand Blanc Comm Schools	7.23	73.81	Hillsdale Comm Public Schools	8.35	70.38
Grand Haven City School District	3.58	84.89	Holly Area School District	12.13	58.93
Grand Ledge Public Schools	4.43	82.83	Holt Public Schools	1.25	94.92
Grandville Schools	4.26	83.94	Holton Public Schools	3.97	85.56
Grant Public School District	1.26	95.20	Homer Schools	5.63	80.42
Grass Lake Community Schools	1.84	93.55	Hopkins Public Schools	6.63	76.49
Greenville Public Schools	1.15	95.91	Houghton Lake Comm Schools	7.90	71.60

Table III-14. Public School Dropout and Graduation Rates(%) in Michigan, by District: 1992-1993 School Year Continued

School District	Dropout Rate(%)	Graduation Rate(%)	School District	Dropout Rate(%)	Graduation Rate(%)
Houghton-Portage Twp Schools	0.46	97.67	Kingston Community School District	10.36	66.34
Howell Public Schools	2.69	89.83	L'Anse Creuse Public Schools	2.48	90.41
Hudson Area Schools	9.79	65.04	Laingsburg Community School Dist	3.73	85.67
Hudsonville Public School District	0.59	97.22	Lake City Area School District	1.52	94.50
Huron School District	8.58	69.87	Lake Fenton Schools	1.25	94.58
Huron Valley Schools	1.14	95.25	Lake Linden Hubbell School District	2.54	89.92
Ida Public School District	1.76	93.37	Lake Orion Community Schools	3.30	87.32
Imlay City Community Schools	3.24	84.37	Lakeshore School District	8.38	72.02
Inkster City School District	17.54	61.10	Lakeview Community Schools	5.13	81.50
Inland Lakes School District	0.00	100.00	Lakeview Public Schools	1.63	93.95
Iron Mountain City School District	2.90	88.08	Lakeview School District	0.69	97.05
Ironwood Area Schools	0.46	98.06	Lakeville Comm School District	4.96	82.31
Ishpeming Public School District	0.51	97.67	Lakewood Public Schools	1.68	93.75
Ithaca Schools	0.23	98.95	Lansing Public School District	9.57	69.22
Jackson Public Schools	0.75	96.91	Lawrence Public School District	3.70	85.49
Jefferson school-Monroe	2.47	90.23	Lawton Community School District	5.93	78.27
Jenison Schools	0.66	97.45	Leland Public School District	7.78	73.29
Johannesburg-Lewiston Schools	2.97	88.64	Les Cheneaux Comm School District	2.92	89.74
Jonesville Community Schools	3.02	88.96	Leslie Public Schools	6.33	77.17
Kalamazoo Public School District	7.41	72.32	Lincoln Cons School District	3.81	87.28
Kaleva Norman Dickson School Dist	4.15	82.81	Linden Comm School District	2.48	87.80
Kalkaska Public Schools	6.53	74.23	Litchfield Community Schools	3.53	91.63
Kearsley Community Schools	8.04	71.52	Littlefield Schools	5.00	77.42
Kelloggsville Public Schools	4.70	82.17	Livonia Public Schools	3.03	88.21
Kenowa Hills Public Schools	1.29	95.20	Loucks School-Roxland #12	5.00	77.42
Kent Intermediate School District	3.28	110.29	Lowell Area School District	1.04	96.47
Kentwood Public Schools	3.31	86.60	Ludington Area School District	3.08	88.52
Kingsley Area School	5.65	81.92	L'Anse Area Schools	4.21	85.51

Table III-14. Public School Dropout and Graduation Rates(%) in Michigan, by District: 1992-1993 School Year Continued

School District	Dropout Rate(%)	Graduation Rate(%)	School District	Dropout Rate(%)	Graduation Rate(%)
Mackinac Island Public Schools	0.00	100.00	Michigan Center School District	4.97	81.54
Mackinaw City Public Schools	5.17	82.36	Mid Peninsula School District	2.94	88.42
Madison Public Schools	4.58	82.94	Midland Public Schools	5.92	77.85
Madison School District	11.83	58.73	Milan Area Schools	3.77	87.17
Mancelona Public Schools	10.55	64.38	Millington Comm Schools	12.48	58.33
Manistee Area Public Schools	1.55	94.36	Mio Au Sable Schools	9.71	66.10
Manistique Area Schools	4.36	85.53	Mona Shores School District	0.57	97.68
Manton Schools	5.05	79.93	Monroe Public Schools	8.27	70.83
Maple Valley School District	2.68	89.07	Montabella Comm Schools	0.59	97.47
Marcellus Community Schools	2.49	90.74	Montague Area Public Schools	4.54	82.97
Marion Public Schools	7.37	73.43	Montrose Community Schools	0.85	96.36
Marlette Community Schools	3.59	85.23	Morenci Area Schools	2.85	89.94
Marquette Area Schools	0.78	96.74	Morley Stanwood Comm Schools	2.09	91.25
Marshall Public Schools	2.69	89.16	Morrice Area Schools	11.94	63.50
Martin Schools	12.95	58.54	Mt Clemens Community School	4.07	82.51
Marysville Public School District	1.61	93.81	Mt. Morris Consolidated Schools	9.11	70.09
Mason Cons (Monroe)	6.30	76.66	Muskegon City School District	5.40	82.10
Mason County Central SD	3.84	85.30	Muskegon Heights Schools	2.41	91.62
Mason County Eastern SD	2.07	94.04	Napoleon Community Schools	2.09	94.42
Mason Public Schools	4.98	81.93	Negaunee Public Schools	0.55	97.71
Mattawan Cons School District	0.72	96.28	New Buffalo Schools	4.48	83.03
Melvindale Northern Allen Park Schls	3.70	86.94	New Haven Community Schools	3.47	85.96
Memphis Community Schools	4.12	86.06	New Lothrop Area Public Schools	3.18	87.41
Mendon Community Schools	6.67	77.24	Newaygo Public School District	4.34	84.78
Menominee Area Public Schools	2.81	88.49	Niles Community School District	3.65	86.57
Meridian Public Schools	1.82	93.31	North Adams Public Schools	4.49	86.07
Merrill Comm School District	1.67	95.53	North Branch Area Schools	5.72	78.81
Mesick Consolidated School District	2.61	88.45	North Central Area Schools	4.81	82.11

Table III-14. Public School Dropout and Graduation Rates(%) in Michigan, by District: 1992-1993 School Year Continued

School District	Dropout Rate(%)	Graduation Rate(%)	School District	Dropout Rate(%)	Graduation Rate(%)
North Dickinson Co School District	2.21	91.78	Pellston Public School District	4.74	82.22
North Huron School District	0.00	98.43	Pennfield School District	7.96	72.74
North Muskegon Public Schools	0.00	100.00	Pentwater Public School District	0.00	100.00
Northport Public School District	4.48	84.44	Perry Public School District	2.85	89.57
Northview Public School District	3.80	85.47	Pewamo Westphalia Comm Schools	0.00	100.00
Northville Public Schools	1.22	94.78	Pickford Public Schools	0.00	100.00
Northwest School District	5.47	78.87	Pinckney Community Schools	1.50	94.06
Norway-Vulcan Area Schools	2.85	88.30	Pinconning Area Schools	0.84	96.40
N.I.C.E. Community Schools	0.18	102.60	Pine River Schools	4.18	84.66
Oak Park City School District	4.99	82.63	Pittsford Area Schools	2.81	86.79
Oakridge Schools	0.00	100.00	Plainwell Community Schools	0.58	97.30
Okemos Public Schools	0.45	98.35	Pontiac City School District	12.53	56.89
Olivet Community Schools	3.85	84.92	Port Hope Community Schools	0.00	100.00
Onaway Area Comm School District	9.06	67.58	Port Huron Area School District	2.17	91.25
Onekama Consolidated Schools	3.50	85.95	Portage Public Schools	0.32	98.63
Onieda Twp School District 3	0.00	0.00	Portland Public School District	0.78	96.47
Onsted Community Schools	6.74	75.44	Posen Consolidated School District	1.27	94.85
Ontonagon Area Schools	4.03	85.96	Potterville Public Schools	1.40	94.76
Orchard View Schools	10.06	66.52	Public Schools of Calumet	4.31	83.84
Osceola Twp School District	0.00	100.00	Public Schools of Petoskey	7.20	76.00
Oscoda School District	31.5	21.76	Quincy Community School District	2.26	90.59
Otsego Public Schools	0.00	100.88	Rapid River Public Schools	1.28	95.09
Ovid Elsie Area Schools	1.87	93.78	Ravenna Public Schools	3.25	87.80
Owendale Gagetown Area S/D	0.00	100.00	Reading Community Schools	1.24	99.62
Owosso Public Schools	4.83	81.57	Redford Union School District	2.56	89.95
Oxford Area Comm School District	1.82	91.73	Reed City Area Public Schools	4.24	99.32
Paw Public School District	5.79	107.96	Reese Public Schools	3.42	87.67
Peck Community School District	1.82	89.74	Reeths Puffer Schools	2.03	96.74

Table III-14. Public School Dropout and Graduation Rates(%) in Michigan, by District: 1992-1993 School Year Continued

School District	Dropout Rate(%)	Graduation Rate(%)	School District	Dropout Rate(%)	Graduation Rate(%)
Republic Michigamme Schools	0.00	100.00	St Charles Comm School	1.60	94.09
Richmond Comm Schools	5.88	79.36	St Johns Public Schools	0.00	100.00
River Rouge School District	6.50	176.78	St Joseph Public Schools	5.02	82.72
Riverview Community School District	4.48	83.76	St Louis Schools	2.72	88.80
Rochester Community School District	3.22	87.79	Standish Sterling Comm S/D	5.97	77.58
Rockford Public Schools	61.75	0.00	Stephenson Area Public Schools	4.82	83.80
Romeo Community Schools	3.23	87.22	Stockbridge Comm Schools	5.13	82.28
Roseville Community Schools	4.98	82.19	Summerfield School District	1.15	95.25
Rudyard Area Schools	5.32	82.45	Superior Central Schools	3.64	85.48
Saginaw City School District	6.33	76.46	Suttons Bay Public School District	3.00	88.26
Saginaw Twp Community School	2.27	91.08	Swan Valley School District	2.64	89.21
Saline Area School District	1.79	93.21	Swartz Creek Community Schools	1.63	93.48
Sand Creek Community Schools	4.02	90.12	Tahquamenon Area Schools	5.66	80.19
Saranac Community Schools	3.92	85.18	Tawas Area Schools	6.69	76.44
Saugatuck Public Schools	3.82	82.77	Taylor School District	9.91	67.54
Sault Ste Marie Area	6.66	76.20	Tecumseh Public Schools	4.45	84.22
School District of Royal Oak	5.19	81.30	Tekonsha Community Schools	3.97	84.71
School District of Ypsilanti	6.09	78.37	Thornapple Kellogg School District	2.98	89.16
Schoolcraft Community Schools	2.84	88.96	Three Rivers Comm School	10.56	63.36
Shelby Public Schools	0.72	97.17	Traverse City Area Public Schools	0.31	98.65
Shepherd Public School District	9.09	78.05	Trenton Public Schools	2.37	90.66
South Haven Public Schools	4.74	81.80	Tri County Area Schools	5.07	81.09
South Lake Schools	1.52	94.26	Troy School District	2.23	91.38
South Lyon Community Schools	0.02	94.05	Ubly Community Schools	3.70	86.41
South Redford School District	2.53	90.44	Union City Comm School District	9.17	70.75
Southgate Community School District	6.34	80.75	Unionville Sebewaing Area SD	1.16	95.13
Spring Lake Public Schools	1.70	93.97	Utica Community Schools	0.20	98.90
Springport Public Schools	6.56	77.22	Van Buren Public Schools	6.21	77.50

Table III-14. Public School Dropout and Graduation Rates(%), by District: 1992-1993 School Year Continued

School District	Dropout Rate(%)	Graduation Rate(%)	School District	Dropout Rate(%)	Graduation Rate(%)
Van Dyke Public Schools	4.58	83.54	Whitefish Schools	4.76	80.00
Vanderbilt Area School	18.39	44.37	Whiteford Agr School District	0.45	97.87
Vandercook Lake Public S/D	3.96	83.75	Whitehall School District	3.19	86.74
Vassar Public Schools	2.78	90.90	Whitmore Lake Pub School District	12.07	69.27
Vestaburg Community Schools	4.44	82.83	Whittemore Prescott Area S/D	9.92	65.21
Vicksburg Schools	2.80	88.66	Williamston Comm Schools	5.30	81.11
Wakefield Twp School District	1.68	95.06	Willow Run Community Schools	3.13	88.50
Waldron Area Schools	5.37	81.54	Wolverine Comm School District	14.46	53.36
Walkerville Rural Comm SD	3.19	87.09	Woodhaven School District	5.50	81.07
Walled Lake Cons Schools	7.35	92.57	Wyandotte City School district	2.84	90.15
Warren Consolidated Schools	5.20	80.58	Wyoming Schools	4.11	84.71
Warren Woods Public School	0.00	100.00	Yale Public Schools	8.75	69.28
Waterford School District	6.05	75.95	Zeeland Public Schools	2.50	91.55
Watersmeet Twp School District	0.00	100.00			
Watervliet School District	16.44	48.23	NOTE: The following school districts report themselves as:		
Waverly Schools	3.30	92.44			
Wayland Union Schools	1.61	93.74	City of Harper Woods Schools		
Webberville Community Schools	0.88	95.81	Public Schools of Calumet		
West Bloomfield School District	1.90	92.07	Public Schools of Petoskey		
West Branch-Rose City Area Schools	51.79	5.34	School District of Royal Oak		
West Iron County School District	0.26	98.88	School District of Ypsilanti		
West Ottawa Public School District	3.36	86.60			
Western School District	7.00	76.90			
Westwood Community Schools	6.36	74.90			
Westwood Heights School District	4.67	83.05			
White Cloud Public Schools	4.12	83.41			
White Pigeon Comm School District	3.38	85.19			
White Pine School District	0.00	103.16			

Source: Michigan Department of Education (Lansing, Michigan) NOTE: The rates in this table were reproduced exactly as reported by each school district. Any questions should be directed to the individual school districts or the Michigan Department of Education. Districts reporting negative rates and the Intermediate School Districts are not included in this table.

Table III-15. Michigan Educational Assessment Program (MEAP) Scores, by School District: 1993-1994 School Year

School District	Math(%)			Reading(%)			Science(%)		
	4th Grade	7th Grade	10th Grade	4th Grade	7th Grade	10th Grade	5th Grade	8th Grade	11th Grade
Adams Twp School District	71.4	52.8	44.7	42.9	36.1	63.0	100.0	76.3	50.0
Addison Community Schools	71.8	41.1	38.1	40.0	34.7	47.4	64.9	67.1	42.2
Adrian City School District	58.8	53.1	36.3	38.2	40.3	48.8	68.3	60.9	46.5
Airport Community School Distr	60.0	41.6	29.3	34.3	36.8	45.3	81.5	64.3	72.1
Akron Fairgrove Schools	59.6	32.7	34.4	40.4	38.5	42.2	84.2	51.1	43.6
Alba Public Schools	27.3	23.5	30.0	18.2	17.6	30.0	56.3	37.5	30.8
Albion Public Schools	54.1	33.6	32.9	33.8	28.9	46.9	69.9	59.6	23.1
Alcona Community Schools	68.0	54.7	46.2	50.7	48.0	65.6	78.8	73.8	49.2
Algonac Community School Distr	68.1	45.6	17.5	49.5	33.0	29.7	86.8	83.1	45.6
Allegan Public Schools	58.7	38.8	31.2	45.3	28.6	37.5	70.7	52.3	41.3
Allen Park Public Schools	55.2	54.2	36.6	54.7	53.8	64.0	79.1	82.8	54.3
Allendale Public School Distri	74.1	71.1	38.0	54.6	40.0	48.0	86.0	53.7	43.2
Alma Public Schools	76.0	50.0	38.5	54.2	41.9	47.8	66.8	65.0	52.5
Alpena Public Schools	63.1	56.2	34.3	48.8	40.9	43.7	79.4	64.6	47.8
Anchor Bay School District	68.3	50.0	40.5	43.5	37.3	45.6	77.0	59.9	49.4
Ann Arbor Public Schools	68.5	65.5	57.1	56.5	58.1	63.6	82.1	74.2	69.1
Arenac Eastern School District	44.7	24.4	29.4	44.7	24.4	29.4	79.4	0.0	45.5
Armada Area Schools	71.6	54.3	44.1	60.6	51.5	56.4	81.7	68.3	65.4
Arvon Township School District	88.9	0.0	0.0	66.7	0.0	0.0	80.0	0.0	0.0
Ashley Community Schools	40.0	44.8	41.9	16.0	28.6	61.3	52.4	58.3	54.1
Athens Area Schools	59.2	50.0	38.1	26.3	34.5	44.2	64.9	62.5	60.9
Atherton Comm School District	55.4	28.2	31.1	37.0	24.4	45.9	75.0	44.3	45.2
Atlanta Community Schools	38.5	43.2	14.8	38.5	15.9	39.2	75.7	55.1	54.1
Au Gres Sims School District	60.5	35.7	33.3	30.2	38.1	41.7	65.1	63.3	62.5
Autrain-Onota Public Schools	40.0	0.0	0.0	30.0	0.0	0.0	62.5	0.0	0.0
Avondale School District	71.1	57.1	32.6	49.8	46.5	49.7	86.3	66.5	50.3
Bad Axe Public Schools	74.5	59.7	50.0	67.0	40.3	63.6	76.8	71.9	57.3
Baldwin Community Schools	46.6	7.9	13.6	37.7	12.7	27.1	40.4	54.9	64.7

117

Table III-15. Michigan Educational Assessment Program (MEAP) Scores, by School District: 1993-1994 School Year Continued

School District	Math(%)			Reading(%)			Science(%)		
	4th Grade	7th Grade	10th Grade	4th Grade	7th Grade	10th Grade	5th Grade	8th Grade	11th Grade
Bangor Public Schools (Van Bur)	38.6	41.3	31.9	33.0	23.1	32.8	67.2	70.3	55.4
Bangor Township Schools	73.1	57.7	24.9	45.5	52.1	46.6	86.9	52.9	60.5
Baraga Area Schools	59.1	65.5	42.2	29.5	35.2	62.2	79.2	68.6	54.0
Bark River Harris School Distr	62.5	63.5	45.2	55.0	54.9	66.7	63.6	69.8	69.6
Bath Community Schools	71.1	66.7	42.5	45.8	48.6	49.3	73.8	71.3	50.0
Battle Creek Public Schools	44.4	27.7	21.1	39.0	23.0	26.8	58.6	53.1	40.6
Bay City School District	66.4	46.7	30.4	42.4	38.9	50.5	69.4	56.4	50.6
Beal City Public Schools	67.7	54.7	34.1	38.7	49.1	39.5	62.5	44.0	56.4
Bear Lake School District	84.2	94.4	45.8	52.6	38.9	50.0	85.0	84.0	73.9
Beaver Island Community School	45.5	60.0	40.0	18.2	80.0	60.0	100.0	75.0	66.7
Beaverton Rural Schools	55.9	36.5	24.8	49.0	34.1	34.5	70.7	67.2	45.5
Bedford Public Schools	62.6	63.7	37.1	48.6	53.7	51.6	83.7	71.7	51.3
Beecher Community School Distr	38.9	11.6	10.8	19.4	14.6	10.4	47.3	27.9	16.0
Belding Area School District	42.4	38.8	32.5	25.6	38.8	43.3	69.7	54.0	51.3
Bellevue Comm School District	58.8	42.7	39.7	48.8	36.0	50.0	52.1	53.7	65.1
Bendle Public Schools	31.0	31.7	18.5	18.6	20.3	27.1	65.6	48.2	24.4
Bentley Community School Distr	76.3	58.9	44.9	44.7	49.3	33.8	77.3	58.4	38.0
Benton Harbor Area Schools	53.1	15.4	3.9	43.8	10.0	13.6	82.6	58.3	24.5
Benzie County Central School	70.9	33.6	34.2	50.0	28.9	51.3	76.4	65.9	49.5
Berkley School District	80.5	74.1	41.7	69.6	61.7	58.6	87.0	77.1	55.0
Berlin Twp School District 3	0.0	0.0	0.0	100.0	0.0	0.0	100.0	0.0	0.0
Berrien Springs Public Schools	75.8	56.1	36.4	53.8	50.4	55.5	90.1	56.8	52.6
Bessemer City School District	68.8	47.8	32.6	43.8	41.3	53.5	80.6	63.4	52.9
Big Bay De Noc School District	31.0	24.3	25.0	27.6	21.6	34.8	95.0	55.6	61.5
Big Jackson School District	75.0	0.0	0.0	50.0	0.0	0.0	100.0	0.0	0.0
Big Rapids Public Schools	65.0	59.6	44.8	55.8	52.2	55.5	86.0	71.9	68.6
Birch Run Area School District	62.7	52.9	31.1	47.6	50.7	47.1	75.3	72.8	53.8
Birmingham City School District	86.5	82.6	61.8	74.3	72.7	72.9	92.8	82.8	77.1

Table III-15. Michigan Educational Assessment Program (MEAP) Scores, by School District: 1993-1994 School Year Continued

School District	Math(%)			Reading(%)			Science(%)		
	4th Grade	7th Grade	10th Grade	4th Grade	7th Grade	10th Grade	5th Grade	8th Grade	11th Grade
Blissfield Community Schools	57.6	43.2	27.7	38.4	41.6	45.5	78.2	62.5	47.7
Bloomfield Hills School Distri	87.8	84.6	66.2	72.2	69.9	70.1	85.1	80.0	70.5
Bloomfield Twp School District	33.3	0.0	0.0	16.7	0.0	0.0	100.0	0.0	0.0
Bloomingdale Public School Dis	51.9	31.6	23.0	36.5	24.1	31.7	77.2	59.5	41.9
Bois Blanc School District	50.0	100.0	0.0	0.0	0.0	0.0	0.0	0.0	0.0
Boyne Falls Public School Dist	39.1	57.1	36.0	21.7	33.3	39.1	53.3	37.0	29.4
Brandon School District	79.5	59.0	34.1	57.8	61.5	43.1	70.9	57.7	55.3
Breckenridge Community Schools	62.0	37.6	36.0	35.4	40.6	38.4	87.1	55.6	31.1
Breitung Twp School District	59.2	65.7	49.4	55.3	48.3	54.0	69.4	58.4	66.7
Bridgeport-Spaulding C S D	59.5	36.0	23.5	46.7	19.3	37.2	60.7	41.3	37.0
Bridgman Public Schools	60.8	55.1	51.6	45.9	37.7	47.5	67.6	60.6	41.3
Brighton Area Schools	78.8	64.9	47.9	60.9	61.6	58.8	90.0	80.0	62.9
Brimley Area Schools	52.6	48.8	13.9	26.3	34.9	48.5	56.9	54.2	40.0
Britton Macon Area School Dist	81.3	48.5	43.5	75.0	21.2	65.2	90.9	51.9	38.5
Bronson Community School Distr	44.6	34.0	32.1	32.2	31.1	49.1	55.6	47.3	34.4
Brown City Comm School Distric	69.3	53.5	48.1	49.3	38.4	67.5	77.6	78.6	53.0
Buchanan Community School Dist	69.5	56.6	34.9	47.7	45.5	53.8	74.2	53.3	54.2
Buckley Comm School District	53.3	52.9	43.3	33.3	29.4	53.3	69.7	69.6	71.4
Buena Vista School District	21.2	27.5	23.5	20.2	14.7	30.7	37.2	64.4	34.2
Bullock Creek School District	79.3	51.3	31.3	55.6	50.4	48.0	85.8	65.6	68.3
Burr Oak Comm School District	34.8	17.4	32.1	13.0	26.1	35.7	56.0	37.0	26.1
Burt Township School District	57.1	16.7	25.0	28.6	33.3	50.0	66.7	33.3	50.0
Byron Area Schools	51.4	50.7	22.0	37.5	33.3	45.1	74.4	58.2	62.4
Byron Center Public Schools	77.1	65.0	47.0	56.2	51.7	44.0	94.0	70.9	78.3
Cadillac Area Public Schools	61.3	41.2	41.4	53.3	44.8	48.5	75.5	60.6	45.9
Caledonia Community Schools	78.6	69.5	43.9	55.5	53.1	52.8	91.3	66.4	72.4
Camden Frontier Schools	67.7	39.2	27.7	56.9	25.5	42.6	78.6	49.1	40.4
Capac Community School Distric	62.7	42.6	27.2	51.8	37.7	38.5	80.2	51.8	66.3

Table III-15. Michigan Educational Assessment Program (MEAP) Scores, by School District: 1993-1994 School Year Continued

School District	Math(%)			Reading(%)			Science(%)		
	4th Grade	7th Grade	10th Grade	4th Grade	7th Grade	10th Grade	5th Grade	8th Grade	11th Grade
Carman-Ainsworth Schools	69.3	61.3	27.1	49.7	48.6	42.1	90.5	59.8	48.3
Carney Nadeau Public Schools	75.0	47.1	61.5	52.0	35.3	65.4	77.8	61.9	38.1
Caro Community Schools	52.0	52.2	44.9	39.1	54.6	58.7	74.7	68.8	54.4
Carrollton School District	41.3	27.2	25.0	29.3	17.5	42.1	65.8	61.0	53.0
Carson City Crystal Area School	54.0	41.1	32.0	38.0	28.6	41.9	79.5	71.4	63.3
Carsonville-Port Sanilac S/D	52.4	68.6	38.3	57.1	35.3	36.2	74.5	62.0	27.8
Caseville Public Schools	52.2	46.2	31.8	30.4	23.1	54.5	89.5	81.0	68.0
Cass City Public Schools	50.9	55.6	33.3	46.4	32.3	46.4	79.7	56.1	56.0
Cassopolis Public Schools	48.8	35.6	27.6	27.9	29.0	49.3	83.8	71.2	65.7
Cedar Springs Public Schools	72.2	48.0	38.0	56.1	36.3	51.8	91.4	61.7	68.8
Center Line Public Schools	63.4	76.3	41.9	48.1	61.3	42.9	76.4	60.5	58.3
Central Lake Public Schools	48.8	64.9	20.7	31.7	21.6	28.6	73.7	54.1	54.8
Central Montcalm Public School	55.8	50.9	35.6	39.4	36.4	47.3	75.1	71.6	54.4
Centreville Public Schools	63.5	42.6	21.4	40.5	27.9	38.6	61.0	61.3	52.3
Charlevoix Public Schools	61.1	67.3	45.2	53.7	59.4	67.6	85.1	78.4	61.0
Charlotte Public Schools	75.7	49.3	37.7	47.4	46.8	42.3	82.0	69.9	52.9
Chassell Twp School District	69.6	36.8	50.0	43.5	38.9	63.3	82.6	72.0	72.7
Cheboygan Area Schools	49.4	47.1	36.4	39.3	44.4	42.1	76.4	49.1	50.3
Chelsea School District	64.2	61.8	59.7	53.4	47.7	62.3	82.0	70.8	66.2
Chesaning Union Schools	64.2	68.7	41.9	38.8	46.9	38.3	87.8	80.4	49.0
Chippewa Hills School District	62.9	37.4	28.9	49.4	35.7	40.8	76.8	59.6	49.6
Chippewa Valley Schools	70.2	74.6	40.6	56.0	62.5	55.3	85.5	81.1	52.5
Church School District	0.0	50.0	0.0	0.0	50.0	0.0	75.0	0.0	0.0
City of Harper Woods Schools	72.1	45.7	29.9	50.0	45.7	31.6	90.4	71.4	69.0
Clare Public Schools	54.2	59.1	29.0	38.3	44.0	36.1	63.5	68.8	48.5
Clarenceville School District	79.5	41.5	29.9	66.1	46.6	46.0	92.0	79.0	57.4
Clarkston Comm School District	75.8	64.7	40.2	59.5	55.8	55.0	85.6	77.8	61.4
Clawson City School District	58.3	65.6	27.4	46.2	48.4	45.7	76.7	87.0	41.2

Table III-15. Michigan Educational Assessment Program (MEAP) Scores, by School District: 1993-1994 School Year Continued

School District	Math(%)			Reading(%)			Science(%)		
	4th Grade	7th Grade	10th Grade	4th Grade	7th Grade	10th Grade	5th Grade	8th Grade	11th Grade
Climax Scotts Community School	65.4	61.4	39.6	34.6	49.1	43.6	96.3	91.7	88.9
Clinton Community Schools	62.9	61.8	42.9	46.4	46.1	43.4	76.7	57.5	47.6
Clintondale Community Schools	73.9	68.6	22.5	65.6	57.9	34.4	97.6	87.8	56.3
Clio Area School District	78.4	56.0	32.3	56.8	45.6	37.5	82.2	57.5	38.5
Coldwater Community Schools	60.0	54.7	43.0	36.2	34.4	39.9	73.2	52.1	54.0
Coleman Community School Distr	49.5	38.6	22.1	37.9	38.9	36.4	61.4	51.6	40.7
Coloma Community Schools	70.1	55.2	21.3	46.9	38.9	26.9	65.9	42.2	34.6
Colon Community School District	54.4	26.7	35.4	38.2	33.7	42.4	74.3	63.8	36.2
Columbia School District	47.4	47.4	30.2	43.7	42.9	47.7	67.1	53.0	57.0
Comstock Park Public Schools	74.6	58.9	51.5	54.2	50.4	59.8	75.3	76.2	84.2
Comstock Public Schools	62.7	56.1	42.3	43.6	34.4	43.0	72.9	59.7	50.3
Concord Community Schools	64.9	67.1	42.4	49.1	52.2	53.1	75.4	70.1	52.2
Constantine Public School Dist	59.5	42.7	33.0	41.5	37.9	38.2	75.0	63.4	47.8
Coopersville Public School Dis	83.2	62.8	32.1	52.4	46.8	56.2	85.4	56.1	58.0
Corunna Public School District	69.2	60.0	32.9	60.0	50.7	46.8	82.7	77.0	54.7
Covert Public Schools	70.3	17.2	17.0	46.9	12.3	15.2	65.4	36.2	45.2
Crawford Ausable Schools	43.3	55.5	31.2	33.7	40.7	41.5	69.0	66.9	56.0
Crestwood School District	73.8	45.9	43.1	46.2	37.1	45.1	81.9	66.5	54.3
Croswell Lexington Comm Sd	59.8	69.7	46.7	52.1	50.3	43.1	84.8	73.7	47.4
Dansville Agricultural Schools	82.4	69.8	44.1	38.2	50.8	57.4	82.9	71.4	54.4
Davison Community Schools	75.7	67.6	45.1	54.4	60.4	60.7	82.2	62.7	52.0
Dearborn City School District	60.9	44.8	29.0	44.0	34.6	39.7	67.5	55.0	34.5
Dearborn Hgts School District	67.6	36.8	20.2	49.6	32.9	29.2	68.6	44.9	39.5
Decatur Public Schools	42.7	40.6	38.5	33.7	35.2	46.0	71.8	54.3	53.8
Deckerville Comm School Distri	55.4	43.2	32.8	46.2	44.4	31.6	67.9	70.4	40.8
Deerfield Public Schools	42.9	37.8	26.5	34.3	35.1	50.0	81.3	72.4	50.0
Delton Kellogg School District	67.1	45.6	24.4	47.2	34.9	39.7	69.3	56.1	50.7
Detour Area Schools	75.0	50.0	38.1	62.5	31.8	27.3	79.2	88.0	85.7

Table III-15. Michigan Educational Assessment Program (MEAP) Scores, by School District: 1993-1994 School Year Continued

School District	Math(%)			Reading(%)			Science(%)		
	4th Grade	7th Grade	10th Grade	4th Grade	7th Grade	10th Grade	5th Grade	8th Grade	11th Grade
Detroit City School District	47.4	21.8	10.5	43.1	26.8	22.4	70.1	41.1	33.6
Dewitt Public Schools	76.6	61.9	67.9	66.5	56.1	69.4	87.1	86.5	80.2
Dexter Community School Distri	75.0	65.7	52.3	59.5	60.1	51.6	86.2	65.9	61.6
Dowagiac Union Schools	61.9	44.0	33.3	37.6	25.5	44.3	66.3	58.9	52.7
Dryden Community Schools	92.2	61.1	49.2	81.8	38.9	52.4	98.2	77.2	66.7
Dundee Community Schools	58.2	36.2	35.1	34.9	34.3	53.0	82.2	64.6	62.6
Durand Area Schools	63.6	37.7	24.0	31.5	37.7	37.7	80.0	63.3	41.3
East China School District	59.0	44.1	38.5	48.3	41.1	50.3	71.0	71.8	53.9
East Detroit Public Schools	62.8	54.1	23.1	45.5	55.7	42.3	78.9	56.2	57.4
East Grand Rapids Public Schoo	90.7	82.0	81.3	82.9	74.6	82.5	93.2	93.8	83.5
East Jackson Community Schools	37.3	60.0	26.8	30.4	32.9	40.0	73.5	54.5	41.0
East Jordan Public Schools	46.4	52.6	20.0	39.2	37.9	31.6	64.4	64.0	36.7
East Lansing School District	70.8	77.0	57.1	59.5	65.3	64.7	84.3	71.4	65.5
Easton Twp School District 6	50.0	0.0	0.0	16.7	0.0	0.0	63.6	0.0	0.0
Eaton Rapids Public Schools	57.4	53.5	34.8	37.0	53.5	55.2	71.2	65.3	55.7
Eau Claire Public Schools	59.6	27.8	17.2	31.9	22.2	19.0	76.3	39.1	18.5
Ecorse Public School District	52.6	8.0	5.6	25.3	13.8	18.4	82.5	16.9	50.0
Edwardsburg Public Schools	53.1	43.1	36.0	38.7	29.2	50.0	81.3	57.1	51.8
Elk Rapids Schools	82.7	39.3	45.5	64.9	44.6	47.5	78.9	67.3	49.0
Elkton-Pigeon-Bay Port Schools	69.0	48.1	35.8	53.6	39.6	50.0	78.9	81.0	63.0
Ellsworth Community Schools	60.9	58.8	30.0	47.8	29.4	22.2	80.0	76.2	56.5
Elm river Twp School District	80.0	0.0	0.0	80.0	0.0	0.0	75.0	100.0	0.0
Engadine Consolidated Schools	47.8	41.7	34.4	34.8	37.5	59.4	79.2	68.6	54.2
Escanaba Area Public Schools	65.7	59.9	41.2	46.4	45.8	51.5	78.9	73.1	59.2
Essexville Hampton School Dist	75.4	52.2	64.5	55.2	46.3	64.5	88.5	68.8	65.2
Evart Public Schools	59.3	50.0	43.0	41.8	46.3	47.1	73.9	60.0	54.2
Ewen-Trout Creek Cons S/D	69.8	57.9	43.9	53.5	44.7	48.8	67.7	64.7	21.3
Excelsior Township District #1	0.0	16.7	0.0	100.0	33.3	0.0	100.0	80.0	0.0

Table III-15. Michigan Educational Assessment Program (MEAP) Scores, by School District: 1993-1994 School Year Continued

School District	Math(%)			Reading(%)			Science(%)		
	4th Grade	7th Grade	10th Grade	4th Grade	7th Grade	10th Grade	5th Grade	8th Grade	11th Grade
Fairview Area School Dist.	64.1	57.5	62.1	46.2	53.8	62.1	94.4	65.6	50.0
Farmington Public School Distr	75.9	63.5	50.0	58.9	57.6	59.4	88.6	71.0	66.4
Farwell Area Schools	42.3	40.9	25.9	41.5	40.9	39.1	62.7	50.0	48.9
Fennville Public Schools	45.7	41.6	29.1	34.5	31.9	28.8	67.5	56.1	48.5
Fenton Area Public Schools	71.1	63.9	49.3	50.4	56.5	64.9	83.8	70.4	54.8
Ferndale City School District	62.9	56.5	21.7	45.7	36.6	34.7	83.2	55.9	40.5
Ferry Community School Distric	34.8	50.0	0.0	13.0	42.9	0.0	88.2	56.3	0.0
Fitzgerald Public Schools	65.3	41.2	24.9	41.6	40.0	31.3	85.8	70.9	63.5
Flat Rock Community Schools	51.3	30.9	9.8	42.6	39.1	28.7	78.2	61.2	39.8
Flint City School District	35.5	18.0	10.9	25.1	18.6	22.5	42.4	28.7	22.7
Flushing Community Schools	77.9	69.8	40.5	60.1	60.5	55.5	87.3	70.2	54.3
Forest Area Community Schools	51.6	32.3	28.9	34.4	24.2	47.8	75.5	59.7	50.0
Forest Hills Public Schools	98.6	89.7	72.2	94.1	78.1	76.9	96.7	95.1	81.4
Forest Park School District	73.3	42.9	42.9	51.7	41.3	44.9	89.5	50.8	64.9
Fowler Public Schools	37.5	76.5	44.4	6.3	41.2	60.0	78.9	63.3	66.1
Fowlerville Community Schools	67.8	58.5	46.7	40.8	45.0	58.4	85.6	76.4	86.8
Frankenmuth School District	89.2	82.2	65.9	75.4	72.6	77.5	89.4	87.9	74.6
Frankfort-Elberta Area Schools	63.4	50.0	36.8	46.3	30.0	38.1	77.8	75.0	57.1
Fraser Public Schools	74.9	56.0	35.2	58.4	46.9	59.9	84.6	76.7	48.1
Free Soil Community School Dis	36.4	17.6	15.4	27.3	11.8	61.5	100.0	47.8	69.2
Freeland Comm School District	69.3	56.2	52.6	43.2	52.1	46.9	75.9	72.1	59.4
Fremont Public School District	46.3	63.1	45.1	27.3	47.0	53.0	79.0	63.0	56.9
Fruitport Community Schools	61.1	41.8	42.6	47.0	45.5	41.5	81.1	68.7	41.1
Fulton Schools	65.0	46.7	39.6	53.3	46.7	45.3	64.5	56.4	51.6
Galesburg Augusta Community	65.4	39.0	34.7	47.4	47.1	42.9	83.7	65.1	70.1
Galien Township School District	40.0	20.9	24.3	45.0	32.6	16.2	77.1	50.0	34.2
Ganges School District No.4	60.0	0.0	0.0	20.0	0.0	0.0	100.0	0.0	0.0
Garden City School District	62.4	40.9	24.9	46.8	35.7	39.3	73.8	54.6	43.6

Table III-15. Michigan Educational Assessment Program (MEAP) Scores, by School District: 1993-1994 School Year Continued

School District	Math(%)			Reading(%)			Science(%)		
	4th Grade	7th Grade	10th Grade	4th Grade	7th Grade	10th Grade	5th Grade	8th Grade	11th Grade
Gaylord Community Schools	58.8	53.5	31.6	44.1	52.7	52.1	77.2	69.1	50.2
Genesee School District	58.5	37.5	42.6	24.6	40.0	43.6	74.5	62.3	47.1
Gerrish Higgins School Distric	50.0	28.1	25.8	44.9	34.9	41.9	73.9	63.2	57.3
Gibraltar School District	76.5	58.3	28.2	70.6	52.7	40.3	83.4	58.7	40.1
Gladstone Area Schools	34.8	49.2	41.9	44.6	47.3	45.7	78.3	55.9	45.6
Gladwin Community Schools	65.9	64.8	26.7	39.5	46.0	40.3	80.5	63.6	51.5
Glen Lake Community School Dis	65.0	56.8	51.8	60.0	56.8	67.9	73.8	65.8	59.2
Gobles Public School District	84.5	43.1	25.8	77.6	40.0	63.9	80.0	62.9	52.7
Godfrey Lee Public Schools	90.1	40.4	12.5	81.3	28.1	12.8	84.2	36.2	25.0
Godwin Heights Public Schools	52.8	58.9	35.5	39.1	45.0	44.9	63.9	71.8	50.5
Goodrich Area School District	65.4	56.9	36.2	50.7	65.0	52.2	83.5	78.4	65.7
Grand Blanc Comm Schools	73.9	64.7	54.3	55.5	60.9	67.4	85.4	81.9	60.3
Grand Haven City School Distri	59.6	57.8	38.0	44.1	53.4	53.1	82.6	70.7	67.8
Grand Ledge Public Schools	78.2	73.1	39.6	64.9	61.7	58.1	92.3	70.3	55.7
Grand Rapids City School Distr	43.3	26.9	20.7	29.4	24.4	31.8	57.1	40.9	40.5
Grandville Public Schools	86.2	69.2	52.5	65.4	61.5	47.4	92.9	78.7	58.2
Grant Public School District	60.6	44.1	38.8	41.7	30.7	42.7	72.7	53.3	41.6
Grass Lake Community Schools	62.2	36.1	36.8	51.7	34.4	44.4	76.7	57.6	48.2
Greenville Public Schools	66.9	49.2	36.2	43.7	39.0	40.7	75.0	58.9	52.5
Grosse Pointe Public Schools	84.7	83.4	62.7	66.6	75.1	72.5	89.6	82.4	72.5
Gull Lake Community Schools	76.7	54.7	49.2	62.4	54.7	59.6	76.9	77.5	66.3
Gwinn Area Community Schools	60.5	45.6	32.9	59.3	41.8	42.4	82.7	70.0	58.6
Hagar Township School District	66.7	25.0	0.0	33.3	62.5	0.0	0.0	40.0	0.0
Hale Area Schools	53.2	41.9	22.2	40.4	33.9	44.7	65.5	32.8	26.8
Hamilton Community Schools	65.3	53.8	43.9	50.3	38.8	47.5	74.3	65.6	62.3
Hamtramck Public Schools	37.7	42.4	16.0	27.7	14.5	27.9	51.8	43.1	42.2
Hancock Public Schools	62.9	60.5	54.1	52.9	55.8	53.3	89.9	63.0	56.9
Hanover Horton Schools	62.0	39.3	21.6	43.0	30.8	33.0	85.7	77.6	33.8

Table III-15. Michigan Educational Assessment Program (MEAP) Scores, by School District: 1993-1994 School Year Continued

School District	Math(%)			Reading(%)			Science(%)		
	4th Grade	7th Grade	10th Grade	4th Grade	7th Grade	10th Grade	5th Grade	8th Grade	11th Grade
Harbor Beach Community Sch	45.7	48.1	42.5	44.4	40.0	52.8	70.0	57.4	53.1
Harbor Springs School District	66.7	63.9	47.4	58.3	52.8	60.0	85.7	83.8	52.9
Harper Creek Community Sch	77.3	48.0	46.2	48.8	42.5	45.5	78.6	57.7	44.7
Harrison Community Schools	39.7	46.3	17.6	30.2	35.6	28.0	58.8	47.5	48.4
Hart Public School District	56.7	46.2	35.6	27.9	45.2	37.1	63.8	58.4	45.6
Hartford Public School Distric	53.8	42.1	19.4	33.7	33.7	43.0	65.3	70.4	35.3
Hartland Consolidated Schools	86.3	66.7	47.6	72.2	56.1	57.7	94.0	80.2	61.9
Haslett Public Schools	72.8	78.2	55.8	62.1	68.6	63.3	80.7	79.4	67.9
Hastings Area School District	68.4	52.9	40.0	39.3	36.4	39.7	82.9	72.1	45.8
Hazel Park City School Distric	73.2	38.9	35.3	48.6	31.8	50.6	61.7	53.6	31.9
Hemlock Public School District	70.4	63.4	23.7	57.4	44.6	52.1	72.8	72.3	30.0
Hesperia Community Schools	58.6	48.1	39.2	36.8	29.6	42.1	57.7	42.3	46.5
Highland Park City Schools	17.9	5.1	6.1	36.3	13.5	24.8	28.2	10.2	8.8
Hillman Community Schools	44.0	34.0	23.1	33.3	37.7	40.4	72.7	44.0	42.2
Hillsdale Community Schools	52.5	32.9	30.1	35.0	30.5	48.8	69.6	33.7	43.7
Holland Cty School District	55.5	49.5	46.5	42.2	41.0	54.7	70.5	54.2	59.9
Holly Area School District	68.8	52.8	35.4	43.0	41.4	47.7	77.4	63.4	44.9
Holt Public Schools	54.8	55.1	45.0	40.0	49.0	48.2	83.5	76.3	51.9
Holton Public Schools	50.6	29.3	21.5	36.6	28.0	40.0	84.3	68.9	30.0
Homer Community Schools	77.4	49.4	33.3	52.4	36.7	46.0	89.2	78.5	57.1
Hopkins Public Schools	58.9	34.2	20.5	42.1	35.9	40.9	77.5	50.5	46.1
Houghton Lake Comm Schools	47.6	34.6	26.7	25.0	35.2	46.2	59.7	47.5	35.6
Houghton-Portage Twp Schools	68.8	65.5	62.8	67.5	58.3	54.0	87.2	73.6	77.7
Howell Public Schools	75.3	62.7	47.3	54.2	41.3	57.8	86.0	69.4	57.9
Hudson Area Schools	51.3	36.0	16.0	40.7	39.0	32.3	65.6	56.5	41.6
Hudsonville Public School Dist	78.5	60.7	47.2	62.1	40.9	46.3	95.2	63.3	61.7
Huron School District	61.2	21.1	19.6	28.8	19.7	36.7	86.4	50.8	47.3
Huron Valley Schools	76.6	72.4	41.4	54.8	54.0	49.7	83.3	75.0	61.9

Table III-15. Michigan Educational Assessment Program (MEAP) Scores, by School District: 1993-1994 School Year Continued

School District	Math(%)			Reading(%)			Science(%)		
	4th Grade	7th Grade	10th Grade	4th Grade	7th Grade	10th Grade	5th Grade	8th Grade	11th Grade
Ida Public School District	65.3	51.7	43.8	48.5	46.7	47.5	75.4	70.4	50.9
Imlay City Community Schools	73.4	45.0	30.5	42.9	42.1	48.0	84.2	66.9	51.7
Inkster City School District	58.2	48.9	16.0	37.1	69.5	0.9	74.3	67.7	50.0
Inland Lakes School District	36.0	33.3	40.5	34.7	24.2	46.5	80.8	66.2	56.5
Ionia Public Schools	62.8	49.6	30.7	43.5	35.2	33.6	77.3	63.2	40.6
Ionia Twp School District 2	33.3	0.0	0.0	33.3	0.0	0.0	85.7	0.0	0.0
Iron Mountain City School Dist	63.0	69.6	49.0	45.2	48.0	61.8	80.0	53.7	59.5
Ironwood Area Schools	68.5	55.4	51.8	49.5	40.8	50.9	76.4	67.8	56.3
Ishpeming Public School Distri	81.4	71.8	33.7	70.9	58.8	42.7	89.8	85.4	49.5
Ithaca Public Schools	54.2	47.3	35.5	47.7	47.3	41.6	75.7	60.5	49.1
Jackson Public Schools	37.0	29.1	28.3	26.1	33.3	33.4	60.2	35.6	42.7
Jefferson Schools (Monroe)	57.9	57.2	11.0	46.3	46.5	43.6	75.8	62.7	42.6
Jenison Public Schools	79.4	64.1	59.8	57.1	50.4	55.7	88.4	81.2	67.2
Johannesburg-Lewiston Schs	59.1	67.8	36.5	49.2	44.1	57.1	61.2	82.1	38.3
Jonesville Community Schools	61.4	43.2	38.2	50.0	22.1	42.9	70.4	56.3	38.8
Kalamazoo Public School Distri	41.0	33.2	29.4	30.9	29.9	34.9	50.4	46.1	37.1
Kaleva Norman Dickson School	75.4	34.8	37.5	46.2	37.7	52.1	81.1	72.5	42.6
Kalkaska Public Schools	49.6	51.2	29.9	35.7	43.5	35.1	72.2	63.0	45.3
Kearsley Community Schools	78.5	42.4	31.6	62.9	46.4	51.5	92.9	65.1	66.0
Kelloggsville Public Schools	67.9	49.4	22.5	54.1	38.5	33.9	82.6	55.3	38.5
Kenowa Hills Public Schools	67.4	55.9	48.8	45.4	49.0	45.5	87.1	78.2	75.3
Kent City Community Schools	52.7	52.8	33.7	38.2	40.0	43.7	61.7	74.0	62.4
Kentwood Public Schools	80.8	62.7	49.6	60.4	50.3	56.9	91.7	79.1	78.7
Kingsley Area Schools	67.9	43.4	44.6	51.9	31.6	45.9	76.9	50.6	61.5
Kingston Community School Dist	47.9	49.2	36.7	41.7	39.3	38.3	74.6	62.3	33.3
L'anse Creuse Public Schools	78.5	59.5	39.4	65.1	62.6	43.4	85.2	80.5	60.8
Laingsburg Community School Di	68.6	43.5	48.0	46.5	31.0	42.2	79.6	77.0	66.2
Lake City Area School District	66.0	36.5	35.4	42.3	38.5	32.0	63.6	52.0	50.0

Table III-15. Michigan Educational Assessment Program (MEAP) Scores, by School District: 1993-1994 School Year Continued

School District	Math(%)			Reading(%)			Science(%)		
	4th Grade	7th Grade	10th Grade	4th Grade	7th Grade	10th Grade	5th Grade	8th Grade	11th Grade
Lake Fenton Schools	70.4	49.1	33.7	48.1	39.8	55.3	69.8	56.6	58.0
Lake Linden Hubbell School Dis	50.0	76.0	36.8	33.3	58.3	44.7	84.0	58.1	71.2
Lake Orion Community Schools	82.2	63.4	41.0	63.9	54.0	53.1	90.6	75.6	57.7
Lake Shore Public Schools	65.9	50.2	31.5	42.8	49.0	38.8	75.1	70.9	62.0
Lakeshore School District	71.2	67.0	47.4	61.9	59.9	55.9	86.9	83.7	69.7
Lakeview Community Schools	61.1	52.8	28.6	43.7	41.6	39.0	74.6	65.4	73.8
Lakeview Public Schools	79.7	55.6	37.1	58.3	51.2	38.5	92.6	59.9	46.3
Lakeview School District	63.8	53.1	50.0	46.3	43.4	52.0	77.1	65.2	53.4
Lakeville Community School Dis	62.8	53.1	33.1	38.4	47.5	42.7	72.7	68.5	62.3
Lakewood Public Schools	66.5	54.8	47.1	49.1	40.2	47.3	84.4	64.8	55.4
Lamphere Public Schools	98.0	65.1	48.8	83.2	53.3	58.8	82.8	74.1	42.4
Lansing Public School District	40.7	29.1	27.3	36.5	27.5	36.6	53.1	39.3	33.9
Lapeer Community Schools	68.2	55.7	33.6	47.8	40.7	48.3	80.5	59.5	48.1
Lawrence Public School Distric	53.8	50.0	45.1	33.8	41.1	52.8	84.6	71.7	64.8
Lawton Community Schools	52.6	48.0	34.3	41.1	40.0	43.3	72.3	63.6	47.5
Leland Public School District	45.5	66.7	63.6	42.4	43.3	50.0	85.7	71.4	52.2
Les Cheneaux Community Sch	46.7	47.1	31.0	46.7	29.4	46.7	63.0	70.0	50.0
Leslie Public Schools	37.4	31.9	41.2	32.2	27.5	49.5	65.7	44.1	57.6
Lincoln Cons School District	57.3	42.1	26.3	48.1	39.4	41.0	68.7	50.8	51.8
Lincoln Park Public Schools	43.3	36.4	15.1	30.7	34.9	26.1	66.5	34.6	38.6
Linden Community Schools	67.2	56.0	43.2	50.2	39.3	44.4	76.8	72.9	64.2
Litchfield Community Schools	32.7	27.3	36.8	22.9	22.7	29.7	77.4	65.8	45.0
Littlefield Public School Dist	60.6	55.9	25.0	56.3	44.1	46.9	70.3	55.3	33.3
Livonia Public Schools	67.2	56.7	39.5	54.0	51.3	51.7	82.6	64.4	56.1
Lowell Area School District	72.5	59.8	44.7	55.1	52.7	52.7	78.7	78.4	59.3
Ludington Area School District	68.0	56.9	54.8	52.8	45.9	60.9	71.5	67.9	66.9
L'anse Area Schools	45.8	35.9	19.4	22.9	21.9	28.0	64.3	51.8	51.6
Mackinac Island Public Schools	80.0	66.7	66.7	40.0	66.7	83.3	75.0	66.7	62.5

Table III-15. Michigan Educational Assessment Program (MEAP) Scores, by School District: 1993-1994 School Year Continued

School District	Math(%)			Reading(%)			Science(%)		
	4th Grade	7th Grade	10th Grade	4th Grade	7th Grade	10th Grade	5th Grade	8th Grade	11th Grade
Mackinaw City Public Schools	52.6	50.0	45.0	57.9	50.0	55.0	77.8	75.0	64.3
Madison Public Schools (Oak.)	55.3	27.9	13.6	37.4	17.5	18.1	74.8	48.9	31.9
Madison School District (Lenaw)	59.5	37.8	29.5	33.3	27.8	47.7	52.0	58.8	28.6
Mancelona Public Schools	60.3	37.5	18.5	43.8	23.4	39.5	68.3	54.1	45.7
Manchester Community Schools	77.2	58.4	60.8	68.4	55.1	59.3	81.1	82.5	71.0
Manistee Area Public Schools	65.0	48.9	38.6	55.7	48.9	53.4	77.9	67.9	52.1
Manistique Area Schools	62.2	50.5	35.4	40.0	26.7	41.5	84.1	53.8	60.2
Manton Consolidated Schools	53.4	33.9	59.6	51.8	30.6	44.2	60.9	68.2	54.2
Maple Valley School District	61.8	47.7	41.1	34.1	40.9	39.8	75.5	48.3	41.4
Marlee School District	45.8	60.9	0.0	37.5	60.9	0.0	54.2	68.8	0.0
Marcellus Community Schools	67.9	64.1	36.3	32.1	39.7	38.0	88.5	65.2	50.0
Marenisco School District	90.0	40.0	0.0	50.0	60.0	12.5	63.6	55.6	55.6
Marion Public Schools	51.8	52.8	39.0	51.8	34.0	37.3	83.3	59.4	36.4
Marlette Community Schools	60.4	42.5	36.4	47.3	41.5	38.8	68.2	76.1	91.8
Marquette Area School District	65.8	73.7	47.2	57.9	59.5	52.8	89.2	78.4	64.4
Marshall Public Schools	77.2	68.4	55.4	60.2	56.5	56.3	86.7	66.5	52.8
Martin Public Schools	49.4	36.6	21.8	49.4	26.8	38.2	76.3	65.2	55.0
Marysville Public School Distr	68.3	54.4	31.5	57.8	50.6	48.5	86.1	76.8	51.9
Mason Consolidated Sch (Mon.)	54.5	54.3	28.0	33.9	33.9	44.7	76.5	53.9	42.9
Mason County Eastern School	55.8	48.0	27.1	34.6	38.8	37.5	89.5	53.3	43.3
Mason Public Schools (Ingham)	85.6	70.4	61.9	65.6	55.3	58.2	92.0	82.8	72.9
Mayville Community School Dist	52.6	43.7	21.2	37.9	50.6	30.6	57.0	52.4	32.9
Mcbain Rural Agricultural Scho	56.3	33.7	25.9	37.6	29.1	36.1	73.0	54.9	60.3
Melvindale North Allen Park	39.9	42.5	21.4	30.3	29.4	47.2	73.1	40.0	31.7
Memphis Community Schools	53.6	50.0	40.0	40.5	42.9	40.4	87.3	64.1	54.2
Mendon Community Schools	56.6	32.1	13.2	47.2	35.7	30.6	71.2	56.1	57.8
Menominee Area Public Schools	67.1	53.9	38.4	47.0	43.9	50.3	77.8	55.0	46.2
Meridian Public Schools	72.6	61.6	33.0	57.5	42.9	40.6	86.8	63.0	52.0

128

Table III-15. Michigan Educational Assessment Program (MEAP) Scores, by School District: 1993-1994 School Year Continued

School District	Math(%)			Reading(%)			Science(%)		
	4th Grade	7th Grade	10th Grade	4th Grade	7th Grade	10th Grade	5th Grade	8th Grade	11th Grade
Merrill Comm School District	64.4	52.2	41.0	37.9	62.3	50.7	55.6	75.3	53.8
Mesick Consolidated School Dis	43.9	32.8	22.4	40.9	15.6	41.8	59.7	64.3	60.3
Michigan Center School Distric	58.8	45.7	31.4	43.5	27.4	37.2	69.2	62.7	52.4
Mid Peninsula School District	64.7	46.2	21.2	52.9	32.0	30.3	85.0	64.9	52.6
Midland Public Schools	77.8	67.5	59.8	65.7	55.9	67.1	92.0	83.0	64.6
Milan Area Schools	65.8	42.6	34.7	34.9	45.4	42.4	69.3	66.0	61.7
Millington Comm Schools	40.6	47.2	25.9	36.7	30.1	35.4	72.0	54.4	43.5
Mio Au Sable Schools	52.2	28.2	31.5	36.4	29.4	32.7	70.1	53.6	40.0
Mona Shores School District	69.9	54.3	52.0	45.4	45.7	55.1	82.1	65.8	48.2
Monroe Public Schools	47.9	45.2	28.2	34.4	31.8	35.4	59.9	56.4	40.4
Montabella Community Schools	74.4	49.5	30.4	65.9	31.9	39.6	68.7	60.4	48.3
Montague Area Public Schools	61.2	39.4	31.7	48.5	39.4	42.6	72.7	76.4	47.8
Montrose Community Schools	68.4	44.7	30.0	47.4	34.1	38.8	73.1	96.9	45.1
Moran Township Schools	58.8	64.7	0.0	41.2	64.7	0.0	76.9	83.3	0.0
Morenci Area Schools	50.0	45.6	20.7	25.8	26.3	28.0	55.7	46.8	38.2
Morley Stanwood Comm Scho	64.2	44.6	26.3	39.4	35.8	26.3	76.5	66.9	44.4
Morrice Area Schools	45.5	47.3	33.3	47.7	19.6	48.9	71.7	72.7	47.6
Mt Clemens Community Schools	70.1	47.4	37.0	63.0	40.0	52.6	76.8	60.7	60.2
Mt Morris Consolidated Schools	68.5	43.3	34.8	42.1	33.9	31.9	87.1	57.8	40.2
Mt Pleasant City School Distri	63.2	52.2	44.6	44.3	44.3	50.3	76.4	61.6	49.4
Munising Public Schools	63.2	63.0	39.3	54.4	46.7	43.8	82.9	78.6	54.7
Muskegon Heights School Distri	36.1	10.0	8.1	15.8	3.6	14.1	32.4	23.7	22.2
Napoleon Community Schools	61.2	24.4	40.9	42.9	35.4	33.0	68.8	64.8	56.7
Negaunee Public Schools	78.0	58.8	43.4	60.0	42.6	59.8	88.2	79.0	78.3
New Buffalo Area School Distri	83.3	51.8	26.1	33.3	35.2	44.7	72.7	68.9	35.1
New Haven Community Schools	40.2	17.6	17.1	26.8	16.7	34.4	50.6	55.6	65.3
New Lothrop Area Public School	55.1	76.5	39.7	38.2	62.7	51.5	80.4	78.6	57.9
Newaygo Public School District	72.9	52.9	43.0	38.0	40.3	47.0	87.1	60.7	48.5

Table III-15. Michigan Educational Assessment Program (MEAP) Scores, by School District: 1993-1994 School Year Continued

School District	Math(%)			Reading(%)			Science(%)		
	4th Grade	7th Grade	10th Grade	4th Grade	7th Grade	10th Grade	5th Grade	8th Grade	11th Grade
Niles Community School Distric	72.4	48.0	31.0	49.6	43.5	47.4	70.9	71.4	45.2
North Adams Public Schools	41.7	30.6	31.9	41.7	25.0	46.8	54.4	63.6	45.7
North Branch Area Schools	66.5	52.5	40.0	40.0	46.4	49.5	75.0	69.8	50.6
North Central Area Schools	42.1	41.2	57.1	28.9	25.5	62.9	70.5	60.5	69.8
North Dickinson Co School Dist	55.0	52.6	26.2	65.0	47.4	33.3	58.5	66.7	49.0
North Huron School District	70.0	30.6	20.4	59.2	27.4	25.9	74.1	84.8	66.0
North Muskegon Public Schs.	79.7	55.1	69.2	70.3	51.0	61.5	86.4	78.0	84.2
Northport Public School Distri	83.3	72.2	50.0	58.3	66.7	43.8	100.0	90.5	93.3
Northview Public School Distri	76.0	64.7	42.3	61.8	57.4	57.8	81.6	74.7	57.0
Northville Public Schools	79.8	83.7	67.3	65.8	69.7	67.8	95.8	84.5	76.8
Northwest School District	54.1	46.6	25.7	43.2	39.4	49.1	67.9	58.4	56.8
Norway-Vulcan Area Schools	74.6	62.7	42.7	64.8	49.3	31.1	86.7	81.9	56.3
Nottawa Community School	55.0	43.8	0.0	25.0	25.0	0.0	69.6	46.7	0.0
Novi Community School District	83.4	65.2	53.1	64.7	54.1	58.6	82.2	80.1	63.6
N.I.C.E. Community Schools	75.6	71.0	59.7	61.1	45.2	55.8	88.3	75.9	57.8
Oak Park City School District	41.9	69.9	12.0	26.9	43.8	32.9	74.9	62.7	72.9
Oakridge Public Schools	55.0	30.3	30.1	37.7	21.3	37.3	75.2	67.0	36.5
Okemos Public Schools	70.1	78.7	69.6	64.8	66.4	75.2	90.5	82.1	81.1
Olivet Community Schools	47.7	45.2	36.3	29.9	40.5	44.2	71.3	61.4	45.9
Onaway Area Comm School	46.3	26.4	39.8	39.4	29.1	41.6	76.1	46.9	53.6
Onekama Consolidated Schools	63.0	59.2	51.3	48.1	57.1	53.8	90.6	84.0	47.5
Onsted Community Schools	62.5	61.3	37.9	43.3	50.4	46.5	76.9	73.0	63.1
Ontonagon Area Schools	55.8	20.5	41.4	38.5	31.8	27.6	66.2	51.6	33.3
Orchard View Schools	73.4	41.8	24.6	49.7	33.3	25.4	89.3	66.1	38.6
Osceola Twp School District	42.9	65.5	37.5	28.6	48.3	50.0	71.0	66.7	38.5
Oscoda Area Schools	38.6	47.5	22.0	24.2	36.7	41.4	67.4	69.0	55.8
Otsego Public Schools	64.6	55.9	44.8	46.6	42.5	44.8	91.4	85.1	67.1
Ovid Elsie Area Schools	69.2	40.0	46.7	44.2	30.1	57.2	68.5	62.1	64.1

Table III-15. Michigan Educational Assessment Program (MEAP) Scores, by School District: 1993-1994 School Year Continued

School District	Math(%)			Reading(%)			Science(%)		
	4th Grade	7th Grade	10th Grade	4th Grade	7th Grade	10th Grade	5th Grade	8th Grade	11th Grade
Owendale Gagetown Area Sch	66.7	51.7	23.8	46.7	34.5	52.2	88.5	47.8	63.6
Owosso Public Schools	53.5	50.6	41.7	35.2	41.5	50.7	64.7	54.8	56.2
Oxford Area Comm School Distri	76.6	61.4	40.6	61.2	49.6	59.9	81.8	73.5	52.9
Palo Community School District	56.3	33.3	0.0	18.8	22.2	0.0	68.2	57.1	0.0
Parchment School District	58.7	65.3	28.9	52.5	50.0	34.7	81.4	63.4	50.0
Paw Public School District	52.7	55.2	39.1	44.5	37.2	43.7	73.8	70.1	50.0
Peck Community School District	63.9	44.4	42.0	47.2	29.5	48.0	90.9	78.9	82.5
Pellston Public School District	35.3	21.6	12.3	27.5	27.5	29.3	79.0	81.6	41.0
Pennfield School District	59.7	61.8	37.8	40.3	58.0	52.0	77.5	75.2	52.5
Pentwater Public School Distri	40.0	36.0	31.0	23.3	28.0	42.3	61.5	81.8	50.0
Perry Public School District	45.8	52.5	39.0	30.3	45.1	38.4	69.7	57.9	51.9
Pewamo Westphalia Comm Sch	71.4	57.1	46.5	28.6	28.6	57.7	55.6	54.7	62.5
Pickford Public Schools	40.7	44.8	26.3	25.9	17.9	50.0	65.0	35.1	36.4
Pinckney Community Schools	69.7	69.0	45.3	57.6	54.0	56.3	91.9	76.5	70.2
Pinconning Area Schools	65.2	53.3	23.3	55.3	39.4	32.7	74.4	63.3	48.5
Pine River Area Schools	41.8	38.7	20.3	42.7	34.2	48.1	54.8	53.8	47.7
Pittsford Area Schools	47.6	38.1	55.6	39.7	31.7	52.8	73.4	66.1	58.3
Plainwell Community Schools	61.9	56.0	45.3	53.5	51.8	49.4	77.2	72.8	60.0
Plymouth Canton Comm Schools	65.3	71.8	50.2	50.5	60.1	58.1	85.0	76.9	59.2
Pontiac City School District	38.2	17.0	11.8	22.0	20.5	26.1	59.1	34.1	23.0
Port Hope Community Schools	31.3	100.0	66.7	12.5	50.0	50.0	72.7	50.0	53.3
Port Huron Area School Distric	61.7	50.9	28.7	44.4	45.3	46.5	76.7	69.8	50.8
Portage Public Schools	75.2	72.4	55.9	65.8	62.2	58.3	83.0	76.6	68.9
Portland Public School Distric	75.8	68.2	46.0	55.0	59.7	52.3	77.1	70.8	57.0
Posen Consolidated School Dist	70.0	66.7	24.4	50.0	66.7	64.4	77.8	80.0	54.1
Potterville Public Schools	68.1	47.2	21.4	44.7	48.1	49.1	82.0	72.9	51.1
Powell Township School Distric	45.5	27.3	0.0	54.5	45.5	0.0	85.7	87.5	0.0
Public Schools of Calumet	59.8	59.4	51.6	47.7	49.2	61.4	88.1	73.4	59.0

Table III-15. Michigan Educational Assessment Program (MEAP) Scores, by School District: 1993-1994 School Year Continued

School District	Math(%)			Reading(%)			Science(%)		
	4th Grade	7th Grade	10th Grade	4th Grade	7th Grade	10th Grade	5th Grade	8th Grade	11th Grade
Public Schools of Petoskey	62.0	60.5	42.9	48.1	47.6	54.0	79.8	77.9	65.1
Quincy Community School Distri	56.9	40.5	44.7	37.6	27.0	40.7	57.0	64.6	46.6
Rapid River Public Schools	36.4	44.1	36.8	40.9	38.2	38.9	80.0	76.2	71.4
Ravenna Public Schools	56.8	27.8	32.9	25.9	31.5	42.1	64.1	70.6	58.2
Reading Community Schools	49.4	42.7	36.5	49.4	32.0	44.4	66.7	57.4	43.8
Redford Union School District	58.3	44.8	21.1	39.8	45.1	37.4	73.9	59.1	27.0
Reed City Area Public Schools	57.6	55.0	30.1	39.9	51.8	58.6	74.0	62.9	48.8
Reese Public Schools	61.1	60.2	47.3	48.6	36.1	49.5	68.4	70.7	60.5
Reeths Puffer Schools	59.7	48.5	44.1	44.8	42.7	49.1	82.6	67.7	50.2
Republic Michigamme Schools	50.0	37.5	45.5	25.0	50.0	60.9	60.0	55.0	75.0
Richmond Community Schools	65.7	44.7	38.9	47.4	50.0	55.9	79.2	69.1	55.6
River Rouge School District	49.7	19.7	16.3	29.8	16.9	24.1	49.7	32.6	25.0
River Valley School District	79.5	44.4	30.2	55.1	36.8	38.3	90.0	65.0	52.7
Riverview Community School Dis	63.4	43.2	39.0	62.8	46.6	50.0	71.3	65.9	53.8
Rochester Community School Dis	82.1	77.8	53.4	67.1	60.3	66.4	89.7	75.2	68.1
Rockford Public Schools	87.5	69.1	48.1	60.1	57.1	56.2	95.5	82.7	81.3
Rogers City Area Schools	74.5	66.7	50.0	49.1	44.4	58.4	83.9	77.0	58.3
Romeo Community Schools	70.2	55.6	42.1	53.1	54.3	47.5	79.2	64.4	46.9
Romulus Community Schools	43.8	23.2	15.7	21.5	26.0	29.3	52.4	38.3	25.6
Roseville Community Schools	73.7	50.1	35.7	54.4	36.5	47.5	88.3	56.8	68.7
Rudyard Area Schools	52.3	41.6	39.0	47.7	37.2	44.7	75.0	57.3	40.9
Saginaw City School District	48.8	24.0	17.2	29.1	22.4	25.3	44.5	26.5	24.4
Saginaw Twp Community School	72.6	52.3	45.7	46.7	53.5	55.9	85.6	71.1	65.2
Saline Area School District	80.6	71.0	59.1	56.6	59.9	71.1	84.0	90.6	66.9
Sand Creek Community Schools	45.3	50.7	30.4	39.1	38.7	43.5	70.5	70.4	55.7
Sandusky Comm School District	64.6	62.7	37.5	43.4	50.8	42.0	67.3	73.7	44.9
Saranac Community Schools	59.4	55.7	69.0	53.5	39.2	53.5	67.9	92.8	66.0
Saugatuck Public Schools	65.4	66.7	45.2	57.7	35.9	35.7	70.9	62.7	66.7

Table III-15. Michigan Educational Assessment Program (MEAP) Scores, by School District: 1993-1994 School Year Continued

School District	Math(%)			Reading(%)			Science(%)		
	4th Grade	7th Grade	10th Grade	4th Grade	7th Grade	10th Grade	5th Grade	8th Grade	11th Grade
Sault Ste Marie Area Schools	51.0	38.0	28.9	42.5	28.3	40.2	65.2	45.1	48.8
Sch District City of Royal Oak	80.2	65.3	45.6	62.4	58.8	53.3	79.6	64.9	49.9
School District of Ypsilanti	51.3	30.5	36.3	35.4	31.0	38.9	64.0	45.7	45.9
Schoolcraft Community Schools	82.3	65.8	52.3	66.7	50.7	66.2	81.0	73.8	80.8
Shelby Public Schools	81.4	49.1	28.9	47.1	42.1	39.8	86.7	62.6	55.0
Shepherd Public School Distric	62.0	37.6	26.1	40.1	37.6	43.3	68.3	58.6	52.8
Sodus Twp School District 5	0.0	50.0	0.0	66.7	50.0	0.0	60.0	100.0	0.0
South Haven Public Schools	66.5	49.8	40.0	40.1	39.4	39.4	74.7	65.2	50.9
South Lake Schools	73.7	65.2	46.1	55.9	49.8	52.2	84.3	76.4	77.5
South Lyon Community Schools	68.4	49.4	43.5	46.7	43.7	53.3	85.2	71.4	56.7
South Redford School District	67.6	64.1	38.6	39.7	50.0	46.6	80.6	67.7	59.1
Southfield Public Sch Dist	65.2	43.1	29.9	55.3	44.0	41.6	79.6	65.6	29.5
Southgate Community Sch Dis	63.0	48.5	35.0	50.2	40.7	45.2	79.5	68.0	57.0
Sparta Area Schools	67.0	76.6	39.6	50.5	68.3	46.1	80.9	77.9	51.4
Spring Lake Public Schools	63.2	60.0	47.7	35.2	57.3	51.6	90.6	82.3	56.0
Springport Public Schools	46.3	41.2	50.8	33.8	29.4	47.0	65.4	43.0	42.9
St Charles Community Schools	74.0	66.7	41.4	40.0	57.5	51.4	77.5	89.2	42.3
St Ignace Area Schools	52.5	38.9	28.0	39.0	35.2	53.9	58.3	63.8	40.6
St Johns Public Schools	70.5	63.0	51.6	48.3	60.3	53.4	85.0	82.3	60.1
St Joseph Public Schools	75.7	71.7	58.1	64.9	62.7	58.1	85.7	81.2	65.8
St Louis Public Schools	62.8	45.0	31.5	45.3	45.0	38.1	64.8	57.6	43.8
Standish Sterling Comm School	51.5	45.5	28.8	42.9	37.0	38.8	68.9	61.4	51.3
Stanton Twp Public Schools	60.9	44.0	0.0	47.8	40.0	0.0	94.4	58.3	0.0
Stephenson Area Public Schools	57.4	41.7	60.9	41.2	36.9	57.5	69.4	76.4	53.3
Stockbridge Community Schools	47.4	30.5	33.1	38.1	30.0	55.8	87.7	50.3	59.1
Sturgis Public Schools	67.2	37.7	39.6	57.6	30.3	50.2	75.7	59.4	56.4
Summerfield School District	66.7	61.8	49.2	47.6	36.4	49.2	73.7	79.7	54.8
Superior Central Schools	50.0	47.7	36.8	42.9	47.7	55.3	76.7	54.3	57.1

Table III-15. Michigan Educational Assessment Program (MEAP) Scores, by School District: 1993-1994 School Year Continued

School District	Math(%)			Reading(%)			Science(%)		
	4th Grade	7th Grade	10th Grade	4th Grade	7th Grade	10th Grade	5th Grade	8th Grade	11th Grade
Suttons Bay Public School Dist	63.5	48.1	48.4	41.9	31.2	46.0	81.2	72.0	70.0
Swan Valley School District	74.4	58.5	36.4	45.5	51.2	68.8	82.8	65.9	61.1
Swartz Creek Comm Schools	69.3	53.3	32.5	46.6	37.5	45.0	87.6	63.7	54.4
Tahquamenon Area Schools	40.5	36.0	31.3	31.6	32.6	51.2	55.6	33.3	34.1
Tawas Area Schools	64.7	59.0	35.2	51.9	44.0	46.1	81.7	65.9	47.7
Taylor School District	53.0	29.3	17.9	30.9	25.2	31.2	61.8	55.1	29.2
Tecumseh Public Schools	61.9	48.0	37.7	51.5	35.1	49.3	67.3	64.5	56.3
Tekonsha Community Schools	86.2	41.4	25.0	58.6	44.8	25.0	69.0	53.1	30.8
Thornapple Kellogg School Dist	53.4	43.1	38.0	40.2	34.5	41.2	85.7	69.6	58.2
Three Rivers Community Schs.	55.1	32.1	29.2	33.5	29.8	39.4	69.9	43.6	51.7
Traverse City Area Public Scho	69.0	65.3	49.3	51.1	49.1	61.3	85.9	78.7	60.7
Trenton Public Schools	62.2	59.4	54.7	57.0	52.6	62.8	83.8	72.1	57.0
Tri County Area Schools	63.1	41.9	50.4	38.2	29.9	42.3	71.6	60.3	49.5
Troy School District	87.4	78.3	60.1	73.4	66.4	66.5	88.6	86.6	66.9
Ubly Community Schools	68.2	76.7	35.0	59.1	31.7	60.0	86.2	77.8	55.7
Union City Comm School Distric	65.0	51.0	34.0	28.2	39.0	29.9	75.0	51.4	47.1
Unionville Sebewaing Area SD	49.2	58.2	41.7	30.2	58.2	57.1	76.6	60.3	51.8
Utica Community Schools	70.2	57.9	50.2	59.1	51.2	57.3	84.2	72.7	53.3
Van Buren Pub Schools	45.4	44.7	27.6	39.2	33.6	37.9	68.5	63.0	35.8
Van Dyke Public Schools	46.6	26.2	19.7	35.8	18.3	29.5	85.2	35.0	32.7
Vanderbilt Area School	50.0	43.5	50.0	41.7	21.7	50.0	66.7	69.6	40.0
Vandercook Lake Public Schools	58.3	38.0	39.0	31.3	39.1	45.6	73.0	83.8	71.0
Vassar Public Schools	56.5	34.5	28.5	41.2	25.0	46.6	63.5	52.8	60.6
Vestaburg Community Schools	61.7	36.2	27.8	36.2	31.9	26.9	76.9	71.7	53.5
Vicksburg Community Schools	74.6	51.7	35.8	69.5	45.4	46.8	89.8	78.7	63.0
Wakefield Twp School District	85.2	65.2	36.4	44.4	30.4	66.7	92.3	75.0	46.5
Waldron Area Schools	57.7	37.5	23.5	42.3	25.0	34.3	66.7	65.5	51.7
Walkerville Rural Comm SD	26.3	42.1	45.5	36.8	42.1	7.7	75.0	47.8	29.4

Table III-15. Michigan Educational Assessment Program (MEAP) Scores, by School District: 1993-1994 School Year Continued

School District	Math(%)			Reading(%)			Science(%)		
	4th Grade	7th Grade	10th Grade	4th Grade	7th Grade	10th Grade	5th Grade	8th Grade	11th Grade
Walled Lake Cons School Distri	74.2	64.3	41.5	53.0	51.1	52.6	80.6	58.5	44.8
Warren Consolidated Schools	64.3	59.5	39.8	51.5	49.9	50.9	78.7	73.6	67.5
Warren Woods Public Schools	69.3	64.2	30.0	49.7	56.3	40.0	80.0	67.3	64.6
Waterford School District	69.2	62.6	39.1	47.6	45.9	41.9	79.1	65.5	67.5
Watersmeet Twp School District	42.9	63.6	36.4	21.4	36.4	41.7	66.7	54.5	66.7
Waverly Community Schools	73.7	64.6	39.1	54.0	49.8	49.5	81.5	72.6	63.9
Wayland Union Schools	62.1	45.9	30.7	40.0	38.5	39.8	81.6	60.4	52.6
Wayne-Westland Community S/D	50.6	33.9	20.4	35.0	29.4	35.0	61.4	46.3	39.8
Webberville Community Schools	63.3	62.0	30.8	51.7	36.0	44.6	81.0	64.4	47.8
Wells Township School District	50.0	66.7	0.0	66.7	66.7	0.0	100.0	0.0	0.0
West Bloomfield School Dist.	86.1	79.2	53.8	71.1	68.2	60.7	94.7	76.3	72.0
West Branch-Rose City Area Sch	52.9	47.2	27.4	29.0	35.8	41.4	70.3	58.7	48.2
West Iron County School District	55.9	48.1	29.3	47.1	36.8	39.7	75.0	59.4	46.2
West Michigan Academy of Envir	57.1	84.6	0.0	52.4	61.5	0.0	0.0	0.0	0.0
West Ottawa Public School Dist	67.9	55.0	42.2	47.9	40.6	50.0	82.2	70.9	49.7
Western School District	63.1	64.2	35.4	49.4	50.3	43.2	72.3	78.6	56.2
Westwood Community Schools	44.9	31.6	15.7	30.4	27.6	6.9	76.9	36.6	20.2
Westwood Heights School Distri	54.8	19.4	20.8	24.7	15.1	20.5	57.1	31.3	43.6
White Cloud Public Schools	57.6	31.3	26.4	41.6	30.8	41.1	71.1	83.8	42.9
White Pigeon Comm School Distr	44.7	39.7	36.5	24.7	38.5	31.6	62.1	56.9	50.8
White Pine School District	69.2	47.6	33.3	38.5	42.9	33.3	62.5	76.5	63.6
Whitefish Schools	77.8	33.3	37.5	11.1	0.0	57.1	0.0	50.0	57.1
Whiteford Agricultural School	56.3	55.6	45.6	31.3	44.4	54.4	74.5	70.2	40.4
Whitehall School District	50.9	46.9	28.5	41.1	43.2	46.5	66.2	66.7	49.2
Whitmore Lake Pub School Distr	55.2	72.3	34.6	45.7	47.0	47.4	81.2	65.5	57.1
Whittemore Prescott Area Sch	41.5	18.0	20.7	32.2	26.0	35.1	69.6	57.4	30.2
Williamston Community Schools	69.7	60.5	50.4	58.5	48.0	67.2	82.1	77.4	63.9
Willow Run Community Schools	55.8	28.1	16.5	38.7	30.0	25.4	83.5	42.9	43.8

Table III-15. Michigan Educational Assessment Program (MEAP) Scores, by School District: 1993-1994 School Year Continued

School District	Math(%)			Reading(%)			Science(%)		
	4th Grade	7th Grade	10th Grade	4th Grade	7th Grade	10th Grade	5th Grade	8th Grade	11th Grade
Wolverine Comm School District	71.4	60.0	43.8	52.4	53.3	37.5	82.4	71.4	47.6
Woodhaven School District	62.6	41.0	40.1	45.2	28.9	50.2	71.9	63.8	51.1
Wyandotte City School Dist	55.8	46.6	28.9	31.5	31.3	42.3	72.7	52.1	49.0
Wyoming Public Schools	78.7	55.1	54.0	44.1	42.0	43.4	85.7	79.6	77.4
Yale Public Schools	56.9	83.9	35.2	35.4	50.0	52.5	78.8	51.7	67.4
Zeeland Public Schools	59.1	50.6	49.8	40.6	38.2	52.3	78.2	65.2	50.0
Total	**61.6**	**48.9**	**35.6**	**46.9**	**41.9**	**45.3**	**75.6**	**61.7**	**51.9**

Source: Michigan Department of Education (Lansing, Michigan: annually).

NOTE: The following school districts report themselves as:
City of Harper Woods Schools
Public Schools of Calumet
Public Schools of Petoskey
School District of Royal Oak
School District of Ypsilanti

Table III-16. Community College Addresses and Telephone Numbers in Michigan: 1994

Community College	Street Address	City	Telephone Number
Alpena Community Coll	666 Johnson St	Alpena, MI 49707	517-356-9021
Bay De Noc Comm. Coll	U.S. 2 & 41 at College Ave	Escanaba, MI 49829	906-786-5802
Mott Community Coll	1401 E. Court Street	Flint, MI 48503	313-762-0387
Delta College	No street address needed	University Center, MI 48710	517-686-9291
Glen Oaks Community Coll	62249 Shimmel Road	Centreville MI 49032	616-467-9945
Gogebic Community Coll	Jackson and Greenbush	Ironwood, MI 49938	906-932-4231
Grand Rapids Junior Coll	143 Bostwick, N.E.	Grand Rapids, MI 49503	616-456-4965
Henry Ford Comm. Coll	5101 Evergreen	Dearborn, MI 48128	313-845-9649
Highland Park Comm. Coll	Glendale at Third	Highland Park, MI 48203	313-252-0475
Jackson Community College	2111 Emmons Road	Jackson, MI 49201	517-787-0800
Kalamazoo Valley C.C.	6767 West "O" Avenue	Kalamazoo, MI 49009	616-372-5223
Kellogg Community Coll	450 North Avenue	Battle Creek, MI 49016	616-965-3931
Kirtland Community Coll	Route 4 Box 59A	Roscommon, MI 48653	517-275-5121
Lake Michigan College	2755 East Napier Avenue	Benton Harbor, MI 49022	616-927-3571
Lansing Community College	P.O. Box 40010, 419 N. Capitol	Lansing, MI 48901	517-483-1848
Macomb Cnty Comm Coll	14500 Twelve Mile Road	Warren, MI 48093	313-445-7000
Mid Michigan Comm. College	1375 S. Clare Avenue	Harrison, MI 48625	517-386-7792
Monroe Community College	1555 South Raisinville Road	Monroe, MI 48161	313-242-7300
Montcalm Comm College	2800 College Drive	Sidney, MI 48885	517-328-2111
Muskegon Comm College	221 S. Quarterline Road	Muskegon, MI 49442	616-773-9131
North Central Michigan CC	Howard Street	Petoskey, MI 49770	616-347-3973
Northwestern Michigan CC	1701 East Front Street	Traverse City, MI 49684	616-922-1015
Oakland Comm College	2480 Opdyke Road	Bloomfield Hills, MI 48013	313-540-1500
Schoolcraft College	18600 Haggerty Road	Livonia, MI 48152	313-591-6400
Southwestern Michigan Coll	Cherry Grove Road	Dowagiac, MI 49047	616-782-5113
St Clair County Comm College	323 Erie Street	Port Huron, MI 48060	313-984-3881
Washtenaw Community Coll	P. O. Box D-1	Ann Arbor, MI 48106	313-973-3543
Wayne County Comm College	801 W. Fort	Detroit, MI 48226	313-496-2588
West Shore Community Coll	P.O. Box 277	Scottville, MI 49454	616-845-6211

Source: The community colleges.

Table III-17. Public University Addresses and Telephone Numbers in Michigan: 1994

University	Street/Building Address	City	Telephone Number
Central Michigan University		Mt Pleasant, MI 48859	517-774-3631
Eastern Michigan University		Ypsilanti, MI 48197	313-487-2240
Ferris State University	Institutional Studies	Big Rapids, MI 49307	616-592-3801
Grand Valley State University	College Landing	Allendale, MI 49401	616-895-2288
Lake Superior State University		Sault Ste. Marie, MI 49783	906-635-2216
Michigan State University	330 Administration Building	East Lansing, MI 48824	517-355-5052
Michigan Tech University	1400 Townsend Drive	Houghton, MI 49931	906-487-2440
Northern Michigan University		Marquette, MI 49855	906-227-2670
Oakland University		Rochester, MI 48309	313-370-2387
Saginaw Valley State University	2250 Pierce Road	University Center, MI 48710	517-790-4293
University of Michigan		Ann Arbor, MI 48109	313-764-6294
University of Michigan - Dearborn	4901 Evergreen Road	Dearborn, MI 48128	313-593-5200
University of Michigan - Flint		Flint, MI 48502	313-762-3327
Wayne State University		Detroit, MI 48202	313-577-2200
Western Michigan University		Kalamazoo, MI 49008	616-387-2000

Source: The universities.

Table III-18. Private College and University Addresses and Telephone Numbers in Michigan: 1994

College/University	Street Address	City	Telephone Number
Calvin Theological Seminary	3233 Burton Street, S. E.	Grand Rapids, MI 49546	616-957-6027
Adrian College	110 S. Madison St	Adrian, MI 49221	517-265-5161
Albion College	611 East Porter St.	Albion, MI 49224	517-629-5511
Alma College	614 West Superior St.	Alma, MI 48801	517-463-7111
Andrews University	Administration Buiding	Berrien Springs, MI 49104	616-471-3404
Aquinas College	1607 Robinson Road, SE.	Grand Rapids, MI 49506	616-459-8281
Baker College of Flint	G-1050 West Bristol Road	Flint, MI 48570	313-767-7600
Calvin College	3201 Burton Street, SE	Grand Rapids, MI 49546	616-957-6102
Center for Creative Studies	245 E. Kirby	Detroit, MI 48202	313-872-3118
Center for Humanistic Studies	40 East Ferry Avenue	Detroit, MI 48202	313-875-7440
Cleary College	2170 Washtenaw	Ypsilanti, MI 48197	313-483-4400
Concordia College	4090 Geddes Road	Ann Arbor, MI 48105	313-995-7325
Cranbrook Academy of Art	500 Lone Pine Road, Box 801	Bloomfield Hills, MI 48013	313-645-3301
Davenport College-Main Campus	415 East Fulton Street	Grand Rapids, MI 49503	616-451-3516
Davenport College-Kalamazoo	4123 West Main	Kalamazoo, MI 49007	616-382-2835
Davenport College-Lansing	220 E Kalamazoo	Lansing, MI 48933	517-484-2600
D'etre University	377 Fisher Rd	Grosse Pointe, MI 48230	313-882-5522
Detroit Baptist Theological Seminary	4801 Allen Road	Allen Park, MI 48101	313-381-0111
Detroit College of Business-Dearborn	4801 Oakman Blvd.	Dearborn, MI 48126	313-581-4400
Detroit College of Law	130 E. Elizabeth	Detroit, MI 48201	313-226-0100
GMI Engineering & Management Institute	1700 W. Third Avenue	Flint, MI 48504	313-762-7862
Grace Bible College	1011 Aldon Street PO Box 910	Grand Rapids, MI 49509	616-538-2330
Grand Rapids Baptist College & Seminary	1001 E. Beltline, N.E.	Grand Rapids, MI 49505	616-949-5300
Great Lakes Bible College	6211 W.Willow,PO Box 40060	Lansing, MI 48901	517-321-0242

Table III-18. Private College and University Addresses and Telephone Numbers in Michigan: 1994 Continued

College/University	Street Address	City	Telephone Number
Hillsdale College	33 East College St.	Hillsdale, MI 49242	517-437-7341
Hope College	No street address needed	Holland, MI 49423	616-394-7760
Jordan College	360 W. Pine St.	Cedar Springs, MI 49319	616-696-1180
Kalamazoo College	1200 Academy Street	Kalamazoo, MI 49007	616-383-8488
Kendall College of Art and Design	111 Division Avenue North	Grand Rapids, MI 49503	616-451-2787
Lawrence Technological University	21000 W. Ten Mile Road	Southfield, MI 48075	313-356-0200
Lewis College of Business	17370 Meyers Road	Detroit, MI 48235	313-862-6300
Madonna University	36600 Schoolcraft Rd.	Livonia, MI 48150	313-591-5042
Marygrove College	8425 W. McNichols	Detroit, MI 48221	313-862-8000
University of Detroit/Mercy-Outer Drive	8200 W. Outer Drive	Detroit, MI 48219	313-592-6160
Michigan Christian College	800 West Avon Rd.	Rochester Hills, MI 48307	313-651-5800
Midrasha College of Jewish Study	21550 W Twelve Mile Road	Southfield, MI 48076	313-352-7117
Baker College of Muskegon	141 Hartford Avenue	Muskegon, MI 49442	616-726-4904
Nazareth College in Kalamazoo	3333 Gull Road	Kalamazoo, MI 49001	616-349-4200
Great Lakes Junior College-Saginaw	310 S Washington Ave	Saginaw, MI 48607	517-755-3457
Northwood Institute	3225 Cook Road	Midland, MI 48640	517-631-1600
Olivet College	No street address needed	Olivet, MI 49076	616-749-7637
Reformed Bible College	3333 E Beltline NE	Grand Rapids, MI 49505	616-363-2050
Sacred Heart Major Seminary	2701 Chicago Blvd.	Detroit, MI 48206	313-883-8500
Siena Heights College	1247 Siena Heights Drive	Adrian, MI 49221	517-263-0731
Spring Arbor College	106 Main Street	Spring Arbor, MI 49283	517-750-1200
SS Cyril and Methodius Seminary	No street address needed	Orchard Lake, MI 48033	313-683-0311
St Johns Provincial Seminary	44011 Five Mile Road	Plymouth, MI 48170	313-453-6200
St Marys College	No street address needed	Orchard Lake, MI 48324	313-683-0504
Suomi College	No street address needed	Hancock, MI 49930	906-482-5300
Thomas M Cooley Law School	217 South Capitol Avenue	Lansing, MI 48933	517-371-5140
University of Detroit/Mercy-McNichols	4001 W. McNichols Road	Detroit, MI 48221	313-927-1313
Walsh College Accounting/Business Admin	3838 Livernois Road	Troy, MI 48084	313-689-8282
Western Theological Seminary	86 East 12th Street	Holland, MI 49423	616-392-8555
William Tyndale College	35700 W. 12 Mile Rd.	Farmington Hills, MI 48331	313-553-7200
Yeshiva Gedola of Greater Detroit	24600 Greenfield Road	Oak Park, MI 48237	313-968-3360
Jordan Energy Institute	155 Seven Mile Road	Comstock Park, MI 49321	616-784-7595
Jordan College-Flint Campus	3488 N. Jennings Rd.	Flint, MI 48504	313-789-0520
Jordan College-Grand Rapids Campus	1925 Breton SE	Grand Rapids, MI 49506	616-957-3999
Detroit College of Business-Warren	27500 Dequindre	Warren, MI 48092	313-558-8700
Baker College of Owosso	1020 S. Washington St	Owosso, MI 48867	517-723-5251
Central Bible College - Detroit Campus	6053 Chase Rd.	Dearborn, MI. 48126	313-846-8565
Jordan college - Detroit campus	15400 Gr River Rower Cntr d1	Detroit, MI 48227	313-835-5100
Jordan College - Newaygo County Campus	6907 West 48th	Fremont, MI 49412	616-924-5480
Jordan College - Thumb Area Campus	6667 Main Street	Cass City, MI 48726	517-872-4394
Jordan College - Berrien County Campus	Vincent Place, 185 East Main	Benton Harbor, MI 49022	616-927-3333
Detroit College of Business-Flint	3115 Lawndale Avenue	Flint, MI 48504	313-239-1443
Ecumenical Theological Center	8425 W McNichols Rd	Detroit, MI 48221	313-342-4600

Source: The colleges and universities.

CHAPTER IV
LABOR MARKET

The statistics in this chapter are mainly compiled from three sources: (1) The Current Population Survey (CPS), and (2) the Current Employment Statistics (CES) survey, and (3) the 1990 Census.

The data collected by the Current Population Survey is based on household interviews conducted each month by the Bureau of the Census for the Bureau of Labor Statistics. The survey provides comprehensive data on the labor force, employment, and the unemployment situation of *households and individuals*. The data collected are based on the activity or status reported for the calendar week including the 12th day of the month and refer to the labor force 16 years of age and over. Table IV-1 to IV-5 and IV-8 to IV-26 are drawn from this survey. Some basic Current Population Survey concepts and definitions are:

Employed persons are all civilians who, during the survey week, did any work at all as paid employees, in their own business, profession, or on their own farm, or who worked 15 hours or more as unpaid workers in an enterprise operated by a member of the family. *Employed persons* also include all those who were not working but who had jobs or businesses from which they were temporarily absent because of illness, bad weather, vacation, labor-management disputes, or personal reasons, whether they were paid for the time off or were seeking other jobs. Each employed person is counted only once, even if they hold more than one job. Multiple jobholders are counted in the job at which they worked the greatest number of hours during the survey week.

The Unemployed are all civilians who had no employment during the survey week, were available for work, except for temporary illness, and had made specific efforts to find employment some time during the prior 4 weeks. Persons who were waiting to be recalled to a job from which they had been laid off or were waiting to report to a new job within 30 days need not be looking for work to be counted as unemployed.

The Civilian Labor Force is the sum of those classified as employed and those classified as unemployed. *The Civilian Unemployment Rate* is the number of unemployed as a percent of the civilian labor force. *The Labor Force Participation Rate* represents the percent of the 16 plus population that is in the labor force.

The data collected by the Current Employment Statistics survey is based on monthly *establishment* payroll data collected by the Michigan Employment Security Commission. The Current Employment Statistics survey is designed to provide *industry* information on nonfarm wage and salary employment, average weekly earnings, average weekly hours, average hourly earnings. The data relate to all workers, full or part time, who receive pay during the payroll period which includes the 12th day of the month. Tables IV-6 and IV-7 are compiled from this survey. The basic concepts and definitions of the *Establishment Survey* are as follows:

Industry Employment data refer to persons on establishment payrolls who received pay for any part of the pay period which includes the 12th day of the month. The persons can be employed full or part time or both (i.e. multiple jobholders are included). The data *exclude* proprietors, the self-employed, unpaid volunteer of family workers, farm workers, and domestic workers. Salaried officers of corporations are included.

Tables IV-27 and IV-28 are compiled from the 1990 Census. Table IV-29 is based on Michigan Employment Security Commission administrative records.

LIST OF TABLES

Table   **Page**

IV-1.   Employment Status of the Civilian Non-Institutional Population 16 Years and
        Older, Michigan and United States: 1956-1995 143

IV-2.   Employment Status of the Civilian Non-Institutional Population 16 Years and
        Older in Michigan, by County, MSA, and Labor Market Area: 1994 145

IV-3.   Employment Status of the Civilian Non-Institutional Population 16 Years and
        Older in Michigan and the United States, by Race and Gender, 1986-1994 . . . 150

IV-4.   Labor Force Participation Rates (%) in Michigan, By Gender, Race, Teen,
        and Adult: 1970-1994 152

IV-5.   Unemployment Rates (%) in Michigan, By Gender, Race, Teen, and Adult:
        1970-1994 153

IV-6.   Nonfarm Wage and Salary Employment in Michigan, by Major Industry:
        1939 -1995 154

IV-7.   Nonfarm Wage and Salary Employment in Michigan, by Detailed Industry:
        Selected Years 1970, 1984, 1994 156

IV-8.   Employment by Major Occupational Group in Michigan, by Gender and
        Race, Selected Years: 1983-1993 158

IV-9.   Female and Black Share (%) of Employment by Major Occupational Group
        in Michigan, Selected Years: 1983-1993 159

IV-10. Unemployment Rates (%) by Major Occupational Group in Michigan,
        Selected Years: 1983-1993 159

IV-11. Occupational Employment by Age Group in Michigan: 1993 160

IV-12. Occupational Employment Distribution (%) by Age Group in Michigan:
        1993 160

IV-13. Labor Force by Education Level in Michigan: 1983-1993 161

IV-14. Labor Force by Education Level in Michigan, Percent Distribution: 1983-
        1993 161

IV-15. Unemployment Rates(%) by Education Level in Michigan: 1983-1994 162

LIST OF TABLES

Table   **Page**

IV-16.   School Enrollment and Labor Force Status of Civilians 16-24 Years Old in
          Michigan, by Selected Characteristics: 1993   163

IV-17.   Full Time and Part Time Employment in Michigan: 1975-1993   164

IV-18.   Employment by Hours Worked in Michigan, by Sex, Age, and Race: 1980-
          1993   165

IV-19.   Median Weekly Earnings by Major Occupational Group, Sex, and Full Time
          or Part Time Status in Michigan: 1984-1993   169

IV-20.   Median Weekly Earnings by Gender and Full Time or Part Time
          Employment Status in Michigan: 1983-1993   170

IV-21.   Median Weekly Earnings and Number of Manufacturing Workers in
          Michigan, by Occupation and Union Affiliation: 1992   171

IV-22.   Full Time Employment in Michigan, by Earnings Category: 1992   171

IV-23.   Detailed Occupational Wage Ranges in Michigan by Level of Responsibility,
          Monthly Dollar Figures: 1994   172

IV-24.   Union Membership by Sector in Michigan: 1979 and 1983-1994   198

IV-25.   Unemployment in Michigan, by Reason of Joblessness: 1983-1993   199

IV-26.   Unemployment Duration in Michigan by Sex, Age, and Race: Percent
          Distribution, 1978-1993   200

IV-27.   Occupational Attachment of the Civilian Labor Force in Michigan, by Race,
          Gender, and Equal Employment Opportunity (E.E.O.) Category: April
          1990   203

IV-28.   Commuting Patterns in Michigan, by County: 1990   204

IV-29.   Michigan Employment Security Commission Job Service Statistics: July
          1984-June 1985 through July 1993-June 1994   206

Table IV-1. Employment Status of the Civilian Non-Institutional Population 16 Years and Older, Michigan and United States: 1956-1995
(Data in Thousands)

Year	Michigan**					United States				
	Labor Force	Labor Force Partici pation Rate(%)	Employ ment	Unemployment		Labor Force	Labor Force Partici pation Rate(%)	Employ ment	Unemployment	
				Number	Rate(%)				Number	Rate(%)
1956	3,141	N.A.	2,922	218	6.9	66,552	60.0	63,799	2,750	4.1
1957	3,076	N.A.	2,874	202	6.6	66,929	59.6	64,071	2,859	4.3
1958	3,045	N.A.	2,627	418	13.7	67,639	59.5	63,036	4,602	6.8
1959	2,968	N.A.	2,717	251	8.4	68,369	59.3	63,630	3,740	5.5
1960	2,959	N.A.	2,760	199	6.7	69,628	59.4	65,778	3,852	5.5
1961	2,954	N.A.	2,656	299	10.1	70,459	59.3	65,746	4,714	6.7
1962	2,939	N.A.	2,734	205	7.0	70,614	58.8	66,702	3,911	5.5
1963	2,967	N.A.	2,801	166	5.6	71,833	58.7	67,762	4,070	5.7
1964	3,071	N.A.	2,923	148	4.8	73,091	58.7	69,305	3,786	5.2
1965	3,211	N.A.	3,036	125	3.9	74,455	58.9	71,088	3,366	4.5
1966	3,369	N.A.	3,253	117	3.5	75,770	59.2	72,895	2,875	3.8
1967	3,450	N.A.	3,296	154	4.5	77,347	59.6	74,372	2,975	3.8
1968	3,501	N.A.	3,350	151	4.3	78,737	59.6	75,920	2,817	3.6
1969	3,594	N.A.	3,449	145	4.0	80,734	60.1	77,902	2,832	3.5
1970	3,591	60.9	3,351	241	6.7	82,771	60.4	78,678	4,093	4.9
1971	3,624	60.3	3,348	276	7.6	84,382	60.2	79,367	5,016	5.9
1972	3,695	60.6	3,438	258	7.0	87,034	60.4	82,153	4,882	5.6
1973	3,803	61.3	3,579	223	5.9	89,429	60.8	85,064	4,365	4.9
1974	3,880	61.5	3,592	288	7.4	91,949	61.3	86,794	5,156	5.6
1975	3,892	61.0	3,406	486	12.5	93,775	61.2	85,846	7,929	8.5
1976	3,990	61.8	3,618	373	9.4	96,158	61.6	88,752	7,406	7.7
1977	4,114	62.9	3,777	337	8.2	99,009	62.3	92,017	6,991	7.1
1978	4,196	63.2	3,908	289	6.9	102,251	63.2	96,048	6,202	6.1
1979	4,314	64.2	3,979	335	7.8	104,962	63.7	98,824	6,137	5.8

Table IV-1. Employment Status of the Civilian Non-Institutional Population 16 Years and Older, Michigan and United States: 1956-1995 Continued

(Data in Thousands)

Year	Michigan**					United States				
	Labor Force	Labor Force Participation Rate(%)	Employ ment	Unemployment		Labor Force	Labor Force Participation Rate(%)	Employ ment	Unemployment	
				Number	Rate(%)				Number	Rate(%)
1980	4,293	63.2	3,759	534	12.4	106,940	63.8	99,303	7,637	7.1
1981	4,306	63.5	3,777	529	12.3	108,670	63.9	100,397	8,273	7.6
1982	4,277	63.3	3,616	661	15.5	110,204	64.0	99,526	10,678	9.7
1983	4,286	63.8	3,678	608	14.2	111,550	64.0	100,834	10,717	9.6
1984	4,347	64.5	3,860	486	11.2	113,544	64.4	105,005	8,539	7.5
1985	4,352	64.1	3,920	433	9.9	115,461	64.8	107,150	8,312	7.2
1986	4,391	64.0	4,005	385	8.8	117,834	65.3	109,597	8,237	7.0
1987	4,524	65.3	4,155	369	8.2	119,865	65.6	112,440	7,425	6.2
1988	4,543	65.2	4,198	345	7.6	121,669	65.9	114,968	6,701	5.5
1989	4,592	65.7	4,267	326	7.1	123,869	66.5	117,342	6,528	5.3
1990	4,583	65.4	4,238	345	7.5	124,787	66.4	117,914	6,874	5.5
1991	4,565	64.7	4,145	420	9.2	125,303	66.0	116,877	8,426	6.7
1992	4,644	65.5	4,236	408	8.8	126,982	66.3	117,598	9,384	7.4
1993	4,690	65.9	4,363	327	7.0	128,040	66.2	119,306	8,734	6.8
1994	4,753	66.6	4,473	280	5.9	131,056	66.6	123,060	7,996	6.1
1995	4,719	65.8	4,467	252	5.3	132,304	66.6	124,900	7,404	5.6

** Beginning in 1970, data for Michigan based on new methodology and not directly comparable to prior years. N.A. data not available.
Source: U.S. Bureau of Labor Statistics, Current Population Survey (Washington, D.C.: monthly/annually), and Michigan Employment Security Commission, Research and Statistics (Detroit, Michigan; monthly/annually)

Table IV-2. Employment Status of the Civilian Non-Institutional Population 16 Years and Older in Michigan, by County, MSA, and Labor Market Area: 1994
(Data in Thousands)

| Counties | Civilian Labor Force (By Place of Residence) | | | | Wage and Salary Employment (By Place of Work) | | | |
| | Total | Employment | Unemployment | | Total | Goods Producing | | Service Producing |
			Level	Rate(%)		Manufacturing	Const/Mining	
Alcona	4,050	3,525	525	13	---	---	---	---
Alger	4,100	3,750	350	8	2,975	750	100	2,150
Allegan	48,875	46,725	2,150	4	---	---	---	---
Alpena	15,050	13,350	1,700	11	12,200	2,250	600	9,350
Antrim	9,225	8,400	850	9	4,875	1,100	275	3,525
Arenac	6,575	5,875	700	11	4,175	650	225	3,325
Baraga	3,900	3,550	350	9	3,225	675	75	2,475
Barry	27,700	26,325	1,375	5	10,475	2,825	625	7,050
Bay	55,050	51,125	3,950	7	---	---	---	---
Benzie	6,725	6,150	575	9	---	---	---	---
Berrien	82,600	77,500	5,100	6	69,200	20,600	1,900	46,700
Branch	20,025	18,925	1,100	6	12,650	3,500	325	8,825
Calhoun	66,775	62,875	3,875	6	---	---	---	---
Cass	25,450	24,225	1,225	5	10,275	3,575	250	6,475
Charlevoix	12,225	11,100	1,125	9	9,325	2,925	500	5,900
Cheboygan	11,650	10,325	1,325	11	7,125	675	575	5,875
Chippewa	17,650	15,925	1,725	10	14,400	850	600	12,950
Clare	10,325	9,275	1,050	10	7,375	1,075	350	5,975
Clinton	31,675	30,375	1,325	4	---	---	---	---
Crawford	5,575	5,050	525	9	4,350	700	125	3,525
Delta	17,900	16,150	1,750	10	14,200	3,000	625	10,575
Dickinson	13,300	12,375	925	7	13,300	2,850	950	9,475

Table IV-2. Employment Status of the Civilian Non-Institutional Population 16 Years and Older in Michigan, by County, MSA, and Labor Market Area: 1994 Continued
(Data in Thousands)

County	Civilian Labor Force (By Place of Residence)				Wage and Salary Employment (By Place of Work)			
	Total	Employment	Unemployment		Total	Goods Producing		Service Producing
			Level	Rate(%)		Manufacturing	Const/Mining	
Eaton	51,950	49,975	1,975	4	---	---	---	---
Emmet	15,425	13,800	1,625	11	13,875	1,650	925	11,325
Genesee	202,300	186,700	15,600	8	174,500	47,400	5,500	121,600
Gladwin	8,675	7,850	850	10	4,600	925	275	3,400
Gogebic	8,150	7,475	675	8	6,225	900	125	5,200
Grand Traverse	41,275	39,025	2,250	6	---	---	---	---
Gratiot	19,350	17,950	1,400	7	13,875	2,850	325	10,700
Hillsdale	22,400	21,175	1,225	6	14,625	6,300	400	7,950
Houghton	16,500	15,275	1,225	7	---	---	---	---
Huron	17,375	15,925	1,450	8	12,350	3,525	425	8,400
Ingham	149,800	143,050	6,750	5	---	---	---	---
Ionia	27,250	25,275	1,975	7	15,150	3,725	525	10,900
Iosco	11,500	10,400	1,100	10	---	---	---	---
Iron	5,475	4,900	575	11	3,850	450	125	3,275
Isabella	28,425	27,050	1,375	5	23,550	2,200	1,325	20,025
Jackson	73,700	69,100	4,700	6	57,000	12,700	1,700	42,500
Kalamazoo	123,250	118,150	5,100	4	---	---	---	---
Kalkaska	7,075	6,425	650	9	---	---	---	---
Kent	287,725	274,900	12,825	0	---	---	---	---
Keweenaw	675	575	100	14	---	---	---	---
Lake	3,475	3,075	375	11	1,650	150	50	1,450

Table IV-2. Employment Status of the Civilian Non-Institutional Population 16 Years and Older in Michigan, by County, MSA, and Labor Market Area: 1994 Continued
(Data in Thousands)

| County | Civilian Labor Force (By Place of Residence) | | | | Wage and Salary Employment (By Place of Work) | | | |
| | Total | Employment | Unemployment | | Total | Goods Producing | | Service Producing |
			Level	Rate(%)		Manufacturing	Const/Mining	
Lapeer	38,350	35,875	2,450	6	---	---	---	---
Leelanau	10,150	9,575	550	6	---	---	---	---
Lenawee	45,225	42,850	2,375	5	---	---	---	---
Livingston	66,500	63,575	2,925	4	---	---	---	---
Luce	2,425	2,100	300	13	2,175	200	75	1,900
Mackinac	7,175	6,300	875	12	5,075	125	325	4,625
Macomb	396,975	374,725	22,250	6	---	---	---	---
Manistee	10,600	9,500	1,100	10	6,950	1,450	325	5,175
Marquette	33,525	31,100	2,400	7	28,625	825	3,425	24,375
Mason	14,650	13,275	1,350	9	10,425	2,875	400	7,125
Mecosta	17,825	16,700	1,150	6	12,250	1,600	225	10,425
Menominee	12,875	12,000	875	7	9,025	3,150	200	5,700
Midland	40,025	37,675	2,350	6	---	---	---	---
Missaukee	6,125	5,675	450	7	---	---	---	---
Monroe	67,925	64,275	3,650	5	---	---	---	---
Montcalm	24,525	22,325	2,200	9	17,900	5,750	625	11,550
Montmorency	3,500	2,950	550	15	2,100	375	200	1,525
Muskegon	78,050	72,325	5,725	7	---	---	---	---
Newaygo	19,650	17,700	1,950	10	9,575	2,025	250	7,300
Oakland	624,075	596,925	27,125	4	---	---	---	---
Oceana	13,050	11,475	1,575	12	5,475	1,150	425	3,900

Table IV-2. Employment Status of the Civilian Non-Institutional Population 16 Years and Older in Michigan, by County, MSA, and Labor Market Area: 1994 Continued
(Data in Thousands)

County	Civilian Labor Force (By Place of Residence)				Wage and Salary Employment (By Place of Work)			
	Total	Employment	Unemployment		Total	Goods Producing		Service Producing
			Level	Rate%		Manufacturing	Const/Mining	
Ogemaw	8,200	7,350	850	10	5,800	1,025	250	4,500
Ontonagon	3,850	3,575	275	7	3,475	500	1,050	1,900
Osceola	10,625	9,750	875	8	7,400	3,325	550	3,525
Oscoda	3,575	3,225	350	10	2,200	525	75	1,600
Otsego	11,350	10,625	750	7	9,575	1,475	1,000	7,125
Ottawa	114,050	109,675	4,400	4	---	---	---	---
Presque Isle	6,475	5,450	1,025	16	3,350	250	450	2,650
Roscommon	8,000	7,200	800	10	6,075	425	325	5,325
Saginaw	98,875	92,800	6,075	6	---	---	---	---
St. Clair	74,025	68,650	5,375	7	---	---	---	---
St. Joseph	32,300	30,775	1,525	5	23,800	10,575	475	12,725
Sanilac	20,300	18,500	1,800	9	11,775	4,025	450	7,300
Schoolcraft	4,075	3,575	500	13	2,600	400	175	2,000
Shiawassee	35,800	33,275	2,525	7	18,700	4,375	675	13,675
Tuscola	27,675	25,575	2,100	8	13,400	2,800	450	10,150
Van Buren	35275	32650	2625	7	---	---	---	---
Washtenaw	163575	158025	5525	3	---	---	---	---
Wayne	929650	869275	60375	7	---	---	---	---
Wexford	13925	12650	1275	9	---	---	---	---
Michigan	4,753,000	4,473,000	281,000	6	4,142,000	949,000	152,000	3,040,000

Table IV-2. Employment Status of the Civilian Non-Institutional Population 16 Years and Older in Michigan, by County, MSA, and Labor Market Area: 1994 Continued
(Data in Thousands)

County/MSA/Labor Market	Civilian Labor Force (By Place of Residence)				Wage and Salary Employment (By Place of Work)			
	Total	Employment	Unemployment		Total	Goods Producing		Service Producing
			Level	Rate(%)		Manufacturing	Const/Mining	
MSA								
Ann Arbor 1	275,300	264,500	10,800	4	247,600	52,100	7,000	188,500
Benton Harbor	82,600	77,500	5,100	6	69,200	20,600	1,900	46,700
Detroit 2	2,131,000	2,010,000	121,000	6	1,958,000	437,000	63,000	1,457,000
Flint	202,300	186,700	15,600	8	174,500	47,400	5,500	121,600
Grand Rapids 3	528,700	503,600	25,100	5	490,900	142,900	20,800	327,200
Jackson	73,700	69,100	4,700	6	57,000	12,700	1,700	42,500
Kalamazoo/Battle Creek 4	225,300	213,700	11,600	5	199,900	49,900	6,800	143,200
Lansing 5	233,400	223,400	10,100	4	217,900	29,800	6,200	181,900
Saginaw/Bay Midland	194,000	181,600	12,400	6	169,200	41,000	7,600	120,600
Labor Market Areas								
Alcona/Iosco	15,550	13,925	1,625	10	10,325	2,075	550	7,725
Grand Traverse 6	65,225	61,175	4,075	6	53,925	7,400	4,675	41,875
Houghton/Keweenaw	17,175	15,850	1,325	8	14,075	925	650	12,525
Missaukee/Wexford	20,075	18,350	1,725	9	16,425	5,000	475	10,950
Upper Peninsula 7	151,600	138,600	12,900	9	123,400	15,500	8,500	99,400

● Notes ●

1. Washtenaw/Lenawee/Livingston
2. Lapeer/Macomb/Monroe/Oakland/ Wayne
3. Kent/Ottawa/Muskegon/Allegan
4. Kalamazoo/Calhoun/Van Buren
5. Clinton/Eaton/Ingham
6. Grand Traverse/Benzie/Kalkaska/Leelanau
7. Alger/Baraga/Chippewa/Delta/Dickinson/Gogebic/Houghton/ Iron/Luce/Mackinac/Marquette/Menominee/Ontonagon/Schoolcraft

--- Data part of multi-county labor market.

Source: Michigan Employment Security Commission, Research and Statistics, Current Population Survey and Establishment Employment Survey (Detroit, Michigan: monthly/annually).

Table IV-3. Employment Status of the Civilian Non-Institutional Population 16 Years and Older in Michigan and the United States, by Race and Gender, 1986-1994 (Data in thousands unless otherwise noted)

Year/Race/Gender	Labor Force	Participation Rate (%)	Employment	Unemployment	Unemployment Rate (%)
	Michigan - Annual Averages				
Male					
1986	2,479	75.7	2,266	212	8.6
1987	2,502	75.8	2,296	207	8.3
1988	2,529	74.9	2,331	198	7.8
1989	2,550	75.6	2,368	182	7.2
1990	2,548	75.3	2,342	206	8.1
1991	2,519	74.4	2,274	245	9.7
1992	2,529	75.0	2,306	223	8.8
1993	2,591	75.2	4,407	183	7.1
1994	2,583	75.2	2,430	153	5.9
Female					
1986	1,914	53.4	1,741	173	9.0
1987	2,021	55.7	1,858	162	8.0
1988	2,051	56.2	1,901	150	7.3
1989	2,042	56.5	1,899	143	7.0
1990	2,029	56.2	1,891	138	6.8
1991	2,023	55.7	1,851	173	8.5
1992	2,081	56.8	1,899	182	8.7
1993	2,111	57.3	1,967	145	6.9
1994	2,133	58.8	2,007	126	5.9
Black					
1986	476	57.0	370	106	22.3
1987	507	60.0	400	107	21.1
1988	503	55.1	418	85	17.0
1989	514	55.5	427	86	16.8
1990	522	55.2	438	84	16.1
1991	530	57.1	420	110	20.7
1992	515	56.8	424	91	17.8
1993	559	58.5	482	77	13.7
1994	559	57.7	492	66	11.9
Youth 16-19					
1986	367	60.0	290	77	21.1
1987	364	61.2	296	68	18.7
1988	374	62.5	309	65	17.5
1989	366	61.3	304	61	16.8
1990	339	58.8	281	59	17.3
1991	308	58.1	240	68	22.2
1992	294	58.8	234	60	20.5
1993	297	58.5	246	51	17.1
1994	313	60.2	246	67	21.4

Table IV-3. Employment Status of the Civilian Non-Institutional Population 16 Years and Older in Michigan and the United States, by Race and Gender, 1986-1994 Continued (Data in thousands unless otherwise noted)

Year/Race/Gender	Labor Force	Participation Rate (%)	Employment	Unemployment	Unemployment Rate (%)
	United States - Annual Averages				
Males					
1986	65,422	76.3	60,892	4,530	6.9
1987	66,207	76.2	62,107	4,101	6.2
1988	66,927	76.2	63,273	3,655	5.5
1989	67,840	76.4	64,315	3,525	5.2
1990	68,234	76.1	64,435	3,799	5.6
1991	68,411	75.5	63,593	4,817	7.0
1992	69,184	75.6	63,805	5,380	7.8
1993	69,633	75.2	64,700	4,932	7.1
1994	70,817	75.1	66,450	4,367	6.2
Females					
1986	52,413	55.3	48,706	3,707	7.1
1987	53,658	56.0	50,334	3,324	6.2
1988	54,742	56.6	51,696	3,046	5.6
1989	56,030	57.4	53,027	3,003	5.4
1990	56,554	57.5	53,479	3,075	5.4
1991	56,893	57.3	53,284	3,609	6.3
1992	57,798	57.8	53,793	4,005	6.9
1993	58,407	57.9	54,606	3,801	6.5
1994	60,239	58.8	56,610	3,629	6.0
Black					
1986	12,654	63.3	10,814	1,840	14.5
1987	12,993	63.8	11,309	1,684	13.0
1988	13,692	63.8	11,658	1,547	11.7
1989	13,497	64.2	11,953	1,544	11.4
1990	13,493	63.3	11,966	1,527	11.3
1991	13,542	62.6	11,863	1,679	12.4
1992	13,891	63.3	11,933	1,958	14.1
1993	13,943	62.4	12,146	1,796	12.9
1994	14,502	63.4	12,835	1,666	11.5
Youth 16-19					
1986	7,496	54.7	6,472	1,454	18.3
1987	7,988	54.7	6,640	1,347	16.9
1988	8,031	55.3	6,805	1,226	15.3
1989	7,954	55.9	6,759	1,194	15.0
1990	7,410	53.7	6,261	1,149	15.5
1991	6,918	51.7	5,528	1,290	18.6
1992	6,751	51.3	5,398	1,352	20.0
1993	6,826	51.5	5,530	1,296	19.0
1994	7,481	52.7	6,161	1,320	17.6

Source: U.S. Bureau of Labor Statistics, Current Population Survey (Washington, D.C.: annually) and Michigan Employment Security Commission, Research and Statistics (Detroit, Michigan: annually).

Table IV-4. Labor Force Participation Rates (%) in Michigan, By Gender, Race, Teen, and Adult: 1970-1994

Year	Labor Force Participation Rates(%)							
	Total	Males 16 Plus	Female 16 Plus	White 16 Plus	Nonwhite 16 Plus	Teen	Adult
1970	60.9	80.3	43.1	60.5	64.1	55.8	61.5
1971	60.3	80.1	42.1	60.3	59.9	56.3	60.8
1972	60.6	79.4	43.0	61.0	57.3	59.3	60.8
1973	61.3	79.5	44.2	61.7	58.3	60.8	61.4
1974	61.5	79.7	45.0	62.1	57.2	56.6	61.9
1975	61.0	77.8	45.4	61.7	55.9	57.3	61.5
1976	61.8	78.0	46.9	62.8	54.6	58.9	62.2
1977	62.9	78.6	48.1	63.6	57.4	61.1	63.1
1978	63.2	78.6	49.1	63.3	63.0	63.9	63.1
1979	64.2	78.9	50.6	64.2	64.3	64.7	64.2
1980	63.2	76.9	50.4	63.9	58.3	60.4	63.5
1981	63.5	77.6	50.5	64.4	57.3	60.6	63.8
1982	63.3	75.9	51.7	64.3	56.9	58.1	63.9
1983	63.8	75.7	52.8	64.7	58.1	59.3	64.3
1984	64.5	76.3	53.8	65.3	59.4	59.9	64.9
1985	64.1	75.4	53.7	65.1	57.7	61.1	64.4
1986	64.0	75.6	53.4	65.1	57.8	59.9	64.4
1987	65.3	75.9	55.7	66.2	60.3	61.3	65.7
1988	65.2	74.9	56.2	66.8	55.7	62.5	65.4
1989	65.7	75.6	56.5	67.4	56.2	61.3	66.2
1990	65.4	75.3	56.2	67.1	55.8	58.8	66.0
1991	64.7	74.4	55.7	66.0	57.5	58.1	65.3
1992	65.5	75.0	56.8	66.8	57.9	58.8	66.0
1993	65.9	75.2	57.3	67.1	59.5	58.5	66.5
1994	66.6	75.2	58.8	68.0	58.9	60.2	72.5

Source: Michigan Employment Security Commission, Research and Statistics, Current Population Survey (Detroit, Michigan; annually).

Table IV-5. Unemployment Rates (%) in Michigan, By Gender, Race, Teen, and Adult: 1970-1994

Year	Unemployment Rates (%)						
	Total	Males 16 Plus	Female 16 Plus	White 16 Plus	Nonwhite 16 Plus	Teen	Adult
1970	6.7	6.0	8.0	6.1	12.2	18.8	5.3
1971	7.6	7.2	8.4	6.9	13.9	21.7	6.0
1972	7.0	6.3	8.3	6.1	14.9	20.8	5.3
1973	5.9	5.0	7.1	4.8	14.2	16.5	4.4
1974	7.4	6.6	8.7	6.6	14.3	19.1	5.9
1975	12.5	12.5	12.4	11.5	21.0	24.7	10.0
1976	9.4	8.2	11.1	8.8	14.2	19.7	8.0
1977	8.2	6.9	10.1	7.3	15.9	20.9	6.6
1978	6.9	5.7	8.6	5.9	14.4	17.1	5.6
1979	7.8	7.2	8.6	6.5	16.3	15.8	6.8
1980	12.4	13.6	11.1	11.1	23.4	20.9	11.7
1981	12.3	12.1	12.6	10.6	26.8	25.5	10.9
1982	15.5	15.7	15.1	13.3	33.3	28.7	14.1
1983	14.2	15.0	13.1	12.2	28.7	27.6	12.9
1984	11.2	10.9	11.6	9.1	25.7	24.5	9.9
1985	9.9	9.5	10.5	7.6	26.2	22.2	8.8
1986	8.8	8.6	9.1	7.1	20.4	21.0	7.7
1987	8.2	8.3	8.1	6.5	19.3	18.7	7.3
1988	7.6	7.8	7.3	6.4	16.1	17.5	6.7
1989	7.1	7.2	7.0	5.8	15.9	16.8	6.3
1990	7.5	8.1	6.8	6.3	15.3	17.3	6.7
1991	9.2	9.7	8.5	7.6	19.5	22.2	8.3
1992	8.8	8.8	8.7	7.6	16.7	20.5	8.0
1993	7.0	7.1	6.9	6.0	12.9	17.1	6.3
1994	5.9	5.9	5.9	5.1	11.2	21.4	5.2

Source: Michigan Employment Security Commission, Research and Statistics, Current Population Survey (Detroit, Michigan; annually).

153

Table IV-6. Nonfarm Wage and Salary Employment in Michigan, by Major Industry: 1939 - 1995
(Data in Thousands)

Year	Total Industry Employment	Mining	Construction	Manufacturing	Transportation/ Communication/ Public Utility	Trade*		Finance/ Insurance/ Real Estate	Services	Government
						Wholesale	Retail			
1939	1,348	16	45	626	86	273		40	118	144
1940	1,478	16	43	717	91	287		43	126	154
1941	1,707	18	52	870	102	315		46	139	165
1942	1,820	19	61	954	104	310		45	146	180
1943	2,034	20	48	1,182	103	303		43	144	191
1944	2,003	19	33	1,172	104	297		41	147	191
1945	1,798	17	37	961	106	293		43	149	194
1946	1,854	14	58	938	122	320		47	160	193
1947	2,014	16	66	1,042	128	343		49	172	199
1948	2,094	16	80	1,058	138	369		51	177	204
1949	2,019	15	75	981	133	373		52	174	215
1950	2,154	17	88	1,063	137	395		54	177	222
1951	2,266	17	102	1,112	143	421		58	189	224
1952	2,275	16	106	1,097	143	427		61	198	226
1953	2,456	18	106	1,222	150	454		66	207	233
1954	2,321	17	118	1,061	142	459		69	213	242
1955	2,479	17	118	1,164	148	481		71	226	254
1956	2,478	17	116	1,109	146	104	367	78	241	313
1957	2,444	17	109	1,084	146	103	359	80	244	316
1958	2,203	15	95	895	135	100	330	81	244	321
1959	2,297	14	98	961	137	101	338	82	253	325
1960	2,350	16	99	976	140	103	348	85	264	333
1961	2,245	13	93	887	128	102	340	87	271	338
1962	2,335	13	89	952	129	105	342	89	287	343
1963	2,410	13	95	990	128	106	345	90	298	360
1964	2,513	13	101	1,032	129	111	365	93	311	373
1965	2,685	13	113	1,112	134	120	391	96	327	395
1966	2,861	14	117	958	140	128	411	102	353	433
1967	2,901	13	122	929	143	133	420	108	377	455
1968	2,960	13	109	950	145	136	434	112	386	471

Table IV-6. Nonfarm Wage and Salary Employment in Michigan, by Major Industry: 1939-1995 Continued
(Data in Thousands)

Year	Total Industry Employment	Mining	Construction	Manufacturing	Transportation/ Communication/ Public Utility	Trade*		Finance/ Insurance/ Real Estate	Services	Government
						Wholesale	Retail			
1969	3,081	12	131	1,204	149	137	456	118	400	494
1970	2,999	12	119	1,081	150	145	458	120	408	507
1971	2,995	11	121	1,059	148	145	461	121	420	510
1972	3,119	12	128	1,097	148	146	479	128	455	526
1973	3,284	13	131	1,179	154	151	503	130	489	534
1974	3,278	13	126	1,114	153	154	511	134	510	563
1975	3,137	14	106	984	145	147	510	134	514	583
1976	3,283	13	110	1,062	146	149	531	137	541	595
1977	3,442	12	123	1,128	151	152	557	142	581	597
1978	3,609	13	139	1,180	156	164	585	147	614	611
1979	3,637	13	140	1,160	161	170	591	155	627	621
1980	3,443	13	117	999	152	162	572	157	645	628
1981	3,364	13	107	979	148	158	557	155	650	618
1982	3,193	10	90	877	143	151	543	152	650	578
1983	3,223	9	87	881	139	155	557	151	675	570
1984	3,381	10	93	963	140	166	580	154	708	567
1985	3,562	10	108	1,002	146	175	617	163	760	581
1986	3,657	10	115	1,000	149	181	639	171	794	599
1987	3,736	10	123	973	152	186	674	180	826	612
1988	3,819	11	132	955	154	191	703	186	863	624
1989	3,922	10	140	971	155	196	727	187	912	623
1990	3,969	9	142	940	158	202	748	191	942	634
1991	3,891	9	129	897	154	199	732	190	946	636
1992	3,927	9	128	897	154	197	728	191	980	639
1993	4,006	9	133	908	157	200	743	195	1,022	639
1994	4,148	9	143	952	163	206	765	197	1,075	639
1995	4,252	8	154	975	166	211	789	196	1,114	639

Source: Michigan Employment Security Commission, Research and Statistics (Detroit, Michigan: annually). * Prior to 1956, wholesale and retail trade data were not reported separately.

Table IV-7. Nonfarm Wage and Salary Employment in Michigan, by Detailed Industry: Selected Years 1970, 1984, 1994
(Data in Thousands)

Industry	Employment			Percent(%) Distribution		
	1970	1984	1994	1970	1984	1994
Total Wage & Salary	**2,999**	**3,381**	**4,141**	**100.0**	**100.0**	**100.0**
Private Wage & Salary	**2,492**	**2,814**	**3,502**	**83.1**	**83.2**	**84.6**
Goods	**1,212**	**1,066**	**1,101**	**40.4**	**31.5**	**26.6**
Mining	**12**	**10**	**9**	**0.4**	**0.3**	**0.2**
Construction	**119**	**98**	**143**	**4.0**	**2.9**	**3.5**
General Contractor	30	22	32	1.0	0.7	0.8
Heavy Construction	22	16	12	0.7	0.5	0.3
Special Trade Contractors	66	55	99	2.2	1.6	2.4
Manufacturing	**1,081**	**963**	**949**	**36.0**	**28.5**	**22.9**
Durable Goods	863	755	707	28.8	22.3	17.1
Lumber & Wood	14	12	17	0.5	0.4	0.4
Furniture & Fixtures	21	25	37	0.7	0.7	0.9
Stone/Clay/Glass	21	17	17	0.7	0.5	0.4
Primary Metals	89	54	37	3.0	1.6	0.9
Fabricated Metals	142	119	126	4.7	3.5	3.0
NonElectric Machines	164	129	126	5.5	3.8	3.0
Electric & Electronic Eq	43	34	32	1.4	1.0	0.8
Transportation Equipment	351	344	289	11.7	10.2	7.0
Motor Vehicles & Equipment	335	325	278	11.2	9.6	6.7
Instruments & Related	9	14	18	0.3	0.4	0.4
Misc Manufacturing	9	8	8	0.3	0.2	0.2
Nondurable Goods	218	208	243	7.3	6.2	5.9
Food & Kindred Products	55	46	44	1.8	1.4	1.1
Textile Mill Products	4	1	2	0.1	0.03	0.05
Apparel & Other Textile	19	19	19	0.6	0.6	0.5
Paper & Allied Products	29	21	21	1.0	0.6	0.5
Printing & Publishing	35	37	45	1.2	1.1	1.1
Chemicals & Allied Prod	45	41	45	1.5	1.2	1.1
Petroleum & Coal Prod	3	2	2	0.1	0.06	0.05
Rubber & Plastic	26	37	61	0.9	1.1	1.5
Leather & Leather Prod	4	3	3	0.1	0.09	0.07
Private Services	**823**	**1,748**	**2,402**	**27.4**	**51.7**	**58.0**
Transport/Communication/Public Utility	**150**	**140**	**163**	**5.0**	**4.1**	**3.9**
Railroad Transportation	20	10	7	0.7	0.3	0.2
Trucking & Warehousing	38	39	50	1.3	1.2	1.2
Air Transportation	6	8	18	0.2	0.2	0.4
Communication	39	36	31	1.3	1.1	0.7
Electrical/Gas/Sanitary Services	34	35	35	1.1	1.0	0.8
Wholesale Trade	**145**	**166**	**205**	**4.8**	**4.9**	**5.0**
Wholesale - Durable Goods	95	106	132	3.2	3.1	3.2
Wholesale - Nondurable Goods	50	61	73	1.7	1.8	1.8

Table IV-7. Nonfarm Wage and Salary Employment in Michigan, by Detailed Industry: Selected Years 1970, 1984, 1994 Continued
(Data in Thousands)

Industry	Employment			Percent(%) Distribution		
	1970	1984	1994	1970	1984	1994
Retail Trade	**458**	**580**	**764**	**15.3**	**17.2**	**18.4**
Building Materials & Garden Supplies	20	21	34	0.7	0.6	0.8
General Merchandise	87	89	123	2.9	2.6	3.0
Food Stores	71	84	102	2.4	2.5	2.5
Auto Dealers & Gas Stations	69	65	80	2.3	1.9	1.9
Apparel & Accessory Stores	33	35	38	1.1	1.0	1.0
Home Furniture & Fixtures	19	21	30	0.6	0.6	0.7
Eating & Drinking Places	111	197	270	3.7	5.8	6.5
Miscellaneous Retail	50	68	87	1.7	2.0	2.1
Finance/Insurance/Real Estate	**120**	**154**	**197**	**4.0**	**4.6**	**4.8**
Banking & Credit Institutions	54	74	82	1.8	2.2	2.0
Insurance Carriers	35	37	42	1.2	1.1	1.0
Insurance Agents/Brokers/Service	10	15	21	0.3	0.4	0.5
Real Estate	17	22	36	0.6	0.7	0.9
Services	**408**	**708**	**1,073**	**13.6**	**20.9**	**25.9**
Hotel & Other Lodging Places	20	26	34	0.7	0.8	0.8
Personal Services	41	33	42	1.4	1.0	1.0
Business / Computer / Engineering Services	57	123	228	1.9	3.6	5.5
Auto Services & Repair	14	24	35	0.5	0.7	0.8
Misc Repair Services	6	11	12	0.2	0.3	0.3
Amusement & Recreation Services	18	26	43	0.6	0.8	1.0
Health Services	138	259	347	4.6	7.7	8.4
Legal Services	7	20	26	0.2	0.6	0.6
Educational Services (Private)	15	33	40	0.5	1.0	1.0
Membership Organizations	54	63	70	1.8	1.9	1.7
Government	**507**	**567**	**639**	**16.9**	**16.8**	**15.4**
Federal	58	56	57	1.9	1.7	1.4
State	116	140	164	3.9	4.1	4.0
Local	333	372	418	11.1	11.0	10.1

Source: Michigan Employment Security Commission, Research and Statistics, Establishment Survey (Detroit, Michigan: monthly/annually).

Table IV-8. Employment by Major Occupational Group in Michigan, by Gender and Race, Selected Years: 1983-1993
(Data in Thousands)

Major Occupational Group	1983	1985	1987	1989	1990	1991	1992	1993
Total, All Sexes & Races	**3,693**	**3,920**	**4,154**	**4,267**	**4,233**	**4,125**	**4,205**	**4,374**
Managerial	336	371	419	472	480	474	480	503
Professional	470	451	508	546	537	553	571	623
Technical	111	114	136	122	136	117	142	142
Sales	409	453	475	525	519	487	480	490
Clerical	550	604	641	632	615	634	642	663
Service	572	574	604	576	591	580	589	621
Precision	443	486	484	516	475	482	493	495
Machine Operative	417	444	427	433	424	381	370	392
Transportation	150	153	180	188	188	161	159	163
Handlers	146	168	177	158	172	169	180	178
Farming	90	100	104	100	96	87	98	102
Total Female	**1,613**	**1,702**	**1,858**	**1,899**	**1,891**	**1,851**	**1,899**	**1,967**
Managerial	106	131	163	175	188	190	201	214
Professional	229	219	236	264	266	260	281	297
Technical	50	54	69	61	65	60	68	67
Sales	197	221	247	282	274	241	249	248
Clerical	452	496	524	507	490	518	515	533
Service	360	352	376	364	368	365	365	376
Precision	37	37	35	37	34	36	38	41
Machine Operative	123	127	137	135	126	115	116	118
Transportation	16	13	22	21	26	18	15	20
Handlers	31	31	31	30	35	32	32	31
Farming	15	23	18	22	19	16	17	18
Total Black	**322**	**346**	**400**	**427**	**438**	**420**	**424**	**482**
Managerial	14	17	24	32	34	30	30	36
Professional	33	33	34	37	43	39	41	51
Technical	9	7	8	13	12	8	11	13
Sales	17	21	34	39	39	39	33	35
Clerical	44	65	76	69	72	75	78	90
Service	79	83	87	97	91	99	91	104
Precision	32	25	23	35	36	33	37	37
Machine Operative	67	57	69	62	67	56	63	72
Transportation	11	15	22	19	19	10	13	17
Handlers	16	20	20	23	22	29	22	23
Farming	2	3	3	2	4	3	5	5

Source: Michigan Employment Security Commission, Research and Statistics, Current Population Survey (Detroit, Michigan: annually).

Table IV-9. Female and Black Share (%) of Employment by Major Occupational Group in Michigan, Selected Years: 1983-1993
(Data in Thousands)

Major Occupational Group	1983	1985	1987	1989	1990	1991	1992	1993
Total Female	**43.7**	**43.4**	**44.7**	**44.5**	**44.7**	**44.9**	**45.2**	**45.0**
Managerial	31.7	35.3	38.9	37.1	39.2	40.1	41.9	42.6
Professional	48.7	48.6	46.5	48.4	49.5	47.0	49.2	47.7
Technical	45.0	47.4	50.7	50.0	47.8	51.3	48.1	47.1
Sales	48.1	48.8	52.0	53.7	52.8	49.5	51.8	50.6
Clerical	82.1	82.1	81.7	80.2	79.7	81.7	80.2	80.4
Service	62.9	61.3	62.3	63.2	62.3	62.9	61.9	60.5
Precision	8.4	7.6	7.2	7.2	7.2	7.5	7.7	8.3
Machine Operative	29.4	28.6	32.1	31.2	29.7	30.2	31.3	30.1
Transportation	10.8	8.5	12.2	11.2	13.8	11.2	9.6	12.1
Handlers	21.0	18.5	17.5	19.0	20.3	18.9	17.9	17.7
Farming	16.1	23.0	17.3	22.0	19.8	18.4	17.4	17.4
Total Black	**8.7**	**8.8**	**9.6**	**10.0**	**10.3**	**10.2**	**10.1**	**11.0**
Managerial	4.1	4.6	5.7	6.8	7.1	6.3	6.2	7.2
Professional	6.9	7.3	6.7	6.8	8.0	7.1	7.2	8.1
Technical	7.8	6.1	5.9	10.7	8.8	6.8	8.1	9.2
Sales	4.2	4.6	7.2	7.4	7.5	8.0	6.8	7.1
Clerical	8.0	10.8	11.9	10.9	11.7	11.8	12.1	13.5
Service	13.7	14.5	14.4	16.8	15.4	17.1	15.4	16.7
Precision	7.2	5.1	4.8	6.8	7.6	6.8	7.6	7.4
Machine Operative	16.0	12.8	16.2	14.3	15.8	14.7	17.1	18.3
Transportation	7.3	9.8	12.2	10.1	10.1	6.2	8.3	10.6
Handlers	11.2	11.9	11.3	14.6	12.8	17.2	12.2	13.0
Farming	1.8	3.0	2.9	2.0	4.2	3.4	4.8	4.7

Source: Michigan Employment Security Commission, Research and Statistics, Current Population Survey (Detroit, Michigan: annually).

Table IV-10. Unemployment Rates (%) by Major Occupational Group in Michigan, Selected Years: 1983-1993

Major Occupational Group	1983	1985	1987	1989	1990	1991	1992	1993
Total, Experienced Workers	**12.7**	**8.5**	**7.2**	**6.2**	**6.8**	**8.2**	**7.9**	**6.2**
Managerial	5.7	3.5	2.8	1.9	2.2	3.9	4.0	2.7
Professional	3.5	2.6	2.7	1.8	2.3	3.0	2.6	2.3
Technical	5.3	3.7	2.5	3.9	3.5	4.5	2.4	3.0
Sales	8.5	7.1	6.1	4.8	6.3	6.7	7.8	6.5
Clerical	10.3	7.0	4.5	4.5	5.1	6.9	6.9	5.2
Service	14.1	12.3	10.1	8.1	8.6	9.3	9.5	7.9
Precision	16.1	8.3	8.0	7.0	8.5	9.5	9.1	6.7
Machine Operative	20.6	11.7	11.9	11.5	11.7	14.4	12.7	8.9
Transportation	17.9	12.1	7.7	9.0	9.2	11.1	12.0	10.9
Handlers	24.1	15.8	16.0	13.5	13.5	18.8	15.5	12.9
Farming	19.5	11.7	10.7	10.5	10.8	11.1	10.4	8.1

Source: Michigan Employment Security Commission, Research and Statistics, Current Population Survey (Detroit, Michigan: annually).

Table IV-11. Occupational Employment by Age Group in Michigan: 1993

Occupational Category	Employment Levels By Age Group						
	Total	16-24	25-34	35-44	45-54	55-64	65 & Over
Total, All Occupations	4,327,218	727,165	1,136,592	1,166,623	792,437	403,498	100,903
Executive & Managerial	494,729	28,780	125,117	151,315	117,999	61,327	10,191
Professional Specialty	617,020	44,474	176,213	200,441	131,195	51,423	13,274
Technician & Related	141,825	21,584	50,747	34,117	24,678	9,306	1,393
Sales	480,019	112,646	130,323	109,625	65,334	43,889	18,202
Administrative Support-Clerical	670,462	105,867	183,163	182,461	124,767	59,219	14,985
Protective Service Workers	72,677	12,473	20,589	16,786	16,790	5,569	470
Other Service Workers	538,947	186,127	114,991	107,447	67,233	47,652	15,497
Precision Prod, Craft & Repair	480,008	40,008	130,073	152,812	95,165	55,960	5,990
Machine Operators,Assem,Inspec	392,261	55,879	97,685	120,539	81,870	32,403	3,885
Transport & Material Moving	164,438	20,760	37,605	44,389	36,309	20,311	5,064
Handlers, Helpers & Laborers	176,779	71,539	45,367	32,724	18,663	4,898	3,588
Farming, Fishing, Forestry	98,053	27,028	24,719	13,967	12,434	11,541	8,364

Source: Michigan Employment Security Commission, Research and Statistics, Current Population Survey (Detroit, Michigan: annually).

Table IV-12. Occupational Employment Distribution (%) by Age Group in Michigan: 1993

Occupational Category	Percent(%) Distribution By Age Group						
	Total	16-24	25-34	35-44	45-54	55-64	65 & Over
Total, All Occupations	100.0	16.8	26.3	27.0	18.3	9.3	2.3
Executive & Managerial	100.0	5.8	25.3	30.6	23.9	12.4	2.1
Professional Specialty	100.0	7.2	28.6	32.5	21.3	8.3	2.2
Technician & Related	100.0	15.2	35.8	24.1	17.4	6.6	1.0
Sales	100.0	23.5	27.1	22.8	13.6	9.1	3.8
Administrative Support-Clerical	100.0	15.8	27.3	27.2	18.6	8.8	2.2
Protective Service Workers	100.0	17.2	28.3	23.1	23.1	7.7	0.6
Other Service Workers	100.0	34.5	21.3	19.9	12.5	8.8	2.9
Precision Prod, Craft & Repair	100.0	8.3	27.1	31.8	19.8	11.7	1.2
Machine Operators,Assem,Inspec	100.0	14.2	24.9	30.7	20.9	8.3	1.0
Transport & Material Moving	100.0	12.6	22.9	27.0	22.1	12.4	3.1
Handlers, Helpers & Laborers	100.0	40.5	25.7	18.5	10.6	2.8	2.0
Farming, Fishing, Forestry	100.0	27.6	25.2	14.2	12.7	11.8	8.5

Source: Michigan Employment Security Commission, Research and Statistics, Current Population Survey (Detroit, Michigan: annually).

Table IV-13. Labor Force by Education Level in Michigan: 1983-1993

Year	Total Labor Force	Level of Schooling			
		Less Than High School	High School Graduate	College	
				1-3 Years	4 Years or More
1983	4,292,188	809,042	1,891,837	874,502	716,805
1984	4,341,992	814,703	1,885,228	951,825	690,236
1985	4,358,546	790,280	1,886,674	943,541	738,050
1986	4,384,494	770,063	1,869,551	937,165	807,715
1987	4,532,505	761,180	1,900,746	1,009,741	860,838
1988	4,575,438	715,066	1,983,313	1,031,185	845,874
1989	4,673,944	697,901	1,989,409	1,073,869	912,765
1990	4,606,638	667,555	1,963,482	1,066,440	909,162
1991	4,563,986	630,312	1,915,754	1,119,653	898,267
1992	4,600,449	582,679	1,673,196	1,428,419	916,156
1993	4,660,692	541,594	1,656,144	1,456,879	1,006,075

Source: Michigan Employment Security Commission, Research and Statistics, Current Population Survey (Detroit, Michigan: annually).

Table IV-14. Labor Force by Education Level in Michigan, Percent Distribution: 1983-1993

Year	Total Labor Force	Level of Schooling - Percent(%) Distribution			
		Less Than High School	High School Graduate	College	
				1-3 Years	4 Years or More
1983	4,292,188	18.8	44.1	20.4	16.7
1984	4,341,992	18.8	43.4	21.9	15.9
1985	4,358,546	18.1	43.3	21.6	16.9
1986	4,384,494	17.6	42.6	21.4	18.4
1987	4,532,505	16.8	41.9	22.3	19.0
1988	4,575,438	15.6	43.3	22.5	18.5
1989	4,673,944	14.9	42.6	23.0	19.5
1990	4,606,638	14.5	42.6	23.2	19.7
1991	4,563,986	13.8	42.0	24.5	19.7
1992	4,600,449	12.7	36.4	31.0	19.9
1993	4,660,692	11.6	35.5	31.3	21.6

Source: Michigan Employment Security Commission, Research and Statistics, Current Population Survey (Detroit, Michigan: annually).

Table IV-15. Unemployment Rates(%) by Education Level in Michigan: 1983-1994

Year	Total Unemployment Rate(%)	Unemployment Rate (%) by Level of Schooling			
		Less Than High School	High School Graduate	College	
				1-3 Years	4 Years or More
1983	14.1	26.2	14.3	11.1	3.4
1984	11.3	23.4	10.7	7.7	3.6
1985	10.3	20.6	10.3	7.0	3.4
1986	9.1	19.1	9.1	6.3	2.9
1987	8.2	17.3	8.3	6.3	2.2
1988	7.9	16.1	8.2	5.8	2.6
1989	7.2	16.0	7.5	4.7	2.5
1990	8.0	17.9	8.1	5.9	2.7
1991	9.1	20.0	10.0	6.1	3.2
1992	8.7	18.0	9.2	7.6	3.5
1993	7.2	15.9	8.1	5.9	2.7
1994	5.9	15.1	6.6	5.2	2.3

Source: Michigan Employment Security Commission, Research and Statistics, Current Population Survey (Detroit, Michigan: annually).

Table IV-16. School Enrollment and Labor Force Status of Civilians 16-24 Years Old in Michigan, by Selected Characteristics: 1993
(Data in Thousands)

Category	Population	Participation Rate (%)	Labor Force	Employed		Unemployment		Not in the Labor Force
				Full Time	Part Time	Number	Rate(%)	
Total, 16-24 years	**1,169**	**71.2**	**833**	**401**	**326**	**105**	**12.6**	**336**
Enrolled in School	**523**	**56.3**	**294**	**50**	**203**	**42**	**14.1**	**229**
16-19 years	326	48.6	158	11	120	28	17.7	167
20-24 years	197	68.9	136	39	83	13	9.9	61
Male	256	55.2	141	25	95	21	14.7	114
Female	267	57.3	153	25	108	21	13.7	114
White	436	59.6	260	43	188	29	11.3	176
Black	71	39.5	28	6	11	11	38.4	43
Not Enrolled in School	**646**	**83.3**	**538**	**351**	**123**	**64**	**11.8**	**108**
16-19 years	176	73.7	130	52	56	22	16.8	46
20-24 years	470	86.9	409	299	67	42	10.3	61
Male	348	90.5	315	216	60	38	12.2	33
Female	298	75.0	224	135	63	25	11.3	75
White	505	86.1	435	291	104	40	9.3	70
Black	125	74.1	93	53	18	22	23.3	32

Source: Michigan Employment Security Commission, Research and Statistics, Current Population Survey (Detroit, Michigan: annually).

Table IV-17. Full Time and Part Time Employment in Michigan: 1975-1993
(Data in Thousands)

Year	Total Employment	Employed Full Time	Part Time - Economic Reasons		Voluntary Part Time		All Part Time as a Percent(%) of Total Employment
			Number	Percent(%) of Total	Number	Percent(%) of Total	
1975	3,431	2,740	155	4.5	536	15.6	20.1
1976	3,622	2,904	157	4.3	561	15.5	19.8
1977	3,782	3,061	157	4.2	564	14.9	19.1
1978	3,913	3,201	148	3.9	564	14.9	18.8
1979	3,978	3,241	148	3.7	589	14.8	18.5
1980	3,758	2,984	195	5.2	579	15.4	20.6
1981	3,774	2,987	211	5.6	576	15.3	20.9
1982	3,615	2,778	273	7.6	564	15.6	23.2
1983	3,693	2,840	300	8.1	553	15	23.1
1984	3,871	3,003	277	7.2	591	15.3	22.5
1985	3,920	3,106	221	5.6	594	15.2	20.8
1986	4,007	3,196	207	5.2	604	15.1	20.3
1987	4,154	3,263	232	5.6	659	15.9	21.5
1988	4,232	3,333	210	5.0	689	16.3	21.3
1989	4,267	3,374	188	4.4	705	16.5	20.9
1990	4,233	3,330	210	5.0	693	16.4	21.4
1991	4,125	3,206	249	6.0	671	16.3	22.3
1992	4,205	3,296	265	6.3	644	15.3	21.6
1993	4,333	3,430	243	5.6	660	15.2	20.8

Source: Michigan Employment Security Commission, Research and Statistics, Current Population Survey (Detroit, Michigan: annually).

Table IV-18. Employment by Hours Worked in Michigan, by Sex, Age, and Race: 1980-1993

Year/ Category	Total at Work	Hours of Work (Data in Thousands)								Average Hours	
		1 to 14 Hours	15 to 29 Hours	30 to 34 Hours	35 Hours and Over	35 to 39 Hours	40 Hours and Over	41 to 48 Hours	49 Hours and Over	Total	Full-Time Schedules
Total											
1980	3,254	191	411	256	2,396	199	1,486	321	390	37.4	43.1
1981	3,539	239	473	353	2,474	226	1,409	348	492	N.A.	N.A.
1982	3,380	248	458	300	2,373	202	1,378	330	463	37.1	43.9
1983	3,481	268	471	265	2,477	218	1,336	361	562	37.5	44.5
1984	3,646	253	485	283	2,626	211	1,347	429	638	38.1	45.0
1985	3,689	237	459	284	2,709	213	1,324	457	714	38.9	45.4
1986	3,770	217	469	292	2,792	214	1,367	469	742	39.1	45.4
1987	3,921	236	527	385	2,774	247	1,340	452	735	38.5	45.4
1988	4,001	234	530	300	2,936	230	1,435	473	798	39.0	45.4
1989	4,026	228	515	297	2,985	204	1,437	490	854	39.3	47.5
1990	4,001	222	544	333	2,902	223	1,455	465	758	38.7	47.6
1991	3,889	229	535	298	2,827	222	1,457	429	719	38.6	47.0
1992	3,974	224	548	407	2,794	233	1,384	429	747	38.5	48.7
1993	4,143	227	527	303	3,077	230	1,486	474	886	39.4	47.4
Male											
1980	N.A.	N.A.	N.A.	N.A.	N.A.	N.A.	N.A.	N.A.	N.A.	N.A.	N.A.
1981	N.A.	N.A.	N.A.	N.A.	N.A.	N.A.	N.A.	N.A.	N.A.	N.A.	N.A.
1982	1,963	91	176	139	1,556	76	868	232	380	40.2	45.0
1983	1,977	101	167	107	1,602	83	804	252	462	41.1	45.9
1984	2,065	88	171	114	1,692	78	794	298	521	41.8	46.4
1985	2,104	85	160	116	1,743	84	765	312	581	42.5	46.9
1986	2,151	78	170	122	1,780	83	791	321	584	42.5	46.8
1987	2,186	79	180	174	1,753	101	776	303	573	42.0	46.7

Table IV-18. Employment by Hours Worked in Michigan, by Sex, Age, and Race: 1980-1993 Continued

Year/ Category	Total at Work	Hours of Work (Data in Thousands)								Average Hours	
		1 to 14 Hours	15 to 29 Hours	30 to 34 Hours	35 Hours and Over	35 to 39 Hours	40 Hours and Over	41 to 48 Hours	49 Hours and Over	Total	Full-Time Schedules
Male-Cont.											
1988	2,218	74	180	113	1,852	88	823	317	624	42.6	46.8
1989	2,251	77	178	109	1,886	70	820	323	674	43.0	48.6
1990	2,231	82	193	145	1,812	77	835	308	592	42.0	48.7
1991	2,160	84	192	125	1,758	83	840	286	549	41.8	48.0
1992	2,195	79	202	184	1,731	93	790	277	571	41.7	49.5
1993	2,294	89	182	124	1,900	83	822	308	687	42.7	48.5
Female											
1980	N.A.	N.A.	N.A.	N.A.	N.A.	N.A.	N.A.	N.A.	N.A.	N.A.	N.A.
1981	N.A.	N.A.	N.A.	N.A.	N.A.	N.A.	N.A.	N.A.	N.A.	N.A.	N.A.
1982	1,417	157	282	161	817	126	510	98	84	32.8	41.9
1983	1,504	167	304	158	875	135	532	108	100	32.9	42.0
1984	1,582	165	313	170	934	133	553	131	117	33.4	42.5
1985	1,585	152	300	168	966	129	559	145	132	34.0	42.7
1986	1,619	139	298	170	1,012	131	576	147	158	34.6	42.9
1987	1,735	157	347	211	1,021	146	564	149	162	34.1	43.1
1988	1,783	160	351	187	1,085	142	612	156	175	34.4	43.1
1989	1,775	151	338	188	1,099	135	617	167	180	34.7	45.5
1990	1,769	140	351	189	1,090	146	620	157	167	34.6	45.7
1991	1,729	145	343	173	1,069	139	617	143	170	34.6	45.4
1992	1,778	146	347	223	1,063	140	594	152	176	34.6	47.3
1993	1,840	139	345	179	1,177	147	664	167	199	35.3	45.6
Teen 16-19 Yrs.											
1980	N.A.	N.A.	N.A.	N.A.	N.A.	N.A.	N.A.	N.A.	N.A.	N.A.	N.A.
1981	N.A.	N.A.	N.A.	N.A.	N.A.	N.A.	N.A.	N.A.	N.A.	N.A.	N.A.

Table IV-18. Employment by Hours Worked in Michigan, by Sex, Age, and Race: 1980-1993 Continued

Year/Category	Total at Work	Hours of Work (Data in Thousands)								Average Hours	
		1 to 14 Hours	15 to 29 Hours	30 to 34 Hours	35 Hours and Over	35 to 39 Hours	40 Hours and Over	41 to 48 Hours	49 Hours and Over	Total	Full-Time Schedules
Teen 16-19 Cont.											
1982	275	77	101	27	70	16	37	9	8	23.2	41.3
1983	272	88	94	22	68	14	38	5	11	22.7	42.3
1984	281	77	109	21	73	10	35	16	12	23.7	43.2
1985	278	72	98	26	82	17	38	13	14	24.8	42.9
1986	279	70	101	31	77	15	36	15	11	24.6	42.3
1987	285	70	107	30	77	17	37	11	12	24.4	42.6
1988	297	66	118	31	83	19	43	12	9	24.6	41.4
1989	294	65	111	34	84	15	47	11	12	25.0	45.1
1990	271	62	102	26	81	17	44	11	10	25.1	44.1
1991	231	66	89	22	54	14	26	8	7	23.1	45.1
1992	224	61	87	24	51	12	27	5	7	23.0	45.4
1993	239	65	95	21	57	13	29	6	10	23.2	45.2
White											
1980	N.A.	N.A.	N.A.	N.A.	N.A.	N.A.	N.A.	N.A.	N.A.	N.A.	N.A.
1981	N.A.	N.A.	N.A.	N.A.	N.A.	N.A.	N.A.	N.A.	N.A.	N.A.	N.A.
1982	3,070	231	422	272	2,144	184	1,213	307	440	37.1	44.1
1983	3,143	246	431	234	2,232	204	1,170	332	526	37.6	44.7
1984	3,275	226	433	251	2,365	192	1,172	401	600	38.3	45.2
1985	3,318	217	419	258	2,425	193	1,135	425	671	39.0	45.7
1986	3,351	196	418	259	2,477	195	1,164	433	685	39.2	45.6
1987	3,481	217	473	349	2,442	225	1,124	413	680	38.5	45.6
1988	3,552	215	475	267	2,595	205	1,207	437	745	39.1	45.8
1989	3,555	207	459	260	2,630	183	1,204	451	792	39.5	47.8
1990	3,533	201	485	293	2,553	202	1,219	428	703	38.8	47.9
1991	3,433	205	469	267	2,492	198	1,228	395	670	38.8	47.4

Table IV-18. Employment by Hours Worked in Michigan, by Sex, Age, and Race: 1980-1993 Continued

| Year/ Category | Total at Work | Hours of Work (Data in Thousands) | | | | | | | | Average Hours | |
		1 to 14 Hours	15 to 29 Hours	30 to 34 Hours	35 Hours and Over	35 to 39 Hours	40 Hours and Over	41 to 48 Hours	49 Hours and Over	Total	Full-Time Schedules
White Cont.											
1992	3,510	203	483	361	2,463	210	1,173	389	692	38.6	48.9
1993	3,602	205	467	266	2,664	202	1,223	428	811	39.5	47.7
Black											
1980	N.A.	N.A.	N.A.	N.A.	N.A.	N.A.	N.A.	N.A.	N.A.	N.A.	N.A.
1981	N.A.	N.A.	N.A.	N.A.	N.A.	N.A.	N.A.	N.A.	N.A.	N.A.	N.A.
1982	271	15	30	25	201	16	151	18	16	36.7	41.8
1983	297	21	36	29	211	11	148	24	28	36.4	42.6
1984	332	24	47	28	234	17	158	25	34	36.4	42.9
1985	322	16	36	23	248	17	170	27	33	37.5	42.5
1986	348	16	41	27	265	17	179	27	41	38.0	43.1
1987	371	13	45	30	283	19	190	31	43	38.4	43.2
1988	389	16	45	28	299	21	205	31	42	37.9	42.6
1989	404	18	47	34	306	18	204	33	52	38.0	45.0
1990	408	15	48	36	309	19	216	31	44	38.1	44.9
1991	395	18	57	26	294	21	205	28	40	37.3	44.1
1992	393	18	50	40	284	21	187	34	43	37.9	47.0
1993	453	18	48	33	353	25	228	40	59	38.9	45.2

N.A. data not available.
Source: Michigan Employment Security Commission, Research and Statistics (Detroit, Michigan: annually).

Table IV-19. Median Weekly Earnings by Major Occupational Group, Sex, and Full Time or Part Time Status in Michigan: 1984-1993

Occupation/Category	1984	1985	1986	1987	1988	1989	1990	1991	1992	1993
Total										
Executive	$462	$481	$500	$500	$550	$550	$600	$614	$625	$675
Professional Specialty	440	460	500	500	562	575	600	620	673	700
Technicians	380	368	373	373	420	400	450	500	450	495
Sales	200	220	212	220	239	240	250	288	293	280
Administrative Support	248	256	280	280	280	297	313	320	336	360
Protect Service	400	444	400	445	375	425	450	442	546	524
Other Service	115	114	130	125	134	156	156	154	170	180
Precision Production	420	453	480	480	491	530	530	524	550	585
Machine Operators	360	382	400	400	400	400	408	400	410	434
Transport Occupations	360	400	393	400	380	400	440	475	440	460
Handlers/Laborers	200	220	220	225	240	250	240	280	250	244
Farm/Forest/Fish	140	145	160	185	200	203	240	240	250	236
Male										
Executive	581	600	620	675	702	720	800	800	800	827
Professional Specialty	550	600	600	615	650	700	750	750	800	780
Technicians	475	500	475	468	520	520	540	600	600	632
Sales	365	400	400	450	430	430	425	450	498	450
Administrative Support	400	440	400	433	380	402	450	440	440	450
Protect Service	400	460	408	480	390	480	480	480	550	560
Other Service	134	140	151	151	189	195	170	184	200	208
Precision Production	440	480	486	480	500	550	550	540	561	600
Machine Operators	392	420	440	450	460	480	492	480	480	480
Transport Occupations	380	400	410	405	400	440	450	490	480	500
Handlers/Laborers	240	234	221	240	260	280	240	276	264	270
Farm/Forest/Fish	160	153	160	200	220	220	240	250	250	250
Female										
Executive	313	350	353	350	365	400	426	455	483	500
Professional Specialty	315	382	400	405	443	450	500	525	550	600
Technicians	272	280	300	332	323	350	389	402	367	390
Sales	123	140	145	144	153	153	160	176	190	193
Administrative Support	230	243	260	260	260	280	300	300	320	345
Protect Service	300	201	300	185	331	200	290	320	480	360
Other Service	104	101	119	110	112	150	150	150	155	163
Precision Production	248	242	246	314	300	300	312	353	360	416
Machine Operators	251	263	262	280	280	280	280	300	320	322
Transport Occupations	223	175	212	237	250	270	317	315	275	243
Handlers/Laborers	150	174	209	160	170	182	214	280	220	220
Farm/Forest/Fish	100	76	150	125	120	90	128	150	170	130

Table IV-19. Median Weekly Earnings by Major Occupational Group, Sex, and Full or Part Time Status in Michigan: 1984-1993 Continued

Occupation/Category	1984	1985	1986	1987	1988	1989	1990	1991	1992	1993
Full Time Schedules										
Executive	$500	$500	$519	$528	$583	$595	$604	$650	$650	$700
Professional Specialty	492	500	548	575	600	606	675	700	731	750
Technicians	400	418	422	419	480	480	500	536	520	557
Sales	325	312	350	352	375	385	374	400	438	420
Administrative Support	287	300	311	320	325	332	360	380	380	400
Protect Service	400	471	420	475	440	500	492	500	580	598
Other Service	192	175	190	200	219	230	240	260	270	260
Precision Production	440	479	486	480	500	550	550	556	563	600
Machine Operators	369	399	404	413	417	429	440	440	435	450
Transport Occupations	386	413	417	425	425	442	475	500	500	520
Handlers/Laborers	300	306	283	280	326	320	320	342	340	350
Farm/Forest/Fish	207	176	225	224	250	275	280	280	303	300
Part Time Schedules										
Executive	96	160	181	164	119	120	120	150	110	96
Professional Specialty	113	228	250	200	200	167	211	175	150	113
Technicians	125	200	228	232	195	162	180	160	164	125
Sales	84	113	102	92	90	92	84	88	80	84
Administrative support	96	150	126	128	126	120	112	102	105	96
Protect Service	91	100	120	77	98	98	80	83	68	91
Other Service	67	100	95	94	85	74	70	70	67	67
Precision Production	150	203	160	180	220	125	197	113	125	150
Machine Operators	116	140	150	140	162	105	160	144	108	116
Transport Occupations	100	158	150	188	158	165	162	137	100	100
Handlers/Laborers	77	95	120	96	97	75	80	81	80	77
Farm/Forest/Fish	25	135	100	75	67	70	53	80	60	25

Source: Michigan Employment Security Commission, Research and Statistics, Current Population Survey (Detroit, Michigan).

Table IV-20. Median Weekly Earnings by Gender and Full Time or Part Time Employment Status in Michigan: 1983-1993

Year	Total	Gender			Employment Status	
		Male	Female	Female/Male Ratio	Full Time	Part Time
1983	$288	$385	$200	0.52	$350	$80
1984	300	400	200	0.50	360	81
1985	315	425	216	0.51	386	84
1986	324	438	240	0.55	400	90
1987	326	440	240	0.55	400	94
1988	349	460	242	0.53	418	98
1989	360	480	259	0.54	440	108
1990	375	500	278	0.56	450	110
1991	400	500	296	0.59	480	120
1992	400	511	300	0.59	491	128
1993	409	525	320	0.61	500	128

Source: Michigan Employment Security Commission, Research and Statistics, Current Population Survey (Detroit, Michigan; annually).

Table IV-21. Median Weekly Earnings and Number of Manufacturing Workers in Michigan, by Occupation and Union Affiliation: 1992

Occupational Category	Total Private Manufacturing		Covered By Collective Bargaining Agreement		Not Covered By Collective Bargaining Agreement	
	Employment	Usual Weekly Earnings	Employment	Usual Weekly Earnings	Employment	Usual Weekly Earnings
Total	929,652	$631	355,024	$608	574,629	$645
Executive/Administrative/Management	93,619	938	4,105	687	89,514	950
Professional	86,324	976	7,130	1,001	79,194	973
Technical and Related	29,631	753	8,193	793	21,437	738
Sales	20,970	819	2,090	549	18,880	849
Administrative Support/Clerical	89,787	513	19,034	576	70,752	496
Protective Services	2,455	765	1,560	992	895	370
Other Services	18,899	494	11,181	614	7,717	321
Precision Production	210,072	651	86,468	680	123,604	631
Machine Operator/Assembly/Inspector	302,169	478	171,232	557	130,937	375
Transportation/Material Moving	37,922	517	24,564	563	13,358	431
Helper/Laborers	35,329	457	18,621	568	16,708	333
Farming/Fishing/Forestry	2,476	319	845	514	1,631	219

Source: Michigan Employment Security Commission, Research and Statistics, Current Population Survey (Detroit, Michigan: annually).

Table IV-22. Full Time Employment in Michigan, by Earnings Category: 1992

Category	Employment - Full Time	Percent(%) Distribution
Total	2,968,671	100.0
Less Than $100 a Week	11,602	0.4
$100 - $149 a Week	33,137	1.1
$150 - $199 a Week	116,727	3.9
$200 - $249 a Week	234,150	7.9
$250 - $299 a Week	204,542	6.9
$300 - $349 a Week	265,327	8.9
$350 - $399 a Week	205,305	6.9
$400 - $499 a Week	425,371	14.3
$500 - $599 a Week	324,518	10.9
$600 - $749 a Week	491,724	16.6
$750 - $999 a Week	342,518	11.5
Greater Than $1,000 a Week	313,750	10.6
$1,000 - $1,199 a Week	144,149	4.9
$1,200 - $1,499 a Week	84,547	2.8
Greater Than $1,500 a Week	85,054	2.9

Source: Michigan Employment Security Commission, Research and Statistics, Current Population Survey (Detroit, Michigan: annually).

Table IV-23. Detailed Occupational Wage Ranges in Michigan by Level of Responsibility, Monthly Dollar Figures: 1994

Occupation	Beginning		Intermediate	
	Minimum	Maximum	Minimum	Maximum
Professional/Technical/Managerial				
Absorption Engineer	$2,130	$2,988	$2,711	$3,611
Accountant	1,871	2,849	2,468	3,265
Accountant, Tax	1,871	2,849	2,468	3,265
Accounting-Systems Expert	1,871	2,849	2,468	3,265
Acoustical Engineer	2,130	2,988	2,884	3,862
Actuaries	--	--	--	--
Adjudicators	--	--	2,711	3,386
Administrative Assistant	1,654	2,373	1,897	3,317
Advertising Photographer	1,853	2,330	2,035	2,979
Agricultural Economist	2,087	2,754	2,356	3,533
Air Pilots & Flight Engineers	--	--	2,330	2,884
Airport Engineer	2,066	3,372	2,709	3,698
Alcohol Addiction Counselor	1,992	2,418	2,217	3,265
Allergist	2,537	7,430	5,291	8,695
Analytical Chemist	2,104	2,676	2,312	3,273
Anatomist	2,061	2,836	2,191	3,403
Anesthesiologist	2,537	7,430	5,291	8,695
Architect, x Landscape & Marine	2,216	2,910	2,711	3,888
Archivists	1,680	2,130	1,793	2,546
Artists	1,853	2,330	2,035	2,979
Assembly Instruction Worker	1,793	2,737	2,234	2,944
Assessors	--	--	--	--
Astronomers	2,061	2,875	2,234	3,464
Attendance Officer	--	--	--	--
Attorneys	2,217	3,507	3,372	5,118
Audiologists-spch	2,494	3,291	2,650	3,594
Audiovisual Librarian	1,888	3,046	2,546	3,551
Auditor	1,871	2,849	2,468	3,265
Auto Design Checker	1,680	2,182	1,853	2,702
Bacteriologist	2,061	2,836	2,191	3,403
Benefits Interviewer	1,827	2,260	2,000	2,442
Biochemist	2,061	2,836	2,191	3,403
Biochemistry Technologist	--	--	--	--
Biological Scientist	2,061	2,836	2,191	3,403
Biologist	2,061	2,836	2,191	3,403
Biophysicists	2,061	2,836	2,191	3,403
Birth Attendant	2,252	2,918	2,494	3,291
Blood Bank Tech Specialist	--	--	1,775	2,468
Blood Bank Technician	--	--	1,775	2,468
Blood-Bank Technologist	--	--	1,775	2,468

172

Table IV-23. Detailed Occupational Wage Ranges in Michigan by Level of Responsibility, Monthly Dollar Figures: 1994 Continued

Occupation	Beginning		Intermediate	
	Minimum	Maximum	Minimum	Maximum
Botanist	$2,061	$2,836	$2,191	$3,403
Budget Analysts	1,675	2,598	2,312	3,308
Building Inspector	1,798	2,702	2,425	3,187
Building-Illuminating Engineer	2,130	2,988	2,884	3,862
Bursar	1,871	2,849	2,468	3,265
Business and Financial Counsel	2,217	3,507	3,372	5,118
Business Programmer	1,680	2,676	2,208	3,412
Business Representative	1,879	2,797	2,546	3,317
Buyer, x Farm Products	1,868	2,763	2,356	3,360
Cable Engineer	2,130	2,988	2,884	3,862
Cad Drafter	1,299	2,208	1,853	2,754
Calibration Laboratory Tech	1,792	2,468	2,135	3,083
Camp Counselor	1,368	2,000	1,897	2,572
Career Counselor	1,879	2,797	2,546	3,317
Cartographer	1,299	2,208	1,853	2,754
Cartographic Technician	1,680	2,130	1,853	2,979
Caseworker	1,845	2,728	2,356	3,698
Central-Office Equip't Engr	2,130	2,988	2,884	3,862
Certified Public Accountant	1,871	2,849	2,468	3,265
Chaplain	2,104	2,693	2,356	3,057
Checker, Drafting	1,299	2,208	1,853	2,754
Chemical Design Engineer	2,130	2,988	2,711	3,611
Chemical Engineers	2,130	2,988	2,711	3,611
Chemical Research Engineer	2,130	2,988	2,711	3,611
Chemical Sales Engineer	2,130	2,988	2,711	3,611
Chemical-Test Engineer	2,130	2,988	2,711	3,611
Chemist, Enzymes	2,061	2,836	2,191	3,403
Chemist, Food	2,104	2,676	2,312	3,273
Chemist, Inorganic	2,104	2,676	2,312	3,273
Chemist, Organic	2,104	2,676	2,312	3,273
Chemist, Pharmaceutical	2,061	2,836	2,191	3,403
Chemist, Steroids	2,061	2,836	2,191	3,403
Chemistry Technologist	--	--	--	--
Chemists	2,104	2,676	2,312	3,273
Chief Dietician	2,087	2,780	2,295	3,005
Chief Drafter	1,299	2,208	1,853	2,754
Chief Librarian, Music Dept	1,888	3,046	2,546	3,551
Chief Librarian, Work / Blind	1,888	3,046	2,546	3,551
Child Health Associate	2,252	2,918	2,494	3,291
Child Psychologist	2,174	3,083	2,693	3,594

Table IV-23. Detailed Occupational Wage Ranges in Michigan by Level of Responsibility, Monthly Dollar Figures: 1994 Continued

Occupation	Beginning		Intermediate	
	Minimum	Maximum	Minimum	Maximum
Chiropodist	--	--	$4,373	$5,664
City Planner	2,052	2,737	2,356	3,533
Civil Eng, Including Traffic	2,066	3,372	2,709	3,698
Civil Engineer	2,066	3,372	2,709	3,698
Claim Attorney	2,217	3,507	3,372	5,118
Claims Examiners, Insurance	1,308	1,836	1,585	2,061
Claims Takers, Unemployment	1,827	2,260	2,000	2,442
Clergy	2,104	2,693	2,356	3,057
Clinical Dietician	2,087	2,780	2,295	3,005
Clinical Lab Technician	--	--	1,775	2,468
Clinical Lab Technologist	--	--	--	--
Clinical Psychologist	2,174	3,083	2,693	3,594
Clinical Social Worker	1,845	2,728	2,356	3,698
Coaches	2,104	2,840	2,217	3,144
Commercial Artist	1,853	2,330	2,035	2,979
Community Organization Worker	1,845	2,728	2,356	3,698
Compliance Officer, Except Cons	--	--	--	--
Computer Analyst	2,122	2,988	2,494	3,559
Computer Engineer	2,130	2,988	2,884	3,862
Computer Programmers	1,680	2,676	2,208	3,412
Computer-Laboratory Technician	1,792	2,468	2,135	3,083
Conservation Scientists	2,064	2,970	2,520	3,369
Construction Engineer	2,066	3,372	2,709	3,698
Construction Inspector	1,798	2,702	2,425	3,187
Contact Representative	1,827	2,260	2,000	2,442
Coordinator of Placement	1,879	2,797	2,546	3,317
Coroner	--	--	--	--
Corporate Counsel	2,217	3,507	3,372	5,118
Cost Accountant	1,871	2,849	2,468	3,265
Counselor-At-Law	2,217	3,507	3,372	5,118
Crystallographer	2,061	2,875	2,546	3,403
Curators	1,680	2,130	1,793	2,546
Cytologist	2,061	2,836	2,191	3,403
Dairy Scientist	2,104	2,676	2,312	3,273
Delineator	1,299	2,208	1,853	2,754
Dental Assistants	--	--	1,585	2,295
Dental Hygienists	1,935	2,485	2,096	2,806
Dental Surgeon	3,984	5,161	4,598	6,036
Dentists	3,984	5,161	4,598	6,036
Design Engineer	2,130	2,988	2,884	3,862

Table IV-23. Detailed Occupational Wage Ranges in Michigan by Level of Responsibility, Monthly Dollar Figures: 1994 Continued

Occupation	Beginning		Intermediate	
	Minimum	Maximum	Minimum	Maximum
Detail Drafter	$1,299	$2,208	$1,853	$2,754
Die Design Drafter	1,299	2,208	1,853	2,754
Dietary Consultant	2,087	2,780	2,295	3,005
Dietician	2,087	2,780	2,295	3,005
Dietician, Teaching	2,087	2,780	2,295	3,005
Dietician, Therapeutic	2,087	2,780	2,295	3,005
Dietician/Nutritionist	2,087	2,780	2,295	3,005
Distribution Field Engineer	2,130	2,988	2,884	3,862
Doctor of Nuclear Medicine	2,537	7,430	5,291	8,695
Drafter, Electrical	1,299	2,208	1,853	2,754
Drafter, Electronic	1,299	2,208	1,853	2,754
Drafters	1,299	2,208	1,853	2,754
Drug Addiction Counselor	1,992	2,418	2,217	3,265
Druggist	2,191	2,970	2,598	3,464
Economists	2,087	2,754	2,356	3,533
Education Counselor	--	--	1,957	2,537
EEG Technician	1,550	2,130	1,853	2,330
Electrical Design Engineer	2,130	2,988	2,884	3,862
Electrical Eng Technologist	1,792	2,468	2,135	3,083
Electrical Engineer	2,130	2,988	2,884	3,862
Electrical Laboratory Tech	1,792	2,468	2,135	3,083
Electrical Product Engineer	2,130	2,988	2,884	3,862
Electrical System Engineer	2,130	2,988	2,884	3,862
Electrical-Research Engineer	2,130	2,988	2,884	3,862
Electrician Eng Technician	1,792	2,468	2,135	3,083
Electroencephalograph Tech.	1,550	2,130	1,853	2,330
Electrol. & Corrosion Ctl Eng.	2,130	2,988	2,884	3,862
Electronic Eng Technician	1,792	2,468	2,135	3,083
Electronic Eng Technologist	1,792	2,468	2,135	3,083
Electronic Engineer	2,130	2,988	2,884	3,862
Elementary Teacher	1,611	2,052	1,848	2,728
Emergency Medical Technician	--	--	1,524	2,459
Employee Relations Admin	1,879	2,797	2,546	3,317
Employment Interviewer	1,871	2,278	2,070	2,728
Endodontist	3,984	5,161	4,598	6,036
Enforcement Inspector	--	--	--	--
Engineer Studio Operations	2,130	2,988	2,884	3,862
Engineer System Developer	2,130	2,988	2,884	3,862
Engineer-in-Charge Transmitter	2,130	2,988	2,884	3,862
Engineering Programmer	1,680	2,676	2,208	3,412

Table IV-23. Detailed Occupational Wage Ranges in Michigan by Level of Responsibility, Monthly Dollar Figures: 1994 Continued

Occupation	Beginning		Intermediate	
	Minimum	Maximum	Minimum	Maximum
Entomologist	$2,061	$2,836	$2,191	$3,403
Environmental Health Program S	--	--	2,130	3,014
Environmental Scientist	2,035	2,702	2,182	3,308
Equipment Design Specialist	2,165	2,884	2,711	3,629
Executive Assistant	1,654	2,373	1,897	3,317
Executive Pilot	--	--	2,330	2,884
Experimental Psychologist	2,174	3,083	2,693	3,594
Experimental Technicians	1,680	2,182	1,853	2,702
Facilities Mech Design Engineer	2,165	2,884	2,711	3,629
Family Counselor	1,845	2,728	2,356	3,698
Family Physician	2,537	7,430	5,291	8,695
Field Agent	--	--	2,128	2,709
Film Librarian	1,888	3,046	2,546	3,551
Financial Analysts	2,087	2,770	2,356	3,265
Fire Protection Engineer	--	--	--	--
Fisheries Technician	1,680	2,130	1,853	2,702
Fitness Plan Coordinator	1,368	2,000	1,897	2,572
Flight Surgeon	2,537	7,430	5,291	8,695
Food Scientist	2,104	2,676	2,312	3,273
Foot Specialist	--	--	4,373	5,664
Forest Ecologist	2,064	2,970	2,520	3,369
Forest Engineer	2,066	3,372	2,709	3,698
Forest Scientists	2,064	2,970	2,520	3,369
General Practitioner	2,537	7,430	5,291	8,695
Geneticists	2,061	2,836	2,191	3,403
Geodesist	2,061	2,875	2,191	3,698
Geologist, Conservation Scienti	2,061	2,875	2,546	3,403
Geologists & Geophysicists	2,061	2,875	2,546	3,403
Graphic Artist	1,853	2,330	2,035	2,979
Group Recreation Worker	1,368	2,000	1,897	2,572
Guidance Counselor	--	--	1,957	2,537
Gynecological Assistant	2,252	2,918	2,494	3,291
Gynecologist	2,537	7,430	5,291	8,695
Head Start Teacher	1,611	2,052	1,848	2,728
Health Officer	2,537	7,430	5,291	8,695
Health Physicist	2,061	2,875	2,234	3,464
Health Specialist Teacher-P	1,585	2,130	1,948	3,014
Hearing Officers	--	--	2,711	3,386
Heart Specialist	2,537	7,430	5,291	8,695
Heat Transfer Engineer Tech	1,680	2,182	1,853	2,702

Table IV-23. Detailed Occupational Wage Ranges in Michigan by Level of Responsibility, Monthly Dollar Figures: 1994 Continued

Occupation	Beginning		Intermediate	
	Minimum	Maximum	Minimum	Maximum
Hematology Technician	--	--	$1,775	$2,468
Hematology Technologist	--	--	1,775	2,468
Highway Engineer	2,066	3,372	2,709	3,698
Histologist	2,061	2,836	2,191	3,403
Historian	2,104	2,719	2,356	3,423
Hospital Librarian	1,888	3,046	2,546	3,551
Human Factors Specialist	2,174	3,083	2,693	3,594
Human Relations Counselor	1,845	2,728	2,356	3,698
Hydraulic Engineer	2,066	3,372	2,709	3,698
Hydrologist	2,061	2,875	2,546	3,403
Illuminating Engineer	2,130	2,988	2,884	3,862
Illustrator	1,853	2,330	2,035	2,979
Industrial Eng, except Safety	--	--	--	--
Industrial Health Engineer	--	--	--	--
Industrial Quality Control Eng	--	--	--	--
Industrial Therapist	1,879	2,459	2,295	3,092
Inhalation Therapist	1,680	2,130	1,853	2,330
Inst Nutrition Consultant	2,087	2,780	2,295	3,005
Insurance Attorney	2,217	3,507	3,372	5,118
Investment Analyst	2,087	2,770	2,356	3,265
Irrigation Engineer	2,066	3,372	2,709	3,698
Job Analyst	1,879	2,797	2,546	3,317
Job Classifier	1,879	2,797	2,546	3,317
Job Development Specialist	1,879	2,797	2,546	3,317
Labor Market Analyst	2,087	2,754	2,356	3,533
Labor Relation Specialist	1,879	2,797	2,546	3,317
Land Planner	2,295	2,910	2,364	3,118
Land Surveyor	2,061	2,875	2,191	3,698
Landscape Architects	2,295	2,910	2,364	3,118
Laryngologist	2,537	7,430	5,291	8,695
Lawyers	2,217	3,507	3,372	5,118
Layout Drafter	1,299	2,208	1,853	2,754
Legal Assistant	1,983	2,537	2,172	2,763
Legal Examiner	2,217	3,507	3,372	5,118
Legal Technicians	1,983	2,537	2,172	2,763
Librarian	1,888	3,046	2,546	3,551
Library Technical Assistant	--	--	--	--
Licensed Practical Nurses	1,490	2,104	1,879	2,615
Lighting Engineer	2,130	2,988	2,884	3,862
Lobbyist	--	--	--	--

Table IV-23. Detailed Occupational Wage Ranges in Michigan by Level of Responsibility, Monthly Dollar Figures: 1994 Continued

Occupation	Beginning		Intermediate	
	Minimum	Maximum	Minimum	Maximum
Lubrication Engineer	$2,165	$2,884	$2,711	$3,629
Management Analysts	--	--	2,442	3,429
Management Consultant	--	--	2,442	3,429
Manpower Planner	2,087	2,754	2,356	3,533
Manufacturing Engineer	--	--	--	--
Map Scientist	2,061	2,875	2,191	3,698
Map Technician	1,680	2,130	1,853	2,979
Map Technologist	1,680	2,130	1,853	2,979
Marine Biologists	2,061	2,836	2,191	3,403
Market Research Analyst	2,087	2,754	2,356	3,533
Mechanical Design Engineer	2,165	2,884	2,711	3,629
Mechanical Drafter	1,299	2,208	1,853	2,754
Mechanical Eng Technician	1,680	2,182	1,853	2,702
Mechanical Eng Technologist	1,680	2,182	1,853	2,702
Mechanical Engineers	2,165	2,884	2,711	3,629
Mechanical Research Engineer	2,165	2,884	2,711	3,629
Mechanical Sales Engineer	2,165	2,884	2,711	3,629
Medical Lab Technician	--	--	1,775	2,468
Medical Lab Technologist	--	--	--	--
Medical Parasitologist	2,061	2,836	2,191	3,403
Medical Physicist	2,061	2,875	2,234	3,464
Medical Physiologist	2,061	2,836	2,191	3,403
Medical Records Librarian	--	--	1,983	2,832
Medical Records Technicians	--	--	1,983	2,832
Medical Technologist, Chem	--	--	--	--
Microbiologist	2,061	2,836	2,191	3,403
Mineralogist	2,061	2,875	2,546	3,403
Minister	2,104	2,693	2,356	3,057
Nurse Anesthetists	2,087	2,771	2,451	3,178
Nurse Practitioner	2,087	2,771	2,451	3,178
Nutritionist	2,087	2,780	2,295	3,005
Nutritionist, Public Health	2,087	2,780	2,295	3,005
Obstetrician	2,537	7,430	5,291	8,695
Occupational Therapist	1,879	2,459	2,295	3,092
Oceanographer, Geological	2,061	2,875	2,546	3,403
Oil & Gas Drafter	1,299	2,208	1,853	2,754
Ophthalmic Medical Assistant	2,252	2,918	2,494	3,291
Opthamologist	2,537	7,430	5,291	8,695
Optomechanical Technician	2,165	2,884	2,711	3,629
Oral Hygienist	1,935	2,485	2,096	2,806

Table IV-23. Detailed Occupational Wage Ranges in Michigan by Level of Responsibility, Monthly Dollar Figures: 1994 Continued

Occupation	Beginning		Intermediate	
	Minimum	Maximum	Minimum	Maximum
Oral Pathologist	$3,984	$5,161	$4,598	$6,036
Oral Surgeon	3,984	5,161	4,598	6,036
Orthodontist	3,984	5,161	4,598	6,036
Orthopedic Physician's Asst	2,252	2,918	2,494	3,291
Osteopath	2,537	7,430	5,291	8,695
Otologist	2,537	7,430	5,291	8,695
Paleontologist	2,061	2,875	2,546	3,403
Paralegal Personnel	1,983	2,537	2,172	2,763
Paramedic	--	--	1,524	2,459
Paraprofessional Teacher Aide	779	1,801	1,550	2,295
Parole Officer	1,845	2,728	2,356	3,698
Pastor	2,104	2,693	2,356	3,057
Pathologist	2,537	7,430	5,291	8,695
Pediatric Dentist	3,984	5,161	4,598	6,036
Pediatric Physical Therapist	2,104	3,057	2,399	3,308
Pediatric Physician's Asst	2,252	2,918	2,494	3,291
Pediatric Surgeon	2,537	7,430	5,291	8,695
Pediatrician	2,537	7,430	5,291	8,695
Pedodontist	3,984	5,161	4,598	6,036
Personnel Recruiter	1,879	2,797	2,546	3,317
Personnel Specialist	1,879	2,797	2,546	3,317
Petrologist	2,061	2,875	2,546	3,403
Pharmacists	2,191	2,970	2,598	3,464
Pharmacy Assistants	1,541	1,905	1,853	2,330
Pharmacy Clerk	1,541	1,905	1,853	2,330
Pharmacy Helper	1,541	1,905	1,853	2,330
Photogrammetrist	2,061	2,875	2,191	3,698
Photographers	1,853	2,330	2,035	2,979
Physiatrist	2,537	7,430	5,291	8,695
Physical Chemist	2,104	2,676	2,312	3,273
Physical Therapists	2,104	3,057	2,399	3,308
Physical Therapy Aide	1,827	2,243	1,957	2,321
Physical Therapy Assistant	1,827	2,243	1,957	2,321
Physical Therapy Attendant	1,827	2,243	1,957	2,321
Physician Assistant	2,252	2,918	2,494	3,291
Physicians	2,537	7,430	5,291	8,695
Physicist, Cryogenics	2,061	2,875	2,234	3,464
Physicist, Light and Optics	2,061	2,875	2,234	3,464
Physicist, Plasma	2,061	2,875	2,234	3,464
Physicists	2,061	2,875	2,234	3,464

Table IV-23. Detailed Occupational Wage Ranges in Michigan by Level of Responsibility, Monthly Dollar Figures: 1994 Continued

Occupation	Beginning		Intermediate	
	Minimum	Maximum	Minimum	Maximum
Physiologists	$2,061	$2,836	$2,191	$3,403
Physiotherapist	2,104	3,057	2,399	3,308
Placement Counselor	--	--	1,957	2,537
Planning Engineer	2,130	2,988	2,884	3,862
Plant Engineer	2,165	2,884	2,711	3,629
Plant Pathologist	2,061	2,836	2,191	3,403
Playground Worker	1,368	2,000	1,897	2,572
Podiatrist, Orthopedic	--	--	4,373	5,664
Podiatrists	--	--	4,373	5,664
Pollution Control Chemist	2,104	2,676	2,312	3,273
Pollution Control Engineer	--	--	--	--
Position Classifier	1,879	2,797	2,546	3,317
Power Distribut/Trans Engineer	2,130	2,988	2,884	3,862
Preschool & Kindergarten Teach	1,611	2,052	1,848	2,728
Priest	2,104	2,693	2,356	3,057
Primary Care Physicians Asst.	2,252	2,918	2,494	3,291
Probation Officer	1,845	2,728	2,356	3,698
Process Description Writer	1,793	2,737	2,234	2,944
Production Engineer	--	--	--	--
Products Mech Design Engineer	2,165	2,884	2,711	3,629
Professional Librarians	1,888	3,046	2,546	3,551
Prosecutor	2,217	3,507	3,372	5,118
Prosthodontist	3,984	5,161	4,598	6,036
Psychiatrist	2,537	7,430	5,291	8,695
Psychologist, Counseling	2,174	3,083	2,693	3,594
Psychologist, Developmental	2,174	3,083	2,693	3,594
Psychologist, Educational	2,174	3,083	2,693	3,594
Psychologist, Physiological	2,174	3,083	2,693	3,594
Psychologist, School	2,174	3,083	2,693	3,594
Psychologists	2,174	3,083	2,693	3,594
Psychometrist	2,174	3,083	2,693	3,594
Public Health Veterinarian	2,797	3,819	2,988	4,096
Public Relations Specialist	--	--	--	--
Public-Health Dentist	3,984	5,161	4,598	6,036
Public-Health Engineer	2,066	3,372	2,709	3,698
Public-Health Microbiologist	2,061	2,836	2,191	3,403
Purchasing Agent, x Farm Produ	1,868	2,763	2,356	3,360
Quality Control Analyst	2,087	2,745	2,537	3,265
Quality Control Technician	866	1,351	1,126	2,018
Rabbi	2,104	2,693	2,356	3,057

Table IV-23. Detailed Occupational Wage Ranges in Michigan by Level of Responsibility, Monthly Dollar Figures: 1994 Continued

Occupation	Beginning		Intermediate	
	Minimum	Maximum	Minimum	Maximum
Radio Operators	$1,680	$2,330	$2,182	$2,979
Radiologic Technician	1,680	2,182	1,853	2,702
Radiologist	2,537	7,430	5,291	8,695
Railroad Engineer	2,066	3,372	2,709	3,698
Real Estate Appraisers	--	--	1,888	2,364
Recreation Leader	1,368	2,000	1,897	2,572
Recreation Worker	1,368	2,000	1,897	2,572
Recreational Therapist	2,035	2,918	2,356	3,057
Recruiter	--	--	--	--
Referee	--	--	2,711	3,386
Refrigeration Engineer	2,165	2,884	2,711	3,629
Regional Planners	2,052	2,737	2,356	3,533
Registered Nurses	2,087	2,771	2,451	3,178
Reinforced Concrete Drafter	1,299	2,208	1,853	2,754
Research Instrumentation Techn	1,792	2,468	2,135	3,083
Research Nutritionist	2,087	2,780	2,295	3,005
Respiratory Therapist	1,680	2,130	1,853	2,330
Restorer	1,680	2,130	1,793	2,546
Retail Buyer, Except Farm Prods	1,868	2,763	2,356	3,360
Revenue Agent	--	--	2,128	2,709
Revenue Officer	--	--	2,128	2,709
Safety Coordinator	--	--	--	--
Safety Eng, Except Mining	--	--	--	--
Safety Engineer	--	--	--	--
Safety Inspector	--	--	--	--
Sanitary Engineer	2,066	3,372	2,709	3,698
Scientific Photographer	1,853	2,330	2,035	2,979
Scientific Programmer	1,680	2,676	2,208	3,412
Secondary Teacher	1,611	2,052	1,848	2,728
Serology Technician	--	--	1,775	2,468
Services Engineer	2,130	2,988	2,884	3,862
Sewage Disposal Engineer	2,066	3,372	2,709	3,698
Signal Engineer	2,130	2,988	2,884	3,862
Site Planner	2,295	2,910	2,364	3,118
Social Psychologist	2,174	3,083	2,693	3,594
Social Service Caseworker	1,845	2,728	2,356	3,698
Social Service Counselor	1,845	2,728	2,356	3,698
Social Worker	1,845	2,728	2,356	3,698
Social Worker, School	1,845	2,728	2,356	3,698
Social Worker, Medical	1,992	2,418	2,217	3,265

Table IV-23. Detailed Occupational Wage Ranges in Michigan by Level of Responsibility, Monthly Dollar Figures: 1994 Continued

Occupation	Beginning		Intermediate	
	Minimum	Maximum	Minimum	Maximum
Social Worker, Phych	$1,992	$2,418	$2,217	$3,265
Software Systems Analyst	2,122	2,988	2,494	3,559
Soil Conservationist	2,064	2,970	2,520	3,369
Special Ed Teacher	--	--	--	--
Special Tools Invest and Plan	2,165	2,884	2,711	3,629
Specialist Physicians Asst	2,252	2,918	2,494	3,291
Speech Therapist	2,494	3,291	2,650	3,594
Standards Laboratory Tech	1,792	2,468	2,135	3,083
Statistician	2,061	2,936	2,312	3,403
Statistician, Analytical	2,061	2,936	2,312	3,403
Statistician, Applied	2,061	2,936	2,312	3,403
Statistician, Engineering	2,061	2,936	2,312	3,403
Statistician, Physical Science	2,061	2,936	2,312	3,403
Stratigrapher	2,061	2,875	2,546	3,403
Structural Drafter	1,299	2,208	1,853	2,754
Structural Engineer	2,066	3,372	2,709	3,698
Surgeons	2,537	7,430	5,291	8,695
Survey Scientist	2,061	2,875	2,191	3,698
Survey Technician	1,680	2,130	1,853	2,979
Survey Technologist	1,680	2,130	1,853	2,979
System Analyst	2,122	2,988	2,494	3,559
Tax Collectors	--	--	2,128	2,709
Tax Examiners	--	--	2,128	2,709
Technical Writers	1,793	2,737	2,234	2,944
Time Study Engineer	--	--	--	--
Tissue Technician	--	--	1,775	2,468
Tool Design Drafter	1,299	2,208	1,853	2,754
Tool Design Engineer	2,165	2,884	2,711	3,629
Tool or Die Drawing Checker	1,680	2,182	1,853	2,702
Tool-Design Specialist	2,165	2,884	2,711	3,629
Tracer	1,299	2,208	1,853	2,754
Traffic Technicians	1,680	2,330	2,182	2,979
Training Specialist	1,879	2,797	2,546	3,317
Truant Officer	--	--	--	--
Umpires	2,104	2,840	2,217	3,144
Underwriters	2,087	2,537	2,122	3,533
Union Contract Representative	1,879	2,797	2,546	3,317
Urban Planners	2,052	2,737	2,356	3,533
Utilization Engineer	2,165	2,884	2,711	3,629
Utilization Officer	1,879	2,797	2,546	3,317

Table IV-23. Detailed Occupational Wage Ranges in Michigan by Level of Responsibility, Monthly Dollar Figures: 1994 Continued

Occupation	Beginning		Intermediate	
	Minimum	Maximum	Minimum	Maximum
Veterinarians	$2,797	$3,819	$2,988	$4,096
Veterinary Inspector	2,797	3,819	2,988	4,096
Vocational Counselor	--	--	1,957	2,537
Water Quality Analyst	2,035	2,702	2,182	3,308
Waterworks Engineer	2,066	3,372	2,709	3,698
Welfare Eligibility Worker	1,940	2,520	2,215	3,002
Wholesale Buyer, Except Farm Pr	1,868	2,763	2,356	3,360
X-Ray Technician	1,680	2,182	1,853	2,702
Zoo Veterinarian	2,797	3,819	2,988	4,096
Zoologist	2,061	2,836	2,191	3,403
Clerical and Sales				
1st Supv-Cler/Admin Support Wk	1,325	2,347	2,044	2,840
Abrasives Sales Representative	1,343	1,845	1,697	2,763
Accounting Clerk	1,065	2,174	1,888	2,581
Accounts Payable Clerk	1,065	2,174	1,888	2,581
Accounts Receivable Clerk	1,065	2,174	1,888	2,581
Actuarial Clerk	1,645	2,139	1,888	2,477
Adjustment Clerks	1,221	1,871	1,645	2,061
Administrative Clerk	1,100	1,585	1,260	2,139
Apparel Trimmings Sales Rep	1,343	1,845	1,697	2,763
Appointment Clerk	1,082	1,683	1,256	1,825
Assignment Clerk	1,527	2,100	2,000	2,573
Attendance Clerk	1,238	1,715	1,412	2,252
Auditing Clerks	1,065	2,174	1,888	2,581
Benefits Clerk	1,221	1,871	1,645	2,061
Bid Clerk	1,871	2,399	2,009	2,832
Billing Mach Operator	788	1,334	1,013	1,819
Bookkeeping Clerk	1,065	2,174	1,888	2,581
Bookkeeping Supervisor	1,325	2,347	2,044	2,840
Bookmobile Driver	840	1,585	1,252	2,177
Braille-and-Talking Book Clerk	840	1,585	1,252	2,177
Budget Clerk	1,645	2,139	1,888	2,477
Card-Punch Operator	1,065	1,936	1,758	2,338
Cash Clerk	901	1,784	1,587	2,338
Cash-Register Operator	901	1,784	1,587	2,338
Cashier	901	1,784	1,587	2,338
Cashier-Checkers	901	1,784	1,587	2,338
Circulation Clerk	840	1,585	1,252	2,177
Classification Clerk	918	1,672	1,481	2,177
Clerk-Typist	1,186	2,139	1,784	2,416

Table IV-23. Detailed Occupational Wage Ranges in Michigan by Level of Responsibility, Monthly Dollar Figures: 1994 Continued

Occupation	Beginning		Intermediate	
	Minimum	Maximum	Minimum	Maximum
Cloths-Room Worker	$1,108	$1,931	$1,654	$2,330
Commission Clerk	1,238	1,715	1,412	2,252
Computer Operators	1,282	2,312	1,819	2,520
Computer Programmer Aide	--	--	--	--
Console Operator	1,282	2,312	1,819	2,520
Controlboard Operator	1,247	1,559	1,308	1,859
Court Clerks	1,074	2,191	1,897	2,745
Court Reporter	753	1,784	1,524	2,390
Crew Scheduler	1,527	2,100	2,000	2,573
Custodian, Blood Bank	1,108	1,931	1,654	2,330
Customer Complaint Clerk	1,221	1,871	1,645	2,061
Customer Service Representative	1,221	1,871	1,645	2,061
Data Entry Keyers	1,065	1,936	1,758	2,338
Data Typist	1,065	1,936	1,758	2,338
Death-Claim Clerk	1,221	1,871	1,645	2,061
Desk Attendant	840	1,585	1,252	2,177
Dining Room Cashier	901	1,784	1,587	2,338
Dispensary Attendant	1,108	1,931	1,654	2,330
Duplicating Machine Operator	1,576	2,191	1,802	2,415
Encoder	1,065	1,936	1,758	2,338
Expediter	1,527	2,100	2,000	2,573
File Clerk, Medical Records	918	1,672	1,481	2,177
File Clerk, X-Rays	918	1,672	1,481	2,177
File Clerks	918	1,672	1,481	2,177
Food Tabulator, Cafeteria	901	1,784	1,587	2,338
Freight-Receiving Clerk	--	--	1,741	2,338
Fuel Sales Representative	1,343	1,845	1,697	2,763
General Office Clerk	1,100	1,585	1,260	2,139
Hospital Cashier	901	1,784	1,587	2,338
Hotel Cashier	901	1,784	1,587	2,338
Hotel Desk Clerks	1,186	1,273	--	--
In-File Operator	1,082	1,683	1,256	1,825
Information Clerk	1,082	1,683	1,256	1,825
Interceptor Operator	1,247	1,559	1,308	1,859
Inventory Clerk	1,108	1,931	1,654	2,330
Invoice Machine Operator	788	1,334	1,013	1,819
Keypunch Operator	1,065	1,936	1,758	2,338
Leather Goods Sales Rep	1,343	1,845	1,697	2,763
Legal Secretaries	1,212	2,174	1,524	2,589
Library Aide	840	1,585	1,252	2,177

Table IV-23. Detailed Occupational Wage Ranges in Michigan by Level of Responsibility, Monthly Dollar Figures: 1994 Continued

Occupation	Beginning		Intermediate	
	Minimum	Maximum	Minimum	Maximum
Library Assistant	$840	$1,585	$1,252	$2,177
Library Clerk	840	1,585	1,252	2,177
Linen Checker	1,108	1,931	1,654	2,330
Meat Sales Representative	1,343	1,845	1,697	2,763
Medical Records Statistical Cl	1,645	2,139	1,888	2,477
Medical Transcriber	1,186	2,139	1,784	2,416
Medical-Record Clerk	1,645	2,139	1,888	2,477
Mileage Clerk	1,645	2,139	1,888	2,477
Office Manager	1,325	2,347	2,044	2,840
Outpatient Receptionist	1,082	1,683	1,256	1,825
Paper Product Sales Rep	1,343	1,845	1,697	2,763
Parts Clerk	1,108	1,931	1,654	2,330
Payroll Clerk	1,238	1,715	1,412	2,252
Payroll Clerk, Data Processing	1,238	1,715	1,412	2,252
Pbx Operator	1,247	1,559	1,308	1,859
Personnel Clerks	1,383	2,191	1,533	2,676
Piggyback Clerk	--	--	1,741	2,338
Posting Mach Operator	788	1,334	1,013	1,819
Prescription Clerk, Len & Fram	1,108	1,931	1,654	2,330
Printing-Punch Operator	1,065	1,936	1,758	2,338
Private-Branch-Exchange Oper	1,247	1,559	1,308	1,859
Procurement Clerks	1,871	2,399	2,009	2,832
Production Expediting Clerk	1,527	2,100	2,000	2,573
Production Plng Clerk	1,527	2,100	2,000	2,573
Production Statistical Clerk	1,645	2,139	1,888	2,477
Program Coder	--	--	--	--
Purchase-Request Editor	1,871	2,399	2,009	2,832
Purchasing Clerk	1,871	2,399	2,009	2,832
Purchasing Contract Clerk	1,871	2,399	2,009	2,832
Receiving Clerk	--	--	1,741	2,338
Receiving Inspector	--	--	1,741	2,338
Reception Clerk	1,082	1,683	1,256	1,825
Receptionist	1,082	1,683	1,256	1,825
Receptionist, Doctor's Office	1,082	1,683	1,256	1,825
Record Clerk	1,645	2,139	1,888	2,477
Refrigerated-Cargo Clerk	--	--	1,741	2,338
Register Clerk	1,082	1,683	1,256	1,825
Registration Clerk	840	1,585	1,252	2,177
Report Clerk	1,645	2,139	1,888	2,477
Reproduction Machine Operator	1,576	2,191	1,802	2,415

Table IV-23. Detailed Occupational Wage Ranges in Michigan by Level of Responsibility, Monthly Dollar Figures: 1994 Continued

Occupation	Beginning		Intermediate	
	Minimum	Maximum	Minimum	Maximum
Reservationist	$1,186	$1,273	$--	$--
Sack Keeper	1,108	1,931	1,654	2,330
Sales Record Clerk	1,645	2,139	1,888	2,477
Sales Rep-Except Sci & Retail	1,343	1,845	1,697	2,763
Schedule Maker	1,527	2,100	2,000	2,573
Scheduler and Planner	1,238	1,715	1,412	2,252
Secretaries	1,169	2,026	1,654	2,840
Shipping Clerk	--	--	1,741	2,338
Shipping/Receiving Clerk	--	--	1,741	2,338
Stack Clerk	840	1,585	1,252	2,177
Station House Clerk	1,221	1,871	1,645	2,061
Statistical Clerks	1,645	2,139	1,888	2,477
Stenographer	1,273	2,122	1,654	2,598
Stenotype Operator	1,273	2,122	1,654	2,598
Stock Clerk,Stockroom,Warehouse	1,108	1,931	1,654	2,330
Stockroom Clerk	1,108	1,931	1,654	2,330
Stockroom Inventory Clerk	1,108	1,931	1,654	2,330
Store Cashier	901	1,784	1,587	2,338
Storekeeper	1,108	1,931	1,654	2,330
Supply Clerk	1,108	1,931	1,654	2,330
Switchboard Operator	1,247	1,559	1,308	1,859
Switchboard Receptionist	1,247	1,559	1,308	1,859
Tabulating Clerk	1,645	2,139	1,888	2,477
Tape Librarian	840	1,585	1,252	2,177
Tax Clerk	1,065	2,174	1,888	2,581
Telephone Operator	1,247	1,559	1,308	1,859
Telephone Solicitor Supervisor	1,325	2,347	2,044	2,840
Telephone-Answering-Service Op	1,247	1,559	1,308	1,859
Tellers	1,057	1,446	1,325	2,243
Textile Sales Rep	1,343	1,845	1,697	2,763
Ticket Cashier	901	1,784	1,587	2,338
Timekeeping Clerk	1,238	1,715	1,412	2,252
Toll Collector	901	1,784	1,587	2,338
Tool Crib Attendant	1,108	1,931	1,654	2,330
Tourist Information Assistant	1,082	1,683	1,256	1,825
Traffic Clerk	--	--	1,741	2,338
Transcriber	1,186	2,139	1,784	2,416
Typing Supervisor	1,325	2,347	2,044	2,840
Typists	1,186	2,139	1,784	2,416
Typists, Word Processing Equip	1,186	2,139	1,784	2,416

Table IV-23. Detailed Occupational Wage Ranges in Michigan by Level of Responsibility, Monthly Dollar Figures: 1994 Continued

Occupation	Beginning		Intermediate	
	Minimum	Maximum	Minimum	Maximum
Uniform Attendant	$1,108	$1,931	$1,654	$2,330
Unloading Checker	--	--	1,741	2,338
Verifier Operator	1,065	1,936	1,758	2,338
Ward Clerk	1,100	1,585	1,260	2,139
Service				
Baker, Bread & Pastry	875	1,386	1,143	2,217
Barbers	1,931	2,381	2,035	2,529
Bartenders	--	--	--	--
Bus, Hall, Babe, Playground Monit	--	--	1,316	2,200
Cafeteria Supervisor	--	--	--	--
Cake Maker	875	1,386	1,143	2,217
Case Aide	1,282	1,853	1,758	2,250
Central-Supply Workers	987	1,490	1,348	1,772
Child Care Attendant	--	--	1,966	2,477
Child Care Workers	--	--	1,966	2,477
Child-Day-Care Center Worker	--	--	1,966	2,477
Conservation Officer	--	--	2,269	3,109
Constable	1,593	2,330	2,026	4,789
Cooks, Institution & Cafe	953	1,732	1,368	2,171
Cooks, Restaurant	944	1,236	1,100	1,905
Correction Officer	1,443	2,330	1,819	2,728
Counter Supervisor	--	--	--	--
Custodian	909	1,888	1,238	2,120
Deputy Sheriff	1,593	2,330	2,026	4,789
Detective Supervisor	--	--	--	--
Dishwasher, Hand	849	1,501	1,203	1,671
Dishwasher, Machine	849	1,501	1,203	1,671
Dispatcher-Pol, Fire, Ambl	979	2,177	1,628	2,511
Dry Cleaner	1,819	2,499	2,078	2,659
Dryclean Cach Opr	1,819	2,499	2,078	2,659
Fire Fighters	1,836	2,321	2,078	3,066
Fire Fighting Supervisor	--	--	--	--
Fire Inspectors	1,706	2,520	2,364	3,083
Fire Prevention Supervisor	--	--	--	--
Fireboat Operator	1,836	2,321	2,078	3,066
Food Preparation Worker	849	1,501	1,203	1,671
Food Service Supervisor	--	--	--	--
Fur Cleaner	1,819	2,499	2,078	2,659
Garbage Porter	849	1,501	1,203	1,671
Guards & Watch Guards	918	1,827	1,593	2,312

Table IV-23. Detailed Occupational Wage Ranges in Michigan by Level of Responsibility, Monthly Dollar Figures: 1994 Continued

Occupation	Beginning		Intermediate	
	Minimum	Maximum	Minimum	Maximum
Highway Patroller	$1,060	$2,014	$1,827	$3,066
Home Health Aides	--	--	1,767	2,260
Homemaker	1,282	1,853	1,758	2,250
House Parent	--	--	1,966	2,477
Housekeeping Cleaners	1,731	2,054	1,821	2,133
Institutional Attendant	987	1,490	1,348	1,772
Jailers	1,443	2,330	1,819	2,728
Janitor & Cleaner	909	1,888	1,238	2,120
Kitchen Hand	849	1,501	1,203	1,671
Kitchen Helper	849	1,501	1,203	1,671
Kitchen Porter	849	1,501	1,203	1,671
Laundry Mach Opr	1,819	2,499	2,078	2,659
Leather Cleaner	1,819	2,499	2,078	2,659
Maids	1,731	2,054	1,821	2,133
Marshall	1,593	2,330	2,026	4,789
Medication Aide	987	1,490	1,348	1,772
Night Baker	875	1,386	1,143	2,217
Nurse Aide, Central Supply	987	1,490	1,348	1,772
Nurse Aide, Surgery	987	1,490	1,348	1,772
Nursery School Attendant	--	--	1,966	2,477
Nursing Aide	987	1,490	1,348	1,772
Nursing Assistant	987	1,490	1,348	1,772
Orderlies, Attd	987	1,490	1,348	1,772
Parking Enforcement Officer	1,498	2,139	1,914	2,330
Pie Baker	875	1,386	1,143	2,217
Plain-Clothes Detective	2,572	3,126	2,970	3,611
Police Cadet	1,060	2,014	1,827	3,066
Police Detectives	2,572	3,126	2,970	3,611
Police Officer	1,060	2,014	1,827	3,066
Police Patrol Officer	1,060	2,014	1,827	3,066
Police Supervisor	--	--	--	--
Rolls Baker	875	1,386	1,143	2,217
Rug Cleaner	1,819	2,499	2,078	2,659
Security Guard	918	1,827	1,593	2,312
Sheriff	1,593	2,330	2,026	4,789
Silverware Washer	849	1,501	1,203	1,671
Social Service Aide	1,282	1,853	1,758	2,250
Utility Hand	849	1,501	1,203	1,671
Waiters	797	1,247	--	--
Waitresses	797	1,247	--	--

Table IV-23. Detailed Occupational Wage Ranges in Michigan by Level of Responsibility, Monthly Dollar Figures: 1994 Continued

Occupation	Beginning		Intermediate	
	Minimum	Maximum	Minimum	Maximum
Welfare Service Aide	$1,282	$1,853	$1,758	$2,250
Window Washer	--	--	1,697	2,312
Farming/Fishery/Forestry				
1st Supv-Agric & Oth	--	--	2,304	2,996
Athletic Field Custodian	1,351	1,792	1,563	2,273
Caretaker, Grounds	1,351	1,792	1,563	2,273
Conservation Worker	1,784	2,719	2,139	3,403
Forest Fire Inspectors	1,923	2,330	1,983	2,702
Forest Fire Prv	1,923	2,330	1,983	2,702
Forest Product Gatherer	1,784	2,719	2,139	3,403
Forest Worker	1,784	2,719	2,139	3,403
Forester Aide	1,784	2,719	2,139	3,403
Gardeners & Groundskeeper	1,351	1,792	1,563	2,273
Gardener, Except Farming	1,351	1,792	1,563	2,273
Greens Planter	1,351	1,792	1,563	2,273
Landscape Laborer	1,351	1,792	1,563	2,273
Landscaper	1,351	1,792	1,563	2,273
Lawn Mower	1,351	1,792	1,563	2,273
Lawn-Service Worker	1,351	1,792	1,563	2,273
Nursery Workers	1,784	2,139	--	--
Seedling Puller	1,784	2,719	2,139	3,403
Tree Planter	1,784	2,719	2,139	3,403
Yard Worker	1,351	1,792	1,563	2,273
Processing				
Air-Furnace Operator	--	--	1,767	2,598
Cupola Tender	--	--	1,767	2,598
First Helper	--	--	1,767	2,598
Furnace Operator & Tender	--	--	1,767	2,598
Pressing Machine Operator	--	--	1,793	2,693
Rotary-Furnace Operator	--	--	1,767	2,598
Machine Trade				
1st Supv-Mech, Installers	1,749	2,744	2,340	3,534
1st Supv-Repairers	1,749	2,744	2,340	3,534
Air Conditioning Mechanic	--	--	1,940	2,693
Air-Conditioning Attendant	--	--	1,940	2,693
Air-Conditioning Erector	--	--	1,940	2,693
Aircraft Mechanics	--	--	2,200	2,693
Automatic Lathe Operator	--	--	1,628	3,074
Automotive Mechanic Helper	--	--	--	--
Automotive Mechanics	1,438	2,066	1,760	2,770

Table IV-23. Detailed Occupational Wage Ranges in Michigan by Level of Responsibility, Monthly Dollar Figures: 1994 Continued

Occupation	Beginning		Intermediate	
	Minimum	Maximum	Minimum	Maximum
Belt Changer	$1,585	$2,295	$1,853	$2,511
Belt Repairer	1,585	2,295	1,853	2,511
Blacksmith	--	--	2,061	2,485
Blade Changer	1,585	2,295	1,853	2,511
Brake Mechanic	1,438	2,066	1,760	2,770
Bus Mechanic	1,533	2,252	2,061	2,858
Chucking Mach Set-Up Oper	--	--	1,628	3,074
Diesel Specialist	1,533	2,252	2,061	2,858
Drill-Press/Brng Mach Oper	1,386	1,897	1,567	2,789
Drillg Mach Tool Setter,M&P	1,386	1,897	1,567	2,789
Engine Lathe Operator	--	--	1,628	3,074
Engine Lathe Set-Up Operator	--	--	1,628	3,074
Engineering-Equip Mechanic	1,533	2,252	2,061	2,858
Floor Layers	--	--	--	--
Furnace Installer	--	--	1,940	2,693
Garage Mechanic	1,438	2,066	1,760	2,770
Greaser and Oiler	1,585	2,295	1,853	2,511
Heating/Air Cond & Refrig Inst	--	--	1,940	2,693
Heating/Air Cond & Refrig Mech	--	--	1,940	2,693
Heavy Equipment Mechanic	1,533	2,252	2,061	2,858
Horizontal Boring-Mill Set-Up	1,386	1,897	1,567	2,789
Industrial Truck Mechanic	1,533	2,252	2,061	2,858
Lathe Setter	--	--	1,628	3,074
Lathe/Turning Mach Oper, Metl	--	--	1,628	3,074
Machine Hostler	1,585	2,295	1,853	2,511
Machine Oiler	1,585	2,295	1,853	2,511
Machinery Erector	1,368	2,096	1,948	2,875
Machinery Maintenance Workers	1,585	2,295	1,853	2,511
Machinists	1,429	2,191	1,845	2,737
Maintenance Machinist	1,429	2,191	1,845	2,737
Mechanic & Repairer Helpers	--	--	--	--
Milling Mach Tool Setter, M&P	--	--	--	--
Millwrights	1,368	2,096	1,948	2,875
Motorcycle Mechanic	1,438	2,066	1,760	2,770
Motorcycle Repairer	1,438	2,066	1,760	2,770
Multiple Spindle Press Oper	1,386	1,897	1,567	2,789
Num Mach Tool Opr & Tender, M&P	1,230	1,862	1,524	2,364
Office Mach Servicers	--	--	--	--
Oil Burner Repairer	--	--	1,940	2,693
Oiler	1,585	2,295	1,853	2,511

Table IV-23. Detailed Occupational Wage Ranges in Michigan by Level of Responsibility, Monthly Dollar Figures: 1994 Continued

Occupation	Beginning		Intermediate	
	Minimum	Maximum	Minimum	Maximum
Print Press Mach Operator	$1,507	$2,176	$2,128	$2,770
Production Machinist	1,429	2,191	1,845	2,737
Profiling Machine Set-Up Opr	--	--	--	--
Punching Mach Setters,M&P	996	1,897	1,689	2,321
Radial Drill Press Operator	1,386	1,897	1,567	2,789
Radial Press Operator	1,386	1,897	1,567	2,789
Refrigeration-Equipment Erecto	--	--	1,940	2,693
Screen Printing Machine Operat	1,507	2,176	2,128	2,770
Screw Machine Set-Up Operator	--	--	1,628	3,074
Sheeter, Ironworkers	--	--	2,563	3,230
Sing Spindle Drill Press Setup	1,386	1,897	1,567	2,789
Soft Tile Setter	--	--	--	--
Spinning Lathe Operator	--	--	1,628	3,074
Stripping Shovel Oiler	1,585	2,295	1,853	2,511
Threading-Machine Operator	--	--	1,628	3,074
Tool & Die Makers	1,723	2,364	2,226	2,754
Tool Sharpen Set-Up Operator	--	--	--	--
Transmission Specialist	1,438	2,066	1,760	2,770
Truck Mechanic	1,533	2,252	2,061	2,858
Tune-Up Mechanic	1,438	2,066	1,760	2,770
Turning Mach Tool Setter	--	--	1,628	3,074
Turret Lathe Set-Up Operator	--	--	1,628	3,074
Benchwork				
Alloy Weigher	1,360	1,619	1,429	2,139
Alteration Tailor	1,739	2,130	1,819	2,252
Assembler & Fabricator, x Mach	1,048	1,862	1,455	2,468
Belt Picker	1,360	1,619	1,429	2,139
Bottle Capper	1,048	1,862	1,455	2,468
Box Maker	1,048	1,862	1,455	2,468
Carton Inspector	1,360	1,619	1,429	2,139
Cigarette Examiner	1,360	1,619	1,429	2,139
Cloth Grader	1,360	1,619	1,429	2,139
Covered-Buckle Assembler	1,048	1,862	1,455	2,468
Custom Tailor & Sewer	1,739	2,130	1,819	2,252
Dental Ceramist	1,680	2,130	1,853	2,330
Dressmaker	1,739	2,130	1,819	2,252
Embroidery Machine Operator	1,195	1,637	1,585	1,810
Filers	--	--	1,923	2,572
Finished Cloth Examiner	1,360	1,619	1,429	2,139
Finisher, Denture	1,680	2,130	1,853	2,330

Table IV-23. Detailed Occupational Wage Ranges in Michigan by Level of Responsibility, Monthly Dollar Figures: 1994 Continued

Occupation	Beginning		Intermediate	
	Minimum	Maximum	Minimum	Maximum
Flour Tester	$1,360	$1,619	$1,429	$2,139
Gas/Water Meter Installers	1,663	2,191	1,948	2,650
Gas/Water Meter Repairers	1,663	2,191	1,948	2,650
Gasoline Tester	1,360	1,619	1,429	2,139
Grinder	--	--	1,897	2,529
Hardness Tester	1,360	1,619	1,429	2,139
Hide Inspector	1,360	1,619	1,429	2,139
Hide Sorter	1,360	1,619	1,429	2,139
Home Entert Equipment Repairer	--	--	2,191	2,696
Leather Sorter	1,360	1,619	1,429	2,139
Lining Feller	1,195	1,637	1,585	1,810
Liquor Inspector	1,360	1,619	1,429	2,139
Locksmith	--	--	2,104	2,988
Log Inspector	1,360	1,619	1,429	2,139
Mech Control Installer	1,663	2,191	1,948	2,650
Mech Control Repairer	1,663	2,191	1,948	2,650
Mech Valve Installer	1,663	2,191	1,948	2,650
Mech Valve Repairer	1,663	2,191	1,948	2,650
Metal Mold Dresser	--	--	1,897	2,529
Orthodontic Technician	1,680	2,130	1,853	2,330
Paper Novelty Maker	1,048	1,862	1,455	2,468
Paperboard Maker	1,048	1,862	1,455	2,468
Petroleum Sampler	1,360	1,619	1,429	2,139
Photo Checkers	1,360	1,619	1,429	2,139
Prec Dental Lab Tech	1,680	2,130	1,853	2,330
Production Inspector	1,360	1,619	1,429	2,139
Safe Repairer	--	--	2,104	2,988
Seamstress	1,739	2,130	1,819	2,252
Sewing Mach Opr, Garment	1,195	1,637	1,585	1,810
Sharpeners	--	--	1,923	2,572
Skin Grader	1,360	1,619	1,429	2,139
Stereo Equipment Repairer	--	--	2,191	2,696
Stone Grader	1,360	1,619	1,429	2,139
Television Servicer	--	--	2,191	2,696
Tool Grinders	--	--	1,923	2,572
Zipper Setter	1,195	1,637	1,585	1,810
Structural Work				
Arc Welder	1,342	2,070	1,706	2,581
Arc-Cutter	1,342	2,070	1,706	2,581
Asbestos Insulation Worker	1,917	2,489	2,413	2,941

Table IV-23. Detailed Occupational Wage Ranges in Michigan by Level of Responsibility, Monthly Dollar Figures: 1994 Continued

Occupation	Beginning		Intermediate	
	Minimum	Maximum	Minimum	Maximum
Asphalt-Paving Machine Operato	$--	$--	$--	$--
Assembly Insp	1,706	2,425	2,174	3,239
Auto Body Repairers	--	--	1,635	2,407
Battery Maintainer	1,897	2,485	2,182	3,187
Boilermakers	--	--	2,156	2,757
Brazer Machine Set-Up Man	--	--	1,438	2,572
Brick Masons	--	--	--	--
Bucker-Up, Ironworkers	--	--	2,771	3,206
Bulldozer Operator	--	--	--	--
Carpenter Inspector	1,706	2,425	2,174	3,239
Carpenters	1,637	2,484	1,940	3,161
Carpentry Maintenance	1,637	2,484	1,940	3,161
Carpentry Repairer	1,637	2,484	1,940	3,161
Carpet Installer	--	--	--	--
Cast-Iron Pipelayer	--	--	2,344	2,840
Casting Inspector	1,706	2,425	2,174	3,239
Cinder Block Mason	--	--	--	--
Combination Carpenter	1,637	2,484	1,940	3,161
Concrete Finishers	1,845	2,425	2,304	2,901
Concrete Paving Machine Operat	--	--	--	--
Coppersmith	--	--	2,018	3,118
Drywall Installers	--	--	2,489	2,946
Elec Powerline Installer	--	--	1,567	2,659
Elec Powerline Repairer	--	--	1,567	2,659
Electrical Repairer	1,897	2,485	2,182	3,187
Electrician, Powerhouse	1,897	2,485	2,182	3,187
Electricians	1,897	2,485	2,182	3,187
Electron Beam Welder Setter	--	--	1,438	2,572
Elevator Examiner & Adjust	1,706	2,425	2,174	3,239
Elevator Installer	--	--	--	--
Elevator Repairer	--	--	--	--
Excavating Machine Opr.	--	--	--	--
Fence Erectors	--	--	--	--
Film Inspector	1,706	2,425	2,174	3,239
Final Assembly Inspector	1,706	2,425	2,174	3,239
Finish Plasterer	1,940	2,745	2,317	3,222
Framing Carpenter	1,637	2,484	1,940	3,161
Gas Line Installer	--	--	2,071	2,245
Gas Welder	1,342	2,070	1,706	2,581
Gauge and Instrument Inspector	1,706	2,425	2,174	3,239

Table IV-23. Detailed Occupational Wage Ranges in Michigan by Level of Responsibility, Monthly Dollar Figures: 1994 Continued

Occupation	Beginning		Intermediate	
	Minimum	Maximum	Minimum	Maximum
General Maintenance Wkr	$1,115	$1,906	$1,663	$2,416
Generators Inspector	1,706	2,425	2,174	3,239
Glaziers	--	--	--	--
Grader, Dozer & Scraper Opr	--	--	--	--
Grading Machine Operator	--	--	--	--
Greeting Card Inspector	1,706	2,425	2,174	3,239
Gypsum Block Setter	--	--	--	--
Hardwood Floor Layer	1,637	2,484	1,940	3,161
Heavy Equipment Operator	--	--	--	--
Helper, Electricians	--	--	1,689	1,931
Highway Maintenance Workers	--	--	--	--
Installation Insp	1,706	2,425	2,174	3,239
Insulation Workers	1,917	2,489	2,413	2,941
Irrigation-System Installer	--	--	2,344	2,840
Joist Setter	--	--	--	--
Lathers	--	--	2,478	3,168
Lead Burner	1,342	2,070	1,706	2,581
Lighting-Equipment Operator	1,897	2,485	2,182	3,187
Maintenance Inspector	1,706	2,425	2,174	3,239
Maintenance Mechanic	1,115	1,906	1,663	2,416
Maintenance Repairer, Genl Utl	1,115	1,906	1,663	2,416
Mechanical Inspector	1,706	2,425	2,174	3,239
Metal Installer	--	--	2,018	3,118
Metal Roofer	--	--	2,018	3,118
Motors Inspector	1,706	2,425	2,174	3,239
Operating Engineers	--	--	--	--
Ornamental Iron Worker	--	--	--	--
Painted Circuit Board Inspector	1,706	2,425	2,174	3,239
Painter	1,351	2,312	2,061	2,927
Paperhanger	1,351	2,312	2,061	2,927
Parts Inspector	1,706	2,425	2,174	3,239
Perishable-Freight Inspector	1,706	2,425	2,174	3,239
Pile Driving Operator	--	--	2,584	3,173
Pipe Setter	--	--	2,344	2,840
Pipefitter	1,940	2,711	2,581	3,152
Plant-Maintenance Worker	1,115	1,906	1,663	2,416
Plaster Mason	1,940	2,745	2,317	3,222
Plasterer	1,940	2,745	2,317	3,222
Plate Glass Glazier	--	--	--	--
Plate Inspector	1,706	2,425	2,174	3,239

Table IV-23. Detailed Occupational Wage Ranges in Michigan by Level of Responsibility, Monthly Dollar Figures: 1994 Continued

Occupation	Beginning		Intermediate	
	Minimum	Maximum	Minimum	Maximum
Plumber	$1,940	$2,711	$2,581	$3,152
Precision Grader	1,706	2,425	2,174	3,239
Precision Inspector	1,706	2,425	2,174	3,239
Protective Signal Install/Repa	1,897	2,485	2,182	3,187
Radio Electrician	--	--	1,567	2,676
Radio Mechanics	--	--	1,567	2,676
Radio-Communications Mechanic	--	--	1,567	2,676
Radio-Maintenance Repairer	--	--	1,567	2,676
Refractory Bricklayer	--	--	--	--
Reinforcing Metal Worker	--	--	--	--
Reinforcing-Bar Setter	--	--	--	--
Reinforcing-Iron Worker	--	--	--	--
Reinforcing-Rod Tier	--	--	--	--
Reinforcing-Steel Erector	--	--	--	--
Residential Wirer	1,897	2,485	2,182	3,187
Resistance Machine Welder Sett	--	--	1,438	2,572
Resistance Welder, Fitter	1,342	2,070	1,706	2,581
Roofers	1,749	2,489	2,030	2,799
Sheet Metal Workers	--	--	2,018	3,118
Sheetrock Applicator	--	--	2,489	2,946
Solderer, Structural	1,342	2,070	1,706	2,581
Special Items Fabricator	--	--	2,018	3,118
Spot Welder	1,342	2,070	1,706	2,581
Spray Gun Plasterer	1,940	2,745	2,317	3,222
Sprinkler-System Installer	--	--	2,344	2,840
Steamfitter	--	--	2,344	2,840
Steel Erector	--	--	--	--
Structural Metal Worker	--	--	--	--
Stucco Mason	1,940	2,745	2,317	3,222
Subassemblies Inspector	1,706	2,425	2,174	3,239
Terrazzo Finishers	1,845	2,425	2,304	2,901
Tinsmith	--	--	2,018	3,118
Tower Erector	--	--	1,567	2,659
Trades Inspector	1,706	2,425	2,174	3,239
Transmitter Repairer	--	--	1,567	2,676
Trench Digging Machine Operato	--	--	--	--
Welder Fitter	1,342	2,070	1,706	2,581
Welder Set-Up Man	--	--	1,438	2,572
Welders & Flamecutters-a	--	--	1,438	2,572
Welding Machine Setter	--	--	1,438	2,572

Table IV-23. Detailed Occupational Wage Ranges in Michigan by Level of Responsibility, Monthly Dollar Figures: 1994 Continued

Occupation	Beginning		Intermediate	
	Minimum	Maximum	Minimum	Maximum
Wirer	$1,897	$2,485	$2,182	$3,187
Miscellaneous				
1st Supv-Production & Operatin	--	--	1,805	2,845
Air Compressor Engineer	--	--	2,491	2,636
Boiler Mechanic	1,940	2,589	2,191	2,944
Boiler Operator, Low Presser	1,833	2,292	2,018	2,711
Boiler Tender	1,833	2,292	2,018	2,711
Boilerhouse Mechanic	1,940	2,589	2,191	2,944
Book Caser	--	--	1,793	2,278
Book Repairer	--	--	1,793	2,278
Bookbinder, Hand	--	--	1,793	2,278
Bookbinders	--	--	1,793	2,278
Bottle Filler	--	--	--	--
Bottle Packer	--	--	--	--
Bridge Operator	--	--	--	--
Bridge, Lock & Lighthouse Tende	1,732	2,174	1,940	2,407
Bus Drivers, School	1,290	1,810	1,372	2,130
Business Forms Packer	--	--	--	--
Capping Machine Operator	--	--	--	--
Car Inspector	--	--	2,364	3,083
Carrier Driver	1,100	1,741	1,567	2,200
Casing Finisher & Stuffer	--	--	--	--
Cement Truck Driver	1,645	2,191	1,758	2,572
Cinder-Crane Operator	--	--	--	--
Clarifying Plant Operator	1,784	2,572	1,992	2,823
Compressed Air, Drum Hoist Op	--	--	--	--
Cooling-System Operator	1,940	2,589	2,191	2,944
Crane & Tower Operator	--	--	--	--
Crane Rigger	--	--	--	--
Crane, Derrick,& Hoist Opr.	--	--	--	--
Dragline Operator	--	--	--	--
Drum Hoist Operator	--	--	--	--
Dumptruck Driver	1,645	2,191	1,758	2,572
Electric Bridge Crane Operator	--	--	--	--
Electric Gantry Crane Operator	--	--	--	--
Electric Monorail Crane Oper	--	--	--	--
Electric Truck Operator	1,100	1,741	1,567	2,200
Electric, Drum Hoist Operator	--	--	--	--
Finishing Bookbinder	--	--	1,793	2,278
Firer, Marine	1,833	2,292	2,018	2,711

Table IV-23. Detailed Occupational Wage Ranges in Michigan by Level of Responsibility, Monthly Dollar Figures: 1994 Continued

Occupation	Beginning		Intermediate	
	Minimum	Maximum	Minimum	Maximum
Firer, Portable Boiler	$1,833	$2,292	$2,018	$2,711
Firer-Watertender	1,833	2,292	2,018	2,711
Forklift Truck Operator	1,100	1,741	1,567	2,200
Forwarder	--	--	1,793	2,278
Front-End Loader Operator	1,100	1,741	1,567	2,200
Fuel House Tender	1,833	2,292	2,018	2,711
Gantry Crane Operator	--	--	--	--
Gasoline Drum Hoist Operator	--	--	--	--
General Laborers	996	1,827	1,386	1,983
Greeting Card Packer	--	--	--	--
Hand Stitcher	--	--	1,793	2,278
Hazardous Waste Remover	--	--	1,946	2,099
Heating-Equipment Repairer	1,940	2,589	2,191	2,944
Hi-Lo Operator	1,100	1,741	1,567	2,200
Hoist & Winch Operator	--	--	--	--
Hook Tender	--	--	--	--
Hydraulic Boom Operator	--	--	--	--
Industrial Truck & Tractor Opr	1,100	1,741	1,567	2,200
Insulation Packer	--	--	--	--
Labeling Machine Operator	--	--	--	--
Library Bookbinder	--	--	1,793	2,278
Liquefaction Plant Operator	1,784	2,572	1,992	2,823
Locomotive Crane Operator	--	--	--	--
Low Pressure Firer	1,833	2,292	2,018	2,711
Magazine Repairer	--	--	1,793	2,278
Mobile Crane Operator	--	--	--	--
Motor Bus Chauffeur	1,290	1,810	1,372	2,130
Operating Eng-Stationary Eng	1,565	2,390	1,892	2,702
Package & Fill Mach Operator	--	--	--	--
Park Lot Attendant	--	--	1,490	1,749
Photographer Helper	1,680	2,130	1,853	2,702
Photographic Service Asst	1,680	2,130	1,853	2,702
Power Generator Plant Operator	1,940	2,589	2,191	2,944
Powerplant Operator	1,940	2,589	2,191	2,944
Production Packager	--	--	--	--
Railroad Car Inspector	--	--	2,364	3,083
Refuse Collectors	--	--	1,611	2,139
Retort Filer	1,833	2,292	2,018	2,711
Retort Firer	1,833	2,292	2,018	2,711
Riggers	--	--	--	--

Table IV-23. Detailed Occupational Wage Ranges in Michigan by Level of Responsibility, Monthly Dollar Figures: 1994 Continued

Occupation	Beginning		Intermediate	
	Minimum	Maximum	Minimum	Maximum
Sewer	$--	$--	$1,793	$2,278
Sewing Room Supervisor	--	--	1,805	2,845
Slinger	--	--	--	--
Spinning Supervisor	--	--	1,805	2,845
Stationary Boler Firer	1,833	2,292	2,018	2,711
Steam Drum Hoist Operator	--	--	--	--
Stoker	1,833	2,292	2,018	2,711
Tractor Crane Operator	--	--	--	--
Transportation Inspector	--	--	2,364	3,083
Truck Crane Operator	--	--	--	--
Truck Driver, Heavy	1,645	2,191	1,758	2,572
Truck Driver, Light	--	--	1,637	2,595
Waste Treat Plant Operator	1,784	2,572	1,992	2,823
Wat-Liq Waste Treat Plant/Sys	1,565	2,390	1,892	2,702
Water Treatment Plant Operator	1,784	2,572	1,992	2,823
Well Pullers	--	--	--	--
Wrapper Layer	--	--	--	--
Wrapper Machine Operator	--	--	--	--
Yard Rigger	--	--	--	--

-- No data available for beginning or intermediate level workers.
Source: Michigan Employment Security Commission, Michigan Occupational Wage Information - June 1994 (Detroit, Michigan: annually).

Table IV-24. Union Membership by Sector in Michigan: 1979 and 1983-1994

Year	Membership			Membership as Percent(%) of All Workers*		
	Total	Private Sector	Public Sector	Total	Private Sector	Public Sector
1979	1,301,000	997,000	304,000	36.7	33.3	55.2
1983	1,005,446	702,208	303,238	30.4	25.3	56.8
1984	1,004,251	738,109	266,142	29.1	25.1	52.4
1985	1,004,466	706,622	297,844	28.4	23.5	56.8
1986	1,016,678	718,561	298,117	28.3	23.6	54.3
1987	997,403	690,745	306,658	26.6	21.5	56.1
1988	1,009,184	697,901	311,283	26.6	21.6	55.1
1989	1,012,804	667,577	345,227	26.0	20.2	58.1
1990	974,033	653,757	320,276	25.4	20.2	54.2
1991	924,302	601,690	322,612	24.7	19.1	55.4
1992	972,153	626,093	346,060	25.6	19.6	57.8
1993	961,528	605,996	355,532	24.6	18.5	56.0
1994	960,609	631,502	329,107	23.8	18.3	56.0

* Wage and Salary workers except owners of incorporated business.
Source: Michigan Employment Security Commission, Research and Statistics, Current Population Survey (Detroit, Michigan).

Table IV-25. Unemployment in Michigan, by Reason of Joblessness: 1983-1993
(Data in Thousands)

Year	Total Unemployment	Indefinite Layoff	Temporary Layoff	Other Job Loser	Job Leaver	Reentrant	New Entrant	Indefinite Layoff & Other Job Losers	
								Number	Percent (%) of Total Unemployment
1983	604.0	137.0	23.4	187.9	31.6	157.0	67.1	324.9	53.8
1984	490.4	81.2	15.7	135.2	38.1	151.4	68.8	216.4	44.1
1985	449.8	68.0	14.3	113.3	37.4	150.8	66.0	181.3	40.3
1986	399.4	45.9	19.1	111.8	45.3	115.1	62.2	157.7	39.5
1987	373.1	59.2	24.6	111.6	37.8	99.5	40.4	170.8	45.8
1988	360.8	60.9	21.0	89.3	47.8	95.7	46.1	150.2	41.6
1989	334.5	55.7	18.6	73.9	41.6	105.2	39.5	129.6	38.7
1990	366.4	62.6	28.0	92.6	45.9	105.0	32.3	155.2	42.4
1991	414.7	76.0	25.8	121.5	36.7	111.0	43.7	197.5	47.6
1992	400.5	80.7	25.2	124.5	39.6	91.2	39.3	205.2	51.2
1993	333.4	63.5	15.4	93.4	33.0	92.0	36.1	156.9	47.1

Source: Michigan Employment Security Commission, Research and Statistics, Current Population Survey (Detroit, Michigan: annually).

Table IV-26. Unemployment Duration in Michigan by Sex, Age, and Race: Percent Distribution, 1978-1993

Year/ Category	Total Unemployed		Duration of Unemployment (Percent(%) of Total)			
	Number (In Thousands)	Percent(%)	Less Than 5 Weeks	5 to 14 Weeks	15 to 26 Weeks	27 Weeks and Over
Total						
1978	289	100.0	47.2	32.3	11.3	9.1
1979	335	100.0	45.8	30.6	13.5	10.2
1980	541	100.0	34.0	30.7	16.4	18.9
1981	528	100.0	32.6	27.8	13.4	25.9
1982	661	100.0	30.6	28.0	16.1	25.3
1983	610	100.0	28.1	24.5	14.9	32.5
1984	488	100.0	36.7	26.2	11.4	25.7
1985	433	100.0	36.4	28.8	12.5	22.3
1986	385	100.0	40.1	28.9	11.7	19.2
1987	369	100.0	41.5	29.2	12.8	16.5
1988	348	100.0	41.5	28.6	13.8	16.1
1989	326	100.0	47.5	29.3	11.2	12.0
1990	344	100.0	48.8	30.4	11.2	9.6
1991	418	100.0	43.4	31.7	12.7	12.2
1992	405	100.0	38.1	29.6	13.0	19.3
1993	328	100.0	40.3	29.8	13.3	16.6
Male						
1978	144	100.0	43.3	32.5	14.2	9.9
1979	183	100.0	41.6	33.5	14.8	10.1
1980	286	100.0	29.2	31.0	17.7	22.1
1981	N.A.	N.A.	N.A.	N.A.	N.A.	N.A.
1982	387	100.0	26.2	28.3	17.1	28.5
1983	368	100.0	23.7	23.2	15.4	37.7
1984	266	100.0	32.6	24.9	11.9	30.6
1985	233	100.0	33.9	28.0	13.5	24.6
1986	212	100.0	36.1	29.7	11.7	22.5
1987	207	100.0	37.7	29.2	14.2	18.9
1988	198	100.0	36.5	29.6	15.2	18.7
1989	182	100.0	43.6	29.4	13.1	13.9
1990	206	100.0	45.5	30.4	11.4	12.6
1991	245	100.0	40.8	32.4	13.2	13.6
1992	223	100.0	37.1	29.7	12.4	20.9
1993	183	100.0	38.9	30.0	13.3	17.8
Female						
1978	146	100.0	51.0	32.2	8.5	8.4
1979	152	100.0	50.7	27.1	11.9	10.2
1980	164	100.0	36.5	28.8	15.5	19.1
1981	N.A.	N.A.	N.A.	N.A.	N.A.	N.A.
1982	274	100.0	36.8	27.6	14.7	20.8

Table IV-26. Unemployment Duration in Michigan by Sex, Age, and Race: Percent Distribution, 1978-1993 Continued

Year/ Category	Total Unemployed		Duration of Unemployment (Percent(%) of Total)			
	Number (In Thousands)	Percent(%)	Less Than 5 Weeks	5 to 14 Weeks	15 to 26 Weeks	27 Weeks and Over
Female - Cont.						
1983	243	100.0	34.6	26.5	14.2	24.7
1984	221	100.0	41.8	27.7	10.9	19.7
1985	200	100.0	39.3	29.7	11.2	19.8
1986	173	100.0	45.1	28.0	11.8	15.1
1987	162	100.0	46.5	29.2	11.0	13.4
1988	150	100.0	48.1	27.4	11.8	12.7
1989	143	100.0	52.4	29.1	9.0	9.4
1990	138	100.0	53.7	30.3	11.0	5.0
1991	173	100.0	47.0	30.8	12.0	10.2
1992	182	100.0	39.3	29.5	13.9	17.3
1993	145	100.0	42.0	29.6	13.2	15.2
Teen 16 - 19 Yrs						
1978	N.A.	N.A.	N.A.	N.A.	N.A.	N.A.
1979	N.A.	N.A.	N.A.	N.A.	N.A.	N.A.
1980	91	100.0	44.5	33.2	13.6	8.6
1981	N.A.	N.A.	N.A.	N.A.	N.A.	N.A.
1982	115	100.0	40.9	29.0	15.0	15.0
1983	107	100.0	39.3	31.4	15.0	14.4
1984	94	100.0	48.7	29.7	11.5	10.2
1985	83	100.0	52.5	30.4	8.9	8.2
1986	77	100.0	55.1	29.3	9.0	6.6
1987	68	100.0	57.7	30.0	8.1	4.2
1988	65	100.0	58.1	31.0	6.6	4.3
1989	61	100.0	66.3	23.7	5.9	4.1
1990	59	100.0	63.4	27.2	7.4	2.0
1991	68	100.0	60.4	28.9	7.7	3.0
1992	60	100.0	53.4	33.9	8.6	4.1
1993	51	100.0	59.9	29.6	7.7	2.7
White						
1978	218	100.0	48.6	32.7	11.2	7.6
1979	247	100.0	47.1	32.3	13.1	7.5
1980	422	100.0	33.9	31.4	17.3	17.5
1981	N.A.	N.A.	N.A.	N.A.	N.A.	N.A.
1982	504	100.0	30.7	29.7	16.7	22.8
1983	463	100.0	28.9	24.8	15.1	31.3
1984	348	100.0	38.7	27.5	12.6	21.2
1985	292	100.0	40.1	29.5	12.4	18.1
1986	271	100.0	40.6	30.3	12.2	16.8
1987	256	100.0	45.0	27.2	12.5	15.3

Table IV-26. Unemployment Duration in Michigan by Sex, Age, and Race: Percent Distribution, 1978-1993 Continued

Year/ Category	Total Unemployed		Duration of Unemployment (Percent(%) of Total)			
	Number (In Thousands)	Percent(%)	Less Than 5 Weeks	5 to 14 Weeks	15 to 26 Weeks	27 Weeks and Over
White - Cont.						
1988	256	100.0	43.3	27.3	13.9	15.5
1989	232	100.0	47.5	29.0	11.4	12.1
1990	253	100.0	47.1	31.0	12.4	9.5
1991	300	100.0	41.4	32.9	13.3	12.4
1992	305	100.0	35.2	30.2	14.3	20.3
1993	244	100.0	38.0	30.2	14.4	17.4
Black						
1978	72	100.0	42.9	31.4	11.6	14.1
1979	88	100.0	42.1	25.8	14.5	17.6
1980	119	100.0	34.3	28.5	13.1	24.2
1981	N.A.	N.A.	N.A.	N.A.	N.A.	N.A.
1982	146	100.0	30.3	21.7	13.5	34.5
1983	134	100.0	26.2	22.4	13.3	38.0
1984	132	100.0	30.8	22.6	8.5	38.2
1985	134	100.0	28.9	27.4	12.3	31.3
1986	106	100.0	38.5	25.8	10.3	25.4
1987	107	100.0	32.8	34.0	13.7	19.5
1988	85	100.0	35.4	32.4	13.8	18.3
1989	86	100.0	48.0	29.4	10.5	12.2
1990	84	100.0	53.8	28.7	7.8	9.7
1991	110	100.0	49.0	28.2	10.6	12.2
1992	91	100.0	47.6	27.6	8.6	16.2
1993	77	100.0	48.1	28.7	9.0	14.2

N.A. data not available.
Source: Michigan Employment Security Commission, Research and Statistics (Detroit, Michigan: annually).

Table IV-27. Occupational Attachment of the Civilian Labor Force in Michigan, by Race, Gender, and Equal Employment Opportunity (E.E.O.) Category: April 1990

E.E.O. Category	Total	Female	White	Total Minority	Black	Native American	Asian and Pacific Is.	Other	Hispanic
Total, All Occupations	**4,540,537**	**2,066,633**	**3,863,877**	**676,660**	**521,331**	**26,152**	**45,867**	**1,501**	**81,809**
	100.0%	45.5%	85.1%	14.9%	11.5%	0.6%	1.0%	0.0%	1.8%
Officials and Managers	475,385	198,095	427,776	47,609	35,114	1,964	5,013	102	5,416
	100.0%	41.7%	90.0%	10.0%	7.4%	0.4%	1.1%	0.0%	1.1%
Professionals	579,288	302,931	507,349	71,939	48,457	1,603	14,698	142	7,039
	100.0%	52.3%	87.6%	12.4%	8.4%	0.3%	2.5%	0.0%	1.2%
Technicians	155,710	74,686	135,555	20,155	13,948	492	3,559	92	2,064
	100.0%	48.0%	87.1%	12.9%	9.0%	0.3%	2.3%	0.1%	1.3%
Sales Workers	508,861	264,903	453,050	55,811	42,818	2,234	3,831	171	6,757
	100.0%	52.1%	89.0%	11.0%	8.4%	0.4%	0.8%	0.0%	1.3%
Clerical and Office Workers	692,221	548,012	585,202	107,019	89,021	3,387	4,200	197	10,214
	100.0%	79.2%	84.5%	15.5%	12.9%	0.5%	0.6%	0.0%	1.5%
Craft Workers	548,785	45,871	495,705	53,080	37,752	3,564	2,238	139	9,387
	100.0%	8.4%	90.3%	9.7%	6.9%	0.6%	0.4%	0.0%	1.7%
Operatives	622,470	160,951	506,724	115,746	90,494	4,711	4,317	193	16,031
	100.0%	25.9%	81.4%	18.6%	14.5%	0.8%	0.7%	0.0%	2.6%
Laborers	195,054	42,795	159,200	35,854	27,159	1,602	1,077	50	5,966
	100.0%	21.9%	81.6%	18.4%	13.9%	0.8%	0.6%	0.0%	3.1%
Service Workers	634,273	385,206	500,368	133,905	107,828	5,306	6,204	350	14,217
	100.0%	60.7%	78.9%	21.1%	17.0%	0.8%	1.0%	0.1%	2.2%
No E.E.O. Category	128,490	43,183	92,948	35,542	28,740	1,289	730	65	4,718

Note: Hispanics are included in total minority, but not in racial groups.
Source: U.S. Bureau of the Census (Washington, D.C.: special release).

Table IV-28. Commuting Patterns in Michigan, by County: 1990

County	Lives and Works in the Same County	Commutes TO a Different County to Work	Commutes FROM a Different County of Residence	Net In-Commuting*
Alcona	1,595	1,605	743	-862
Alger	2,472	1,064	1,292	228
Allegan	19,562	20,190	9,142	-11,048
Alpena	10,794	1,000	1,535	535
Antrim	4,131	2,810	1,304	-1,506
Arenac	3,035	2,169	1,290	-879
Baraga	2,245	748	838	90
Barry	8,416	12,927	2,212	-10,715
Bay	30,309	15,924	6,429	-9,495
Benzie	2,855	1,935	851	-1,084
Berrien	58,815	10,712	10,093	-619
Branch	11,492	5,262	2,370	-2,892
Calhoun	48,904	7,299	12,351	5,052
Cass	8,599	13,202	3,470	-9,732
Charlevoix	7,221	2,113	1,893	-220
Cheboygan	5,621	3,033	3,352	319
Chippewa	11,282	725	1,021	296
Clare	5,152	2,744	2,521	-223
Clinton	7,480	21,254	5,515	-15,739
Crawford	3,278	1,768	8,984	7,216
Delta	12,625	1,503	991	-512
Dickinson	9,714	1,364	4,106	2,742
Eaton	18,336	26,975	15,468	-11,507
Emmet	10,013	1,180	3,041	1,861
Genesee	151,269	20,945	27,234	6,289
Gladwin	3,739	3,752	2,141	-1,611
Gogebic	4,910	1,620	1,022	-598
Grand Traverse	26,742	2,622	8,632	6,010
Gratiot	11,025	4,519	3,345	-1,174
Hillsdale	12,042	5,576	2,638	-2,938
Houghton	11,361	1,155	1,203	48
Huron	10,864	1,645	1,394	-251
Ingham	112,331	20,502	56,428	35,926
Ionia	11,246	10,804	4,548	-6,256
Iosco	10,787	925	1,934	1,009
Iron	3,696	793	510	-283
Isabella	17,823	4,892	4,799	-93
Jackson	49,195	14,450	11,111	-3,339
Kalamazoo	94,584	11,732	21,886	10,154
Kalkaska	2,990	2,055	1,255	-800
Kent	218,372	18,138	56,029	37,891
Keweenaw	198	383	176	-207

Table IV-28. Commuting Patterns in Michigan, by County: 1990 Continued

County	Lives and Works in the Same County	Commutes TO a Different County to Work	Commutes FROM a Different County of Residence	Net In-Commuting*
Lake	1,128	1,321	658	-663
Lapeer	14,468	17,294	5,710	-11,584
Leelanau	3,133	4,044	1,419	-2,625
Lenawee	27,872	11,678	6,046	-5,632
Livingston	23,031	32,991	10,040	-22,951
Luce	1,826	5,950	15,395	9,445
Mackinac	2,823	1,137	1,089	-48
Macomb	201,469	144,161	105,598	-38,563
Manistee	6,100	1,470	1,005	-465
Marquette	29,163	1,473	1,440	-33
Mason	8,376	1,250	1,138	-112
Mecosta	10,149	3,775	2,420	-1,355
Menominee	6,718	3,536	2,268	-1,268
Midland	25,708	7,219	10,657	3,438
Missaukee	2,038	2,500	965	-1,535
Monroe	30,101	28,309	8,474	-19,835
Montcalm	12,766	6,524	5,386	-1,138
Montmorency	1,909	826	998	172
Muskegon	51,154	11,309	8,729	-2,580
Newaygo	7,890	6,406	2,318	-4,088
Oakland	365,902	169,067	224,337	55,270
Oceana	4,701	3,836	1,015	-2,821
Ogemaw	4,559	1,170	1,271	101
Ontonagon	2,880	397	759	362
Osceola	4,514	2,575	1,660	-915
Oscoda	1,658	787	260	-527
Otsego	6,832	834	1,666	832
Ottawa	57,732	33,895	25,060	-8,835
Presque Isle	3,387	3,619	8,917	5,298
Roscommon	4,217	1,563	1,195	-368
Saginaw	71,069	12,559	21,476	8,917
St. Clair	40,189	21,305	4,940	-16,365
St. Joseph	18,154	6,733	3,840	-2,893
Sanilac	9,990	4,707	3,654	-1,053
Schoolcraft	2,195	612	271	-341
Shiawassee	15,667	14,430	3,563	-10,867
Tuscola	10,965	10,552	2,758	-7,794
Van Buren	15,286	12,800	4,786	-8,014
Washtenaw	117,815	26,148	57,535	31,387
Wayne	623,455	189,333	223,779	34,446
Wexford	8,453	1,467	3,704	2,237

Source: Southeast Michigan Council of Governments (Detroit, Michigan: special tabulation from 1990 census). * A negative sign indicates outcommuters exceed in commuters.

Table IV-29. Michigan Employment Security Commission Job Service Statistics: July 1984-June 1985 through July 1993-June 1994

Time Period	New Applicants	Job Openings	Referrals	Placements
July 1984 - June 1985	466,114	219,848	218,975	128,143
July 1985 - June 1986	399,127	136,723	219,848	126,980
July 1986 - June 1987	376,412	140,055	208,631	117,371
July 1987 - June 1988	368,147	181,715	218,305	116,708
July 1988 - June 1989	371,524	157,952	204,986	106,439
July 1989 - June 1990	430,021	160,867	223,320	103,630
July 1990 - June 1991	450,276	126,726	180,888	84,201
July 1991 - June 1992	449,876	129,158	184,162	85,011
July 1992 - June 1993	428,819	154,866	215,262	89,391
July 1993 - June 1994	401,442	155,723	263,841	102,478

Source: Michigan Employment Security Commission, Research and Statistics (Detroit, Michigan: annually).

The system used to develop the employment projections is generally referred to as the Occupational Employment Statistics (OES) Matrix system. This system is a methodology used nationally by all states to develop employment forecasts. The system can be separated into two major components: (1) Industry projections; and (2) The occupation by industry distribution, or "matrix," which transforms the industry employment figures into occupational employment. Projections were developed for nearly 350 three-digit Standard Industrial Code (SIC) industries. The industry projections serve as inputs for the industry/occupation matrix. The matrix consists of industry staffing patterns for each of the 350 industries and serves as the basis for converting the industry estimates into occupational terms. Information is available for up to 500 detail occupational cells for each industry.

In broad terms, the projections of industry employment were developed by analyzing the impact on employment of the major variables determining Michigan's economic climate. More specifically, industry forecasts were developed using an econometric forecasting methodology. The manufacturing sector of the model is based on the relationships between manufacturing output and employment. The employment projections, therefore, reflect assumptions about future U.S. output trends by industry. Since more than half of the state's manufacturing work force works directly for the motor vehicle producers or for supplier industries, special attention is focused on this sector in developing the forecasts. The key factors that are considered are the outlook for vehicle sales, foreign imports, productivity, and the impact of auto industry output on the supplier industries.

The private nonmanufacturing and government components of the model are based on the assumption that total local economic activity is the primary direct stimulus to employment in these sectors. For modeling purposes, total wage and salary employment is used as the gauge of local activity. In the model, employment in local market oriented industries is broadly influenced by activity in all industries. Two important variables in the total employment forecast are population and labor force participation.

The matrix process essentially consists of distributing industry employment on the basis of each industry's occupational staffing patterns. The staffing patterns are based on the Occupational Employment Statistics (OES) survey of employers conducted by the MESC. Approximately 30,000 Michigan employers are surveyed over a three year cycle. The base year (1992) matrix is adjusted for technological effects, changes in workplace organization and other staffing trends to arrive at a projected year (2005) matrix. The estimates for both 1992 and 2005 were extensively reviewed and adjustments made where necessary based on analyst judgment.

CHAPTER V
EMPLOYMENT PROJECTIONS

LIST OF TABLES

Table   **Page**

V-1. Occupational Employment Projections for Michigan, by Broad Group: 1992-2005 209

V-2. Industry Employment Projections for Michigan, by Broad Group: 1992-2005 . . . 209

V-3. Detailed Industry Employment Projections for Michigan: 1992-2005 210

V-4. Detailed Occupational Employment Projections for Michigan: 1992-2005 213

Table V-1. Occupational Employment Projections for Michigan, by Broad Group: 1992-2005

Occupational Title	Employment		Change		Average Annual Openings
	1992	2005	Level	Rate (%)	
TOTAL, ALL OCCUPATIONS	**4,319,075**	**4,966,175**	**647,100**	**15**	**147,685**
Executive/Managerial	441,550	522,700	81,150	18	13,530
Professional/Paraprofess/Technical	755,850	955,050	199,200	26	28,405
Marketing & Sales	441,125	507,150	66,025	15	1,330
Administrative Support/Clerical	753,150	805,950	52,800	7	20,400
Service	690,875	839,350	148,475	21	3,011
Agriculture/Forestry/Fishing	110,900	105,475	-5,425	-5	2,595
Precision Production/Craft/Repair	465,650	515,900	50,250	11	15,660
Operators/Fabricators/Laborers	660,000	714,600	54,600	8	20,585

Source: Michigan Employment Security Commission, Research and Statistics (Detroit, Michigan: special release).

Table V-2. Industry Employment Projections for Michigan, by Broad Group: 1992-2005

Industry	Employment		Change	
	1992	2005	Level	Percent(%)
TOTAL, WAGE & SALARY EMPLOYMENT	**3,926,300**	**4,593,200**	**666.9**	**17.0**
Goods Producing	1,036,000	1,098,800	62.8	6.1
Mining	8,800	8,7000	-200.0	-1.7
Construction	127,700	151,100	23.3	18.3
Manufacturing	899,600	939,200	39.6	4.4
Durable Goods	669,100	678,700	9.6	1.4
Motor Vehicles	270,604	254,000	-16,600	-6.0
Non-Durable Goods	230,500	260,500	30.0	13.0
Private Service Producing	2,252,000	2,811,300	559.3	24.8
Transportation/Communication/Utilities	153,800	161,900	8.1	5.3
Wholesale Trade	200,400	226,500	26.1	13.0
Retail Trade	730,200	858,600	128.5	17.6
Finance/Insurance/Real Estate	189,700	219,900	30.3	16.0
Services	978,200	1,344,200	366.0	37.4
Government	638,200	683,500	45.3	7.1

Source: Michigan Employment Security Commission, Research and Statistics (Detroit, Michigan: special release).

Table V-3. Detailed Industry Employment Projections for Michigan: 1992-2005

Industry	SIC Code	Employment (Data in Thousands)		Employment Change	
		1992	2005	Level	Percent(%)
Total, Wage & Salary Employment		3,926.3	4,593.2	666.9	17.0
Goods Producing		1,036.0	1,098.8	62.8	6.1
Mining		8.8	8.7	-0.2	-1.7
Metal Mining	10	3.2	3.3	0	0.4
Oil and Gas Extraction	13	3.1	2.8	-0.3	-10.2
Nonmetallic Minerals, Except Fuels	14	2.6	2.8	0.2	5.7
Construction		127.7	151.1	23.3	18.3
General Building Contractors	15	30.2	34	3.7	12.3
General Contractors, Exc. Bldg.	16	11.5	14.6	3	26.3
Special Trade Contractors	17	86.1	102.7	16.6	19.3
Manufacturing		899.6	939.2	39.6	4.4
Durable Goods		669.1	678.7	9.6	1.4
Lumber and Wood Products	24	14.7	15.6	0.9	6.3
Furniture and Fixtures	25	33.8	38.6	4.8	14.2
Stone, Clay, and Glass	32	16.5	17	0.5	2.9
Primary Metal Industries	33	37.1	34.4	-2.7	-7.2
Fabricated Metal Products	34	113.1	123.2	10.1	9.0
Industrial Machinery and Equipment	35	116.2	124.6	8.3	7.1
Electronic & Other Electrical Equip	36	29.4	32.1	2.7	9.1
Transportation Equipment	37	284	266.1	-17.9	-6.3
Instruments and Related Products	38	17.3	19.3	2	11.3
Misc. Manufacturing Industries	39	7.5	8.5	0.9	12.0
Non-Durable Goods		230.5	260.5	30	13.0
Food and Kindred Products	20	44.9	46.4	1.5	3.3
Textile Mill Products	22	1.6	1.7	0.1	7.9
Apparel and Textile Products	23	16.4	16.5	0.1	0.6
Paper and Allied Products	26	21.1	23	1.9	8.9
Printing and Publishing	27	44.9	48.5	3.6	7.9
Chemicals and Allied Products	28	44.9	49.1	4.1	9.1
Petroleum and Coal Products	29	2.1	1.8	-0.3	-14.8
Rubber and Misc Plastics Products	30	51.8	70.3	18.4	35.5
Leather and Leather Products	31	3.1	3.7	0.6	19.4

Table V-3. Detailed Industry Employment Projections for Michigan: 1992-2005 Continued

Industry	SIC Code	Employment (Data in Thousands)		Employment Change	
		1992	2005	Level	Percent(%)
Private Service Producing		**2252**	**2811.3**	**559.3**	**24.8**
Transportation/Communication/Utilities		**153.8**	**161.9**	**8.1**	**5.3**
Railroad Transportation	40	7.1	6.6	-0.5	-7.1
Local & Suburban Passenger Transpor	41	6.3	7.2	0.9	14.0
Trucking and Warehousing	42	45.3	50.1	4.8	10.6
Water Transportation	44	1.9	2.1	0.3	15.4
Transportation by Air	45	16.6	19.4	2.8	16.7
Pipe Lines, Except Natural Gas	46	0.3	0.3	0	-10.7
Transportation Services	47	11.1	15.3	4.1	37.2
Communications	48	32.2	28.2	-4	-12.3
Utilities and Sanitary Services	49	33.5	33.3	-0.3	-0.8
Wholesale Trade		**200.4**	**226.5**	**26.1**	**13.0**
Wholesale Trade, Durable Goods	50	128.2	144	15.8	12.3
Wholesale Trade, Nondurable Goods	51	72.2	82.6	10.3	14.3
Retail Trade		**730.2**	**858.6**	**128.5**	**17.6**
Building Materials & Garden Supplies	52	30.8	34.4	3.6	11.8
General Merchandise Stores	53	117.2	136.3	19.1	16.3
Food Stores	54	99.5	115.4	15.9	16.0
Auto Dealers and Service Stations	55	75	80	4.9	6.6
Apparel and Accessories Stores	56	38.3	43.5	5.2	13.6
Furniture & Homefurnishings Stores	57	27.8	31.2	3.4	12.1
Eating and Drinking Places	58	256.5	322.6	66.1	25.8
Miscellaneous Retail Stores	59	85.5	95.8	10.3	12.0
Finance/Insurance/Real Estate		**189.7**	**219.9**	**30.3**	**16.0**
Depository Institutions	60	70	74.1	4.1	5.8
Nondepository Institutions	61	11.6	14.6	2.9	25.1
Security and Commodity Brokers	62	6.1	7.6	1.5	24.5
Insurance Carriers	63	41.9	48.6	6.7	16.0
Insurance Agents, Brokers, & Services	64	19.9	26.1	6.2	31.0
Real Estate	65	34.2	39.5	5.3	15.5
Holding & Other Investment Offices	67	6.2	9.9	3.6	58.1

Table V-3. Detailed Industry Employment Projections for Michigan: 1992-2005 Continued

Industry	SIC Code	Employment (Data in Thousands)		Employment Change	
		1992	2005	Level	Percent(%)
Services		**978.2**	**1,344.2**	**366**	**37.4**
Hotels and Other Lodging Places	70	33.6	38.6	5	15.0
Personal Services	72	40.4	48.9	8.5	21.1
Business Services	73	191.3	302.3	111.1	58.1
Auto Repair Services and Parking	75	32.1	40.7	8.6	26.8
Miscellaneous Repair Services	76	12.5	15.1	2.6	21.3
Motion Pictures	78	12.3	15.2	3	24.3
Amusement and Recreation Services	79	36.6	49.1	12.4	34.0
Health Services	80	321.8	423.4	101.6	31.6
Legal Services	81	25.7	29.7	3.9	15.3
Educational Services	82	35.2	43.1	7.9	22.4
Social Services	83	68.4	117.4	48.9	71.5
Museums, Botanical, Zoological Garden	84	1.8	2.2	0.4	24.3
Membership Organizations	86	66	76.4	10.4	15.8
Engineering and Management Services	87	81.8	118.1	36.3	44.3
Services, Not Elsewhere Classified	89	1.6	2	0.3	19.9
Agricultural Services	**7**	**17.9**	**23**	**5.1**	**28.4**
Government		**638.2**	**683.5**	**45.3**	**7.1**
Federal	91	58.2	57.7	-0.5	-0.9
State	92	163	178.8	15.8	9.7
Local	93	417	447	30	7.2

Source: Michigan Employment Security Commission, Research and Statistics (Detroit, Michigan: special release).

Table V-4. Detailed Occupational Employment Projections for Michigan: 1992-2005

Occupation	Employment		Employment Change	
	1992	2005	Level	Percent(%)
Total, All Occupations	**4,319,075**	**4,966,175**	**647,100**	**15**
Executive, Admin, & Managerial Occ	**441,550**	**522,700**	**81,150**	**18**
Admin. Specialty Managers	74,700	92,075	17,375	23
Administrative Service Managers	6,200	6,875	675	11
Engineer., Math., Nat. Sci. Mgr.	10,850	14,950	4,100	38
Financial Managers	25,125	29,825	4,700	19
Marketing, Adv., Public Rel. Mgrs	14,775	19,275	4,500	30
Personnel, Training, Labor Rel. Mgr	7,500	9,750	2,250	30
Purchasing Managers	10,250	11,375	1,125	11
Line & Middle Management	59,575	72,775	13,200	22
Communication, Transp., Util. Mgrs	3,900	4,250	350	9
Construction Managers	5,125	7,075	1,950	38
Education Administrators	11,300	12,175	875	8
Food Service & Lodging Managers	21,625	29,000	7,375	34
Industrial Production Managers	10,725	11,900	1,175	11
Lawn Service Managers	550	725	175	32
Nursery & Greenhouse Managers	125	175	50	40
Property & Real Estate Managers	6,225	7,500	1,275	20
Other Managers & Administrators	184,550	205,125	20,575	11
General Managers and Top Exec.	106,200	115,050	8,850	8
Gvmt Chief Exec. & Legislators	2,650	2,500	-150	-6
All Other Managers & Administ.	75,725	87,575	11,850	16
Management Support Occupations	122,725	152,725	30,000	24
Accountants, Auditors, Fin. Spec	42,725	52,625	9,900	23
Accountants and Auditors	32,525	39,700	7,175	22
Budget Analysts	1,525	1,875	350	23
Credit Analysts	1,000	925	-75	-8
Loan Officers and Counselors	4,825	6,750	1,925	40
Underwriters	2,825	3,375	550	19
Purchasing Agents and Buyers	13,600	14,400	800	6
Purchasing Agent Ex.Who/Ret/Farm	9,250	9,725	475	5
Wholesale, Retail Buyers, ex. Farm	4,350	4,675	325	7

Table V-4. Detailed Occupational Employment Projections for Michigan: 1992-2005 Continued

Occupation	Employment		Employment Change	
	1992	2005	Level	Percent(%)
Personnel Specialists & Related	12,750	16,825	4,075	32
Employment Interviewers	2,775	3,425	650	23
Personnel, Train., Labor Rel. Spec	9,975	13,400	3,425	34
All Other Management Support Occ	53,675	68,875	15,200	28
Claims Examiners, Insurance	750	975	225	30
Construction, Building Inspector	2,350	2,875	525	22
Cost Estimators	7,575	9,325	1,750	23
Inspectors & Compliance Officers	2,550	3,150	600	24
Management Analysts	6,500	7,700	1,200	18
Tax Examiner, Collector, Rev. Agent	1,150	1,275	125	11
All Other Management Support Wks	32,750	43,600	10,850	33
Professional, Paraprofess., Tech.	**755,850**	**955,050**	**199,200**	**26**
Engineers & Related	99,575	123,475	23,900	24
Engineers	64,650	81,275	16,625	26
Aeronautical & Astro. Engineers	200	250	50	25
Chemical Engineers	1,375	1,675	300	22
Civil Engineers, Incl. Traffic	3,275	3,950	675	21
Electrical & Electronic Engineer	9,075	13,000	3,925	43
Industrial Engineers, Exc. Safety	7,475	8,000	525	7
Mechanical Engineers	31,200	39,000	7,800	25
Metallurgists and Rel. Engineers	1,150	1,500	350	30
Mining Engineers, Inc. Safety	25	25	0	0
Nuclear Engineers	150	100	-50	-33
Petroleum Engineers	125	125	0	0
All Other Engineers	10,575	13,625	3,050	29
Architects and Surveyors	5,150	6,025	875	17
Architects, Exc. Land. & Marine	1,600	1,600	0	0
Landscape Architects	925	1,225	300	32
Surveyors, Map Scientists & Tech	2,625	3,200	575	22
Engineering Technicians	29,775	36,150	6,375	21
Drafters	21,700	25,450	3,750	17
Electrical & Electronic Techn.	8,100	10,700	2,600	32

Table V-4. Detailed Occupational Employment Projections for Michigan: 1992-2005 Continued

Occupation	Employment		Employment Change	
	1992	2005	Level	Percent(%)
Natural Scientists & Related Occ	18,950	23,050	4,100	22
Physical Scientists	5,825	7,250	1,425	24
Atmospheric & Space Scientists	75	100	25	33
Chemists	3,575	4,400	825	23
Geologist, Geophysicist, Oceanog	775	975	200	26
Physicists and Astronomers	475	450	-25	-5
All Other Physical Scientists	900	1,300	400	44
Life Scientists	4,900	5,675	775	16
Agricultural and Food Scientists	675	700	25	4
Biological Scientists	2,100	2,525	425	20
Forester, Conservation Scientist	725	725	0	0
Medical Scientists	950	1,175	225	24
All Other Life Scientists	450	550	100	22
Phys & Life Science Technicians	8,225	10,125	1,900	23
Computer and Mathematical Occ.	44,325	76,575	32,250	73
Computer and Related Occupations	40,275	71,375	31,100	77
Computer Engineers & Scientists	6,050	13,975	7,925	131
Computer Programmers and Aides	17,325	21,525	4,200	24
Programmers: Numerical, Tool	375	450	75	20
Systems Analysts	16,500	35,400	18,900	115
Comp, Math Scient, & Op Res Anal	4,050	5,200	1,150	28
Actuaries	400	525	125	31
Mathematicians & Math Scientists	175	200	25	14
Operations and Research Analysts	2,025	3,225	1,200	59
Statisticians	1,475	1,275	-200	-14
Social Scientists, Recr., Religion	54,375	69,575	15,200	28
Social Scientists	10,100	11,700	1,600	16
Economists	1,075	1,450	375	35
Psychologists	5,150	6,275	1,125	22
Urban and Regional Planners	500	525	25	5
All Other Social Scientists	3,375	3,450	75	2

Table V-4. Detailed Occupational Employment Projections for Michigan: 1992-2005 Continued

Occupation	Employment		Employment Change	
	1992	2005	Level	Percent(%)
Social, Recreation, Religion Wks	44,275	57,900	13,625	31
Clergy	10,800	11,850	1,050	10
Directors, Religious Activ./Educ.	3,500	4,250	750	21
Human Services Workers	5,650	12,100	6,450	114
Recreation Workers	6,625	7,650	1,025	15
Social Workers	17,725	22,025	4,300	24
Law and Related Occupations	23,575	26,350	2,775	12
Lawyers and Judicial Workers	19,750	21,450	1,700	9
Judges, Magistrates, & Jud. Wks	2,125	2,600	475	22
Lawyers	17,625	18,850	1,225	7
Legal Assistants & Technicians	3,825	4,900	1,075	28
Paralegals	1,825	2,725	900	49
Title Examiners and Searchers	700	675	-25	-4
All Other Legal Assistants	1,300	1,500	200	15
Teachers, Librarians, Counselors	206,075	243,850	37,775	18
College and University Faculty	33,525	40,050	6,525	19
Teachers and Instructors	158,775	188,825	30,050	19
Farm & Home Management Advisors	75	75	0	0
Instructors, Nonvocational Educ.	6,350	7,100	750	12
Instructors and Coaches, Sports	10,025	12,475	2,450	24
Teachers, Elementary	45,500	47,750	2,250	5
Teachers, Secondary School	48,375	56,350	7,975	16
Teachers, Special Education	13,250	19,700	6,450	49
Teachers, Vocational Education	10,975	13,575	2,600	24
Teachers, Preschool & Kindergartn	9,625	12,950	3,325	35
All Other Teachers, Instructors	14,625	18,825	4,200	29
Librarians, Archivists & Rel Wks	13,775	14,950	1,175	9
Counselors	6,625	7,375	750	11
Curators, Archivists, Museum Tech.	450	525	75	17
Librarians, Professional	4,225	4,200	-25	-1
Technical Assistants, Library	2,500	2,850	350	14

Table V-4. Detailed Occupational Employment Projections for Michigan: 1992-2005 Continued

Occupation	Employment		Employment Change	
	1992	2005	Level	Percent(%)
Health Practitioners, Technicians	198,925	251,300	52,375	26
Health Treating Practitioners	35,400	43,400	8,000	23
Chiropractors	1,525	2,400	875	57
Dentists	7,675	8,200	525	7
Optometrists	1,375	1,500	125	9
Physicians	22,825	29,000	6,175	27
Podiatrists	600	600	0	0
Veterinarians, Vet. Inspectors	1,400	1,700	300	21
Therapists	11,500	16,575	5,075	44
Occupational Therapists	1,925	2,800	875	45
Physical Therapists	2,325	3,625	1,300	56
Recreational Therapists	800	1,200	400	50
Respiratory Therapists	2,850	3,775	925	32
Speech Pathologists, Audiologists	2,325	3,075	750	32
All Other Therapists	1,275	2,100	825	65
Health Assessment & Treatment	104,100	128,100	24,000	23
Dieticians and Nutritionists	1,475	1,675	200	14
Emergency Medical Technicians	3,575	4,475	900	25
Licensed Practical Nurses	23,775	25,500	1,725	7
Opticians, Dispensing & Measur.	2,600	3,300	700	27
Pharmacists	5,875	6,400	525	9
Physician Assistants	2,300	2,550	250	11
Registered Nurses	64,500	84,200	19,700	31
Health Technicians, Technologists	47,925	63,225	15,300	32
Cardiology Technologists	550	675	125	23
Clinical Lab Technol & Techn	10,100	12,450	2,350	23
Dental Hygienists	5,550	7,950	2,400	43
EEG Technologists	250	350	100	40
EKG Technicians	425	325	-100	-24
Medical Records Techn.	2,700	3,875	1,175	44
Nuclear Medicine Technologists	450	600	150	33
Psychiatric Technicians	2,300	2,750	450	20

Table V-4. Detailed Occupational Employment Projections for Michigan: 1992-2005 Continued

Occupation	Employment		Employment Change	
	1992	2005	Level	Percent(%)
Radiologic Technol. & Technician	5,675	8,025	2,350	41
Surgical Technicians	1,300	1,650	350	27
Veterinary Tech & Technologists	575	725	150	26
All Other Health Prof., Para, Tech	18,075	23,825	5,750	32
Writer, Artist, Enter., Athlete	50,350	59,325	8,975	18
Artists and Commercial Artists	8,050	8,700	650	8
Athlete, Coach, Umpire & Related	2,175	2,500	325	15
Broadcast Technicians	700	675	-25	-4
Camera Operators, TV & Movies	400	450	50	13
Dancers and Choreographers	50	50	0	0
Designers, Exc. Interior Design.	12,275	17,000	4,725	38
Interior Designers	2,650	2,900	250	9
Musicians	4,700	5,275	575	12
Photographers	3,275	3,350	75	2
Prod., Direct., Actors, Entertainer	1,225	1,600	375	31
Public Relations Specialists	3,675	4,075	400	11
Radio & TV Announcer & Newscast.	1,650	1,825	175	11
Reporters and Correspondents	1,975	2,175	200	10
Writers, Editors, Incl Technical	7,550	8,750	1,200	16
Engineering & Science Techs.	19,750	23,050	3,300	17
All Other Prof. Paraprof., Tech.	39,975	58,475	18,500	46
Air Traffic Controllers	550	625	75	14
Funeral Directors and Morticians	900	1,125	225	25
All Other Technicians	500	550	50	10
All Other Professional Workers	38,025	56,175	18,150	48
Marketing & Sales Occupations	**441,125**	**507,150**	**66,025**	**15**
First Line Supervisors - Sales	58,400	66,250	7,850	13
Sales Occupations, Services	49,875	55,475	5,600	11
Brokers, Real Estate	2,700	2,875	175	6
Insurance Sales Workers	19,475	20,400	925	5
Real Estate Appraisers	1,050	1,200	150	14
Sales Agents, Real Estate	19,300	20,850	1,550	8

Table V-4. Detailed Occupational Employment Projections for Michigan: 1992-2005 Continued

Occupation	Employment		Employment Change	
	1992	2005	Level	Percent(%)
Securities, Financial Serv. Sales	3,950	5,125	1,175	30
Travel Agents	3,375	5,050	1,675	50
Commodity Sales Occupations	332,850	385,425	52,575	16
Cashiers	104,200	145,000	40,800	39
Counter and Rental Rlerks	8,125	10,825	2,700	33
Salespersons, Retail	118,225	119,000	775	1
All Other Sales & Related Occ.	102,300	110,600	8,300	8
Admin. Support Occ., Clerical	**753,150**	**805,950**	**52,800**	**7**
First Line Supervisors, Clerical	38,100	44,650	6,550	17
Industry Specific Support Occ.	108,250	124,425	16,175	15
Banking, Security, Finance, Credit	39,975	42,275	2,300	6
Adjustment Clerks	10,750	13,625	2,875	27
Bank Tellers	20,075	18,000	-2,075	-10
Brokerage Clerks	1,150	1,350	200	17
Credit Authorizers	375	450	75	20
Credit Checkers	950	1,000	50	5
Loan and Credit Clerks	3,675	4,475	800	22
Loan Interviewers	500	625	125	25
New Accounts Clerks	2,075	2,350	275	13
Statement Clerks	425	350	-75	-18
Selected Insurance Workers	13,275	17,450	4,175	31
Insurance Adjusters, Investigator	3,925	5,800	1,875	48
Insurance Claims Clerks	3,850	5,225	1,375	36
Insurance Policy Process. Clerks	5,500	6,425	925	17
Investigative & Related Workers	11,350	12,950	1,600	14
Bill and Account Collectors	6,400	8,000	1,600	25
Welfare Eligibility Workers	4,950	4,950	0	0
Municipal Workers	3,400	3,500	100	3
Court Clerks	1,175	1,375	200	17
Municipal Clerks	750	800	50	7
All Other Adjust & Investigators	1,450	1,300	-150	-10

Table V-4. Detailed Occupational Employment Projections for Michigan: 1992-2005 Continued

Occupation	Employment		Employment Change	
	1992	2005	Level	Percent(%)
Lodging and Travel Workers	6,725	7,625	900	13
Hotel Desk Clerks	3,775	4,200	425	11
Res. & Ticket Agt., Travel Cons.	2,950	3,425	475	16
Other Industry Specific Workers	33,525	40,625	7,100	21
Advertising Clerks	800	975	175	22
Library Assistants & Bookmobile	5,425	6,000	575	11
Proofreaders and Copy Markers	700	700	0	0
Real Estate Clerks	325	425	100	31
Teacher Aides & Educ. Assistants	26,275	32,525	6,250	24
Secretarial & General Office Occ	377,850	395,400	17,550	5
Secretarial Workers	115,200	119,500	4,300	4
Legal Secretaries	8,525	10,475	1,950	23
Medical Secretaries	9,050	11,275	2,225	25
All Other Secretaries	97,625	97,775	150	0
General Office Occupations	262,650	275,875	13,225	5
Billing, Cost and Rate Clerks	11,400	12,350	950	8
Bookkeeping & Account & Auditing	59,450	58,525	-925	-2
Correspondence Clerks	625	675	50	8
Customer Service Reps, Utilities	2,975	3,350	375	13
File Clerks	7,700	8,875	1,175	15
General Office Clerks	91,250	94,000	2,750	3
Interviewing Clerks, ex. Personnel	3,600	4,250	650	18
Order Clerks: Materials, Service	9,450	9,650	200	2
Payroll and Timekeeping Clerks	5,225	5,175	-50	-1
Personnel Clerks, Except Payroll	3,375	4,225	850	25
Procurement Clerks	2,275	2,175	-100	-4
Receptionists, Information Clerk	30,925	44,000	13,075	42
Statistical Clerks	3,925	3,275	-650	-17
Stenographers	4,050	3,575	-475	-12
Typists and Word Processors	26,450	21,750	-4,700	-18

Table V-4. Detailed Occupational Employment Projections for Michigan: 1992-2005 Continued

Occupation	Employment		Employment Change	
	1992	2005	Level	Percent(%)
Elec Data Proc & Off Machine Occ	29,800	29,100	-700	-2
Bill, Post, Calculate Mach Oper.	2,900	1,875	-1,025	-35
Computer Operators, Exc. Periph.	7,750	5,500	-2,250	-29
Data Entry Keyers, Composing	550	350	-200	-36
Data Entry Keyers, Ex. Composing	12,900	15,950	3,050	24
Dupl., Mail, & Other Office Equ.	4,925	5,100	175	4
Peripheral EDP Equip. Operators	800	325	-475	-59
Communications, Mail, Distrib.	30,650	29,950	-700	-2
Communications Equip. Operators	9,550	6,700	-2,850	-30
Central Office Operators	1,175	575	-600	-51
Directory Assistance Operators	650	325	-325	-50
Switchboard Operators	7,500	5,625	-1,875	-25
All Other Communication Operator	225	175	-50	-22
Mail & Message Distrib. Worker	21,100	23,250	2,150	10
Mail Clerks, Exc. Mail Machine	3,675	4,350	675	18
Messengers	4,350	5,000	650	15
Postal Mail Carriers	11,425	12,175	750	7
Postal Service Clerks	1,650	1,725	75	5
Mat. Record., Sched., Dist. Occ.	136,875	151,175	14,300	10
Dispatcher: Exc. Pol.,Fire, amb.	4,525	5,375	850	19
Dispatcher: Police, Fire, Ambulance	2,525	2,675	150	6
Meter Readers, Utilities	1,125	975	-150	-13
Order Fillers, Sales	5,025	5,625	600	12
Production, Expediting Clerks	8,450	10,000	1,550	18
Stock Clerks	78,175	82,400	4,225	5
Traffic, Shipping, & Rec. Clerks	29,375	35,250	5,875	20
Weighers, Measurers, Checkers	3,350	3,875	525	16
All Other Material Workers	4,300	4,975	675	16
All Other Clerical Occupations	31,600	31,300	-300	-1

Table V-4. Detailed Occupational Employment Projections for Michigan: 1992-2005 Continued

Occupation	Employment		Employment Change	
	1992	2005	Level	Percent(%)
Service Occupations	**690,875**	**839,350**	**148,475**	**21**
First Line Supervisors, Service	9,200	10,250	1,050	11
Fire Fighting & Prev. Supervisors	1,125	1,200	75	7
Housekeepers Supv, Institutional	5,575	6,475	900	16
Police and Detective Supervisors	2,500	2,600	100	4
Private Household Occupations	28,500	22,000	-6,500	-23
Child Care Wkrs., Pvt. Household	11,425	8,475	-2,950	-26
Cleaners & Servants, Pvt. House.	15,000	11,575	-3,425	-23
Cooks, Private Household	450	400	-50	-11
Housekeepers and Butlers	1,650	1,550	-100	-6
Protective Service Occupations	74,700	91,100	16,400	22
Correction Officers and Jailers	5,975	9,000	3,025	51
Crossing Guards	1,950	2,125	175	9
Detectives and Investigators	1,400	2,000	600	43
Fire Fighters	10,925	11,625	700	6
Fire Inspection Occupations	825	850	25	3
Guards	24,650	35,075	10,425	42
Other Protective Service Workers	925	975	50	5
Police Detectives & Investigator	2,325	2,300	-25	-1
Police Patrol Officers	18,900	19,625	725	4
Sheriffs and Deputy Sheriffs	1,525	1,575	50	3
All Other Protective Service	5,325	5,950	625	12
Food & Beverage Service Occ.	290,075	346,475	56,400	19
Bakers, Bread and Pastry	6,875	9,300	2,425	35
Bartenders	15,100	12,700	-2,400	-16
Cooks, Fast Food and Short Order	37,675	55,000	17,325	46
Cooks, Institution or Cafeteria	11,425	11,975	550	5
Cooks, Restaurant	24,750	33,800	9,050	37
Dining Room & Bartender Helpers	14,925	15,000	75	1
Food Counter, Fountain & Related	47,300	51,925	4,625	10
Food Preparation Workers	49,925	65,250	15,325	31
Hosts & Hostesses: Rest., Lounge	8,950	13,200	4,250	47

Table V-4. Detailed Occupational Employment Projections for Michigan: 1992-2005 Continued

Occupation	Employment		Employment Change	
	1992	2005	Level	Percent(%)
Waiters and Waitresses	66,975	70,000	3,025	5
All Other Food Service Workers	6,150	8,350	2,200	36
Health Service Occupations	91,225	131,675	40,450	44
Ambulance Drivers & Attendants	275	300	25	9
Dental Assistants	8,200	11,550	3,350	41
Home Health Aides	12,150	30,175	18,025	148
Medical Assistants	8,425	11,850	3,425	41
Nursing Aides and Orderlies	47,475	54,000	6,525	14
Occupational Therapy Assistants	325	600	275	85
Pharmacy Assistants	2,725	3,400	675	25
Physical, Correct.Therapy Assist	1,675	2,675	1,000	60
Psychiatric Aides	1,350	1,700	350	26
All Other Health Service Workers	8,650	15,425	6,775	78
Clean & Bldg. Serv Occup ex. Priv	101,350	111,625	10,275	10
Janitor, Cleaners, Maids	92,500	101,550	9,050	10
Pest Controllers and Assistants	875	1,000	125	14
All Other Clean, Building Service	7,975	9,100	1,125	14
Selected Personal Serv Occ.	63,725	83,725	20,000	31
Amusement & Recreation Attendant	7,175	8,775	1,600	22
Baggage Porters and Bellhops	400	475	75	19
Barbers	1,125	1,100	-25	-2
Child Care Workers	22,100	28,450	6,350	29
Flight Attendants	2,575	2,900	325	13
Hairdressers and Cosmetologists	21,650	26,225	4,575	21
Manicurists	1,050	1,400	350	33
Personal Home Care Aides	5,775	12,125	6,350	110
Shampooers	200	225	25	13
Ushers, Lobby Att., Ticket Taker	1,675	2,050	375	22
All Other Service Occupations	32,125	42,475	10,350	32

223

Table V-4. Detailed Occupational Employment Projections for Michigan: 1992-2005 Continued

Occupation	Employment		Employment Change	
	1992	2005	Level	Percent(%)
Agriculture, Forestry, Fishing	**110,900**	**105,475**	**-5,425**	**-5**
Farm Operators and Managers	46,600	37,600	-9,000	-19
Farm Managers	1,275	1,300	25	2
Farmers	45,325	36,300	-9,025	-20
Supervisors, Farm, Forest, Ag. Rel	1,250	1,575	325	26
Forestry and Logging Occupations	1,950	2,175	225	12
Fallers and Buckers	725	775	50	7
Log Handling Equipment Operators	250	275	25	10
Logging Tractor Operators	750	900	150	20
All Other Timber Cutting Workers	225	225	0	0
Farm Workers	30,300	26,000	-4,300	-14
Fishing, Hunting, Trapping Occ.	225	225	0	0
Captains & Officers, Fish. Vessel	25	25	0	0
Fishers, Hunters, and Trappers	175	175	0	0
Other Agriculture & Forestry Occ	30,575	37,900	7,325	24
Animal Breeders	25	25	0	0
Animal Caretakers, Except Farm	2,300	2,950	650	28
Animal Trainers	50	75	25	50
Forest and Conservation Workers	700	775	75	11
Gardeners and Groundskeepers	350	400	50	14
Gardeners & Groundskeep, Excp Farm	17,200	19,900	2,700	16
General Farm Workers	100	150	50	50
Lawn Maintenance Workers	2,600	3,375	775	30
Nursery Workers	2,775	4,525	1,750	63
Pruners	1,050	1,375	325	31
Sprayers/Applicators	575	750	175	30
Veterinary Assistants	725	925	200	28
All Other Agric., Forest, Fish.	2,125	2,700	575	27
Prec. Prod, Craft, & Repr Occ	**465,650**	**515,900**	**50,250**	**11**
Blue Collar Worker Supervisors	59,575	66,000	6,425	11
Inspectors, Testers & Graders	26,900	28,200	1,300	5
Mechanics, Installers, Repairers	169,700	191,075	21,375	13

Table V-4. Detailed Occupational Employment Projections for Michigan: 1992-2005 Continued

Occupation	Employment		Employment Change	
	1992	**2005**	**Level**	**Percent(%)**
Mech., Install., Repairer, Wrkrs	65,025	77,525	12,500	19
Industrial Machinery Mechanics	15,250	15,725	475	3
Maintenance Repairers, Gen. Util.	42,275	54,000	11,725	28
Millwrights	7,525	7,800	275	4
Vehicle & Mobile Equip. Mechanic	51,825	57,800	5,975	12
Aircraft Engine Specialists	275	300	25	9
Aircraft Mechanics	1,800	1,925	125	7
Automotive Body, Related Repairer	7,750	9,000	1,250	16
Automotive Mechanics	27,000	29,425	2,425	9
Bus, Truck, Diesel Eng. Mechanic	9,375	10,900	1,525	16
Farm Equipment Mechanics	900	950	50	6
Mobile Heavy Equipment Mechanics	2,650	2,775	125	5
Motorcycle Repairers	300	300	0	0
Small Engine Specialists	1,800	2,200	400	22
Communications Equip. Mechanics	2,525	1,525	-1,000	-40
Central Office & PBX Instal/Rpr.	1,725	1,100	-625	-36
Frame Wirers, Central Office	250	50	-200	-80
Radio Mechanics	200	175	-25	-13
Signal or Track Switch Maint.	100	25	-75	-75
All Other Commun. Equip. Mechanics	250	175	-75	-30
Electrical & Electronic Eq.Mech.	16,675	16,450	-225	-1
Data Processing Equip. Repairers	2,725	3,675	950	35
Electrical Powerline Instal/Rpr.	3,025	3,075	50	2
Electronics Repairers, Comm. & Ind.	1,850	2,400	550	30
Elec.Home Entertainment Eq. Rpr.	1,425	1,200	-225	-16
Home Appli.& Power Tool Repairer	1,875	1,900	25	1
Station Install & Repair, Tele	975	475	-500	-51
Telephone & Cable TV Instal/Rpr.	3,675	2,550	-1,125	-31
All Oth.Elec&Electronic Eq.Mech	1,150	1,200	50	4
Other Mechanics,Installers,Rpr.	33,650	37,750	4,100	12
Bicycle Repairers	800	1,050	250	31
Camera & Photographic Repairers	200	225	25	13

Table V-4. Detailed Occupational Employment Projections for Michigan: 1992-2005 Continued

Occupation	Employment		Employment Change	
	1992	2005	Level	Percent(%)
Coin & Vending Machine Servicers	425	425	0	0
Electric Meter Installers/Repair	200	175	-25	-13
Electromedical & Biomed. Repair.	250	325	75	30
Elevator Installers & Repairers	600	650	50	8
Heating, A/C, Refrig. Mechanics	6,225	7,725	1,500	24
Locksmiths and Safe Repairers	450	550	100	22
Musical Instrument Repair & Tune	225	200	-25	-11
Office Machine, Register Servicer	1,650	1,750	100	6
Precision Instrument Repairers	1,575	1,750	175	11
Riggers	400	425	25	6
Tire Repairers and Changers	2,175	2,525	350	16
Watchmakers	300	200	-100	-33
All Other Mechanics, Installers	18,125	19,850	1,725	10
Const. Trades & Extractive Occ.	120,800	136,375	15,575	13
Construction Trades Workers	115,850	130,600	14,750	13
Bricklayers and Stone Masons	4,550	5,250	700	15
Carpenters	29,050	32,225	3,175	11
Carpet Installers	1,575	1,675	100	6
Ceiling Tile Installers	200	175	-25	-13
Concrete and Terrazzo Finishers	2,375	2,675	300	13
Drywall Installers & Finishers	1,850	2,325	475	26
Electricians	22,975	25,150	2,175	9
Glaziers	1,325	1,600	275	21
Hard Tile Setters	600	675	75	13
Highway Maintenance Workers	4,575	5,600	1,025	22
Insulation Workers	1,550	1,775	225	15
Painters and Paperhangers	11,200	13,075	1,875	17
Paving, Surfacing, Tamping	1,750	2,575	825	47
Pipelayers & Pipelaying Fitters	1,350	1,550	200	15
Plasterers	275	300	25	9
Plumber, Pipefitter, Steamfitter	11,275	11,725	450	4
Roofers	3,575	3,650	75	2

Table V-4. Detailed Occupational Employment Projections for Michigan: 1992-2005 Continued

Occupation	Employment		Employment Change	
	1992	2005	Level	Percent(%)
Sheet Metal Workers, Duct Install	9,925	11,600	1,675	17
Struct. & Reinforc. Metal Worker	1,925	2,150	225	12
All Other Construction Workers	3,925	4,825	900	23
Extractive and Blasting Workers	4,975	5,800	825	17
Mining Quarrying & Tunneling Occ	50	75	25	50
Roustabouts	275	200	-75	-27
All Other Extractive & Related	4,125	5,150	1,025	25
All Other Oil & Gas Extract Occ	500	375	-125	-25
Precision Production Occupations	88,650	94,275	5,625	6
Precision Metal Workers	52,725	55,400	2,675	5
Boilermakers	400	450	50	13
Jewelers and Silversmiths	825	1,000	175	21
Machinists	24,700	28,000	3,300	13
Shipfitters	25	25	0	0
Tool and Die Makers	21,175	20,150	-1,025	-5
All Other Precision Metal Worker	5,600	5,775	175	3
Precision Woodworkers	9,375	11,700	2,325	25
Cabinetmakers & Bench Carpenters	3,325	4,150	825	25
Furniture Finishers	1,550	1,875	325	21
Wood Machinists	1,850	2,500	650	35
All Other Precision Woodworkers	2,675	3,175	500	19
Textile, Apparel, Furnish, Precision	7,325	7,300	-25	0
Custom Tailors and Sewers	3,750	3,400	-350	-9
Patternmaker, Layout Workers, Fab	150	175	25	17
Shoe and Leather Workers	100	125	25	25
Upholsterers	1,900	2,150	250	13
All Other Precision Textile, Appa	1,400	1,475	75	5
Precision Printing Workers	4,850	5,475	625	13
Bookbinders	75	75	0	0
Camera Operators	425	450	25	6
Electronic Pagination Sys Oprts	575	950	375	65
Hand Compositors, Typesetters,	175	100	-75	-43

Table V-4. Detailed Occupational Employment Projections for Michigan: 1992-2005 Continued

Occupation	Employment		Employment Change	
	1992	2005	Level	Percent(%)
Job Printers	400	250	-150	-38
Paste-Up Workers	700	525	-175	-25
Photoengravers	300	350	50	17
Platemakers	550	550	0	0
Strippers, Printing	1,225	1,450	225	18
All Other Printing Workers, Prec	450	775	325	72
Precision Food Workers	8,275	7,675	-600	-7
Bakers, Manufacturing	675	775	100	15
Butchers and Meatcutters	6,550	5,675	-875	-13
All Other Precision Food,Tobacco	1,025	1,225	200	20
Other Precision Workers	6,100	6,725	625	10
Dental Laboratory Technicians	1,475	1,400	-75	-5
Optical Goods Workers	175	200	25	14
Photographic Process Workers	225	225	0	0
All Other Precision Workers	4,250	4,900	650	15
Operators, Fabricators, & Laborers	**660,000**	**714,600**	**54,600**	**8**
Mach. Setters Set-Up Oper, Tenders	205,925	201,975	-3,950	-2
Selected Mach. Set, Oper, Tenders	29,875	25,775	-4,100	-14
Drilling,Boring Mach.Set/Op.,M/P	4,775	4,300	-475	-10
Grinding Mach.Set/Op.M/P	5,550	5,075	-475	-9
Lathe,Turning Mach.Setter/Op,M/P	6,025	5,325	-700	-12
Machine Tool Cutting Oper., M/P	13,500	11,075	-2,425	-18
Machine Forming Setters/Oper M/P	31,450	29,050	-2,400	-8
Machine Forming Operators, M/P	13,225	10,850	-2,375	-18
Punching Mach. Setter/Oper., M/P	3,775	3,650	-125	-3
All Other Mach. Tool Cut & Form	14,450	14,550	100	1
Numerical & Comb. Mach Set, Op	14,075	18,075	4,000	28
Combin. Mach.Tool Set/Oper. M/P	9,575	12,525	2,950	31
Numerical Control Mach.Tool, M/P	4,500	5,550	1,050	23
Metal Fabricating Setters & Oper	9,850	9,200	-650	-7
Metal Fabricators, Structural Met	1,225	1,325	100	8
Soldering, Brazing Mach. Set/Ops	175	200	25	14

Table V-4. Detailed Occupational Employment Projections for Michigan: 1992-2005 Continued

Occupation	Employment		Employment Change	
	1992	2005	Level	Percent(%)
Welding Machine Set/Ops/Tenders	8,450	7,675	-775	-9
Metal & Plastic Process.Mach.Set	21,025	23,050	2,025	10
Electrolytic Plating Mach.Opers.	1,775	1,900	125	7
Foundry Mold Assembly/Shakeout	625	675	50	8
Furnace Operators and Tenders	875	900	25	3
Heat Treating, Tempering Mach.Op.	1,225	1,100	-125	-10
Heaters, Metal and Plastic	100	100	0	0
Heating Equip. Setter/Oper. M/P	550	500	-50	-9
Metal Molding Mach.Ops/Tend/Set	2,425	2,275	-150	-6
Nonelectrolytic Plating Mach.Opr	325	350	25	8
Plastic Molding, Casting Oper.	13,150	15,225	2,075	16
All Other Met.& Plas.Mach.Set/Ops	10,900	11,275	375	3
Woodworking Machine Setters, Op.	3,975	3,350	-625	-16
Head Sawyers & Saw Mach.Opr/Tend	1,650	1,350	-300	-18
Woodworking Machine Operators	2,350	2,000	-350	-15
Printing, Binding, & Related Occ	10,800	12,700	1,900	18
Bindery Mach. Operators/Set/Tend	2,500	2,800	300	12
Letterpress Setter/Operator	425	325	-100	-24
Offset Lithographic Press Setter	3,350	4,400	1,050	31
Photoengraving & Lithog. Oper.	175	200	25	14
Printing Press Mach.Ops/Set/Tend	1,750	1,925	175	10
Screen Printing Mach. Setter/Op.	475	725	250	53
Typesetting Mach. Operator/Tend.	650	525	-125	-19
All Other Printing, Binding, Rel	1,000	1,275	275	28
All Other Printing Press Set/Op.	450	500	50	11
Textile Mach. Operators & Related	13,575	15,325	1,750	13
Extruding Mach. Operator, Fibers	500	625	125	25
Laundry, Drycleaning Mach. Oper.	4,125	5,400	1,275	31
Pressing Mach. Operator, Textiles	1,450	1,725	275	19
Sewing Mach. Operator, Garment	1,500	1,550	50	3
Sewing Mach. Oper., Non-Garment	5,100	5,050	-50	-1
Shoe Sewing Machine Operator	250	275	25	10

Table V-4. Detailed Occupational Employment Projections for Michigan: 1992-2005 Continued

Occupation	Employment		Employment Change	
	1992	2005	Level	Percent(%)
Textile Machine Setter/Operator	200	225	25	13
Text.Drawout & Wind.Mach.Ops/Set	450	500	50	11
Other Mach. Set,Operators,Tender	60,400	54,150	-6,250	-10
Boiler Operator,Tender Low Press	725	700	-25	-3
Cementing & Gluing Machine Oper.	1,125	925	-200	-18
Chemical Equipment Tender	2,475	2,850	375	15
Cooking Machine Oper., Food/Tob.	675	825	150	22
Crushing & Mixing Machine Oper.	5,850	5,350	-500	-9
Cutting & Slicing Mach. Set/Ops	2,275	1,875	-400	-18
Dairy Processing Equip. Operator	200	275	75	38
Electronic Semiconductor	25	25	0	0
Extruding & Forming Mach.Set/Ops	4,025	4,725	700	17
Furnace, Kiln, Oven,Kettle Oper.	625	625	0	0
Motion Picture Projectionists	425	300	-125	-29
Packaging & Filling Machine Oper	8,225	6,800	-1,425	-17
Painters, Transportation Equip.	2,325	2,000	-325	-14
Painting Machine Operators	5,025	5,850	825	16
Paper Goods Machine Setter/Oper.	1,425	1,825	400	28
Photographic Processing Mach.Op.	1,225	1,400	175	14
Separating, Filtering Mach. Op.	450	350	-100	-22
All Other Machine Operators	23,300	17,475	-5,825	-25
Hand Working Occ., Inc.Assembler	140,400	151,075	10,675	8
Precision Assemblers	12,825	13,525	700	5
Aircraft Structure Assembly	100	75	-25	-25
Electrical, Electronic Assembler	2,275	2,325	50	2
Electromechanical Eq. Assembler	2,150	2,200	50	2
Fitters, Struc. Metal, Precision	425	500	75	18
Machine Builders, Assemblers	6,700	7,000	300	4
All Other Precision Assemblers	1,200	1,400	200	17
Other Hand Workers & Assemblers	127,575	137,550	9,975	8
Cannery Workers	2,675	2,850	175	7
Coil Winders, Tapers, Finishers	675	550	-125	-19

Table V-4. Detailed Occupational Employment Projections for Michigan: 1992-2005 Continued

Occupation	Employment		Employment Change	
	1992	2005	Level	Percent(%)
Cutters and Trimmers, Hand	2,025	2,475	450	22
Electrical, Electronic Assembler	5,000	5,725	725	15
Grinding and Polishing, Hand	3,800	4,075	275	7
Machine Assemblers	1,350	1,425	75	6
Meat, Poultry, Fish Cutters	875	1,150	275	31
Metal Pourers, Basic Shapes	525	525	0	0
Painting and Coating, Hand	1,500	2,225	725	48
Portable Machine Cutters	50	50	0	0
Pressers, Hand	350	350	0	0
Sewers, Hand	375	475	100	27
Solderers and Brazers	825	1,025	200	24
Welders and Cutters	14,075	15,900	1,825	13
All Other Assemblers, Fabricator	66,675	62,175	-4,500	-7
All Other Hand Workers	26,825	36,600	9,775	36
Plant & System Occupations	10,900	11,500	600	6
Chemical Plant and System Oper.	1,350	1,425	75	6
Gas & Petroleum Plant,System Occ	300	225	-75	-25
Power Distributors & Dispatchers	250	225	-25	-10
Power & Reactor Plant Operators	950	925	-25	-3
Stationary Engineers	725	725	0	0
Water & Waste Treat. Plant Oper.	3,925	4,200	275	7
All Other Plant and System Occ.	3,375	3,750	375	11
Transp. & Mat. Moving Mach.Oper.	155,800	172,500	16,700	11
Motor Vehicle Operators	100,800	115,725	14,925	15
Bus Drivers	4,175	4,225	50	1
Bus Drivers, School	13,625	15,300	1,675	12
Driver/Sales Workers	10,600	12,050	1,450	14
Taxi Drivers and Chauffeurs	2,825	3,400	575	20
Truck Drivers, Light & Heavy	68,425	79,250	10,825	16
All Other Motor Vehicle Operator	1,125	1,525	400	36
Rail Transportation Workers	2,400	2,600	200	8
Locomotive Engineers	400	400	0	0

Table V-4. Detailed Occupational Employment Projections for Michigan: 1992-2005 Continued

Occupation	Employment		Employment Change	
	1992	2005	Level	Percent(%)
Rail Yard Engineers, Dinkey Oper.	300	300	0	0
Railroad Brake, Signal, Switch	725	750	25	3
Railroad Conductors, Yardmasters	900	1,100	200	22
All Other Rail Vehicle Operators	75	50	-25	-33
Water Transportation & Related	225	300	75	33
Able Seamen, Marine Oilers	100	100	0	0
Captains and Pilots, Ship	100	125	25	25
Mates: Ship, Boat, and Barge	25	25	0	0
Ship Engineers	25	25	0	0
Aircraft Pilots, Flight Engineers	3,150	3,775	625	20
Other Transportation Workers	10,650	10,675	25	0
Parking Lot Attendants	1,075	1,250	175	16
Service Station Attendants	7,375	6,950	-425	-6
All Other Transportation Workers	2,200	2,475	275	13
Material Moving Equipment Opers.	38,550	39,450	900	2
Crane and Tower Operators	2,175	2,475	300	14
Excavation Loading Machine Oper.	1,950	2,175	225	12
Grader, Dozer, Scraper Operators	2,075	2,450	375	18
Hoist and Winch Operators	300	325	25	8
Industrial Truck & Tractor Oper.	21,875	20,000	-1,875	-9
Operating Engineers	4,225	4,950	725	17
Other Material Moving Equip.Oper	5,950	7,075	1,125	19
Helpers, Laborers, and Hand Movers	146,975	177,550	30,575	21
Construction Trades Helpers	7,800	8,675	875	11
Machine Feeders and Offbearers	7,525	8,000	475	6
Freight & Material Movers, Hand	29,950	36,625	6,675	22
Refuse Collectors	3,700	3,900	200	5
Hand Packers and Packagers	21,725	25,375	3,650	17
Vehicle, Equipment Cleaners	10,575	12,750	2,175	21
All Other Helper, Laborer, Mover	65,725	82,200	16,475	25

Source: Michigan Employment Security Commission, Research and Statistics (Detroit, Michigan: special release).

The Bureau of Economic Analysis (BEA) prepares estimates of personal income for the nation, states, the District of Columbia, and counties. The BEA also makes estimates of Gross State Product which is a more inclusive concept of the economic activity that has taken place.

The BEA defines *Personal Income* as current income of residents of an area from all sources, after deduction of contributions for Social Security and similar government-mandated social insurance programs. The wages and salaries component of personal income is based largely on the administrative records of state agencies, such as the Michigan Employment Security Commission, that administer state unemployment compensation programs. Fringe benefits, self-employment income, rental income, interest and dividends received, and other personal income estimates are developed from a variety of other sources. Rental income includes imputed rent, the rental value of owner occupied housing. Interest income also has an imputed component, namely interest from private noninsured pension funds.

Personal income is estimated on a where received basis while wages and salaries are reported on a where earned basis. Therefore a residence adjustment is applied to the unemployment insurance data so that personal income figures are published on the basis of where recipients reside and not on where they work.

Per Capita Personal Income simply is total personal income divided by population.

Gross State Product is patterned after gross domestic product for the nation. The BEA bases these numbers on the state unemployment insurance data along with other sources.

BEA state and county income data are available electronically and are published in the <u>Survey of Current Business</u>. Local Area Personal Income contains more detailed county income accounts than those published in the Survey.

The Bureau of the Census also produces income data on a per capita basis (see Tables I-4 and I-5) as part of the decennial <u>Census of Population</u>. These are developed from reports of income received by households and do not, like the BEA personal income data, include imputed items nor the fringe benefits that are not actually received by households. Also, the Census data are subject to sampling error.

The Bureau of the Census produces annual income estimates for the nation based on its Current Population Survey. Some state data are developed from the CPS and published in <u>Current Population Reports, Series P-60</u>.

The Bureau of Labor Statistics is responsible for preparing Consumer Price Indices for the nation and for various urban areas. These indexes are derived by pricing a market basket of goods and services each month in each of the areas. The annual CPIs are averages of the twelve monthly figures. <u>Monthly Labor Review</u> is a source of national and metropolitan CPIs.

CHAPTER VI
INCOME / OUTPUT / PRICES

LIST OF TABLES

Table   **Page**

VI-1. Total and Per-Capita Personal Income in Michigan and the United States: 1929-1994 235

VI-2. Total Personal Income in Michigan, by County: 1992, and Percentage Change, 1991-1992 and 1982-1992 237

VI-3. Per-Capita Personal Income in Michigan, by County: 1992, and Percentage Change, 1991-1992 and 1982-1992 239

VI-4. Consumer Price Index for All Urban Consumers, Detroit Area and United States: 1950-1994 241

VI-5. Percentage Change in Consumer Price Index for All Urban Consumers, Detroit Area and United States: 1950-1994 243

VI-6. Purchasing Power of the Dollar, Detroit Area: 1950-1994 (Base Year: 1982-1984) 243

VI-7. Gross State Product in Michigan, by Industry: Current Dollar 1979-1992 244

VI-8. Gross State Product in Michigan, by Industry: Constant Dollar(1987) 1979-1992 247

Table VI-1. Total and Per-Capita Personal Income in Michigan and the United States: 1929-1994

Year	Total Personal Income (In Millions)			Per Capita Personal Income		
	Michigan	United States	Mich % U.S.	Michigan	United States	Mich % U.S.
1929	$3,770	$84,894	4.4	$786	$697	112.8
1930	3,165	76,173	4.2	655	619	105.8
1931	2,590	65,377	4.0	540	527	102.5
1932	1,888	50,050	3.8	395	401	98.5
1933	1,664	46,916	3.6	348	374	93.0
1934	2,173	53,648	4.1	453	425	106.6
1935	2,560	60,239	4.3	529	473	111.8
1936	3,017	68,405	4.4	617	534	115.5
1937	3,382	73,721	4.6	681	572	119.1
1938	2,874	67,918	4.2	568	523	108.6
1939	3,199	72,301	4.4	620	552	112.3
1940	3,586	77,739	4.6	675	589	114.6
1941	4,493	95,103	4.7	822	713	115.3
1942	5,780	121,496	4.8	1,041	902	115.4
1943	7,242	147,772	4.9	1,342	1,097	122.3
1944	7,529	158,959	4.7	1,379	1,186	116.3
1945	7,190	163,359	4.4	1,315	1,225	107.3
1946	7,743	175,411	4.4	1,318	1,247	105.7
1947	8,829	188,539	4.7	1,453	1,312	110.7
1948	9,550	207,582	4.6	1,537	1,421	108.2
1949	9,516	204,918	4.6	1,503	1,378	109.1
1950	10,811	225,684	4.8	1,687	1,492	113.1
1951	12,066	252,485	4.8	1,857	1,647	112.8
1952	12,908	268,983	4.8	1,941	1,728	112.3
1953	14,663	284,866	5.2	2,149	1,800	119.4
1954	14,257	286,953	5.0	2,018	1,781	113.3
1955	15,825	307,601	5.1	2,172	1,872	116.0
1956	16,472	329,933	5.0	2,206	1,972	111.9
1957	16,917	348,309	4.9	2,235	2,044	109.3
1958	16,602	358,913	4.7	2,165	2,061	105.0
1959	17,625	382,548	4.6	2,269	2,160	105.0
1960	18,328	398,843	4.6	2,339	2,216	105.6
1961	18,281	414,285	4.4	2,316	2,264	102.3
1962	19,560	440,023	4.5	2,466	2,369	104.1
1963	20,887	462,406	4.5	2,592	2,454	105.6
1964	22,904	495,188	4.6	2,798	2,592	107.9
1965	25,511	536,152	4.8	3,053	2,772	110.1
1966	27,844	582,630	4.8	3,271	2,980	109.8
1967	28,967	623,757	4.6	3,357	3,161	106.2
1968	32,010	683,561	4.7	3,681	3,430	107.3

Table VI-1. Total and Per-Capita Personal Income in Michigan and the United States: 1929-1994 Continued

Year	Total Personal Income (In Millions)			Per Capita Personal Income		
	Michigan	United States	Mich % U.S.	Michigan	United States	Mich % U.S.
1969	$35,620	$767,608	4.6	$4,057	$3,813	106.4
1970	36,713	824,823	4.5	4,127	4,047	102.0
1971	39,937	888,002	4.5	4,451	4,294	103.7
1972	44,312	974,938	4.5	4,910	4,659	105.4
1973	49,709	1,092,217	4.6	5,480	5,168	106.0
1974	53,197	1,200,575	4.4	5,840	5,628	103.8
1975	56,122	1,302,532	4.3	6,162	6,045	101.9
1976	63,523	1,442,221	4.4	6,967	6,629	105.1
1977	71,750	1,596,944	4.5	7,835	7,267	107.8
1978	80,100	1,802,663	4.4	8,705	8,117	107.2
1979	88,160	2,024,812	4.4	9,532	9,017	105.7
1980	93,977	2,259,006	4.2	10,154	9,940	102.2
1981	100,388	2,526,009	4.0	10,901	11,009	99.0
1982	101,882	2,683,456	3.8	11,177	11,583	96.5
1983	108,026	2,857,710	3.8	11,939	12,223	97.7
1984	119,335	3,144,363	3.8	13,186	13,332	98.9
1985	129,110	3,368,069	3.8	14,223	14,155	100.5
1986	137,887	3,579,783	3.9	15,104	14,906	101.3
1987	143,404	3,789,297	3.8	15,607	15,638	99.8
1988	152,142	4,061,806	3.7	16,502	16,610	99.3
1989	162,359	4,366,135	3.7	17,546	17,690	99.2
1990	169,808	4,655,420	3.6	18,237	18,666	97.7
1991	175,250	4,841,078	3.6	18,703	19,201	97.4
1992	184,702	5,135,452	3.6	19,707	20,137	97.7
1993	194,718	5,361,968	3.6	20,584	20,800	99.0
1994	212,080	5,677,780	3.7	22,333	21,809	102.4

Source: U.S. Department of Commerce, Economics & Statistics Administration, Bureau of Economic Analysis, Regional Economic Measurement Division, R.E.I.S. May 1994 Compact Disc (Washington, D.C.: annually).

Table VI-2. Total Personal Income in Michigan, by County: 1992, and Percentage Change, 1991-1992 and 1982-1992

County	Personal Income (In Thousands)	Percent(%) Change		County	Personal Income (In Thousands)	Percent(%) Change	
		1992-1991	1992-1982			1992-1991	1992-1982
Alcona	$143,065	4.6	79.5	Gogebic	$263,275	3.5	64.7
Alger	122,915	6.4	93.9	Grand Traverse	1,270,697	7.7	122.4
Allegan	1,604,998	7.2	106.7	Gratiot	609,741	6.0	67.1
Alpena	491,420	5.7	77.3	Hillsdale	669,789	8.5	80.8
Antrim	285,687	6.3	96.0	Houghton	494,740	3.6	69.2
Arenac	217,511	3.7	75.1	Huron	595,741	4.6	75.7
Baraga	106,274	3.7	69.5	Ingham	5,254,541	4.7	77.8
Barry	859,329	5.1	88.5	Ionia	808,329	4.9	83.4
Bay	2,011,227	5.0	64.0	Iosco	428,717	-0.7	78.3
Benzie	205,216	5.9	103.5	Iron	185,284	3.9	59.3
Berrien	2,836,260	6.2	69.8	Isabella	821,921	4.2	77.8
Branch	621,066	2.8	65.0	Jackson	2,523,189	5.0	63.6
Calhoun	2,475,355	6.3	70.8	Kalamazoo	4,628,287	5.3	93.7
Cass	782,534	7.1	70.3	Kalkaska	188,911	5.8	115.0
Charlevoix	373,795	5.9	110.2	Kent	10,249,088	5.7	103.7
Cheboygan	314,815	4.5	81.6	Keweenaw	27,425	4.7	86.6
Chippewa	445,143	6.9	94.5	Lake	110,160	7.1	97.7
Clare	340,983	6.9	83.3	Lapeer	1,332,632	2.8	90.3
Clinton	1,012,964	5.2	83.4	Leelanau	330,780	7.7	126.5
Crawford	161,468	5.8	121.8	Lenawee	1,621,958	6.0	79.7
Delta	601,801	6.0	67.5	Livingston	2,549,604	6.4	121.0
Dickinson	462,431	6.3	75.0	Luce	91,328	-7.4	60.4
Eaton	1,763,655	5.3	87.2	Mackinac	179,061	6.1	103.1
Emmet	515,911	4.9	120.1	Macomb	15,962,749	5.7	96.5
Genesee	7,893,104	2.5	59.0	Manistee	341,620	5.8	73.6
Gladwin	305,334	6.8	90.8	Marquette	1,127,086	4.9	78.9

Table VI-2. Total Personal Income in Michigan, by County: 1992, and Percentage Change, 1991-1992 and 1982-1992 Continued

County	Personal Income (In Thousands)	Percent(%) Change		County	Personal Income (In Thousands)	Percent(%) Change	
		1992-1991	1992-1982			1992-1991	1992-1982
Mason	$409,172	7.1	82.2	Tuscola	$867,326	4.3	67.4
Mecosta	476,954	6.8	97.7	Van Buren	1,096,833	6.2	85.4
Menominee	401,822	6.8	78.1	Washtenaw	6,747,480	5.7	93.5
Midland	1,747,709	7.4	97.8	Wayne	39,380,467	5.2	56.1
Missaukee	171,924	7.4	123.9	Wexford	405,277	8.3	97.9
Monroe	2,441,465	6.3	75.0	**Michigan**	**184,765,000**	**5.6**	**81.4**
Montcalm	737,576	7.8	66.1				
Montmorency	115,438	7.5	91.4				
Muskegon	2,541,620	5.4	67.0				
Newaygo	570,258	6.5	92.1				
Oakland	32,071,985	6.6	109.3				
Oceana	348,562	5.9	85.9				
Ogemaw	237,377	5.0	93.9				
Ontonagon	132,203	3.1	51.8				
Osceola	285,244	10.9	100.3				
Oscoda	93,779	6.2	88.5				
Otsego	298,689	6.8	117.3				
Ottawa	3,853,360	8.1	127.5				
Presque Isle	194,825	2.7	63.4				
Roscommon	297,010	5.8	103.1				
Saginaw	3,672,511	4.0	58.0				
St. Clair	2,700,621	5.4	83.8				
St. Joseph	968,909	7.4	82.5				
Sanilac	614,958	5.5	70.1				
Schoolcraft	121,472	2.4	67.6				
Shiawassee	1,140,803	4.1	65.0				

Source: U.S. Department of Commerce, Economics & Statistics Administration, Bureau of Economic Analysis, Regional Economic Measurement Division, R.E.I.S. May 1994 Compact Disc (Washington, D.C.: annually).

238

Table VI-3. Per-Capita Personal Income in Michigan, by County: 1992, and Percentage Change, 1991-1992 and 1982-1992

County	Per Capita Income	Percent(%) Change 1992-1991	Percent(%) Change 1992-1982	County	Per Capita Income	Percent(%) Change 1992-1991	Percent(%) Change 1992-1982
Alcona	$13,952	4.4	68.4	Gogebic	$14,715	3.8	80.7
Alger	13,147	5.5	89.4	Grand Traverse	18,884	5.3	84.5
Allegan	17,244	5.8	82.8	Gratiot	15,456	5.9	66.4
Alpena	15,852	5.2	81.1	Hillsdale	15,083	7.6	68.5
Antrim	15,118	4.8	71.2	Houghton	13,808	2.5	79.4
Arenac	13,921	2.1	64.7	Huron	17,032	4.8	80.0
Baraga	13,576	5.9	80.5	Ingham	18,646	4.8	71.9
Barry	16,785	3.7	68.7	Ionia	13,940	4.3	63.7
Bay	17,936	4.6	71.4	Iosco	14,191	1.4	70.2
Benzie	16,266	4.1	79.4	Iron	14,105	3.1	64.4
Berrien	17,566	6.1	72.5	Isabella	14,622	2.2	69.4
Branch	14,833	2.5	54.7	Jackson	16,628	4.6	59.7
Calhoun	17,888	5.6	70.8	Kalamazoo	20,511	4.6	84.4
Cass	15,934	7.5	67.8	Kalkaska	13,457	4.8	72.4
Charlevoix	16,819	4.4	85.5	Kent	20,018	4.9	80.3
Cheboygan	14,454	2.7	72.6	Keweenaw	16,076	3.0	112.1
Chippewa	12,490	5.8	63.1	Lake	12,201	4.7	75.3
Clare	12,924	4.7	64.6	Lapeer	16,971	0.7	67.3
Clinton	17,054	4.5	69.6	Leelanau	19,129	4.4	89.4
Crawford	12,447	3.0	67.9	Lenawee	17,231	5.2	68.7
Delta	15,751	5.7	72.6	Livingston	20,786	3.7	79.3
Dickinson	17,118	6.0	65.0	Luce	16,297	-5.2	76.1
Eaton	18,515	4.5	71.8	Mackinac	16,654	5.8	92.0
Emmet	19,799	3.4	95.7	Macomb	21,920	5.0	85.7
Genesee	18,208	2.3	61.6	Manistee	15,581	3.4	75.3
Gladwin	13,271	4.8	66.5	Marquette	15,779	4.5	83.3

Table VI-3. Per-Capita Personal Income in Michigan, by County: 1992, and Percentage Change, 1991-1992 and 1982-1992 Continued

County	Per Capita Income	Percent(%) Change	
		1992-1991	1992-1982
Mason	$15,487	5.1	81.3
Mecosta	12,371	6.2	87.4
Menominee	16,339	7.1	86.6
Midland	22,421	5.8	87.0
Missaukee	13,496	5.1	82.9
Monroe	17,957	5.6	68.4
Montcalm	13,303	6.3	44.0
Montmorency	12,340	4.8	52.6
Muskegon	15,691	4.6	59.2
Newaygo	13,992	2.7	65.6
Oakland	28,671	5.0	87.5
Oceana	15,185	5.2	75.0
Ogemaw	12,086	3.1	64.3
Ontonagon	15,090	4.1	75.5
Osceola	13,821	9.5	86.7
Oscoda	11,406	3.5	61.1
Otsego	15,641	4.0	73.4
Ottawa	19,531	6.1	84.4
Presque Isle	14,052	2.4	63.2
Roscommon	14,238	3.5	65.4
Saginaw	17,284	4.0	65.5
St. Clair	17,994	4.3	67.7
St. Joseph	16,315	6.9	74.2
Sanilac	15,069	4.2	64.8
Schoolcraft	14,328	-0.4	68.7
Shiawassee	16,106	3.4	61.0

County	Per Capita Income	Percent(%) Change	
		1992-1991	1992-1982
Tuscola	$15,452	3.5	65.1
Van Buren	15,164	4.7	70.0
Washtenaw	23,427	5.0	77.1
Wayne	18,787	5.5	67.5
Wexford	14,955	6.7	85.3
Michigan	19,586	4.9	75.2

Source: U.S. Department of Commerce, Economics & Statistics Administration, Bureau of Economic Analysis, Regional Economic Measurement Division, R.E.I.S. May 1994 Compact Disc (Washington, D.C.: annually).

Table VI-4. Consumer Price Index for All Urban Consumers, Detroit Area and United States: 1950-1994 (Base Year: 1982-1984)

Year	Detroit Consumer Price Index				United States Consumer Price Index			
	Total CPI	CPI for Food	CPI for Energy	CPI for Housing	Total CPI	CPI for Food	CPI for Energy	CPI for Housing
1950	24.6	---	---	---	24.1	---	---	---
1951	26.5	31.2	---	---	26.0	28.2	---	---
1952	27.1	31.6	---	---	26.5	28.7	---	---
1953	27.6	30.9	---	---	26.7	28.3	---	---
1954	27.7	30.9	---	---	26.9	28.2	---	---
1955	27.7	30.3	---	---	26.8	27.8	---	---
1956	28.2	30.6	---	---	27.2	28.0	---	---
1957	29.0	31.4	---	---	28.1	28.9	---	---
1958	29.4	32.4	---	---	28.9	30.2	21.5	---
1959	29.4	31.5	---	---	29.1	29.7	21.9	---
1960	29.7	31.8	---	---	29.6	30.0	22.4	---
1961	29.8	32.2	---	---	29.9	30.4	22.5	---
1962	29.9	32.1	---	---	30.2	30.6	22.6	---
1963	30.2	32.3	---	---	30.6	31.1	22.6	---
1964	30.4	32.4	---	---	31.0	31.5	22.5	---
1965	31.2	33.3	---	---	31.5	32.2	22.9	---
1966	32.5	35.6	---	---	32.4	33.8	23.3	---
1967	33.6	36.2	---	---	33.4	34.1	23.8	30.8
1968	35.1	37.4	---	---	34.8	35.3	24.2	32.0
1969	37.2	39.5	---	---	36.7	37.1	24.8	34.0
1970	39.5	41.7	---	---	38.8	39.2	25.5	36.4
1971	40.9	42.5	---	---	40.5	40.4	26.5	38.0
1972	42.5	44.5	---	---	41.8	42.1	27.2	39.4
1973	45.2	52.0	---	---	44.4	48.2	29.4	41.2
1974	50.1	59.5	---	---	49.3	55.1	38.1	45.8
1975	53.9	62.2	---	---	53.8	59.8	42.1	50.7
1976	56.8	63.6	---	52.3	56.9	61.6	45.1	53.8
1977	60.7	67.6	---	55.8	60.6	65.5	49.4	57.4

Table VI-4. Consumer Price Index for All Urban Consumers, Detroit Area and United States: 1950-1994 (Base Year: 1982-1984) Continued

Year	Detroit Consumer Price Index				United States Consumer Price Index			
	Total CPI	CPI for Food	CPI for Energy	CPI for Housing	Total CPI	CPI for Food	CPI for Energy	CPI for Housing
1978	65.3	74.5	52.6	60.3	65.2	72.0	52.5	62.4
1979	73.6	82.1	65.5	70.3	72.6	79.9	65.7	70.1
1980	85.3	88.9	83.8	85.5	82.4	86.8	86.0	81.1
1981	93.2	95.7	94.5	93.4	90.9	93.6	97.7	90.4
1982	97.0	99.4	96.3	96.3	96.5	97.4	99.2	96.9
1983	99.8	99.2	100.7	100.4	99.6	99.4	99.9	99.5
1984	103.2	101.4	103.0	103.3	103.9	103.2	100.9	103.6
1985	106.8	103.1	106.6	107.5	107.6	105.6	101.6	107.7
1986	108.3	107.1	93.1	109.8	109.6	109.0	88.2	110.9
1987	111.7	110.3	93.8	113.0	113.6	113.5	88.6	114.2
1988	116.1	114.4	92.6	116.1	118.3	118.2	89.3	118.5
1989	122.3	120.5	98.1	121.2	124.0	125.1	94.3	123.0
1990	128.6	126.3	103.5	126.4	130.7	132.4	102.1	128.5
1991	133.1	130.5	102.5	128.6	136.2	136.3	102.5	133.6
1992	135.9	132.9	102.4	131.8	140.3	137.9	103.0	137.5
1993	139.6	134.5	100.5	134.4	144.5	140.9	104.2	141.2
1994	144.0	137.8	100.4	137.6	148.2	144.3	104.6	144.8

--- No data.
Source: U.S. Bureau of Labor Statistics (Washington, D.C.: annually).

Table VI-5. Percentage Change in Consumer Price Index for All Urban Consumers, Detroit Area and United States: 1950-1994

Year	Percent(%) Change		Year	Percent(%) Change		Year	Percent(%) Change	
	Michigan	U. S.		Michigan	U. S.		Michigan	U. S.
1950	---	---	1965	2.6	1.6	1980	15.9	13.5
1951	7.7	7.9	1966	4.2	2.9	1981	9.3	10.3
1952	2.3	1.9	1967	3.4	3.1	1982	4.1	6.2
1953	1.8	0.8	1968	4.5	4.2	1983	2.9	3.2
1954	0.4	0.7	1969	6.0	5.5	1984	3.4	4.3
1955	0.0	-0.4	1970	6.2	5.7	1985	3.5	3.6
1956	1.8	1.5	1971	3.5	4.4	1986	1.4	1.9
1957	2.8	3.3	1972	3.9	3.2	1987	3.1	3.6
1958	1.4	2.8	1973	6.4	6.2	1988	3.9	4.1
1959	0.0	0.7	1974	10.8	11.0	1989	5.3	4.8
1960	1.0	1.7	1975	7.6	9.1	1990	5.2	5.4
1961	0.3	1.0	1976	5.4	5.8	1991	3.5	4.2
1962	0.3	1.0	1977	6.9	6.5	1992	2.1	3.0
1963	1.0	1.3	1978	7.6	7.6	1993	2.7	3.0
1964	0.7	1.3	1979	12.7	11.3	1994	3.2	2.6

Source: U.S. Bureau of Labor Statistics (Washington, D.C.: annually).

Table VI-6. Purchasing Power of the Dollar, Detroit Area: 1950-1994 (Base Year: 1982-1984)

Year	Value of Dollar	Year	Value of Dollar	Year	Value of Dollar	Year	Value of Dollar	Year	Value of Dollar
1950	4.07	1960	3.37	1970	2.53	1980	1.36	1990	0.78
1951	3.77	1961	3.36	1971	2.44	1981	1.17	1991	0.75
1952	3.69	1962	3.34	1972	2.35	1982	1.07	1992	0.74
1953	3.62	1963	3.31	1973	2.21	1983	1.03	1993	0.72
1954	3.61	1964	3.29	1974	2.00	1984	1.00	1994	0.69
1955	3.61	1965	3.21	1975	1.86	1985	0.97		
1956	3.55	1966	3.08	1976	1.76	1986	0.94		
1957	3.45	1967	2.98	1977	1.65	1987	0.92		
1958	3.40	1968	2.85	1978	1.53	1988	0.90		
1959	3.40	1969	2.69	1979	1.36	1989	0.86		

Source: Bureau of Labor Statistics data, Michigan Employment Security Commission special calculation (Detroit, Michigan).

Table VI-7. Gross State Product in Michigan, by Industry: Current Dollar 1979-1992
(Data in Millions of Dollars)

Industry	1979	1980	1981	1982	1983	1984	1985	1986	1987	1988	1989	1990	1991	1992
TOTAL GSP	105,322	103,081	112,703	111,128	123,683	139,998	152,336	160,294	167,001	176,091	184,636	187,160	191,113	204,421
Private Industries	95,113	91,840	101,068	98,910	110,848	126,455	137,900	144,703	150,678	158,592	165,962	166,922	169,786	181,818
Agricult/Forest/Fish	1,624	1,711	1,837	1,796	1,535	1,858	2,033	1,744	1,852	1,831	2,334	2,381	2,335	2,404
Farms	1,399	1,482	1,592	1,552	1,251	1,534	1,673	1,349	1,358	1,328	1,810	1,776	1,690	1,702
AgServ/Forest/Fish	225	229	245	244	284	324	361	395	494	503	524	604	644	702
Mining	887	1,207	1,568	1,325	1,208	1,276	1,129	881	1,011	1,193	1,116	1,237	1,071	989
Metal Mining	265	266	237	133	142	153	120	138	138	235	241	247	292	295
Coal Mining	1	1	1	0	0	0	0	0	0	0	0	0	0	0
Oil/Gas Extraction	495	813	1,220	1,109	963	974	860	551	663	721	634	763	557	467
NonMetalic Minerals	127	128	110	83	103	149	150	192	210	236	241	227	223	228
Construction	4,398	3,920	3,757	3,376	3,426	3,826	4,665	5,541	5,917	6,704	7,069	7,114	6,547	6,598
Manufacturing	38,783	32,874	37,856	34,860	41,372	49,406	53,521	53,683	52,414	54,727	53,576	51,360	50,384	55,704
Durable Goods	31,960	26,247	30,661	27,627	33,340	40,360	43,493	43,107	41,167	41,956	40,151	37,852	36,159	40,973
Lumber & Wood	336	280	248	252	309	342	389	447	598	594	666	679	675	723
Furniture & Fixtures	529	623	707	748	879	1,052	1,227	1,256	1,480	1,571	1,675	1,696	1,499	1,544
Stone/Clay/Glass	680	603	586	485	570	748	858	936	894	978	1,018	989	865	935
Primary Metals	3,231	2,797	3,096	2,197	2,050	2,503	2,422	2,422	2,235	2,340	2,382	2,164	2,006	1,967
Fabricated Metals	3,775	3,348	3,627	3,164	3,751	4,664	5,241	5,173	5,258	5,401	5,765	5,536	5,224	5,742
NonElect. Machines	5,007	5,047	5,237	4,438	4,388	5,338	5,779	5,495	4,903	5,487	6,060	6,274	5,690	5,840
Elect./Electronic Eq	1,330	1,320	1,000	919	1,095	1,329	1,438	1,692	1,342	1,284	1,393	1,392	1,343	1,330
Motor Veh. & Eq	16,259	11,443	15,255	14,413	19,177	23,017	24,714	24,141	22,838	22,476	19,212	17,036	16,671	20,692
Trans Eq ex Mot Veh	343	267	364	491	571	713	765	823	794	777	760	765	807	717
Instruments & Rel	268	301	327	326	365	404	416	471	566	768	952	1,013	1,060	1,151
Misc Manufacturing	204	218	214	193	185	250	244	251	258	280	268	309	318	331
Nondurable Goods	6,823	6,627	7,195	7,233	8,032	9,045	10,028	10,576	11,247	12,771	13,426	13,509	14,225	14,731
Food/Kindred Prod	1,792	1,838	1,996	2,113	2,186	2,393	2,525	2,550	2,757	3,295	3,416	3,461	3,460	3,621
Tobacco Mfgs.	0	0	0	0	0	0	0	0	0	0	0	0	0	0
Textile Mill Products	51	49	53	61	64	63	63	54	54	64	63	60	58	74
Apparel/Other Text.	552	479	526	514	622	733	852	927	912	956	988	872	823	709

Table VI-7. Gross State Product in Michigan, by Industry: Current Dollar 1979-1992 Continued
(Data in Millions of Dollars)

Industry	1979	1980	1981	1982	1983	1984	1985	1986	1987	1988	1989	1990	1991	1992
Paper/Allied Prod	698	647	682	694	790	989	1,053	1,157	1,171	1,279	1,324	1,255	1,276	1,313
Printing/Publishing	832	824	850	894	982	1,052	1,245	1,287	1,280	1,479	1,822	1,875	2,000	2,140
Chemical/Allied Prod.	1,750	1,704	1,872	1,763	2,028	2,289	2,453	2,775	3,125	3,267	3,423	3,517	4,142	4,302
Petroleum/Coal Prod.	352	330	381	345	299	279	321	406	406	747	479	477	454	384
Rubber/Plastic	720	664	741	762	973	1,165	1,428	1,351	1,468	1,594	1,815	1,866	1,892	2,052
Leather/Leather Prod.	76	91	92	85	88	84	87	68	74	89	96	124	120	137
Trans/Comm/Pub Util	7,395	7,689	8,208	8,412	9,673	10,596	11,353	12,131	13,378	12,971	14,325	13,662	13,799	13,814
Transportation	2,757	2,531	2,587	2,507	2,730	3,100	3,360	3,650	4,035	4,192	4,417	4,469	4,597	4,838
Railroad Trans.	535	518	493	459	455	467	448	461	490	498	450	425	394	414
Local Passenger Trans	85	88	87	86	88	93	101	122	125	157	155	163	179	184
Trucking/Warehousing	1,581	1,415	1,461	1,415	1,537	1,710	1,872	2,040	2,014	2,083	2,163	2,208	2,222	2,314
Water Transportation	46	37	36	33	43	49	65	58	80	80	83	79	86	81
Air Transportation	278	272	265	258	338	421	458	532	816	891	1,011	1,019	1,033	1,069
Pipelines ex Nat. Gas	55	49	48	54	57	67	73	65	86	73	68	57	62	65
Transport Services	177	153	196	201	213	293	343	371	424	410	488	517	622	710
Communication	1,955	2,123	2,170	2,166	2,462	2,535	2,854	3,159	3,339	3,666	3,740	3,926	4,018	3,934
Electric/Gas/San. Serv.	2,683	3,036	3,452	3,739	4,480	4,961	5,139	5,322	6,004	5,113	6,168	5,267	5,185	5,043
Wholesale Trade	6,393	6,359	6,774	6,537	6,815	8,256	8,864	9,621	10,323	11,195	11,998	12,206	12,636	13,449
Retail Trade	9,561	9,534	10,131	10,216	11,217	12,431	13,336	14,488	15,219	15,954	17,129	17,213	17,851	18,941
Finance/Insur./Real Est.	13,827	15,103	16,375	16,940	18,611	20,133	21,825	23,543	25,224	26,987	28,751	29,830	31,860	33,650
Banking	1,480	1,676	1,734	1,934	2,153	2,452	2,726	2,856	3,817	3,998	4,212	4,403	5,368	5,749
Credit Agncy ex Banks	353	247	295	141	377	408	558	704	513	563	621	627	684	750
Hold. Co/Invest. Serv.	67	128	320	284	445	374	515	655	611	513	631	752	631	716
Insurance Carriers	1,179	1,235	1,106	949	1,026	1,055	1,143	1,410	1,497	1,803	1,881	1,906	2,329	2,340
Insur Agnts/Brkrs/Serv	470	505	513	523	540	549	591	711	827	922	953	1,032	1,050	1,122
Real Estate	10,278	11,312	12,408	13,110	14,070	15,295	16,291	17,208	17,959	19,187	20,453	21,110	21,799	22,974
Services	12,247	13,442	14,561	15,447	16,991	18,675	21,175	23,070	25,339	27,032	29,664	31,919	33,301	36,268
Hotel/Other Lodging	404	393	399	403	421	456	518	606	673	711	802	798	824	825
Personal Services	658	684	692	698	735	790	930	1,012	1,019	1,155	1,198	1,219	1,229	1,309

Table VI-7. Gross State Product in Michigan, by Industry: Current Dollar 1979-1992 Continued
(Data in Millions of Dollars)

Industry	1979	1980	1981	1982	1983	1984	1985	1986	1987	1988	1989	1990	1991	1992
Business Services	1,761	1,910	2,103	2,337	2,780	3,401	4,578	5,174	5,000	5,443	5,889	6,422	6,447	7,325
Auto Repr/Serv/Gas St.	703	669	683	716	805	913	1,122	1,223	1,250	1,325	1,412	1,535	1,578	1,619
Misc Repair Services	284	304	295	285	325	404	444	482	493	552	596	608	536	566
Motion Pictures	122	111	93	114	127	175	202	245	290	259	335	331	332	399
Amuse./Recreat Serv.	413	432	452	451	492	478	534	579	643	697	852	961	1,079	1,219
Health Services	4,504	5,105	5,687	6,178	6,684	6,921	7,225	7,724	8,615	9,064	9,784	10,746	11,861	12,850
Legal Services	648	773	836	974	1,060	1,178	1,279	1,444	1,574	1,774	1,838	1,935	2,017	2,148
Educational Services	283	322	344	376	405	445	474	498	567	668	713	724	811	855
Soc Serv/Member Org	915	1,015	1,083	1,140	1,222	1,285	1,385	1,480	1,621	1,798	2,001	2,165	2,279	2,483
Misc Prof Serv	1,412	1,592	1,759	1,637	1,797	2,068	2,323	2,435	3,423	3,402	4,048	4,268	4,109	4,449
Private Households	139	133	135	137	138	160	161	169	169	182	195	206	200	220
Government	10,209	11,241	11,635	12,218	12,836	13,543	14,436	15,591	16,322	17,499	18,674	20,238	21,327	22,604
Federal Civilian	1,119	1,197	1,350	1,414	1,492	1,564	1,681	1,718	1,765	1,947	2,061	2,214	2,331	2,488
Federal Military	267	303	360	415	457	486	516	536	574	599	628	650	669	639
State and Local	8,822	9,741	9,925	10,389	10,887	11,493	12,240	13,338	13,983	14,953	15,985	17,375	18,327	19,476

Source: U.S. Department of Commerce, Economics & Statistics Administration, Bureau of Economic Analysis, Regional Economic Measurement Division, R.E.I.S. May 1994 Compact Disc (Washington, D.C.)

Table VI-8. Gross State Product in Michigan, by Industry: Constant Dollar(1987) 1979-1992
(Data in Millions of Dollars)

Industry	1979	1980	1981	1982	1983	1984	1985	1986	1987	1988	1989	1990	1991	1992
TOTAL GSP	**158,824**	**164,367**	**161,163**	**144,791**	**144,250**	**134,323**	**142,076**	**154,157**	**162,375**	**165,005**	**167,001**	**171,147**	**172,516**	**168,449**
Private Industries	**142,865**	**147,945**	**143,775**	**127,038**	**127,363**	**118,070**	**126,029**	**138,317**	**146,446**	**148,636**	**150,678**	**154,552**	**155,701**	**151,120**
Agricult/Forest/Fish	**1,536**	**1,308**	**1,361**	**1,611**	**1,646**	**1,704**	**1,675**	**1,583**	**1,970**	**1,804**	**1,852**	**1,716**	**1,959**	**2,037**
Farms	1,303	1,050	1,095	1,347	1,385	1,435	1,366	1,234	1,600	1,378	1,358	1,241	1,478	1,495
AgServ/Forest/Fish	233	258	266	264	261	269	309	349	370	426	494	475	481	542
Mining	**1,004**	**978**	**834**	**808**	**800**	**694**	**711**	**821**	**782**	**920**	**1,011**	**1,225**	**1,073**	**1,107**
Metal Mining	117	114	110	94	132	108	118	131	120	164	138	208	231	262
Coal Mining	1	1	0	0	0	0	0	0	0	0	0	0	0	0
Oil/Gas Extraction	713	670	538	564	552	493	480	525	501	557	663	787	606	624
NonMetalic	173	194	186	149	116	92	113	165	161	200	210	230	237	221
Construction	**6,683**	**7,211**	**7,059**	**5,649**	**5,072**	**4,301**	**4,223**	**4,529**	**5,439**	**5,740**	**5,917**	**6,236**	**6,387**	**6,228**
Manufacturing	**59,593**	**60,724**	**55,517**	**42,326**	**44,109**	**38,335**	**44,132**	**51,557**	**55,215**	**53,243**	**52,414**	**54,579**	**51,784**	**49,096**
Durable Goods	**50,815**	**51,304**	**46,238**	**34,120**	**35,806**	**30,101**	**35,256**	**42,102**	**44,861**	**42,706**	**41,167**	**42,661**	**39,839**	**37,338**
Lumber & Wood	373	349	363	314	279	294	325	360	411	461	598	569	599	612
Furniture & Fixtures	777	754	785	863	909	887	1,012	1,174	1,291	1,264	1,480	1,520	1,565	1,522
Stone/Clay/Glass	1,028	1,015	971	798	730	563	654	806	888	922	894	1,005	1,048	1,016
Primary Metals	4,497	4,547	3,892	3,114	3,194	2,284	2,046	2,407	2,399	2,524	2,235	1,858	1,732	1,730
Fabricated Metals	5,071	5,044	4,919	4,022	4,088	3,372	4,019	4,851	5,261	5,065	5,258	5,313	5,301	4,967
NonElect. Machines	5,968	6,256	6,080	5,342	4,959	3,805	3,703	4,513	5,180	5,107	4,903	5,317	5,845	5,888
Elect./Electronic Eq	1,296	1,658	1,765	1,690	1,185	1,015	1,145	1,336	1,436	1,669	1,342	1,348	1,457	1,477
Motor Veh. & Eq	30,636	30,424	26,272	16,985	19,396	16,770	21,198	25,287	26,593	24,191	22,838	23,882	20,337	18,187
Trans Eq x Mot Veh	563	600	537	389	465	562	599	701	741	787	794	804	775	753
Instruments & Rel	314	356	385	373	377	353	384	408	414	466	566	767	926	904
Misc Manufacturing	293	301	271	230	223	196	171	258	248	250	258	279	253	282
Nondurable Goods	**8,778**	**9,420**	**9,279**	**8,206**	**8,303**	**8,235**	**8,876**	**9,456**	**10,354**	**10,537**	**11,247**	**11,918**	**11,946**	**11,757**
Food/Kindred Prod	2,179	2,327	2,338	2,281	2,275	2,458	2,424	2,439	2,628	2,529	2,757	3,274	3,091	2,989
Tobacco Mfgs.	1	1	1	1	1	1	0	0	0	0	0	0	0	0
Textile Mill Products	95	70	62	57	58	66	68	66	66	54	54	62	62	58
Apparel/Other Text.	659	697	695	565	566	511	624	732	846	906	912	955	964	829

247

Table VI-8. Gross State Product in Michigan, by Industry: Constant Dollar(1987) 1979-1992 Continued
(Data in Millions of Dollars)

Industry	1979	1980	1981	1982	1983	1984	1985	1986	1987	1988	1989	1990	1991	1992
Paper/Allied Prod	1,148	1,148	1,070	879	851	844	992	1,113	1,143	1,217	1,171	1,148	1,107	1,139
Printing/Publishing	1,376	1,402	1,441	1,330	1,298	1,256	1,270	1,271	1,397	1,331	1,280	1,433	1,650	1,610
Chemical/Allied Prod.	2,290	2,710	2,502	2,062	2,085	1,987	2,228	2,349	2,454	2,827	3,125	2,874	2,885	2,975
Petroleum/Coal Prod.	239	217	287	204	287	266	249	266	318	305	406	549	382	307
Rubber/Plastic	675	734	787	723	781	754	929	1,134	1,415	1,298	1,468	1,535	1,713	1,740
Leather/Leather Prod.	116	113	97	105	100	91	91	88	87	69	74	87	91	111
Trans/Comm/Pub Util	11,595	11,781	11,764	11,140	10,470	9,639	10,437	11,164	11,512	11,891	13,378	12,886	13,944	13,146
Transportation	3,482	3,599	3,601	2,985	2,724	2,634	2,982	3,289	3,468	3,692	4,035	4,005	4,224	4,271
Railroad Trans.	434	473	507	464	402	375	387	402	395	416	490	502	479	462
Local Passenger Trans	180	168	172	141	125	110	109	109	114	125	125	145	141	142
Trucking/Warehousing	2,183	2,222	2,173	1,783	1,618	1,543	1,775	1,941	2,032	2,078	2,014	2,006	2,074	2,079
Water Transportation	65	68	65	48	44	41	47	53	65	58	80	69	66	63
Air Transportation	280	353	366	289	274	293	374	417	429	548	816	804	944	1,015
Pipelines ex Nat. Gas	128	63	62	49	47	51	50	55	64	59	86	80	79	61
Transport Services	212	252	256	212	215	221	239	311	369	408	424	398	440	447
Communication	2,591	2,685	2,736	2,911	2,704	2,470	2,690	2,812	2,936	3,101	3,339	3,666	3,627	3,769
Electric/Gas/San. Serv.	5,522	5,497	5,427	5,244	5,042	4,536	4,765	5,064	5,107	5,098	6,004	5,215	6,093	5,107
Wholesale Trade	6,039	6,638	7,011	6,323	6,611	6,588	6,834	8,290	8,751	10,155	10,323	10,530	11,074	10,743
Retail Trade	13,458	14,137	13,725	12,474	12,436	12,005	12,752	13,681	14,374	15,683	15,219	15,885	16,495	15,957
Finance/Insur./Real Est.	22,350	23,406	24,521	24,794	24,653	23,972	23,996	24,740	24,886	24,857	25,224	26,149	26,595	26,203
Banking	3,107	2,989	3,084	3,207	3,186	3,078	3,101	3,184	3,151	3,164	3,817	3,937	3,922	3,748
Credit Agncy ex Banks	667	715	743	795	986	989	785	842	869	922	513	528	530	541
Hold. Co/Invest. Serv.	203	224	155	226	385	315	453	401	504	496	611	613	747	791
Insurance Carriers	1,814	1,926	1,968	2,045	1,816	1,596	1,524	1,690	1,717	1,659	1,497	1,678	1,767	1,638
Insur Agnts/Brkrs/Serv	752	780	777	778	769	774	757	733	719	769	827	868	852	878
Real Estate	15,806	16,772	17,795	17,744	17,510	17,221	17,377	17,890	17,925	17,847	17,959	18,525	18,777	18,607
Services	20,607	21,763	21,984	21,913	21,566	20,831	21,268	21,951	23,518	24,344	25,339	25,346	26,391	26,604
Hotel/Other Lodging	840	859	762	621	557	533	542	547	569	635	673	686	748	721
Personal Services	1,202	1,193	1,134	1,080	1,018	937	926	930	1,037	1,067	1,019	1,110	1,089	1,041

248

Table VI-8. Gross State Product in Michigan, by Industry: Constant Dollar(1987) 1979-1992 Continued
(Data in Millions of Dollars)

Industry	1979	1980	1981	1982	1983	1984	1985	1986	1987	1988	1989	1990	1991	1992
Business Services	2,490	2,748	2,855	2,865	2,881	2,912	3,225	3,785	4,831	5,303	5,000	5,111	5,478	5,591
Auto Repr/Serv/Gas St.	1,278	1,360	1,257	1,109	1,047	1,002	1,038	1,123	1,326	1,315	1,250	1,266	1,259	1,290
Misc Repair Services	423	464	471	461	419	373	392	455	455	496	493	544	584	568
Motion Pictures	160	222	189	166	136	157	162	208	226	261	290	247	298	276
Amuse./Recreat Serv.	563	566	584	594	594	567	590	546	588	604	643	663	773	828
Health Services	8,205	8,572	8,805	8,981	8,954	8,742	8,732	8,443	8,286	8,298	8,615	8,385	8,363	8,520
Legal Services	1,557	1,568	1,536	1,599	1,546	1,549	1,475	1,479	1,507	1,575	1,574	1,703	1,655	1,607
Educational Services	455	477	498	515	495	495	501	516	520	523	567	631	632	610
Soc Serv/Member Org	1,338	1,405	1,438	1,466	1,459	1,431	1,454	1,457	1,507	1,549	1,621	1,727	1,871	1,964
Misc Prof Serv	1,893	2,125	2,277	2,300	2,312	1,990	2,087	2,296	2,500	2,548	3,423	3,093	3,451	3,393
Private Households	204	205	177	156	147	144	144	165	164	171	169	180	190	195
Government	15,959	16,421	17,387	17,754	16,887	16,253	16,048	15,840	15,929	16,368	16,322	16,595	16,815	17,329
Federal Civilian	1,747	1,872	1,889	1,892	1,881	1,789	1,818	1,783	1,802	1,797	1,765	1,864	1,882	1,936
Federal Military	516	462	444	453	479	501	528	541	548	553	574	574	575	566
State and Local	13,696	14,087	15,054	15,408	14,527	13,963	13,702	13,516	13,579	14,018	13,983	14,157	14,359	14,826

Source: U.S. Department of Commerce, Economics & Statistics Administration, Bureau of Economic Analysis, Regional Economic Measurement Division, R.E.I.S. May 1994 Compact Disc (Washington, D.C.)

CHAPTER VII
SOCIAL INSURANCE AND HUMAN SERVICES

Data on state income maintenance programs are prepared by the Michigan Department of Social Services and published in its Program Statistics. The DSS also publishes an Information Packet as well as compilations relating to Medicaid, foster homes, and other programs that they administer.

The Social Security Administration publishes an annual supplement to its Social Security Bulletin which has data for various programs in the various states. Various other federal agencies, such as the Railroad Retirement Board and the Veterans Administration also publish data on their programs.

Unemployment insurance data are prepared by the Michigan Employment Security Commission and published in its Handbook of Unemployment Insurance Program Statistics. The Bureau of Workers' Disability Compensation publishes an Annual Report. In August 1993, the Michigan Department of Commerce released its Final Report on the State of Competition in the Workers' compensation insurance market.

The Association of Statisticians of American Religious Bodies (ASARB) provided the material on churches and church membership. The data is published by the Glenmary Research Center.

In the material that follows, O.A.S.D.H.I. stands for Old-Age Survivors, Disability and Health Insurance, more commonly known as Social Security. AFDC stands for Aid to Families with Dependent Children.

LIST OF TABLES

Table   **Page**

VII-1. Number of Social Security (O.A.S.D.H.I.) Current-Pay Benefits in Michigan: 1974-1993 253

VII-2. Medical Assistance Recipients and Expenditures in Michigan, by Type of Service: Fiscal Year 1993 254

VII-3. Average Number of Medical Assistance Cases and Recipients in Michigan: October 1992 - September 1993 254

VII-4. Recipients of AFDC, State Assistance, State Emergency Relief, Emergency Assistance, and Food Stamps in Michigan, by County: Fiscal Year 1993 255

VII-5. Aid to Families with Dependent Children (AFDC) in Michigan, by County: Fiscal Year 1993 256

VII-6. State Assistance Cases, Recipients, and Payments in Michigan, by County: Fiscal Year 1993 257

VII-7. Food Stamp Cases, Recipients, and Payments in Michigan, by County: Fiscal Year 1993 258

VII-8. Medical Assistance Recipients and Payments in Michigan, by County: Fiscal Year 1993 259

Table		Page
VII-9.	Supplemental Security Income Recipients and Payments in Michigan, by County: Fiscal Year 1993	260
VII-10.	Home Help Cases and Payments in Michigan, by County: Fiscal Year 1993	261
VII-11.	Unduplicated Recipients of General Assistance Payments and Recipient Rates in Michigan, by County: September 1993	262
VII-12.	Number and Percent of Individuals Receiving Financial Payments in Michigan: Fiscal Years 1980-1994	263
VII-13.	Children's Protective Services Referrals Studied and Number of Child Sexual Abuse Victims in Michigan: Fiscal Years 1983-1994	263
VII-14.	Statewide Abuse and Neglect Caseload and Type of Placement in Michigan: Fiscal Years 1983-1994	263
VII-15.	Number of Neglected Children in Foster Care Homes and Private Institutions in Michigan: 9-84 thru 9-94	264
VII-16.	Child Support Collections, AFDC and Non-AFDC Case Related In-State Collections, Michigan: Fiscal Years 1983-1994	264
VII-17.	Department of Social Services' Domestic Violence Program Statistics in Michigan: 1989-1994	264
VII-18.	Workers' Compensation Policies, Premiums, and Payroll in Michigan, Voluntary Market: 1982-1994	265
VII-19.	Employer Basic Report of Injury and Number of Contested Cases in Michigan: 1968-1993	265
VII-20.	Annual Workers' Compensation Paid in Michigan, Not Including Medical: 1977-1993	266
VII-21.	Status of Michigan's Unemployment Insurance Trust Fund: 1937-1995	267
VII-22.	Federal Advances Received from Unemployment Trust Fund, Michigan: 1958-1994	269

LIST OF TABLES

Table   **Page**

VII-23.   Relationship of Average Weekly Benefit Claims to Total
            Unemployment in Michigan: 1975-1995 Annual Averages 270

VII-24.   Unemployment Compensation Benefit Payments Programs in
            Michigan: 1938-1994 271

VII-25.   Average, Minimum and Maximum Unemployment Insurance
            Contribution Rates and Taxable Wage Base in Michigan:
            1970-1996 273

VII-26.   Relationship of Average Weekly Wage to Average
            Unemployment Insurance Benefit Amount in Michigan:
            1937-1994 274

VII-27.   Relationship of Average Weekly Unemployment Insurance
            Benefit Amount to Maximum Weekly Benefit Amount in
            Michigan: 1956-1994 276

VII-28.   Average Weekly Insured Unemployment and Rate, Average
            Duration of Unemployment, and Total Unemployment Rate in
            Michigan: 1956-1995 277

VII-29.   Churches and Church Membership in Michigan, by
            Denomination: 1990 278

VII-30.   Churches and Church Membership in Michigan, by
            Denomination and County: 1990 281

Table VII-1. Number of Social Security (O.A.S.D.H.I.) Current-Pay Benefits in Michigan: 1974-1993
(Data in Thousands)

| Year | Total | Retired Workers | Disabled Workers | Spouses of | | Children of | | | Widowed Parents | Widows and Widowers |
				Retired Workers	Disabled Workers	Retired Workers	Deceased Workers	Disabled Workers		
1974	1,213	603	95	112	17	22	122	53	23	157
1975	1,258	625	105	113	19	23	123	59	24	161
1976	1,291	643	112	114	19	23	123	62	24	164
1977	1,317	662	116	115	20	25	120	62	24	168
1978	1,325	678	116	115	19	23	115	60	23	171
1979	1,334	689	115	114	19	23	115	59	23	173
1980	1,359	723	113	116	18	23	108	54	23	177
1982	1,365	771	103	117	14	20	94	39	20	184
1983	1,379	796	105	117	12	19	87	38	16	188
1984	1,391	814	107	117	12	17	80	38	---	---
1985	1,409	830	109	117	12	16	76	40	---	---
1986	1,427	848	112	116	12	16	73	40	---	---
1987	1,439	863	112	117	11	16	71	40	---	---
1988	1,453	878	113	117	11	16	70	40	---	---
1989	1,468	895	114	117	10	15	69	40	---	---
1990	1,490	913	117	117	10	16	68	40	---	---
1991	1,515	930	122	117	9	15	67	43	---	---
1992	1,546	945	131	118	10	16	68	47	---	---
1993	1,569	953	141	118	10	15	68	51	---	---

Source: Social Security Administration, Social Security Bulletin, Annual Statistical Supplement (Washington D.C.: annually).   --- No data.

Table VII-2. Medical Assistance Recipients and Expenditures in Michigan, by Type of Service: Fiscal Year 1993

Type of Service	Recipients	Expenditures($)	Average per Recipient($)
Total Services (Unduplicated)	**1,171,548**	**$3,077,140,672**	**$2,626.56**
Inpatient General Hospital Services	188,111	804,095,156	4,274.58
Mental Hospital Services for the Aged	336	11,078,147	32,970.68
SNF/ICF Services for the Aged	66	1,322,800	20,042.42
Inpatient Psych Services Ages < 22	2,628	49,172,384	18,710.95
ICF/MR Services	2,564	145,539,794	56,762.79
Nursing Facility Services	43,575	641,548,931	14,722.87
Physician's Services	873,013	229,250,394	262.60
Dental Services	362,796	33,023,992	91.03
Other Practitioners' Services	167,446	9,290,769	55.49
Outpatient Hospital Services	555,280	206,024,320	371.03
Clinic Services	241,979	305,684,147	1,263.27
Lab and Radiological	556,640	41,763,546	75.03
Home Health Services	69,974	238,972,672	3,415.16
Prescribed Drugs	855,328	259,324,929	303.19
Family Planning Services	146,378	21,619,184	147.69
Rural Health Services	9,441	1,018,107	107.84
Early and Periodic Screening	193,218	14,497,644	75.03
Other Care	213,125	63,913,757	299.89

Source: Social Security Administration, Social Security Bulletin, Annual Statistical Supplement (Washington D.C.: annually).

Table VII-3. Average Number of Medical Assistance Cases and Recipients in Michigan: October 1992 - September 1993

Type of Case	Number of Cases	Number of Recipients
Total	**202,862**	**300,852**
Age 65 and over	48,600	48,600
Families with Dependent Children	34,630	96,376
Blind	286	286
Disabled	35,026	35,026
Other Children Under Age 21	41,620	47,451
Pregnant Women	42,700	73,113

Source: Social Security Administration, Social Security Bulletin, Annual Statistical Supplement (Washington D.C.: annually).

Table VII-4. Recipients of AFDC, State Assistance, State Emergency Relief, Emergency Assistance, and Food Stamps in Michigan, by County: Fiscal Year 1993

County	Recipients	County	Recipients
Alcona	1,074	Lake	2,115
Alger	660	Lapeer	4,665
Allegan	6,464	Leelanau	1,000
Alpena	3,604	Lenawee	7,502
Antrim	1,609	Livingston	3,579
Arenac	2,512	Luce	946
Baraga	1,127	Mackinac	748
Barry	3,703	Macomb	29,919
Bay	12,977	Manistee	2,965
Benzie	1,071	Marquette	4,666
Berrien	21,127	Mason	3,037
Branch	3,891	Mecosta	4,291
Calhoun	17,780	Menominee	1,830
Cass	5,501	Midland	6,414
Charlevoix	1,687	Missaukee	1,559
Cheboygan	2,812	Monroe	9,505
Chippewa	3,258	Montcalm	6,435
Clare	5,101	Montmorency	1,198
Clinton	2,703	Muskegon	22,927
Crawford	1,744	Newaygo	4,870
Delta	3,684	Oakland	51,756
Dickinson	1,681	Oceana	3,592
Eaton	4,866	Ogemaw	3,388
Emmet	1,860	Ontonagon	774
Genesse	72,932	Osceola	2,945
Gladwin	3,529	Oscoda	1,178
Gogebic	1,782	Otsego	1,234
Grand Traverse	3,444	Ottawa	7,115
Gratiot	4,012	Presque Isle	1,368
Hillsdale	3,817	Roscommon	3,055
Houghton	4,084	Saginaw	34,249
Huron	3,723	St. Clair	13,530
Ingham	30,176	St. Joseph	5,617
Ionia	4,548	Sanilac	4,535
Iosco	2,919	Schoolcraft	1,188
Iron	1,079	Shiawassee	6,497
Isabella	5,020	Tuscola	5,723
Jackson	15,107	Van Buren	10,775
Kalamazoo	20,779	Washtenaw	14,215
Kalkaska	1,856	Wayne	405,833
Kent	38,322	Wexford	3,745
Keweenaw	161	**Michigan**	**1,032,262**

Source: Michigan Department of Social Services, Data Reporting Unit, Program Statistics Fiscal 1993 (Lansing, Michigan: 1994).

Table VII-5. Aid to Families with Dependent Children (AFDC) in Michigan, by County: Fiscal Year 1993

County	Cases	Recipients	Payments	County	Cases	Recipients	Payments
Alcona	174	556	$880,845.17	Lake	399	1,241	$1,905,593.81
Alger	109	355	522,839.45	Lapeer	976	2,889	5,149,646.01
Allegan	1,234	3,775	6,326,477.49	Leelanau	140	468	726,177.55
Alpena	661	1,961	3,218,472.47	Lenawee	1,610	4,806	8,397,933.22
Antrim	270	829	1,340,707.72	Livingston	779	2,192	4,166,137.00
Arenac	436	1,353	2,031,839.09	Luce	150	481	719,321.96
Baraga	195	653	968,576.25	Mackinac	122	365	542,860.82
Barry	724	2,225	3,807,189.78	Macomb	6,699	18,799	35,475,183.78
Bay	2,667	8,178	14,145,577.40	Manistee	487	1,560	2,379,410.51
Benzie	178	535	811,823.92	Marquette	935	2,717	4,574,231.25
Berrien	4,694	13,851	23,640,234.05	Mason	557	1,717	2,735,262.14
Branch	737	2,267	3,776,089.90	Mecosta	848	2,502	3,958,318.41
Calhoun	3,764	11,104	18,595,033.73	Menominee	285	850	1,311,525.29
Cass	1,139	3,504	5,995,924.28	Midland	1,316	4,202	6,971,883.22
Charlevoix	306	896	1,466,425.65	Missaukee	280	924	1,439,181.30
Cheboygan	468	1,447	2,270,299.35	Monroe	2,148	6,479	11,780,644.21
Chippewa	581	1,809	2,744,369.34	Montcalm	1,246	3,931	6,352,224.41
Clare	1,023	3,290	5,398,299.62	Montmorency	211	664	1,063,775.30
Clinton	536	1,614	2,819,017.65	Muskegon	4,954	14,719	24,514,172.72
Crawford	289	940	1,478,453.09	Newaygo	879	2,721	4,217,862.11
Delta	718	2,150	3,450,371.63	Oakland	11,788	34,320	64,258,009.01
Dickinson	303	884	1,473,054.51	Oceana	563	1,839	2,753,706.09
Eaton	1,014	2,893	5,165,555.31	Ogemaw	635	2,043	3,152,715.00
Emmet	287	852	1,417,538.46	Ontonagon	133	404	640,944.53
Genesee	17,939	53,118	99,068,993.80	Osceola	535	1,699	2,702,912.92
Gladwin	687	2,237	3,555,377.53	Oscoda	202	654	1,004,536.23
Gogebic	324	951	1,483,071.29	Otsego	215	636	1,091,998.30
Grand Traverse	616	1,725	3,105,485.97	Ottawa	1,399	4,058	7,046,653.52
Gratiot	818	2,537	4,239,538.04	Presque Isle	214	655	1,013,182.12
Hillsdale	712	2,232	3,563,885.13	Roscommon	625	1,982	3,226,886.94
Houghton	639	2,020	3,094,988.06	Saginaw	7,955	24,152	42,743,730.85
Huron	620	1,985	2,996,932.21	St. Clair	2,980	8,831	16,171,790.83
Ingham	6,733	2,574	37,474,537.38	St. Joseph	1,077	3,306	5,612,267.41
Ionia	916	2,853	4,728,491.52	Sanilac	806	2,614	4,091,748.03
Iosco	495	1,520	2,323,421.70	Schoolcraft	216	684	1,088,458.00
Iron	176	542	802,750.98	Shiawassee	1,307	3,895	6,601,370.30
Isabella	1,015	3,093	5,275,284.33	Tuscola	1,079	3,465	5,608,841.09
Jackson	3,335	9,881	16,605,286.29	Van Buren	1,965	6,076	10,264,522.07
Kalamazoo	4,571	13,342	24,309,734.37	Washtenaw	3,372	9,480	18,051,157.18
Kalkaska	312	981	1,471,687.24	Wayne	95,858	289,476	516,273,977.35
Kent	8,317	23,299	43,146,670.92	Wexford	659	2,076	3,331,090.41
Keweenaw	17	56	80,071.68	**Michigan**	**229,349**	**687,428**	**1,216,183,066.95**

Source: Michigan Department of Social Services, Data Reporting Unit, Program Statistics Fiscal 1993 (Lansing, Michigan: 1994).

Table VII-6. State Assistance Cases, Recipients, and Payments in Michigan, by County: Fiscal Year 1993

County	Cases	Recipients	Payments	County	Cases	Recipients	Payments
Alcona	8	10	$22,821.41	Lake	32	36	$89,284.54
Alger	5	6	19,852.74	Lapeer	41	51	115,860.03
Allegan	49	64	157,634.37	Leelanau	6	8	19,057.70
Alpena	54	60	115,492.14	Lenawee	54	70	158,364.10
Antrim	6	9	18,576.70	Livingston	31	36	90,820.58
Arenac	22	24	66,344.34	Luce	9	10	25,778.52
Baraga	23	23	24,438.76	Mackinac	N.A.	1	1,168.00
Barry	33	42	103,891.53	Macomb	382	460	1,189,239.88
Bay	153	203	461,815.01	Manistee	27	37	81,782.56
Benzie	9	13	27,591.00	Marquette	71	74	131,799.71
Berrien	154	200	456,474.90	Mason	32	37	93,840.85
Branch	39	47	137,396.86	Mecosta	41	48	125,113.42
Calhoun	209	257	630,760.91	Menominee	12	19	41,657.08
Cass	37	49	122,994.52	Midland	104	119	325,664.27
Charlevoix	15	15	39,681.02	Missaukee	10	13	40,831.96
Cheboygan	24	28	68,574.04	Monroe	101	140	357,038.87
Chippewa	48	55	73,266.73	Montcalm	47	60	146,863.68
Clare	55	75	193,962.24	Montmorency	14	15	37,536.36
Clinton	37	49	117,209.49	Muskegon	180	211	545,308.27
Crawford	8	11	27,406.46	Newaygo	69	86	212,518.88
Delta	38	47	87,375.76	Oakland	666	1,242	2,275,345.11
Dickinson	24	27	29,716.07	Oceana	19	23	55,095.70
Eaton	50	60	154,971.15	Ogemaw	34	47	105,757.12
Emmet	52	55	56,253.83	Ontonagon	7	8	26,220.86
Genesee	728	964	2,199,316.49	Osceola	38	50	119,019.24
Gladwin	38	54	125,464.03	Oscoda	10	17	33,276.18
Gogebic	16	22	68,617.30	Otsego	6	8	23,280.50
Grand Traverse	50	54	94,687.96	Ottawa	110	123	374,199.03
Gratiot	32	51	106,367.02	Presque Isle	19	24	48,982.23
Hillsdale	34	40	92,840.34	Roscommon	35	37	101,624.66
Houghton	54	60	177,668.66	Saginaw	310	482	1,037,733.51
Huron	32	38	103,420.58	St. Clair	187	215	566,915.11
Ingham	379	511	1,141,605.83	St. Joseph	66	75	200,808.51
Ionia	36	54	133,576.69	Sanilac	45	54	121,294.42
Iosco	25	34	78,019.29	Schoolcraft	8	10	30,963.52
Iron	10	10	31,387.85	Shiawassee	60	74	193,175.80
Isabella	34	46	105,193.07	Tuscola	59	77	182,889.58
Jackson	141	177	447,209.49	Van Buren	93	114	293,753.76
Kalamazoo	300	468	1,066,088.20	Washtenaw	201	230	487,242.61
Kalkaska	9	11	25,758.00	Wayne	5,183	8,264	18,453,939.09
Kent	650	1,051	1,978,311.71	Wexford	22	37	74,814.37
Keweenaw	N.A.	N.A.	246.00	**Michigan**	**12,161**	**17,812**	**39,763,140.64**

Source: Michigan Department of Social Services, Data Reporting Unit, Program Statistics Fiscal 1993 (Lansing, Michigan: 1994). N.A. data not available.

Table VII-7. Food Stamp Cases, Recipients, and Payments in Michigan, by County: Fiscal Year 1993

County	Cases	Recipients	Payments	County	Cases	Recipients	Payments
Alcona	425	1,060	$845,076	Lake	872	2,103	$1,615,030
Alger	323	626	461,586	Lapeer	1,677	4,424	3,455,833
Allegan	2,309	6,224	4,715,347	Leelanau	131	941	653,089
Alpena	1,525	3,557	2,672,027	Lenawee	2,734	7,261	5,536,609
Antrim	587	1,556	11,115,330	Livingston	1,373	3,395	2,722,784
Arenac	934	2,492	1,931,282	Luce	346	935	687,375
Baraga	458	1,125	838,220	Mackinac	266	727	520,762
Barry	1,361	3,574	2,737,457	Macomb	12,404	28,571	23,611,876
Bay	5,199	12,798	9,833,429	Manistee	1,100	2,908	2,242,556
Benzie	384	1,044	798,681	Marquette	1,839	4,549	3,407,837
Berrien	8,253	21,175	16,323,584	Mason	1,135	2,993	2,294,587
Branch	1,390	3,743	2,888,547	Mecosta	1,750	4,229	3,309,447
Calhoun	7,354	17,709	14,432,318	Menominee	723	1,785	1,324,442
Cass	1,955	5,287	4,151,949	Midland	2,267	6,262	4,768,861
Charlevoix	653	1,639	1,214,721	Missaukee	564	1,571	1,204,756
Cheboygan	1,041	2,758	2,031,223	Monroe	3,376	9,106	7,025,802
Chippewa	1,215	3,183	2,310,267	Montcalm	2,330	6,392	4,958,428
Clare	1,819	5,054	3,942,753	Montmorency	472	1,184	912,234
Clinton	983	2,585	2,015,705	Muskegon	9,168	22,872	18,165,309
Crawford	604	1,709	1,219,092	Newaygo	1,691	4,741	3,521,725
Delta	1,466	3,585	2,824,432	Oakland	20,435	49,899	40,869,011
Dickinson	687	1,621	1,224,678	Oceana	1,181	3,553	2,581,695
Eaton	1,850	4,664	3,710,237	Ogemaw	1,280	3,373	2,626,765
Emmet	765	1,786	1,332,422	Ontonagon	326	754	552,547
Genesee	29,687	72,258	60,447,199	Osceola	1,061	2,926	2,182,080
Gladwin	1,303	3,486	2,771,058	Oscoda	450	1,178	913,031
Gogebic	743	1,754	1,267,920	Otsego	468	1,197	850,278
Grand Traverse	1,411	3,332	2,506,247	Ottawa	2,571	6,806	5,234,204
Gratiot	1,431	3,922	2,904,662	Presque Isle	548	1,353	1,008,356
Hillsdale	1,336	3,723	2,755,465	Roscommon	1,186	3,022	2,381,315
Houghton	1,806	4,003	2,913,045	Saginaw	13,590	31,041	26,536,481
Huron	1,485	3,684	2,841,622	St. Clair	5,403	13,102	10,352,316
Ingham	11,988	29,630	23,762,565	St. Joseph	2,080	5,444	4,146,693
Ionia	1,611	4,390	3,365,019	Sanilac	1,678	4,406	3,444,623
Iosco	1,095	2,862	2,248,948	Schoolcraft	449	1,157	847,232
Iron	473	1,055	815,221	Shiawassee	2,464	60,280	4,892,533
Isabella	1,907	4,976	3,695,554	Tuscola	1,913	5,524	4,217,582
Jackson	6,002	14,984	11,967,849	Van Buren	3,971	10,514	8,125,577
Kalamazoo	8,557	20,301	16,240,767	Washtenaw	5,797	13,716	11,046,801
Kalkaska	602	1,757	1,272,991	Wayne	169,985	400,185	350,422,845
Kent	15,294	38,752	30,769,267	Wexford	1,400	3,718	2,775,399
Keweenaw	82	162	102,768	**Michigan**	**414,879**	**1,014,679**	**836,192,236**

Source: Michigan Department of Social Services, Data Reporting Unit, <u>Program Statistics Fiscal 1993</u> (Lansing, Michigan: 1994).

Table VII-8. Medical Assistance Recipients and Payments in Michigan, by County: Fiscal Year 1993

County	Recipients	Payments	County	Recipients	Payments
Alcona	1,395	$4,244,958	Lake	2,576	$6,326,999
Alger	1,097	3,272,925	Lapeer	6,823	19,158,115
Allegan	9,730	23,689,135	Leelanau	1,642	4,093,839
Alpena	4,967	12,720,901	Lenawee	11,156	24,669,068
Antrim	2,506	7,745,366	Livingston	5,745	16,648,547
Arenac	3,098	8,466,079	Luce	1,510	4,820,856
Baraga	1,479	3,735,472	Mackinac	1,229	4,367,493
Barry	5,154	11,882,695	Macomb	43,057	139,532,489
Bay	15,566	39,638,617	Manistee	3,845	10,827,002
Benzie	1,835	6,207,957	Marquette	6,560	19,484,950
Berrien	27,654	57,260,121	Mason	4,313	9,534,915
Branch	5,789	14,215,054	Mecosta	5,625	13,029,619
Calhoun	22,727	49,693,640	Menominee	2,707	8,487,931
Cass	7,336	14,940,537	Midland	8,458	18,886,981
Charlevoix	2,638	7,558,896	Missaukee	2,131	4,219,879
Cheboygan	3,823	9,135,967	Monroe	13,247	32,384,724
Chippewa	4,856	12,055,610	Montcalm	8,296	15,562,720
Clare	6,370	13,673,913	Montmorency	1,576	4,844,154
Clinton	3,919	11,535,254	Muskegon	26,291	57,302,143
Crawford	2,427	5,272,080	Newaygo	7,022	14,336,096
Delta	5,417	15,826,655	Oakland	72,156	235,164,069
Dickinson	2,911	8,227,238	Oceana	4,893	9,024,257
Eaton	6,780	17,885,173	Ogemaw	4,175	9,757,691
Emmet	2,916	7,817,476	Ontonagon	1,191	4,310,179
Genesee	78,857	171,282,935	Osceola	3,879	8,021,052
Gladwin	4,262	9,034,222	Oscoda	1,511	3,713,050
Gogebic	2,913	8,822,319	Otsego	2,278	6,619,022
Grand Traverse	6,300	19,298,018	Ottawa	11,961	33,464,390
Gratiot	5,841	15,587,302	Presque Isle	1,796	5,441,375
Hillsdale	5,842	16,369,089	Roscommon	3,937	9,020,241
Houghton	5,158	17,351,669	Saginaw	38,792	74,812,590
Huron	5,001	14,586,397	St. Clair	17,823	44,256,581
Ingham	35,985	80,180,916	St. Joseph	7,927	19,024,908
Ionia	6,339	13,029,166	Sanilac	6,053	18,222,463
Iosco	3,807	9,090,683	Schoolcraft	1,637	5,144,391
Iron	1,830	7,041,240	Shiawassee	8,700	20,343,572
Isabella	6,830	34,477,192	Tuscola	7,969	29,599,099
Jackson	20,309	49,748,749	Van Buren	14,057	32,035,944
Kalamazoo	26,059	69,941,185	Washtenaw	20,092	51,933,079
Kalkaska	2,551	6,375,505	Wayne	343,855	962,957,896
Kent	57,461	145,630,858	Wexford	5,113	10,619,693
Keweenaw	209	596,447	**Michigan**	**1,171,548**	**3,077,140,672**

Source: Michigan Department of Social Services, Data Reporting Unit, Program Statistics Fiscal 1993 (Lansing, Michigan: 1994).

Table VII-9. Supplemental Security Income Recipients and Payments in Michigan, by County: Fiscal Year 1993

County	Recipients	Payments	County	Recipients	Payments
Alcona	208	$740,835.05	Lake	381	$1,315,333.72
Alger	192	658,198.94	Lapeer	681	2,424,422.01
Allegan	1,072	3,651,205.14	Leelanau	131	405,837.60
Alpena	773	2,667,036.85	Lenawee	1,560	5,844,115.26
Antrim	366	1,222,826.29	Livingston	495	1,704,520.95
Arenac	369	1,238,993.96	Luce	196	711,523.03
Baraga	211	689,944.68	Mackinac	225	669,806.84
Barry	499	1,815,079.84	Macomb	5,865	20,793,753.67
Bay	1,926	7,136,384.86	Manistee	406	1,346,467.42
Benzie	2,032	753,063.30	Marquette	928	3,099,769.76
Berrien	4,302	16,228,283.75	Mason	496	1,743,600.10
Branch	622	2,228,679.93	Mecosta	597	2,084,888.97
Calhoun	3,406	13,046,629.71	Menominee	386	1,107,028.26
Cass	773	2,657,254.21	Midland	874	3,295,194.42
Charlevoix	316	1,132,201.95	Missaukee	216	805,595.57
Cheboygan	406	1,415,273.34	Monroe	1,641	5,697,525.27
Chippewa	655	2,250,598.06	Montcalm	1,112	4,109,956.95
Clare	790	2,850,277.18	Montmorency	196	608,734.80
Clinton	340	1,230,162.65	Muskegon	4,471	17,078,742.86
Crawford	203	703,094.85	Newaygo	805	2,827,687.71
Delta	744	2,350,828.48	Oakland	10,887	39,679,237.73
Dickinson	395	1,173,479.71	Oceana	489	1,770,552.89
Eaton	676	2,351,736.54	Ogemaw	441	1,470,632.15
Emmet	387	1,286,904.66	Ontonagon	231	744,564.64
Genesee	9,444	37,973,829.34	Osceola	545	1,968,908.66
Gladwin	452	1,660,688.44	Oscoda	163	538,591.17
Gogebic	479	1,418,103.89	Otsego	257	959,387.09
Grand Traverse	1,169	4,082,633.58	Ottawa	1,276	4,446,800.64
Gratiot	865	3,048,684.13	Presque Isle	295	987,849.53
Hillsdale	849	3,274,676.29	Roscommon	432	1,567,822.62
Houghton	789	2,419,997.93	Saginaw	5,931	24,369,962.64
Huron	673	2,445,710.33	St. Clair	2,166	7,989,220.44
Ingham	4,829	18,443,495.44	St. Joseph	895	3,263,998.61
Ionia	708	2,550,644.22	Sanilac	603	2,117,914.49
Iosco	405	1,350,928.85	Schoolcraft	205	758,426.75
Iron	288	816,969.23	Shiawassee	1,052	3,852,733.23
Isabella	1,163	4,040,281.87	Tuscola	900	3,168,735.63
Jackson	2,910	11,204,738.48	Van Buren	1,732	6,154,405.49
Kalamazoo	3,647	13,241,132.05	Washtenaw	2,937	11,034,658.93
Kalkaska	276	974,929.56	Wayne	60,709	237,486,430.49
Kent	8,775	33,395,077.45	Wexford	667	2,259,417.11
Keweenaw	35	114,649.23	**Michigan**	**172,083**	**648,209,258.34**

Source: Michigan Department of Social Services, Data Reporting Unit, Program Statistics Fiscal 1993 (Lansing, Michigan: 1994).

Table VII-10. Home Help Cases and Payments in Michigan, by County: Fiscal Year 1993

County	Cases	Payments	County	Cases	Payments
Alcona	53	$616,128.39	Lake	110	$409,063.51
Alger	25	47,135.95	Lapeer	101	337,719.82
Allegan	165	591,361.43	Leelanau	39	118,220.37
Alpena	194	805,987.75	Lenawee	135	571,644.51
Antrim	62	193,890.78	Livingston	111	403,205.75
Arenac	80	234,543.57	Luce	20	36,941.06
Baraga	59	176,385.34	Mackinac	20	52,051.92
Barry	50	161,774.87	Macomb	1,451	4,927,388.46
Bay	269	930,113.68	Manistee	115	352,750.39
Benzie	24	81,718.43	Marquette	172	532,300.75
Berrien	423	1,225,544.66	Mason	58	141,284.51
Branch	77	219,145.99	Mecosta	91	238,562.24
Calhoun	240	742,338.24	Menominee	57	181,197.38
Cass	185	654,647.77	Midland	158	869,806.17
Charlevoix	87	295,072.58	Missaukee	28	116,929.46
Cheboygan	109	325,911.60	Monroe	231	829,738.85
Chippewa	51	121,429.19	Montcalm	112	294,820.50
Clare	77	229,009.43	Montmorency	46	162,005.98
Clinton	61	206,852.49	Muskegon	460	1,200,948.72
Crawford	48	152,531.16	Newaygo	124	446,521.52
Delta	97	281,401.75	Oakland	2,022	6,757,638.62
Dickinson	45	151,715.29	Oceana	90	348,510.62
Eaton	89	376,122.12	Ogemaw	104	346,624.79
Emmet	76	275,937.19	Ontonagon	30	65,391.82
Genesee	1,056	3,675,168.05	Osceola	81	270,974.65
Gladwin	91	285,707.08	Oscoda	37	148,950.16
Gogebic	60	265,688.71	Otsego	36	112,822.68
Grand Traverse	66	213,274.61	Ottawa	204	787,446.61
Gratiot	66	263,541.74	Presque Isle	92	272,418.76
Hillsdale	116	406,110.36	Roscommon	67	238,983.59
Houghton	124	396,903.95	Saginaw	506	1,627,937.80
Huron	97	261,275.77	St. Clair	355	1,202,936.61
Ingham	731	2,862,154.45	St. Joseph	70	189,500.60
Ionia	53	200,477.52	Sanilac	128	626,193.58
Iosco	38	90,695.78	Schoolcraft	68	242,739.52
Iron	69	247,740.77	Shiawassee	157	627,313.17
Isabella	146	592,098.93	Tuscola	112	508,337.96
Jackson	451	1,468,675.01	Van Buren	238	877,926.77
Kalamazoo	589	2,331,111.75	Washtenaw	540	2,268,541.68
Kalkaska	33	100,052.24	Wayne	11,899	38,565,426.77
Kent	1,196	3,744,356.97	Wexford	78	258,282.91
Keweenaw	10	35,442.23	**Michigan**	**28,184**	**94,587,177.11**

Source: Michigan Department of Social Services, Data Reporting Unit, Program Statistics Fiscal 1993 (Lansing, Michigan: 1994).

Table VII-11. Unduplicated Recipients of General Assistance Payments and Recipient Rates in Michigan, by County: September 1993

County	Unduplicated Recipients of Payments	Recipient Rate(%)	County	Unduplicated Recipients of Payments	Recipient Rate(%)
Alcona	1,012	9.8	Lake	2,010	22.8
Alger	628	6.8	Lapeer	4,230	5.5
Allegan	6,291	6.8	Leelanau	1,090	6.5
Alpena	3,386	11.0	Lenawee	7,261	7.9
Antrim	1,357	7.3	Livingston	3,469	2.9
Arenac	2,662	17.3	Luce	968	16.7
Baraga	1,048	13.1	Mackinac	634	5.9
Barry	3,545	7.0	Macomb	29,852	4.1
Bay	12,538	11.2	Manistee	3,111	14.5
Benzie	1,001	8.1	Marquette	4,510	6.3
Berrien	21,658	13.4	Mason	2,758	10.6
Branch	3,762	9.0	Mecosta	4,276	11.2
Calhoun	17,520	12.8	Menominee	1,835	7.4
Cass	5,465	11.1	Midland	6,294	8.2
Charlevoix	1,609	7.3	Missaukee	1,502	12.1
Cheboygan	2,499	11.7	Monroe	9,267	6.9
Chippewa	3,161	9.1	Montcalm	6,270	11.6
Clare	5,019	19.4	Montmorency	1,133	12.5
Clinton	2,596	4.4	Muskegon	22,179	13.8
Crawford	1,708	13.6	Newaygo	4,482	11.4
Delta	3,588	9.4	Oakland	52,223	4.7
Dickinson	1,592	5.9	Oceana	3,717	16.3
Eaton	4,918	5.2	Ogemaw	3,153	16.3
Emmet	1,672	6.5	Ontonagon	717	8.1
Genesee	72,427	16.8	Osceola	2,687	13.2
Gladwin	3,292	14.6	Oscoda	1,125	14.1
Gogebic	1,772	9.8	Otsego	1,106	5.9
Grand Traverse	3,280	5.0	Ottawa	7,018	3.6
Gratiot	3,905	9.9	Presque Isle	1,249	9.0
Hillsdale	3,601	8.2	Roscommon	2,844	13.9
Houghton	3,809	10.7	Saginaw	33,850	15.9
Huron	3,466	9.8	St. Clair	12,940	8.7
Ingham	30,302	10.7	St. Joseph	5,062	8.6
Ionia	4,471	7.8	Sanilac	4,309	10.7
Iosco	2,878	9.3	Schoolcraft	1,170	14.3
Iron	1,038	7.9	Shiawassee	6,208	8.8
Isabella	4,870	8.8	Tuscola	5,417	9.7
Jackson	14,939	9.9	Van Buren	10,938	15.4
Kalamazoo	20,626	9.2	Washtenaw	14,436	5.0
Kalkaska	1,608	11.6	Wayne	406,635	19.3
Kent	38,991	7.7	Wexford	3,486	13.1
Keweenaw	137	8.1	**Michigan**	**1,023,068**	**10.9**

Source: Michigan Department of Social Services, Data Reporting Unit, Program Statistics Fiscal 1993 (Lansing, Michigan: 1994).

Table VII-12. Number and Percent of Individuals Receiving Financial Payments in Michigan: Fiscal Years 1980-1994

Fiscal Year	Individuals Receiving Payments (Rounded To Nearest 25,000)	Percent(%) of State Population	Fiscal Year	Individuals Receiving Payments (Rounded To Nearest 25,000)	Percent(%) of State Population
1980	1,200,000	13.0	1988	1,200,000	13.0
1981	1,300,000	14.1	1989	1,200,000	12.9
1982	1,300,000	14.3	1990	1,200,000	13.0
1983	1,400,000	15.5	1991	1,300,000	13.9
1984	1,400,000	15.5	1992	1,225,000	13.0
1985	1,300,000	14.3	1993	1,275,000	13.5
1986	1,225,000	13.4	1994	1,300,000	13.7
1987	1,200,000	13.0			

Source: Michigan Department of Social Services, Data Reporting Unit (Lansing, Michigan).

Table VII-13. Children's Protective Services Referrals Studied and Number of Child Sexual Abuse Victims in Michigan: Fiscal Years 1983-1994

Fiscal Year	Referrals Studied	Non-Substantiated	Substantiated	Child Sexual Abuse Victims
1983	---	---	---	2,030
1984	40,210	24,836	15,374	2,928
1985	42,982	27,367	15,615	3,518
1986	49,367	31,211	18,156	4,025
1987	49,392	33,083	16,309	3,457
1988	47,934	31,970	15,964	3,115
1989	48,970	32,811	16,159	3,145
1990	50,997	35,116	15,881	2,689
1991	49,074	33,134	15,940	2,553
1992	51,601	36,177	15,424	2,570
1993	53,302	41,819	11,483	2,111
1994	57,394	44,639	12,755	1,934

Source: Michigan Department of Social Services, Policy Analysis Div., Information Packet May 1995 (Lansing, Michigan: 1995) --- No Data.

Table VII-14. Statewide Abuse and Neglect Caseload and Type of Placement in Michigan: Fiscal Years 1983-1994

Fiscal Year	Total Caseload	Out-of-Home Placement*	Relative Placements	Own Home/ Legal Guardian	Other**
1983	10,532	7,011	1,526	1,693	302
1984	11,273	7,517	1,545	1,867	344
1985	11,981	7,963	1,587	2,040	391
1986	13,166	8,111	2,356	2,330	369
1987	14,113	8,625	2,550	2,503	435
1988	15,319	9,364	2,824	2,663	468
1989	15,692	9,711	2,851	2,702	428
1990	16,735	10,645	3,057	2,581	452
1991	17,179	10,935	3,214	2,524	506
1992	16,974	10,797	3,284	2,397	496
1993	15,797	10,101	3,127	2,118	451
1994	16,238	10,273	3,382	2,105	478

* Includes DSS foster homes, private agency foster homes, DSS group homes, public shelter homes, residential care centers, detention facility, jail, private institutions, DSS training schools, DSS camps, mental health facility, court treatment facility, out-of-state placements, and Arbor Heights. ** Includes independent living, boarding school, runaway services, and AWOL.

Source: Michigan Department of Social Services, Policy Analysis Division, Information Packet May 1995 (Lansing, Michigan: 1995).

Table VII-15. Number of Neglected Children in Foster Care Homes and Private Institutions in Michigan: 9-84 thru 9-94

Fiscal Year	Total	DSS Foster Homes	Private Agency FH	Private Institutions
9-84	7,143	3,344	2,648	1,151
9-85	7,616	3,423	3,000	1,193
9-86	7,734	3,238	3,350	1,146
9-87	8,264	3,212	3,903	1,149
9-88	8,973	3,282	3,504	1,187
9-89	9,391	3,385	4,853	1,153
9-90	10,141	3,682	5,350	1,109
9-91	10,630	3,712	5,850	1,068
9-92	10,520	3,440	6,110	970
9-93	9,802	3,108	5,797	897
9-94	9,946	3,090	5,906	950

Source: Michigan Department of Social Services, Policy Analysis Division, Information Packet May 1995 (Lansing, Michigan: 1995).

Table VII-16. Child Support Collections, AFDC and Non-AFDC Case Related In-State Collections, Michigan: Fiscal Years 1983-1994

Fiscal Year	Total	AFDC	Non-AFDC
1983	$273,800,000	$977,000	$176,100
1984	305,400,000	106,800	198,600
1985	341,100,000	111,900	229,200
1986	424,600,000	125,400	299,200
1987	531,000,000	127,500	403,500
1988	579,200,000	131,700	447,500
1989	610,700,000	138,000	472,700
1990	644,700,000	145,200	499,500
1991	697,600,000	153,700	543,900
1992	778,500,000	164,000	614,500
1993	865,500,000	162,000	703,500
1994	885,500,000	166,200	719,300

Note: Totals are year end amounts. Source: Michigan Department of Social Services, Policy Analysis Division, Information Packet May 1995 (Lansing, Michigan: 1995).

Table VII-17. Department of Social Services' Domestic Violence Program Statistics in Michigan: 1989-1994

Program Summary	1994	1993	1992	1991	1990	1989
Number of Shelters	45	44	42	42	42	42
Counties Served	81	80	78	77	77	77
Number of Residential Adults*	6,340	6,343	6,058	6,265	5,600	6,056
Number of Residential Children*	9,181	8,732	8,776	8,978	7,743	9,038
Average Shelter Days	14.3	12.6	11.5	11.6	13.7	11.4
Total Shelter Days	222,168	190,921	171,026	176,968	182,326	172,573
Number of Crisis Calls	70,246	59,651	53,176	51,401	50,148	39,339
Number Denied Shelter Due to Lack of Space	2,205	2,299	2,354	1,780	1,423	1,735
Number of Non-Residents Served	9,168	8,785	7,318	7,651	N.A.	N.A.

* In 1990, the method of counting the number of shelter residents changed so that those with multiple shelter stays were only counted once. N.A. data not available. Source: Michigan Department of Social Services, Policy Analysis Division, Information Packet May 1995 (Lansing, Michigan: 1995).

Table VII-18. Workers' Compensation Policies, Premiums, and Payroll in Michigan, Voluntary Market: 1982-1994

| Year | Policies | Standard Premiums (In Thousands) | Payroll (In Thousands) | Average Rate per $100 Pay | | Manual Rate | Rate Difference |
| | | | | Standard | | | |
				Rate	Index		
1982	120,097	$589,283	$23,833,497	2.5	100.0	2.7	-8.4
1983	126,310	572,079	26,648,607	2.2	86.9	2.5	-17.2
1984	129,620	556,273	28,166,790	2.0	80.0	2.4	-19.3
1985	127,750	634,036	29,697,705	2.1	86.4	2.4	-12.9
1986	125,439	767,884	31,819,528	2.4	97.7	2.6	-6.8
1987	126,329	871,985	33,870,928	2.6	104.2	2.9	-10.7
1988	130,730	934,035	36,448,015	2.6	103.8	2.9	-12.1
1989	135,148	1,010,806	38,974,961	2.6	105.0	2.9	-10.2
1990	138,275	1,093,277	41,327,945	2.7	107.1	3.0	-12.1
1991	137,063	1,171,189	42,571,896	2.8	111.3	3.0	-9.5
1992	135,236	1,158,091	43,422,865	2.7	107.9	3.2	-16.1
1993	138,989	1,107,687	42,632,297	2.6	105.1	3.4	-24.2
1994	140,827	1,098,286	43,874,142	2.5	101.2	3.6	-30.5

Source: Michigan Department of Commerce, Insurance Bureau, Final Report on the State of Competition in the Workers' Compensation Insurance Market (Lansing, Michigan: 1995).

Table VII-19. Employer Basic Report of Injury and Number of Contested Cases in Michigan: 1968-1993

Year	Employer Basic Report of Injury	Contested Cases	Year	Employer Basic Report of Injury	Contested Cases
1968	59,483	20,451	1981	77,203	44,054
1969	63,581	22,247	1982	66,676	32,674
1970	71,981	21,563	1983	67,450	28,615
1971	72,437	23,769	1984	75,045	21,867
1972	69,045	26,336	1985	84,513	22,072
1973	69,204	25,982	1986	90,790	21,751
1974	69,847	28,107	1987	89,580	21,541
1975	62,786	28,776	1988	95,736	24,230
1976	70,397	29,681	1989	93,549	23,015
1977	76,934	29,636	1990	89,064	22,277
1978	85,078	30,636	1991	89,963	23,534
1979	97,088	37,865	1992	92,476	20,071
1980	88,307	40,232	1993	88,259	22,496

Source: Michigan Department of Labor, Bureau of Workers' Disability Compensation (Lansing, Michigan: 1994).

Table VII-20. Annual Workers' Compensation Paid in Michigan, Not Including Medical: 1977-1993

Year	Total Payments	Insurance Companies	Self-Insured Employers
1977	$276,379,146	$170,611,790	$105,767,356
1978	286,536,927	172,262,034	114,274,893
1979	399,893,431	247,838,475	152,054,955
1980	431,243,399	256,196,737	175,046,662
1981	500,064,989	300,724,668	199,340,321
1982	467,072,152	270,339,899	196,732,252
1983	450,574,606	256,599,150	193,975,456
1984	453,983,583	249,474,286	204,509,297
1985	523,640,905	302,504,526	221,136,278
1986	547,690,078	317,260,634	230,429,444
1987	588,674,899	348,323,667	240,351,232
1988	688,092,909	392,853,121	295,239,788
1989	770,791,025	440,073,189	330,717,836
1990	870,733,560	496,749,876	373,983,684
1991	907,254,906	499,617,302	407,637,604
1992	974,075,716	553,563,944	420,511,773
1993	934,060,557	504,827,116	429,233,441

Source: Michigan Department of Labor, Bureau of Workers' Disability Compensation (Lansing, Michigan: 1994).

Table VII-21. Status of Michigan's Unemployment Insurance Trust Fund: 1937-1995

Year	Benefits Charged To Fund		Employer Contribution	Interest Earned On Fund	Total Available For Benefits
	Regular	State Share Of EB			
1937	$ 0	---	$43,128,416	$176,080	$43,304,496
1938	39,903,200	---	32,904,180	1,186,186	37,491,662
1939	37,113,553	---	45,156,850	996,468	46,531,427
1940	27,191,492	---	50,870,924	1,349,568	69,628,941
1941	15,316,185	---	67,537,385	2,131,530	123,981,671
1942	40,952,428	---	57,149,743	2,997,128	143,176,114
1943	3,218,935	---	62,806,826	3,391,914	206,155,919
1944	6,163,979	---	53,576,037	4,175,315	257,743,292
1945	77,228,381	---	62,179,962	5,104,368	247,799,241
1946	79,219,621	---	39,437,347	4,381,178	212,398,145
1947	33,508,714	---	59,656,846	4,212,059	242,758,336
1948	34,342,023	---	77,976,899	5,242,800	291,636,012
1949	80,782,987	---	78,261,198	6,347,800	295,462,023
1950	48,812,574	---	63,156,825	6,351,825	316,158,099
1951	47,119,684	---	78,763,108	7,098,995	354,900,518
1952	61,987,036	---	76,533,186	7,858,261	377,304,929
1953	39,485,105	---	90,799,289	9,244,297	437,863,410
1954	147,842,084	---	69,185,903	10,044,822	369,252,051
1955	67,045,468	---	54,169,188	8,449,183	364,824,954
1956	150,076,923	---	73,391,698	8,138,247	298,125,596
1957	132,316,631	---	115,808,198	7,648,875	293,021,042
1958	323,912,683	---	107,793,491	5,816,062	197,422,403
1959	133,000,920	---	137,492,773	2,480,021	204,394,277
1960	147,391,056	---	159,113,022	3,043,312	219,159,555
1961	210,589,794	---	147,687,355	2,261,767	158,518,883
1962	113,798,796	---	160,305,104	1,686,245	206,711,436
1963	91,534,912	---	184,421,382	3,755,153	303,353,059
1964	78,490,472	---	187,156,162	7,784,611	411,671,860
1965	58,966,871	---	172,199,394	12,556,118	511,360,501
1966	77,900,629	---	180,591,079	17,173,430	602,424,381
1967	124,444,720	---	136,711,106	21,187,721	592,205,153
1968	113,777,040	---	117,704,575	22,838,254	577,783,644
1969	111,584,894	---	130,973,741	25,888,416	623,060,907
1970	282,187,339	---	120,983,852	28,752,898	484,129,447
1971	294,622,200	$ 6,480,871	133,287,482	21,762,871	308,319,180
1972	245,397,215	36,238,420	310,221,438	15,262,387	379,105,801
1973	183,017,067	9,299,989	338,702,497	21,959,511	556,750,742
1974	458,359,440	36,196,426	296,240,887	29,701,290	388,137,053

267

Table VII-21. Status of Michigan's Unemployment Insurance Trust Fund: 1937-1995 Continued

Year	Benefits Charged To Fund		Employer Contributions	Interest Earned On Fund	Total Available For Benefits
	Regular	State Share Of EB			
1975	$835,929,776	$132,475,186	$283,800,953	$10,854,796	$37,642,203
1976	487,645,946	88,044,106	470,121,669	15,426	148,161,854
1977	406,690,499	67,605,021	591,873,538	0	339,556,980
1978	392,903,898	31,480,518	690,760,910	248,807	597,103,340
1979	596,681,951	21,267,483	724,109,860	9,889,124	117,559,600
1980	1,142,458,666	150,764,944	617,516,567	393,142	208,512,026
1981	936,226,157	128,303,250	624,164,088	0	8,822,082
1982	1,524,272,973	178,723,970	598,996,399	0	0
1983	939,776,378	78,284,427	833,591,498	0	0
1984	599,604,165	4,528,431	1,146,189,065	0	0
1985	648,937,483	1,176,862	1,330,473,204	0	454,009,223
1986	727,486,115	-117,479	1,329,593,215	0	935,167,223
1987	921,065,123	-12,208	1,179,237,833	5,989,988	978,224,505
1988	923,791,331	-2,870	1,071,163,749	11,799,594	981,921,038
1989	914,372,688	1,049	1,052,287,877	28,600,271	972,496,273
1990	1,129,434,315	0	1,050,913,432	29,975,312	713,500,000
1991	1,491,126,083	51,675,113	1,050,860,222	4,931,780	251,000,000
1992	1,221,010,903	254,684	1,133,105,245	1,119,815	140,231,663
1993	988,472,854	41,022	1,165,385,331	21,672,680	364,530,473
1994	819,740,544	0	1,283,617,606	40,763,717	866,906,368
1995	842,047,540	0	1,389,721,843	84,256,625	4,497,688,281

--- No program. EB stands for extended benefit.
Source: Michigan Employment Security Commission, Handbook of Unemployment Insurance Program Statistics (Detroit, Michigan: 1994).

Table VII-22. Federal Advances Received from Unemployment Trust Fund*, Michigan: 1958 - 1994
(Data in Millions of Dollars)

Year	Federal Advances During Year	Repayments During Year	FUTA Reduction Offset	Balance Outstanding End of Year
1958	$113.0	$---	$---	$113.0
1959-1962	---	---	---	113.0
1963	---	---	7.3	105.7
1964	---	8.1	8.1	89.5
1965	---	8.7	---	80.8
1966	---	9.6	---	71.2
1967	---	30.0	---	41.2
1968	---	41.2	---	---
1969-1974	---	---	---	---
1975	326.0	---	---	326.0
1976	245.0	---	---	571.0
1977	53.0	---	---	624.0
1978	---	---	---	624.0
1979	---	624.0	---	0.0
1980	842.0	---	---	842.0
1981	233.0	---	---	1,075.0
1982	1,181.6	70.8	---	2,185.8
1983	789.8	613.0	40.4	2,322.3
1984	429.2	983.0	102.7	1,665.8
1985	192.6	438.4	131.4	1,288.7
1986	---	166.0	1.9	1,120.8
1987	---	168.0	0.2	952.6
1988	---	71.0	0.1	781.5
1989	---	179.0	---	602.5
1990	---	185.0	---	417.5
1991	---	0.0	---	417.5
1992	210.0	210.0	204.8	212.7
1993	75.5	75.5	238.7	0.0
1994	0.0	0.0	1.7	0.0

*Federal Unemployment Account of the Unemployment Trust Fund, Section 1201, Title XII, of the Social Security Act. --- No data.
Source: Michigan Employment Security Commission, Handbook of Unemployment Insurance Program Statistics (Detroit, Michigan: 1994).

Table VII-23. Relationship of Average Weekly Benefit Claims to Total Unemployment in Michigan: 1975-1995 Annual Averages
(Data in Thousands)

Calendar Year	Benefit Claims*		Total Unemployment	Percent(%) of Total Unemployment	
	Regular Program	All Programs**		Regular Program	All Programs
1975	249.6	391.3	486.0	51.4	80.5
1976	155.8	276.1	373.0	41.8	74.0
1977	140.4	216.9	337.0	41.7	64.4
1978	128.5	145.4	289.0	44.5	50.3
1979	162.9	173.5	335.0	48.6	51.8
1980	284.1	352.7	534.0	53.2	66.0
1981	192.7	242.0	529.0	36.4	45.7
1982	230.1	298.3	661.0	34.8	45.1
1983	144.2	241.3	608.0	23.7	39.7
1984	102.1	123.1	488.0	20.9	25.2
1985	103.4	110.9	433.0	23.9	25.6
1986	108.6	108.6	385.0	28.2	28.2
1987	121.4	121.4	369.0	32.9	32.9
1988	116.0	116.0	348.0	33.3	33.3
1989	109.4	109.9	326.0	33.6	33.7
1990	121.1	121.1	344.0	35.2	35.2
1991	154.4	168.1	418.0	37.0	40.2
1992	133.1	205.8	405.0	32.9	50.8
1993	108.4	157.3	328.0	33.0	48.0
1994	92.0	96.7	282.0	32.6	34.2
1995	88.3	88.3	252.0	35.0	35.0

* Includes Intrastate and Interstate Agent Weeks Claimed. Excludes Unemployment Compensation for Ex-Service Personnel and Interstate Liable Weeks Claimed. Adjusted for Working Days in Year. **Includes Regular Benefits, Extended Benefits, Federal Supplemental Compensation, Emergency Unemployment Compensation, Federal Supplemental Benefits, Additional Federal Supplemental Benefits and Supplemental Unemployment Assistance. Source: Michigan Employment Security Commission, Handbook of Unemployment Insurance Program Statistics (Detroit, Michigan: 1994).

Table VII-24. Unemployment Compensation Benefit Payments Programs in Michigan: 1938-1994

Year	Total Payments Regular Benefits Program	Total Payments Extended Benefits Program	Federal Supplemental Compensation Program	Emergency Unemployment Compensation Program	Temporary Benefit Programs (TUC/TEC)
1938	$39,907,305	$---	$---	$---	$---
1939	37,160,876	---	---	---	---
1940	27,232,423	---	---	---	---
1941	15,348,516	---	---	---	---
1942	40,987,638	---	---	---	---
1943	3,272,816	---	---	---	---
1944	6,175,312	---	---	---	---
1945	78,507,028	---	---	---	---
1946	78,808,184	---	---	---	---
1947	32,923,558	---	---	---	---
1948	34,575,622	---	---	---	---
1949	79,176,946	---	---	---	---
1950	50,498,316	---	---	---	---
1951	46,648,871	---	---	---	---
1952	63,827,413	---	---	---	---
1953	38,572,261	---	---	---	---
1954	148,501,057	---	---	---	---
1955	68,552,016	---	---	---	---
1956	149,897,741	---	---	---	---
1957	131,144,591	---	---	---	---
1958	326,428,009	---	---	---	60,808,000
1959	134,667,084	---	---	---	14,269,227
1960	146,136,385	---	---	---	---
1961	213,601,418	---	---	---	43,181,651
1962	115,150,807	---	---	---	10,448,083
1963	92,666,244	---	---	---	---
1964	79,633,150	---	---	---	---
1965	59,914,356	---	---	---	---
1966	78,350,639	---	---	---	---
1967	125,259,322	---	---	---	---
1968	115,228,981	---	---	---	---
1969	112,015,489	---	---	---	---
1970	280,303,326	---	---	---	---
1971	304,584,651	74,490,145	---	---	---
1972	249,788,826	18,975,152	---	---	---
1973	187,378,387	---	---	---	---
1974	464,260,065	73,174,772	---	---	---
1975	867,385,847	245,393,057	---	---	---
1976	526,985,506	186,874,811	---	---	---

Table VII-24. Unemployment Compensation Benefit Payments Programs in Michigan: 1938-1994 Continued

Year	Total Payments Regular Benefits Program	Total Payments Extended Benefits Program	Federal Supplemental Compensation Program	Emergency Unemployment Compensation Program	Temporary Benefit Programs (TUC/TEC)
1977	$436,322,708	$147,882,228	$---	$---	$---
1978	417,788,085	68,930,834	---	---	---
1979	622,475,394	46,331,082	---	---	---
1980	1,183,481,416	314,581,597	---	---	---
1981	1,005,917,583	248,080,125	---	---	---
1982	1,593,270,291	353,203,366	131,595,662	---	---
1983	977,089,578	153,039,639	521,140,447	---	---
1984	629,238,738	268,202	148,068,252	---	---
1985	676,030,002	88,634	59,717,026	---	---
1986	754,661,831	1,118	54,196	---	---
1987	956,728,668	1,750	17,592	---	---
1988	958,455,833	---	2,601	---	---
1989	938,913,234	---	---	---	---
1990	1,165,835,850	---	---	---	---
1991	1,547,832,094	91,580,453	---	44,374,762	---
1992	1,287,613,689	87,339	---	749,148,201	---
1993	1,050,078,596	3,395	---	535,284,669	---
1994	880,180,282	0	---	51,146,976	---

--- No data.

Source: Michigan Employment Security Commission, Handbook of Unemployment Insurance Program Statistics (Detroit, Michigan: 1994).

Table VII-25. Average, Minimum and Maximum Unemployment Insurance Contribution Rates and Taxable Wage Base in Michigan: 1970 - 1996

Year	Taxable Wage Base	Minimum Contribution Rate(%)	Maximum Contribution Rate(%)	Median Contribution Rate(%)	Average Contribution Rate as Percent(%) of:	
					Taxable Payroll	Total Payroll
1970	3,600	0.0	6.0	---	1.29	0.59
1971	3,600	0.0	6.0	---	1.51	0.63
1972	4,200	0.1	6.6	---	3.10	1.38
1973	4,200	0.2	6.6	---	2.95	1.24
1974	4,200	0.1	6.6	---	2.53	1.02
1975	4,200	0.1	6.6	---	2.74	1.05
1976	5,400	0.2	6.6	---	3.61	1.53
1977	5,400	0.2	6.6	2.68	4.08	1.63
1978	6,000	1.0	7.5	2.65	4.11	1.68
1979	6,000	1.0	8.0	2.65	4.03	1.56
1980	6,000	1.0	8.5	2.61	3.73	1.37
1981	6,000	1.0	9.0	2.62	3.83	1.31
1982	6,000	1.0	9.0	2.65	3.92	1.30
1983	8,000	1.0	10.0	2.85	4.64	1.82
1984	8,500	1.0	10.0	3.32	5.42	2.12
1985	9,000	1.0	10.0	2.98	5.71	2.22
1986	9,500	1.0	10.0	2.70	5.44	2.14
1987	9,500	1.0	10.0	2.69	4.59	1.79
1988	9,500	1.0	10.0	2.65	3.97	1.47
1989	9,500	1.0	10.0	2.61	3.73	1.37
1990	9,500	1.0	10.0	2.52	3.63	1.33
1991	9,500	1.0	10.0	2.20	3.70	1.34
1992	9,500	1.0	10.0	2.30	3.90	1.36
1993	9,500	0.5	10.0	2.50	4.15	1.33
1994	9,500	0.5	10.0	2.42	4.33	1.37
1995	9,500	0.5	10.0	2.35	4.28	1.36
1996*	9,500	0.5	10.0	N.A.	4.01	1.18

---No data. N.A. not avalable for this printing. * Forecast

Source: Michigan Employment Security Commission, <u>Handbook of Unemployment Insurance Program Statistics</u> (Detroit, Michigan: 1995).

Table VII-26. Relationship of Average Weekly Wage to Average Unemployment Insurance Benefit Amount in Michigan: 1937-1994

Year	Average Weekly Wage	Average Weekly Benefit Amount**	Average Weekly Benefit Amount as a(%) of Average Weekly Wage
1937	$30.28	$---	---
1938	31.68	13.49	42.6
1939	30.82	13.31	43.2
1940	32.66	12.56	38.5
1941	37.35	12.75	34.1
1942	45.88	16.50	36.0
1943	53.45	16.75	31.3
1944	55.02	19.01	34.6
1945	53.33	20.70	38.8
1946	53.45	20.35	38.1
1947	58.94	19.77	33.5
1948	64.26	20.34	31.7
1949	66.36	22.68	34.2
1950	71.90	24.21	33.7
1951	77.50	25.68	33.1
1952	83.33	27.21	32.7
1953	89.24	27.15	30.4
1954	90.12	29.73	33.0
1955	95.62	31.65	33.1
1956	97.24	34.12	35.1
1957	99.26	34.55	34.8
1958	100.93	36.55	36.2
1959	106.99	35.89	33.5
1960	109.70	36.19	33.0
1961	110.12	36.86	33.5
1962	115.98	35.86	30.9
1963	121.71	35.65	29.3
1964	127.86	37.38	29.2
1965	133.94	38.87	29.0
1966	135.21	46.54	34.4
1967	139.18	47.60	34.2
1968	150.67	49.71	33.0
1969	158.95	50.42	31.7
1970	163.38	56.49	34.6
1971	175.77	59.27	33.7
1972	189.63	59.79	31.5
1973	203.55	59.39	29.2
1974	212.58	67.09	31.6
1975	225.10	79.22	35.2

Table VII-26. Relationship of Average Weekly Wage to Average Unemployment Insurance Benefit Amount in Michigan: 1937-1994 Continued

Year	Average Weekly Wage	Average Weekly Benefit Amount**	Average Weekly Benefit Amount as a (%) of Average Weekly Wage
1976	$248.07	$87.82	35.4
1977	269.33	89.56	33.3
1978	289.54	92.86	32.1
1979	311.40	99.04	31.8
1980	333.26	101.87	30.6
1981	358.26	128.08	35.7
1982	369.13	154.74	41.9
1983	386.59	150.38	38.9
1984	411.48	143.73	34.9
1985	431.18	145.83	33.8
1986	446.08	154.92	34.7
1987	452.69	173.31	38.3
1988	475.94	183.82	38.6
1989	483.72	189.74	39.2
1990	491.86	203.94	41.5
1991	504.43	212.42	42.1
1992	529.44	211.29	39.9
1993	544.05	215.02	39.5
1994	571.34	212.77	37.2

Note: **Regular UI Claimants. ---No data.
Source: Michigan Employment Security Commission, Handbook of Unemployment Insurance Program Statistics (Detroit, Michigan: 1994)

Table VII-27. Relationship of Average Weekly Unemployment Insurance Benefit Amount to Maximum Weekly Benefit Amount in Michigan: 1956-1994

Year	Average Weekly Benefit Amount	Maximum Weekly Benefit Amount (WBA)		Effective Date For New Maximums
		Zero Dependent	Four or More Dependent	
1956	$34.12	$30	$54	
1957	34.55	30	55	6/21/57
1958	36.55	30	55	
1959	35.89	30	55	
1960	36.19	30	55	
1961	36.86	30	55	
1962	35.86	30	55	
1963	35.65	33	60	9/6/63
1964	37.38	33	60	
1965	38.87	43	72	9/5/65
1966	46.54	43	72	
1967	47.60	46	76	8/27/67
1968	49.71	46	76	
1969	50.42	46	76	
1970	56.49	53	87	5/10/70
1971	59.27	53	87	
1972	59.79	56	92	1/31/72
1973	59.39	56	92	
1974	67.09	67	106	6/9/74
1975	79.22	97	136	6/8/75
1976	87.82	97	136	
1977	89.56	97	136	
1978	92.86	97	136	
1979	99.04	97	136	
1980	101.87	97	136	
		Minimum WBA	Maximum WBA	
1981	128.08	17	182	3/1/81
1982	154.74	41	197	1/1/82
1983	150.38	54	197	
1984	143.73	54	197	
1985	145.83	54	197	
1986	154.92	54	197	
1987	173.31	58	229	1/4/87
1988	183.82	58	242	1/4/88
1989	189.74	59	263	1/1/89
1990	203.94	59	275	1/7/90
1991	212.42	59	276	1/6/91
1992	211.29	42	293	1/1/92
1993	215.02	42	293	1/2/93
1994	212.77	42	293	1/3/94

Source: Michigan Employment Security Commission, Handbook of Unemployment Insurance Program Statistics (Detroit, Michigan: 1994).

Table VII-28. Average Weekly Insured Unemployment and Rate, Average Duration of Unemployment, and Total Unemployment Rate in Michigan: 1956-1995

Year	Average Weekly Insured Unemployment	Insured Unemployment Rate(%) (IUR)	Average Duration of Unemployment Weeks	Total Unemployment Rate(%) (TUR)	IUR/TUR Ratio(%)
1956	98,601	5.24	12.3	6.9	75.9
1957	90,112	4.79	11.3	6.6	72.6
1958	201,381	12.22	17.7	13.7	89.2
1959	88,075	5.07	10.3	8.4	60.4
1960	93,891	5.31	11.3	6.7	79.3
1961	131,382	7.86	14.9	10.1	77.8
1962	76,125	4.39	10.5	7.0	62.7
1963	62,287	3.49	9.7	5.6	62.3
1964	51,675	2.75	9.0	4.8	57.3
1965	38,193	1.89	7.6	3.9	48.5
1966	40,468	1.79	8.2	3.5	51.1
1967	61,979	2.73	9.8	4.5	60.7
1968	55,465	2.38	9.8	4.3	55.3
1969	52,569	2.17	9.8	4.0	54.3
1970	116,969	5.05	13.0	6.7	75.4
1971	123,201	5.35	14.2	7.6	70.4
1972	102,588	3.92	12.8	7.0	56.0
1973	78,834	2.84	12.1	5.9	48.1
1974	162,949	5.92	11.4	7.4	80.0
1975	248,663	8.74	16.2	12.5	69.9
1976	160,207	5.34	13.2	9.4	56.8
1977	139,336	4.40	12.2	8.2	53.8
1978	127,573	3.75	10.8	6.9	54.3
1979	162,071	4.70	11.4	7.8	60.3
1980	283,091	8.76	18.1	12.4	70.6
1981	191,897	6.03	13.8	12.3	49.1
1982	229,703	7.63	17.3	15.5	49.2
1983	143,909	4.72	17.7	14.2	33.2
1984	101,752	3.18	12.8	11.2	28.4
1985	102,982	3.05	13.6	9.9	30.8
1986	108,267	3.12	12.3	8.8	35.5
1987	121,011	3.41	15.5	8.2	41.6
1988	116,044	3.18	16.0	7.6	41.8
1989	109,434	2.90	12.8	7.1	40.8
1990	121,120	3.16	12.5	7.5	42.3
1991	154,886	4.13	14.5	9.2	44.9
1992	133,187	3.51	12.8	8.8	39.9
1993	108,445	2.81	12.7	7.0	40.1
1994	92,009	2.29	13.2	5.9	38.8
1995	88,304	2.15*	11.2	5.6	38.3*

* Estimated
Source: Michigan Employment Security Commission, <u>Handbook of Unemployment Insurance Program Statistics</u> (Detroit, Michigan: 1994).

Table VII-29. Churches and Church Membership in Michigan, by Denomination: 1990

Denomination	Number of Churches	Communicant, Confirmed, Full Members	Total Adherents*		
			Number	Percent(%) of Total Population	Percent(%) of Total Adherents
Michigan	**7,229**	**1,583,261**	**4,686,550***	**50.4**	**100.0**
Advent Church of Christ	3	111	135*	---	---
African Methodist Episcopal Zion	18	38,774	47,183	0.5	1.0
Albanian Orthodox Arc	1	N.R.	N.R	---	---
Allegheny Wesleyan Methodist Connection	2	0	0*	---	---
American Baptist USA	176	53,812	67,895*	0.7	1.4
Apostolic Christian Church (Naz)	2	84	105*	---	---
Apostolic Christian Church-Amer	3	328	583	---	---
Apostolic Lutheran	19	1,133	2,154	---	---
Armenian Apostolic Church Am	1	1,000	5,000	0.1	0.1
Assemb of God	268	34,307	67,404	0.7	1.4
Baptist General Conference	53	7,528	9,544*	0.1	0.2
Baptist Missionary Association	15	1,663	2,118*	---	---
Beachy Amish	1	44	57*	---	---
Brethren (ASH)	1	10	13*	---	---
Brethren IN CR	7	216	340	---	---
Catholic	915	N.A.	2,338,608	25.2	49.9
Armenian	1	N.A.	600	---	---
Byzan Ruth	7	N.A.	2,447	---	---
Chaldean	5	N.A.	31,000	0.3	0.7
Latin	888	N.A.	2,292,593	24.7	48.9
Maronite	2	N.A.	3,457	---	0.1
Melkite-Greek	3	N.A.	2,274	---	---
Romanian	2	N.A.	644	---	---
Ukraninian	7	N.A.	5,593	0.1	0.1
Christian & Missionary Alliance	32	2,312	4,313	---	0.1
Christian Church (Disciples of Christ)	39	6,326	9,170	0.1	0.2
Christian Churches & Churches Christ	114	16,521	20,930*	0.2	0.4
Christian Reformed	235	65,792	100,680	1.1	2.1
Church of Christ, Scientst	79	N.R.	N.R.	---	---
Church of God (Abraham)	7	428	544*	---	---
Church of God (Anderson)	131	12,553	14,901	0.2	0.3
Church of God (Cleveland)	110	15,865	20,024	0.2	0.4
Church of God (7th) Den	11	341	431	---	---
Congregation in Christ(Menn)	2	355	453*	---	---
Church of God of Prophecy	29	1,025	1,297*	---	---
Church of God Mountain Assembly	8	410	522*	---	---

Table VII-29. Churches and Church Membership in Michigan, by Denomination: 1990 Continued

Denomination	Number of Churches	Communicant, Confirmed, Full Members	Total Adherents*		
			Number	Percent(%) of Total Population	Percent(%) of Total Adherents
Latter-Day Saints	77	N.A.	23,475	0.3	0.5
Church of Brethren	26	1,428	1,794	---	---
Church of Lutheran Conf	6	711	943	---	---
Church of Nazarene	197	20,242	34,214	0.4	0.7
Churches of Christ	198	23,075	30,591	0.3	0.7
Church of God-General Congregation	8	200	253*	---	---
Congregational Christian Churches	52	13,924	17,571*	0.2	0.4
Congregational Christian Churches, Not Nat'l	6	2,322	2,967*	---	0.1
Conservative Baptist	28	N.R.	N.R.	---	---
Conservative Congregational	21	2,182	2,768*	---	0.1
Cumberland Presbyterian	3	232	245	---	---
Episcopal	246	47,929	71,727	0.8	1.5
Estonian Evangelical Lutheran Church	1	90	111*	---	---
Evangelical Free Church	26	1,976	3,791	---	0.1
Evangelical Lutheran Church in America	362	123,952	167,598	1.8	3.6
Evangelical Lutheran Syn	9	1,109	1,549	---	---
Fellowship of Evangelical Bible Churches	1	12	20	---	---
Evangelical Menn Inc	3	257	331*	---	---
Evangelical Methodist Church	1	4	5*	---	---
Evan Presbyterian Church	17	9,360	9,711	0.1	0.2
Free Lutheran	7	534	712	---	---
Free Methodist	137	9,369	14,465	0.2	0.3
Free Will Baptist	33	3,998	5,007*	0.1	0.1
Friends-USA	21	1,142	1,497*	---	---
Evangelical Friends International	8	653	845	---	---
Friends General Conference	9	343	446*	---	---
Friends United Meeting	4	146	206*	---	---
Greek Orthodox	22	N.R.	N.R.	---	---
Apostolic Catholic Assyrian	2	131	680	---	---
Independent Fundamental Churches of America	109	N.R.	N.R.	---	---
International Foursquare Gospel	10	659	825*	---	---
Internation Pentecostal Church	8	215	308	---	---
Lat Evangelical Lutheran	6	1,492	1,640	---	---
Lutheran-Missouri Synod	404	185,240	250,141	2.7	5.3
Lutheran Church, The American Association of	2	61	86	---	---
Mennonite Church	56	3,246	5,230	0.1	0.1

Table VII-29. Churches and Church Membership in Michigan, by Denomination: 1990 Continued

Denomination	Number of Churches	Communicant, Confirmed, Full Members	Total Adherents*		
			Number	Percent(%) of Total Population	Percent(%) of Total Adherents
Menn Gen Conf	5	142	207	---	---
Missionary Ch	69	4,015	7,192	0.1	0.2
Morav Ch-North	4	633	798	---	---
Neth Ref Congr	3	1,025	1,817	---	---
N AM Bapt Conf	22	5,353	6,692*	0.1	0.1
*Old MB Ascs	1	121	149*	---	---
Old Order Amish	38	N.A.	5,250	0.1	0.1
Old Reg Bapt	11	412	517*	---	---
Open Bible Std	3	N.R.	N.R.	---	---
Orthodox Church in Amercia	9	N.R.	N.R.	---	---
Pentecostal Church of God	53	1,813	4,729	0.1	0.1
Pentecostal Holiness	6	136	173*	---	---
Christian Brethren	50	3,322	5,424	0.1	0.1
Presbyterian Church (USA)	275	100,122	126,324*	1.4	2.7
Presbyterian Church in America	5	908	1,116	---	---
Primitive Baptists Ascs	4	138	176*	---	---
Prot Conf (Lu)	1	50	65	---	---
Reformed Church in Amercia	162	53,029	88,399	1.0	1.9
Romanian Orthodox	6	N.R.	N.R.	---	---
Salvation Army	56	6,873	7,896	0.1	0.2
Seventh Day Adeventists	185	29,905	37,949*	0.4	0.8
S-D Baptist Gc	2	217	277*	---	---
Southern Baptist Convention	236	49,133	61,953*	0.7	1.3
Syrian Antioch	2	N.A.	1,700	---	---
Ukranian American	2	N.R.	N.R.	---	---
Unitarian-Universalist	21	3,075	4,266	---	0.1
United Baptist	1	26	31*	---	---
United Bretheren in Christ	48	3,935	4,803	0.1	0.1
United Church of Christ	200	58,740	74,302*	0.8	1.6
United Methodist	938	199,321	252,129*	2.7	5.4
Wesleyan	142	12,026	39,404	0.4	0.8
Wisconsin Evangel Lutheran Synod	138	36,051	47,357	0.5	1.0
Jewish Est-1	73	N.A.	107,116	1.2	2.3
Black Baptest-2	N.A.	295,710	374,325	4.0	8.0
Independent Charis-3	21	N.A.	20,830	0.2	0.4
Indep Non-Char-3	50	N.A.	38,525	0.4	0.8

Note: N.A.- not applicable, N.R.- not reported. *Total adherents estimated from known number of communicants, confirmed, and full members. --- Represents a percentage of less than 0.1, Source: Association of Statisticians of American Religious Bodies, Churches and Church Membership in the United States 1990 Published by Glenmary Research Company (Atlanta, Georgia: 1990).

Table VII-30. Churches and Church Membership in Michigan, by Denomination and County: 1990

County and Denomination	Number of Churches	Communicant, Confirmed, Full Members	Total Adherents*		
			Number	Percent(%) of Total Population	Percent(%) of Total Adherents
MICHIGAN	**7,229**	**1,583,261**	**4,686,550**	**50.4**	**100.0**
African Methodist Episcopal Zion	18	38,774	47,183	0.5	1.0
American Baptist USA	176	53,812	67,895	0.7	1.4
Assembly of God	268	34,307	67,404	0.7	1.4
Black Baptist	N.A.	295,710	374,325	4.0	8.0
Catholic	915	N.A.	2,338,608	25.2	49.9
Christian Reformed	235	65,792	100,680	1.1	2.1
Episcopal	246	47,929	71,727	0.8	1.5
Evangelical Lutheran Church in America	362	123,952	167,598	1.8	3.6
Jewish	73	N.A.	107,116	1.2	2.3
Lutheran-Missouri Synod	404	185,240	250,141	2.7	5.3
Presbyterian Church (USA)	275	100,122	126,324	1.4	2.7
Reformed Church in America	162	53,029	88,399	1.0	1.9
Southern Baptist Convention	236	49,133	61,953	0.7	1.3
United Church of Christ	200	58,740	74,302	0.8	1.6
United Methodist	938	199,321	252,129	2.7	5.4
Wisconsin Evangel Lutheran Synod	138	36,051	47,357	0.5	1.0
Alcona	**19**	**1,040**	**2,410**	**23.8**	**100.0**
American Baptist USA	1	100	119	1.2	4.9
Catholic	4	N.A.	1,175	11.6	48.8
Episcopal	1	35	35	0.3	1.5
Evangelical Lutheran Church in America	2	185	225	2.2	9.3
Lutheran-Missouri Synod	1	30	36	0.4	1.5
Presbyterian Church (USA)	2	168	200	2.0	8.3
United Methodist	4	330	392	3.9	16.3
Wisconsin Evangel Lutheran Synod	1	113	134	1.3	5.6
Alger	**18**	**1,410**	**3,993**	**44.5**	**100.0**
Catholic	4	N.A.	2,032	22.6	50.9
Episcopal	1	49	110	1.2	2.8
Evangelical Lutheran Church in America	3	498	686	7.6	17.2
Lutheran-Missouri Synod	2	322	424	4.7	10.6
Presbyterian Church (USA)	1	105	130	1.4	3.3
United Methodist	3	173	214	2.4	5.4
Allegan	**140**	**25,568**	**47,504**	**52.5**	**100.0**
American Baptist USA	1	130	170	0.2	0.4
Assembly of God	4	162	303	0.3	0.6
Black Baptist	N.A	332	435	0.5	0.9
Catholic	8	N.A	8,983	9.9	18.9
Christian Reformed	31	7,695	11,540	12.8	24.3
Episcopal	3	311	421	0.5	0.9
Evangelical Lutheran Church in America	2	482	714	0.8	1.5
Presbyterian Church (USA)	2	259	339	0.4	0.7

281

Table VII-30. Churches and Church Membership in Michigan, by Denomination and County: 1990 Continued

County and Denomination	Number of Churches	Communicant, Confirmed, Full Members	Total Adherents*		
			Number	Percent(%) of Total Population	Percent(%) of Total Adherents
Reformed Church in America	25	9,914	15,192	16.8	32.0
Southern Baptist Convention	1	39	51	0.1	0.1
United Church of Christ	2	251	329	0.4	0.7
United Methodist	20	2,650	3,471	3.8	7.3
Wisconsin Evangel Lutheran Synod	5	952	1,299	1.4	2.7
Alpena	**42**	**7,421**	**20,104**	**65.7**	**100.0**
American Baptist USA	2	225	283	0.9	1.4
Assembly of God	1	126	150	0.5	0.7
Catholic	6	N.A.	10,233	33.4	50.9
Episcopal	2	781	1,000	3.3	5.0
Evangelical Lutheran Church in America	5	2,507	3,468	11.3	17.3
Jewish	1	N.A.	0	---	---
Lutheran-Missouri Synod	3	1,606	2,216	7.2	11.0
Presbyterian Church (USA)	1	174	218	0.7	1.1
Southern Baptist Convention	1	43	54	0.2	0.3
United Church of Christ	1	336	422	1.4	2.1
United Methodist	5	669	840	2.7	4.2
Antrim	**36**	**2,702**	**5,640**	**31.0**	**100.0**
Catholic	4	N.A.	1,537	8.5	27.3
Christian Reformed	2	206	318	1.7	5.6
Episcopal	1	117	184	1.0	3.3
Evangelical Lutheran Church in America	1	87	113	0.6	2.0
Lutheran-Missouri Synod	3	309	412	2.3	7.3
Presbyterian Church (USA)	2	303	378	2.1	6.7
Reformed Church in America	1	173	296	1.6	5.2
United Methodist	8	706	881	4.8	15.6
Arenac	**27**	**2,110**	**7,751**	**51.9**	**100.0**
Assembly of God	1	74	166	1.1	2.1
Catholic	3	N.A.	4,700	31.5	60.6
Episcopal	1	58	81	0.5	1.0
Evangelical Lutheran Church in America	1	156	195	1.3	2.5
Lutheran-Missouri Synod	2	446	609	4.1	7.9
Presbyterian Church (USA)	1	51	64	0.4	0.8
Southern Baptist Convention	1	38	48	0.3	0.6
United Church of Christ	1	49	62	0.4	0.8
United Methodist	6	652	823	5.5	10.6
Wisconsin Evangel Lutheran Synod	2	117	150	1.0	1.9
Baraga	**13**	**2,141**	**4,613**	**58.0**	**100.0**
Catholic	3	N.A.	1,892	23.8	41.0
Evangelical Lutheran Church in America	5	1,607	2,043	25.7	44.3
Lutheran-Missouri Synod	1	250	324	4.1	7.0
United Methodist	2	167	210	2.6	4.6

Table VII-30. Churches and Church Membership in Michigan, by Denomination and County: 1990 Continued

County and Denomination	Number of Churches	Communicant, Confirmed, Full Members	Total Adherents*		
			Number	Percent(%) of Total Population	Percent(%) of Total Adherents
Barry	**6**	**5,867**	**12,077**	**24.1**	**100.0**
Assembly of God	3	170	423	0.8	3.5
Catholic	4	N.A.	2,410	4.8	20.0
Christian Reformed	1	93	158	0.3	1.3
Episcopal	1	158	243	0.5	2.0
Evangelical Lutheran Church in America	2	457	605	1.2	5.0
Lutheran-Missouri Synod	1	71	105	0.2	0.9
Presbyterian Church (USA)	1	605	775	1.5	6.4
Reformed Church in America	1	604	1,172	2.3	9.7
Southern Baptist Convention	2	87	111	0.2	0.9
United Methodist	15	2,291	2,933	5.9	24.3
Bay	**9**	**21,254**	**74,064**	**66.3**	**100.0**
American Baptist USA	3	863	1,085	1.0	1.5
Assembly of God	3	233	605	0.5	0.8
Black Baptist	N.A	351	441	0.4	0.6
Catholic	23	N.A.	44,406	39.7	60.0
Episcopal	2	1,146	1,326	1.2	1.8
Evangelical Lutheran Church in America	1	577	745	0.7	1.0
Jewish	1	N.A	280	0.3	0.4
Lutheran-Missouri Synod	11	9,112	11,961	10.7	16.1
Presbyterian Church (USA)	5	1,875	2,357	2.1	3.2
Southern Baptist Convention	2	215	270	0.2	0.4
United Church of Christ	2	194	244	0.2	0.3
United Methodist	10	2,288	2,877	2.6	3.9
Wisconsin Evangel Lutheran Synod	5	2,651	3,403	3.0	4.6
Benzie	**28**	**2,528**	**3,977**	**32.6**	**100.0**
Assembly of God	1	88	90	0.7	2.3
Catholic	1	N.A.	588	4.8	14.8
Episcopal	1	111	150	1.2	3.8
Evangelical Lutheran Church in America	1	311	409	3.4	10.3
Lutheran-Missouri Synod	1	184	264	2.2	6.6
United Church of Christ	1	369	457	3.7	11.5
United Methodist	5	675	835	6.8	21.0
Berrien	**179**	**46,456**	**83,979**	**52.0**	**100.0**
American Baptist USA	3	1,091	1,382	0.9	1.6
Assembly of God	5	1,068	1,985	1.2	2.4
Black Baptist	N.A.	7,039	8,914	5.5	10.6
Catholic	12	N.A.	22,424	13.9	26.7
Christian Reformed	1	192	332	0.2	0.4
Episcopal	4	489	654	0.4	0.8
Evangelical Lutheran Church in America	4	1,085	1,397	0.9	1.7
Jewish	1	N.A.	500	0.3	0.6

Table VII-30. Churches and Church Membership in Michigan, by Denomination and County: 1990 Continued

County and Denomination	Number of Churches	Communicant, Confirmed, Full Members	Total Adherents*		
			Number	Percent(%) of Total Population	Percent(%) of Total Adherents
Lutheran-Missouri Synod	10	7,434	9,768	6.1	11.6
Presbyterian Church (USA)	5	1,576	1,996	1.2	2.4
Reformed Church in America	2	160	293	0.2	0.3
Southern Baptist Convention	7	730	924	0.6	1.1
United Church of Christ	15	3,515	4,451	2.8	5.3
United Methodist	26	5,506	6,972	4.3	8.3
Wisconsin Evangel Lutheran Synod	6	3,886	4,910	3.0	5.8
Branch	**45**	**4,786**	**11,997**	**28.9**	**100.0**
American Baptist USA	2	644	827	2.0	6.9
Assembly of God	2	176	396	1.0	3.3
Black Baptist	N.A.	162	208	0.5	1.7
Catholic	3	N.A.	4,372	10.5	36.4
Episcopal	1	139	166	0.4	1.4
Evangelical Lutheran Church in America	1	182	243	0.6	2.0
Lutheran-Missouri Synod	3	392	520	1.3	4.3
Presbyterian Church (USA)	2	481	618	1.5	5.2
United Church of Christ	3	440	565	1.4	4.7
United Methodist	6	1,069	1,373	3.3	11.4
Calhoun	**137**	**25,883**	**52,105**	**38.3**	**100.0**
African Methodist Episcopal Zion	1	435	492	0.4	0.9
American Baptist USA	6	901	1,138	0.8	2.2
Assembly of God	6	803	1,537	1.1	2.9
Black Baptist	N.A.	4,070	5,140	3.8	9.9
Catholic	5	N.A.	15,654	11.5	30.0
Christian Reformed	1	208	344	0.3	0.7
Episcopal	4	934	1,408	1.0	2.7
Evangelical Lutheran Church in America	2	478	661	0.5	1.3
Jewish	1	N.A.	180	0.1	0.3
Lutheran-Missouri Synod	6	2,766	3,908	2.9	7.5
Presbyterian Church (USA)	6	2,402	3,034	2.2	5.8
Reformed Church in America	1	118	186	0.1	0.4
Southern Baptist Convention	8	1,543	1,949	1.4	3.7
United Church of Christ	4	1,628	2,056	1.5	3.9
United Methodist	18	4,175	5,273	3.9	10.1
Wisconsin Evangel Lutheran Synod	1	108	146	0.1	0.3
Cass	**50**	**5,028**	**11,219**	**22.7**	**100.0**
American Baptist USA	2	335	424	0.9	3.8
Black Baptist	N.A.	854	1,082	2.2	9.6
Catholic	5	N.A.	4,077	8.2	36.3
Episcopal	1	101	177	0.4	1.6
Lutheran-Missouri Synod	1	167	239	0.5	2.1
Presbyterian Church (USA)	2	321	407	0.8	3.6

Table VII-30. Churches and Church Membership in Michigan, by Denomination and County: 1990 Continued

County and Denomination	Number of Churches	Communicant, Confirmed, Full Members	Total Adherents*		
			Number	Percent(%) of Total Population	Percent(%) of Total Adherents
United Church of Christ	2	255	323	0.7	2.9
United Methodist	9	1,080	1,368	2.8	12.2
Wisconsin Evangel Lutheran Synod	1	347	497	1.0	4.4
Cheboygan	**32**	**2,616**	**9,291**	**43.4**	**100.0**
Assembly of God	2	160	361	1.7	3.9
Catholic	6	N.A.	5,425	25.4	58.4
Episcopal	2	248	332	1.6	3.6
Evangelical Lutheran Church in America	1	544	782	3.7	8.4
Lutheran-Missouri Synod	1	267	371	1.7	4.0
Presbyterian Church (USA)	1	105	132	0.6	1.4
Southern Baptist Convention	1	22	28	0.1	0.3
United Church of Christ	2	152	191	0.9	2.1
United Methodist	3	672	843	3.9	9.1
Wisconsin Evangel Lutheran Synod	1	55	73	0.3	0.8
Chippewa	**6**	**5,386**	**12,196**	**65.2**	**100.0**
American Baptist USA	1	110	135	0.4	1.1
Assembly of God	3	90	203	0.6	1.7
Black Baptist	N.A.	501	615	1.8	5.0
Catholic	14	N.A.	5,079	14.7	41.6
Christian Reformed	2	220	370	1.1	3.0
Episcopal	4	252	307	0.9	2.5
Evangelical Lutheran Church in America	2	660	862	2.5	7.1
Lutheran-Missouri Synod	1	40	49	0.1	0.4
Presbyterian Church (USA)	8	955	1,171	3.4	9.6
Southern Baptist Convention	2	617	757	2.2	6.2
United Church of Christ	1	37	45	0.1	0.4
United Methodist	5	867	1,064	3.1	8.7
Wisconsin Evangel Lutheran Synod	1	176	240	0.7	2.0
Clare	**33**	**3,172**	**6,992**	**28.0**	**100.0**
Assembly of God	2	226	490	2.0	7.0
Catholic	2	N.A.	1,982	7.9	28.3
Lutheran-Missouri Synod	2	370	480	1.9	6.9
Southern Baptist Convention	1	80	101	0.4	1.4
United Church of Christ	2	531	669	2.7	9.6
United Methodist	2	736	928	3.7	13.3
Wisconsin Evangel Lutheran Synod	3	297	364	1.5	5.2
Clinton	**49**	**6,397**	**21,076**	**36.4**	**100.0**
American Baptist USA	2	178	230	0.4	1.1
Assembly of God	1	73	138	0.2	0.7
Catholic	4	N.A.	11,964	20.7	56.8
Christian Reformed	1	145	286	0.5	1.4
Episcopal	2	118	219	0.4	1.0

Table VII-30. Churches and Church Membership in Michigan, by Denomination and County: 1990 Continued

County and Denomination	Number of Churches	Communicant, Confirmed, Full Members	Total Adherents*		
			Number	Percent(%) of Total Population	Percent(%) of Total Adherents
Jewish	0	N.A.	281	0.5	1.3
Lutheran-Missouri Synod	4	1,291	1,681	2.9	8.0
Reformed Church in America	1	186	255	0.4	1.2
Southern Baptist Convention	1	150	193	0.3	0.9
United Church of Christ	1	256	330	0.6	1.6
United Methodist	16	2,232	2,879	5.0	13.7
Crawford	**12**	**1,406**	**3,309**	**27.0**	**100.0**
Assembly of God	1	63	200	1.6	6.0
Catholic	1	N.A.	1,150	9.4	34.8
Episcopal	1	171	310	2.5	9.4
Evangelical Lutheran Church in America	1	129	173	1.4	5.2
Lutheran-Missouri Synod	1	356	465	3.8	14.1
Southern Baptist Convention	1	82	104	0.8	3.1
United Methodist	1	453	572	4.7	17.3
Delta	**58**	**7,283**	**24,054**	**63.7**	**100.0**
Assembly of God	1	160	265	0.7	1.1
Catholic	13	N.A.	14,545	38.5	60.5
Episcopal	3	292	499	1.3	2.1
Evangelical Lutheran Church in America	10	3,542	4,362	11.5	18.1
Lutheran-Missouri Synod	1	122	181	0.5	0.8
Presbyterian Church (USA)	1	337	425	1.1	1.8
Southern Baptist Convention	1	12	15	0.0	0.1
United Church of Christ	2	57	72	0.2	0.3
United Methodist	4	1,197	1,510	4.0	6.3
Wisconsin Evangel Lutheran Synod	4	546	685	1.8	2.8
Dickinson	**35**	**5,217**	**16,084**	**59.9**	**100.0**
Assembly of God	1	117	187	0.7	1.2
Catholic	9	N.A.	8,955	33.4	55.7
Episcopal	1	157	397	1.5	2.5
Evangelical Lutheran Church in America	5	2,209	2,922	10.9	18.2
Jewish	1	N.A.	0	0.0	0.0
Lutheran-Missouri Synod	1	269	350	1.3	2.2
Presbyterian Church (USA)	2	594	748	2.8	4.7
Southern Baptist Convention	1	131	165	0.6	1.0
United Methodist	4	972	1,224	4.6	7.6
Wisconsin Evangel Lutheran Synod	1	107	151	0.6	0.9
Eaton	**81**	**13,685**	**25,248**	**27.2**	**100.0**
American Baptist USA	1	581	739	0.8	2.9
Assembly of God	7	2,411	5,842	6.3	23.1
Black Baptist	N.A.	937	1,193	1.3	4.7
Catholic	1	N.A.	2,990	3.2	11.8
Christian Reformed	1	34	53	0.1	0.2

Table VII-30. Churches and Church Membership in Michigan, by Denomination and County: 1990 Continued

County and Denomination	Number of Churches	Communicant, Confirmed, Full Members	Total Adherents*		
			Number	Percent(%) of Total Population	Percent(%) of Total Adherents
Episcopal	3	401	561	0.6	2.2
Evangelical Lutheran Church in America	2	410	560	0.6	2.2
Jewish	0	N.A.	451	0.5	1.8
Lutheran-Missouri Synod	2	683	935	1.0	3.7
Presbyterian Church (USA)	1	240	305	0.3	1.2
Southern Baptist Convention	2	384	489	0.5	1.9
United Church of Christ	4	958	1,219	1.3	4.8
United Methodist	17	3,522	4,483	4.8	17.8
Wisconsin Evangel Lutheran Synod	2	282	365	0.4	1.4
Emmet	**43**	**4,480**	**12,493**	**49.9**	**100.0**
Assembly of God	1	121	240	1.0	1.9
Catholic	6	N.A.	5,917	23.6	47.4
Episcopal	1	264	300	1.2	2.4
Evangelical Lutheran Church in America	1	141	205	0.8	1.6
Jewish	1	N.A.	0	0.0	0.0
Lutheran-Missouri Synod	1	537	686	2.7	5.5
Presbyterian Church (USA)	2	738	937	3.7	7.5
Southern Baptist Convention	2	193	245	1.0	2.0
United Church of Christ	1	42	53	0.2	0.4
United Methodist	6	1,071	1,360	5.4	10.9
Wisconsin Evangel Lutheran Synod	1	31	42	0.2	0.3
Genesee	**316**	**81,940**	**182,431**	**42.4**	**100.0**
African Methodist Episcopal Zion	1	539	646	0.2	0.4
American Baptist USA	11	2,902	3,715	0.9	2.0
Assembly of God	16	1,680	3,114	0.7	1.7
Black Baptist	N.A.	23,845	30,523	7.1	16.7
Catholic	29	N.A.	67,251	15.6	36.9
Christian Reformed	1	84	152	0.0	0.1
Episcopal	7	1,708	2,405	0.6	1.3
Evangelical Lutheran Church in America	6	1,276	1,713	0.4	0.9
Jewish	2	N.A.	1,825	0.4	1.0
Lutheran-Missouri Synod	17	7,968	10,423	2.4	5.7
Presbyterian Church (USA)	16	5,964	7,634	1.8	4.2
Reformed Church in America	1	219	368	0.1	0.2
Southern Baptist Convention	27	7,610	9,741	2.3	5.3
United Church of Christ	3	1,327	1,699	0.4	0.9
United Methodist	41	10,728	13,733	3.2	7.5
Wisconsin Evangel Lutheran Synod	6	1,251	1,702	0.4	0.9
Gladwin	**31**	**2,885**	**6,451**	**29.5**	**100.0**
Assembly of God	2	110	240	1.1	3.7
Catholic	2	N.A.	1,824	8.3	28.3
Episcopal	1	127	165	0.8	2.6

Table VII-30. Churches and Church Membership in Michigan, by Denomination and County: 1990 Continued

County and Denomination	Number of Churches	Communicant, Confirmed, Full Members	Total Adherents*		
			Number	Percent(%) of Total Population	Percent(%) of Total Adherents
Evangelical Lutheran Church in America	2	338	478	2.2	7.4
Lutheran-Missouri Synod	1	527	653	3.0	10.1
Presbyterian Church (USA)	1	85	107	0.5	1.7
United Methodist	5	632	795	3.6	12.3
Wisconsin Evangel Lutheran Synod	1	120	154	0.7	2.4
Gogebic	**29**	**4,675**	**10,788**	**59.8**	**100.0**
Assembly of God	1	53	122	0.7	1.1
Catholic	6	N.A.	4,687	26.0	43.4
Episcopal	1	61	83	0.5	0.8
Evangelical Lutheran Church in America	6	2,849	3,555	19.7	33.0
Lutheran-Missouri Synod	4	889	1,144	6.3	10.6
Presbyterian Church (USA)	3	155	187	1.0	1.7
United Methodist	2	408	493	2.7	4.6
Grand Traverse	**60**	**9,615**	**27,413**	**42.7**	**100.0**
American Baptist USA	2	107	137	0.2	0.5
Assembly of God	1	60	80	0.1	0.3
Catholic	7	N.A.	13,747	21.4	50.1
Christian Reformed	1	63	113	0.2	0.4
Episcopal	1	280	460	0.7	1.7
Evangelical Lutheran Church in America	3	1,328	1,744	2.7	6.4
Jewish	2	N.A.	0	0.0	0.0
Lutheran-Missouri Synod	4	1,423	2,062	3.2	7.5
Presbyterian Church (USA)	1	812	1,037	1.6	3.8
Reformed Church in America	1	587	943	1.5	3.4
Southern Baptist Convention	3	253	323	0.5	1.2
United Church of Christ	2	1,139	1,454	2.3	5.3
United Methodist	9	2,229	2,846	4.4	10.4
Wisconsin Evangel Lutheran Synod	1	71	94	0.1	0.3
Gratiot	**71**	**7,964**	**15,117**	**38.8**	**100.0**
American Baptist USA	1	111	141	0.4	0.9
Assembly of God	2	79	150	0.4	1.0
Catholic	5	N.A.	4,036	10.4	26.7
Episcopal	1	237	283	0.7	1.9
Lutheran-Missouri Synod	2	636	835	2.1	5.5
Presbyterian Church (USA)	5	858	1,088	2.8	7.2
Southern Baptist Convention	1	123	156	0.4	1.0
United Church of Christ	1	130	165	0.4	1.1
United Methodist	13	2,107	2,671	6.9	17.7
Wisconsin Evangel Lutheran Synod	2	351	454	1.2	3.0
Hillsdale	**63**	**5,830**	**10,163**	**23.4**	**100.0**
American Baptist USA	4	469	602	1.4	5.9
Assembly of God	1	314	418	1.0	4.1

Table VII-30. Churches and Church Membership in Michigan, by Denomination and County: 1990 Continued

County and Denomination	Number of Churches	Communicant, Confirmed, Full Members	Total Adherents*		
			Number	Percent(%) of Total Population	Percent(%) of Total Adherents
Catholic	1	N.A.	1,666	3.8	16.4
Episcopal	2	169	197	0.5	1.9
Evangelical Lutheran Church in America	1	127	172	0.4	1.7
Lutheran-Missouri Synod	1	233	329	0.8	3.2
Presbyterian Church (USA)	3	774	994	2.3	9.8
Southern Baptist Convention	1	212	272	0.6	2.7
United Church of Christ	2	270	347	0.8	3.4
United Methodist	13	1,367	1,756	4.0	17.3
Houghton	**59**	**6,076**	**15,018**	**42.4**	**100.0**
Assembly of God	1	116	246	0.7	1.6
Catholic	12	N.A.	6,594	18.6	43.9
Episcopal	2	193	265	0.7	1.8
Evangelical Lutheran Church in America	8	2,503	3,311	9.3	22.0
Jewish	1	N.A.	0	0.0	0.0
Lutheran-Missouri Synod	3	696	871	2.5	5.8
Presbyterian Church (USA)	2	104	126	0.4	0.8
Southern Baptist Convention	1	32	39	0.1	0.3
United Church of Christ	2	208	252	0.7	1.7
United Methodist	7	1,045	1,266	3.6	8.4
Wisconsin Evangel Lutheran Synod	2	279	370	1.0	2.5
Huron	**71**	**9,427**	**25,756**	**73.7**	**100.0**
American Baptist USA	2	215	272	0.8	1.1
Assembly of God	3	82	189	0.5	0.7
Catholic	15	N.A.	13,358	38.2	51.9
Episcopal	2	94	133	0.4	0.5
Evangelical Lutheran Church in America	1	446	591	1.7	2.3
Lutheran-Missouri Synod	9	4,089	5,325	15.2	20.7
Presbyterian Church (USA)	5	331	419	1.2	1.6
United Methodist	18	2,389	3,027	8.7	11.8
Wisconsin Evangel Lutheran Synod	3	768	959	2.7	3.7
Ingham	**199**	**47,311**	**113,481**	**40.3**	**100.0**
American Baptist USA	12	3,783	4,703	1.7	4.1
Assembly of God	7	629	1,152	0.4	1.0
Black Baptist	N.A.	7,878	9,794	3.5	8.6
Catholic	17	N.A.	43,976	15.6	38.8
Christian Reformed	2	628	948	0.3	0.8
Episcopal	5	1,322	1,808	0.6	1.6
Evangelical Lutheran Church in America	9	3,372	4,591	1.6	4.0
Jewish	2	N.A.	1,368	0.5	1.2
Lutheran-Missouri Synod	8	2,463	3,393	1.2	3.0
Presbyterian Church (USA)	10	3,674	4,567	1.6	4.0
Reformed Church in America	1	206	416	0.1	0.4

Table VII-30. Churches and Church Membership in Michigan, by Denomination and County: 1990 Continued

County and Denomination	Number of Churches	Communicant, Confirmed, Full Members	Total Adherents*		
			Number	Percent(%) of Total Population	Percent(%) of Total Adherents
Southern Baptist Convention	4	1,552	1,929	0.7	1.7
United Church of Christ	9	3,527	4,385	1.6	3.9
United Methodist	28	7,695	9,566	3.4	8.4
Wisconsin Evangel Lutheran Synod	3	1,782	2,311	0.8	2.0
Ionia	**61**	**6,022**	**19,951**	**35.0**	**100.0**
American Baptist USA	3	330	424	0.7	2.1
Assembly of God	2	66	187	0.3	0.9
Black Baptist	N.A.	689	884	1.6	4.4
Catholic	6	N.A.	11,461	20.1	57.4
Christian Reformed	3	257	438	0.8	2.2
Episcopal	1	121	179	0.3	0.9
Lutheran-Missouri Synod	3	689	940	1.6	4.7
Presbyterian Church (USA)	2	279	358	0.6	1.8
United Church of Christ	3	507	651	1.1	3.3
United Methodist	12	1,883	2,417	4.2	12.1
Wisconsin Evangel Lutheran Synod	1	58	80	0.1	0.4
Iosco	**39**	**5,056**	**12,302**	**40.7**	**100.0**
American Baptist USA	2	148	189	0.6	1.5
Assembly of God	3	234	410	1.4	3.3
Black Baptist	N.A.	145	185	0.6	1.5
Catholic	5	N.A.	5,200	17.2	42.3
Episcopal	2	282	364	1.2	3.0
Evangelical Lutheran Church in America	2	373	464	1.5	3.8
Lutheran-Missouri Synod	4	1,097	1,437	4.8	11.7
Southern Baptist Convention	2	511	651	2.2	5.3
United Methodist	7	1,404	1,790	5.9	14.6
Wisconsin Evangel Lutheran Synod	1	456	576	1.9	4.7
Iron	**25**	**2,434**	**5,913**	**44.9**	**100.0**
Assembly of God	1	41	75	0.6	1.3
Catholic	5	N.A.	2,762	21.0	46.7
Episcopal	2	86	104	0.8	1.8
Evangelical Lutheran Church in America	4	1,251	1,662	12.6	28.1
Lutheran-Missouri Synod	2	179	236	1.8	4.0
Presbyterian Church (USA)	1	342	413	3.1	7.0
United Methodist	3	257	310	2.4	5.2
Wisconsin Evangel Lutheran Synod	1	49	57	0.4	1.0
Isabella	**53**	**5,618**	**19,099**	**35.0**	**100.0**
American Baptist USA	1	45	55	0.1	0.3
Assembly of God	1	24	50	0.1	0.3
Black Baptist	N.A.	146	179	0.3	0.9
Catholic	6	N.A.	10,988	20.1	57.5
Christian Reformed	1	66	103	0.2	0.5

Table VII-30. Churches and Church Membership in Michigan, by Denomination and County: 1990 Continued

County and Denomination	Number of Churches	Communicant, Confirmed, Full Members	Total Adherents*		
			Number	Percent(%) of Total Population	Percent(%) of Total Adherents
Episcopal	1	209	257	0.5	1.3
Evangelical Lutheran Church in America	1	499	707	1.3	3.7
Jewish	0	N.A.	120	0.2	0.6
Lutheran-Missouri Synod	2	375	519	1.0	2.7
Presbyterian Church (USA)	2	506	619	1.1	3.2
Southern Baptist Convention	1	31	38	0.1	0.2
United Methodist	11	1,862	2,278	4.2	11.9
Wisconsin Evangel Lutheran Synod	2	189	263	0.5	1.4
Jackson	**114**	**21,023**	**59,486**	**39.7**	**100.0**
American Baptist USA	4	768	963	0.6	1.6
Assembly of God	5	258	387	0.3	0.7
Black Baptist	N.A.	3,391	4,253	2.8	7.1
Catholic	10	N.A.	29,459	19.7	49.5
Christian Reformed	1	75	123	0.1	0.2
Episcopal	5	1,275	2,144	1.4	3.6
Evangelical Lutheran Church in America	3	981	1,324	0.9	2.2
Jewish	1	N.A.	325	0.2	0.5
Lutheran-Missouri Synod	2	1,618	2,282	1.5	3.8
Presbyterian Church (USA)	4	1,767	2,216	1.5	3.7
Southern Baptist Convention	5	1,535	1,925	1.3	3.2
United Church of Christ	5	802	1,006	0.7	1.7
United Methodist	18	3,979	4,991	3.3	8.4
Wisconsin Evangel Lutheran Synod	2	205	287	0.2	0.5
Kalamazoo	**163**	**39,611**	**85,521**	**38.3**	**100.0**
American Baptist USA	5	2,030	2,521	1.1	2.9
Assembly of God	6	987	2,217	1.0	2.6
Black Baptist	N.A.	5,626	6,986	3.1	8.2
Catholic	9	N.A.	26,642	11.9	31.2
Christian Reformed	17	4,022	6,163	2.8	7.2
Episcopal	5	1,722	2,517	1.1	2.9
Evangelical Lutheran Church in America	6	1,876	2,577	1.2	3.0
Jewish	2	N.A.	1,000	0.4	1.2
Lutheran-Missouri Synod	5	1,711	2,231	1.0	2.6
Presbyterian Church (USA)	5	2,347	2,914	1.3	3.4
Reformed Church in America	16	5,417	8,977	4.0	10.5
Southern Baptist Convention	4	544	676	0.3	0.8
United Church of Christ	6	1,399	1,737	0.8	2.0
United Methodist	21	6,329	7,859	3.5	9.2
Wisconsin Evangel Lutheran Synod	1	172	246	0.1	0.3
Kalkaska	**17**	**1,440**	**2,669**	**19.8**	**100.0**
American Baptist USA	1	160	208	1.5	7.8
Assembly of God	2	91	123	0.9	4.6

Table VII-30. Churches and Church Membership in Michigan, by Denomination and County: 1990 Continued

County and Denomination	Number of Churches	Communicant, Confirmed, Full Members	Total Adherents*		
			Number	Percent(%) of Total Population	Percent(%) of Total Adherents
Catholic	1	N.A.	750	5.6	28.1
Lutheran-Missouri Synod	1	250	351	2.6	13.2
Southern Baptist Convention	1	9	12	0.1	0.4
United Methodist	3	157	204	1.5	7.6
Kent	**381**	**105,814**	**258,043**	**51.5**	**100.0**
African Methodist Episcopal Zion	2	1,670	1,912	0.4	0.7
American Baptist USA	2	162	210	0.0	0.1
Black Baptist	N.A.	11,409	14,821	3.0	5.7
Catholic	38	N.A.	86,135	17.2	33.4
Christian Reformed	78	28,511	43,473	8.7	16.8
Episcopal	9	2,270	3,218	0.6	1.2
Evangelical Lutheran Church in America	12	5,906	8,246	1.6	3.2
Jewish	3	N.A.	1,090	0.2	0.4
Lutheran-Missouri Synod	16	5,325	7,351	1.5	2.8
Presbyterian Church (USA)	7	4,243	5,512	1.1	2.1
Reformed Church in America	38	13,138	20,738	4.1	8.0
Southern Baptist Convention	4	1,540	2,001	0.4	0.8
United Church of Christ	16	7,731	10,043	2.0	3.9
United Methodist	32	8,578	11,143	2.2	4.3
Wisconsin Evangel Lutheran Synod	2	477	702	0.1	0.3
Keweenaw	**4**	**320**	**720**	**42.3**	**100.0**
Catholic	2	N.A.	284	16.7	39.4
Evangelical Lutheran Church in America	1	257	361	21.2	50.1
United Methodist	1	63	75	4.4	10.4
Lake	15	1,046	2,290	26.7	100.0
Black Baptist	N.A.	257	320	3.7	14.0
Catholic	3	N.A.	735	8.6	32.1
Lutheran-Missouri Synod	1	87	128	1.5	5.6
United Church of Christ	1	167	208	2.4	9.1
United Methodist	3	187	233	2.7	10.2
Lapeer	**60**	**8,040**	**28,646**	**38.3**	**100.0**
American Baptist USA	2	219	284	0.4	1.0
Assembly of God	3	302	469	0.6	1.6
Catholic	6	N.A.	14,932	20.0	52.1
Christian Reformed	1	293	513	0.7	1.8
Episcopal	3	494	683	0.9	2.4
Jewish	0	N.A.	1,604	2.1	5.6
Lutheran-Missouri Synod	4	1,807	2,515	3.4	8.8
Presbyterian Church (USA)	1	540	700	0.9	2.4
Southern Baptist Convention	1	26	34	0.0	0.1
United Church of Christ	1	140	182	0.2	0.6
United Methodist	14	1,908	2,474	3.3	8.6

Table VII-30. Churches and Church Membership in Michigan, by Denomination and County: 1990 Continued

County and Denomination	Number of Churches	Communicant, Confirmed, Full Members	Total Adherents*		
			Number	Percent(%) of Total Population	Percent(%) of Total Adherents
Wisconsin Evangel Lutheran Synod	2	258	366	0.5	1.3
Leelanau	**3**	**1,952**	**6,053**	**36.6**	**100.0**
Catholic	8	N.A.	3,329	20.1	55.0
Evangelical Lutheran Church in America	2	246	333	2.0	5.5
Lutheran-Missouri Synod	3	405	523	3.2	8.6
Presbyterian Church (USA)	1	17	21	0.1	0.3
Reformed Church in America	1	218	334	2.0	5.5
Southern Baptist Convention	1	18	23	0.1	0.4
United Church of Christ	1	195	246	1.5	4.1
United Methodist	3	386	488	3.0	8.1
Lenawee	**112**	**17,008**	**35,789**	**39.1**	**100.0**
American Baptist USA	6	1,031	1,315	1.4	3.7
Assembly of God	3	800	1,485	1.6	4.1
Black Baptist	N.A.	328	418	0.5	1.2
Catholic	8	N.A.	11,058	12.1	30.9
Episcopal	4	571	1,208	1.3	3.4
Evangelical Lutheran Church in America	5	1,446	1,990	2.2	5.6
Lutheran-Missouri Synod	6	1,762	2,503	2.7	7.0
Presbyterian Church (USA)	6	1,158	1,477	1.6	4.1
Southern Baptist Convention	6	910	1,161	1.3	3.2
United Church of Christ	4	810	1,033	1.1	2.9
United Methodist	17	3,413	4,354	4.8	12.2
Wisconsin Evangel Lutheran Synod	4	1,360	1,719	1.9	4.8
Livingston	**68**	**12,059**	**38,616**	**33.4**	**100.0**
American Baptist USA	3	638	819	0.7	2.1
Black Baptist	N.A.	190	544	0.2	0.6
Catholic	7	N.A.	18,498	16.0	47.9
Episcopal	3	443	644	0.6	1.7
Evangelical Lutheran Church in America	5	1,924	2,797	2.4	7.2
Jewish	1	N.A.	2,481	2.1	6.4
Lutheran-Missouri Synod	6	2,232	3,183	2.8	8.2
Presbyterian Church (USA)	3	1,186	1,523	1.3	3.9
Southern Baptist Convention	2	202	259	0.2	0.7
United Church of Christ	1	245	315	0.3	0.8
United Methodist	8	2,335	2,998	2.6	7.8
Wisconsin Evangel Lutheran Synod	1	143	214	0.2	0.6
Luce	**11**	**879**	**1,978**	**34.3**	**100.0**
Assembly of God	1	50	85	1.5	4.3
Catholic	1	N.A.	848	14.7	42.9
Episcopal	1	52	55	1.0	2.8
Evangelical Lutheran Church in America	1	283	378	6.6	19.1
Lutheran-Missouri Synod	1	182	228	4.0	11.5

Table VII-30. Churches and Church Membership in Michigan, by Denomination and County: 1990 Continued

County and Denomination	Number of Churches	Communicant, Confirmed, Full Members	Total Adherents*		
			Number	Percent(%) of Total Population	Percent(%) of Total Adherents
Presbyterian Church (USA)	1	107	134	2.3	6.8
United Methodist	2	153	192	3.3	9.7
Mackinac	**28**	**1,208**	**3,446**	**32.3**	**100.0**
Assembly of God	1	24	40	0.4	1.2
Catholic	7	N.A.	1,849	17.3	53.7
Episcopal	4	79	123	1.2	3.6
Evangelical Lutheran Church in America	4	296	380	3.6	11.0
Lutheran-Missouri Synod	1	207	235	2.2	6.8
Presbyterian Church (USA)	2	55	69	0.6	2.0
United Methodist	2	369	461	4.3	13.4
Wisconsin Evangel Lutheran Synod	1	14	14	0.1	0.4
Macomb	**271**	**66,047**	**484,786**	**67.6**	**100.0**
African Methodist Episcopal Zion	1	400	448	0.1	0.1
American Baptist USA	3	607	747	0.1	0.2
Assembly of God	14	2,292	4,136	0.6	0.9
Black Baptist	N.A.	2,943	3,621	0.5	0.7
Catholic	59	N.A.	373,485	52.1	77.0
Christian Reformed	1	55	85	0.0	0.0
Episcopal	7	1,202	1,908	0.3	0.4
Evangelical Lutheran Church in America	23	8,795	12,896	1.8	2.7
Jewish	2	N.A.	15,388	2.1	3.2
Lutheran-Missouri Synod	25	21,884	30,290	4.2	6.2
Presbyterian Church (USA)	10	4,039	4,970	0.7	1.0
Reformed Church in America	1	120	210	0.0	0.0
Southern Baptist Convention	12	4,138	5,091	0.7	1.1
United Church of Christ	9	2,878	3,541	0.5	0.7
United Methodist	22	5,692	7,003	1.0	1.4
Wisconsin Evangel Lutheran Synod	5	591	799	0.1	0.2
Manistee	**32**	**4,837**	**12,037**	**56.6**	**100.0**
Assembly of God	1	61	120	0.6	1.0
Catholic	5	N.A.	5,512	25.9	45.8
Episcopal	1	159	165	0.8	1.4
Evangelical Lutheran Church in America	2	1,347	1,838	8.6	15.3
Lutheran-Missouri Synod	4	1,587	2,132	10.0	17.7
Southern Baptist Convention	1	46	57	0.3	0.5
United Church of Christ	2	325	399	1.9	3.3
United Methodist	4	599	736	3.5	6.1
Wisconsin Evangel Lutheran Synod	1	115	133	0.6	1.1
Marquette	**83**	**13,539**	**32,745**	**46.2**	**100.0**
American Baptist USA	1	100	126	0.2	0.4
Assembly of God	1	191	350	0.5	1.1
Black Baptist	N.A.	268	338	0.5	1.0

Table VII-30. Churches and Church Membership in Michigan, by Denomination and County: 1990 Continued

County and Denomination	Number of Churches	Communicant, Confirmed, Full Members	Total Adherents*		
			Number	Percent(%) of Total Population	Percent(%) of Total Adherents
Catholic	15	N.A.	13,961	19.7	42.6
Episcopal	5	486	837	1.2	2.6
Evangelical Lutheran Church in America	15	6,670	8,988	12.7	27.4
Jewish	1	N.A.	150	0.2	0.5
Lutheran-Missouri Synod	2	747	1,119	1.6	3.4
Presbyterian Church (USA)	3	582	733	1.0	2.2
Southern Baptist Convention	3	525	661	0.9	2.0
United Methodist	10	2,444	3,078	4.3	9.4
Wisconsin Evangel Lutheran Synod	2	141	186	0.3	0.6
Mason	**38**	**4,762**	**11,290**	**44.2**	**100.0**
Assembly of God	1	112	150	0.6	1.3
Catholic	7	N.A.	4,799	18.8	42.5
Episcopal	1	117	125	0.5	1.1
Evangelical Lutheran Church in America	3	972	1,218	4.8	10.8
Lutheran-Missouri Synod	2	513	661	2.6	5.9
Reformed Church in America	1	186	285	1.1	2.5
United Methodist	5	1,017	1,280	5.0	11.3
Wisconsin Evangel Lutheran Synod	1	129	156	0.6	1.4
Mecosta	**51**	**5,249**	**12,140**	**32.5**	**100.0**
Assembly of God	1	91	195	0.5	1.6
Black Baptist	N.A.	224	271	0.7	2.2
Catholic	4	N.A.	4,700	12.6	38.7
Christian Reformed	1	116	164	0.4	1.4
Episcopal	1	201	227	0.6	1.9
Evangelical Lutheran Church in America	1	318	407	1.1	3.4
Lutheran-Missouri Synod	3	1,037	1,394	3.7	11.5
Presbyterian Church (USA)	1	251	303	0.8	2.5
Southern Baptist Convention	1	186	225	0.6	1.9
United Church of Christ	1	225	272	0.7	2.2
United Methodist	9	1,231	1,487	4.0	12.2
Wisconsin Evangel Lutheran Synod	2	231	299	0.8	2.5
Menominee	**39**	**4,817**	**15,192**	**61.0**	**100.0**
Assembly of God	2	65	142	0.6	0.9
Catholic	11	N.A.	8,686	34.9	57.2
Episcopal	2	121	192	0.8	1.3
Evangelical Lutheran Church in America	5	2,207	2,937	11.8	19.3
Presbyterian Church (USA)	1	396	499	2.0	3.3
Southern Baptist Convention	1	28	35	0.1	0.2
United Methodist	4	552	696	2.8	4.6
Wisconsin Evangel Lutheran Synod	4	763	979	3.9	6.4
Midland	**81**	**17,036**	**38,239**	**50.5**	**100.0**
American Baptist USA	1	385	490	0.6	1.3

Table VII-30. Churches and Church Membership in Michigan, by Denomination and County: 1990 Continued

County and Denomination	Number of Churches	Communicant, Confirmed, Full Members	Total Adherents*		
			Number	Percent(%) of Total Population	Percent(%) of Total Adherents
Assembly of God	3	553	932	1.2	2.4
Black Baptist	N.A.	203	258	0.3	0.7
Catholic	7	N.A.	12,568	16.6	32.9
Episcopal	2	725	984	1.3	2.6
Evangelical Lutheran Church in America	2	1,399	1,858	2.5	4.9
Jewish	1	N.A.	200	0.3	0.5
Lutheran-Missouri Synod	4	2,616	3,409	4.5	8.9
Presbyterian Church (USA)	2	2,060	2,623	3.5	6.9
Reformed Church in America	1	193	338	0.4	0.9
Southern Baptist Convention	5	613	781	1.0	2.0
United Church of Christ	1	422	537	0.7	1.4
United Methodist	13	4,323	5,505	7.3	14.4
Wisconsin Evangel Lutheran Synod	1	191	305	0.4	0.8
Missaukee	**25**	**2,433**	**4,397**	**36.2**	**100.0**
Assembly of God	1	19	28	0.2	0.6
Catholic	1	N.A.	700	5.8	15.9
Christian Reformed	6	1,088	1,758	14.5	40.0
Evangelical Lutheran Church in America	1	204	266	2.2	6.0
Presbyterian Church (USA)	2	192	252	2.1	5.7
Reformed Church in America	3	404	708	5.8	16.1
Southern Baptist Convention	1	37	49	0.4	1.1
United Methodist	5	297	390	3.2	8.9
Monroe	**117**	**22,725**	**82,215**	**61.5**	**100.0**
American Baptist USA	4	674	866	0.6	1.1
Assembly of God	3	147	271	0.2	0.3
Black Baptist	N.A.	662	851	0.6	1.0
Catholic	13	N.A.	47,781	35.8	58.1
Episcopal	2	346	426	0.3	0.5
Evangelical Lutheran Church in America	11	4,231	5,951	4.5	7.2
Jewish	0	N.A.	2,866	2.1	3.5
Lutheran-Missouri Synod	6	4,043	5,695	4.3	6.9
Presbyterian Church (USA)	5	804	1,033	0.8	1.3
Southern Baptist Convention	16	3,682	4,733	3.5	5.8
United Methodist	17	3,166	4,070	3.0	5.0
Wisconsin Evangel Lutheran Synod	3	925	1,296	1.0	1.6
Montcalm	**80**	**7,857**	**13,543**	**25.5**	**100.0**
African Methodist Episcopal Zion					
American Baptist USA	2	186	240	0.5	1.8
Assembly of God	3	193	352	0.7	2.6
Black Baptist	N.A.	220	283	0.5	2.1
Catholic	5	N.A.	2,782	5.2	20.5
Christian Reformed	1	93	156	0.3	1.2

Table VII-30. Churches and Church Membership in Michigan, by Denomination and County: 1990 Continued

County and Denomination	Number of Churches	Communicant, Confirmed, Full Members	Total Adherents*		
			Number	Percent(%) of Total Population	Percent(%) of Total Adherents
Episcopal	1	89	107	0.2	0.8
Evangelical Lutheran Church in America	6	1,246	1,698	3.2	12.5
Lutheran-Missouri Synod	5	1,058	1,400	2.6	10.3
United Church of Christ	6	760	979	1.8	7.2
United Methodist	13	1,612	2,077	3.9	15.3
Montmorency	**20**	**1,732**	**3,709**	**41.5**	**100.0**
Assembly of God	2	60	105	1.2	2.8
Catholic	3	N.A.	1,517	17.0	40.9
Episcopal	2	133	161	1.8	4.3
Jewish	1	N.A.	235	0.1	0.4
Lutheran-Missouri Synod	2	714	887	9.9	23.9
Southern Baptist Convention	2	56	69	0.8	1.9
United Church of Christ	2	374	458	5.1	12.3
United Methodist	1	120	147	1.6	4.0
Muskegon	**133**	**32,565**	**62,706**	**39.4**	**100.0**
African Methodist Episcopal Zion	1	1,510	1,812	1.1	2.9
American Baptist USA	2	683	880	0.6	1.4
Assembly of God	6	962	1,926	1.2	3.1
Black Baptist	N.A.	6,118	7,882	5.0	12.6
Catholic	12	N.A.	16,181	10.2	25.8
Christian Reformed	7	1,909	2,781	1.7	4.4
Episcopal	4	900	1,609	1.0	2.6
Evangelical Lutheran Church in America	10	3,317	4,425	2.8	7.1
Jewish	1	N.A.	235	0.1	0.4
Lutheran-Missouri Synod	5	2,434	3,226	2.0	5.1
Presbyterian Church (USA)	1	457	589	0.4	0.9
Reformed Church in America	15	3,196	5,715	3.6	9.1
Southern Baptist Convention	1	10	13	0.0	0.0
United Church of Christ	3	1,496	1,927	1.2	3.1
United Methodist	13	3,506	4,517	2.8	7.2
Wisconsin Evangel Lutheran Synod	1	247	335	0.2	0.5
Newaygo	**47**	**5,822**	**13,490**	**35.3**	**100.0**
Assembly of God	3	186	410	1.1	3.0
Catholic	6	N.A.	4,206	11.0	31.2
Christian Reformed	7	1,545	2,243	5.9	16.6
Episcopal	2	139	185	0.5	1.4
Lutheran-Missouri Synod	2	507	693	1.8	5.1
Reformed Church in America	3	897	1,488	3.9	11.0
Southern Baptist Convention	1	54	71	0.2	0.5
United Church of Christ	3	587	767	2.0	5.7
United Methodist	6	1,166	1,523	4.0	11.3

Table VII-30. Churches and Church Membership in Michigan, by Denomination and County: 1990 Continued

County and Denomination	Number of Churches	Communicant, Confirmed, Full Members	Total Adherents*		
			Number	Percent(%) of Total Population	Percent(%) of Total Adherents
Oakland	522	139,125	481,835	44.5	100.0
American Baptist USA	13	4,111	5,105	0.5	1.1
Assembly of God	18	3,379	6,028	0.6	1.3
Black Baptist	N.A.	21,930	27,230	2.5	5.7
Catholic	63	N.A.	269,878	24.9	56.0
Christian Reformed	2	269	474	0.0	0.1
Episcopal	23	7,974	12,714	1.2	2.6
Evangelical Lutheran Church in America	30	11,444	15,575	1.4	3.2
Jewish	36	N.A.	23,243	2.1	4.8
Lutheran-Missouri Synod	33	18,661	25,211	2.3	5.2
Presbyterian Church (USA)	30	17,240	21,406	2.0	4.4
Reformed Church in America	2	92	244	0.0	0.1
Southern Baptist Convention	26	4,995	6,202	0.6	1.3
United Church of Christ	8	3,097	3,845	0.4	0.8
United Methodist	59	22,564	28,017	2.6	5.8
Wisconsin Evangel Lutheran Synod	3	471	632	0.1	0.1
Oceana	38	3,200	7,370	32.8	100.0
Assembly of God	1	28	67	0.3	0.9
Catholic	8	N.A.	2,753	12.3	37.4
Christian Reformed	2	247	371	1.7	5.0
Episcopal	1	78	85	0.4	1.2
Evangelical Lutheran Church in America	1	244	332	1.5	4.5
Lutheran-Missouri Synod	1	237	284	1.3	3.9
Presbyterian Church (USA)	1	153	200	0.9	2.7
Reformed Church in America	1	205	334	1.5	4.5
United Church of Christ	2	429	560	2.5	7.6
United Methodist	9	1,061	1,384	6.2	18.8
Wisconsin Evangel Lutheran Synod	1	112	158	0.7	2.1
Ogemaw	24	2,465	6,329	33.9	100.0
Assembly of God	1	30	57	0.3	0.9
Catholic	3	N.A.	2,897	15.5	45.8
Episcopal	2	137	218	1.2	3.4
Evangelical Lutheran Church in America	1	166	223	1.2	3.5
Lutheran-Missouri Synod	2	791	1,039	5.6	16.4
Southern Baptist Convention	2	272	343	1.8	5.4
United Methodist	3	656	826	4.4	13.1
Ontonagon	31	2,163	4,433	50.1	100.0
Assembly of God	2	71	108	1.2	2.4
Catholic	6	N.A.	1,663	18.8	37.5
Episcopal	2	57	126	1.4	2.8
Evangelical Lutheran Church in America	7	906	1,156	13.1	26.1
Lutheran-Missouri Synod	2	411	484	5.5	10.9

Table VII-30. Churches and Church Membership in Michigan, by Denomination and County: 1990 Continued

County and Denomination	Number of Churches	Communicant, Confirmed, Full Members	Total Adherents*		
			Number	Percent(%) of Total Population	Percent(%) of Total Adherents
United Methodist	6	374	455	5.1	10.3
Wisconsin Evangel Lutheran Synod	1	134	165	1.9	3.7
Osceola	**48**	**3,500**	**6,707**	**33.3**	**100.0**
Assembly of God	2	113	234	1.2	3.5
Catholic	5	N.A.	1,548	7.7	23.1
Christian Reformed	1	257	446	2.2	6.6
Evangelical Lutheran Church in America	4	665	893	4.4	13.3
Lutheran-Missouri Synod	1	412	547	2.7	8.2
Presbyterian Church (USA)	1	14	18	0.1	0.3
United Church of Christ	2	113	147	0.7	2.2
United Methodist	12	1,239	1,607	8.0	24.0
Oscoda	**17**	**1,291**	**2,586**	**33.0**	**100.0**
Assembly of God	1	39	60	0.8	2.3
Catholic	1	N.A.	637	8.1	24.6
Episcopal	1	29	31	0.4	1.2
United Church of Christ	1	39	48	0.6	1.9
United Methodist	1	182	226	2.9	8.7
Wisconsin Evangel Lutheran Synod	1	111	129	1.6	5.0
Otsego	**19**	**2,071**	**10,141**	**56.5**	**100.0**
Assembly of God	1	85	200	1.1	2.0
Catholic	3	N.A.	7,025	39.1	69.3
Christian Reformed	1	52	91	0.5	0.9
Episcopal	1	115	127	0.7	1.3
Evangelical Lutheran Church in America	1	240	351	2.0	3.5
Lutheran-Missouri Synod	1	323	447	2.5	4.4
Presbyterian Church (USA)	1	70	91	0.5	0.9
Southern Baptist Convention	1	80	104	0.6	1.0
United Church of Christ	1	226	293	1.6	2.9
United Methodist	1	540	699	3.9	6.9
Wisconsin Evangel Lutheran Synod	1	20	29	0.2	0.3
Ottawa	**162**	**47,114**	**100,790**	**53.7**	**100.0**
Assembly of God	6	547	792	0.4	0.8
Black Baptist	N.A.	282	369	0.2	0.4
Catholic	10	N.A.	22,146	11.8	22.0
Christian Reformed	50	15,959	24,506	13.1	24.3
Episcopal	2	689	901	0.5	0.9
Evangelical Lutheran Church in America	1	567	727	0.4	0.7
Jewish	0	N.A.	410	0.2	0.4
Lutheran-Missouri Synod	10	4,481	6,178	3.3	6.1
Presbyterian Church (USA)	4	2,406	3,150	1.7	3.1
Reformed Church in America	33	15,038	26,514	14.1	26.3
Southern Baptist Convention	1	130	170	0.1	0.2

Table VII-30. Churches and Church Membership in Michigan, by Denomination and County: 1990 Continued

County and Denomination	Number of Churches	Communicant, Confirmed, Full Members	Total Adherents*		
			Number	Percent(%) of Total Population	Percent(%) of Total Adherents
United Church of Christ	2	792	1,037	0.6	1.0
United Methodist	5	2,834	3,711	2.0	3.7
Presque Isle	**23**	**3,229**	**8,701**	**63.3**	**100.0**
Assembly of God	2	53	117	0.9	1.3
Catholic	4	N.A.	4,593	33.4	52.8
Episcopal	1	55	62	0.5	0.7
Evangelical Lutheran Church in America	4	338	436	3.2	5.0
Lutheran-Missouri Synod	6	1,883	2,369	17.2	27.2
Presbyterian Church (USA)	1	282	352	2.6	4.0
Southern Baptist Convention	2	188	235	1.7	2.7
United Methodist	2	354	442	3.2	5.1
Roscommon	**30**	**2,586**	**6,828**	**34.5**	**100.0**
American Baptist USA	2	254	304	1.5	4.5
Assembly of God	3	131	320	1.6	4.7
Catholic	5	N.A.	3,179	16.1	46.6
Episcopal	2	168	325	1.6	4.8
Evangelical Lutheran Church in America	1	167	194	1.0	2.8
Lutheran-Missouri Synod	2	577	686	3.5	10.0
Presbyterian Church (USA)	1	85	102	0.5	1.5
Southern Baptist Convention	3	275	330	1.7	4.8
United Methodist	2	503	603	3.0	8.8
Saginaw	**181**	**51,771**	**121,646**	**57.4**	**100.0**
American Baptist USA	6	1,682	2,150	1.0	1.8
Assembly of God	12	1,293	2,984	1.4	2.5
Black Baptist	N.A.	10,429	13,328	6.3	11.0
Catholic	36	N.A.	52,068	24.6	42.8
Christian Reformed	1	84	140	0.1	0.1
Episcopal	6	952	1,620	0.8	1.3
Evangelical Lutheran Church in America	12	5,620	7,292	3.4	6.0
Jewish	2	N.A.	200	0.1	0.2
Lutheran-Missouri Synod	15	13,789	17,898	8.4	14.7
Presbyterian Church (USA)	8	2,657	3,396	1.6	2.8
Southern Baptist Convention	1	215	275	0.1	0.2
United Church of Christ	4	1,302	1,664	0.8	1.4
United Methodist	18	4,897	6,258	3.0	5.1
Wisconsin Evangel Lutheran Synod	12	5,206	6,667	3.1	5.5
St. Clair	**109**	**18,042**	**81,566**	**56.0**	**100.0**
American Baptist USA	3	369	471	0.3	0.6
Assembly of God	3	314	436	0.3	0.5
Black Baptist	N.A.	845	1,079	0.7	1.3
Catholic	17	N.A.	52,261	35.9	64.1
Episcopal	8	1,187	1,972	1.4	2.4

Table VII-30. Churches and Church Membership in Michigan, by Denomination and County: 1990 Continued

County and Denomination	Number of Churches	Communicant, Confirmed, Full Members	Total Adherents*		
			Number	Percent(%) of Total Population	Percent(%) of Total Adherents
Evangelical Lutheran Church in America	8	2,539	3,797	2.6	4.7
Jewish	1	N.A.	3,123	2.1	3.8
Lutheran-Missouri Synod	6	3,084	4,351	3.0	5.3
Presbyterian Church (USA)	4	924	1,180	0.8	1.4
Southern Baptist Convention	2	143	183	0.1	0.2
United Church of Christ	5	1,430	1,826	1.3	2.2
United Methodist	20	3,380	4,317	3.0	5.3
Wisconsin Evangel Lutheran Synod	2	356	461	0.3	0.6
St. Joseph	**91**	**10,120**	**22,236**	**37.7**	**100.0**
American Baptist USA	2	237	307	0.5	1.4
Assembly of God	3	239	430	0.7	1.9
Black Baptist	N.A.	367	475	0.8	2.1
Catholic	6	N.A.	6,138	10.4	27.6
Christian Reformed	1	45	80	0.1	0.4
Episcopal	2	376	540	0.9	2.4
Evangelical Lutheran Church in America	3	829	1,187	2.0	5.3
Lutheran-Missouri Synod	6	1,427	1,952	3.3	8.8
Presbyterian Church (USA)	3	1,173	1,519	2.6	6.8
United Church of Christ	1	74	96	0.2	0.4
United Methodist	13	2,205	2,855	4.8	12.8
Wisconsin Evangel Lutheran Synod	1	202	255	0.4	1.1
Sanilac	**81**	**6,578**	**15,219**	**38.1**	**100.0**
American Baptist USA	2	252	323	0.8	2.1
Assembly of God	3	119	278	0.7	1.8
Catholic	9	N.A.	5,616	14.1	36.9
Episcopal	3	242	312	0.8	2.1
Evangelical Lutheran Church in America	2	410	605	1.5	4.0
Lutheran-Missouri Synod	7	1,527	1,975	4.9	13.0
Presbyterian Church (USA)	6	778	998	2.5	6.6
United Church of Christ	1	31	40	0.1	0.3
United Methodist	25	2,137	2,741	6.9	18.0
Schoolcraft	**19**	**874**	**2,715**	**32.7**	**100.0**
American Baptist USA	1	247	307	3.7	11.3
Catholic	4	N.A.	1,509	18.2	55.6
Episcopal	1	35	43	0.5	1.6
Lutheran-Missouri Synod	1	67	89	1.1	3.3
Presbyterian Church (USA)	1	126	157	1.9	5.8
United Church of Christ	1	40	50	0.6	1.8
United Methodist	2	178	221	2.7	8.1
Shiawassee	**86**	**10,452**	**26,550**	**38.1**	**100.0**
American Baptist USA	2	281	360	0.5	1.4

Table VII-30. Churches and Church Membership in Michigan, by Denomination and County: 1990 Continued

County and Denomination	Number of Churches	Communicant, Confirmed, Full Members	Total Adherents*		
			Number	Percent(%) of Total Population	Percent(%) of Total Adherents
Assembly of God	3	144	246	0.4	0.9
Catholic	6	N.A.	10,333	14.8	38.9
Episcopal	2	219	314	0.5	1.2
Evangelical Lutheran Church in America	1	193	298	0.4	1.1
Lutheran-Missouri Synod	1	24	43	0.1	0.2
Southern Baptist Convention	3	356	456	0.7	1.7
United Church of Christ	3	897	1,150	1.6	4.3
United Methodist	23	2,567	3,291	4.7	12.4
Wisconsin Evangel Lutheran Synod	3	1,556	2,145	3.1	8.1
Tuscola	**84**	**12,831**	**24,145**	**43.5**	**100.0**
American Baptist USA	1	21	27	0.0	0.1
Assembly of God	4	220	498	0.9	2.1
Catholic	8	N.A.	6,564	11.8	27.2
Evangelical Lutheran Church in America	2	312	414	0.7	1.7
Lutheran-Missouri Synod	8	5,353	7,103	12.8	29.4
Presbyterian Church (USA)	4	829	1,061	1.9	4.4
Southern Baptist Convention	1	35	45	0.1	0.2
United Methodist	19	2,965	3,795	6.8	15.7
Wisconsin Evangel Lutheran Synod	2	809	1,087	2.0	4.5
Van Buren	**86**	**9,349**	**20,387**	**29.1**	**100.0**
African Methodist Episcopal Zion					
American Baptist USA	1	160	207	0.3	1.0
Assembly of God	2	56	99	0.1	0.5
Black Baptist	N.A.	1,075	1,394	2.0	6.8
Catholic	7	N.A.	7,412	10.6	36.4
Christian Reformed	3	151	245	0.3	1.2
Episcopal	2	192	298	0.4	1.5
Evangelical Lutheran Church in America	1	469	570	0.8	2.8
Jewish	1	N.A.	0	0.0	0.0
Lutheran-Missouri Synod	1	633	849	1.2	4.2
Presbyterian Church (USA)	3	728	944	1.3	4.6
Reformed Church in America	3	620	1,090	1.6	5.3
Southern Baptist Convention	3	189	245	0.3	1.2
United Church of Christ	2	513	665	0.9	3.3
United Methodist	14	1,888	2,448	3.5	12.0
Wisconsin Evangel Lutheran Synod	3	507	687	1.0	3.4
Washtenaw	**187**	**48,432**	**104,216**	**36.8**	**100.0**
American Baptist USA	9	3,411	4,128	1.5	4.0
Assembly of God	8	938	1,897	0.7	1.8
Black Baptist	N.A.	8,977	10,863	3.8	10.4
Catholic	14	N.A.	34,376	12.1	33.0
Christian Reformed	3	448	645	0.2	0.6

Table VII-30. Churches and Church Membership in Michigan, by Denomination and County: 1990 Continued

County and Denomination	Number of Churches	Communicant, Confirmed, Full Members	Total Adherents*		
			Number	Percent(%) of Total Population	Percent(%) of Total Adherents
Episcopal	8	1,743	3,386	1.2	3.2
Evangelical Lutheran Church in America	10	4,796	6,112	2.2	5.9
Jewish	3	N.A.	4,500	1.6	4.3
Lutheran-Missouri Synod	11	3,024	4,132	1.5	4.0
Presbyterian Church (USA)	7	3,695	4,471	1.6	4.3
Reformed Church in America	1	45	105	0.0	0.1
Southern Baptist Convention	6	2,851	3,450	1.2	3.3
United Church of Christ	12	4,650	5,627	2.0	5.4
United Methodist	19	6,200	7,503	2.7	7.2
Wisconsin Evangel Lutheran Synod	6	1,543	1,995	0.7	1.9
Wayne	**923**	**401,097**	**1,367,836**	**64.8**	**100.0**
African Methodist Episcopal Zion	12	35,220	41,873	2.0	3.1
American Baptist USA	33	21,018	26,658	1.3	1.9
Assembly of God	30	4,968	8,783	0.4	0.6
Black Baptist	N.A.	173,017	219,448	10.4	16.0
Catholic	186	N.A.	778,340	36.9	56.9
Christian Reformed	2	494	769	0.0	0.1
Episcopal	44	10,759	15,284	0.7	1.1
Evangelical Lutheran Church in America	56	18,303	24,474	1.2	1.8
Jewish	5	N.A.	45,296	2.1	3.3
Lutheran-Missouri Synod	61	26,752	36,873	1.7	2.7
Presbyterian Church (USA)	44	22,668	28,751	1.4	2.1
Reformed Church in America	8	759	1,631	0.1	0.1
Southern Baptist Convention	41	10,416	13,211	0.6	1.0
United Church of Christ	24	9,796	12,425	0.6	0.9
United Methodist	62	19,396	24,601	1.2	1.8
Wisconsin Evangel Lutheran Synod	12	4,020	5,432	0.3	0.4
Wexford	**47**	**5,033**	**9,812**	**37.2**	**100.0**
American Baptist USA	2	781	1,011	3.8	10.3
Assembly of God	1	120	260	1.0	2.6
Catholic	3	N.A.	2,400	9.1	24.5
Christian Reformed	1	188	299	1.1	3.0
Episcopal	1	71	134	0.5	1.4
Evangelical Lutheran Church in America	2	736	1,083	4.1	11.0
Lutheran-Missouri Synod	2	354	528	2.0	5.4
Presbyterian Church (USA)	1	383	496	1.9	5.1
Southern Baptist Convention	1	78	101	0.4	1.0
United Church of Christ	1	148	192	0.7	2.0
United Methodist	5	766	992	3.8	10.1

Note: * Total adherents estimated from known number of communicants, confirmed, and full members.

Source: Association of Statisticians of American Religious Bodies, <u>Churches and Church Membership in the United States 1990</u> Published by Glenmary Research Center (Atlanta, Georgia: 1990).

The Michigan Department of State Police tabulates data on crime from its own files as well as from local police and sheriffs offices. Its Uniform Crime Report is an annual summary of these data developed from reports by law enforcement agencies. At the national level the Federal Bureau of Investigation assembles data from the states and publishes them in its annual Crime in the United States.

Uniform crime reporting is a national system. Offenses are divided into Index and Non-index categories. Because of their seriousness and frequency of occurrence, *Index Crimes* (murder, rape, robbery, aggravated assault, burglary, larceny, motor vehicle theft, and arson) comprise the crime index and serve as indicators of the nation's crime experience. *Non-index crimes* include negligent manslaughter, non-aggravated assaults, forgery, fraud, counterfeiting, violation of drug and liquor laws, drunken driving, and a host of other non-index offenses.

The *Crime Rate* is the number of index crimes per 100,000 population. *Offenses* are crimes reported. *Arrests* pertain to the number of individuals charged.

The Michigan Department of Corrections issues an annual Statistical Report highlighting the number of people incarcerated in state correctional institutions. There also is one federal prison in this state, near Milan. For data on this facility, as well as on city and county jails, it is necessary to contact the institutions themselves.

The activities of Michigan courts are reported in The Michigan State Courts Annual Report, prepared by the Michigan Supreme Court. Federal court data are available from each of the federal courts.

Michigan's court system consists of:

Supreme Court: The highest court in the state. Consists of seven judges who hear cases appealed from other state courts. Also in charge of general administrative supervision of all courts in the state.

Court of Appeals: Acts as an intermediate appellate court between the lower courts and the Supreme Court. There are 24 judgeships. Appeals on criminal and civil cases are heard in Lansing, Detroit, Grand Rapids, and Marquette.

Circuit Court: The trial court of general jurisdiction. Currently, there are 56 Circuit Courts with 177 judgeships. Generally speaking, this circuit has original jurisdiction in all civil cases involving more than $10,000, in all criminal felony cases or certain serious misdemeanors, and in all domestic relation cases.

Probate Court: There are 78 probate courts with 107 judgeships. This court has exclusive jurisdiction in cases involving juvenile delinquency, neglect, abuse, and adoption. This court also hears cases pertaining to wills, administration of estates and trusts, condemnation of land, guardianships, and the commitment for hospital care of mentally ill, mentally handicapped, and addicted persons.

District Court: There are 101 district courts with 260 judgeships. The District Court has exclusive jurisdiction in civil litigation up to $10,000, garnishments, eviction, land contracts, and mortgage foreclosures. District courts also handle criminal misdemeanors where punishment does not exceed one year and conduct preliminary examinations in felony cases.

Municipal Court: Jurisdiction is limited to claims not exceeding $1,000 in civil cases. Criminal traffic case jurisdiction is the same as in District Court.

List of Tables

Table | | Page

VIII-1. Criminal Index Offenses in Michigan, by Type: 1966-1993 307

VIII-2. Percentage Distribution of Juvenile and Adult Arrests in Michigan, by Offense: 1990-1992 308

VIII-3. Criminal Index Offenses in Michigan, by Type of Offense and County: 1992 309

VIII-4. Selected Murder Statistics for the State of Michigan: 1985-1992 312

VIII-5. Prison Commitments in Michigan, by Age, Race and Sex: As of December 1992 313

VIII-6. Age Breakdown of the Total Prison Population in Michigan, by Institution: As of December 1992 314

VIII-7. Descriptions of Michigan Correctional Institutions: As of January 1993 316

VIII-8. Prison Commitments in Michigan, by Minimum Sentence: 1991 318

VIII-9. Department of Corrections Supervision Workloads in Michigan: June 12, 1992 318

VIII-10. Court Sentences in Michigan, by Major Crime Category: 1991 318

VIII-11. Trends in Dispositions, by Opinion or Order, Michigan Court of Appeals: 1978-1992 319

VIII-12. Trends in Court of Appeals Filings per Judge in Michigan: 1965-1992 319

VIII-13. Michigan Court of Claims Cases Referred to Mediation: 1988-1992 320

VIII-14. Michigan Court of Claims Summary Report: 1992 320

VIII-15. Probate Court Pending Cases in Michigan, by Type: 1992 321

VIII-16. Juvenile Division Caseload Information in Michigan: 1992 321

VIII-17. Juvenile Division Activity Information in Michigan: 1992 322

List of Tables

Table		Page
VIII-18.	Municipal Court Pending Cases in Michigan: End of 1992	323
VIII-19.	District Court Cases Pending in Michigan: End of 1992	323
VIII-20.	Circuit Court Cases Pending in Michigan: End of 1992	324
VIII-21.	Average Number of Filings per Circuit Court Judge in Michigan, by Circuit Court: 1992	325
VIII-22.	Trends in Circuit Court Filings in Michigan, by Circuit Court: 1988-1992 . . .	327
VIII-23.	Circuit Court Summary Report for Michigan: 1992	329
VIII-24.	Average Number of Filings per Judge in Michigan, by Probate Court: 1992 . .	331
VIII-25.	Trends in Probate Court Filings in Michigan, Estate and Mental Division: 1988-1992	334
VIII-26.	Probate Court Summary Reports for Michigan: 1992	337
VIII-27.	Average Number of Filings per Judge, by Michigan District Court: 1992	338
VIII-28.	Trends in District Court Filings in Michigan, by Court: 1988-1992	342
VIII-29.	District Court Summary Report for Michigan, by District Court: 1992	346
VIII-30.	Municipal Court Summary Report for Michigan: 1992	347

Table VIII-1. Criminal Index Offenses in Michigan, by Type: 1966-1993

Year	Total Crime Index	Murder & Nonnegligent Manslaughter	Rape	Robbery	Aggravated Assault	Burglary	Larceny & Theft	Motor Vehicle Theft	Arson
1966	279,113	365	1,844	12,423	10,641	72,333	153,895	27,612	N.A.
1967	329,036	517	1,848	16,071	12,826	91,264	173,095	33,415	N.A.
1968	324,878	614	2,105	17,608	13,802	88,234	167,783	34,732	N.A.
1969	388,154	726	2,231	22,880	15,080	104,177	201,466	41,594	N.A.
1970	484,930	831	2,402	30,758	17,099	139,398	253,258	41,184	N.A.
1971	512,745	938	2,405	29,698	18,647	151,357	264,980	44,720	N.A.
1972	484,429	964	2,652	26,248	20,440	143,034	248,201	42,890	N.A.
1973	492,092	1,163	3,166	25,521	23,001	142,304	247,785	49,234	N.A.
1974	591,664	1,170	3,370	30,657	24,739	172,828	302,301	56,599	N.A.
1975	622,880	1,042	3,477	32,354	25,751	173,134	327,367	59,755	N.A.
1976	586,764	1,001	3,281	30,241	24,154	151,207	321,192	55,688	N.A.
1977	532,011	853	3,537	23,834	24,828	138,299	285,432	49,539	N.A.
1978	511,301	862	3,614	20,192	28,661	130,716	279,261	47,995	N.A.
1979	562,183	810	4,085	20,168	31,261	138,074	312,643	55,142	N.A.
1980	608,446	941	4,267	22,363	30,760	158,944	337,609	53,562	N.A.
1981	635,903	863	4,353	23,644	29,970	170,372	339,676	58,213	N.A.
1982	615,423	870	4,083	24,470	28,952	162,952	326,283	61,252	7,056
1983	601,832	917	4,553	26,208	31,001	156,525	307,159	67,235	8,234
1984	592,143	865	5,687	27,694	30,806	147,948	295,114	78,006	6,023
1985	582,270	1,019	6,131	26,548	32,941	138,518	296,808	75,123	5,182
1986	586,708	1,028	6,077	27,319	38,017	135,734	300,967	72,021	5,545
1987	591,913	1,118	6,144	25,271	38,668	132,233	314,567	68,415	5,497
1988	558,292	1,003	6,370	22,077	38,461	119,893	298,157	67,211	5,120
1989	541,210	982	6,467	20,325	36,668	110,640	296,238	65,297	4,593
1990	549,344	959	7,094	21,484	42,691	104,292	303,145	65,220	4,459
1991	568,194	1,003	7,248	22,574	43,378	109,368	317,248	62,636	4,739
1992	524,304	939	7,451	20,731	42,792	96,822	293,018	58,037	4,514
1993	505,497	922	7,335	22,261	43,659	90,878	279,515	56,670	4,257

Source: Michigan Department of State Police, Uniform Crime Report, (East Lansing, Michigan: annually). N.A. data not available.

Table VIII-2. Percentage Distribution of Juvenile and Adult Arrests in Michigan, by Offense: 1990-1992

Offense	Adult Share (%)			Juvenile Share (%)		
	1990	1991	1992	1990	1991	1992
Murder	95.4	93.8	95.0	4.6	6.2	5.0
Rape	88.0	90.6	85.5	12.0	9.4	14.5
Robbery	90.9	88.1	87.3	9.1	11.9	12.7
Aggravated Assault	90.1	90.7	88.8	9.9	9.3	11.2
Burglary	78.7	77.9	74.3	21.3	22.1	25.7
Larceny/Theft	74.4	74.7	73.3	25.6	25.3	26.7
Motor Vehicle Theft	68.1	66.1	63.4	31.9	33.9	36.6
Arson	73.9	71.3	60.0	26.1	28.7	40.0
Nonaggravated Assault	89.1	89.9	89.9	10.9	10.1	10.1
Forgery/Counterfeiting	95.9	96.1	95.5	4.1	3.9	4.5
Fraud	94.6	95.2	95.6	5.4	4.8	4.4
Embezzlement	97.7	96.9	97.8	2.3	3.1	2.3
Stolen Property	88.9	88.8	89.8	11.1	11.2	10.2
Vandalism	70.8	69.5	66.1	29.2	30.5	33.9
Weapons	90.2	89.1	87.2	9.8	10.9	12.8
Prostitution	99.5	99.8	99.7	0.5	0.2	0.3
Sex Offenses	86.0	85.9	84.4	14.0	14.1	15.6
Narcotic Laws	94.4	95.5	95.6	5.6	4.5	4.2
Gambling	97.1	93.8	95.5	2.9	6.2	4.5
Driving Under The Influence	99.6	99.7	99.7	0.4	0.3	0.3
Liquor Laws	94.9	95.6	95.0	5.1	4.4	5.0
Drunkenness	96.8	92.8	93.1	3.2	7.2	6.9
Disorderly Conduct	95.2	94.6	94.7	4.8	5.4	5.3
Vagrancy	92.1	94.1	92.1	7.9	5.9	7.9
Curfew/Loitering	0.0	0.1	0.1	100.0	99.9	99.9
Runaway	0.1	0.2	0.1	99.9	99.8	99.9

Note: Adult and Juvenile shares sum to 100 percent for each year.
Source: Michigan Department of State Police, Uniform Crime Report, (East Lansing, Michigan: annually), special release.

Table VIII-3. Criminal Index Offenses in Michigan, by Type of Offense and County: 1992

County	Total Crime Index	Murder & Nonnegligent Manslaughter	Rape	Robbery	Aggravated Assault	Burglary	Larceny & Theft	Motor Vehicle Theft	Arson
Alcona	249	0	6	0	9	108	122	3	1
Alger	187	0	7	1	19	72	74	11	3
Allegan	2,695	0	126	5	150	721	1,573	86	34
Alpena	1,152	0	37	2	35	242	789	27	20
Antrim	454	0	14	0	13	169	225	21	12
Arenac	531	0	11	4	24	178	293	14	7
Baraga	183	0	2	1	5	45	117	5	8
Barry	1,430	2	42	6	66	469	771	55	19
Bay	4,281	1	80	62	214	748	2,938	298	30
Benzie	439	1	7	1	28	90	288	16	8
Berrien	11,174	13	167	232	1,322	2,369	6,435	526	110
Branch	1,557	2	83	9	78	312	1,008	50	15
Calhoun	8,729	10	142	266	795	2,076	4,936	436	68
Cass	1,842	2	43	22	141	563	950	89	32
Charlevoix	494	0	11	1	28	81	357	11	5
Cheboygan	739	0	20	0	28	184	465	21	21
Chippewa	1,315	1	35	6	60	298	864	45	6
Clare	1,227	0	7	0	28	502	670	16	4
Clinton	1,395	0	25	10	46	270	991	48	5
Crawford	517	0	13	2	10	218	254	12	8
Delta	1,183	0	19	0	27	205	887	39	6
Dickinson	625	0	8	1	21	104	460	25	6
Eaton	4,160	0	86	34	210	635	2,957	218	20
Emmet	1,270	3	22	7	28	204	974	29	3
Genesee	32,573	57	407	1,196	3,311	6,966	16,593	3,607	436
Gladwin	650	0	19	3	20	224	346	31	7
Gogebic	557	2	13	0	14	137	365	23	3
Grand Traverse	2,157	0	76	13	52	322	1,617	48	29

Table VIII-3. Criminal Index Offenses in Michigan, by Type of Offense and County: 1992 Continued

County	Total Crime Index	Murder & Nonnegligent Manslaughter	Rape	Robbery	Aggravated Assault	Burglary	Larceny & Theft	Motor Vehicle Theft	Arson
Gratiot	1,211	0	27	4	59	221	849	30	21
Hillsdale	1,104	2	41	0	59	222	734	37	9
Houghton	701	1	11	0	25	119	521	15	9
Huron	873	2	43	2	23	177	597	24	5
Ingham	16,894	13	315	357	1,547	2,551	10,839	1,140	132
Ionia	1,501	0	58	2	105	324	946	52	14
Iosco	1,035	1	27	1	62	303	598	29	14
Iron	431	0	4	1	26	87	289	20	4
Isabella	2,097	1	37	7	58	325	1,592	54	23
Jackson	7,382	5	180	98	1,463	1,167	4,104	310	55
Kalamazoo	14,894	3	139	360	1,528	2,600	9,498	632	134
Kalkaska	563	0	13	1	27	196	304	18	4
Kent	30,106	22	572	892	2,387	6,177	18,185	1,701	170
Keweenaw	64	0	0	0	1	23	39	0	1
Lake	441	0	15	2	35	192	182	11	4
Lapeer	1,614	5	43	2	74	346	1,051	83	10
Leelanau	299	0	13	1	10	61	203	8	3
Lenawee	2,805	1	60	17	101	496	1,982	133	15
Livingston	3,605	3	54	21	166	799	2,376	158	28
Luce	153	0	4	2	2	57	79	7	2
Mackinac	669	1	7	3	17	110	512	13	6
Macomb	34,000	18	332	540	2,004	4,389	22,891	3,688	138
Manistee	541	0	7	1	28	155	330	17	3
Marquette	2,106	1	90	5	65	260	1,595	73	17
Mason	1,193	0	26	2	44	253	801	58	9
Mecosta	1,791	0	32	6	49	325	1,336	37	6
Menominee	830	0	19	1	29	265	472	32	12
Midland	2,009	2	49	5	168	256	1,457	55	17

Table VIII-3. Criminal Index Offenses in Michigan, by Type of Offense and County: 1992 Continued

County	Total Crime Index	Murder & Nonnegligent Manslaughter	Rape	Robbery	Aggravated Assault	Burglary	Larceny & Theft	Motor Vehicle Theft	Arson
Missaukee	223	0	7	0	7	87	109	9	4
Monroe	5,912	2	112	71	459	1,039	3,813	353	63
Montcalm	1,998	2	75	8	137	532	1,133	90	21
Montmorency	327	2	8	2	18	179	106	11	1
Muskegon	11,254	8	111	209	806	2,817	6,609	639	55
Newaygo	1,263	1	61	7	107	464	574	38	11
Oakland	51,656	31	454	1,212	4,052	8,193	32,207	5,237	270
Oceana	619	0	32	4	42	181	330	22	8
Ogemaw	753	1	18	7	47	285	350	37	8
Ontonagon	155	0	4	1	7	60	76	7	0
Osceola	538	2	16	0	26	201	264	24	5
Oscoda	411	0	2	0	5	192	199	12	1
Otsego	624	0	11	5	24	152	413	12	7
Ottawa	6,931	6	96	32	224	1,074	5,222	241	36
Presque Isle	260	0	8	0	8	82	153	7	2
Roscommon	1,216	1	32	5	41	443	590	97	7
Saginaw	14,806	34	247	594	1,846	3,061	8,003	754	267
St. Clair	5,679	7	122	70	368	1,119	3,663	259	71
St. Joseph	1,977	1	77	14	159	411	1,222	68	25
Sanilac	761	2	31	6	38	225	424	31	4
Schoolcraft	244	0	7	2	14	77	134	7	3
Shiawassee	1,774	1	44	7	121	388	1,137	63	13
Tuscola	1,034	0	38	2	59	299	578	51	7
Van Buren	3,689	5	93	24	260	1,176	1,930	152	49
Washtenaw	16,995	7	211	405	1,149	2,905	11,279	873	166
Wayne	177,283	650	1,755	13,823	15,745	30,024	78,939	34,736	1,611
Wexford	1,245	1	33	4	79	188	880	52	8

Source: Michigan Department of State Police, Uniform Crime Report, (East Lansing, Michigan: annually), special release.

Table VIII-4. Selected Murder Statistics for the State of Michigan: 1985-1992

Category	1985	1986	1987	1988	1989	1990	1991	1992
RACE OF VICTIM								
White	336	273	301	281	242	272	302	281
Black	677	751	815	717	732	687	695	655
American Indian/Alaskan Native	N.A.	1	1	0	5	1	1	1
Asian/Pacific Islander	N.A.	N.A.	3	3	0	5	3	2
Race Unknown	N.A.	N.A.	2	0	0	2	2	0
SEX OF VICTIM								
Male	773	797	847	780	763	745	775	717
Female	246	231	271	223	219	215	228	222
AGE OF VICTIM								
16 Years and Younger	90	88	100	78	82	80	78	65
Between 17 and 24 Years	238	264	318	251	253	282	307	299
Between 25 and 39 Years	437	412	439	439	418	393	371	359
40 Years and Older	244	261	250	231	220	201	242	198
Age Unknown	10	3	11	4	9	3	0	18
RELATIONSHIP OF VICTIM TO OFFENDER								
Spouse (Includes Common Law)	63	54	41	48	43	30	37	40
Parent	23	20	33	8	11	15	24	16
Son/Daughter	N.A.	N.A.	N.A.	17	22	20	23	20
Brother/Sister	N.A.	N.A.	N.A.	13	6	7	11	9
Other Family Member	48	35	44	20	21	24	15	14
Acquaintance/Neighbor	N.A.	N.A.	N.A.	368	328	316	324	260
Boyfriend/Girlfriend	N.A.	N.A.	N.A.	29	31	25	30	26
Other - Known to Victim	N.A.	N.A.	N.A.	31	46	36	37	46
Homosexual Relationship	N.A.	N.A.	N.A.	5	2	2	2	3
Stranger	N.A.	N.A.	N.A.	92	80	99	107	119
Relationship Unknown	N.A.	N.A.	N.A.	372	392	385	393	386

Source: Michigan Department of State Police, Uniform Crime Report, (East Lansing, Michigan: annually). N.A. data not available.

Table VIII-5. Prison Commitments in Michigan, by Age, Race and Sex: As of December 1992

Race/Gender	Age Group						
	Total	19 and Under	20 - 24 Years	25 - 29 Years	30 - 39 Years	40 and Over	Subtotals As Percent(%) of Total Commitments
Total Commitments							100.0
Number	12,170	1,472	3,079	2,531	3,634	1,454	
Percent(%)	100.0	12.1	25.3	20.8	29.9	11.9	
Total Males							92.6
Number	11,267	1,452	2,926	2,298	3,257	1,334	
Percent(%)	100.0	12.9	26.0	20.4	28.9	11.8	
White Males							39.9
Number	4,860	528	1,136	957	1,535	704	
Percent(%)	43.1	4.7	10.1	8.5	13.6	6.2	
Non-White Males							52.6
Number	6,407	924	1,790	1,341	1,722	630	
Percent(%)	56.9	8.2	15.9	11.9	15.3	5.6	
Total Females							7.4
Number	903	20	153	233	377	120	
Percent(%)	100.0	2.2	16.9	25.8	41.7	13.3	
White Females							2.8
Number	343	10	55	83	147	48	
Percent(%)	38.0	1.1	6.1	9.2	16.3	5.3	
Non-White Females							4.6
Number	560	10	98	150	230	72	
Percent(%)	62.0	1.1	10.9	16.6	25.5	8.0	

Source: Michigan Department of Corrections, Annual Report (Lansing, Michigan: annually).

Table VIII-6. Age Breakdown of the Total Prison Population in Michigan, by Institution: As of December 1992

Institution	Less than 20	20 - 24 Years	25 - 29 Years	30 - 34 Years	35 - 39 Years	40 - 44 Years	45 - 49 Years	50 - 54 Years	55 - 59 Years	60 - 64 Years	65 - 69 Years	70 - 74 Years	80 Plus
Adrian Regional	12	237	285	277	184	96	45	19	15	5	0	0	0
Adrian Temporary	2	153	205	204	176	129	66	14	5	2	2	0	0
Brooks Regional	37	239	272	235	193	104	48	20	11	7	0	1	0
Carson City Reg	39	221	297	263	177	90	47	20	8	6	2	0	0
Carson City Temp	18	155	167	209	173	116	74	27	9	6	2	0	1
Chippewa Regional	48	249	265	219	136	81	31	12	7	1	1	0	0
Chippewa Temporary	27	196	207	211	157	87	39	19	8	4	5	1	0
Cotton Corr Facil	16	202	278	293	279	196	110	57	39	22	16	11	5
Female Camps	2	13	22	29	21	16	11	0	0	0	0	0	0
Female Corr Centers	2	34	60	53	60	23	12	2	0	2	0	0	0
Female Res Homes	0	9	17	18	19	7	3	0	1	1	0	0	0
Florence Crane Corr	9	53	133	158	132	80	35	15	12	4	2	1	0
Hiawatha Temporary	28	174	243	189	145	101	34	21	13	3	4	1	1
Huron Valley Men	3	47	99	108	103	53	24	13	6	2	3	0	0
Ionia Max Corr	4	106	139	141	96	59	14	10	6	0	2	0	0
Ionia Reformatory	222	690	261	27	6	2	2	0	0	0	0	0	0
Ionia Temp Facil	60	225	128	176	153	108	46	36	6	12	7	1	0
Jackson SPSM	33	549	1,068	1,118	898	631	337	177	107	73	65	16	6
Kinross Corr Fac	19	185	226	229	204	158	83	47	20	10	7	1	0
Lakeland Corr	3	53	115	103	136	96	45	55	31	33	25	15	2
Male Camps	119	857	829	726	520	263	98	30	8	7	4	1	0

Table VIII-6. Age Breakdown of the Total Prison Population in Michigan, by Institution: As of December 1992 Continued

Institution	Age Group												
	Less than 20	20 - 24 Years	25 - 29 Years	30 - 34 Years	35 - 39 Years	40 - 44 Years	45 - 49 Years	50 - 54 Years	55 - 59 Years	60 - 64 Years	65 - 69 Years	70 - 74 Years	80 Plus
Male Corr Centers	105	649	535	451	348	192	89	38	21	4	2	1	0
Male Resident Homes	19	170	159	148	90	43	15	15	14	0	0	0	0
Manistee Close Cus	13	192	119	67	23	17	5	2	1	0	1	0	0
Marquette Branch Pr	9	135	197	181	123	80	44	23	11	7	3	3	0
Mental Health Fac	0	0	4	6	6	6	1	1	2	0	0	0	0
Mich Training Unit	292	761	177	35	22	14	7	3	0	0	0	0	0
Mid-Mich Temporary	27	164	184	196	177	119	50	19	11	9	2	0	0
Munising Maximum	9	104	117	105	49	18	11	4	0	1	0	0	0
Muskegon Corr Fac	17	194	319	264	216	149	74	41	19	10	2	3	0
Muskegon Temp Facil	23	103	173	174	185	137	74	46	16	14	8	1	1
Non-Dept. Prisons	0	12	27	25	24	14	9	7	1	0	0	1	0
Riverside Corr Fac	23	45	42	51	47	30	26	11	9	4	1	0	0
Riverside Reception Ctr	117	49	0	0	0	0	0	0	0	0	0	0	0
Ryan Regional Corr Fac	4	174	232	201	191	113	64	27	8	6	5	1	2
Scott Corr Facil	10	95	180	161	143	88	40	17	2	1	0	1	0
SPSM Reception Ctr	1	120	130	112	62	49	19	12	8	2	2	1	0
Thumb Corr Facil	42	197	201	188	140	85	46	33	14	4	0	0	0
Western Wayne Corr	2	70	79	102	111	77	33	11	3	2	0	1	0
TOTAL NUMBER	1,416	7,881	8,191	7,453	5,925	3,727	1,811	904	452	264	173	61	18

Source: Michigan Department of Corrections, Annual Report (Lansing, Michigan: annually).

315

Table VIII-7. Descriptions of Michigan Correctional Institutions: As of January 1993

Institution	Warden	Year Opened	Capacity	Population	Age Limits	Security Level
Adrian Temporary Correctional Facility	William S. Overton	1989	640	958	Men, 21 or older	II (medium)
Alger Maximum Correctional Facility	Wayne Stine	1990	440	416	Men, all ages	V (maximum)
E. C. Brooks Regional Facility	Joseph Abramajtys	1989	612	1,076	Men, all ages	I, III and IV (minimum, medium, close)
Carson City Regional Facility	Richard E. Johnson	1989	634	1,156	Men, all ages	I, III and IV (minimum, medium, close)
Carson City Temporary Facility	Richard E. Johnson	1987	640	955	Men, 21 and older	II (medium)
Chippewa Regional Correctional Facility	Patricia Caruso	1989	612	1,056	Men, all ages	I, III, and IV (minimum, medium, close)
Chippewa Temporary Correctional Facility	Patricia Caruso	1988	640	960	Men, 21 and older	II (medium)
Corrections Camps	Denise Quarles	15*	1,760	3,815	17 and older	I (minimum)
Cotton Regional Correctional Facility	Gene E. Borgert	1985	1,088	1,129	Men, all ages	I, II, III, and IV (minimum, medium, close)
Florence Crane Women's Facility	Carol Howes	1985	650	650	Women, 17 and older	II (medium)
Charles E. Egeler Correctional Facility	H. N. Grayson	1988	1,006	959	Men, 21 and older	III (medium)
Gus Harrison Regional Facility	William S. Overton	1991	612	1,032	Men, all ages	I, III and IV
Handlon Michigan Training Unit	James C. Yarborough	1958	1,207	1,150	Men under 26	II and III (medium)
Hiawatha Temporary Correctional Facility	Robert E. LeCureux	1989	960	946	Men, 21 and older	II (medium)
Huron Valley Men's Facility	William F. Grant	1981	396	450	Men, all ages	IV (close)
Huron Valley Women's Facility	Joan Yukins	1977	369	586	Women, 17 and older	III and IV (medium, close)
Ionia Maximum Correctional Facility	Ray Toombs	1987	461	570	Men, all ages	II, VI (medium, special maximum)
Ionia Temporary Facility	Stanley Adams	1985	640	953	Men, 21 and older	I (minimum)
Kinross Correctional Facility	Robert E. LeCureux	1978	1,108	1,226	Men, 21 and older	II (medium)
Lakeland Correctional Facility	Robert Redman	1985	86	720	Men, 17 and older	II (medium)
Marquette Branch Prison	John W. Hawley	1889	809	888	Men, 21 and older	I and V (minimum, maximum)
Michigan Reformatory	Pamela K. Withrow	1877	1,260	1,234	Men, 17 to 26	I and IV (minimum, close)
Mid-Michigan Temporary Correctional Facility	John Prelesnik	1990	640	957	Men, 21 and older	I (minimum)
Muskegon Correctional Facility	Martin Makel	1974	660	1,310	Men, 21 and older	III (medium)
Muskegon Temporary Facility	Joseph Abramajtys	1987	640	960	Men, 21 and older	I (minimum)
Oaks Correctional Facility	Terry Pitcher	1992	456	456	Males, all ages	V (maximum)
Riverside Correctional Facility	John Makowski	1977	795	917	Men, 17 and older	IV (close)

Table VIII-7. Descriptions of Michigan Correctional Institutions: As of January 1993 Continued

Institution	Warden	Year Opened	Capacity	Population	Age Limits	Security Level
Riverside Reception Center	Adria Libolt	1979	103	184	All male under 21	III, and IV (medium, close)
Ryan Regional Correctional Facility	Sherry Burt	1991	528	1,032	Men, all ages	
Scott Regional Correctional Facility	Joan N. Yukins	1986	862	743	Females, all ages	I, III, and IV (minimum, medium, close)
Standish Maximum Correctional Facility	Robert Kapture	1990	440	400	Men, all ages	V (maximum)
State Prison of Southern Michigan	John Jabe	1839	3,732	4,124	Men, 21 and older	I, IV, and V (minimum, close, maximum)
Reception and Guidance Center - SPSM	Jim Pogats	1956	538	510	All male 21 or older	
Thumb Regional Correctional Facility	David Trippett	1987	480	954	Men, all ages	III and IV (medium, close)
Western Wayne Correctional Facility	Luella Burke	1985	500	450	Men, all ages	III (medium)

* There are currently 15 camps. There is no single year to report.
Source: Michigan Department of Corrections, <u>Annual Report</u> (Lansing, Michigan: annually).

Table VIII-8. Prison Commitments in Michigan, by Minimum Sentence: 1991

Minimum Sentence	Number	Percent(%) of Total	Cumulative Percentage(%)
0 Months to 6 Months	723	6.0	6.0
7 Months to 12 Months	2,446	20.2	26.2
13 Months to 18 Months	1,603	13.2	39.4
19 Months to 24 Months	2,017	16.7	56.1
25 Months to 36 Months	1,987	16.3	72.4
37 Months to 48 Months	885	7.3	79.7
49 Months to 25 or More Years	2,233	18.5	98.2
Life	220	1.8	100.0

Source: Michigan Department of Corrections, Annual Report (Lansing, Michigan: annually).

Table VIII-9. Department of Corrections Supervision Workloads in Michigan: June 12, 1992

Type of Supervision	Number of Offenders	Percent of Total (%)
Probation	46,798	48.2
Parole	13,094	13.5
CRP	3,502	3.6
Total Community	63,394	65.2
Total Prison & Camps	33,790	34.8
Total Supervised	97,184	100.0

Source: Michigan Department of Corrections, Annual Report (Lansing, Michigan: annually).

Table VIII-10. Court Sentences in Michigan, by Major Crime Category: 1991

Sentence Category	Total	Assaultive	Non-Assaultive	Drug
Total Sentences	47,967	10,291	26,808	10,868
Percent(%) of Total	100.0	100.0	100.0	100.0
Prison	16,716	6,161	7,042	3,513
Percent(%) of Total	34.8	60.0	26.3	32.3
Probation	23,264	3,328	13,786	6,150
Percent(%) of Total	48.5	32.3	51.5	56.6
Probation/Jail	4,842	464	3,460	918
Percent(%) of Total	10.1	4.5	13.0	8.4
Jail/Fine	3,145	338	2,520	287
Percent(%) of Total	6.6	3.3	9.4	2.6

Source: Michigan Department of Corrections, Annual Report (Lansing, Michigan: annually).

Table VIII-11. Trends in Dispositions, by Opinion or Order, Michigan Court of Appeals: 1978-1992

Year	Number Disposed	Disposed By Opinion	Percent(%) Opinion	Disposed By Order	Percent(%) Orders
1978	4,937	2,550	51.7	2,387	48.3
1979	5,159	2,790	54.1	2,369	45.9
1980	5,193	2,657	51.2	2,536	48.8
1981	5,977	3,052	51.1	2,925	48.9
1982	5,946	3,246	54.6	2,700	45.4
1983	6,690	3,791	56.7	2,899	43.3
1984	6,605	3,775	57.2	2,899	43.9
1985	6,308	3,694	57.8	2,614	40.9
1986	6,573	3,858	58.7	2,715	41.3
1987	7,502	4,179	55.7	3,323	44.3
1988	8,508	4,874	57.3	3,628	42.7
1989	8,983	4,976	55.4	4,007	44.6
1990	10,503	4,729	45.0	5,774	55.0
1991	10,237	4,627	45.0	5,610	55.0
1992	11,662	5,300	45.4	6,362	54.6

Source: Michigan Supreme Court, The Michigan State Courts Annual Report (Lansing, Michigan: 1992).

Table VIII-12. Trends in Court of Appeals Filings per Judge in Michigan: 1965-1992

Year	Number Filed	Number Disposed	Judges	Filings per Judge
1965	1,235	642	9	137.2
1966	1,475	1,250	9	163.9
1967	1,795	1,375	9	199.4
1968	1,894	1,712	9	210.4
1969	1,959	1,884	12	163.3
1970	2,214	2,133	12	184.5
1971	2,336	2,334	12	194.7
1972	2,799	2,459	12	233.3
1973	3,076	2,950	12	256.3
1974	3,579	2,824	12	298.3
1975	4,435	3,503	18	246.4
1976	4,544	4,584	18	252.4
1977	5,274	4,788	18	293.0
1978	5,248	4,937	18	291.6
1979	5,499	5,159	18	305.5
1980	5,980	5,193	18	332.2
1981	6,318	5,977	18	351.0
1982	6,911	5,946	18	383.9
1983	6,994	6,690	18	388.6
1984	6,554	6,605	18	364.1

Table VIII-12. Trends in Court of Appeals Filings per Judge in Michigan: 1965-1992 Continued

Year	Number Filed	Number Disposed	Judges	Filings per Judge
1985	7,436	6,386	18	413.1
1986	7,966	6,573	18	442.6
1987	8,186	7,502	18	454.8
1988	8,546	8,508	18	475.5
1989	10,951	8,983	24	456.3
1990	12,369	10,503	24	514.2
1991	11,825	10,237	24	492.7
1992	13,352	11,662	24	556.3

Source: Michigan Supreme Court, The Michigan State Courts Annual Report (Lansing, Michigan: 1992).

Table VIII-13. Michigan Court of Claims Cases Referred to Mediation: 1988-1992

Category	1988	1989	1990	1991	1992
Referrals to Mediation	195	217	147	193	185
Percentage(%) of Filed Cases	30.7	24.9	28.2	37.5	32.7

Source: Michigan Supreme Court, The Michigan State Courts Annual Report (Lansing, Michigan: 1992).

Table VIII-14. Michigan Court of Claims Summary Report: 1992

Category	Number
Cases Pending at Beginning of Year	405
New Cases Filed	636
Re-Opened	31
Total Caseload	1,072
Disposition Resulting From	
Non-Jury Verdicts	21
Defaults, Uncontested, Settled	61
Removal/Transfers	127
No Progress Dismissals	15
Non-Service Dismissals	31
Dismissals	165
Other Dispositions	310
Total Cases Disposed of During Year	730
Total Cases Pending at End of Year	342
Cases Pending Over Two Years	37

Source: Michigan Supreme Court, The Michigan State Courts Annual Report (Lansing, Michigan: 1992).

Table VIII-15. Probate Court Pending Cases in Michigan, by Type: 1992

Case Type	Pending at End of Year	Percent(%) Total
Decedent Estates - Supervised	31,878	17.5
Decedent Estates - Independent	19,922	11.0
Trust - Inter Vivos	263	0.1
Trusts - Testamentary	7,318	4.0
Guardians Developmentally Disabled Persons	17,348	9.5
Guardians - Limited	9,442	5.2
Guardians - Other	62,819	34.6
Conservators	31,214	17.2
Escheated Property	1,499	0.8
Total	**181,703**	**100.0**

Source: Michigan Supreme Court, The Michigan State Courts Annual Report (Lansing, Michigan: 1992).

Table VIII-16. Juvenile Division Caseload Information in Michigan: 1992

Category	Delinquency Proceedings			Child Protective Proceedings
	Criminal Statute & Ordinance	Status Offense	Traffic & Ordinance	
Beginning Petitions	19,881	3,744	1,303	8,457
Original Petitions Offered	49,657	6,153	15,554	7,207
Suppl. Petitions Offered	4,032	3,223	54	1,536
Disposed Petitions	50,463	8,220	15,222	8,532
Ending Petitions	23,111	4,900	1,689	8,664

Source: Michigan Supreme Court, The Michigan State Courts Annual Report (Lansing, Michigan: 1992).

Table VIII-17. Juvenile Division Activity Information in Michigan: 1992

Category	Delinquency Proceedings			Child Protective Proceedings
	Criminal Statute & Ordinance	Status Offense	Traffic & Ordinance	
Preliminary Inquires	23,887	2,374	2,955	1,210
Preliminary Hearings	16,433	2,251	664	9,091
Pretrials	16,681	3,545	161	6,962
Pre-Disposition Motion Hearings	610	31	6	588
Pleas of Admission/No Contest Hearings	17,762	1,655	2,769	1,929
Trials				
Bench	4,321	110	91	3,770
Jury	225	13	9	106
Original Dispositional Hearings	16,514	1,248	1,819	3,669
Post - Disposition Motion Hearings	472	42	12	451
Dispositional Review Hearings	9,711	897	38	21,127
Supplemental Dispositional Hearings	2,295	182	10	N.A.
Waiver Hearings				
Phase I	105	6	0	N.A.
Phase II	87	6	0	N.A.
Progress Review Hearings	6,667	1,323	0	2,695
Commitment/Other Commitment Review Hearings	572	55	2	N.A.
Termination of Parental Rights	N.A.	N.A.	N.A.	1,301
Post - Termination Review	N.A.	N.A.	N.A.	3,823
Rehearings	393	58	4	211
Show Cause Hearings	1,483	131	10	597
Other	4,766	465	1,542	2,146

N.A. data not available.
Source: Michigan Supreme Court, The Michigan State Courts Annual Report (Lansing, Michigan: 1992).

Table VIII-18. Municipal Court Pending Cases in Michigan: End of 1992

Case Type	Pending at End of Year	Percent(%) Within Case Type	Percent(%) of Total
Criminal			
Felony	113	8.0	3.3
Misdemeanor	1,296	92.0	38.1
Criminal Total	1,409	100.0	41.4
Traffic	1,665	100.0	48.9
Civil			
Civil	271	82.4	8.0
Small Claims	49	14.9	1.4
Summary Proceedings	9	2.7	0.3
Civil Total	329	100.0	9.7
Grand Total	**3,403**	**100.0**	**100.0**

Source: Michigan Supreme Court, The Michigan State Courts Annual Report (Lansing, Michigan: 1992).

Table VIII-19. District Court Cases Pending in Michigan: End of 1992

Case Type	Pending at End of Year	Percent(%) Within Case Type	Percent(%) of Total
Criminal			
Felony	35,288	18.2	3.3
Misdemeanor	159,116	81.8	14.9
Criminal Total	194,404	100.0	18.2
Traffic	772,822	100.0	72.5
Civil			
Civil	50,387	51.1	4.7
Small Claims	29,131	29.5	2.7
Summary Proceedings	19,079	19.4	1.8
Civil Total	98,597	100.0	9.3
Grand Total	**1,065,823**	**100.0**	**100.0**

Source: Michigan Supreme Court, The Michigan State Courts Annual Report (Lansing, Michigan: 1992).

Table VIII-20. Circuit Court Cases Pending in Michigan: End of 1992

Case Type	Pending at End of Year	Percent(%) Within Case Type	Percent(%) of Total
Appeals			
Criminal	644	16.4	0.5
Civil	717	18.2	0.6
Agency	1,998	51.0	1.6
Other	566	14.4	0.5
Total Appeals	**3,925**	**100.0**	**3.2**
Domestic Relations			
Divorce	30,747	64.7	25.4
Paternity	10,070	21.2	8.3
Unifrom Reciprocal Enforcement Support Action	437	0.9	0.4
Support	3,637	7.6	3.0
Other	2,659	5.6	2.2
Total Domestic	**47,550**	**100.0**	**39.2**
Civil			
General	22,164	43.9	18.3
Damage	27,537	54.5	22.7
Other	832	1.6	0.7
Total Civil	**50,533**	**100.0**	**41.7**
Criminal			
Capital	2,687	14.2	2.2
Non-Capital	16,205	85.8	13.4
Total Criminal	**18,892**	**100.0**	**15.6**
Court of Claims	**342**	**100.0**	**0.3**
Total	**121,142**	**100.0**	**100.0**

Source: Michigan Supreme Court, The Michigan State Courts Annual Report (Lansing, Michigan: 1992).

Table VIII-21. Average Number of Filings per Circuit Court Judge in Michigan, by Circuit Court: 1992

Court	Circuit	Filed 1992	Number of Judges	Average per Judge
Region I				
Recorder's Court	R	1,494	29	486
Wayne County	3	54,552	35	1,559
County Summary	3/RC	68,646	64	1,073
Oakland County	6	30,492	16	1,906
Genesee County	7	12,308	7	1,758
Macomb County	16	13,977	9	1,553
Washtenaw County	22	5,242	5	1,048
St. Clair County	31	3,230	3	1,077
Monroe County	38	3,007	3	1,002
Region I Total		**136,902**	**107**	**1,280**
Region II				
Hillsdale County	1	974	1	974
Berrien County	2	4,696	4	1,174
Jackson County	4	3,688	4	922
Barry County	5	866	1	866
Kalamazoo County	9	5,455	5	1,091
Muskegon County	14	4,672	4	1,168
Branch County	15	960	1	960
Kent County	17	11,973	7	1,710
Ottawa County	20	2,899	2	1,450
Ingham County & Court of Claims	30	8,551	7	1,222
Van Buren County	36	1,749	2	875
Calhoun County	37	3,737	3	1,246
Lenawee County	39	1,689	2	845
Cass County	43	987	1	987
Livingston County	44	2,390	2	1,195
St. Joseph County	45	1,341	1	1,341
Allegan County	48	1,467	2	734
Eaton County	56	1,763	2	882
Region II Total		**59,857**	**51**	**1,174**
Region III				
Ionia/Montcalm Counties	8	2,143	2	1,072
Saginaw County	10	6,816	5	1,363
Bay County	18	2,121	3	707
Isabella County	21	916	1	916
Iosco/Oscoda Counties	23	778	1	778
Sanilac County	24	735	1	735
Newaygo/Oceana Counties	27	1,400	2	700
Clinton/Gratiot Counties	29	1,572	2	786

Table VIII-21. Average Number of Filings per Circuit Court Judge in Michigan, by Circuit Court: 1992 Continued

Court	Circuit	Filed 1992	Number of Judges	Average per Judge
Arenac/Ogemaw/Roscommon Counties	34	1,335	2	668
Shiawassee County	35	1,391	1	1,391
Lapeer County	40	1,441	2	721
Midland County	42	1,340	2	670
Mecosta/Osceola Counties	49	1,069	1	1,069
Lake/Mason Counties	51	843	1	843
Huron County	52	496	1	496
Tuscola County	54	822	1	822
Clare/Gladwin Counties	55	1,100	1	1,100
Region III Total		**26,318**	**29**	**908**
Region IV				
Alger/Luce/Schoolcraft Counties	11	444	1	444
Baraga/Houghton/Keweenaw Counties	12	576	1	576
Antrim/Grand Traverse/Leelanau Counties	13	1,981	2	991
Benzie/Manistee Counties	19	675	1	675
Marquette County	25	1,391	2	696
Alcona/Alpena/Montmorency/Presque Isle Cntys	26	1,244	2	622
Missaukee/Wexford Counties	28	898	1	898
Gogebic/Ontonagon Counties	32	366	1	366
Charlevoix/Emmet Counties	33	1,041	1	1,041
Dickinson/Iron/Menominee Counties	41	1,249	2	625
Crawford/Kalkaska/Otsego Counties	46	1,157	2	579
Delta County	47	613	1	613
Chippewa/Mackinac Counties	50	896	1	896
Cheboygan County	53	538	1	538
Region IV Total		**13,069**	**19**	**688**
Michigan Total		**236,146**	**206**	**1,146**

Source: Michigan Supreme Court, The Michigan State Courts Annual Report (Lansing, Michigan: 1992).

Table VIII-22. Trends in Circuit Court Filings in Michigan, by Circuit Court: 1988-1992

Court	Circuit	1988	1989	1990	1991	1992
Region I						
Recorder's Court	R	12,756	13,585	12,276	13,388	14,094
Wayne County	3	52,023	52,890	55,029	54,794	54,552
County Summary	3/RC	64,779	66,475	67,305	68,182	68,646
Oakland County	6	26,638	27,973	29,053	30,762	30,492
Genesee County	7	11,109	12,103	11,891	10,969	12,308
Macomb County	16	12,389	12,461	12,726	13,668	13,977
Washtenaw County	22	4,951	4,883	5,322	5,557	5,242
St. Clair County	31	2,927	2,982	3,318	3,162	3,230
Monroe County	38	2,222	2,455	2,573	2,801	3,007
Region I Total		**125,015**	**129,332**	**132,188**	**135,101**	**136,902**
Region II						
Hillsdale County	1	725	854	922	948	974
Berrien County	2	3,987	4,174	4,317	4,523	4,696
Jackson County	4	3,419	3,504	3,642	3,499	3,688
Barry County	5	2,204	2,101	2,394	860	866
Kalamazoo County	9	4,733	5,232	5,207	5,356	5,455
Muskegon County	14	4,007	4,012	4,091	4,394	4,672
Branch County	15	835	856	932	934	960
Kent County	17	10,120	11,226	11,921	11,852	11,973
Ottawa County	20	2,428	2,522	2,638	2,730	2,899
Ingham County & Court of Claims	30	7,400	7,934	8,156	8,469	8,551
Van Buren County	36	1,627	1,546	1,823	1,678	1,749
Calhoun County	37	3,221	3,389	3,571	3,613	3,737
Lenawee County	39	1,674	1,663	1,820	1,739	1,689
Cass County	43	943	1,070	1,167	1,119	987
Livingston County	44	1,816	2,005	2,102	2,222	2,390
St. Joseph County	45	1,158	1,175	1,346	1,225	1,341
Allegan County	48	1,237	1,374	1,349	1,444	1,467
Eaton County	56	---	---	---	1,831	1,763
Region II Total		**51,534**	**54,637**	**57,398**	**58,436**	**59,857**
Region III						
Ionia/Montcalm Counties	8	1,789	1,802	1,956	2,136	2,143
Saginaw County	10	4,987	5,276	5,594	6,197	6,816
Bay County	18	1,921	1,930	2,037	2,082	2,121
Isabella County	21	827	838	850	902	916
Iosco/Oscoda Counties	23	705	690	712	776	778
Sanilac County	24	651	667	697	760	735
Newaygo/Oceana Counties	27	1,329	1,360	1,390	1,409	1,400
Clinton/Gratiot Counties	29	1,289	1,351	1,411	1,376	1,572

Table VIII-22. Trends in Circuit Court Filings in Michigan, by Circuit Court: 1988-1992 Continued

Court	Circuit	1988	1989	1990	1991	1992
Arenac/Ogemaw/Roscommon Counties	34	1,100	1,113	1,086	1,249	1,335
Shiawassee County	35	1,215	1,257	1,187	1,303	1,391
Lapeer County	40	1,400	1,370	1,531	1,494	1,441
Midland County	42	1,051	1,221	1,225	1,304	1,340
Mecosta/Osceola Counties	49	927	1,002	1,121	1,126	1,069
Lake/Mason Counties	51	640	676	716	790	843
Huron County	52	442	430	476	429	496
Tuscola County	54	744	888	881	990	822
Clare/Gladwin Counties	55	842	965	983	1,051	1,100
Region III Total		**21,859**	**22,836**	**23,853**	**25,374**	**26,318**
Region IV						
Alger/Luce/Schoolcraft Counties	11	390	337	423	392	444
Baraga/Houghton/Keweenaw Counties	12	483	482	589	635	576
Antrim/Grand Traverse/Leelanau Counties	13	1,798	1,827	1,849	1,948	1,981
Benzie/Manistee Counties	19	608	599	635	606	675
Marquette County	25	1,142	1,284	1,267	1,272	1,391
Alcona/Alpena/Montmorency/Presque Isle Counties	26	1,059	1,083	1,061	1,134	1,244
Missaukee/Wexford Counties	28	791	849	926	897	898
Gogebic/Ontonagon Counties	32	339	378	397	399	366
Charlevoix/Emmet Counties	33	888	945	1,036	1,031	1,041
Dickinson/Iron/Menominee Counties	41	1,083	1,148	1,216	1,199	1,249
Crawford/Kalkaska/Otsego Counties	46	986	1,052	1,110	1,110	1,157
Delta County	47	633	643	690	594	613
Chippewa/Mackinac Counties	50	899	848	838	881	896
Cheboygan County	53	435	524	493	551	538
Region IV Total		**11,534**	**11,999**	**12,530**	**12,649**	**13,069**
Michigan Total		**209,942**	**218,804**	**225,969**	**231,560**	**236,146**

--- No data provided by the source.
Source: Michigan Supreme Court, The Michigan State Courts Annual Report (Lansing, Michigan: 1992).

Table VIII-23. Circuit Court Summary Report for Michigan: 1992

Category	Appeals				Domestic Relations					
	Criminal	Civil	Agency	Other	Divorce No Child	Divorce With Child	Paternity	Initiate URESA	Support	Other
Beginning Pending	584	668	2,205	539	10,308	22,348	12,678	342	4,184	2,722
New Cases Filed	791	1,102	6,757	2,153	23,988	29,612	24,867	4,621	13,743	7,196
Re-Opened Cases	18	68	819	34	1,004	2,167	664	16	73	867
Total Caseload	1,393	1,838	9,781	2,726	35,300	54,127	38,209	4,979	18,000	10,785
Dispositions										
Jury Verdicts	1	0	2	0	1	0	4	0	0	0
Non-Jury Verdicts	9	24	126	12	361	670	178	2	15	61
Guilty Pleas, Defaults Uncontested, Settled	26	42	688	126	19,153	22,387	17,410	530	5,038	1,820
Removal/Transfers	124	59	36	19	24	40	11	245	7	66
No Progress Dismissals	18	28	328	44	891	1,424	336	35	246	307
Non Service Dismissals	3	5	90	44	1,268	2,279	4,805	11	2,201	538
Dismissals	232	525	2,696	396	3,533	5,276	3,657	183	1,358	3,215
Other Dispositions	336	438	3,817	1,519	457	916	1,738	3,536	5,498	2,118
Total Dispositions	749	1,121	7,783	2,160	25,688	32,992	28,139	4,542	14,363	8,126
Ending Pending	644	717	1,998	566	9,612	21,135	10,070	437	3,637	2,659
Cases Pending Over Two Years	21	19	95	34	152	462	110	13	43	99

Table VIII-23. Circuit Court Summary Report for Michigan: 1992 Continued

Category	Civil				Criminal		Court of Claims	Total
	General	Damage Suit		Other	Capital	Non-Capital		
		Auto Neg.	Other					
Beginning Pending	**24,273**	**11,464**	**15,713**	**887**	**2,651**	**16,631**	**405**	**128,602**
New Cases Filed	30,665	13,275	15,545	1,805	4,857	54,533	636	236,146
Re-Opened Cases	4,200	1,592	4,085	200	341	6,727	31	22,906
Total Caseload	**59,138**	**26,331**	**35,343**	**2,892**	**7,849**	**77,891**	**1,072**	**387,654**
Dispositions								
Jury Verdicts	285	276	605	0	1,010	1,586	0	3,771
Non-Jury Verdicts	673	41	88	24	688	2,464	21	5,457
Guilty Pleas, Defaults Uncontested, Settled	12,811	2,509	2,767	853	2,523	37,278	61	126,022
Removal/Transfers	2,675	1,592	2,228	47	99	1,352	127	8,751
No Progress Dismissals	1,013	220	190	85	1	11	15	5,192
Non Service Dismissals	2,098	790	1,071	90	0	0	31	15,324
Dismissals	14,077	9,121	11,049	655	576	6,520	165	63,234
Other Dispositions	3,342	437	1,153	306	265	12,475	310	38,661
Total Dispositions	**36,974**	**14,986**	**19,151**	**2,060**	**5,162**	**61,686**	**730**	**266,412**
Ending Pending	**22,164**	**11,345**	**16,192**	**832**	**2,687**	**16,205**	**342**	**121,242**
Cases Pending Over Two Years	**1,422**	**402**	**1,006**	**23**	**54**	**401**	**37**	**4,393**

Note: URESA stands for Uniform Reciprocal Enforcement of Support Action.
Source: Michigan Supreme Court, The Michigan State Courts Annual Report (Lansing, Michigan: 1992).

Table VIII-24. Average Number of Filings per Judge in Michigan, by Probate Court: 1992

Court	Estate Filed in 1992	Juvenile Petitions 1992	Total Filings and Petitions 1992	Number of Judges 1992	Average per Judge
Region I					
Genesee	4,196	3,354	7,550	3	2,516.7
Macomb	5,784	1,706	7,490	3	2,496.7
Monroe	716	481	1,197	2	598.5
Oakland	8,227	7,113	15,340	4	3,835.0
St. Clair	1,245	1,157	2,402	2	1,201.0
Washtenaw	1,580	1,982	3,562	2	1,781.0
Wayne	21,581	25,630	47,211	9	5,245.7
Region I Total	**43,329**	**41,423**	**84,752**	**25**	**3,390.1**
Region II					
Allegan	625	1,091	1,716	1	1,716.0
Barry	298	378	676	1	676.0
Berrien	811	1,899	2,710	2	1,355.0
Branch	272	218	490	1	490.0
Calhoun	1,345	2,762	4,107	2	2,053.5
Cass	250	481	731	1	731.0
Eaton	497	1,082	1,579	1	1,579.0
Hillsdale	173	225	398	1	398.0
Ingham	2,126	3,147	5,273	2	2,636.5
Jackson	930	1,630	2,560	2	1,280.0
Kalamazoo	1,435	3,700	5,135	3	1,711.7
Kent	3,192	5,001	8,193	4	2,048.3
Lenawee	639	868	1,507	1	1,507.0
Livingston	832	613	1,445	1	1,445.0
Muskegon	1,070	2,827	3,897	2	1,948.5
Ottawa	735	1,946	2,681	1	2,681.0
St. Joseph	319	799	1,118	1	1,118.0
Van Buren	549	973	1,522	1	1,522.0
Region II Total	**16,098**	**29,640**	**45,738**	**2**	**1,633.5**

Table VIII-24. Average Number of Filings per Judge in Michigan, by Probate Court: 1992 Continued

Court	Estate Filed in 1992	Juvenile Petitions 1992	Total Filings and Petitions 1992	Number of Judges 1992	Average per Judge
Region III					
Alcona	101	34	135	1	135.0
Arenac	193	82	275	1	275.0
Bay	750	1,527	2,277	1	2,277.0
Clare/Gladwin	387	615	1,002	1	1,002.0
Clinton	362	424	786	1	786.0
Gratiot	268	303	571	1	571.0
Huron	462	140	602	1	602.0
Ionia	382	198	580	1	580.0
Iosco	289	218	507	1	507.0
Isabella	357	376	733	1	733.0
Lake	85	173	258	1	258.0
Lapeer	681	573	1,254	1	1,254.0
Mason	190	217	407	1	407.0
Mecosta/Osceola	361	463	824	1	824.0
Midland	632	368	1,000	1	1,000.0
Montcalm	335	383	718	1	718.0
Newaygo	376	349	725	1	725.0
Oceana	169	177	346	1	346.0
Ogemaw	185	360	545	1	545.0
Oscoda	74	39	113	1	113.0
Saginaw	1,664	1,557	3,221	2	1,610.5
Sanilac	435	275	710	1	710.0
Shiawassee	421	634	1,055	1	1,055.0
Tuscola	428	228	656	1	656.0
Region III Total	**9,587**	**9,713**	**19,305**	**25**	**772.0**
Region IV					
Alger/Schoolcraft	136	145	281	1	281.0
Alpena	281	370	651	1	651.0

Table VIII-24. Average Number of Filings per Judge in Michigan, by Probate Court: 1992 Continued

Court	Estate Filed in 1992	Juvenile Petitions 1992	Total Filings and Petitions 1992	Number of Judges 1992	Average per Judge
Antrim	171	264	435	1	435.0
Baraga	47	77	124	1	124.0
Benzie	122	175	297	1	297.0
Charlevoix/Emmet	417	670	1,087	1	1,087.0
Cheboygan	228	229	457	1	457.0
Chippewa	283	409	692	1	692.0
Crawford	102	175	277	1	277.0
Delta	161	323	484	1	484.0
Dickinson	140	281	421	1	421.0
Gogebic	116	87	203	1	203.0
Grand Traverse	475	476	951	1	951.0
Houghton	316	213	529	1	529.0
Iron	95	140	235	1	235.0
Kalkaska	158	228	386	1	386.0
Keweenaw	19	0	19	1	19.0
Leelanau	130	145	275	1	275.0
Luce/Mackinac	230	191	421	1	421.0
Manistee	240	226	466	1	466.0
Marquette	280	746	1,026	1	1,026.0
Menominee	209	202	411	1	411.0
Missaukee	107	86	193	1	193.0
Montmorency	121	74	195	1	195.0
Ontonagon	51	60	111	1	111.0
Otsego	207	151	358	1	358.0
Presque Isle	93	136	229	1	229.0
Roscommon	279	185	464	1	464.0
Wexford	258	175	433	1	433.0
Region IV Total	**5,472**	**6,639**	**12,111**	**29**	**417.6**
Michigan Total	**74,486**	**87,415**	**161,901**	**107**	**1,513.1**

Source: Michigan Supreme Court, The Michigan State Courts Annual Report (Lansing, Michigan: 1992).

Table VIII-25. Trends in Probate Court Filings in Michigan, Estate and Mental Division: 1988-1992

Court	Filed in 1988	Filed in 1989	Filed in 1990	Filed in 1991	Filed 1992
Region I					
Genesee	3,294	3,054	3,483	3,949	4,196
Macomb	4,889	5,140	5,318	5,613	5,784
Monroe	597	586	707	716	716
Oakland	6,637	7,590	8,017	9,071	8,227
St. Clair	1,111	1,091	1,188	1,472	1,245
Washtenaw	1,328	1,361	1,482	1,546	1,580
Wayne	23,772	22,652	23.228	20,578	21,581
Region I Total	**41,628**	**41,474**	**43,423**	**42,945**	**43,329**
Region II					
Allegan	598	530	531	582	625
Barry	239	269	307	325	298
Berrien	932	895	870	786	811
Branch	208	247	263	208	272
Calhoun	1,213	1,211	1,378	1,254	1,345
Cass	273	201	286	268	250
Eaton	433	456	613	550	497
Hillsdale	213	211	230	219	173
Ingham	1,590	1,710	1,396	2,006	2,126
Jackson	851	762	972	710	930
Kalamazoo	1,155	1,002	985	1,211	1,435
Kent	2,988	3,442	3,534	3,017	3,192
Lenawee	547	580	625	564	639
Livingston	710	600	611	696	832
Muskegon	1,004	987	1,098	978	1,070
Ottawa	526	571	676	749	735
St. Joseph	264	253	273	273	319
Van Buren	633	651	579	593	549
Region II Total	**14,377**	**14,578**	**15,227**	**14,989**	**16,098**

Table VIII-25. Trends in Probate Court Filings in Michigan, Estate and Mental Division: 1988-1992 Continued

Court	Filed in 1988	Filed in 1989	Filed in 1990	Filed in 1991	Filed in 1992
Region III					
Alcona	77	78	99	128	101
Arenac	143	127	162	147	193
Bay	603	706	667	641	750
Clare/Gladwin	327	284	287	388	387
Clinton	244	259	276	350	362
Gratiot	266	287	259	367	268
Huron	381	367	347	362	462
Ionia	343	325	275	344	382
Iosco	238	246	305	304	289
Isabella	275	305	262	257	357
Lake	80	73	89	105	85
Lapeer	516	592	628	591	681
Mason	182	191	258	238	190
Mecosta/Osceola	379	334	354	287	361
Midland	522	373	528	504	632
Montcalm	321	272	282	293	335
Newaygo	299	269	305	284	376
Oceana	171	166	180	178	169
Ogemaw	141	131	94	185	185
Oscoda	51	53	75	94	74
Saginaw	1,344	1,458	1,406	1,494	1,664
Sanilac	263	334	415	449	435
Shiawassee	375	344	342	408	421
Tuscola	304	313	340	321	428
Region III Total	**7,845**	**7,887**	**8,235**	**8,719**	**9,587**
Region IV					
Alger/Schoolcraft	100	120	122	129	136
Alpena	229	235	226	289	281

Table VIII-25. Trends in Probate Court Filings in Michigan, Estate and Mental Division: 1988-1992 Continued

Court	Filed in 1988	Filed in 1989	Filed in 1990	Filed in 1991	Filed in 1992
Antrim	183	184	159	162	171
Baraga	39	38	43	76	47
Benzie	83	117	114	150	122
Charlevoix/Emmet	419	410	487	449	417
Cheboygan	179	192	157	234	228
Chippewa	225	216	195	276	283
Crawford	76	84	87	96	102
Delta	168	166	146	190	161
Dickinson	109	115	101	111	140
Gogebic	114	156	130	134	116
Grand Traverse	291	371	391	424	475
Houghton	174	253	210	281	316
Iron	86	81	108	110	95
Kalkaska	103	113	116	117	158
Keweenaw	7	9	7	16	19
Leelanau	103	127	130	95	130
Luce/Mackinac	86	79	96	112	230
Mackinac	123	129	91		128
Manistee	257	296	278	290	240
Marquette	257	263	338	358	280
Menominee	146	149	129	151	209
Missaukee	73	79	106	103	107
Montmorency	56	71	83	90	121
Ontonagon	28	38	43	55	51
Otsego	128	136	140	145	207
Presque Isle	99	104	124	167	93
Roscommon	199	182	257	240	279
Wexford	249	223	275	229	258
Region IV Total	**4,389**	**4,736**	**4,889**	**5,407**	**5,472**
Michigan	**68,239**	**68,675**	**71,774**	**72,060**	**74,486**

Source: Michigan Supreme Court, The Michigan State Courts Annual Report (Lansing, Michigan: 1992).

Table VIII-26. Probate Court Summary Reports for Michigan: 1992

Case Type	Cases Pending Beginning of Year	Cases Filed	Cases Closed	Cases Pending End of Year
Decedent Estates-Supervised	32,383	9,958	10,463	31,878
Decedent Estates-Independent	18,84	12,138	11,065	19,922
Trusts-Inter vivos	180	202	119	263
Trusts-Testamentary	7,675	429	786	7,318
Adoption	N.A.	6,092	N.A.	N.A.
Mentally Ill Petitions	N.A.	15,351	N.A.	N.A.
Guardians-Developmentally				
Disabled Persons	16,532	2,161	1,345	17,348
Guardian-Limited	7,730	3,956	2,244	9,442
Guardian-Other	60,832	15,527	13,540	62,819
Conservators	30,156	7,012	5,954	31,214
Escheated Property	1,288	1,660	1,449	1,449
Totals	175,625	74,486	46,965	181,703
Assignments of Property under $5,000	N.A.	7,256	N.A.	N.A.
Judicial and Administrative				
Admissions--DDP	N.A.	8	N.A.	N.A.
Protective Orders	N.A.	360	N.A.	N.A.
Change of Name	N.A.	5,543	N.A.	N.A.
Marriage--Secret	N.A.	48	N.A.	N.A.
Marriage--Ceremonies	N.A.	642	N.A.	N.A.
Acknowledgements of Paternity	N.A.	25,917	N.A.	N.A.
Safe Deposit Box	N.A.	282	N.A.	N.A.
Trust Registration and Wills for Safe Keeping	N.A.	29,125	N.A.	N.A.
Appeals to Probate Court	N.A.	25	N.A.	N.A.
Inheritance Tax	N.A.	3,387	N.A.	N.A.
Determination of Heirs	N.A.	74	N.A.	N.A.
Infectious Diseases	N.A.	6	N.A.	N.A.
Emancipation of Minors	N.A.	165	N.A.	N.A.
Waiver of Parental Rights	N.A.	597	N.A.	N.A.
Totals	**N.A.**	**73,435**	**N.A.**	**N.A.**

Source: Michigan Supreme Court, <u>The Michigan State Courts Annual Report</u> (Lansing, Michigan: 1992) N.A. data not available.

Table VIII-27. Average Number of Filings per Judge, by Michigan District Court: 1992

Court	District	Filed 1992	Judges	Average per Judge
Region I				
Monroe County	1	42,912	3	14,304.0
Washtenaw County	14A	42,888	3	14,296.0
Ypsilanti Township	14B	22,785	1	22,785.0
City of Ann Arbor	15	32,109	3	10,703.0
Livonia	16	32,489	2	16,244.5
Redford Township	17	13,655	2	6,827.5
Westland	18	26,426	2	13,213.0
Dearborn	19	32,457	3	10,819.0
Dearborn Heights	20	19,917	2	9,958.5
Garden City	21	7,887	1	7,887.0
Inkster	22	12,229	1	12,229.0
Taylor	23	31,931	2	15,965.5
Allen Park/Melvindale	24	22,585	2	11,292.5
Lincoln Park	25	13,070	2	6,535.0
River Rouge	26-1	5,401	1	5,401.0
Ecorse	26-2	4,638	1	4,638.0
Court Summary	26	10,039	2	5,019.5
Wyandotte	27-1	9,135	1	9,135.0
Riverview	27-2	3,378	1	3,378.0
Court Summary	27	12,513	2	6,256.5
Southgate	28	7,190	1	7,190.0
Wayne(City)	29	8,439	1	8,439.0
Highland Park	30	12,431	2	6,215.5
Hamtramck	31	21,559	2	10,779.5
Harper Woods	32A	6,457	1	6,457.0
Woodhaven, et al	33	22,795	2	11,397.5
Romulus, et al	34	36,118	3	12,039.3
Plymouth, et al	35	40,237	2	20,118.5
Detroit	36	398,013	31	12,839.1
Center Line/Warren	37	54,296	4	13,574.0
Fraser/Roseville	39	30,753	3	10,251.0
St. Clair Shores	40	12,105	2	6,052.5
Shelby Township/Sterling Heights	41A	50,720	4	12,680.0
Mt. Clemens/Clinton Township	41B	39,866	3	13,288.7
Macomb County-Memphis, et al	42-1	8,708	1	8,708.0
Macomb County-New Baltimore	42-2	14,113	1	14,113.0
Court Summary	42	22,821	2	11,410.5

Table VIII-27. Average Number of Filings per Judge, by Michigan District Court: 1992 Continued

Court	District	Filed 1992	Judges	Average per Judge
Ferndale/Hazel Park/Madison Heights	43	41,849	3	13,949.7
Royal Oak	44	20,818	2	10,409.0
Berkley	45A	5,577	1	5,577.0
Oak Park	45B	31,286	2	15,643.0
Southfield	46	40,279	3	13,426.3
Farmington/Farmington Hills	47	30,349	2	15,174.5
Bloomfield Hills	48	48,117	3	16,039.0
Pontiac	50	23,742	4	5,935.5
Waterford Township	51	24,034	2	12,017.0
Oakland County-Walled Lake	52-1	41,512	3	13,837.3
Oakland County-Clarkson	52-2	21,205	1	21,205.0
Oakland County-Rochester	52-3	57,679	3	19,226.3
Oakland County-Troy & Clawson	52-4	23,306	3	7,768.7
Court Summary	52	143,702	1	14,370.2
Genesee County	67	60,291	6	10,048.5
Flint	68	47,010	6	7,835.0
St. Clair County	72	33,968	3	11,322.7
Region I Total		**1,690,714**	**143**	**11,823.2**
Region II				
Lenawee County	2-1	31,614	2	15,807.0
Hillsdale County	2-2	10,733	1	10,733.0
Court Summary	2	42,347	3	14,115.7
Branch County	3A	12,712	1	12,712.0
St. Joseph County	3B	15,436	2	7,718.0
Cass County	4	8,221	1	8,221.0
Berrien County	5	54,656	5	10,931.2
Van Buren County	7	21,620	2	10,810.0
Kalmazoo County	8	23,450	2	11,725.0
Kalamazoo (City)	9-1	45,076	4	11,269.0
Portage	9-2	8,145	1	8,145.0
Court Summary	9	53,221	5	10,644.2
Calhoun County	10	42,079	4	10,519.7
Jackson County	12	47,045	4	11,761.2
Livingston County	53	29,530	3	9,843.3
Lansing	54A	46,457	6	7,742.8
East Lansing	54B	13,355	2	6,677.5
Ingham County	55	30,646	2	15,323.0
Barry County	56-1	8,603	1	8,603.0
Eaton County	56-2	21,141	2	10,570.5
Court Summary	56	29,744	3	9,914.7

Table VIII-27. Average Number of Filings per Judge, by Michigan District Court: 1992 Continued

Court	District	Filed 1992	Judges	Average per Judge
Allegan County	57	21,179	2	10,589.5
Ottawa County	58	47,083	4	11,770.7
Grandville/Walker	59	10,792	1	10,792.0
Muskegon County	60	43,926	5	8,785.2
Grand Rapids	61	59,275	6	9,879.2
Wyoming	62A	20,923	2	10,461.5
Kentwood	62B	10,164	1	10,164.0
Kent County	63	43,378	2	21,689.0
Region II Total		**727,239**	**6**	**10,649.7**
Region III				
Ionia County	64A	15,083	1	15,083.0
Montcalm County	64B	14,621	1	14,621.0
Gratiot County	65-1	15,333	1	15,333.0
Clinton County	65-2	17,236	1	17,236.0
Court Summary	65	32,569	2	16,284.5
Shiawassee County	66	13,195	2	6,597.5
Saginaw County	70	51,571	6	8,595.2
Lapeer County	71A	24,517	2	12,258.5
Tuscola County	71B	13,437	1	13,437.0
Huron County	73-1	8,871	1	8,871.0
Sanilac County	73-2	9,817	1	9,817.0
Bay County	74	26,169	3	8,723.0
Midland County	75	20,860	2	10,430.0
Isabella County	76	14,770	1	14,770.0
Mecosta/Osceola Counties	77	15,362	1	15,362.0
Lake/Newaygo Counties	78	12,066	1	12,066.0
Mason/Oceana Counties	79	11,934	1	11,934.0
Clare/Gladwin Counties	80	14,196	1	14,196.0
Arenac/Iosco Counties	81	11,191	1	11,191.0
Alcona/Oscoda/Ogemaw Counties	82	13,997	1	13,997.0
Region III Total		**324,226**	**2**	**11,180.2**
Region IV				
Crawford/Roscommon Counties	83	9,234	1	9,234.0
Missaukee/Wexford Counties	84	11,657	1	11,657.0
Benzie/Manistee Counties	85	6,834	1	6,834.0
Grand Traverse/Leelanau Counties	86	25,365	2	12,682.5
Antrim/Kalkaska Otsego Counties	87	16,248	2	8,124.0
Alpena/Montmorency Counties	88	9,635	1	9,635.0

Table VIII-27. Average Number of Filings per Judge, by Michigan District Court: 1992 Continued

Court	District	Filed 1992	Judges	Averages per Judge
Cheboygan/Presque Isle Counties	89	10,294	1	10,294.0
Charlevoix/Emmet Counties	90	11,011	1	11,011.0
Chippewa County	91	7,177	1	7,177.0
Luce/Mackinac Counties	92	7,018	1	7,018.0
Alger/Schoolcraft Counties	93	4,658	1	4,658.0
Delta County	94	7,892	1	7,892.0
Menominee County	95A	5,736	1	5,736.0
Dickinson/Iron Counties	95B	7,678	1	7,678.0
Marquette County	96	16,443	2	8,221.5
Baraga/Houghton/Keweenaw Counties	97	7,141	1	7,141.0
Gogebic/Ontonagon Counties	98	4,790	1	4,790.0
Region IV Total		**168,811**	**20**	**8,440.6**
Michigan Total		**2,910,990**	**260**	**11,196.1**

Source: Michigan Supreme Court, The Michigan State Courts Annual Report (Lansing, Michigan: 1992).

Table VIII-28. Trends in District Court Filings in Michigan, by Court: 1988-1992

Court	District	1988	1989	1990	1991	1992
Region I						
Monroe County	1	32,445	35,075	45,736	47,912	42,912
Washtenaw County	14A	41,437	41,552	43,157	41,785	42,888
Ypsilanti Township	14B	14,109	13,918	20,026	23,488	22,785
City of Ann Arbor	15	39,127	33,632	33,280	27,599	32,109
Livonia	16	31,273	33,157	31,645	30,869	32,489
Redford Township	17	15,249	12,932	14,370	13,311	13,655
Westland	18	23,294	22,781	25,624	26,550	26,426
Dearborn	19	45,121	47,967	49,401	43,617	32,457
Dearborn Heights	20	21,690	20,905	22,702	21,410	19,917
Garden City	21	5,574	9,199	11,887	9,946	7,887
Inkster	22	11,407	11,684	13,249	11,483	12,229
Taylor	23	16,949	15,422	18,875	24,586	31,931
Allen Park/ Melvindale	24	24,626	19,202	14,975	18,423	22,585
Lincoln Park	25	17,875	19,188	15,801	13,455	13,070
River Rouge	26-1	3,983	4,796	4,695	5,669	5,401
Ecorse	26-2	3,884	6,223	5,491	4,595	4,638
Court Summary	26	7,867	11,019	10,186	10,264	10,039
Wyandotte	27-1	10,721	10,363	7,431	7,334	9,135
Riverview	27-2	3,312	3,863	3,695	3,145	3,378
Court Summary	27	14,033	14,226	11,126	10,479	12,513
Southgate	28	8,801	8,983	10,153	13,024	7,190
Wayne(City)	29	8,245	8,701	9,047	8,248	8,439
Highland Park	30	7,830	8,755	7,955	7,963	12,431
Hamtramck	31	17,805	15,530	22,953	22,984	21,559
Harper Woods	32A	8,812	6,336	5,844	6,035	6,457
Woodhaven, et al	33	28,274	26,928	26,845	26,977	22,795
Romulus, et al	34	32,775	26,576	30,520	32,609	36,118

Table VIII-28. Trends in District Court Filings in Michigan: 1988-1992 Continued

Court	District	1988	1989	1990	1991	1992
Plymouth, et al	35	34,982	36,120	34,479	36,879	40,237
Detroit	36	436,811	451,407	471,416	447,274	398,013
Center Line/Warren	37	41,818	40,193	42,805	43,520	54,296
Fraser/Roseville	39	30,715	27,435	34,788	34,242	30,753
St. Clair Shores	40	11,029	10,521	11,119	14,809	12,105
Shelby Township/Sterling Heights	41A	39,002	41,831	48,038	47,876	50,720
Mt. Clemens/Clinton	41B	29,386	31,593	38,499	43,501	39,866
Macomb County-Memphis, et al	42-1	7,590	8,787	9,872	10,844	8,708
Macomb County-New Baltimore	42-2	14,147	12,767	13,383	17,200	14,113
Court Summary	42	21,737	21,554	23,255	28,044	22,821
Ferndale/Hazel Park/Madison Township	43	40,885	41,179	43,045	42,623	41,849
Royal Oak	44	12,416	18,171	15,760	19,423	20,818
Berkley	45A	6,320	6,777	6,654	6,005	5,577
Oak Park	45B	18,563	15,302	16,586	27,204	31,286
Southfield	46	42,962	42,505	43,635	38,667	40,279
Farmington/Farmington Hills	47	30,564	33,853	34,260	34,572	30,349
Bloomfield Hills	48	45,502	50,585	44,450	49,337	48,117
Pontiac	50	23,093	25,780	24,540	28,623	23,742
Waterford Township	51	24,593	28,200	26,273	24,229	24,034
Oakland County-Walled Lake	52-1	41,257	43,468	50,701	47,427	41,512
Oakland County-Clarkson	52-2	17,209	18,013	18,530	18,584	21,205
Oakland County-Rochester	52-3	47,962	51,708	53,348	51,781	57,679
Oakland County-Troy & Clawson	52-4	27,118	25,440	22,600	25,648	23,306
Court Summary	52	133,546	138,629	145,179	143,440	143,702
Genesee County	67	71,655	71,412	69,010	68,374	60,291
Flint	68	83,937	73,455	52,660	49,012	47,010
St. Clair County	72	36,687	37,677	37,181	35,677	33,968
Region I Total		**1,690,821**	**1,707,847**	**1,758,989**	**1,756,348**	**1,690,714**
Region II						
Lenawee County	2-1	24,929	28,852	29,036	29,524	31,614

Table VIII-28. Trends in District Court Filings in Michigan: 1988-1992 Continued

Court	District	1988	1989	1990	1991	1992
Hillsdale County	2-2	11,280	11,314	11,807	10,986	10,733
Court Summary	2	36,209	40,166	40,843	40,510	42,347
Branch County	3A	11,954	12,493	14,820	14,048	12,712
St. Joseph County	3B	13,879	18,393	15,302	15,641	15,436
Cass County	4	10,297	13,154	10,922	7,692	8,221
Berrien County	5	57,471	60,276	54,423	52,967	54,656
Van Buren County	7	24,853	22,443	22,228	23,446	21,620
Kalamazoo County	8	26,147	24,053	27,539	27,661	23,450
Kalamazoo (City)	9-1	51,132	44,271	48,693	50,871	45,076
Portage	9-2	9,382	12,038	9,945	8,728	8,145
Court Summary	9	60,514	56,309	58,638	59,599	53,221
Calhoun County	10	46,255	48,511	45,010	46,739	42,079
Jackson County	12	40,158	47,902	50,552	49,340	47,045
Livingston County	53	29,552	29,047	27,744	29,187	29,530
Lansing	54A	58,125	54,305	57,230	53,634	46,457
East Lansing	54B	20,193	19,733	17,521	15,297	13,355
Ingham County	55	23,614	26,687	34,900	37,193	30,646
Barry County	56-1	9,700	10,367	10,336	9,540	8,603
Eaton County	56-2	26,482	22,693	24,434	21,739	21,141
Court Summary	56	46,470	33,060	34,770	31,279	29,744
Allegan County	57	22,943	23,775	21,369	23,500	21,179
Ottawa County	58	41,827	49,620	51,832	48,246	47,083
Grandville/Walker	59	12,191	11,613	12,709	11,141	10,792
Muskegon County	60	43,522	47,616	50,288	47,717	43,926
Grand Rapids	61	66,369	52,865	58,931	56,381	59,275
Wyoming	62A	21,376	23,451	26,035	22,849	20,923
Kentwood	62B	8,810	10,394	9,844	8,505	10,164
Kent County	63	39,038	41,603	40,365	39,990	43,378
Region II Total		**751,479**	**767,469**	**783,815**	**763,215**	**727,239**
Region III						
Ionia County	64A	25,430	18,528	17,286	16,379	15,083
Montcalm County	64B	15,036	15,241	13,793	14,440	14,621
Gratiot County	65-1	14,627	14,231	12,193	12,588	15,333
Clinton County	65-2	13,099	15,010	14,068	15,340	17,236
Court Summary	65	18,173	17,901	19,405	27,928	32,569
Shiawassee County	66	18,463	17,403	15,963	14,271	13,195
Saginaw County	70	59,014	64,177	63,914	62,719	51,571

Table VIII-28. Trends in District Court Filings in Michigan: 1988-1992 Continued

Court	District	1988	1989	1990	1991	1992
Lapeer County	71A	21,959	24,631	28,197	29,296	24,517
Tuscola County	71B	13,717	13,011	12,166	12,181	13,437
Huron County	73-1	8,703	7,524	9,177	9,862	8,871
Sanilac County	73-2	9,470	10,377	10,228	11,737	9,817
Court Summary	73	18,173	17,901	19,405	21,599	18,688
Bay County	74	28,752	29,080	31,402	28,363	26,169
Midland County	75	13,867	14,108	13,560	15,829	20,860
Isabella County	76	12,049	13,452	13,160	14,238	14,770
Mecosta/Osceola Counties	77	17,665	17,017	19,693	18,928	15,362
Lake/Newaygo Counties	78	10,516	11,677	11,981	10,733	12,066
Mason/Oceana Counties	79	9,968	12,027	11,813	11,912	11,934
Clare/Gladwin Counties	80	11,776	12,796	14,938	15,941	14,196
Arenac/Iosco Counties	81	11,962	13,164	13,312	10,481	11,191
Alcona/Oscoda/Ogemaw Counties	82	13,401	13,557	13,939	12,763	13,997
Region III Total		**329,474**	**337,011**	**340,783**	**338,001**	**324,226**
Region IV						
Crawford/Roscommon Counties	83	11,181	12,995	12,060	9,486	9,234
Missaukee/Wexford Counties	84	15,336	13,008	14,391	12,646	11,657
Benzie/Manistee Counties	85	7,106	7,355	7,969	7,390	6,834
Grand Traverse/Leelanau Counties	86	18,691	20,750	23,657	23,957	25,365
Antrim/Kalkaska /Otsego Counties	87	15,666	15,378	17,257	18,055	16,248
Alpena/Montmorency Counties	88	9,185	8,005	9,892	8,092	9,635
Cheboygan/Presque Isle Counties	89	9,658	10,750	13,537	12,008	10,294
Charlevoix/Emmet Counties	90	12,228	12,882	13,138	11,317	11,011
Chippewa County	91	5,781	7,589	7,953	8,503	7,177
Luce/Mackinac Counties	92	8,501	8,402	9,628	7,860	7,018
Alger/Schoolcraft Counties	93	5,296	5,183	5,256	4,403	4,658
Delta County	94	6,644	8,603	8,952	8,618	7,892
Menominee County	95A	3,829	4,399	4,787	4,834	5,736
Dickinson/Iron Counties	95B	6,882	7,917	7,929	8,057	7,678
Marquette County	96	15,473	16,299	16,355	18,277	16,443
Baraga/Houghton/Keweenaw Counties	97	7,220	8,284	7,551	6,065	7,141
Gogebic/Ontonagon Counties	98	4,751	5,393	5,080	5,573	4,790
Region IV Total		**163,428**	**173,192**	**185,392**	**175,141**	**168,811**
Michigan Total		**2,930,202**	**2,985,519**	**3,068,979**	**3,032,052**	**2,910,990**

Source: Michigan Supreme Court, The Michigan State Courts Annual Report (Lansing, Michigan: 1992).

Table VIII-29. District Court Summary Report for Michigan, by District Court: 1992

Category	Criminal Felony	Criminal Misdemeanor	Traffic		Civil			Total
			Misd/Civil	OUIL/OWI	Civil	Small Claims	Summary	
Beginning Pending	35,373	169,111	722,485	10,946/431	61,423	33,852	15,388	1,049,009
New Cases Filed	77,395	214,804	2,140,443	60,659	162,553	114,253	140,883	2,910,990
Traffic Misdemeanor			523,783	57,891				
Traffic Civil (Felonies for OUIL/OWI)			1,616,660	2,768				
Total Caseload	112,768	383,915	2,862,928	72,036	223,976	148,105	156,271	3,959,999
Dispositions								
Guilty Pleas/Admissions of Responsibility	9,426	106,443	211,919	47,552/1,812	---	---	---	377,152
Non-Jury Trials, Hearings, Informal	310	9,327	52,867	667/85	7,044	19,493	23,954	113,747
Jury Trials	33	1,448	788	565/21	557	---	56	3,468
Preliminary Exams Waived	37,712	---	---	985	---	---	---	38,697
Preliminary Exams Conducted	17,894	---	---	242	---	---	---	18,136
Magistrate Informal Hearings	---	---	113,392	---	---	9,499	---	122,891
Magistrate Other Dispositions	---	28,971	284,984	---	---	---	---	313,955
Violations Bureau Dispositions	---	20,652	879,470	---	---	---	---	900,122
No Progress Dismissal, Non-Service	---	---	---	---	31,953	14,806	4,102	50,861
Other Dispositions	12,105	57,958	561,797	4,743/253	134,035	75,176	109,080	955,147
Total Dispositions	77,480	224,799	2,105,217	56,925	173,589	118,974	137,192	2,894,176
Ending Pending	35,288	159,116	757,711	15,111	50,387	29,131	19,079	1,065,823

--- Not applicable

Note: In OUIL/OWI column, the first number is for misdemeanor cases, the second number is for felony cases.

Note: Courts were instructed to begin 1992 OUIL/OWI column with "0" beginning pending cases. However, some courts chose to report ending pending cases from previous years.

Source: Michigan Supreme Court, The Michigan State Courts Annual Report (Lansing, Michigan: 1992).

Table VIII-30. Municiple Court Summary Report for Michigan: 1992

Category	Criminal		Traffic		Civil			Total
	Felony	Misdemeanor	Misd./Civil	OUIL/OWI	Civil	Small Claims	Summary	
Beginning Pending	85	1,104	2,518	0/0	195	62	8	3,972
New Cases Filed	593	2,365	28,924	472	465	193	138	33,150
Traffic Misdemeanor			5,523	439				
Traffic Civil (Felonies for OUIL/OWI)			23,401	33				
Total Caseload	678	3,469	31,442	472	660	255	146	37,122
Dispositions								
Guilty Pleas/Admissions of Responsibility	197	348	3,978	263/20	---	---	---	4,806
Non-Jury Trials, Hearings, Informal Hearings	0	1,258	5,527	55/0	173	175	93	7,281
Jury Trials	1	8	12	6/1	0	---	0	28
Preliminary Exams Waived	245	---	---	9	---	---	---	254
Preliminary Exams Conducted	73	---	---	1	---	---	---	74
Magistrate Informal Hearings	---	---	0	---	---	0	---	0
Magistrate Other Dispositions	---	0	6	---	---	---	---	6
Violations Bureau Dispositions	---	512	13,958	---	---	---	---	14,470
No Progress Dismissal,Non-Service Dismissal	---	---	---	---	86	14	16	116
Other Dispositions	49	47	6,367	45/1	130	17	28	6,684
Total Dispositions	565	2,173	29,848	401	389	206	137	33,719
Ending Pending	113	1,296	1,594	71	271	49	9	3,403

--- Not applicable

Note: In OUIL/OWI column, the first number is for misdemeanor cases, the second number is for felony cases.

Source: Michigan Supreme Court, The Michigan State Courts Annual Report (Lansing, Michigan: 1992).

The Michigan Department of Management and Budget publishes the <u>Michigan Manual</u>. This is a definitive source of data on Michigan elections as well as of historical information such as the names of Governors, dates of incorporation of cities and villages, and dates of organization of counties in this state. The DMB also issues the <u>Comprehensive Annual Financial Report</u>, which contains details on State of Michigan revenue and expenditure and the Budget of The State of Michigan, which is the Governor's revenue and spending plan sent to the Legislature each year.

The State Tax Commission of the Michigan Department of Treasury is responsible for preparing and disseminating data on state equalized valuations and property tax revenues for jurisdictions in the state. This agency issues two reports: <u>Ad Valorem Property Tax Levy Report and Assessed Valuation, State Equalized Valuation, Assessment Level</u>, and <u>S.E.V. Multiplier (Factor) for Separately Equalized Classifications</u>.

The Bureau of the Census collects and publishes data in its annual <u>Government Finances</u> and <u>State Government Finances</u>. Summary data for each state are published in these reports. A more ambitious undertaking, the <u>U.S. Census of Governments</u> is done for years ending in 2 and 7 (i.e., 1982, 1987, and so forth). Reports from this Census have detailed information for counties, not just on finances but on employment as well.

The Census Bureau definition of government includes state and local institutions of higher education. Thus tuition and items such as fees for living in dormitories are included on the revenue side, and other items, such as faculty salaries and other labor costs are listed as government expenditures. For these and other reasons the Census tabulations differ from the official reports of the state and its local units of government.

At the federal level, the Internal Revenue Service compiles estimates of personal income taxes, by state, in its <u>Statistics of Income</u> annual reports. A wide range of other U.S. government reports on revenue as well as on spending, by state, are available.

The Michigan Employment Security Commission prepares monthly and annual estimates of federal, state, and local governmental employment for Michigan as a whole as well as for each labor market within the state. Annual figures are averages of the twelve monthly estimates.

The Tax Foundation, Inc., a private sector agency domiciled in New York, assembles a host of data on government for its annual <u>Facts and Figures on Government Finance</u>. Among other items, it estimates the federal tax burden for each state.

The Citizens' Research Council, in Detroit, also assembles and publishes data on Michigan governments, and conducts special studies in this regard.

List of Tables

Table   **Page**

IX-1. Average Employment in Government in Michigan and the United States:
1957-1994 350

IX-2. State and Local Tax Collections and Federal Tax Burden in Michigan and the
United States, Fiscal Years: 1966-1992 351

IX-3. Percentage of General Revenue of State and Local Governments Originating at
Federal, State, and Local Level in Michigan and the United States, Fiscal Years:
1966-1992 352

IX-4. Local Government Revenue in Michigan, Defined by the Bureau of Census, Fiscal
Years: 1972, 1977, 1984, 1990, 1991, 1992 353

IX-5. Revenue of the State of Michigan as Defined by the State of Michigan, Fiscal
Years: 1988, 1990, 1991, 1992, 1994 354

IX-6. Local Government Revenue in Michigan as Defined by the Bureau of Census, by
Level of Government: Fiscal Year 1992 357

IX-7. Federal, State, and Local Government Direct General Expenditures in Michigan
and the United States: Fiscal Years 1966-1992 358

IX-8. Local Government Expenditures in Michigan as Defined by the Bureau of Census:
Fiscal Years 1972, 1977, 1984, 1990, 1991, 1992 359

IX-9. General Fund Expenditures by the State of Michigan as Defined by the State of
Michigan: Fiscal Years 1988, 1990, 1991, 1992, 1994 360

IX-10. Selected Federal Individual Income Tax Statistics for Michigan, by Adjusted
Gross Income Group: Tax Year 1992 361

IX-11. First Governors and Officers of Michigan Territory: 1805-1835 364

IX-12. Governors of the State of Michigan: 1835-1995 365

Table IX-1. Average Employment in Government in Michigan and the United States: 1957-1994

Year	Michigan (In Thousands)				United States (In Thousands)		
	Federal Government	State Government		Local Government	Federal Government	State Government	Local Government
		Total	Civil Service				
1957	43	65	29	207	2,217	1,328	4,071
1958	44	67	30	209	2,191	1,415	42,322
1959	45	70	30	211	2,233	1,484	4,366
1960	47	73	30	214	2,270	1,536	4,547
1961	48	74	32	216	2,279	1,607	4,708
1962	48	74	31	222	2,340	1,668	4,881
1963	50	75	32	235	2,358	1,747	5,121
1964	49	78	33	246	2,348	1,856	5,392
1965	51	85	34	259	2,378	1,996	5,700
1966	54	96	38	283	2,564	2,141	6,080
1967	57	100	N.A.	298	2,719	2,302	6,371
1968	59	104	42	3087	2,737	2,442	6,660
1969	57	112	44	326	2,758	2,533	6,904
1970	58	116	46	333	2,731	2,664	7,158
1971	55	118	47	337	2,696	2,747	7,437
1972	55	122	50	349	2,684	2,859	7,790
1973	55	124	53	355	2,663	2,923	8,146
1974	56	128	54	379	2,724	3,039	8,407
1975	56	133	56	394	2,748	3,179	8,758
1976	56	135	59	404	2,733	3,273	8,865
1977	55	137	60	405	2,727	3,377	9,023
1978	55	144	64	413	2,753	3,474	9,446
1979	57	148	68	417	2,773	3,541	9,633
1980	58	152	70	417	2,866	3,610	9,765
1981	56	148	67	395	2,772	3,640	9,619
1982	56	142	62	380	2,739	3,640	9,458
1983	56	141	60	373	2,774	3,662	9,434
1984	56	140	58	372	2,807	3,734	9,482
1985	58	144	58	379	2,875	3,832	9,687
1986	60	148	60	391	2,899	3,893	9,901
1987	60	154	61	397	2,943	3,967	10,100
1988	60	158	63	406	2,971	4,076	10,339
1989	60	162	65	401	2,988	4,182	10,609
1990	61	166	67	406	3,085	4,305	10,914
1991	58	166	65	412	2,966	4,355	11,081
1992	58	163	62	417	2,969	4,403	11,281
1993	57	164	61	418	2,915	4,467	11,459
1994	57	164	63	418	2,870	4,553	11,618

Source: Michigan Employment Security Commission, and Michigan Department of Civil Service, Fourteenth Annual Work Force Report, FY 1992-1993 (Lansing, Michigan: annually), and U.S. Bureau of Labor Statistics, Employment and Earnings (Washington, D.C.: monthly).

Table IX-2. State and Local Tax Collections and Federal Tax Burden in Michigan and the United States, Fiscal Years: 1966-1992

Year	Total (In Millions of Dollars)		Federal (In Millions of Dollars)		State (In Millions of Dollars)		Local (In Millions of Dollars)	
	Michigan	U.S.	Michigan	U.S.	Michigan	U.S.	Michigan	U.S.
1966	$8,185	$180,143	$5,590	$123,402	$1,468	$29,380	$1,128	$27,361
1967	N.A.	N.A.	N.A.	N.A.	1,531	31,926	1,184	29,074
1968	10,187	211,522	6,982	143,950	1,886	36,400	1,319	31,171
1969	N.A.	N.A.	N.A.	N.A.	2,241	41,931	1,505	34,781
1970	12,979	273,742	8,936	186,947	2,345	47,962	1,698	38,833
1971	N.A.	N.A.	N.A.	N.A.	2,544	51,541	1,877	43,434
1972	14,196	303,306	8,949	193,687	3,062	58,870	2,185	49,739
1973	N.A.	N.A.	N.A.	N.A.	3,528	68,069	2,217	53,032
1974	17,671	374,189	11,492	243,467	3,681	74,207	2,498	56,515
1975	N.A.	N.A.	N.A.	N.A.	3,486	80,155	2,757	61,310
1976	19,738	435,233	12,919	278,420	3,770	89,256	3,050	67,557
1977	N.A.	N.A.	N.A.	N.A.	4,844	101,084	3,138	84,852
1978	26,168	582,806	17,357	389,164	5,445	113,261	3,366	80,381
1979	30,401	656,385	20,737	450,816	6,018	124,963	3,646	80,606
1980	33,350	724,413	23,394	500,950	5,948	137,075	4,009	86,388
1981	N.A.	N.A.	N.A.	N.A.	6,177	149,738	4,505	94,776
1982	35,429	863,771	24,032	597,472	6,307	162,658	5,090	103,641
1983	N.A.	N.A.	N.A.	N.A.	7,023	171,440	5,405	113,145
1984	38,311	965,237	24,014	645,043	8,569	196,795	5,728	123,399
1985	40,832	1,059,193	26,213	709,400	8,684	215,320	5,935	134,473
1986	44,111	1,117,629	28,534	744,578	9,314	228,054	6,263	144,997
1987	49,294	1,235,685	32,959	830,536	9,857	246,933	6,478	158,216
1988	51,554	1,318,039	34,147	884,364	10,515	262,080	6,892	171,595
1989	55,090	1,432,023	36,626	963,376	11,124	284,169	7,340	184,478
1990	56,893	1,501,092	37,674	999,473	11,343	300,489	7,876	201,130
1991	57,944	1,552,265	38,213	1,026,910	11,103	310,561	8,628	214,794
1992	59,590	1,614,755	39,087	1,059,276	11,279	328,380	9,224	227,099

Source: Bureau of the Census, Government Finances (Washington, D.C.: annually); Tax Foundation, Inc., Facts and Figures on Government Finance (Washington, D.C.: biannually). N.A. data not available.

Table IX-3. Percentage of General Revenue of State and Local Governments Originating at Federal, State, and Local Level in Michigan and the United States, Fiscal Years: 1966-1992

Year	Originating Level of Government						Final Recipient Level of Government			
	Michigan			United States			Michigan		United States	
	Federal(%)	State(%)	Local(%)	Federal(%)	State(%)	Local(%)	State(%)	Local(%)	State(%)	Local(%)
1965-66	12.7	46.3	41.0	15.8	41.6	42.6	36.2	63.8	36.6	63.4
1966-67	14.6	45.3	40.1	16.9	41.4	41.7	35.4	64.6	36.9	63.1
1967-68	13.6	47.7	38.5	16.9	42.6	40.3	40.0	59.9	38.3	61.6
1968-69	13.1	48.8	37.9	16.7	43.2	40.0	39.9	60.0	37.9	62.0
1969-70	13.8	46.7	39.3	16.7	43.9	39.3	38.2	61.7	38.8	61.1
1970-71	15.4	45.6	38.9	18.0	42.2	39.6	37.6	62.3	37.2	62.7
1971-72	16.5	45.1	38.4	18.7	42.2	39.1	39.4	60.6	37.9	62.1
1972-73	19.7	45.8	34.5	20.6	42.3	37.1	42.5	57.5	38.5	61.5
1973-74	18.8	45.1	36.1	20.1	42.9	36.9	39.7	60.3	37.4	62.6
1974-75	20.5	41.3	38.2	20.6	42.4	37.0	37.2	62.8	36.6	63.4
1975-76	23.0	39.7	37.3	21.7	41.9	36.4	37.3	62.7	38.1	61.9
1976-77	21.5	43.7	34.7	21.9	42.4	35.7	39.4	60.6	38.3	61.7
1977-78	21.6	45.3	33.1	22.0	42.9	35.0	39.4	60.6	40.8	59.2
1978-79	21.1	45.3	33.6	21.9	44.0	34.1	41.0	59.0	39.0	61.0
1979-80	22.3	42.7	35.0	21.7	44.3	34.0	39.9	60.1	39.8	60.2
1980-81	21.7	41.9	36.4	21.3	44.3	34.4	42.1	57.9	39.9	60.1
1981-82	19.6	40.6	39.9	19.1	45.2	35.8	41.3	58.7	39.5	60.5
1982-83	19.1	42.3	38.6	18.5	44.7	36.8	44.4	55.6	39.5	60.5
1983-84	18.2	45.0	36.8	17.9	45.9	36.2	46.6	53.4	41.4	58.6
1984-85	17.4	45.5	36.8	17.8	46.1	36.2	45.9	54.1	41.7	58.3
1985-86	18.0	46.0	37.1	17.6	46.0	36.4	45.7	54.3	41.6	58.4
1986-87	17.1	47.0	36.0	16.8	46.2	37.0	45.5	54.5	41.2	58.8
1987-88	15.9	48.2	35.8	16.2	46.5	37.3	46.3	53.7	41.2	58.8
1988-89	15.6	48.1	36.0	16.0	46.7	37.3	45.8	54.2	41.3	58.7
1989-90	14.9	47.9	37.2	16.1	46.0	37.9	44.3	55.7	40.6	59.4
1990-91	16.8	45.7	37.6	17.1	45.2	37.7	43.1	56.9	40.9	59.1
1991-92	17.8	44.4	37.8	18.4	44.9	36.7	42.8	57.2	41.0	59.0

Source: Bureau of the Census, Governmental Finances (Washington, D.C.: annually).

Table IX-4. Local Government Revenue in Michigan, Defined by the Bureau of Census, Fiscal Years: 1972, 1977, 1984,1990,1991, 1992

Item	Year (Data in Millions of Dollars)					
	1972	1977	1984	1990	1991	1992
Total	**$5,211**	**$8,461**	**$14,435**	**$20,092**	**$21,534**	**$22,769**
General Revenue	**4,854**	**7,887**	**13,117**	**17,965**	**19,515**	**20,557**
Federal Government	249	799	819	482	479	502
State Government	1,566	2,656	3,530	5,812	6,294	6,489
Own Sources	3,396	4,431	8,768	11,671	12,742	13,565
Taxes	**2,185**	**3,138**	**5,728**	**7,876**	**8,628**	**9,224**
Property	2,005	2,875	5,285	7,293	8,046	8,842
Individual Income	135	188	313	390	388	388
Other	44	75	130	194	194	195
Charges & Miscellaneous	**854**	**1,294**	**3,039**	**3,796**	**4,115**	**4,361**
Current Charges	587	951	2,027	2,362	2,517	2,776
Education	135	204	369	433	470	502
School Lunch	63	71	---	---	---	---
Other	72	133	884	1,371	1,451	412
Hospitals	207	347	774	558	596	671
Sewerage	85	151	---	---	---	---
Airports	18	40	---	---	---	---
Other Current Charges	142	209	---	---	---	---
Misc. Revenue	---	---	1,012	1,434	1,598	1,585
Interest Earnings	103	143	437	817	840	734
Other	90	155	575	617	758	851
Utility Revenue	**252**	**411**	**823**	**1,182**	**1,204**	**1,222**
Water Supply	153	239	---	---	---	---
Electric Power	60	137	---	---	---	---
Transit	39	35	---	---	---	---
Insurance Trust Revenue						
Total	**---**	**---**	**496**	**945**	**816**	**990**
Employee Retirement	105	163	496	945	816	990

Source: Bureau of the Census, Governmental Finances, (Washington, D.C.: annually). --- No data.

Table IX-5. Revenue of the State of Michigan as Defined by the State of Michigan, Fiscal Years: 1988, 1990, 1991, 1992, 1994

Source of Revenue	Years (Data in Millions of Dollars)				
	1988	1990	1991	1992	1994
Revenue From Taxes					
Sales tax	$2,474,963	$1,022,949	$1,026,500	$1,062,490	$1,192,143
Personal income tax	3,573,727	3,907,700	3,810,263	4,892,631	5,529,116
Corporation income tax	1,225	1,535	671	---	---
Single business tax	1,828,702	1,798,604	1,573,665	1,685,052	2,035,394
Use tax	418,969	473,918	474,278	479,978	593,139
Tobacco products tax	264,496	234,912	238,427	226,324	232,592
Beer and wine tax	53,273	52,105	51,677	49,087	48,570
Liquor tax	59,631	41,941	43,335	43,975	44,252
Horse race wagering tax	20,172	20,627	19,940	19,972	19,606
Intangibles tax	79,782	119,805	123,625	123,907	123,495
Estate and Inheritance tax	93,799	24,402	119,581	207,774	56,981
Telephone and telegraph company tax	128,589	142,271	143,695	145,198	122,477
Insurance company taxes	43,881	78,647	175,973	178,303	194,442
Motor vehicle weight tax	363,183	---	---	---	---
Gasoline tax	628,543	52,176	50,571	---	---
Aviation fuel tax	5,659	---	---	---	---
Diesel fuel tax	52,171	---	---	---	---
Gas and oil severance tax	43,581	45,570	48,895	41,331	33,483
Industrial facilities tax	68,717	---	---	---	---
Penalties and interest - various taxes	65,496	77,320	92,773	86,859	114,560
Watercraft registration tax	---	---	---	---	---
Convention hotel accommodation tax	9,167	10,304	9,633	9,559	11,413
Airport parking tax	5,167	7,378	7,026	8,465	8,492
Other taxes	2,634	2,103	2,062	2,353	1,972
Revenue From Federal Agencies					
Department of Health and Human Services	2,488,224	2,836,609	3,331,363	3,639,943	4,458,045
Department of Education	268,159	259,913	300,348	350,020	460,234
Department of Agriculture	224,135	262,900	277,875	301,529	248,495
Department of Labor	266,910	164,297	166,189	195,445	155,894
Department of Housing and Urban Development	34,168	21,364	26,001	24,439	49,540
Environmental Protection Agency	19,323	24,410	24,633	21,776	23,588
Department of Energy	12,638	13,059	11,670	11,982	10,089
Department of Transportation	340,455	7,016	7,516	8,149	9,474
Department of Interior	11,611	11,139	10,254	11,089	13,541
Department of Defense	12,891	19,294	17,713	18,243	26,318
Department of Justice	8,767	9,339	18,012	20,340	18,669
Other federal agencies	27,439	24,560	30,411	28,669	35,092

Table IX-5. Revenue of the State of Michigan as Defined by the State of Michigan, Fiscal Years 1988, 1990, 1991, 1992, 1994 Continued

Source of Revenue	Years (Data in Millions of Dollars)				
	1988	1990	1991	1992	1994
Revenue From Local Agencies					
Counties	$91,864	$86,988	$74,669	$74,203	$70,826
Cities, villages, and townships	18,355	20,540	20,509	19,824	18,836
Colleges and universities	5,191	6,000	6,421	6,654	7,622
School districts	6,011	7,328	7,927	8,848	9,752
Multi-level governmental units	10,406	1,708	1,643	1,733	1,680
Other local agencies	19,982	4,410	5,351	7,195	7,788
Revenue From Hospitals					
Contributions for medical services	---	---	400,934	451,581	900,461
Revenue From Services					
Charges for furnishing vehicle driver records	21,302	25,582	25,922	27,912	26,752
Revenue for patient, ward, and inmate care	70,383	62,979	73,403	65,621	59,696
Other services	11,879	13,012	15,439	14,125	26,977
Revenue From Licenses and Permits					
Liquor retailers'/manufacturers'/wholesalers' licenses	11,541	11,745	11,679	11,516	11,797
Motor vehicle operators' and chauffeurs' licenses	26,445	17,340	20,608	37,415	21,224
Examination fees - financial inst./insurance inst	8,340	9,463	9,647	10,588	11,157
Dept of Licensing and Regulation licenses & permits	18,781	20,393	20,737	---	---
Concession and privilege fees - State parks	10,002	11,004	12,509	12,896	13,899
Motor vehicle related	50,370	9,084	10,260	10,927	12,605
Public utility assessment fees	41,412	15,625	16,124	17,085	17,633
Department of Commerce licenses and permits	15,007	7,376	8,157	29,264	43,844
Department of Agriculture licenses and permits	4,332	1,775	1,884	2,022	4,599
Auto repair facilities , mechanics licenses and fees	1,197	3,955	4,138	4,264	4,316
Corporation franchise fees	3,077	6,360	6,317	8,390	9,314
Underground storage tank program fees	5,646	4,201	4,904	4,039	---
Other licenses and permits	20,334	16,527	19,031	23,621	30,376
Revenue From Miscellaneous Sources					
Income from investments	71,059	8,040	7,535	13,504	2,021
Various fines, fees, and assessments	16,298	16,813	19,904	26,810	32,629
Court fines, fees, and assessments	17,040	18,528	20,620	20,909	35,419
Oil and gas royalties, fees, assignments, and rentals	47,413	6,132	5,687	5,891	6,021
International Bridge Authority reimbursements	---	---	---	---	---
Sale of forest products on tax reverted land	1,426	7,279	7,997	8,285	11,796

Table IX-5. Revenue of the State of Michigan as Defined by the State of Michigan, Fiscal Years 1988, 1990, 1991, 1992, 1994 Continued

Source of Revenue	Years (Data in Millions of Dollars)				
	1988	1990	1991	1992	1994
Child support	$6,489	$153,324	$157,598	$161,786	$171,098
Sale of land	130,231	549	335	1,385	1,132
Third party	3,711	5,192	4,844	6,929	9,965
State agency office rentals	4,543	4,950	---	3,995	2,350
Other	84,304	119,548	141,134	171,030	161,656
Total Revenues	**14,854,652**	**12,571,947**	**14,235,273**	**15,165,160**	**17,714,156**
Other Financing Sources					
Proceeds from bond issues and bond anticipation notes	300	---	---	---	---
Capital lease acquisitions	26,490	61,877	35,229	24,215	8,778
Settlement from local unit	33,995	---	---	---	---
Operating transfers in:					
From special revenue funds:	1,287,509	245,937	---	---	229,589
Budget Stabilization Fund	---	---	230,000	170,134	---
Other special revenue funds	---	---	192,166	218,745	---
From Liquor Purchase Revolving Fund	64,632	63,518	68,237	73,009	104,992
From State Lottery Fund	489,112	1,234	2,369	3,555	5,429
From Escheats Fund	11,244	18,725	13,834	43,631	54,981
From Gifts, Bequests, and Deposits Investment Fund	37,649	12,262	6,855	9,361	2,756
From State Building Authority	13,000	2,237	6,949	392	---
From Michigan Strategic Fund	---	13,091	---	7,525	9,113
From other funds	16,076	14,113	16,564	38,976	11,957
Total Other Financing Sources	**1,980,011**	**432,998**	**572,206**	**589,549**	**427,505**
Total Revenue and Other Financing Sources	---	**13,004,945**	**14,807,479**	**15,754,709**	**18,141,661**
Budgetary Basis Adjustments					
Capital lease acquisitions	---	-61,877	-35,229	-24,215	-8,778
State Building Authority Equip. Refinancing	---	---	-6,864	---	---
Tax expenditures reported as revenue reductions	---	---	-894,770	---	---
Total Revenue and Other Financing Sources	**16,834,664**	**12,943,068**	**13,870,616**	**15,730,492**	**18,132,883**

Source: Michigan Department of Management and Budget, Comprehensive Annual Financial Report, (Lansing, Michigan: annually). --- No data.

Table IX-6. Local Government Revenue in Michigan as Defined by the Bureau of Census, by Level of Government: Fiscal Year 1992

Item	Level of Government(Data in Thousands of Dollars)					
	All Local Governments	Counties	Municipalities	Townships	Special Districts	School Districts
TOTAL REVENUE	$22,769,554	$4,717,362	$6,671,272	$1,010,254	$552,910	$10,659,815
General Revenue	20,557,010	4,438,179	4,995,386	902,780	402,910	10,559,815
Intergovernmental Revenue	6,991,547	2,182,390	1,573,881	242,854	153,547	3,581,264
Federal Government	502,288	191,038	229,881	8,684	19,039	53,668
State Government	6,489,281	1,666,476	1,244,428	224,082	67,538	3,287,760
Revenue From Own Sources	13,565,463	2,255,789	3,421,724	660,128	249,263	6,978,551
Tax Revenue	9,224,181	948,139	1,883,294	320,321	29,125	6,123,302
Property Tax	8,841,950	913,652	1,317,511	295,496	29,014	6,088,078
Other Taxes	194,998	34,287	98,550	24,826	111	37,224
Current Charges	2,776,087	901,394	1,054,135	147,908	170,338	502,312
Miscellaneous	1,585,195	406,258	564,295	191,897	49,800	352,947
Utility System	1,222,178	50,187	925,880	96,154	149,977	---
Employee Retirement	990,388	229,018	750,007	11,320	23	---

--- No data.
Source: U.S Bureau of the Census, State and Local Government Finances (Washington, D.C.) and Michigan Information Center (Lansing, Michigan).

Table IX-7. Federal, State, and Local Government Direct General Expenditures in Michigan and the United States: Fiscal Years 1966-1992

Year	Total (In Millions)		Federal (In Millions)		State (In Millions)		Local (In Millions)	
	Michigan	U.S.	Michigan	U.S.	Michigan	U.S.	Michigan	U.S.
1966	N.A.	N.A.	N.A.	N.A.	1,242	29,162	2,503	53,680
1967	N.A.	N.A.	N.A.	N.A.	1,553	34,249	2,771	59,101
1968	N.A.	N.A.	N.A.	N.A.	1,742	38,446	2,960	63,966
1969	N.A.	N.A.	N.A.	N.A.	1,929	43,244	3,459	73,483
1970	10,063	299,483	4,053	168,152	2,146	48,749	3,864	82,582
1971	11,341	333,376	4,531	182,702	2,481	56,478	4,329	94,196
1972	12,677	364,222	4,813	195,672	2,913	62,051	4,981	106,499
1973	14,034	402,440	5,452	221,354	3,280	67,264	5,302	113,822
1974	15,625	438,254	6,249	239,636	3,630	73,950	5,746	124,688
1975	18,443	509,146	7,538	279,672	4,269	86,326	6,636	143,148
1976	19,691	558,833	7,787	303,281	4,510	95,832	7,391	158,720
1977	21,990	606,041	9,466	333,212	4,801	101,891	7,723	170,938
1978	23,436	658,779	9,745	363,269	5,291	112,515	8,400	182,995
1979	26,312	720,611	10,928	394,582	5,938	124,588	9,446	201,470
1980	29,612	812,998	12,211	445,659	6,934	143,718	10,467	223,621
1981	35,790	967,795	17,614	562,219	7,178	160,474	10,998	245,102
1982	37,088	1,037,106	18,016	603,576	7,682	170,747	11,390	262,783
1983	40,274	1,161,436	19,978	696,780	8,312	183,732	11,984	280,924
1984	41,967	1,228,033	20,297	724,749	9,358	201,310	12,312	301,974
1985	44,926	1,340,704	22,221	788,488	9,634	223,562	13,071	328,654
1986	48,762	1,434,714	23,402	830,259	10,759	244,553	14,601	359,902
1987	50,010	1,501,418	23,348	847,810	11,360	262,513	15,302	391,095
1988	52,501	1,586,370	23,651	884,131	12,255	280,516	16,595	421,723
1989	55,746	1,691,280	25,973	931,900	12,619	303,853	17,154	455,527
1990	60,337	1,833,243	29,205	1,001,703	13,247	333,256	17,885	498,284
1991	65,323	2,001,135	31,565	1,096,493	14,162	368,360	19,596	536,282
1992	71,341	2,163,272	35,752	1,191,087	14,868	409,343	20,721	562,842

Source: Bureau of the Census, Governmental Finances (Washington, D.C.: annually); and Executive Office of the President, Federal Expenditures by State (Washington, D.C.: annually). N.A. Not available.

Table IX-8. Local Government Expenditures in Michigan as Defined by the Bureau of Census: Fiscal Years 1972, 1977, 1984, 1990, 1991, 1992

Item	Years (Data in Millions of Dollars)					
	1972	1977	1984	1990	1991	1992
Total	**$5,478**	**$8,411**	**$14,055**	**$20,048**	**$21,908**	**$22,996**
General Expenditure	5,046	7,744	12,339	17,885	19,597	20,721
Intergovernmental - Net	95	21	26	189	176	196
Direct Expenditure	4,951	7,723	12,313	17,696	19,420	22,800
Education	2,397	3,623	5,799	8,668	9,572	10,296
Higher	100	239	428	680	711	738
Local Schools	2,297	3,384	5,371	7,986	8,861	9,558
Highways	351	508	738	1,146	1,205	1,135
Capital Outlay	160	194	173	228	240	193
Other	.2	.3	1	1	1	1
Public Welfare	142	229	190	353	386	360
Health/Hospitals	256	416	1,140	1,481	1,614	1,732
Police Protection	245	426	699	983	1,045	1,083
Fire Protection	108	184	308	389	412	433
Sewerage	317	292	495	704	709	832
Other Sanitation	68	93	146	261	274	312
Parks & Recreation	87	153	294	340	357	348
Urban Renewal	81	89	132	105	103	124
Airports	27	49	49	136	129	192
Correction	32	68	292	183	231	273
Libraries	29	42	74	113	122	147
Financial Administration	60	98	235	262	281	284
General Control	140	233	417	250	266	270
General Public Buildings	39	70	91	168	208	185
Interest on General Debt	202	299	490	570	676	711
Other	304	678	837	1,221	1,385	1,383
Utility Expenditure	334	513	1,408	1,471	1,586	1,525
Insurance Trust Expenditure, Employee Retirement	98	153	309	503	549	554

Source: Bureau of the Census, Governmental Finances (Washington, D.C.: annually).

Table IX-9. General Fund Expenditures by the State of Michigan as Defined by the State of Michigan, Fiscal Years: 1988, 1990, 1991, 1992, 1994

Item	Years (Data in Millions of Dollars)				
	1988	1990	1991	1992	1994
Total General Fund Expenditures	$11,830,040	$13,460,214	$14,554,098	$15,536,987	$18,038,344
Executive	3,799	3,943	3,654	4,175	4,286
Legislative	106,736	116,509	116,351	125,103	129,105
Judicial	131,350	154,403	150,200	159,465	186,330
Management & Budget	1,200,333	1,329,710	1,414,672	1,244,709	743,176
Attorney General	28,222	31,488	31,477	33,642	36,053
Civil Rights	12,280	12,256	11,976	12,594	13,294
Civil Service	17,051	22,051	22,229	22,698	22,819
State	102,996	118,303	121,112	128,003	133,229
Treasury	222,819	228,858	259,315	1,218,591	2,443,460
Education	1,153,263	1,373,145	1,656,272	1,599,198	1,470,658
Grants to College/University	1,266,460	1,343,101	1,287,615	1,447,715	1,483,220
Public Health	314,120	407,327	435,480	421,705	515,546
Mental Health	1,117,871	1,260,761	1,328,877	1,308,564	1,438,781
Social Services	4,498,988	5,128,104	5,807,424	5,823,455	7,111,832
Corrections	614,502	774,172	811,878	893,727	1,088,398
Military Affairs	25,737	30,849	28,986	61,800	69,386
State Police	191,158	228,782	235,383	252,045	271,741
Transportation	100	0	0	0	4,562
Commerce	205,534	210,769	191,168	184,587	219,502
Labor	281,486	315,036	288,109	277,794	70,801
Licensing	22,974	24,891	25,000	0	0
Natural Resources	255,710	279,534	269,108	264,478	292,582
Agriculture	56,539	66,210	57,802	52,930	52,897

Source: Michigan Department of Management and Budget, Comprehensive Annual Financial Report, (Lansing, Michigan: annually).

Table IX-10. Selected Federal Individual Income Tax Statistics for Michigan, by Adjusted Gross Income Group: Tax Year 1992

Item	All Returns	Adjusted Gross Income							
		Under $15,000	$15,000 to $29,999	$30,000 to $49,999	$50,000 to $74,999	$75,000 to $99,999	$100,000 to $199,999	$200,000 or More	
TOTAL NUMBER OF RETURNS	4,122,250	1,600,262	914,377	814,700	501,581	168,902	94,661	27,767	
Number with Paid Preparer's Signature	2,022,806	649,886	449,900	450,850	285,970	97,862	63,752	24,586	
Number of Exemption	8,909,268	2,249,080	2,004,164	2,168,329	1,551,025	541,062	305,527	90,081	
Adjusted Gross Income (less deficit)	**$131,883,866**	**$9,799,293**	**$1,989,244**	**$32,135,685**	**$30,278,140**	**$14,375,004**	**$12,180,205**	**$13,223,094**	
Salaries and Wages									
Number of returns	3,487,824	1,212,260	767,533	756,385	478,771	161,254	86,958	24,663	
Amount (Thousands)	$104,918,398	$7,384,652	$14,953,260	$27,259,793	$26,422,353	$12,377,144	$9,137,354	$7,686,841	
Interest Income									
Number of returns	2,567,167	702,515	533,892	610,154	442,653	159,100	91,485	27,368	
Amount (Thousands)	$5,116,691	$977,562	$1,005,660	$904,484	$707,010	$350,167	$435,746	$736,081	
Dividends									
Number of returns	968,936	209,088	178,093	213,985	194,747	87,331	62,652	23,040	
Amount (Thousands)	$2,532,348	$268,704	$336,656	$376,219	$344,564	$203,563	$301,477	$701,166	
Net Capital Gain (less loss)									
Number of returns	481,083	91,112	85,188	99,238	90,566	46,052	47,297	21,630	
Amount (Thousands)	$2,914,450	$213,435	$152,675	$257,029	$321,912	$233,026	$450,189	$1,286,183	
Taxable Pension and Annuities									
Number of returns	706,707	253,169	198,765	128,618	77,915	26,781	16,923	4,536	
Amount (Thousands)	$6,874,053	$1,495,573	$2,051,790	$1,507,191	$961,313	$370,790	$326,474	$160,923	
Unemployment compensation									
Number of returns	558,742	126,847	143,959	172,553	91,353	19,757	4,012	261	
Amount (Thousands)	$1,702,213	$407,418	$521,424	$489,454	$222,519	$47,057	$12,970	$1,371	
Number of Sole Proprietorship Returns	493,550	134,729	104,559	116,653	78,034	28,991	22,902	7,682	
Number of Farm Returns (Schedule F)	49,349	15,231	11,833	11,873	6,819	1,945	1,179	469	

Table IX-10. Selected Federal Individual Income Tax Statistics for Michigan, by Adjusted Gross Income Group: Tax Year 1992 Continued

Item	All Returns	Adjusted Gross Income						
		Under $15,000	$15,000 to $29,999	$30,000 to $49,999	$50,000 to $74,999	$75,000 to $99,999	$100,000 to $199,999	$200,000 or More
Total Itemized Deductions								
Number of returns	1,346,127	69,475	176,554	412,240	407,179	160,596	92,619	27,464
Amount (Thousands)	$17,054,265	$800,468	$1,499,382	$3,863,678	$4,819,718	$2,540,321	$2,122,989	$1,407,709
Average (whole dollars)	$12,669	$11,522	$8,492	$9,372	$11,837	$15,818	$22,922	$51,257
Medical and Dental Expenses								
Number of returns	143,925	40,796	50,349	35,788	12,891	2,715	1,200	186
Amount (Thousands)	$738,876	$336,879	$187,157	$120,760	$53,254	$17,479	$16,446	$6,900
Tax Paid and Deductions								
Number of returns	1,339,682	65,512	175,030	411,571	406,989	160,568	92,591	27,451
Amount (Thousands)	$7,480,161	$182,737	$522,915	$1,572,706	$2,151,710	$1,160,186	$991,602	$878,304
Interest Paid Deductions								
Number of returns	1,144,755	38,367	133,395	357,888	366,766	144,627	80,963	22,749
Amount (Thousands)	$5,893,072	$184,682	$472,510	$1,430,774	$17,545,302	$897,584	$749,831	$403,388
Contributions								
Number of returns	1,241,650	49,056	151,290	378,117	389,493	156,669	90,189	26,836
Amount (Thousands)	$2,361,920	$54,258	$189,470	$496,473	$622,167	$336,686	$301,500	$359,366
Taxable Income								
Number of returns	3,345,506	845,977	893,942	813,129	501,293	168,830	94,583	27,752
Amount (Thousands)	$87,656,880	$2,621,100	$10,785,974	$21,341,249	$21,444,813	$10,574,487	$2,343,855	$11,785,559
Total Tax Liability								
Number of returns	3,399,340	897,100	896,586	813,213	501,312	168,839	94,617	27,763
Amount (Thousands)	$17,823,074	$479,057	$1,732,690	$3,598,146	$3,952,226	$2,264,151	$2,343,855	$3,452,951
Average (whole dollars)	$5,243	$534	$1,933	$4,425	$7,884	$13,410	$24,772	$124,372

Table IX-10. Selected Federal Individual Income Tax Statistics for Michigan, by Adjusted Gross Income Group: Tax Year 1992 Continued

Item	All Returns	Adjusted Gross Income						
		Under $15,000	$15,000 to $29,999	$30,000 to $49,999	$50,000 to $74,999	$75,000 to $99,999	$100,000 to $199,999	$200,000 or More
Earned Income Credit								
Number of returns	388,166	243,702	124,464	---	---	---	---	---
Amount (Thousands)	$316,447	$250,217	$66,230	---	---	---	---	---
Excess Earned Income Credit								
Number of returns	279,250	235,099	44,151	---	---	---	---	---
Amount (Thousands)	$231,438	$211,358	$20,079	---	---	---	---	---
Overpayment								
Number of returns	2,940,354	1,213,559	678,054	581,907	325,633	90,995	41,766	8,340
Amount (Thousands)	$2,953,030	$645,344	$558,525	$749,383	$564,216	$197,862	$147,584	$90,116
Tax Due at Time of Filing								
Number of returns	923,006	226,609	202,106	207,569	159,850	70,204	43,346	13,322
Amount (Thousands)	$1,356,060	$83,418	$154,400	$224,326	$251,391	$164,924	$215,955	$291,646

Source: Internal Revenue Service (Washington, D.C.). --- Category does not apply to income group.

Table IX-11. First Governors and Officers of Michigan Territory: 1805 - 1835

Governor/Officer	Date of Appointment	Governor/Officer	Date of Appointment
General William Hull - Governor	March 1, 1805	General Lewis Cass - Governor	December 22, 1825
General William Hull - Governor	April 1, 1808	William Woodbridge Secretary/Acting Governor	August 31, 1826/ October 23, 1826/ July 25, 1827
Reuben Atwater Acting Governor	1811 - 1812	General Lewis Cass - Governor	December 24, 1828
General Lewis Cass - Governor	January 21, 1817	James Witherell Secretary/Acting Governor	January 1, 1830 to April 2, 1830
Stanly Griswold Secretary/Acting Governor	1806	General John T. Mason Secretary/Acting Governor	September 24, 1830 to October 4, 1830 & April 4, to May 27, 1831
General William Hull - Governor	January 11, 1811	Stevens T. Mason Secretary/Acting Governor	August 1, 1831 to September 17, 1831
General Lewis Cass - Governor	October 29, 1813	George B. Porter - Governor	August 6, 1831
William Woodbridge Secretary/Acting Governor	August 17, 1818	Stevens T. Mason Secretary/Acting Governor	October 30, 1831 to June 11, 1832; May 23 to July 14, 1833; August 13 - 28, 1833; September 5 to December 14, 1833; February 1 - 7, 1834
General Lewis Cass - Governor	January 24, 1820	Stevens T. Mason - ex officio Governor as Secretary of Territory	July 6, 1834
William Woodbridge Secretary/Acting Governor	August 8, 1820/ September 18, 1821	Charles Shaler	August 29, 1835
General Lewis Cass - Governor	December 20, 1822	John S. Norner Secretary/Acting Governor	September 8, 1835
William Woodbridge Secretary/Acting Governor	September 29, 1823/ May 28, 1825		

Source: Michigan Department of Management and Budget, Michigan Manual, 1979-1980 (Lansing, Michigan: annually).

Table IX-12. Governors of the State of Michigan: 1835-1995

Governor	Appointment	Governor	Appointment
Steven T. Mason	1835 to 1840	Hazen S. Pingree	1897 - 1900
Edward Mundy, Lt. Gov.	Served during Gov. Mason's absences.	Aaron T. Bliss	1901 - 1904
William Woodbridge	1840 to 1841: Resigned February 24, 1841 to be U.S. Senator.	Fred M. Warner	1905 - 1910
James Write Gorden, Lt. Gov.	1841	Chase S. Osborn	1911 - 1912
John S. Barry	1842 - 1846	Woodbridge N. Ferris	1913 - 1916
Alpheus Felch	1846 - 1847: Resigned March 3, 1847 to be U.S. Senator.	Albert E. Sleeper	1917 - 1920
Wm. L. Greenly, Lt. Gov.	1847	Alexander J. Groesbeck	1921 - 1926
Epaphroditus Ransom	1848 - 1850	Fred W. Green	1927 - 1930
John S. Barry	1850 - 1851	Wilber M. Brucker	1931 - 1932
Robert McClelland	1852 - 1853: Resigned March 7, 1853 to become Secretary of Interior.	William A. Comstock	1933 - 1934
Andrew Parsons, Lt Gov.	1853 - 1854	Frank D. Fitzgerald	1935 - 1936
Kingsley S. Bingham	1855 - 1858	Frank Murphy	1937 - 1938
Moses Wisner	1859 - 1860	Frank D. Fitzgerald	1939: Died March 16, 1939.
Austin Blair	1861 - 1864	Luren D. Dickinson	1939 - 1940: Became Governor March 17, 1939.
Henry H. Crapo	1865 - 1868	Murray D. Van Wagoner	1941 - 1942
Henry P. Baldwin	1869 - 1872	Harry F. Kelly	1943 - 1946
John J. Bagley	1873 - 1876	Kim Sigler	1947 - 1948
Charles M. Croswell	1877 - 1880	G. Mennen Williams	1949 - 1960
David H. Jerome	1881 - 1882	John B. Swainson	1961 - 1962
Josiah W. Begole	1883 - 1884	George Romney	1963 - 1969: Resigned January 22, 1969 to become U.S. Secretary of Housing and Urban Development.
Russell A. Alger	1885 - 1886	William G. Milliken	1969 - 1982: Became Governor January 22, 1969.
Cyrus G. Luce	1887 - 1890	James J. Blanchard	1983 - 1991
Edwin B. Winans	1891 - 1892	John Engler	1991 - Present
John T. Rich	1893 - 1896		

Source: Michigan Department of Management and Budget, Michigan Manual (Lansing, Michigan: annually).

According to the latest <u>Inventory Report on Real Property Owned by the United States Throughout the World</u> the state of Michigan covered 36,492,000 acres of the earth's surface. Of this, 4,589,000, or 12.6 percent, was owned by the federal government. This Inventory is maintained by the General Services Administration in Washington, D.C.

The U.S. Geological Survey, in its Elevations and Distances: 1990, reports that Michigan's highest point, 1,979 feet above sea level, is at Mount Avron. Our lowest point, 571 feet, is Lake Erie.

The Michigan Weather Service, located at Michigan State University, is the repository of data on Michigan weather. There, <u>Climate of Michigan, by Stations</u>, and a host of other publications are available.

The Michigan Department of Natural Resources maintains extensive files on state park and campground use as well as on recreational hunting and fishing activity. The Forest Management Division should be contacted for information on commercial taking of timber and on forest fires.

Tourism data are maintained at the Michigan Department of Commerce as well as at Michigan State University's Travel, Tourism, and Recreation Center. Comerica Bank in Detroit produces and publishes a Michigan tourism index. The U.S. Travel Data Center, a private company, also produces data on the impact of tourism. The National Sporting Goods Association compiles estimates of participation in various activities.

For data on air quality users of this Abstract can look to the Department of Natural Resources. The DNR also publishes <u>Michigan Sites of Environmental Contamination</u>. A private organization, SCS Engineers of Cincinnati, Ohio, has prepared a report, <u>Disposal Capacity and Disposal Requirements in the State of Michigan</u>.

Land area information is reported in the latest Census of Population, published by the Bureau of the Census. The Michigan Information Center in Lansing has tabulations of land and water areas for Michigan counties. An office of the National Oceanic and Atmospheric Administration, domiciled on the campus at Michigan State University in East Lansing is a repository of data on Michigan climate.

LIST OF TABLES

Table		Page
X-1.	Michigan Tourism Index and Component Indicators: 1980-1994	369
X-2.	The Impact of Travel on Michigan's Economy: 1987-1992	369
X-3.	Person-Trips in Michigan, by Quarter: 1994	369
X-4.	Top 15 States in Domestic Travel Expenditures: 1992	370
X-5.	Domestic Travel Generated Employment and Expenditures in Michigan: 1992	370

LIST OF TABLES

Table **Page**

X-6. Trips to Michigan by the State of Origin, Top 15 States: January to September 1994 371

X-7. Primary Purpose of a Trip in Michigan and the United States 371

X-8. International Visitor Expenditures, Top 15 States: 1992 372

X-9. International Travel Generated Employment in Michigan: 1992 372

X-10. International Arrivals to Michigan: 1993 372

X-11. Travel Related Expenditures, Payroll, and Employment in Michigan, by County: 1990 373

X-12. Sports Participation in Michigan: 1992 374

X-13. State Park Use and Turnaway in Michigan: 1971-1993 376

X-14. Location, Acreage, Number of Campsites, and Usage of Michigan State Parks: 1991-1993 377

X-15. Number of Resident and Nonresident Hunting and Fishing Licenses Issued in Michigan: 1970-1992 381

X-16. Land Areas and Inland Water Areas of Michigan Counties: 1992 382

X-17. Total Precipitation and Departures from Normal in Michigan, by Weather Station: 1992 383

X-18. Average Temperatures and Departures from Normal in Michigan, by Weather Station: 1992 396

X-19. State-Wide Stationary Source Emission Trends, Tons per Year: 1974-1992 407

X-20. Geographical Designation of Attainment Status for Ozone in Michigan, by County: 1990 and 1992 408

X-21. Geographical Designation of Attainment Status for Carbon Monoxide in Michigan: 11/15/1990 409

X-22. Geographical Designation of Attainment Status for Particle Matter with a Nominal Diameter of 10 Micrometers or Less (PM-10) in Michigan: 11/15/1990 409

CHAPTER X
TOURISM AND THE ENVIRONMENT

LIST OF TABLES

Table   **Page**

X-23. Geographical Designation of Attainment Status for Nitrogen Dioxide in
Michigan: 11/15/1990 409

X-24. Geographical Designation of Attainment Status for Sulfur Dioxide in Michigan:
11/15/1990 410

X-25. Geographical Designation of Attainment Status for Lead in Michigan:
11/15/1990 410

X-26. Total Annual Solid Waste Disposal Requirements in Michigan, by County:
1993 411

X-27. Permitted Solid Waste Disposal Capacity in Michigan, by County: 1993 413

X-28. Sites of Environmental Contamination in Michigan, by County: 1994 414

X-29. Number of Reported Forest Fires in Michigan, and Acreage Burned:
1970-1992 418

Table X-1. Michigan Tourism Index and Component Indicators: 1980-1994

Year	Total Index	Mackinac Bridge Crossings	Occupancy Rate at Lodgings	Airline Traffic	Vehicle Traffic
1980	99.98	100.02	99.98	99.99	100.00
1981	97.11	100.51	96.01	91.10	100.86
1982	90.98	97.92	88.18	89.19	88.21
1983	95.07	104.81	91.91	89.84	93.80
1984	101.05	109.33	97.00	99.91	97.97
1985	111.92	111.37	99.32	147.21	100.45
1986	121.44	119.01	95.60	167.94	104.56
1987	135.05	133.49	92.24	206.31	108.17
1988	140.01	142.4	92.42	213.98	111.26
1989	148.08	148.8	89.23	237.04	117.28
1990	148.68	140.85	86.81	239.50	127.60
1991	149.82	158.31	84.83	224.84	131.31
1992	156.81	165.82	81.34	236.60	140.83
1993	165.23	179.14	87.16	255.34	139.34
1994	177.30	194.50	94.90	279.30	140.50

Source: Comerica Bank, Economic Research Unit (Detroit, Michigan: quarterly/annually).

Table X-2. The Impact of Travel on Michigan's Economy: 1987-1992

Category	1987	1988	1989	1990	1991	1992
Direct Travel Expenditures	$5,302,3000	$6,000,100	$6,426,800	$6,763,600	$6,740,400	$6,975,900

Source: U.S. Travel Data Center, Impact of Travel on State Economies (Washington, D.C.).

Table X-3. Person-Trips in Michigan, by Quarter: 1994

Category	1st Quarter 1994	2nd Quarter 1994	3rd Quarter 1994	4th Quarter 1994	3 Quarter Total
Person-Trips	5,210	8,188	14,058	N.A.	27,456

Source: U.S. Travel Data Center, TravelScope (Washington, D.C.). N.A. Data not available.

Table X-4. Top 15 States in Domestic Travel Expenditures: 1992

State	1992 Travel Expenditures (In Millions of Dollars)	Percent (%) Share of U.S. Total
California	$41,397.7	13.6
Florida	27,060.8	8.9
New York	18,980.2	6.2
Texas	18,676.3	6.2
Illinois	12,793.6	4.2
Nevada	11,610.8	3.8
New Jersey	10,479.9	3.4
Pennsylvania	9,648.7	3.2
Virginia	8,558.5	2.8
Georgia	8,434.0	2.8
Ohio	8,162.2	2.7
North Carolina	7,417.1	2.4
Michigan	**6,975.9**	**2.3**
Massachusetts	6,767.2	2.2
Tennessee	6,384.9	2.1

Source: U.S. Travel Data Center, 1992 Impact of Travel on State Economies (Washington, D.C.).

Table X-5. Domestic Travel Generated Employment and Expenditures in Michigan: 1992

Category	Employment (In Thousands)		Expenditures (In Billions of Dollars)	
	Number	Percent (%)	Level($)	Percent(%)
Public Transportation	18.9	16.6	$1,704.5	24.4
Auto Transportation	6.4	5.6	1,768.4	25.4
Lodging	25.0	21.9	935.1	13.4
Food Service	41.6	36.5	1,616.0	23.2
Entertainment & Recreation	11.5	10.1	444.1	6.4
General Retail	5.0	4.4	507.7	7.3
Travel Planning	5.5	4.8	---	---
Totals	**113.9**	**100.0**	**6,975.9**	**100.0**

Source: U.S. Travel Data Center, 1992 Impact of Travel on State Economies (Washington, D.C.). --- Does not apply.

Table X-6. Trips to Michigan by the State of Origin, Top 15 States: January to September 1994

State of Origin	Number of Trips	Percent of Total (%)
Michigan	15,962,000	58.0
Illinois	2,710,000	9.9
Ohio	2,216,000	8.1
Wisconsin	1,322,000	4.8
Indiana	1,034,000	3.8
Florida	463,000	1.7
New York	445,000	1.6
California	382,000	1.4
Minnesota	368,000	1.3
Pennsylvania	361,000	1.3
Texas	327,000	1.2
North Carolina	288,000	1.0
New Jersey	234,000	0.9
Missouri	202,000	0.7
Washington	198,000	0.7
All Other	974,000	3.5
Totals	27,456,000	100.0

Source: U.S. Travel Data Center, TravelScope (Washington, D.C.).

Table X-7. Primary Purpose of a Trip in Michigan and the United States

Trip Purpose	Percent(%) of Michigan Trips	Percent(%) of U.S. Trips
Visit Friends and Relatives	25.0	36.0
Outdoor Recreation	20.4	13.3
Entertainment	13.6	18.0
Business/Pleasure	2.9	4.2
Conference/Seminar	2.8	3.7
Business	11.8	13.0
Personal	8.8	8.6
Other	3.6	3.1
Totals	100.0	100.0

Source: U.S. Travel Data Center, TravelScope (Washington, D.C.).

Table X-8. International Visitor Expenditures, Top 15 States: 1992

State	1992 Travel Expenditures (In Millions of Dollars)	Percent (%) Share of U.S. Total
Florida	$11,378.6	22.1
California	10,055.6	19.5
New York	6,588.8	12.8
Hawaii	4,855.7	9.4
Texas	2,990.8	5.8
Massachusetts	1,331.3	2.6
Washington, D.C.	1,305.9	2.5
Arizona	1,280.7	2.5
Nevada	1,222.3	2.4
Illinois	1,168.2	2.3
Washington	718.3	1.4
New Jersey	672.5	1.3
Pennsylvania	597.6	1.2
Michigan	**493.2**	**1.0**
Louisiana	480.9	0.9
U.S. Total	**51,596.7**	**100.0**

Source: U.S. Department of Commerce, U.S. Travel and Tourism Administration Impact of International Visitor Spending on State Economies: 1991 (Washington, D.C.).

Table X-9. International Travel Generated Employment in Michigan: 1992

Category	Employment	Percent of State Total
Public Transportation	600	5.0
Auto Transportation	100	0.8
Lodging	4,400	40.8
Food Service	3,000	29.2
Entertainment & Recreation	1,400	11.7
General Retail	1,500	12.5
Totals	**11,000**	**100.0**

Source: U.S. Department of Commerce, U.S. Travel and Tourism Administration Impact of International Visitor Spending on State Economies: 1991 (Washington, D.C.).

Table X-10. International Arrivals to Michigan: 1993

Region/Country	Arrivals (In Thousands)	Region/Country	Arrivals (In Thousands)
Overseas	261	Canada	1,768
Western Europe	134	Ontario	1,644
France	22	Manitoba	34
Germany	29	Quebec	31
United Kingdom	51	Alberta	25
South America	12	British Columbia	18
Far East	72	Mexico	18
Japan	35	**Total**	**2,047**

Source: U.S. Department of Commerce, U.S. Travel and Tourism Administration Abstract of Internation Travel to and from the U.S. - 1993 (Washington, D.C.).

Table X-11. Travel Related Expenditures, Payroll, and Employment in Michigan, by County: 1990

County	Expenditures ($ Millions)	Payroll ($ Millions)	Employment (Thousands)	County	Expenditures ($ Millions)	Payroll ($ Millions)	Employment (Thousands)
Alcona	13.39	2.30	170	Lake	15.08	2.64	190
Alger	26.50	5.90	580	Lapeer	15.54	2.54	220
Allegan	30.96	6.48	560	Leelanau	42.00	9.34	890
Alpena	24.53	4.84	430	Lenawee	22.29	4.60	360
Antrim	52.01	11.05	1,100	Livingston	31.78	6.15	520
Arenac	19.77	2.57	180	Luce	8.08	1.69	140
Baraga	9.10	2.14	180	Mackinac	93.47	21.97	2,140
Barry	9.30	2.02	140	Macomb	195.53	35.05	3,220
Bay	24.44	4.53	410	Manistee	24.99	7.44	580
Benzie	16.33	4.25	340	Marquette	54.74	11.30	1,060
Berrien	102.78	23.69	1,940	Mason	27.39	8.10	650
Branch	24.07	8.25	600	Mecosta	18.72	3.45	300
Calhoun	55.55	9.68	890	Menominee	11.94	3.24	240
Cass	17.93	8.60	530	Midland	44.88	9.41	950
Charlevoix	56.30	13.00	1,240	Missaukee	6.65	1.06	80
Cheboygan	38.62	8.31	770	Monroe	45.10	11.45	990
Chippewa	46.56	11.62	990	Montcalm	16.88	2.15	150
Clare	21.76	3.05	220	Montmorency	13.37	2.57	210
Clinton	34.71	11.73	430	Muskegon	49.74	9.82	860
Crawford	32.79	6.85	680	Newaygo	14.72	3.39	230
Delta	38.48	8.77	820	Oakland	624.67	124.89	11,820
Dickinson	23.60	5.93	520	Oceana	14.49	3.08	240
Eaton	49.01	9.85	1,030	Ogemaw	8.48	1.48	120
Emmet	107.57	24.44	2,420	Ontonagon	22.68	5.30	510
Genesee	168.63	29.77	2,480	Osceola	7.09	0.99	70
Gladwin	12.90	1.76	130	Oscoda	9.63	1.44	110
Gogebic	46.84	15.92	1,220	Otsego	57.13	13.15	1,240
Grnd Traverse	227.18	47.15	4,790	Ottawa	95.51	18.19	1,780
Gratiot	21.08	3.72	370	Presque Isle	9.97	1.81	140
Hillsdale	10.70	3.14	220	Roscommon	38.98	7.63	630
Houghton	24.44	4.85	450	Saginaw	145.38	35.46	2,600
Huron	19.84	3.22	270	St. Clair	59.60	12.76	1,220
Ingham	141.42	34.39	2,800	St. Joseph	25.00	7.53	570
Ionia	10.09	1.49	120	Sanilac	11.48	1.86	150
Iosco	40.55	8.50	770	Schoolcraft	32.52	8.35	740
Iron	15.11	5.76	390	Shiawassee	13.05	2.21	200
Isabella	43.37	8.42	850	Tuscola	7.81	1.26	100
Jackson	44.50	8.76	780	Van Buren	34.11	7.60	620
Kalamazoo	94.30	22.41	1,430	Washtenaw	225.21	44.52	4,550
Kalkaska	9.21	1.53	120	Wayne	2310.58	730.24	32,600
Kent	405.04	97.05	7,090	Wexford	39.90	9.74	870
Keweenaw	5.89	1.28	110	**Michigan**	**6,763.30**	**1,696.40**	**116,440**

Source: U.S. Travel Data Center, Michigan Travel Bureau, The Economic Impact of U.S. Travel on Michigan Counties 1990 (Wash. D.C.).

Table X-12. Sports Participation in Michigan: 1992

Sport (Data in Thousands)	Total Participants For Sport	Total Participants in Michigan	Degree of Participation in Michigan				Total Days of Participation
			Frequent (110 + Days)	Occasional (25-109 Days)	Infrequent (6-24 Days)		
Aerobic Exercising	26,875	1,101	268	549	283		84,365
Backpacking/Wilderness Camping	10,033	358	56	170	132		3,383
Baseball	15,844	670	111	413	146		18,740
Basketball	27,165	1,331	314	660	357		39,995
Bicycle Riding	54,302	2,437	403	1,166	868		151,956
Billiards/Pool	29,348	1,047	136	523	388		15,272
Boating-Motor/Power	22,309	1,076	373	396	306		15,266
Bowling	41,432	2,181	579	866	736		43,643
Calisthenics	11,898	439	115	178	145		35,085
Camping (Vacation/Overnight)	47,202	2,285	456	1,205	624		25,147
Dart Throwing	18,778	897	173	383	341		17,802
Exercise Walking	68,690	2,380	993	840	546		254,177
Exercising With Equipment	39,274	1,701	510	688	502		143,966
Fishing - Fresh Water	41,717	1,959	727	735	498		36,403
Fishing - Salt Water	12,291	131	15	52	64		1,346
Football	13,391	576	98	227	251		10,882
Golf	24,375	1,419	291	637	491		34,485
Hiking	22,141	606	76	316	214		8,309
Horseback Riding	8,444	285	8	113	164		1,621
Hunting With Firearms	17,465	1,051	295	580	177		15,747
Miniature Golf	35,287	1,766	332	731	703		8,399
Roller Skating/In-Line Wheels	9,717	459	155	107	197		7,041
Roller Skating/Traditional 2x2 Wheels	16,754	811	95	354	362		6,761
Running/Jogging	22,202	798	177	324	297		53,675
Skiing-Alpine/Downhill	10,604	361	64	160	136		3,504
Soccer	10,305	477	176	217	84		17,163
Softball	19,416	959	261	477	221		22,861
Step Aerobics	9,171	337	29	181	127		18,455

Table X-12. Sports Participation in Michigan: 1992 Continued

Sport (Data in Thousands)	Total Participants For Sport	Total Participants in Michigan	Degree of Participation in Michigan				Total Days of Participation
			Frequent (110 + Days)	Occasional (25-109 Days)	Infrequent (6-24 Days)		
Swimming	64,664	2,385	32	1,278	1,075		88,637
Table Tennis	9,531	553	104	216	233		5,999
Target Shooting	11,914	553	143	189	221		6,615
Tennis	17,012	696	140	218	338		13,912
Volleyball	22,358	874	263	334	277		13,350
Work-Out at Club	19,202	670	130	306	234		44,717

Source: National Sporting Goods Association: Sports Participation in 1992, State-By-State (Mt. Prospect, Illinois: 1992).

Table X-13. State Park Use and Turnaway in Michigan: 1971-1993

| Year | State Park Use and Turnaway | | | | Vehicles Turned Away | |
	Total Attendance (Data in Thousands)	Number of Day Users (Data in Thousands)	Number of Camper Days (Data in Thousands)	Number of Camp Permits	Day Use	Camping
1971	21,914	15,419	6,495	491,807	52,465	84,258
1972	19,191	12,941	6,251	485,616	27,719	59,730
1973	19,848	13,606	6,248	496,812	25,378	57,445
1974	19,486	13,358	6,128	471,313	31,973	71,711
1975	20,366	14,768	5,598	462,123	46,708	70,962
1976	22,014	16,132	5,882	482,787	35,085	77,218
1977	22,344	N.A.	N.A.	480,133	40,154	79,107
1978	23,656	N.A.	N.A.	475,551	65,708	66,613
1979	21,426	N.A.	N.A.	422,371	38,227	51,128
1980	20,784	15,598	5,187	403,450	47,527	55,333
1981	20,812	20,812	5,257	398,404	29,219	49,205
1982	20,677	15,342	5,334	405,402	26,890	50,650
1983	23,029	17,729	5,300	403,562	40,811	51,944
1984	22,283	17,030	5,254	393,073	37,154	49,541
1985	22,728	17,459	5,269	399,128	N.A.	N.A.
1986	22,845	17,574	5,271	391,000	39,000	43,000
1987	25,354	19,939	5,209	448,000	50,000	49,000
1988	23,011	17,803	5,416	432,000	52,000	44,000
1989	22,490	17,334	5,155	423,000	N.A.	N.A.
1990	25,246	19,686	5,378	446,000	N.A.	N.A.
1991	25,292	19,917	5,378	448,269	36,486	43,612
1992	21,160	16,251	4,906	402,537	18,185	25,627
1993	22,396	17,413	5,030	413,208	26,912	31,377

Source: Michigan Department of Natural Resources, Parks Division (Lansing, Michigan: annually). N.A. Data not available.

Table X-14. Location, Acreage, Number of Campsites, and Usage of Michigan State Parks: 1991-1993

Park Name	Post Office Location	Acreage	Number of Campsites	Attendance		
				1991	1992	1993
STATEWIDE TOTAL				**25,292,232**	**21,160,402**	**22,394,564**
Upper Peninsula				**2,421,202**	**2,113,990**	**2,252,343**
Baraga	Baraga US-41	56	119	45,289	42,725	51,406
Bewabic	Crystal Falls US-2	315	144	89,121	69,067	74,001
Brimley	Brimley US-221	151	270	224,941	157,569	134,655
Fayette	Fayette US-2	711	80	110,383	98,683	93,140
Fort Wilkins	Copper Harbor US-41	203	165	178,415	153,571	161,308
Indian Lake	Manistique M-149	897	302	110,000	89,788	88,392
Lake Gogebic	Marenisco M-64	361	125	63,162	51,970	52,007
McLain	Hancock M-203	417	103	179,627	161,500	157,522
Muskallonge Lake	Newberry M-123	217	179	76,832	63,843	72,306
Palms Book	Manistique M-149	388	No Camping	69,178	58,407	57,137
Porcupine Mountains	Ontonagon M-107	58,335	183	361,249	361,556	432,591
Straits	St. Ignace I-75	181	322	171,520	152,515	170,347
Tahquamenon Falls	Paradise M-123	35,733	319	487,225	441,478	484,846
Twin Lakes	Winona M-26	175	62	46,669	34,899	36,860
Van Riper	Champion US-41	1,044	226	102,018	87,124	100,451
J.W. Wells	Cedar River M-35	694	178	105,573	89,295	85,374
Northern Lower Peninsula				**4,826,758**	**4,078,023**	**4,199,499**
Aloha	Cheboygan M-212	91	300	175,665	161,453	133,168
Bay City	Bay City M-247	196	264	493,447	373,284	408,183
Burt Lake	Indian River I-75	405	375	190,304	172,640	183,700
Cheboygan	Cheboygan US-23	932	78	58,355	50,494	56,990

Table X-14. Location, Acreage, Number of Campsites, and Usage of Michigan State Parks: 1991-1993 Continued

Park Name	Post Office Location	Acreage	Number of Campsites	Attendance		
				1991	1992	1993
Northern Lower Peninsula - Continued						
Clear Lake	Atlanta M-33	290	200	91,754	72,916	78,168
Fisherman's Island	N.A.	2,678	90	61,175	54,575	54,693
Harrisville	Harrisville US-23	94	229	149,111	147,887	163,099
Hartwick Pines	Grayling M-93	9,672	100	206,862	201,468	187,531
Hoeft	Rogers City US-23	301	144	64,919	47,240	52,984
Interlochen	Interlochen M-137	187	550	262,218	249,804	291,579
Leelanau	Glen Arbor CR-201	1,300	50	137,121	136,683	109,530
Ludington	Ludington M-116	5,202	400	732,984	715,897	779,212
Mears	Pentwater US-31	50	179	350,853	254,635	253,770
Mitchell	Cadillac M-115	334	270	268,974	269,878	195,106
Newaygo	Newaygo M-37	257	99	38,861	47,233	36,870
North Higgins Lake	Roscommon M-18, M-76	429	218	209,748	167,319	205,673
Onaway	Onaway M-211	158	101	58,404	52,579	56,127
Orchard Beach	Manistee M-110	201	175	104,981	91,843	95,075
Otsego Lake	Gaylord I-75	62	203	143,273	99,235	133,710
Petoskey	Petoskey US-31	305	190	287,547	237,651	245,364
Rifle River	Lupton M-33	4,329	181	129,700	112,869	122,532
Silver Lake	Mears US-31	2,860	249	703,712	727,230	780,029
South Higgins Lake	Roscommon US-27	962	512	633,936	389,506	422,637
Tawas Point	E. Tawas US-23	183	210	305,467	288,867	278,391
Traverse City	Traverse City US-31	45	343	246,480	196,789	209,969
Wilderness	Carp Lake US-31	7,514	210	153,078	145,715	154,096
Wilson	Harrison I-75	36	160	130,025	120,116	107,711
Young	Boyne City M-75	563	293	140,878	129,125	135,338
Southern Lower Peninsula				18,044,272	14,968,389	15,942,722
Algonac	Algonac M-29	1,037	300	209,517	181,644	203,331
Bald Mountain	Lake Orion M-24	4,637	N.A.	476,347	415,457	429,831

Table X-14. Location, Acreage, Number of Campsites, and Usage of Michigan State Parks: 1991-1993 Continued

Park Name	Post Office Location	Acreage	Number of Campsites	Attendance		
				1991	1992	1993
Southern Lower Peninsula - Continued						
Brighton	Howell I-96	4,913	222	273,872	237,603	246,300
Dodge #4	Pontiac M-59	139	No Camping	508,342	191,118	281,154
Duck Lake	Muskegon	704	N.A.	150,496	110,118	96,891
Fort Custer	Augusta I-94	2,962	112	334,378	316,950	345,980
Grand Haven	Grand Haven US-31	48	182	1,226,091	1,076,524	1,259,722
Grand Mere	Sawyer Red Arrow Hwy.	985	No Camping	49,208	100,012	92,434
W.J. Hayes	Onsted US-12	654	200	685,714	209,479	286,518
Highland	Milford M-59	5,524	30	232,035	170,545	188,714
Hoffmaster	Muskegon US-31	1,043	333	425,778	380,639	390,358
Holland	Holland US-31	142	368	1,425,733	1,271,480	1,140,352
Holly	Holly I-75	7,670	161	374,712	321,140	283,293
Ionia	Saranac M-66	4,085	100	197,768	194,312	237,716
Island Lake	Brighton I-96	3,466	45	488,870	435,922	482,038
Lake Hudson	Clayton M-156	2,650	50	232,457	68,501	38,860
Lakeport	Port Huron US-23	565	315	231,909	207,889	200,029
Maybury	Northville	944	N.A.	428,386	432,779	398,730
Metamora-Hadley	Metamora M-24	683	220	364,226	179,855	188,792
Muskegon	North Muskegon M-213	1,357	348	844,796	730,590	740,809
Ortonville	Ortonville M-75	4,875	25	168,685	88,698	83,888
Pinckney	Pinckney M-36	9,994	245	733,244	677,805	735,538
Pontiac Lake	Pontiac M-59	3,700	176	440,511	483,939	558,239
Port Crescent	Port Austin M-25	569	181	213,233	175,042	146,111
Proud Lake	Milford I-96	3,614	130	400,117	413,638	501,371
Saugatuck	Saugatuck	866	No Camping	41,459	42,500	47,618
Seven Lakes	Fenton US-23, I-75	1,410	78	125,404	124,770	127,327
Sleeper	Caseville M-25	723	280	244,031	157,195	149,384
Sleepy Hollow	Lansing US-27	2,678	181	280,550	252,243	275,916

Table X-14. Location, Acreage, Number of Campsites, and Usage of Michigan State Parks: 1991-1993 Continued

Park Name	Post Office Location	Acreage	Number of Campsites	Attendance		
				1991	1992	1993
Southern Lower Peninsula - Continued						
Sterling	Monroe I-75	1,000	288	904,147	824,370	1,047,351
Van Buren	South Haven I-196	326	220	439,765	193,719	224,472
Warren Dunes	Sawyer I-94	1,950	197	1,095,264	1,023,884	1,253,873
Waterloo	Chelsea I-94	19,962	434	622,702	570,627	587,248
Yankee Springs	Middleville M-37	5,014	345	747,237	705,457	793,528

Source: Michigan Department of Natural Resources, Parks Division (Lansing, Michigan: annually). N.A. Data not available.

Table X-15. Number of Resident and Nonresident Hunting and Fishing Licenses Issued in Michigan: 1970-1992

Year	Hunting						Fishing			
	Small Game		Deer-Firearm		Deer-Bow		Resident		Nonresident	Trout Stamp
	Resident	Nonresident	Resident	Nonresident	Resident	Nonresident	Senior	Annual	Annual	
1970	581,855	6,202	616,173	12,729	58,234	3,584	92,932	807,703	133,196	303,774
1971	465,201	5,683	457,349	10,189	35,514	2,985	97,169	837,462	137,460	313,432
1972	445,389	6,396	422,089	9,108	29,378	2,576	99,540	811,393	127,218	308,630
1973	515,101	7,803	475,885	10,169	38,053	2,735	103,805	832,539	131,671	311,565
1974	552,028	8,609	530,540	11,820	46,146	2,851	91,938	871,557	131,516	324,865
1975	543,762	8,866	562,738	13,710	54,199	3,582	95,206	916,571	137,919	352,207
1976	488,463	7,601	511,158	13,781	56,915	4,287	95,331	817,088	106,028	278,130
1977	421,700	7,847	482,002	14,990	62,013	5,464	94,659	770,299	99,971	253,235
1978	353,073	7,059	522,520	16,388	NA	6,793	95,469	738,324	94,089	239,601
1979	318,799	6,900	519,505	16,030	NA	7,300	94,069	718,779	91,278	223,622
1980	378,982	5,571	651,333	10,597	152,521	4,039	98,943	712,813	114,522	236,386
1981	365,951	5,839	668,146	10,714	168,556	4,401	125,333	865,394	72,078	354,703
1982	335,895	5,795	649,018	10,339	177,620	4,903	127,551	870,664	73,909	365,954
1983	349,005	5,220	609,834	10,210	192,563	4,133	127,365	839,582	72,836	364,873
1984	346,288	5,537	619,330	10,103	193,543	4,469	128,203	851,298	74,288	387,511
1985	344,318	6,262	651,999	12,383	202,709	4,917	132,163	879,534	78,358	401,223
1986	332,715	3,554	739,046	11,544	227,615	4,344	131,246	1,002,134	113,938	370,494
1987	321,760	3,821	759,353	12,901	242,358	4,704	135,965	1,010,203	137,880	363,362
1988	304,594	3,848	737,864	13,634	252,947	5,094	134,612	987,040	139,820	348,533
1989	311,329	4,242	697,400	14,854	268,926	5,456	134,266	967,877	137,614	327,683
1990	316,053	4,312	711,451	15,407	279,405	5,980	135,317	962,646	138,897	300,094
1991	314,069	4,282	707,079	17,939	297,097	6,238	138,101	966,202	140,731	286,738
1992	295,421	4,442	680,657	18,159	300,206	6,444	134,617	915,823	136,751	275,472

Source: Michigan Department of Natural Resources, License Control Section (Lansing, Michigan: annually).

Table X-16. Land Areas and Inland Water Areas of Michigan Counties: 1992

County	Land (In Square Miles)	Water (In Square Miles)	County	Land (In Square Miles)	Water (In Square Miles)
Alcona	1,746,875	2,890,674	Lake	1,470,032	18,281
Alger	2,377,489	10,687,435	Lapeer	1,694,712	22,772
Allegan	2,143,325	2,605,468	Leelanau	902,597	5,658,810
Alpena	1,487,098	2,903,089	Lenawee	1,943,986	27,985
Antrim	1,235,298	323,737	Livingston	1,472,163	44,185
Arenac	950,196	812,954	Luce	2,338,946	2,612,870
Baraga	2,341,770	427,239	Mackinac	2,645,953	2,794,588
Barry	1,440,454	53,798	Macomb	1,244,271	231,545
Bay	1,150,643	483,591	Manistee	1,408,609	1,908,909
Benzie	832,267	1,394,401	Marquette	4,717,202	4,158,479
Berrien	1,478,981	2,617,039	Mason	1,282,545	1,934,194
Branch	1,314,215	31,342	Mecosta	1,439,491	39,758
Calhoun	1,836,004	24,886	Menominee	2,703,073	762,694
Cass	1,274,899	42,149	Midland	1,349,954	17,346
Charlevoix	1,079,643	2,522,707	Missaukee	1,467,955	18,329
Cheboygan	1,853,408	439,426	Monroe	1,427,436	334,018
Chippewa	4,043,192	2,944,630	Montcalm	1,833,945	33,499
Clare	1,468,168	21,731	Montmorency	1,418,370	38,401
Clinton	1,480,146	8,071	Muskegon	1,318,828	2,460,743
Crawford	1,445,648	13,572	Newaygo	2,181,891	49,255
Delta	3,030,794	2,127,834	Oakland	2,260,323	91,589
Dickinson	1,985,034	27,921	Oceana	1,399,866	1,984,836
Eaton	1,493,262	6,525	Ogemaw	1,461,695	26,706
Emmet	1,212,002	1,073,233	Ontonagon	3,397,117	6,293,037
Genesee	1,656,731	25,134	Osceola	1,466,242	18,216
Gladwin	1,312,728	24,913	Oscoda	1,463,435	17,002
Gogebic	2,854,012	970,224	Otsego	1,332,813	29,539
Grand Traverse	1,204,593	352,435	Ottawa	1,465,203	2,761,982
Gratiot	1,476,719	3,837	Presque Isle	1,709,541	4,955,109
Hillsdale	1,551,043	21,555	Roscommon	1,350,454	151,378
Houghton	2,620,414	1,268,799	Saginaw	2,095,229	17,737
Huron	2,166,754	3,368,722	St. Clair	1,876,337	279,960
Ingham	1,448,414	4,535	St. Joseph	1,304,695	45,153
Ionia	1,484,690	18,177	Sanilac	2,496,393	1,623,377
Iosco	1,422,298	3,474,669	Schoolcraft	3,051,482	1,827,542
Iron	3,021,204	115,697	Shiawassee	1,395,595	5,015
Isabella	1,487,450	9,011	Tuscola	2,104,621	262,202
Jackson	1,830,215	44,470	Van Buren	1,582,506	1,241,319
Kalamazoo	1,455,312	47,471	Washtenaw	1,839,079	32,421
Kalkaska	1,453,093	25,244	Wayne	1,590,632	150,515
Kent	2,217,651	41,382	Wexford	1,464,762	26,778
Keweenaw	1,401,710	14,294,962	**Michigan**	**147,135,821**	**103,602,763**

Source: U.S. Bureau of the Census, Michigan Information Center (Lansing, Michigan).

Table X-17. Total Precipitation and Departures from Normal in Michigan, by Weather Station: 1992

Station	January Precip	January Deprt	February Precip	February Deprt	March Precip	March Deprt	April Precip	April Deprt	May Precip	May Deprt	June Precip	June Deprt
West Upper												
Alberta Ford For Cen	1.37	N.A.	1.45	N.A.	0.94	N.A.	1.11	N.A.	2.35	N.A.	M1.02	N.A.
Bergland Dam	2.47	0.14	2.66	0.9	1.60	-0.74	1.73	-1.01	2.33	-1.51	1.83	-2.27
Big Bay	0.83	N.A.	0.97	N.A.	0.78	N.A.	1.78	N.A.	M1.29	N.A.	M.37	N.A.
Champion van Riper Prk	1.11	-0.38	1.44	0.08	1.56	-0.57	1.87	-0.58	2.16	-1.27	1.35	-2.51
Copper Harbor Ft Wilki	M2.13	N.A.	M1.57	N.A.	0.67	N.A.	2.34	N.A.	2.55	N.A.	1.39	N.A.
Herman	1.8	N.A.	1.72	N.A.	1.24	N.A.	1.42	N.A.	2.23	N.A.	0.82	N.A.
Houghton FAA Airport	2.98	-0.72	2.02	-0.04	0.93	-1.29	1.23	-0.65	2.20	-0.87	1.61	-1.42
Iron MTN-Kingsford WWT	1.08	-0.05	0.88	-0.08	1.04	-0.68	2.48	-0.14	2.87	-0.48	2.04	-1.81
Ironwood	1.84	0.07	1.43	0.12	M1.37	N.A.	2.04	-0.23	1.89	-1.82	2.39	-1.81
Kenton	1.08	-0.01	M1.38	N.A.	0.99	-0.47	1.23	-0.92	M2.20	N.A.	0.81	-3.07
Marquette	1.15	-0.58	M1.71	N.A.	1.74	-0.31	M1.49	N.A.	1.51	-1.51	1.23	-2.03
Marquette WSO	1.28	-0.72	2.66	0.79	2.57	-0.26	2.12	-1.51	1.76	-2.2	0.61	-3.24
Mott Island Isle Royal	N.A.	N.A.	N.A.	N.A.	N.A.	N.A.	N.A.	N.A.	N.A.	N.A.	1.66	N.A.
Ontonagon 6 SE	2.43	-0.58	1.7	-0.17	0.83	N.A.	0.97	N.A.	1.54	-0.52	1.07	-1.23
Spalding 1 SSE	0.73	-0.34	0.89	0.11	1.86	0	2.57	-0.17	2.84	-1.49	2.31	-2.47
Stambaugh 2 SSE	0.86	N.A.	1.14	N.A.	1.71	-0.06	1.72	-0.74	2.20	-1.25	1.7	-1.83
Stephenson 8 WNW	M0.94	N.A.	0.85	-0.48	1.55	-0.59	2.87	0.2	2.32	N.A.	1.89	N.A.
Watersmeet	1.07	N.A.	1.41	N.A.	1.40	N.A.	1.85	N.A.	2.66	N.A.	1.56	N.A.
Divisional Data	1.53	-0.25	1.56	0.2	1.30	-0.66	1.78	-0.6	2.18	-1.23	1.46	-2.29
East Upper												
Chatham Exp Farm 2	1.32	-0.65	1.4	-0.25	M1.23	N.A.	M1.38	N.A.	1.16	-1.99	2.12	-1.49
Cornell 5 SE	1.06	N.A.	M0.73	N.A.	1.22	N.A.	M2.18	N.A.	2.41	N.A.	1.9	N.A.
Detour Village	M2.39	N.A.	1.14	-0.18	1.15	-0.8	2.0	-0.54	0.34	-2.31	1.21	-1.73
Escanaba	1.39	0.02	0.76	-0.31	1.63	-0.15	2.14	-0.28	2.47	-0.54	2.83	-0.54
Fayette 4 SW	1.27	-0.37	0.73	-0.56	2.33	0.41	M1.87	N.A.	2.34	-0.79	3.22	0.23
Grand Marais 2 E	2.32	0.04	0.83	-0.71	M0.16	N.A.	0.27	-1.8	1.55	-1.33	4.21	1.07

Table X-17. Total Precipitation and Departures from Normal in Michigan, by Weather Station: 1992 Continued

Station	July Precip	July Deprt	August Precip	August Deprt	September Precip	September Deprt	October Precip	October Deprt	November Precip	November Deprt	December Precip	December Deprt	Annual Precip	Annual Deprt
West Upper														
Alberta Ford For Cen	6.94	N.A.	4.15	N.A.	3.23	N.A.	2.26	N.A.	3.71	N.A.	M2.61	N.A.	M31.14	N.A.
Bergland Dam	7.36	3.49	3.69	-0.7	3.22	-0.75	3.01	0.01	3.53	0.06	M3.58	N.A.	M37.01	N.A.
Big Bay	M3.9	N.A.	2.74	N.A.	M2.01	N.A.	1.94	N.A.	2.87	N.A.	M	N.A.	N.A.	N.A.
Champion van Riper Prk	7.50	3.7	3.14	-0.4	3.97	-0.30	1.69	-1.20	3.84	1.32	2.66	0.75	32.29	-1.36
Copper Harbor Ft Wilki	3.60	N.A.	1.95	N.A.	3.07	N.A.	2.52	N.A.	2.86	N.A.	M3.80	N.A.	M28.45	N.A.
Herman	6.89	N.A.	4.83	N.A.	3.56	N.A.	2.56	N.A.	3.68	N.A.	3.13	N.A.	33.88	N.A.
Houghton FAA Airport	4.20	1.3	1.41	-1.96	3.46	-0.03	2.22	-0.16	2.50	-0.45	3.30	0.22	28.06	-6.07
Iron MTN-Kingsford WWT	2.76	-0.89	3.22	-0.79	4.04	0.5	1.47	-0.81	4.89	3.11	2.27	0.80	29.04	-1.32
Ironwood	7.34	3.39	2.96	-1.53	3.27	-0.19	3.66	0.91	3.50	0.58	1.67	-0.31	M33.36	N.A.
Kenton	9.35	5.65	3.04	-0.83	M3.90	N.A.	2.50	-0.13	3.29	1.16	2.24	0.91	M32.01	N.A.
Marquette	5.19	2.36	3.10	0.23	3.64	-0.06	1.39	-1.36	3.50	0.97	M2.28	N.A.	M27.93	N.A.
Marquette WSO	4.93	1.72	3.28	0.03	3.35	-0.57	1.98	-1.27	4.27	1.35	2.46	0.02	31.27	-5.86
Mott Island Isle Royal	2.91	N.A.	3.41	N.A.	4.49	N.A.	N.A.	N.A.	N.A.	N.A.	N.A.	N.A.	N.A.	N.A.
Ontonagon 6 SE	5.51	N.A.	2.39	N.A.	3.18	N.A.	3.49	N.A.	2.94	N.A.	M3.08	N.A.	M29.13	N.A.
Spalding 1 SSE	4.77	1.07	3.29	-0.54	4.15	0.65	1.36	-0.96	5.09	3.12	2.42	0.81	32.29	1.48
Stambaugh 2 SSE	3.23	-0.55	2.85	-1.43	4.68	1.19	1.52	-0.88	3.67	1.69	M1.93	N.A.	M27.21	N.A.
Stephenson 8 WNW	2.51	-1.12	3.74	-0.12	5.53	1.93	1.24	-1.05	4.79	2.74	M2.00	N.A.	M30.23	N.A.
Watersmeet	5.92	N.A.	4.51	N.A.	3.35	N.A.	3.03	N.A.	M3.33	N.A.	M1.88	N.A.	M31.97	N.A.
Divisional Data	5.38	1.94	3.20	-0.5	3.74	0.10	2.28	-0.34	3.59	1.11	2.53	0.54	30.53	-1.98
East Upper														
Chatham Exp Farm 2	5.73	2.17	2.56	-1	M3.71	N.A.	2.05	-1.19	M3.14	N.A.	M1.45	N.A.	M	N.A.
Cornell 5 SE	4.84	N.A.	2.83	N.A.	4.88	N.A.	1.25	N.A.	3.93	N.A.	1.94	N.A.	M29.17	N.A.
Detour Village	3.11	0.17	1.85	-1.09	4.50	0.44	1.94	-0.39	2.80	0.19	1.91	-0.12	M24.34	N.A.
Escanaba	3.61	0.03	3.87	0.55	3.98	0.82	1.19	-0.80	4.77	2.78	2.07	0.46	30.71	2.04
Fayette 4 SW	3.08	-0.20	4.78	1.42	3.61	0.22	2.69	0.57	M5.05	N.A.	2.16	0.26	M33.13	N.A.
Grand Marais 2 E	5.73	2.89	2.54	-0.59	4.44	0.84	1.60	-1.17	1.52	-1.38	M1.08	N.A.	M26.25	N.A.

Table X-17. Total Precipitation and Departures from Normal in Michigan, by Weather Station: 1992 Continued

Station	January Precip	January Deprt	February Precip	February Deprt	March Precip	March Deprt	April Precip	April Deprt	May Precip	May Deprt	June Precip	June Deprt
Manistique	M	N.A.	M	N.A.	M1.49	N.A.	2.86	N.A.	1.95	N.A.	2.87	N.A.
Munising	2.45	N.A.	2.34	N.A.	M2.33	N.A.	1.61	N.A.	1.66	N.A.	2.27	N.A.
Newberry State Hospital	M1.71	N.A.	1.44	-0.24	1.0	-1.12	M1.12	N.A.	1.71	-1.33	4.39	0.98
Rudyard 4 N	M1.95	N.A.	0.81	N.A.	M	N.A.	M.45	N.A.	1.19	N.A.	1.54	N.A.
St Ignace Mackinac Br	1.82	N.A.	1.52	N.A.	1.38	N.A.	1.87	N.A.	0.45	N.A.	0.96	N.A.
Sault Ste Marie WSO	2.86	0.66	1.07	-0.62	1.52	-0.51	2.5	0.12	1.46	-1.44	1.55	-1.71
Seney Wildlife Refuge	M1.18	N.A.	M	N.A.	1.60	-0.5	M.35	N.A.	M1.13	N.A.	4.74	1.20
Tahquamenon Falls Stpk	M	N.A.	M	N.A.	M	N.A.	M.98	N.A.	2.08	N.A.	3.47	N.A.
Trout Lake	1.51	N.A.	1.52	N.A.	1.01	N.A.	1.59	N.A.	1.40	N.A.	M2.44	N.A.
Whitefish Point	M	N.A.	1.52	N.A.	1.22	N.A.	2.18	N.A.	1.22	N.A.	4.16	N.A.
Divisional Data	1.78	-0.25	1.26	-0.32	1.41	-0.56	1.89	-0.54	1.56	-1.47	2.76	-0.56
Northwest Lower												
Boyne Falls	1.92	N.A.	1.26	N.A.	1.73	N.A.	2.15	N.A.	0.92	N.A.	1.83	N.A.
Cadillac	M1.27	N.A.	1.88	0.51	2.15	0.12	3.72	0.69	0.68	-1.86	2.66	-0.41
Charlevoix	2.35	0.32	1.76	0.36	1.66	-0.37	2.68	0.19	0.92	-1.78	2.27	-0.61
Cross Village	M1.73	N.A.	M1.66	N.A.	0.86	N.A.	M2.67	N.A.	0.47	N.A.	1.28	N.A.
East Jordan	M1.86	N.A.	1.34	0.07	1.81	0.25	2.11	-0.44	0.94	-1.72	2.56	-0.39
Frankfort 2 NE	2.98	N.A.	2.07	N.A.	1.92	N.A.	3.62	N.A.	0.94	N.A.	2.55	N.A.
Houghton Lake 6 WSW	1.03	-0.41	1.78	0.59	1.07	-0.61	2.60	0.05	0.61	-2.15	2.03	-1.06
Kalkaska	1.42	-0.22	1.67	0.28	2.01	0.50	2.64	-0.21	0.33	-2.26	1.96	-1.28
Lake City Exp Farm	1.09	-0.17	1.61	0.46	2.19	0.49	M4.00	N.A.	0.56	-2.11	2.08	-1.01
Manistee 3 SE	1.70	-0.37	1.76	0.17	1.96	-0.06	M3.49	N.A.	0.74	-1.65	2.25	-0.70
Maple City	1.88	N.A.	2.34	N.A.	1.81	N.A.	M1.29	N.A.	M.94	N.A.	2.50	N.A.
Northport 2 W	1.86	N.A.	M1.65	N.A.	1.99	N.A.	2.42	N.A.	0.80	N.A.	1.82	N.A.
Old Mission 3 SSW	M	N.A.	0.99	N.A.	1.83	N.A.	2.50	N.A.	0.99	N.A.	2.72	N.A.
Pellston Airport	1.55	-0.73	1.44	-0.09	1.64	-0.41	2.72	0.02	0.38	-2.57	1.19	-1.72
Petoskey	2.26	N.A.	1.58	N.A.	1.61	N.A.	2.41	N.A.	0.72	N.A.	1.61	N.A.

385

Table X-17. Total Precipitation and Departures from Normal in Michigan, by Weather Station: 1992 Continued

Station	July Precip	July Deprt	August Precip	August Deprt	September Precip	September Deprt	October Precip	October Deprt	November Precip	November Deprt	December Precip	December Deprt	Annual Precip	Annual Deprt
Manistique	4.24	N.A.	1.76	N.A.	4.80	N.A.	M2.79	N.A.	M5.33	N.A.	M	N.A.	N.A.	N.A.
Munising	6.44	N.A.	3.71	N.A.	4.09	N.A.	3.24	N.A.	M3.97	N.A.	4.10	N.A.	M38.21	N.A.
Newberry State Hospital	M4.22	N.A.	1.58	-2.09	4.86	1.19	2.58	-0.20	3.85	1.11	2.73	.44	M31.19	N.A.
Rudyard 4 N	3.81	N.A.	M.79	N.A.	5.52	N.A.	3.01	N.A.	3.32	N.A.	M2.16	N.A.	N.A.	N.A.
St Ignace Mackinac Br	2.57	N.A.	1.77	N.A.	4.75	N.A.	3.03	N.A.	4.49	N.A.	1.76	N.A.	26.37	N.A.
Sault Ste Marie WSO	4.09	1.09	3.27	-0.19	5.72	1.82	3.29	0.40	5.03	1.83	3.45	0.88	35.81	2.33
Seney Wildlife Refuge	5.86	2.85	1.69	-1.64	3.28	-0.45	2.71	-0.13	M3.59	N.A.	2.85	0.48	N.A.	N.A.
Tahquamenon Falls Stpk	5.66	N.A.	1.50	N.A.	3.60	N.A.	M2.01	N.A.	M	N.A.	M	N.A.	N.A.	N.A.
Trout Lake	3.34	N.A.	1.37	N.A.	4.60	N.A.	2.72	N.A.	3.95	N.A.	M	N.A.	N.A.	N.A.
Whitefish Point	5.71	N.A.	1.94	N.A.	3.54	N.A.	2.97	N.A.	3.76	N.A.	M3.63	N.A.	N.A.	N.A.
Divisional Data	4.52	1.33	2.47	-1.02	4.41	0.66	2.40	-0.28	3.74	0.94	2.55	0.26	30.75	-1.81
Northwest Lower														
Boyne Falls	2.79	N.A.	2.56	N.A.	4.78	N.A.	3.25	N.A.	M5.37	N.A.	2.27	N.A.	M30.83	N.A.
Cadillac	3.55	0.35	2.38	-0.68	6.22	2.74	2.94	0.06	M5.74	N.A.	M1.91	N.A.	M35.10	N.A.
Charlevoix	3.33	0.27	1.97	-1.32	6.89	3.09	2.91	0.35	4.56	1.80	2.74	0.64	34.04	2.94
Cross Village	2.24	N.A.	2.18	N.A.	4.20	N.A.	3.92	N.A.	4.74	N.A.	1.94	N.A.	M27.89	N.A.
East Jordan	2.78	-0.41	2.08	-1.08	5.79	1.60	3.53	0.62	3.80	0.75	1.49	-0.78	M30.09	N.A.
Frankfort 2 NE	3.42	N.A.	2.83	N.A.	6.39	N.A.	2.69	N.A.	6.48	N.A.	3.07	N.A.	38.96	N.A.
Houghton Lake 6 WSU	3.11	-0.15	3.18	0.24	4.68	1.54	3.06	0.25	5.30	2.97	1.69	-0.28	30.14	0.98
Kalkaska	2.70	-0.43	1.38	-1.64	5.42	1.56	3.01	-0.17	5.78	2.89	2.10	0.0	30.42	-0.98
Lake City Exp Farm	3.47	0.21	2.71	-0.30	6.77	3.52	2.65	0.0	4.99	2.66	1.57	-0.04	M33.69	N.A.
Manistee 3 SE	4.49	1.68	1.31	-1.88	5.57	2.29	2.00	-0.96	6.55	3.95	2.49	0.28	M34.31	N.A.
Maple City	2.40	N.A.	1.50	N.A.	6.31	N.A.	2.99	N.A.	5.35	N.A.	M3.63	N.A.	M32.94	N.A.
Northport 2 W	3.66	N.A.	2.03	N.A.	6.15	N.A.	2.88	N.A.	3.71	N.A.	2.33	N.A.	M31.30	N.A.
Old Mission 3 SSW	1.83	N.A.	1.83	N.A.	4.53	N.A.	2.51	N.A.	M4.62	N.A.	1.45	N.A.	30.11	N.A.
Pellston Airport	2.40	-0.53	2.24	-1.06	5.60	1.60	3.39	0.79	5.36	2.35	2.20	-0.38	N.A.	-2.73
Petoskey	3.33	N.A.	2.64	N.A.	5.62	N.A.	2.47	N.A.	4.48	N.A.	1.73	N.A.	30.46	N.A.

Table X-17. Total Precipitation and Departures from Normal in Michigan, by Weather Station: 1992 Continued

Station	January Precip	January Deprt	February Precip	February Deprt	March Precip	March Deprt	April Precip	April Deprt	May Precip	May Deprt	June Precip	June Deprt
St James 2 S Beaver IS	M1.63	N.A.	1.82	N.A.	1.28	N.A.	M	N.A.	1.21	N.A.	2.09	N.A.
Traverse City FAA Ap	2.30	0.44	1.53	0.12	1.94	0.16	2.95	0.44	0.41	-2.07	1.58	-1.57
Wellston Tippy Dam	M1.16	N.A.	2.26	0.74	2.16	0.33	3.85	0.86	0.65	-1.92	2.39	-0.99
Divisional Data	1.81	-0.15	1.65	0.20	1.72	-0.14	2.74	0.03	0.71	-1.91	2.06	-0.95
Northeast Lower												
Alpena WSO Airport	1.70	0.05	1.70	0.36	1.50	-0.43	2.61	0.11	1.10	-1.73	1.69	-1.47
Alpena Wastewater Pl	M	N.A.	1.13	-0.01	0.75	-0.90	M	N.A.	1.40	-1.44	1.17	-1.78
Atlanta 5 WNW	M0.72	N.A.	M0.48	N.A.	M0.16	N.A.	1.82	N.A.	0.86	N.A.	1.85	N.A.
Cheboygan	1.82	0.41	1.47	0.29	1.66	0.03	2.91	0.47	0.26	-2.28	2.36	-0.32
East Tawas	1.59	-0.02	1.93	0.65	1.78	-0.28	4.26	1.65	1.24	-1.61	2.43	-0.78
Gaylord	2.49	0.24	2.86	1.22	2.60	0.54	1.73	-0.94	0.84	-2.08	1.68	-1.31
Grayling	1.29	-0.41	1.68	0.32	M1.79	N.A.	4.59	1.88	0.59	-2.44	2.23	-1.15
Hale Loud Dam	1.27	-0.25	1.58	0.36	M	N.A.	3.19	0.66	1.39	-1.35	2.69	-0.07
Houghton Lake WSO AP	1.29	-0.20	1.35	0.05	1.84	-0.04	3.13	0.55	0.49	-2.10	1.91	-1.19
Lupton 1 S	M1.22	N.A.	M2.44	N.A.	M1.38	N.A.	3.89	1.32	0.92	-2.07	4.39	1.57
Mio Hydro Plant	1.08	-0.42	M1.39	N.A.	M	N.A.	3.63	1.25	M.44	N.A.	3.89	1.05
Onaway State Park	M1.77	N.A.	M1.61	N.A.	1.39	-0.57	3.75	1.10	0.50	-2.36	1.25	-1.83
Rogers City	M1.61	N.A.	M1.71	N.A.	1.47	N.A.	2.69	N.A.	0.76	N.A.	1.62	N.A.
Vanderbilt 11 Ene	M2.10	N.A.	M2.01	N.A.	1.75	-0.13	3.24	0.68	0.68	-2.16	1.53	-1.36
West Branch 3 SE	1.32	-0.11	1.22	-0.10	1.89	0.01	M4.33	N.A.	0.35	-2.43	2.65	-0.15
Divisional Data	1.54	-0.08	1.66	0.35	1.66	-0.18	3.19	0.66	0.81	-1.99	2.22	-0.79
West Central Lower 05												
Baldwin	1.97	-0.32	1.97	0.29	2.17	-0.01	3.49	0.30	0.53	-2.4	2.33	-0.94
Hart	1.93	-0.62	M2.61	N.A.	2.42	0.16	3.53	0.28	0.39	-2.24	2.52	-0.76
Hesperia 4 WNW	0.98	-1.42	1.61	-0.03	M	N.A.	M	N.A.	M	N.A.	M	N.A.
Ludington 4 SE	M0.93	N.A.	M	N.A.	M0.88	N.A.	M1.47	N.A.	0.47	-2.00	1.54	-1.39
Montague 4 NW	1.06	-1.56	0.76	-0.87	2.45	0.12	4.06	0.66	0.37	-2.26	3.28	0.53

Table X-17. Total Precipitation and Departures from Normal in Michigan, by Weather Station: 1992 Continued

Station	July Precip	July Deprt	August Precip	August Deprt	September Precip	September Deprt	October Precip	October Deprt	November Precip	November Deprt	December Precip	December Deprt	Annual Precip	Annual Deprt
St James 2 S Beaver IS	1.77	N.A.	2.60	N.A.	4.71	N.A.	4.30	N.A.	5.64	N.A.	2.91	N.A.	N.A.	N.A.
Traverse City FAA Ap	1.87	-1.01	1.31	-1.62	4.79	1.19	2.21	-0.38	4.02	1.51	2.53	0.52	27.44	-2.27
Wellston Tippy Dam	4.68	1.54	1.85	-1.44	7.56	4.07	2.88	0.00	6.05	3.43	2.44	0.32	M37.93	N.A.
Divisional Data	2.81	-0.18	2.18	-0.97	5.43	1.73	2.99	0.30	5.21	2.48	2.11	-0.06	31.42	0.38
Northeast Lower														
Alpena WSO Airport	3.37	0.26	2.65	-0.52	2.53	-0.39	2.34	0.35	4.01	1.80	1.24	-0.71	26.44	-2.32
Alpena Wastewater Pl	3.21	0.24	2.33	-0.83	2.60	-0.37	M2.64	N.A.	4.13	1.93	M1.05	N.A.	N.A.	N.A.
Atlanta 5 WNW	2.14	N.A.	M1.46	N.A.	3.86	N.A.	M1.83	N.A.	1.47	N.A.	M.43	N.A.	M	N.A.
Cheboygan	3.37	0.38	1.68	-1.22	5.70	1.93	M1.89	N.A.	4.53	2.15	1.81	-0.05	M29.46	N.A.
East Tawas	2.56	-0.38	4.06	1.01	4.31	1.33	2.94	0.64	5.93	3.52	1.40	-0.82	34.43	4.91
Gaylord	2.44	-0.98	2.03	-1.23	4.49	0.56	3.77	0.94	5.25	2.14	3.16	0.64	33.34	-0.26
Grayling	3.90	0.25	2.33	-1.15	4.99	1.38	3.23	0.55	5.41	N.A.	1.55	-0.34	M33.58	N.A.
Hale Loud Dam	3.11	-0.01	4.09	1.03	3.85	0.90	M	N.A.	4.82	2.56	1.47	-0.32	N.A.	N.A.
Houghton Lake WSO Ap	2.86	-0.03	3.45	0.49	3.63	0.86	2.75	0.47	4.65	2.39	1.98	0.09	29.33	1.34
Lupton 1 S	M	N.A.	M	N.A.	3.48	0.36	3.20	0.89	4.71	2.33	M1.59	N.A.	N.A.	N.A.
Mio Hydro Plant	2.53	-0.65	1.82	-1.20	3.63	0.69	2.07	0.04	3.77	1.70	1.17	-0.52	N.A.	N.A.
Onaway State Park	3.90	0.60	2.14	-1.07	3.75	0.00	2.60	0.22	M3.33	N.A.	M1.57	N.A.	M	N.A.
Rogers City	2.96	N.A.	2.44	N.A.	2.94	N.A.	2.39	N.A.	3.54	N.A.	M1.57	N.A.	M25.70	N.A.
Vanderbilt 11 ENE	2.16	-1.07	2.17	-0.98	3.67	0.08	2.00	-0.44	M4.95	N.A.	2.01	-0.12	M28.27	N.A.
West Branch 3 SE	3.62	0.37	3.62	0.52	4.04	1.00	2.94	0.46	5.09	2.64	1.67	-0.19	M32.74	N.A.
Divisional Data	3.01	-0.18	2.68	-0.47	3.83	0.51	2.75	0.41	4.33	1.92	1.75	-0.23	29.43	-0.07
West Central Lower 05														
Baldwin	2.11	-0.77	1.49	-2.13	4.36	1.07	2.40	-0.60	5.71	2.54	1.88	-0.56	30.41	-3.53
Hart	3.39	0.48	2.27	-1.12	3.84	0.48	3.20	-0.10	5.35	2.34	2.10	-0.50	M33.55	N.A.
Hesperia 4 WNW	M	N.A.	1.54	-2.25	N.A.	N.A.	1.97	-1.08	4.68	1.90	3.31	0.81	N.A.	N.A.
Ludington 4 SE	2.68	0.50	1.76	-2.03	M4.26	N.A.	M3.14	N.A.	6.57	3.80	2.10	N.A.	N.A.	N.A.
Montague 4 NW	4.52	1.62	2.43	-1.16	3.50	0.36	M2.14	N.A.	M6.68	N.A.	2.05	-0.49	M33.30	N.A.

Table X-17. Total Precipitation and Departures from Normal in Michigan, by Weather Station: 1992 Continued

Station	January		February		March		April		May		June	
	Precip	Deprt	Precip	Deprt	Precip	Deprt	Precip	Deprt	Precip	Deprt	Precip	Deprt
Muskegon WSO Airport	1.36	-1.01	1.33	-0.32	2.30	-0.24	3.30	0.14	0.33	-2.21	1.50	-1.02
White Cloud 4 SE	1.71	N.A.	1.64	N.A.	3.60	N.A.	M3.99	N.A.	0.62	N.A.	M	N.A.
Divisional Data	**1.46**	**-0.90**	**1.42**	**-0.24**	**2.34**	**0.05**	**3.60**	**0.39**	**0.42**	**-2.26**	**2.23**	**-0.77**
Central Lower												
Alma	1.26	-0.20	1.65	0.46	2.86	0.80	4.76	1.78	1.29	-1.50	1.34	-1.64
Beaverton 1 ESE	1.38	N.A.	1.10	N.A.	2.77	N.A.	4.87	N.A.	0.16	N.A.	2.36	N.A.
Big Rapids Waterworks	M1.50	N.A.	1.67	0.17	2.76	0.64	4.35	1.22	0.68	-2.20	M	N.A.
Evart	1.13	-0.64	1.65	0.29	2.03	0.08	3.18	0.15	0.22	-2.46	2.38	-0.96
Gladwin	1.41	-0.29	1.91	0.60	3.16	1.08	4.47	1.60	0.74	-2.08	3.03	-0.46
Greenville 2 NNE	1.31	-0.56	1.28	-0.28	2.63	0.11	3.74	0.46	0.69	-2.19	1.13	-2.30
Midland	1.40	-0.06	1.63	0.32	2.02	-0.16	5.42	2.56	1.09	-1.38	2.88	-0.04
Mt Pleasant Univ	1.15	-0.22	1.69	0.57	1.67	-0.32	6.22	3.03	0.22	-2.62	1.67	-1.53
Vestaburg	M	N.A.	M	N.A.	2.00	N.A.	4.73	N.A.	0.48	N.A.	1.52	N.A.
Divisional Data	1.28	-0.38	1.64	0.31	2.45	0.33	4.59	1.55	0.70	-2.07	2.07	-1.14
East Central Lower 07												
Bad Axe	1.63	-0.16	1.54	-0.02	1.77	-0.42	5.03	2.41	M1.38	N.A.	2.65	-0.23
Caro Regional Center	M1.42	N.A.	0.51	-0.67	1.87	-0.23	4.23	1.71	1.49	-1.06	3.45	0.36
Cass City 1 SSW	2.06	N.A.	1.64	N.A.	1.98	N.A.	5.73	N.A.	1.34	N.A.	3.27	N.A.
Essexville	M1.45	N.A.	0.53	N.A.	1.95	N.A.	6.23	N.A.	1.20	N.A.	1.66	N.A.
Harbor Beach 1 SSE	2.16	-0.49	1.69	-0.52	2.04	-0.39	5.07	2.17	1.31	-1.37	3.16	0.03
Millington 3 SW	1.80	0.40	1.56	0.30	1.53	-0.52	5.30	2.78	1.57	-1.32	1.30	-1.81
Saginaw #3	1.76	N.A.	M1.80	N.A.	2.86	N.A.	M4.72	N.A.	1.30	N.A.	1.67	N.A.
Saginaw FAA Airport	1.86	0.07	1.37	-0.15	2.46	0.15	5.15	2.15	0.89	-1.56	2.26	-0.51
St Charles	M1.35	N.A.	1.65	0.31	1.91	-0.22	4.46	2.03	1.29	-1.20	1.94	-1.15
Sandusky	M	N.A.	M	N.A.	M	N.A.	M	N.A.	M.37	N.A.	M0.35	N.A.
Sebewaing	M1.02	N.A.	M.36	N.A.	M1.27	N.A.	M	N.A.	0.87	-1.60	2.29	-0.42
Standish 5 SW	1.25	-0.05	1.30	0.15	1.33	-5.20	4.19	1.69	1.19	-1.50	3.59	0.44

Table X-17. Total Precipitation and Departures from Normal in Michigan, by Weather Station: 1992 Continued

Station	July		August		September		October		November		December		Annual	
	Precip	Deprt	Precip	Deprt	Precip	Deprt	Precip	Deprt	Precip	Deprt	Precip	Deprt	Precip	Deprt
Muskegon WSO Airport	2.68	0.26	1.97	-1.16	3.54	0.62	2.46	-0.32	6.26	3.39	2.69	0.09	29.72	-1.78
White Cloud 4 SE	3.74	N.A.	2.25	N.A.	5.44	N.A.	M1.50	N.A.	6.52	N.A.	1.80	N.A.	N.A.	N.A.
Divisional Data	**3.08**	**0.33**	**1.91**	**-1.67**	**3.81**	**0.65**	**2.51**	**-0.52**	**5.71**	**2.82**	**2.41**	**-0.08**	**30.90**	**-2.20**
Central Lower														
Alma	3.75	1.13	3.33	-0.33	4.63	1.59	2.51	0.04	4.87	2.56	1.99	0.00	34.24	4.69
Beaverton 1 WSW	3.61	N.A.	4.08	N.A.	4.92	N.A.	2.83	N.A.	4.73	N.A.	1.54	N.A.	34.35	N.A.
Big Rapids Waterworks	3.10	0.52	2.43	-1.00	6.25	2.95	2.94	0.10	5.49	2.72	1.75	N.A.	N.A.	N.A.
Evart	2.04	-0.92	2.84	-0.78	5.42	2.14	2.50	0.04	5.15	2.72	M	N.A.	N.A.	N.A.
Gladwin	3.53	0.32	3.31	-0.26	4.99	1.87	2.87	0.14	5.19	2.82	1.47	-0.74	36.08	4.60
Greenville 2 NNE	4.64	2.13	2.68	-1.16	4.90	1.78	1.95	-0.78	4.82	2.02	2.48	-0.06	32.25	-0.83
Midland	3.86	1.30	3.39	0.02	5.87	3.04	2.33	-0.24	5.37	3.18	1.79	-0.24	37.05	8.30
Mt Pleasant Univ	4.44	1.22	3.63	0.06	6.58	3.63	2.11	-0.49	4.97	2.64	1.53	-0.33	35.88	5.64
Vestaburg	M2.32	N.A.	3.24	N.A.	4.56	N.A.	2.72	N.A.	5.09	N.A.	M1.58	N.A.	N.A.	N.A.
Divisional Data	**3.62**	**0.79**	**3.09**	**-0.51**	**5.52**	**2.42**	**2.46**	**-0.17**	**5.12**	**2.66**	**1.85**	**-0.26**	**34.39**	**3.53**
East Central Lower 07														
Bad Axe	5.42	2.49	5.84	2.83	3.27	0.60	2.15	-0.34	3.69	1.31	1.23	-0.95	M35.60	N.A.
Caro Regional Center	5.90	2.98	3.86	0.90	3.23	0.25	2.22	-0.09	4.46	2.19	1.91	0.04	M34.55	N.A.
Cass City 1 SSW	M	N.A.	3.38	N.A.	4.02	N.A.	2.60	N.A.	4.45	N.A.	1.77	N.A.	N.A.	N.A.
Essexville	3.41	N.A.	4.51	N.A.	M	N.A.	2.59	8.00	5.19	N.A.	1.36	N.A.	N.A.	N.A.
Harbor Beach 1 SSE	4.88	1.79	4.11	0.74	2.45	-0.59	1.53	-1.20	4.50	1.59	1.30	-1.84	34.20	-0.08
Millington 3 SW	5.46	2.76	3.42	0.35	4.36	1.51	2.71	0.46	3.77	1.55	2.30	0.46	35.08	6.92
Saginaw #3	4.39	N.A.	3.69	N.A.	4.05	N.A.	2.78	N.A.	5.34	N.A.	M2.13	N.A.	M36.49	N.A.
Saginaw FAA Airport	4.25	1.65	3.55	0.51	4.00	1.02	2.75	0.09	4.33	1.99	2.05	-0.26	34.92	5.15
St Charles	4.77	1.94	3.39	0.10	4.43	1.67	M2.43	N.A.	4.23	2.06	2.33	0.42	M34.18	N.A.
Sandusky	M	N.A.	6.02	3.42	M	N.A.	M0.10	N.A.	M	N.A.	M	N.A.	N.A.	N.A.
Sebewaing	3.12	0.18	3.73	0.97	3.06	0.25	2.51	0.20	M3.46	N.A.	M1.49	N.A.	N.A.	N.A.
Standish 5 SW	3.24	0.32	3.63	0.74	3.65	0.66	1.98	-0.55	5.05	2.94	1.28	-0.45	31.68	3.87
Divisional Data	**1.73**	**0.03**	**1.23**	**-0.17**	**1.90**	**-2.4**	**4.91**	**2.23**	**1.23**	**-1.37**	**2.67**	**-0.38**	**N.A**	**N.A**

Table X-17. Total Precipitation and Departures from Normal in Michigan, by Weather Station: 1992 Continued

Station	January		February		March		April		May		June	
	Precip	Deprt	Precip	Deprt	Precip	Deprt	Precip	Deprt	Precip	Deprt	Precip	Deprt
Southwest Lower												
Allegan 5 NE	M2.02	N.A.	M1.46	N.A.	1.59	-1.11	3.20	-0.17	1.35	-1.58	1.59	-2.31
Benton Harbor Arpt	1.16	-1.83	1.36	-0.51	1.99	-0.60	3.13	-0.63	1.05	-1.95	2.58	-0.82
Bloomingdale	1.87	-0.86	1.73	-0.16	2.30	-0.50	3.39	-0.38	1.18	-1.92	1.53	-2.51
Dowagiac 1 W	2.19	N.A.	1.71	N.A.	2.53	N.A.	2.06	N.A.	1.73	N.A.	1.72	N.A.
Eau Claire 4 NE	1.30	-1.02	1.40	-0.18	3.23	0.78	2.28	-1.42	1.26	-1.92	1.53	-1.93
Grand Haven Fire Dept	1.52	-0.54	M1.21	N.A.	2.03	-0.17	4.01	1.03	M0.50	N.A.	2.28	-0.80
Grand Rapids WSO Arpt	1.52	-0.39	1.06	-0.47	3.51	1.03	3.98	0.42	1.45	-1.58	1.61	-2.25
Gull Lake Biol Sta	M1.36	N.A.	1.05	-0.40	2.67	0.64	2.86	-0.65	0.98	-2.18	1.21	-2.99
Holland	1.36	-0.92	1.17	-0.31	2.03	-0.42	M2.58	N.A.	1.39	-1.41	2.56	-1.36
Kalamazoo State Hosp	M	N.A.	M	N.A.	M	N.A.	M	N.A.	M	N.A.	M	N.A.
Kent City 2 SW	1.71	-0.36	1.29	-0.26	2.97	0.58	4.89	1.58	0.67	-2.26	1.68	-1.49
Lowell 2 SE	M1.15	N.A.	0.62	N.A.	2.56	N.A.	1.66	N.A.	0.87	N.A.	0.72	N.A.
Lowell	2.25	0.12	1.45	-0.09	3.13	0.51	4.73	1.49	2.03	-0.83	1.26	-2.45
Niles	1.69	-0.82	1.71	-0.29	2.87	-0.05	2.14	-2.00	1.22	-1.94	1.46	-2.59
South Haven	M	N.A.	M	N.A.	M0.48	N.A.	2.40	-1.07	0.87	-1.98	2.50	-1.31
Divisional Data	**1.56**	**-0.74**	**1.35**	**-0.26**	**2.43**	**-0.05**	**3.03**	**-0.52**	**1.25**	**-1.76**	**1.91**	**-1.86**
South Central Lower												
Albion	1.21	-0.57	M0.96	N.A.	2.40	-0.07	2.31	-1.15	1.95	-1.31	3.50	0.11
Battle Creek 5 NW	1.20	-0.65	1.04	-0.54	2.03	-0.45	2.56	-0.88	1.41	-1.74	1.64	-2.22
Burlington 3 E	1.28	N.A.	M0.88	N.A.	2.60	N.A.	M2.45	N.A.	1.63	N.A.	2.33	N.A.
Charlotte	1.24	-0.66	0.96	-0.57	2.54	0.15	3.27	-0.10	1.85	-1.13	2.00	-1.84
Coldwater State School	0.96	-0.76	1.15	-0.41	2.78	0.42	2.13	-1.35	2.82	-0.21	2.95	-0.72
Dimondale 1 WSW	1.49	N.A.	0.70	N.A.	2.73	N.A.	3.83	N.A.	2.44	N.A.	2.25	N.A.
East Lansing 4 S	M0.82	N.A.	1.05		M1.62	N.A.	3.84	N.A.	M0.73	N.A.	M1.77	N.A.
Eaton Rapids	M1.35	N.A.	0.97	-0.32	2.65	0.41	3.40	0.24	1.45	-1.46	2.32	-1.36
Grand Ledge 1 NW	1.48	-0.12	1.30	-0.11	2.86	0.50	4.18	1.07	1.53	-1.31	1.88	-1.99

Table X-17. Total Precipitation and Departures from Normal in Michigan, by Weather Station: 1992 Continued

Station	July Precip	July Deprt	August Precip	August Deprt	September Precip	September Deprt	October Precip	October Deprt	November Precip	November Deprt	December Precip	December Deprt	Annual Precip	Annual Deprt
Southwest Lower														
Allegan 5 NE	M	N.A.	3.04	-0.27	M6.10	N.A.	2.75	-0.07	5.56	2.55	M2.82	N.A.	N.A.	N.A.
Benton Harbor Arpt	7.80	4.74	2.38	-0.79	4.38	1.03	1.76	-1.44	5.12	2.22	2.91	-0.21	35.62	-0.79
Bloomingdale	4.66	1.15	2.43	-0.92	4.51	1.03	2.49	-0.54	4.86	1.58	2.75	-0.52	33.70	-4.55
Dowagiac 1 W	11.47	N.A.	2.53	N.A.	5.35	N.A.	3.09	N.A.	5.60	N.A.	4.05	N.A.	44.03	N.A.
Eau Claire 4 NE	7.84	4.58	2.25	-0.89	4.75	1.39	1.42	-1.76	4.92	2.16	3.19	0.48	35.37	0.27
Grand Haven Fire Dept	M	N.A.	2.16	-0.85	3.57	0.30	2.23	-0.60	5.97	3.30	2.61	0.25	N.A.	N.A.
Grand Rapids WSO Arpt	8.83	5.81	3.55	0.10	5.60	2.46	2.34	-0.55	5.64	2.71	3.27	0.72	42.36	8.01
Gull Lake Biol Sta	6.03	2.63	3.37	-0.17	5.48	2.50	2.87	-0.02	4.42	1.71	M3.03	N.A.	M35.33	N.A.
Holland	M4.89	N.A.	2.25	-1.07	4.87	1.48	2.05	-1.08	6.37	3.24	M2.41	N.A.	M33.93	N.A.
Kalamazoo State Hosp	M4.85	N.A.	M	N.A.	N.A.	N.A.	N.A.	N.A.	N.A.	N.A.	N.A.	N.A.	N.A.	N.A.
Kent City 2 SW	3.38	1.01	2.82	-0.94	3.54	0.24	1.91	-0.88	5.92	3.07	3.15	0.67	33.93	0.96
Lowell 2 SE	4.92	N.A.	2.92	N.A.	4.08	N.A.	1.64	N.A.	3.55	N.A.	1.71	N.A.	M26.40	N.A.
Lowell	5.71	2.89	3.83	0.26	5.26	1.97	2.50	-0.13	5.29	2.57	2.51	-0.03	39.95	6.28
Niles	6.21	2.57	1.70	-2.07	7.85	4.59	2.83	-0.74	5.40	2.42	4.01	0.83	39.09	-0.09
South Haven	5.43	2.13	2.69	-0.78	5.21	1.84	2.05	-0.97	4.70	2.01	M	N.A.	N.A.	N.A.
Divisional Data	**7.44**	**4.18**	**2.67**	**-0.60**	**4.86**	**1.55**	**2.31**	**-0.70**	**5.32**	**2.45**	**3.13**	**0.38**	**37.26**	**2.07**
South Central Lower														
Albion	7.86	4.21	2.24	-0.92	4.59	2.07	3.04	0.50	4.99	2.61	2.38	0.04	M37.43	N.A.
Battle Creek 5 NW	6.19	2.71	3.07	-0.21	5.57	2.78	3.30	0.47	4.06	1.40	2.45	N.A.	M34.52	N.A.
Burlington 3 E	7.27	N.A.	2.57	N.A.	5.22	N.A.	3.40	N.A.	5.61	N.A.	2.81	N.A.	M38.05	N.A.
Charlotte	5.21	2.01	2.86	-0.38	5.81	2.78	2.86	0.30	4.51	1.89	2.51	0.21	35.62	2.66
Coldwater State School	9.57	5.56	3.50	0.10	4.47	1.44	3.57	0.97	5.30	2.92	2.88	0.69	42.08	8.65
Dimondale 1 WSW	6.29	N.A.	2.73	N.A.	5.35	N.A.	2.81	N.A.	4.52	N.A.	2.40	N.A.	37.54	N.A.
East Lansing 4 S	7.29	N.A.	M1.50	N.A.	M2.30	N.A.	M1.94	N.A.	4.47	N.A.	M1.22	N.A.	M	N.A.
Eaton Rapids	6.33	3.44	2.57	-0.65	4.94	2.17	3.57	1.27	4.25	2.14	2.39	0.50	M36.19	N.A.
Grand Ledge 1 NW	6.42	3.31	2.01	-1.02	4.59	1.76	2.34	-0.08	3.79	1.35	1.92	-0.26	34.3	3.10

Table X-17. Total Precipitation and Departures from Normal in Michigan, by Weather Station: 1992 Continued

Station	January Precip	January Deprt	February Precip	February Deprt	March Precip	March Deprt	April Precip	April Deprt	May Precip	May Deprt	June Precip	June Deprt
Hastings	M1.61	N.A.	1.41	0.03	2.87	0.79	M3.01	N.A.	2.19	-0.55	1.97	-1.98
Hillsdale	1.19	-1.08	0.63	-1.38	2.53	-0.58	3.09	-0.64	1.42	-2.03	2.02	-2.19
Ionia 2 SSW	1.21	-0.54	1.06	-0.36	2.97	0.82	4.44	1.16	1.40	-1.50	1.03	-2.78
Jackson FAA Arpt	1.06	-0.54	0.97	0.57	1.64	-0.50	1.84	-1.12	1.25	-1.63	3.04	-0.39
Lansing WSO Airport	1.38	-0.36	1.36	-0.20	2.68	0.38	4.64	1.76	2.09	-0.48	2.07	-1.43
Nottawa 3 SE	M1.12	N.A.	1.28	N.A.	2.86	N.A.	2.27	N.A.	2.24	N.A.	2.02	N.A.
Owosso 3 NNW	M	N.A.	M1.10	N.A.	M	N.A.	M	N.A.	M	N.A.	3.46	0.14
St Johns	M	N.A.	M	N.A.	3.15	1.10	4.81	1.80	0.86	-1.98	1.63	-1.76
Three Rivers	1.41	-0.43	1.00	-0.49	2.78	0.34	1.28	-2.07	2.04	-1.08	1.30	-2.65
Divisional Data	**1.21**	**-0.54**	**1.06**	**-0.43**	**2.60**	**0.29**	**3.19**	**0.00**	**1.73**	**-1.19**	**2.10**	**-1.60**
Southeast Lower												
Adrian 2 NNE	1.65	-0.09	1.02	-0.68	2.69	0.04	3.21	-0.18	2.06	-0.98	2.82	-0.48
Ann Arbor Univ of Mich	3.00	1.26	1.36	-0.18	3.44	1.05	M4.10	N.A.	1.24	-1.54	2.73	-0.71
Chelsea	1.71	N.A.	1.06	N.A.	2.90	N.A.	3.72	N.A.	1.70	N.A.	2.78	N.A.
Dearborn	2.48	N.A.	1.50	N.A.	3.07	N.A.	3.55	N.A.	1.37	N.A.	2.82	N.A.
Detroit City Airport	M	N.A.	M	N.A.	M	N.A.	M	N.A.	M	N.A.	M	N.A.
Detroit Metro WSO Ap	1.78	-0.08	1.54	-0.15	3.34	0.80	4.34	1.19	1.33	-1.44	2.35	-1.08
Flint WSO Ap	1.15	-0.44	1.59	0.13	2.56	0.42	3.80	0.75	1.64	-1.14	2.26	-0.97
Flint 7 W	M1.22	N.A.	1.56	N.A.	2.30	N.A.	3.86	N.A.	1.05	N.A.	1.57	N.A.
Grosse Pointe Farms	1.92	0.05	1.47	-0.14	M1.73	N.A.	3.83	0.71	1.43	-1.35	3.46	-0.03
Howell WWTP	1.08	-0.57	0.69	-0.80	M1.72	N.A.	3.08	0.18	1.13	-1.50	1.77	-1.60
Hudson 3 E	1.22	N.A.	1.25	N.A.	2.78	N.A.	2.69	N.A.	1.45	N.A.	3.09	N.A.
Lapeer	M0.98	N.A.	1.35	0.11	1.47	-0.37	4.31	1.39	1.66	-1.09	1.94	-1.40
Milan 4 ESE	2.33	0.56	0.70	-0.97	2.15	-0.46	2.53	-0.72	1.57	-1.31	3.34	-0.22
Milford GM Proving Gr	M0.87	N.A.	1.08	-0.68	1.63	-0.91	3.44	0.18	M1.17	N.A.	2.09	-1.28
Monroe	M2.38	N.A.	1.60	0.01	3.26	0.69	3.81	0.67	2.25	-0.74	1.64	-1.96
Morenci	M1.83	N.A.	1.18	N.A.	3.53	N.A.	3.27	N.A.	2.57	N.A.	M	N.A.

Table X-17. Total Precipitation and Departures from Normal in Michigan, by Weather Station: 1992 Continued

Station	July Precip	July Deprt	August Precip	August Deprt	September Precip	September Deprt	October Precip	October Deprt	November Precip	November Deprt	December Precip	December Deprt	Annual Precip	Annual Deprt
Hastings	6.33	3.52	3.99	0.85	4.74	1.64	2.16	-0.52	4.45	2.11	2.82	0.74	37.55	N.A.
Hillsdale	7.94	3.81	3.80	0.53	4.64	1.72	3.07	0.28	3.90	0.96	1.24	-1.69	35.47	-2.29
Ionia 2 SSW	5.35	2.91	4.71	1.03	5.04	2.00	2.36	-0.04	4.28	1.86	2.19	-0.15	36.04	4.41
Jackson FAA Arpt	6.48	3.36	2.46	-0.52	3.65	1.34	2.90	0.79	3.89	1.75	1.77	-0.13	30.95	1.84
Lansing WSO Airport	6.43	3.65	2.79	-0.25	3.21	0.67	2.18	0.05	3.88	1.55	2.16	-0.05	34.87	5.29
Nottawa 3 SE	10.49	N.A.	3.67	N.A.	M5.29	N.A.	M4.37	N.A.	5.13	N.A.	3.30	N.A.	M44.04	N.A.
Owosso 3 NNW	2.99	0.29	3.13	-0.08	M2.29	N.A.	M	N.A.	1.93	-0.34	M1.15	N.A.	N.A.	N.A.
St Johns	5.18	2.55	3.95	0.13	4.88	2.09	2.33	-0.11	3.36	1.05	1.89	-0.12	N.A.	N.A.
Three Rivers	9.40	5.61	2.14	-1.02	4.92	1.91	2.26	-0.45	3.17	0.79	2.48	0.16	34.18	0.62
Divisional Data	6.53	3.34	3.31	0.03	4.69	1.89	2.70	0.24	3.93	1.52	2.22	0.00	35.27	3.55
Southeast Lower														
Adrian 2 NNE	7.08	3.35	2.58	-0.62	5.83	3.21	2.58	0.15	5.14	2.65	2.46	-0.04	39.12	6.33
Ann Arbor Univ of Mich	5.01	2.08	3.54	0.70	4.70	2.34	3.03	0.82	4.36	1.98	2.53	0.13	M39.04	N.A.
Chelsea	6.75	N.A.	3.32	N.A.	4.31	N.A.	3.00	N.A.	4.06	N.A.	2.21	N.A.	37.52	N.A.
Dearborn	4.97	N.A.	M1.39	N.A.	5.64	N.A.	2.27	N.A.	3.75	N.A.	2.15	N.A.	M34.96	N.A.
Detroit City Airport	M	N.A.	M	N.A.	M	N.A.	M	N.A.	M	N.A.	M	N.A.	N.A.	N.A.
Detroit Metro WSO Ap	5.91	2.81	2.50	-0.71	5.55	3.30	2.01	-0.11	4.33	2.00	2.35	-0.17	37.33	6.36
Flint WSO Ap	9.35	6.54	3.50	0.12	2.50	0.15	2.46	0.33	4.05	1.76	2.01	0.01	36.87	7.66
Flint 7 W	7.39	N.A.	3.85	N.A.	3.46	N.A.	2.97	N.A.	3.74	N.A.	M2.08	N.A.	M35.05	N.A.
Grosse Pointe Farms	5.55	2.33	3.82	0.38	6.71	4.15	2.39	0.15	4.75	2.28	1.68	-0.71	M38.74	N.A.
Howell WWTP	6.07	3.11	3.64	0.50	5.56	3.04	2.61	0.34	3.01	N.A.	1.85	-0.21	M32.21	N.A.
Hudson 3 E	7.57	N.A.	2.34	N.A.	4.75	N.A.	3.25	N.A.	5.02	N.A.	2.45	N.A.	37.86	N.A.
Lapeer	5.48	3.02	4.60	1.26	4.49	2.15	2.34	0.09	3.67	1.52	M0.56	N.A.	M32.85	N.A.
Milan 4 ESE	8.71	5.98	3.87	0.57	5.76	3.32	2.35	0.18	4.65	2.21	1.61	-0.86	39.57	8.28
Milford GM proving Gr	6.29	3.46	3.65	0.21	4.08	1.58	2.37	0.01	3.65	1.22	2.12	-0.30	M32.44	N.A.
Monroe	5.30	2.42	2.51	-0.49	5.07	2.49	2.48	0.29	5.46	3.23	3.30	0.95	M39.06	N.A.
Morenci	10.34	N.A.	2.18	N.A.	4.41	N.A.	2.47	N.A.	5.97	N.A.	3.30	N.A.	N.A.	N.A.

Table X-17. Total Precipitation and Departures from Normal in Michigan, by Weather Station: 1992 Continued

Station	January Precip	January Deprt	February Precip	February Deprt	March Precip	March Deprt	April Precip	April Deprt	May Precip	May Deprt	June Precip	June Deprt
Mount Clemens Ang Base	2.24	N.A.	1.69	N.A.	3.07	N.A.	3.20	N.A.	1.34	N.A.	2.76	N.A.
Pontiac State Hospital	M1.54	N.A.	1.30	-0.06	M3.19	N.A.	3.97	1.10	M1.24	N.A.	2.23	-1.29
Port Huron	2.46	0.70	1.28	-0.15	2.23	-0.03	4.02	0.85	1.97	-0.82	2.56	-0.91
Yale 1 NNE	1.15	-0.53	1.21	-0.17	1.85	-0.16	4.00	1.18	1.88	-0.89	2.15	-1.04
Ypsilanti E Mich Univ	1.48	-0.25	1.24	-0.34	2.92	0.45	4.11	1.01	1.33	-1.36	2.61	-0.52
Divisional Data	2.05	0.31	1.34	-0.21	2.65	0.26	3.70	0.58	1.60	-1.20	2.54	-0.85

Table X-17. Total Precipitation and Departures from Normal in Michigan, by Weather Station: 1992 Continued

Station	July Precip	July Deprt	August Precip	August Deprt	September Precip	September Deprt	October Precip	October Deprt	November Precip	November Deprt	December Precip	December Deprt	Annual Precip	Annual Deprt
Mount Clemens Ang Base	7.21	N.A.	3.37	N.A.	4.14	N.A.	M	N.A.	4.65	N.A.	1.74	N.A.	N.A.	N.A.
Pontiac State Hospital	6.59	3.77	4.00	0.95	M3.83	N.A.	2.77	0.46	M4.43	N.A.	M2.00	N.A.	N.A.M	N.A.
Port Huron	5.68	2.77	3.82	0.80	3.65	1.28	1.75	-0.75	4.96	2.36	1.85	-0.49	36.23	5.61
Yale 1 NNE	6.38	3.58	3.79	0.87	5.06	2.64	1.67	-0.73	M	N.A.	1.62	-0.52	N.A.	N.A.
Ypsilanti E Mich Univ	5.63	2.72	3.25	0.35	5.14	2.71	2.77	0.70	4.45	2.13	2.35	-0.06	37.28	7.54
Divisional Data	6.34	3.40	3.46	0.27	4.87	2.43	2.43	0.21	4.45	2.10	2.18	-0.15	37.61	7.15

Source: National Oceanic and Atmospheric Administration, Climatological Data Annual Summary - Michigan 1992 (Asheville, North Carolina: annually). Notes: An M denotes insufficient or partial data. M is appended to average and/or total values computed with 1-9 daily values missing. M appears alone if 10 or more daily values are missing. N.A. Data not available.

Table X-18. Average Temperatures and Departures from Normal in Michigan, by Weather Station: 1992

Station	January		February		March		April		May		June	
	Temp	Deprt	Temp	Deprt	Temp	Deprt	Temp	Deprt	Temp	Deprt	Temp	Deprt
West Upper												
Alberta Ford For Cen	17.6	N.A.	18.9	N.A.	22.6	N.A.	36.5	N.A.	53.3	N.A.	57.7	N.A.
Bergland Dam	16.6	6.7	18.5	6.0	22.0	-0.6	35.6	-2.3	53.0	2.2	56.9	-3.5
Big Bay	21.8	N.A.	24.2	N.A.	26.7	N.A.	38.3	N.A.	55.8	N.A.	58.0	N.A.
Champion van Riper Prk	17.2	6.3	19.5	6.3	21.9	-1.0	36.2	-1.2	53.6	3.2	56.7	-2.8
Copper Harbor Ft Wilki	20.8	N.A.	22.6	N.A.	25.9	N.A.	37.0	N.A.	53.2	N.A.	55.3	N.A.
Herman	17.2	N.A.	20.3	N.A.	23.7	N.A.	36.6	N.A.	54.7	N.A.	57.2	N.A.
Houghton FAA Airport	19.1	5.7	21.5	7.1	24.5	1.3	36.0	-1.1	53.7	4.3	57.4	-1.5
Iron MTN-Kingsford WWT	18.5	5.4	20.4	3.8	26.9	0.4	39.1	-2.3	54.5	0.8	60.8	-1.8
Ironwood	16.2	5.9	19.8	5.5	23.3	-1.2	35.2	-5.3	53.8	0.8	57.2	-4.9
Kenton	MN.A.	N.A.	MN.A.	N.A.	MN.A.	N.A.	MN.A.	N.A.	55.7	N.A.	59.3	N.A.
Marquette	22.4	5.2	24.7	5.6	28.1	0.8	38.2	-1.5	54.0	3.6	56.9	-3.0
Marquette WSO	17.0	4.9	19.8	5.5	22.6	-0.6	34.6	-2.8	52.6	2.4	56.3	-3.3
Mott Island Isle Royal	N.A.	N.A.	N.A.	N.A.	N.A.	N.A.	N.A.	N.A.	N.A.	N.A.	53.0	N.A.
Ontonagon 6 SE	20.5	N.A.	22.9	N.A.	27.1	N.A.	39.2	N.A.	56.9	N.A.	57.6	N.A.
Stambaugh 2 SSE	14.9	3.5	16.9	2.0	21.6	-3.6	35.6	-4.7	51.5	-0.9	55.9	-5.0
Stephenson 8 WNW	19.5	5.2	21.0	3.3	27.2	-0.5	38.7	-3.6	52.8	-0.9	59.7	-3.0
Watersmeet	18.0	6.8	M21.6	7.7	24.5	0.2	37.2	-2.0	53.7	2.0	58.0	-2.8
Divisional Data	**18.5**	**5.6**	**20.8**	**5.5**	**24.6**	**-0.3**	**36.9**	**-2.4**	**53.9**	**2.7**	**57.3**	**-2.7**
East Upper												
Chatham Exp Farm 2	20.8	4.9	23.4	5.8	26.6	1.0	38.8	-0.5	54.3	3.3	58.0	-1.9
Cornell 5 SE	20.1	N.A.	21.4	N.A.	25.4	N.A.	37.0	N.A.	51.5	N.A.	58.0	N.A.
Detour Village	19.2	N.A.	19.6	N.A.	23.2	N.A.	35.6	N.A.	50.3	N.A.	58.3	N.A.
Escanaba	21.2	5.1	23.2	5.4	26.6	0.2	36.6	-2.4	50.4	0.1	58.4	-2.1
Fayette 4 SW	22.3	4.8	24.3	5.3	27.5	0.0	37.9	-1.4	50.7	0.5	58.3	-1.0
Grand Marais 2 E	21.8	4.3	22.5	4.8	25.4	0.5	37.3	-0.5	52.4	3.6	55.4	-2.1
Manistique	20.2	N.A.	21.8	N.A.	24.0	N.A.	35.4	N.A.	47.3	N.A.	55.3	N.A.

Table X-18. Average Temperatures and Departures from Normal in Michigan, by Weather Station: 1992 Continued

Station	July		August		September		October		November		December		Annual	
	Temp	Deprt	Temp	Deprt	Temp	Deprt	Temp	Deprt	Temp	Deprt	Temp	Deprt	Temp	Deprt
West Upper														
Alberta Ford For Cen	59.2	N.A.	60.2	N.A.	54.7	N.A.	42.1	N.A.	28.4	N.A.	19.5	N.A.	39.2	N.A.
Bergland Dam	58.7	-6.5	59.4	-3.2	53.7	-0.6	42.5	-2.7	27.4	-2.6	17.7	1.1	38.5	-0.5
Big Bay	M60.8	N.A.	62.6	N.A.	56.3	N.A.	43.6	N.A.	MN.A	N.A.	MN.A	N.A.	MN.A.	N.A.
Champion van Riper Prk	58.8	-5.4	59.3	-3.0	55.5	1.6	42.1	-2.0	28.0	-1.7	18.7	1.9	39.0	0.2
Copper Harbor Ft Wilki	58.2	N.A.	62.2	N.A.	57.1	N.A.	44.3	N.A.	32.4	N.A.	24.2	N.A.	41.1	N.A.
Herman	58.5	N.A.	59.4	N.A.	54.7	N.A.	42.1	N.A.	27.7	N.A.	19.0	N.A.	39.3	N.A.
Houghton FAA Airport	59.4	-5.3	60.6	-2.5	M55.4	1.1	42.9	-2.1	30.2	-0.9	21.8	2.2	M40.2	0.7
Iron MTN-Kingsford WWT	62.2	-5.0	62.7	-2.3	55.4	-0.8	44.5	-2.1	29.6	-2.7	20.4	1.1	41.3	-0.5
Ironwood	58.6	-8.2	59.0	-5.6	53.0	-2.8	41.9	-4.3	27.0	-3.4	17.0	0.2	38.5	-1.9
Kenton	M59.7	N.A.	MN.A	N.A.	MN.A	N.A.	MN.A	N.A.	MN.A	N.A.	MN.A	N.A.	MN.A.	N.A.
Marquette	59.7	-6.6	63.0	-2.3	57.3	0.1	45.5	-2.5	32.6	-1.9	24.7	1.4	42.3	-0.1
Marquette WSO	58.4	-6.2	59.2	-3.4	53.5	-0.5	41.4	-2.9	28.4	-1.7	20.2	2.3	38.7	-0.5
Mott Island Isle Royal	54.7	N.A.	61.1	N.A.	54.2	N.A.	N.A.	N.A.	N.A.	N.A.	N.A.	N.A.	N.A.	N.A.
Ontonagon 6SE	60.1	N.A.	61.5	N.A.	58.4	N.A.	45.4	N.A.	31.5	N.A.	22.6	N.A.	42.0	N.A.
Stambaugh 2 SSE	56.8	-8.6	56.7	-6.6	52.0	-2.8	41.1	-4.6	25.9	-4.8	17.5	-0.1	37.2	-3.0
Stephenson 8 WNW	61.5	-5.9	61.5	-4.0	54.9	-2.2	44.3	-3.1	30.3	-3.2	21.1	0.3	41.0	-1.5
Watersmeet	59.8	-5.9	59.7	-3.6	55.8	0.8	42.6	-3.2	M27.2	-3.3	19.2	1.7	M39.8	-0.1
Divisional Data	**59.1**	**-6.2**	**60.5**	**-3.3**	**55.1**	**-0.4**	**43.1**	**-3.0**	**29.0**	**-2.7**	**20.3**	**1.2**	**39.9**	**-0.4**
East Upper														
Chatham Exp Farm 2	60.1	-5.3	61.8	-2.5	56.5	0.1	44.0	-3.	31.4	-2.2	23.3	1.6	41.6	0.1
Cornell 5 SE	60.2	N.A.	60.7	N.A.	54.5	N.A.	44.3	N.A.	30.5	N.A.	22.5	N.A.	40.5	N.A.
Detour Village	59.2	N.A.	62.6	N.A.	54.8	N.A.	43.6	N.A.	33.5	N.A.	27.2	N.A.	40.6	N.A.
Escanaba	61.5	-5.0	62.6	-2.3	56.5	-0.5	45.4	-2.0	32.3	-2.6	25.3	2.5	41.7	-0.3
Fayette 4 SW	61.2	-4.6	62.9	-2.3	56.5	-1.4	46.5	-1.8	33.4	-2.8	26.1	1.9	42.3	-0.2
Grand Marais 2 E	57.2	-5.6	61.4	-1.1	56.4	0.7	44.2	-2.3	31.6	-2.5	25.3	2.1	40.9	0.2
Manistique	57.9	N.A.	60.3	N.A.	54.6	N.A.	42.8	N.A.	31.5	N.A.	24.8	N.A.	39.7	N.A.

Table X-18. Average Temperatures and Departures from Normal in Michigan, by Weather Station: 1992 Continued

Station	January Temp	Deprt	February Temp	Deprt	March Temp	Deprt	April Temp	Deprt	May Temp	Deprt	June Temp	Deprt
Munising	21.0	N.A.	M23.3	N.A.	26.3	N.A.	M37.4	N.A.	53.0	N.A.	57.0	N.A.
Newberry State Hospital	18.1	2.6	19.6	2.9	22.7	-2.7	35.7	-3.2	50.8	0.5	56.5	-2.8
Rudyard 4 N	18.4	N.A.	19.3	N.A.	MN.A.	N.A.	39.3	N.A.	52.7	N.A.	57.2	N.A.
St Ignace Mackinac Br	22.6	N.A.	20.7	N.A.	25.0	N.A.	36.3	N.A.	50.7	N.A.	57.7	N.A.
Sault Ste Marie WSO	16.6	3.3	17.7	3.4	21.8	-2.1	35.6	-2.5	51.9	2.2	56.4	-2.0
Seney Wildlife Refuge	MN.A.	N.A.	MN.A.	N.A.	MN.A.	N.A.	M36.8	-3.3	51.7	-0.6	58.9	-2.3
Tahquamenon Falls Stpk	19.0	N.A.	19.1	N.A.	21.7	N.A.	35.0	N.A.	50.2	N.A.	54.0	N.A.
Trout Lake	17.6	N.A.	17.3	N.A.	20.9	N.A.	35.3	N.A.	50.4	N.A.	56.6	N.A.
Whitefish Point	MN.A.	N.A.	19.2	N.A.	22.4	N.A.	34.1	N.A.	47.9	N.A.	53.5	N.A.
Divisional Data	**19.9**	**4.0**	**20.8**	**4.0**	**24.3**	**-1.1**	**36.5**	**-2.2**	**51.0**	**0.9**	**56.8**	**-2.3**
Northwest Lower												
Boyne Falls	24.3	N.A.	23.8	N.A.	28.1	N.A.	41.4	N.A.	55.6	N.A.	61.3	N.A.
Cadillac	22.6	5.4	23.8	6.2	27.3	0.4	38.3	-3.0	52.0	-0.9	58.3	-4.0
Cross Village	24.5	N.A.	22.9	N.A.	27.5	N.A.	39.5	N.A.	54.3	N.A.	59.2	N.A.
East Jordan	26.2	6.0	25.4	5.7	28.3	-0.4	41.2	-1.4	54.5	0.5	60.9	-2.2
Frankfort 2 NE	26.4	N.A.	27.8	N.A.	30.4	N.A.	40.1	N.A.	M54.2	N.A.	60.1	N.A.
Houghton Lake 6 WSW	21.7	3.8	23.9	5.0	27.5	-0.9	38.7	-4.1	52.4	-2.2	58.3	-5.3
Kalkaska	21.1	N.A.	20.7	N.A.	25.3	N.A.	37.2	N.A.	53.0	N.A.	58.4	N.A.
Lake City Exp Farm	21.9	4.4	23.7	5.4	27.4	0.0	38.2	-4.2	52.7	-1.2	59.5	-3.5
Manistee 3 SE	24.1	1.4	25.4	1.7	28.5	-3.4	37.8	-6.6	49.9	-5.1	53.9	-10.3
Maple City	25.2	N.A.	25.8	N.A.	29.6	N.A.	MN.A.	N.A.	55.1	N.A.	60.5	N.A.
Old Mission 3 SSW	MN.A.	N.A.	24.8	N.A.	28.5	N.A.	38.6	N.A.	51.7	N.A.	58.6	N.A.
Pellston Airport	21.3	5.3	20.5	5.0	25.9	0.9	38.8	-0.9	53.9	2.5	58.9	-1.9
Petoskey	23.4	N.A.	23.8	N.A.	26.2	N.A.	37.5	N.A.	51.2	N.A.	57.5	N.A.
St James 2 S Beaver Is	MN.A.	N.A.	22.5	N.A.	26.0	N.A.	MN.A.	N.A.	52.6	N.A.	58.2	N.A.
Traverse City FAA Ap	25.8	6.1	26.9	7.3	30.5	2.1	41.4	-1.0	55.6	2.1	60.5	-3.2
Divisional Data	**23.7**	**4.1**	**24.1**	**4.4**	**27.8**	**-0.7**	**39.1**	**-2.8**	**53.2**	**0.2**	**58.9**	**-3.6**

Table X-18. Average Temperatures and Departures from Normal in Michigan, by Weather Station: 1992 Continued

Station	July Temp	July Deprt	August Temp	August Deprt	September Temp	September Deprt	October Temp	October Deprt	November Temp	November Deprt	December Temp	December Deprt	Annual Temp	Annual Deprt
Munising	M59.2	N.A.	62.1	N.A.	56.5	N.A.	M44.7	N.A.	31.7	N.A.	24.1	N.A.	M41.4	N.A.
Newberry State Hospital	57.5	-7.1	59.7	-3.6	53.4	-1.5	41.9	-3.5	29.7	-3.1	23.2	2	39.1	-1.6
Rudyard 4 N	58.1	N.A.	59.9	N.A.	53.7	N.A.	42.3	N.A.	31.2	N.A.	27.1	N.A.	MN.A.	N.A.
St Ignace Mackinac Br	60.2	N.A.	62.4	N.A.	56.1	N.A.	45.2	N.A.	33.5	N.A.	27.8	N.A.	41.5	N.A.
Sault Ste Marie WSO	57.4	-6.1	60.4	-2.5	54.0	-0.8	43.4	-1.9	30.9	-1.9	23.7	4	39.2	-0.6
Seney Wildlife Refuge	59.1	-7.2	60.6	-4.3	56.4	-0.6	45.4	-1.8	31.6	-2.5	24.5	2.7	MN.A.	N.A.
Tahquamenon Falls Stpk	55.8	N.A.	58.8	N.A.	52.9	N.A.	41.8	N.A.	M28.0	N.A.	23.1	N.A.	M38.2	N.A.
Trout Lake	56.8	N.A.	58.5	N.A.	53.0	N.A.	40.7	N.A.	28.3	N.A.	22.5	N.A.	38.2	N.A.
Whitefish Point	55.3	N.A.	59.6	N.A.	55.3	N.A.	44.5	N.A.	32.6	N.A.	25.7	N.A.	MN.A.	N.A.
Divisional Data	**58.5**	**-6.2**	**60.9**	**-2.9**	**55.1**	**-1.0**	**43.8**	**-2.8**	**31.4**	**-2.7**	**24.8**	**2.8**	**40.3**	**-0.7**
Northwest Lower														
Boyne Falls	63.0	N.A.	63.1	N.A.	58.4	N.A.	46.6	N.A.	33.8	N.A.	27.8	N.A.	43.9	N.A.
Cadillac	61.3	-4.9	60.5	-4.0	55.8	-1.0	44.0	-2.8	32.2	-2.2	26.1	3.5	41.9	-0.6
Cross Village	60.7	N.A.	63.7	N.A.	58.6	N.A.	47.1	N.A.	35.4	N.A.	29.1	N.A.	43.5	N.A.
East Jordan	62.0	-5.4	62.1	-3.8	58.0	-0.8	47.1	-2.3	36.2	-0.9	29.5	3.7	44.3	-0.1
Frankfort 2 NE	63.5	N.A.	64.0	N.A.	59.1	N.A.	M47.5	N.A.	35.3	N.A.	29.4	N.A.	M44.8	N.A.
Houghton Lake 6 WSW	61.1	-6.4	59.7	-6.0	54.5	-3.3	43.3	-4.5	32.6	-2.9	25.8	2.4	41.6	-2
Kalkaska	60.3	N.A.	60.5	N.A.	55.0	N.A.	43.9	N.A.	31.5	N.A.	25.1	N.A.	41	N.A.
Lake City Exp Farm	61.6	-5.6	60.5	-4.9	55.1	-2.5	43.8	-3.5	32.0	-2.9	25.4	2.7	41.8	-1.3
Manistee 3 SE	57.0	-12.4	55.5	-12.7	50.9	-10.5	39.4	-12.1	27.6	-11.5	M27.2	-1.0	M39.8	-6.9
Maple City	64.1	N.A.	63.9	N.A.	59.3	N.A.	47.3	N.A.	34.7	N.A.	29.0	N.A.	MN.A.	N.A.
Old Mission 3 SSW	61.6	N.A.	62.8	N.A.	57.4	N.A.	46.0	N.A.	35.1	N.A.	29.7	N.A.	MN.A.	N.A.
Pellston Airport	60.6	-4.9	61.6	-2.2	55.8	0.1	44.5	-1.9	33.5	-1.0	27.3	5.0	41.9	0.5
Petoskey	59.8	N.A.	62.5	N.A.	57.5	N.A.	46.6	N.A.	34.7	N.A.	29.4	N.A.	42.5	N.A.
St James 2 S bBaver Is	M59.7	N.A.	63.7	N.A.	56.9	N.A.	46.4	N.A.	34.4	N.A.	27.7	N.A.	MN.A.	N.A.
Traverse City FAA Ap	63.4	-5.4	64.4	-2.9	58.1	-1.3	46.8	-2.4	35.0	-1.9	28.2	2.6	44.7	0.2
Divisional Data	**61.3**	**-6.0**	**61.9**	**-4.2**	**56.7**	**-2.0**	**45.4**	**-3.5**	**33.6**	**-3.0**	**27.8**	**2.6**	**42.8**	**-1.1**

Table X-18. Average Temperatures and Departures from Normal in Michigan, by Weather Station: 1992 Continued

Station	January		February		March		April		May		June	
	Temp	Deprt	Temp	Deprt	Temp	Deprt	Temp	Deprt	Temp	Deprt	Temp	Deprt
Northeast Lower												
Alpena WSO Airport	22.3	4.9	23.5	5.5	26.8	0.0	38.5	-1.8	52.6	1.1	58.5	-2.7
Alpena Wastewater Pl	MN.A.	N.A.	22.7	2.4	26.2	-2.1	MN.A.	N.A.	50.9	-0.8	58.1	-3.5
Atlanta 5 WNW	20.5	N.A.	21.0	N.A.	25.3	N.A.	36.5	N.A.	M54.4	N.A.	60.0	N.A.
Cheboygan	21.4	2.4	20.8	1.7	25.2	-2.5	36.9	-3.8	51.8	-0.4	59.6	-2.3
East Tawas	25.1	5.1	26.2	5.0	28.8	-0.9	40.3	-2.3	54.4	1.1	59.3	-3.6
Gaylord	21.0	3.5	21.5	3.2	25.0	-2.7	38.5	-3.6	54.6	0.6	60.1	-3.1
Grayling	20.0	2.4	20.0	2.0	24.8	-2.6	37.3	-4.9	52.2	-2.1	59.1	-4.3
Hale Loud Dam	24.6	7.0	24.2	5.2	MN.A.	N.A.	41.3	-0.8	55.0	1.4	60.9	-2.2
Houghton Lake WSO Ap	22.8	5.8	24.1	6.1	28.6	1.2	39.4	-2.5	54.3	0.6	60.4	-2.4
Lupton 1 S	MN.A.	N.A.	22.8	4.2	MN.A.	N.A.	38.0	-4.4	53.0	-0.6	58.9	-3.7
Mio Hydro Plant	22.5	5.0	22.7	4.1	MN.A.	N.A.	39.4	-2.6	54.7	1.2	60.6	-2.1
Onaway State Park	23.6	5.4	23.2	4.3	27.0	-1.2	39.5	-2.6	56.0	1.8	61.5	-1.8
Rogers city	23.0	N.A.	22.8	N.A.	26.1	N.A.	37.6	N.A.	53.1	N.A.	59.2	N.A.
Vanderbilt 11 ENE	19.6	3.7	19.2	3.4	23.0	-2.7	36.5	-3.8	52.0	-0.1	58.5	-2.8
West Branch 3 SE	22.3	4.5	23.8	4.1	27.6	-1.2	39.6	-3.2	54.3	0.0	60.2	-3.4
Divisional Data	**22.2**	**4.1**	**22.6**	**3.7**	**26.2**	**-1.8**	**38.5**	**-3.2**	**53.6**	**0.5**	**59.7**	**-2.8**
West Central Lower 05												
Baldwin	24.0	4.1	25.5	4.8	29.7	-0.6	40.3	-3.9	55.2	-1.0	60.4	-4.7
Hart	25.3	2.8	26.9	3.3	30.8	-1.3	39.6	-5.6	52.9	-3.1	60.0	-5.3
Hesperia 4 WNW	29.1	8.4	28.5	6.6	MN.A.	N.A.	MN.A.	N.A.	MN.A.	N.A.	MN.A.	MN.A.
Ludington 4 SE	26.9	4.7	30.0	6.8	32.4	0.8	42.3	-2.0	55.0	0.7	61.4	-2.4
Montague 4 NW	26.6	3.3	27.8	3.3	32.4	-0.4	41.2	-3.7	52.9	-2.4	59.0	-5.1
Muskegon WSO Airport	28.8	5.7	29.9	5.8	33.6	0.8	43.1	-2.1	55.4	-0.6	61.7	-3.8
Divisional Data	**26.8**	**5.2**	**28.1**	**5.3**	**31.8**	**0.2**	**41.3**	**-3.4**	**54.3**	**-1.3**	**60.5**	**-4.3**
Central Lower												
Alma	24.7	3.5	27.2	4.0	30.6	-2.2	41.7	-4.8	56.5	-1.4	63.6	-4.0

Table X-18. Average Temperatures and Departures from Normal in Michigan, by Weather Station: 1992 Continued

Station	July Temp	July Deprt	August Temp	August Deprt	September Temp	September Deprt	October Temp	October Deprt	November Temp	November Deprt	December Temp	December Deprt	Annual Temp	Annual Deprt
Northeast Lower														
Alpena WSO Airport	61.3	-4.7	62.0	-2.5	55.7	-0.9	44.3	-2.8	34.1	-1.0	27.9	4.4	42.3	0.0
Alpena Wastewater Pl	60.9	-6.4	62.8	-3.2	57.3	-1.2	44.7	-3.9	34.6	-2.2	28.7	3.1	MN.A.	N.A.
Atlanta 5 WNW	61.3	N.A.	62.1	N.A.	57.5	N.A.	41.1	N.A.	30.1	N.A.	23.0	N.A.	M41.1	N.A.
Cheboygan	60.2	-7.8	62.7	-4.1	56.3	-2.9	44.6	-4.7	33.9	-3.0	27.9	2.9	41.8	-2.0
East Tawas	63.2	-4.7	62.8	-3.8	58.3	-0.9	46.1	-2.8	37.0	-0.3	29.8	4.0	44.3	-0.3
Gaylord	61.9	-5.5	62.0	-3.7	56.1	-1.7	44.0	-4.0	31.4	-3.4	24.8	2.0	41.7	-1.5
Grayling	60.9	-6.6	60.2	-5.5	54.1	-3.7	42.6	-5.2	30.8	-4.4	24.1	1.2	40.5	-2.8
Hale Loud Dam	63.8	-3.8	62.7	-3.1	57.2	-0.9	MN.A.	N.A.	34.8	-1.2	28.5	4.6	MN.A.	N.A.
Houghton Lake WSO Ap	63.0	-4.0	62.0	-3.2	56.8	-0.5	44.8	-2.3	33.6	-1.3	26.1	3.2	43.0	0.1
Lupton 1 S	MN.A.	N.A.	MN.A.	N.A.	M54.5	-2.4	42.6	-4.2	32.3	-2.6	25.4	2.7	MN.A.	N.A.
Mio Hydro Plant	62.5	-4.9	62.3	-3.1	56.6	-0.8	44.8	-2.9	33.6	-2.2	27.4	4.1	MN.A.	N.A.
Onaway State Park	63.2	-4.9	64.5	-1.9	59.3	0.6	46.9	-2.2	34.6	-1.7	M28.4	4.1	M44.0	0.0
Rogers City	60.7	N.A.	M63.7	N.A.	56.9	N.A.	45.1	N.A.	35.0	N.A.	28.4	N.A.	M42.6	N.A.
Vanderbilt 11 ENE	60.2	-4.8	59.8	-3.3	53.9	-1.5	42.1	-3.6	30.8	-2.7	25.4	4.1	40.1	-1.2
West Branch 3 SE	62.7	-5.1	61.3	-4.6	55.7	-2.2	44.2	-3.5	33.9	-1.4	27.5	4.1	42.8	-1.0
Divisional Data	**61.8**	**-5.5**	**62.2**	**-3.4**	**56.4**	**-1.6**	**44.1**	**-4.0**	**33.4**	**-2.4**	**26.9**	**3.1**	**42.3**	**-1.0**
West Central Lower 05														
Baldwin	63.2	-5.7	61.4	-5.7	57.0	-2.2	44.6	-4.2	34.5	-2.1	27.2	2.2	43.6	-1.6
Hart	63.6	-6.2	62.9	-5.5	57.7	-3.6	46.0	-5.1	35.9	-2.8	28.6	0.8	44.2	-2.6
Hesperia 4 WNW	MN.A.	N.A.	63.6	-3.8	N.A.	N.A.	49.0	-0.5	37.4	0.0	29.6	3.6	MN.A.	N.A.
Ludington 4 SE	65.1	-3.5	64.7	-2.6	60.5	0.0	47.1	-3.1	35.8	-2.5	28.8	1.4	45.8	-0.1
Montague 4 NW	64.3	-4.2	62.6	-4.8	59.2	-1.3	47.6	-3.1	36.7	-2.5	29.8	1.3	45.0	-1.6
Muskegon WSO Airport	66.2	-3.9	64.5	-4.4	59.9	-1.5	49.0	-2.0	38.3	-0.9	31.0	2.7	46.8	-0.4
Divisional Data	**64.5**	**-4.6**	**63.3**	**-4.3**	**58.9**	**-1.4**	**47.2**	**-2.8**	**36.4**	**-1.7**	**29.2**	**2.2**	**45.2**	**-0.8**
Central Lower														
Alma	65.6	-6.0	63.4	-6.1	58.3	-3.7	46.1	-5.1	35.7	-2.9	29.1	2.3	45.2	-2.2

Table X-18. Average Temperatures and Departures from Normal in Michigan, by Weather Station: 1992 Continued

Station	January Temp	January Deprt	February Temp	February Deprt	March Temp	March Deprt	April Temp	April Deprt	May Temp	May Deprt	June Temp	June Deprt
Big Rapids Waterworks	24.7	5.1	27.3	6.1	30.8	0.3	41.4	-2.7	55.5	0.0	MN.A.	N.A.
Evart	MN.A.	N.A.	MN.A.	N.A.	MN.A.	N.A.	MN.A.	N.A.	MN.A.	N.A.	MN.A.	N.A.
Gladwin	23.4	4.4	26.2	5.3	29.0	-1.5	40.9	-3.4	56.2	0.8	62.6	-2.3
Greenville 2 NNE	25.6	4.3	28.2	4.9	31.8	-1.0	42.5	-4.0	57.0	-0.8	63.3	-3.9
Midland	26.6	4.6	28.9	5.1	32.0	-0.9	44.0	-2.6	58.6	0.7	64.6	-2.9
Mt Pleasant Univ	24.5	3.7	27.0	4.4	29.5	-2.4	40.9	-4.9	55.8	-1.3	62.5	-4.1
Divisional Data	**24.9**	**4.6**	**27.5**	**5.4**	**30.6**	**-1.0**	**41.9**	**-3.4**	**56.6**	**0.0**	**63.3**	**-2.8**
East Central Lower 07												
Bad Axe	23.8	3.2	25.2	3.2	28.9	-2.2	40.3	-4.0	54.4	-0.7	60.0	-4.9
Caro Regional Center	25.5	4.6	27.8	5.1	32.0	-0.7	43.7	-2.3	57.4	0.7	62.5	-3.9
Essexville	25.2	N.A.	27.0	N.A.	31.1	N.A.	42.3	N.A.	57.5	N.A.	63.9	N.A.
Harbor Beach 1 SSE	25.1	3.9	26.7	4.2	28.9	-1.9	38.8	-4.3	51.7	-1.5	M57.6	-5.6
Saginaw FAA Airport	25.1	4.4	27.7	5.2	30.8	-1.3	42.9	-2.9	57.2	0.3	64.5	-2.2
St Charles	24.2	2.0	27.2	2.9	30.3	-3.6	41.8	-5.7	55.3	-3.4	61.6	-6.6
Sandusky	23.3	2.0	MN.A.	N.A.	30.1	-2.0	41.5	-3.6	54.9	-1.1	60.2	-5.6
Standish 5 SW	23.7	4.6	25.8	5.1	27.8	-2.5	40.1	-3.7	53.3	-1.4	59.7	-4.9
Divisional Data	**24.5**	**3.4**	**26.8**	**4.1**	**30.0**	**-2.1**	**41.4**	**-3.9**	**55.2**	**-1.0**	**61.3**	**-4.8**
Southwest Lower												
Allegan 5 NE	27.0	3.7	30.1	4.9	35.2	0.7	44.5	-3.0	57.9	-0.5	62.7	-4.8
Benton Harbor Arpt	28.4	3.7	31.7	4.5	35.8	-0.1	44.1	-3.8	55.8	-2.3	61.6	-6.3
Bloomingdale	28.4	N.A.	30.6	N.A.	34.4	N.A.	43.6	N.A.	56.5	N.A.	61.7	N.A.
Dowagiac 1 W	28.1	N.A.	31.9	N.A.	35.7	N.A.	44.7	N.A.	57.8	N.A.	62.4	N.A.
Eau Claire 4 NE	28.5	5.1	32.2	5.8	37.5	1.7	46.2	-2.4	59.8	0.6	65.4	-3.4
Grand Haven Fire Dept	27.2	2.5	28.5	2.4	33.2	-1.2	41.2	-5.0	55.2	-1.4	61.0	-4.8
Grand Rapids WSO Arpt	27.5	5.5	30.3	6.6	33.7	0.6	44.0	-2.3	57.4	-0.1	64.3	-2.8
Gull Lake Biol Sta	27.8	5.2	31.5	6.6	36.8	2.4	46.3	-1.2	59.4	0.7	64.7	-3.3
Holland	30.0	5.9	31.6	5.8	36.5	1.9	44.1	-3.0	58.8	1.0	63.4	-3.6
Kalamazoo State Hosp	MN.A.	N.A.	MN.A.	N.A.	MN.A.	N.A.	MN.A.	N.A.	MN.A.	N.A.	MN.A.	N.A.

Table X-18. Average Temperatures and Departures from Normal in Michigan, by Weather Station: 1992 Continued

Station	July Temp	July Deprt	August Temp	August Deprt	September Temp	September Deprt	October Temp	October Deprt	November Temp	November Deprt	December Temp	December Deprt	Annual Temp	Annual Deprt
Big Rapids Waterworks	64.5	-4.4	62.6	-4.4	57.2	-1.7	45.1	-3.2	34.8	-1.7	27.3	2.2	MN.A.	N.A.
Evart	MN.A.	N.A.	MN.A	N.A.	MN.A	N.A.	MN.A	N.A.	MN.A	N.A.	MN.A	N.A.	MN.A.	N.A.
Gladwin	65.0	-4.1	63.2	-3.9	57.1	-1.8	44.7	-3.8	34.7	-1.4	27.9	3.2	44.2	-0.7
Greenville 2 NNE	65.4	-5.7	63.0	-6.3	58.4	-3.3	47.2	-3.6	35.6	-2.5	28.0	1.5	45.5	-1.7
Midland	66.8	-4.7	65.1	-4.3	60.9	-1.1	48.6	-2.8	37.3	-1.8	31.2	3.8	47.1	-0.6
Mt Pleasant Univ	64.9	-5.9	63.4	-5.6	58.4	-2.9	46.5	-4.1	35.4	-2.8	29.2	2.7	44.8	-1.9
Divisional Data	**65.4**	**-4.7**	**63.5**	**-4.7**	**58.4**	**-2.0**	**46.4**	**-3.4**	**35.6**	**-1.9**	**28.8**	**2.9**	**45.2**	**-0.8**
East Central Lower 07														
Bad Axe	64.2	-5.1	M62.6	-5.2	58.6	-2.3	M46.1	-4.5	M36.7	-1.8	29.4	2.8	M44.2	-1.8
Caro Regional Center	66.2	-4.3	64.3	-4.3	60.2	-1.2	47.1	-3.7	37.8	-1.0	30.7	3.8	46.3	-0.6
Essexville	M66.4	N.A.	65.3	N.A.	MN.A	N.A.	M47.7	N.A.	37.9	N.A.	30.6	N.A.	MN.A.	N.A.
Harbor Beach 1 SSE	62.4	-6.0	63.3	-4.5	58.4	-2.8	M47.3	-3.6	37.7	-1.1	30.4	3.2	M44.0	-1.7
Saginaw FAA Airport	66.2	-4.8	64.6	-4.4	59.4	-1.9	47.1	-3.5	37.1	-1.3	30.2	3.8	46.1	-0.7
St Charles	64.5	-7.7	62.1	-8.0	56.9	-5.9	45.5	-6.3	36.7	-2.6	29.6	1.9	44.6	-3.6
Sandusky	MN.A.	N.A.	64.7	-4.0	MN.A	N.A.	47.8	-3.0	38.3	-0.5	29.8	2.9	MN.A.	N.A.
Standish 5 SW	62.6	-6.2	61.2	-5.6	56.1	-3.2	44.8	-3.9	35.1	-1.6	29.0	3.9	43.3	-1.6
Divisional Data	**64.6**	**-5.8**	**63.5**	**-5.2**	**58.3**	**-3.2**	**46.7**	**-4.1**	**37.2**	**-1.4**	**30.0**	**3.1**	**45.0**	**-1.6**
Southwest Lower														
Allegan 5 NE	MN.A.	N.A.	64.2	-5.5	60.2	-2.5	48.6	-2.9	37.5	-2.3	29.8	1.2	MN.A.	N.A.
Benton Harbor Arpt	67.1	-4.7	64.3	-5.8	60.4	-3.5	48.9	-4.5	37.7	-3.4	30.0	-0.1	47.2	-2.2
Bloomingdale	66.6	N.A.	63.6	N.A.	59.7	N.A.	48.6	N.A.	38.5	N.A.	30.5	N.A.	46.9	N.A.
Dowagiac 1 W	67.7	N.A.	64.7	N.A.	60.5	N.A.	48.6	N.A.	39.4	N.A.	30.3	N.A.	47.7	N.A.
Eau Claire 4 NE	69.3	-3.3	67.3	-3.8	62.3	-2.1	51.0	-2.4	38.5	-1.8	31.0	2.0	49.1	-0.3
Grand Haven Fire Dept	MN.A.	N.A.	65.3	-4.0	61.8	-1.0	50.0	-2.7	38.3	-2.4	31.0	1.1	MN.A.	N.A.
Grand Rapids WSO Arpt	67.2	-4.2	65.0	-4.6	59.7	-2.4	48.2	-2.7	38.2	-0.3	30.5	3.2	47.2	-0.3
Gull Lake Biol Sta	68.4	-3.8	66.0	-4.6	61.3	-2.3	49.8	-2.8	38.5	-1.2	31.5	3.4	48.5	-0.1
Holland	67.7	-3.3	66.2	-3.3	61.9	-1.2	50.5	-2.0	38.9	-1.4	31.9	2.8	48.5	0.0
Kalamazoo State Hosp	M69.3	-3.9	MN.A	N.A.	N.A.	N.A.	N.A.	N.A.	N.A.	N.A.	N.A.	N.A.	N.A.	N.A.

Table X-18. Average Temperatures and Departures from Normal in Michigan, by Weather Station: 1992 Continued

Station	January		February		March		April		May		June	
	Temp	Deprt	Temp	Deprt	Temp	Deprt	Temp	Deprt	Temp	Deprt	Temp	Deprt
South Haven	30.1	5.3	32.3	5.4	36.8	1.5	44.4	-1.9	55.9	-0.4	61.6	-4.2
Divisional Data	**28.3**	**4.7**	**31.1**	**5.3**	**35.6**	**0.7**	**44.3**	**-3.2**	**57.5**	**-0.7**	**62.9**	**-4.6**
South Central Lower												
Battle Creek 5 NW	26.7	4.3	30.7	5.9	34.8	0.5	44.7	-2.5	57.5	-0.7	63.1	-4.6
Charlotte	25.3	3.6	29.1	5.5	32.1	-1.4	42.8	-3.9	55.8	-1.8	62.5	-4.3
Coldwater State School	27.3	4.9	31.3	6.3	34.6	0.1	45.4	-1.6	57.4	-0.4	64.3	-3.0
East Lansing 4 S	26.4	N.A.	29.5	N.A.	33.2	N.A.	43.1	N.A.	56.7	N.A.	63.1	N.A.
Hastings	26.8	4.5	29.9	5.7	33.2	-0.7	43.0	-4.2	55.7	-2.6	62.7	-4.8
Hillsdale	25.7	3.4	29.2	4.4	32.9	-1.4	43.2	-3.9	55.5	-2.2	62.2	-4.7
Ionia 2 SSW	25.4	3.3	28.6	4.7	31.5	-2.2	41.9	-5.2	56.7	-1.4	63.5	-3.8
Jackson FAA Arpt	26.7	5.1	29.8	5.8	34.1	0.4	44.1	-2.8	56.5	-1.4	63.2	-4.5
Lansing WSO Airport	25.9	4.3	29.5	6.2	32.2	-0.8	43.4	-2.9	56.2	-1.0	63.3	-3.5
Owosso 3 NNW	MN.A.	N.A.	27.6	4.0	MN.A.	N.A.	MN.A.	N.A.	MN.A.	N.A.	61.9	-4.9
St Johns	MN.A.	N.A.	MN.A.	N.A.	31.7	-2.0	41.9	-5.2	56.7	-1.4	63.4	-4.3
Three Rivers	27.5	4.5	31.6	5.7	35.2	-0.5	44.8	-3.8	56.6	-2.6	63.2	-5.3
Divisional Data	**26.4**	**4.3**	**29.7**	**5.5**	**33.2**	**-0.7**	**43.5**	**-3.5**	**56.5**	**-1.4**	**63.0**	**-4.3**
Southeast Lower												
Adrian 2 NNE	27.4	4.4	30.3	4.9	34.6	-0.3	45.0	-2.4	56.2	-2.2	62.9	-5.1
Ann Arbor Univ of Mich	27.1	3.3	30.5	4.4	35.3	-0.3	46.6	-1.9	58.9	-0.8	64.8	-4.3
Dearborn	27.5	N.A.	30.1	N.A.	34.9	N.A.	45.3	N.A.	57.9	N.A.	64.4	N.A.
Detroit City Airport	MN.A.	N.A.	30.7	N.A.	35.2	N.A.	45.7	N.A.	M59.1	N.A.	65.6	N.A.
Detroit Metro WSO Ap	28.3	4.9	30.8	5.0	35.5	0.5	46.3	-1.1	58.3	0.2	65.5	-2.2
Flint WSO Ap	25.8	4.5	29.4	6.1	32.9	0.8	43.6	-2.2	57.3	0.9	64.2	-1.7
Grosse Pointe Farms	28.6	3.6	M31.0	4.1	34.8	-0.6	45.2	-2.8	58.1	-1.0	64.2	-4.7
Lapeer	26.0	4.6	29.0	5.5	32.6	-0.4	43.8	-2.5	58.0	1.1	63.8	-2.6
Milan 4 ESE	26.8	4.8	30.0	5.5	34.8	0.6	46.4	-0.3	57.2	-0.3	63.7	-3.1

Table X-18. Average Temperatures and Departures from Normal in Michigan, by Weather Station: 1992 Continued

Station	July Temp	July Deprt	August Temp	August Deprt	September Temp	September Deprt	October Temp	October Deprt	November Temp	November Deprt	December Temp	December Deprt	Annual Temp	Annual Deprt
South Haven	67.5	-2.7	65.9	-3.3	63.0	-0.4	51.9	-1.5	40.3	-1.0	32.7	2.6	48.5	-0.1
Divisional Data	**67.9**	**-3.6**	**65.3**	**-4.7**	**61.1**	**-2.2**	**49.6**	**-2.9**	**38.6**	**-1.5**	**30.9**	**2.0**	**47.8**	**-0.8**
South Central Lower														
Battle Creek 5 NW	66.7	-5.0	64.3	-5.7	59.4	-3.3	48.0	-3.5	36.9	-2.1	29.9	2.2	46.9	-1.2
Charlotte	65.6	-4.9	63.0	-5.5	59.1	-2.7	47.0	-3.7	36.7	-1.6	29.3	2.4	45.7	-1.5
Coldwater State School	68.0	-2.9	65.4	-3.8	60.4	-2.0	49.0	-2.4	39.0	0.0	30.4	2.7	47.7	-0.2
East Lansing 4 S	66.5	N.A.	64.0	N.A.	59.4	N.A.	47.4	N.A.	37.9	N.A.	30.8	N.A.	46.5	N.A.
Hastings	66.3	-4.9	63.6	-6.0	59.8	-2.7	47.7	-3.8	37.6	-1.5	29.9	2.5	46.4	-1.5
Hillsdale	67.1	-3.2	63.8	-5.0	59.3	-2.7	47.6	-3.5	37.5	-1.2	29.5	2.1	46.1	-1.5
Ionia 2 SSW	66.4	-4.7	63.4	-5.9	59.0	-3.0	46.8	-4.4	36.8	-2.1	29.3	2.0	45.8	-1.9
Jackson FAA Arpt	66.7	-5.2	64.7	-5.3	59.5	-3.2	48.0	-3.4	38.0	-0.8	30.9	3.7	46.9	-1.0
Lansing WSO Airport	66.1	-4.7	63.9	-5.3	58.8	-2.9	47.3	-3.4	37.7	-0.8	30.8	3.8	46.3	-0.9
Owosso 3 NNW	65.1	-5.6	62.8	-6.0	M60.8	-0.9	MN.A.	N.A.	37.0	-1.9	29.4	2.3	MN.A.	N.A.
St Johns	66.0	-5.6	63.7	-6.0	60.7	-2.0	48.0	-3.9	36.8	-2.3	29.4	2.1	MN.A.	N.A.
Three Rivers	68.1	-3.9	64.9	-5.3	60.3	-3.1	48.6	-3.6	38.9	-0.9	30.1	1.5	47.5	-1.4
Divisional Data	**66.6**	**-4.5**	**64.0**	**-5.4**	**59.7**	**-2.6**	**47.8**	**-3.5**	**37.6**	**-1.3**	**30.0**	**2.6**	**46.5**	**-1.1**
Southeast Lower														
Adrian 2 NNE	67.6	-4.1	64.9	-5.0	59.4	-3.3	47.7	-3.7	38.3	-0.7	30.8	2.7	47.1	-1.2
Ann Arbor Univ of Mich	68.6	-4.3	66.5	-4.7	61.8	-2.4	49.8	-3.3	38.4	-2.0	31.5	2.6	48.3	-1.1
Dearborn	69.5	N.A.	66.1	N.A.	61.9	N.A.	49.2	N.A.	39.8	N.A.	32.1	N.A.	48.2	N.A.
Detroit City Airport	M69.7	N.A.	68.2	N.A.	63.0	N.A.	50.5	N.A.	40.6	N.A.	33.4	N.A.	MN.A.	N.A.
Detroit Metro WSO Ap	68.8	-3.1	66.7	-3.8	61.4	-1.9	49.7	-2.2	40.5	1.0	33.2	4.7	48.8	0.2
Flint WSO Ap	66.9	-3.2	65.2	-3.3	60.2	-1.0	48.1	-2.5	38.3	-0.5	31.5	4.3	47.0	0.2
Grosse Pointe Farms	69.3	-4.0	68.2	-3.4	64.2	-0.9	50.9	-3.0	40.5	-1.2	33.2	2.8	M49.0	-0.9
Lapeer	66.7	-3.6	65.3	-3.1	61.3	-0.2	48.5	-2.3	38.0	-0.7	30.3	3.3	46.9	-0.1
Milan 4 ESE	67.8	-2.6	65.2	-3.5	60.7	-1.0	48.5	-2.1	39.1	0.5	31.6	4.2	47.7	0.2

Table X-18. Average Temperatures and Departures from Normal in Michigan, by Weather Station: 1992 Continued

Station	January Temp	January Deprt	February Temp	February Deprt	March Temp	March Deprt	April Temp	April Deprt	May Temp	May Deprt	June Temp	June Deprt
Milford GM proving Gr	25.2	4.3	28.2	5.3	32.5	-0.1	43.1	-2.6	M55.7	-1.2	62.7	-4.0
Monroe	28.3	3.7	31.7	4.8	35.1	-0.6	46.0	-2.3	58.9	-0.5	66.5	-2.9
Mount Clemens Ang Base	27.1	N.A.	29.2	N.A.	33.0	N.A.	43.7	N.A.	57.0	N.A.	63.0	N.A.
Pontiac State Hospital	26.4	4.0	29.5	4.8	34.1	0.0	44.9	-2.3	58.3	-0.1	64.1	-3.8
Port Huron	25.9	2.3	28.0	2.7	32.5	-1.5	43.0	-3.0	55.8	-0.7	63.0	-3.8
Ypsilanti E Mich Univ	28.5	5.0	31.4	5.5	37.1	1.9	47.6	-0.3	59.9	1.0	66.6	-2.0
Divisional Data	**27.1**	**3.9**	**30.0**	**4.7**	**34.3**	**-0.2**	**45.1**	**-2.1**	**57.8**	**-0.3**	**64.3**	**-3.5**

Table X-18. Average Temperatures and Departures from Normal in Michigan, by Weather Station: 1992 Continued

Station	July Temp	July Deprt	August Temp	August Deprt	September Temp	September Deprt	October Temp	October Deprt	November Temp	November Deprt	December Temp	December Deprt	Annual Temp	Annual Deprt
Milford GM proving Gr	66.5	-4.3	64.3	-4.9	59.8	-1.9	47.0	-3.6	36.6	-1.5	30.1	3.0	M46.0	-0.9
Monroe	71.1	-2.4	68.9	-3.0	63.8	-1.3	49.7	-3.7	40.2	-0.9	32.0	2.2	49.4	-0.6
Mount Clemens Ang Base	68.0	N.A.	66.5	N.A.	61.4	N.A.	MN.	N.A.	M39.	N.A.	33.1	N.A.	MN.A.	N.A.
Pontiac State Hospital	67.6	-4.5	65.6	-4.9	61.6	-1.9	48.6	-3.7	38.0	-1.5	31.0	3.2	47.5	-0.9
Port Huron	67.5	-4.5	67.0	-3.8	62.7	-1.2	49.8	-3.1	39.4	-1.2	31.9	2.9	47.2	-1.2
Ypsilanti E Mich Univ	69.7	-3.1	68.2	-2.9	63.4	-0.3	51.0	-1.5	39.8	-0.1	33.0	4.3	49.7	0.6
Divisional Data	**68.4**	**-3.6**	**66.5**	**-3.9**	**61.8**	**-1.6**	**49.2**	**-3.0**	**39.1**	**-0.8**	**31.9**	**3.4**	**48.0**	**-0.5**

Source: National Oceanic and Atmospheric Administration, Climatological Data Annual Summary - Michigan 1992 (Asheville, North Carolina: annually). Notes: An M denotes insufficient or partial data. M is appended to average and/or total values computed with 1-9 daily values missing. M appears alone if 10 or more daily values are missing. N.A. Data not available.

Table X-19. State-Wide Stationary Source Emission Trends,* Tons per Year: 1974-1992

Year	Particulate	Sulfur Dioxide	Nitrogen Dioxide	Carbon Monoxide	Hydrocarbon
1974	331,539	1,562,715	437,571	334,893	260,487
1975	264,050	1,319,654	353,299	496,363	213,402
1976	230,401	1,189,189	332,206	518,337	251,124
1977	116,327	1,175,069	341,745	642,680	252,694
1978	115,401	1,077,301	350,914	651,775	257,272
1979	108,301	1,111,546	368,866	393,832	367,655
1980	99,702	768,150	340,966	187,681	214,708
1981	78,380	811,569	338,393	198,696	175,436
1982	73,651	713,918	308,862	147,749	151,641
1983	65,283	718,121	315,223	160,421	145,885
1984	60,415	739,777	320,128	173,378	149,902
1985	43,154	532,274	329,575	146,854	144,847
1986	48,319	591,122	353,393	134,347	135,486
1987	51,628	632,103	391,745	138,298	126,230
1988	50,642	566,811	353,531	126,137	107,082
1989	47,637	574,740	382,518	97,272	102,904
1990**	69,755	608,020	426,896	116,823	101,381
1991	46,958	581,756	377,060	113,433	83,160
1992	44,442	513,762	360,546	96,410	84,220

Source: Michigan Department of Natural Resources, Air Quality Division (Lansing, Michigan). * Does not include transportation, residential and commercial sources. ** Base line year for emission inventory has been quality assured.

Table X-20. Geographical Designation of Attainment Status for Ozone in Michigan, by County: 1990 and 1992*

County	Designation	Classification	County	Designation	Classification
Alcona	Attainment		Lake	Attainment	
Alger	Attainment		Lapeer	Nonattainment	Not Classified/Inc. Data
Allegan	Nonattainment	Not Classified/Inc. Data	Leelanau	Attainment	
Alpena	Attainment		Lenawee	Nonattainment	Not Classified/Inc. Data
Antrim	Attainment		Livingston	Nonattainment	Moderate
Arenac	Attainment		Luce	Attainment	
Baraga	Attainment		Mackinac	Attainment	
Barry	Nonattainment	Not Classified/Inc. Data	Macomb	Nonattainment	Moderate
Bay	Nonattainment	Not Classified/Inc. Data	Manistee	Attainment	
Benzie	Attainment		Marquette	Attainment	
Berrien	Nonattainment	Not Classified/Inc. Data	Mason	Attainment	
Branch	Nonattainment	Not Classified/Inc. Data	Mecosta	Attainment	
Calhoun	Nonattainment	Not Classified/Inc. Data	Menominee	Attainment	
Cass	Nonattainment	Not Classified/Inc. Data	Midland	Nonattainment	Not Classified/Inc. Data
Charlevoix	Attainment		Missaukee	Attainment	
Cheboygan	Attainment		Monroe	Nonattainment	Moderate
Chippewa	Attainment		Montcalm	Nonattainment	Not Classified/Inc. Data
Clare	Attainment		Montmorency	Attainment	
Clinton	Nonattainment	Transitional	Muskegon	Nonattainment	Moderate
Crawford	Attainment		Newaygo	Attainment	
Delta	Attainment		Oakland	Nonattainment	Moderate
Dickinson	Attainment		Oceana	Attainment	
Eaton	Nonattainment	Transitional	Ogemaw	Attainment	
Emmet	Attainment		Ontonagon	Attainment	
Genesee	Nonattainment	Transitional	Osceola	Attainment	
Gladwin	Attainment		Oscoda	Attainment	
Gogebic	Attainment		Otsego	Attainment	
Grand Traverse	Attainment		Ottawa	Nonattainment	Moderate
Gratiot	Nonattainment	Not Classified/Inc. Data	Presque Isle	Attainment	
Hillsdale	Nonattainment	Not Classified/Inc. Data	Roscommon	Attainment	
Houghton	Attainment		Saginaw	Nonattainment	Not Classified/Inc. Data
Huron	Nonattainment	Not Classified/Inc. Data	St. Clair	Nonattainment	Moderate
Ingham	Nonattainment	Transitional	St. Joseph	Nonattainment	Not Classified/Inc. Data
Ionia	Nonattainment	Not Classified/Inc. Data	Sanilac	Nonattainment	Not Classified/Inc. Data
Iosco	Attainment		Schoolcraft	Attainment	
Iron	Attainment		Shiawassee	Nonattainment	Not Classified/Inc. Data
Isabella	Attainment		Tuscola	Nonattainment	Not Classified/Inc. Data
Jackson	Nonattainment	Not Classified/Inc. Data	Van Buren	Nonattainment	Not Classified/Inc. Data
Kalamazoo	Nonattainment	Not Classified/Inc. Data	Washtenaw	Nonattainment	Moderate
Kalkaska	Attainment		Wayne	Nonattainment	Moderate
Kent	Nonattainment	Moderate	Wexford	Attainment	
Keweenaw	Attainment				

Source: Department of Natural Resources, Air Quality Division, Geographical Designation of Attainment Status - June 1994 (Lansing, Michigan).
* All date 11/15/90 except for Muskegon county which is 11/30/92.

Table X-21. Geographical Designation of Attainment Status for Carbon Monoxide in Michigan: 11/15/1990

Geographic Region	Designation	Classification
South Bend-Elkhart-Benton Harbor Air Quality Control Region 82 (Michigan Portion)	Attainment	
Central Michigan Air Quality Control Region 122	Attainment	
Detroit-Port Huron Air Quality Control Region 123 Except Portion Listed Below:	Attainment	
Macomb, Oakland, Wayne Counties-area within the following (Counterclockwise): Lake St. Clair to 14 Mile Rd. to Kelly Rd., north to 15 Mile Rd. to Hayes Rd. South to 14 Mile Rd to Clawson City Boundary, following north Clawson City boundary to north Royal Oak City boundary to 13 Mile Rd. to Evergreen Rd. to Southern Bingham Farms City boundary to southern Franklin City boundary to Inkster Rd., south to Pennsylvania Rd. extending east to the Detroit River.	Nonattainment	Not Classified
Monroe/Toledo Air Quality Control Region 124 (Michigan Portion)	Attainment	
South Central Air Quality Control Region 125	Attainment	
Upper Michigan Air Quality Control Region 126	Attainment	

Source: Department of Natural Resources, Air Quality Division, Geographical Designation of Attainment Status - June 1994 (Lansing, Michigan).

Table X-22. Geographical Designation of Attainment Status for Particle Matter with a Nominal Diameter of 10 Micrometers or Less (PM-10) in Michigan: 11/15/1990

Geographic Region	Designation	Classification
South Bend-Elkhart-Benton Harbor Air Quality Control Region 82 (Michigan Portion)	Unclassifiable	
Central Michigan Air Quality Control Region 122	Unclassifiable	
Detroit-Port Huron Air Quality Control Region 123 Except Portion Listed Below:	Unclassifiable	
Wayne County portion of: area bounded by Michigan Ave. from its intersection with I-75 west to I-94, I-94 southwest to Greenfield Rd., Greenfield Rd. south to Schaefer Rd., Schaefer Rd. south and east to Jefferson Ave., Jefferson Ave. (Biddle through the city of Wyandotte), south to Sibley Ave., Sibley Ave. west to Fort St. Fort St. south to King Rd., King Rd. east to Jefferson Ave., Jefferson Ave. south to Helen Rd., Helen Rd. east extended to Trenton Channel, Trenton Channel north to the Detroit River, the Detroit River north to the Ambassador Bridge, Ambassador Bridge to I-75, I-75 to Michigan Ave.	Nonattainment	Moderate
Monroe/Toledo Air Quality Control Region 124 (Michigan Portion)	Unclassifiable	
South Central Air Quality Control Region 125	Unclassifiable	
Upper Michigan Air Quality Control Region 126	Unclassifiable	

Source: Department of Natural Resources, Air Quality Division, Geographical Designation of Attainment Status - June 1994 (Lansing, Michigan).

Table X-23. Geographical Designation of Attainment Status for Nitrogen Dioxide in Michigan: 11/15/1990

Geographic Region	Designation	Classification
South Bend-Elkhart-Benton Harbor Air Quality Control Region 82 (Michigan Portion)	Attainment	None Given
Central Michigan Air Quality Control Region 122	Attainment	None Given
Detroit-Port Huron Air Quality Control Region 123	Attainment	None Given
Monroe/Toledo Air Quality Control Region 124 (Michigan Portion)	Attainment	None Given
South Central Air Quality Control Region 125	Attainment	None Given
Upper Michigan Air Quality Control Region 126	Attainment	None Given

Source: Department of Natural Resources, Air Quality Division, Geographical Designation of Attainment Status - June 1994 (Lansing, Michigan).

Table X-24. Geographical Designation of Attainment Status for Sulfur Dioxide in Michigan: 11/15/1990

Geographic Region	Designation	Classification
South Bend-Elkhart-Benton Harbor Air Quality Control Region 82 (Michigan Portion)	Attainment	None Given
Central Michigan Air Quality Control Region 122	Attainment	None Given
Detroit-Port Huron Air Quality Control Region 123	Attainment	None Given
Monroe/Toledo Air Quality Control Region 124 (Michigan Portion)	Attainment	None Given
South Central Air Quality Control Region 125	Attainment	None Given
Upper Michigan Air Quality Control Region 126	Attainment	None Given

Source: Department of Natural Resources, Air Quality Division, Geographical Designation of Attainment Status - June 1994 (Lansing, Michigan).

Table X-25. Geographical Designation of Attainment Status for Lead in Michigan: 11/15/1990

Geographic Region	Designation	Classification
South Bend-Elkhart-Benton Harbor Air Quality Control Region 82 (Michigan Portion)	Not Designated	None Given
Central Michigan Air Quality Control Region 122	Not Designated	None Given
Detroit-Port Huron Air Quality Control Region 123	Not Designated	None Given
Monroe/Toledo Air Quality Control Region 124 (Michigan Portion)	Not Designated	None Given
South Central Air Quality Control Region 125	Not Designated	None Given
Upper Michigan Air Quality Control Region 126	Not Designated	None Given

Source: Department of Natural Resources, Air Quality Division, Geographical Designation of Attainment Status - June 1994 (Lansing, Michigan).

Table X-26. Total Annual Solid Waste Disposal Requirements in Michigan, by County: 1993

County	Total (Tons per Year=TPY)	Residential/ Commercial (TPY)	Industrial (TPY)	County	Total (TPY)	Residential/ Commercial (TPY)	Industrial (TPY)
Alcona	8,525	7,961	564	Hillsdale	55,152	34,082	21,069
Alger	12,971	7,041	5,930	Houghton	33,431	27,816	5,615
Allegan	171,832	71,027	100,805	Huron	45,088	27,428	17,659
Alpena	38,444	24,017	14,427	Ingham	305,892	221,230	84,661
Antrim	19,122	14,271	4,852	Ionia	65,449	44,750	20,699
Arenac	13,824	11,717	2,106	Iosco	30,996	23,707	7,289
Baraga	9,976	6,242	3,734	Iron	12,801	10,339	2,462
Barry	46,914	39,282	7,632	Isabella	48,180	42,866	5,313
Bay	126,679	87,675	39,004	Jackson	171,974	117,521	54,453
Benzie	12,257	9,574	2,683	Kalamazoo	379,688	175,322	204,366
Berrien	224,828	126,641	98,187	Kalkaska	15,153	10,592	4,561
Branch	50,866	32,569	18,298	Kent	746,908	392,870	354,038
Calhoun	227,751	106,712	121,039	Keweenaw	1,502	1,335	167
Cass	58,169	38,827	19,342	Lake	7,642	6,736	907
Charlevoix	33,906	16,847	17,059	Lapeer	77,419	58,674	18,745
Cheboygan	19,451	16,792	2,659	Leelanau	14,185	12,970	1,216
Chippewa	30,827	27,155	3,672	Lenawee	129,994	71,788	58,208
Clare	25,041	19,581	5,460	Livingston	123,695	90,752	32,943
Clinton	52,650	45,424	7,227	Luce	5,373	4,523	851
Crawford	13,386	9,621	3,765	Mackinac	8,590	8,376	213
Delta	47,061	29,648	17,413	Macomb	906,069	562,980	343,089
Dickinson	41,783	21,056	20,728	Manistee	29,611	16,688	12,924
Eaton	88,487	72,887	15,600	Marquette	60,890	55,629	5,261
Emmet	29,236	19,650	9,586	Mason	38,755	20,040	18,715
Genesee	455,978	337,803	118,175	Mecosta	34,315	29,277	5,037
Gladwin	19,450	17,183	2,277	Menominee	36,000	19,556	16,444
Gogebic	18,522	14,166	4,356	Midland	168,949	59,367	109,582
Grand Traverse	71,042	50,438	20,604	Missaukee	11,416	9,532	1,884
Gratiot	45,778	30,591	15,187	Monroe	158,487	104,843	53,644

Table X-26. Total Annual Solid Waste Disposal Requirements in Michigan, by County: 1993 Continued

County	Total (Tons per Year=TPY)	Residential/Commercial (TPY)	Industrial (TPY)
Montcalm	57,977	41,638	16,339
Montmorency	8,391	7,013	1,379
Muskegon	233,605	124,762	108,843
Newaygo	38,931	29,979	8,952
Oakland	1,258,196	850,349	407,847
Oceana	25,707	17,621	8,086
Ogemaw	18,537	14,660	3,877
Ontonagon	28,440	6,948	21,492
Osceola	28,801	15,810	12,992
Oscoda	7,909	6,154	1,755
Otsego	20,902	14,092	6,811
Ottawa	273,015	147,351	125,664
Presque Isle	11,510	10,785	11,510
Roscommon	16,940	15,519	4,421
Saginaw	321,610	166,325	155,286
St. Clair	175,231	114,265	60,966
St. Joseph	87,036	46,232	40,804
Sanilac	48,463	31,333	17,130
Schoolcraft	8,794	6,515	2,279
Shiawassee	71,844	54,752	17,092
Tuscola	60,583	43,552	17,031
Van Buren	85,750	54,980	30,771
Washtenaw	318,853	222,035	96,818
Wayne	2,500,527	1,657,146	843,381
Wexford	35,594	20,686	14,908
Michigan	**11,481,517**	**7,294,484**	**4,187,033**

Source: SCS Engineers, Disposal Capacity and Disposal Requirements In The State of Michigan, March 1994 (Cincinnati, Ohio).

Table X-27. Permitted Solid Waste Disposal Capacity in Michigan, by County: 1993 (Data in Cubic Yards)

Rank	County	Remaining Permitted	Rank	County	Remaining Permitted
1	Wayne	70,921,877	43	Alcona	0
2	Ottawa	27,412,890	44	Allegan	0
3	Leelanau	18,000,000	45	Alpena	0
4	Genesee	15,426,000	46	Antrium	0
5	Berrien	15,300,000	47	Arenac	0
6	Washtenaw	12,500,000	48	Baraga	0
7	Sanilac	11,130,000	49	Benzie	0
8	Oakland	10,970,000	50	Branch	0
9	St. Clair	10,700,000	51	Cass	0
10	Macomb	10,000,000	52	Cheboygan	0
11	Clara	9,527,500	53	Dickinson	0
12	Saginaw	8,720,000	54	Eaton	0
13	St. Joseph	7,734,540	55	Emmet	0
14	Clinton	6,500,000	56	Gladwin	0
15	Bay	5,300,000	57	Gogebic	0
16	Shiawassee	4,500,000	58	Grand Traverse	0
17	Ingham	4,000,000	59	Gratiot	0
18	Presque Isle	3,500,000	60	Hillsdale	0
19	Manistee	3,282,660	61	Houghton	0
20	Monroe	3,000,000	62	Huron	0
21	Marquette	2,956,000	63	Iosco	0
22	Kent	2,500,000	64	Iron	0
23	Lenawee	2,416,532	65	Isabella	0
24	Muskegon	2,250,000	66	Kalamazoo	0
25	Osceola	1,703,910	67	Kalkaska	0
26	Wexford	1,517,904	68	Keweenaw	0
27	Calhoun	1,500,000	69	Lake	0
28	Lapeer	1,500,000	70	Livingston	0
29	Montcalm	1,500,000	71	Luce	0
30	Ontonogon	1,250,000	72	Mackinac	0
31	Barry	1,164,000	73	Mecosta	0
32	Crawford	1,151,000	74	Missaukee	0
33	Delta	998,000	75	Newaygo	0
34	Montmorency	900,000	76	Ogemaw	0
35	Charlevoix	775,000	77	Oscoda	0
36	Chippewa	745,000	78	Otsego	0
37	Iona	717,000	79	Oceana	0
38	Menominee	480,000	80	Roscommon	0
39	Alger	400,000	81	Schoolcraft	0
40	Jackson	134,000	82	Tuscola	0
41	Mason	100,000	83	Washtenaw	0
42	Midland	100,000		**Michigan**	**285,204,668**

Source: SCS Engineers, <u>Disposal Capacity and Disposal Requirements In The State of Michigan, March 1994</u> (Cincinnati, Ohio).

Table X-28. Sites of Environmental Contamination** in Michigan, by County: 1994 (For category headings please see page 417.)

| County | Public Act #307 | | | | | | | Leaking Underground Storage Tanks (LUST) | | Total |
	Category 1	Category 2	Category 3	Category 4	Category 5	Category 6	Category 7	Category 8	Category 9	
Alcona	4	2	2	0	0	0	0	4	6	18
Alger	6	4	2	0	0	0	0	5	12	29
Allegan	11	8	20	0	2	0	0	1	48	90
Alpena	21	4	11	0	0	0	0	5	41	82
Antrim	15	3	4	0	3	0	1	2	26	54
Arenac	7	0	5	0	0	0	0	1	17	30
Baraga	2	1	1	0	0	0	0	2	11	17
Barry	2	7	9	0	0	0	0	2	19	39
Bay	7	3	30	1	2	0	3	5	93	144
Benzie	3	0	3	1	0	0	0	1	22	30
Berrien	11	10	34	1	6	0	0	7	101	170
Branch	7	3	13	0	0	0	0	1	30	54
Calhoun	19	18	30	0	0	0	1	0	116	184
Cass	7	6	6	1	1	0	0	5	27	53
Charlevoix	5	4	8	1	0	2	0	1	28	49
Cheboygan	12	0	5	0	0	1	1	3	37	59
Chippewa	13	5	13	0	1	0	0	4	66	102
Clare	10	3	14	0	1	0	1	6	20	55
Clinton	12	0	9	0	1	0	0	9	59	90
Crawford	3	2	9	1	6	0	0	2	26	49
Delta	6	7	6	0	1	0	0	5	36	61
Dickinson	3	2	6	0	0	0	0	1	17	29
Eaton	9	4	7	0	1	0	0	11	72	104
Emmet	3	3	2	0	0	0	0	6	17	31
Genesee	22	20	24	0	2	0	1	10	343	422
Gladwin	11	3	6	0	0	0	0	5	22	47
Gogebic	4	0	2	0	0	0	0	0	19	25
Grand Traverse	14	3	37	0	4	0	1	0	73	132

Table X-28. Sites of Environmental Contamination** in Michigan, by County: 1994 Continued (For category headings please see page 417.)

County	Public Act #307							Leaking Underground Storage Tanks (LUST)		Total
	Category 1	Category 2	Category 3	Category 4	Category 5	Category 6	Category 7	Category 8	Category 9	
Gratiot	2	5	17	1	0	0	1	4	49	79
Hillsdale	14	17	8	0	0	0	0	0	39	78
Houghton	2	1	7	1	0	0	0	2	21	34
Huron	6	0	7	0	0	0	0	0	28	41
Ingham	15	4	33	1	4	0	0	37	241	335
Ionia	9	2	4	0	4	0	0	3	36	58
Iosco	3	3	20	1	2	0	2	6	30	67
Iron	6	2	3	0	0	1	0	1	3	16
Isabella	15	2	11	0	1	0	0	1	55	85
Jackson	17	7	29	0	2	0	0	1	127	183
Kalamazoo	11	23	43	0	5	0	0	12	131	225
Kalkaska	13	4	18	0	3	0	0	0	12	50
Kent	1	15	66	1	5	2	4	4	365	463
Keweenaw	1	0	1	0	0	0	0	0	5	7
Lake	4	1	5	1	0	0	0	1	10	22
Lapeer	12	28	4	1	1	0	0	1	73	108
Leelanau	5	3	14	0	2	0	0	1	18	43
Lenawee	4	3	21	0	0	0	0	0	80	108
Livingston	6	8	27	1	2	1	0	4	46	95
Luce	2	1	1	0	0	0	0	1	11	16
Mackinac	4	2	2	0	1	0	0	4	26	39
Macomb	18	9	25	0	5	0	0	17	446	520
Manistee	19	8	43	0	6	0	4	6	16	102
Marquette	13	9	33	0	1	0	0	2	67	125
Mason	6	1	23	0	1	0	0	7	37	75
Mecosta	7	0	11	0	0	0	0	6	25	49
Menominee	7	7	4	0	1	0	0	8	15	42
Midland	18	6	13	0	1	0	1	1	52	92

Table X-28. Sites of Environmental Contamination** in Michigan, by County: 1994 Continued (For category headings please see page 417.)

County	Public Act #307							Leaking Underground Storage Tanks (LUST)		Total
	Category 1	Category 2	Category 3	Category 4	Category 5	Category 6	Category 7	Category 8	Category 9	
Missaukee	4	2	9	0	3	0	2	0	13	33
Monroe	13	11	15	2	0	0	0	1	79	121
Montcalm	15	1	14	1	0	0	0	0	39	70
Montmorency	3	2	3	0	0	0	1	0	16	25
Muskegon	10	14	46	5	4	0	0	0	85	164
Newaygo	10	4	4	1	1	0	0	0	29	49
Oakland	31	25	62	0	1	1	0	8	707	835
Oceana	15	3	10	1	0	0	0	0	26	55
Ogemaw	5	2	4	0	2	0	0	4	25	42
Ontonagon	9	0	2	0	0	0	0	0	6	17
Osceola	6	10	14	1	1	0	0	1	13	46
Oscoda	2	2	3	0	0	0	0	4	4	15
Otsego	11	1	9	0	7	0	1	1	7	37
Ottawa	11	8	35	1	0	1	1	0	108	165
Presque Isle	1	0	3	0	0	0	0	1	16	21
Roscommon	4	6	11	1	1	0	2	13	23	61
Saginaw	18	2	36	0	5	0	1	7	208	277
St. Clair	13	2	11	0	0	0	0	0	115	141
St. Joseph	4	3	15	0	4	0	1	0	30	57
Sanilac	5	0	5	0	0	0	1	1	49	61
Schoolcraft	6	4	4	0	0	0	0	0	17	31
Shiawassee	3	2	14	1	1	0	0	1	49	71
Tuscola	4	3	11	1	1	0	0	0	41	61
Van Buren	11	9	18	0	2	0	0	1	41	82
Washtenaw	12	7	49	0	3	0	0	1	205	277
Wayne	54	16	115	0	11	1	0	3	1,109	1,309
Wexford	3	3	20	0	3	0	3	0	43	75
Michigan	772	438	1,353	29	128	10	34	281	6,571	9,616

Source: Michigan Department of Natural Resources - Michigan Sites of Environmental Contamination FY-1996 (Lansing, Michigan: annually).

TABLE X-28. SITES OF ENVIRONMENTAL CONTAMINATION IN MICHIGAN, BY COUNTY: 1994
Definition of Category Headings

Public Act #307:   The Michigan Environmental Response Act (MERA)

Category 1:   Inactive - No actions taken

Category 2:   Cleanup actions taken or in progress - Evaluation/Interim Response Fund

Category 3:   Cleanup actions taken or in progress - Evaluation/Interim Response Potentially Responsible Party/Other

Category 4:   Cleanup actions taken or in progress - Final Cleanup-Fund

Category 5:   Cleanup actions taken or in progress - Final Cleanup-Potentially Responsible Party/Other

Category 6:   Cleanup Complete / Long Term Maintenance-Operations & Maintenance Fund

Category 7:   Cleanup Complete / Long Term Maintenance-Operations & Maintenance Fund-Potentially Responsible Party/Other

Category 8:   Inactive

Category 9:   Cleanup actions taken or in progress

Table X-29. Number of Reported Forest Fires in Michigan, and Acreage Burned: 1970-1992

Year	Total		Lightning		Campfire		Tobacco Smoking		Debris Burning		Incendiary		Equipment Use		All Other	
	Fires	Acres	Fires	Acres	Fires	Acres	Fires	Acres	Fires	Acres	Fires	Acres	Fires	Acres	Fires	Acres
1970	1,395	6,492	39	56	64	255	203	741	461	2,844	152	581	239	947	237	1,069
1971	1,210	5,597	25	60	79	449	212	1,344	347	1,630	91	831	293	993	163	287
1972	1,060	5,654	17	24	66	630	166	1,151	324	1,628	77	553	223	804	187	864
1973	832	2,664	7	7	47	160	142	615	295	1,069	83	322	139	241	119	250
1974	1,029	6,087	20	80	45	195	176	1,566	343	2,176	109	999	196	608	140	464
1975	853	16,775	40	143	77	342	204	1,041	225	1,467	79	4,788	42	275	186	8,715
1976	1,341	25,470	99	19,264	159	645	258	1,626	296	1,122	131	923	103	505	295	1,385
1977	1,433	12,109	72	805	122	710	223	1,396	329	3,911	169	1,563	155	2,074	363	1,650
1978	721	2,639	8	17	68	207	120	513	160	420	95	420	47	159	223	795
1979	472	2,299	7	15	44	113	67	152	113	410	73	1,049	52	391	116	169
1980	843	9,279	16	68	65	353	96	1,211	303	1,733	116	1,410	88	1,347	159	3,157
1981	824	7,607	14	102	64	258	108	404	224	2,821	132	2,620	87	410	195	1,892
1982	486	3,989	11	151	36	672	52	231	178	816	52	581	44	362	113	1,187
1983	547	4,375	38	177	38	75	60	342	147	824	72	1,351	60	397	132	1,209
1984	613	4,070	18	29	34	87	51	180	227	1,495	85	800	71	436	127	1,033
1985	359	3,117	10	7	25	100	25	127	111	397	43	317	40	175	105	1,994
1986	493	9,701	13	65	40	94	36	251	157	715	86	623	56	7,370	105	583
1987	849	9,533	37	187	50	258	59	292	279	1,941	117	1,798	100	1,348	207	3,709
1988	1,094	8,049	145	448	75	1,681	90	420	248	1,259	156	2,516	165	702	215	1,023
1989	712	4,570	52	586	57	157	70	594	231	1,057	94	847	93	1,034	115	295
1990	483	9,158	15	18	37	229	38	215	168	6,929	60	494	46	226	119	1,047
1991	412	1,472	19	176	41	57	27	126	123	549	48	265	56	145	98	154
1992	551	1,975	13	61	46	296	21	85	188	598	92	459	58	226	133	250

Source: Michigan Department of Natural Resources, Forest Management Division (Lansing, Michigan).

CHAPTER XI
AGRICULTURE / FORESTRY / FISHING / MINING

The Office of Management and Budget in the Executive Office of the President is responsible for maintaining the Standard Industrial Classification system. The SIC is used in all federal statistical programs and in most other programs where the focus is on economic activity.

According to the latest <u>Standard Industrial Classification Manual,</u>

> agricultural production covers establishments (e.g., farms, ranches, dairies, greenhouses,nurseries, orchards, hatcheries) primarily engaged in the production of crops, plants, vines, or trees (excluding forestry operations); and the keeping, grazing, or feeding of livestock for the sale of livestock or livestock products (including serums), for livestock increase or for value increase. Livestock as used here includes cattle, sheep, goats, hogs, and poultry. Also included are animal specialties, such as horses, rabbits, bees, pets, fur-bearing animals in captivity, and fish in captivity. Agricultural production also includes establishments engaged in the operation of sod farms, cranberry bogs, and poultry hatcheries; in the production of mushrooms, bulbs, flower seeds, and vegetable seeds; and in the growing of hydroponic crops.

> Agricultural services includes establishments engaged primarily in rendering soil preparation services, landscape and horticultural services, veterinary and other animal services, and farm labor and management services.

> Under the classification, forestry, are establishments that operate timber tracts, tree farms, and forest nurseries. It also includes those that gather forest products and perform forestry services.

> Fishing (i.e. fishing, hunting, and trapping) includes commercial fishing, fish hatcheries and preserves, and hunting, trapping, and game propagation.

> The term mining is used in the broad sense to include the extraction of minerals occurring naturally, such as coals and ores; liquids, such as crude petroleum; and gases, such as natural gas. The term mining also is used in the broad sense to include quarrying, well operations, milling (e.g., the crushing, screening, washing, flotation), and other preparation customarily done at the mine site, or as part of mining activity.

> Exploration and development of mineral properties are included.

The Michigan Department of Agriculture maintains extensive files on farming activity in Michigan. Some of these data are published in the annual <u>Michigan Agricultural Statistics</u>. This state Department also works closely with the United States Department of Agriculture in its Crop Reporting System, and with the Bureau of the Census. The Census Bureau is responsible for the quinquennial <u>Census of Agriculture</u> as well as of the <u>Census of Mining</u>, conducted in years ending in 2 and 7 (i.e., 1987 and 1992).

The Michigan Department of Natural Resources, The U.S. Department of Interior and the Bureau of the Census compile data on mining in this state. In cooperation with the DNR, the Interior Department publishes an annual <u>Minerals Yearbook</u> which has a Michigan chapter. Material for this chapter was reproduced from a pre-print entitled "The Mineral Industry of Michigan".

CHAPTER XI
AGRICULTURE / FORESTRY / FISHING / MINING

The Independent Petroleum Association of America publishes an annual compilation entitled, <u>The Oil & Natural Gas Producing Industry in Your State</u>. Their sources include Baker Hughs, Inc., the U.S. Energy Information Administration, the Interstate Oil & Gas Compact Commission, the National Stripper Well Association, the American Petroleum Institute, and World Oil.

In connection with its quinquennial economic censuses the Census Bureau issues reports on Michigan mining industries.

Current data on mining employment, hours, and earnings are collected and disseminated by the Michigan Employment Security Commission in Detroit and by the Bureau of Labor Statistics in Washington, D.C.

Some terms found in this chapter are defined as follows:

Units, Employment, Average Weekly Wage: See the notes at the beginning of chapter XVI on Trade or chapter XVIII on Services.

Rotary Drilling Rig: A derrick equipped with modern rotary equipment capable of drilling a bore hole with a bit attached to a rotating column of steel pipe, in contrast to a cable tool rig which drills on the percussion principle.

Wildcat Well: A type of exploratory well drilled in an unproven area where there has been no previous production.

Exploratory Well: A crude oil, natural gas, or dry hole drilled to discover a petroleum formation or its limits.

Development Well: A crude oil, natural gas or dry hole drilled within an area known to be productive.

Stripper Well: A producing well which pumps less than 10 barrels of crude oil or 60 Mcf of natural gas per day.

LIST OF TABLES

Table		Page
XI-1.	Michigan's Rank in the Nation's Agriculture: 1993	422
XI-2.	Acreage and Production of Major Crops in Michigan: 1993	423
XI-3.	Major Livestock Inventory and Production of Major Livestock Products in Michigan: 1993	424
XI-4.	Gross Farm Income, Production Expenses, and Realized Net Farm Income in Michigan and the United States: 1950-1992	424

420

LIST OF TABLES

Table   **Page**

XI-5.   Agriculture, Forestry and Fishery Income as a Percentage of Total Personal
        Income in Michigan, by County: 1992 425

XI-6.   Cash Receipts from Farming in Michigan, by County: 1992 426

XI-7.   Total Employment in Farm Production, Agricultural Services, Forestry, and
        Fishing in Michigan, by County: 1992 427

XI-8.   Michigan Tree Volumes, by Species Group: 1993 428

XI-9.   Michigan's Timberland Acreage, by Forest Type and Ownership Group: 1993 . . 429

XI-10. Nonfuel Mineral Production in Michigan: 1990-1992 429

XI-11. Number of Mining Establishments, Employment, and Average Weekly Wage in
        Michigan and the United States: 1970-1994 430

XI-12. Number of Mining Establishments, Employment, and Average Weekly Wage in
        Michigan, by County: 1992 431

XI-13. Number and Type of Petroleum Rigs Operating and Wells Drilled in Michigan
        and the United States: 1983-1992 432

XI-14. Number of Producing Wells, by Type, in Michigan and the United States:
        1983-1992 432

XI-15. Production from Oil and Gas Wells in Michigan and the United States:
        1983-1992 433

XI-16. Cost of Drilling and Equipping Oil and Gas Wells in Michigan and the United
        States: 1991 433

XI-17. Crude Oil and Natural Gas Revenues in Michigan and the United States:
        1983-1992 433

Table XI-1. Michigan's Rank in the Nation's Agriculture: 1993

Commodity	Rank	Michigan Production	Units	Percent(%) U.S. Production	Leading State
Cranberry Beans	1	575	Cwt.	95.4	Michigan
Black Turtle Beans	1	1,040	Cwt.	77.7	Michigan
Tart Cherries	1	270,000	Lbs.	83.5	Michigan
Navy Beans	1	4,060	Cwt.	77.1	Michigan
Blueberries	1	87,000	Lbs.	50.4	Michigan
Cucumbers for Pickles	1	128	Tons	21.8	Michigan
Geraniums, Potted	1	18,290	Pots	18.0	Michigan
Easter Lilies, Potted	1	1,170	Pots	13.6	Michigan
Summer Potatoes	1	3,500	Cwt	17.1	Michigan
All Dry Beans	1	6,080	Cwt	27.8	Michigan
Apples	2	1,020,000	Lbs.	9.4	Washington
Bedding Plants	2	9,805	Flats	11.1	California
Gladioli	2	42,140	Spikes	26.0	Florida
Hanging Flowers	2	2,155	Baskets	8.5	North Carolina
Asparagus	3	285	Cwt.	12.9	California
Snap Beans	3	70	Tons	10.7	Wisconsin
Lilies, other	3	160	Pots	10.4	Pennsylvania
Celery	3	1,134	Cwt.	6.2	California
Carrots	3	2,016	Cwt.	6.3	California
Sweet Cherries	3	30	Tons	17.8	Washington
Prunes & Plums	3	7	Tons	2.1	California
Tomatoes	3	182	Tons	1.9	California
Dark Red Kidney Beans	4	105	Cwt.	13.2	Minnesota
Light Red Kidney Beans	4	115	Cwt.	10.1	California
Small White Beans	4	30	Cwt.	21.3	Idaho
Cucumbers, Fresh Market	4	918	Cwt.	9.2	Florida
Grapes, All	4	55	Tons	1.0	California
Grapes, Concord	4	46	Tons	9.5	Washington
Hay, Alfalfa	4	5,040	Tons	6.2	California
Sugarbeets	4	3,179	Tons	12.0	Minnesota
Beans, Dry, Other	5	45	Cwt.	9.4	California
Cauliflower	5	91	Cwt.	1.4	California
Floriculture	5	145,574	Dollars	4.7	California
Maple Syrup	5	75	Gallons	7.4	Vermont
Mohair	5	74	lbs.	0.5	Texas
Mushrooms	5	15,411	lbs.	2.0	Pennsylvania
Peppers, Bell, Fresh	5	368	Cwt.	2.7	California
Strawberries	5	114	Cwt.	0.8	California
Corn, Sweet, Freshmarket	6	863	Cwt.	5.1	Florida
Milk Sherbet	6	2,147	Gallons	4.2	Iowa

Table XI-1. Michigan's Rank in the Nation's Agriculture: 1993 Continued

Commodity	Rank	Michigan Production	Units	Percent(%) U.S. Production	Leading State
Peaches	6	48,000	Lbs.	3.1	California
Pears	6	6	Tons	0.6	Washington
Poinsettias	6	3,085	Pots	5.5	California
Spearmint	6	90	Lbs.	3.3	Washington
Trout	6	2,986	Fish	4.3	Idaho
Corn, for grain	7	236,500	Bushels	3.7	Illinois
Corn, Sweet	7	44	Cwt.	1.6	Wisconsin
Ice Milk	7	12,168	Gallons	3.7	California
Milk	7	5,435,000	Lbs.	3.6	Wisconsin
Milk Cows	7	339	Head	3.5	Wisconsin
Corn, for silage	8	3,960	Tons	4.8	Wisconsin
Potatoes, all	8	15,280	Cwt.	3.6	Idaho
Beans, snap, fresh market	9	84	Cwt.	2.0	Florida
Butter	9	20,312	Lbs.	1.4	California
Cantaloupes, fresh market	9	99	Cwt.	0.5	California
Hay, all	9	5,790	Tons	3.9	S. Dakota
Oats	9	7,150	Bushels	3.5	N. Dakota
Onions	9	2,201	Cwt.	3.9	California
Potatoes, Fall	9	11,780	Cwt.	3.1	Idaho
Rye	9	420	Bushels	4.1	S. Dakota
Soybeans	9	54,720	Bushels	3.0	Illinois
Honey	10	6,930	Lbs.	3.0	California
Mink	10	56	Pelts	2.2	Utah
Cash Receipts From Marketings	19	3,749,135	Dollars	2.2	California

Source: Michigan Department of Agriculture, Michigan Agricultural Statistics 1993 (Lansing, Michigan: annually).

Table XI-2. Acreage and Production of Major Crops in Michigan: 1993

Crop	Harvested acreage (Thousands of Acreage)	Crop	Production (Thousands of Units)
All Corn	2,150	All Corn	236,500 bushels
Winter Wheat	540	Winter Wheat	22,140 bushels
Oats	130	Oats	7,150 bushels
Tame Hay	1,500	Tame Hay	5,790 tons
Soybeans	1,440	Soybeans	54,720 bushels
Dry Beans	380	Dry Beans	6,080 cwt.
Sugar Beets	187	Sugar Beets	3,179 tons
Potatoes	51	Potatoes	15,280 cwt.
Vegetables	122,800	Vegetables	17,659 cwt.
Fruit	131,500*	Fruit	1,620,000 lbs.

Source: Michigan Department of Agriculture - Michigan Agricultural Statistics 1993 (Lansing, Michigan: annually). *Fruit harvest does not include prunes and plums due to disclosure constraints.

Table XI-3. Major Livestock Inventory and Production of Major Livestock Products in Michigan: 1993

Livestock or Product	Inventory (Thousands)	Livestock or Product	Production (Millions of Units)
Milk Cows	339	Milk	5,435
Beef Cows	126	Cattle & Calves	411,780
Total Cows	1,225	Hogs	458,025
Hogs & Pigs	1,220	Sheep & Lambs	6,100
Sheep & Lambs	94	Eggs	1,401
Chickens (All)	6,915	Chickens	15,510
		Commercial Broilers	2,750

Source: Michigan Department of Agriculture, Michigan Agricultural Statistics 1993 (Lansing, Michigan: annually).

Table XI-4. Gross Farm Income, Production Expenses, and Realized Net Farm Income in Michigan and the United States: 1950-1992

Year	Total (Data in Millions of Dollars)			Per Farm (Data in Actual Dollars)	
	Gross Income	Production Expenses	Net Farm Income	Gross Income	Net Farm Income
Michigan					
1950 - 1954	$833	$208	$325	$5,507	$2,165
1955 - 1959	835	571	244	6,365	1,887
1960 - 1964	919	663	256	8,386	2,333
1965 - 1969	1,033	754	279	11,265	3,030
1970 - 1974	1,411	1,028	383	17,396	4,735
1975 - 1979	2,326	1,892	443	34,094	6,518
1980 - 1984	3,386	2,915	505	52,772	7,333
1985 - 1989	3,319	2,675	645	57,781	11,293
1990	3,725	3,101	625	68,981	11,569
1991	3,756	3,239	517	69,561	9,578
1992	3,787	3,206	581	70,130	10,754
United States					
1950 - 1954	34,996	21,574	13,422	6,739	2,683
1955 - 1959	35,571	24,309	11,262	8,168	2,637
1960 - 1964	41,258	29,931	11,327	11,193	3,126
1965 - 1969	50,791	37,996	12,795	16,073	4,162
1970 - 1974	76,949	56,376	20,574	26,971	7,506
1975 - 1979	121,358	93,918	27,440	45,730	9,571
1980 - 1984	161,218	135,511	25,707	67,407	10,749
1985 - 1989	170,460	132,360	38,100	76,890	17,385
1990	196,000	145,100	51,000	91,586	23,807
1991	189,500	144,900	44,600	90,019	21,191
1992	197,741	149,094	48,647	94,439	23,233

Source: Michigan Department of Agriculture, Michigan Agricultural Statistics 1993 (Lansing, Michigan: annually); and U.S. Department of Agriculture, Economic Indicators of the Farm Sector (Washington, D.C.: 1993).

Table XI-5. Agriculture, Forestry and Fishing Income as a Percentage of Total Personal Income in Michigan, by County: 1992

County	Total Ag./Forest/Fish Income	Percent(%) of County Income	County	Total Ag./Forest/Fish Income	Percent(%) of County Income
Alcona	$295,000	0.2	Lake	$209,000	0.2
Alger	817,000	0.7	Lapeer	16,548,000	1.2
Allegan	44,183,000	2.8	Leelanau	5,761,000	1.7
Alpena	1,611,000	0.3	Lenawee	12,305,000	0.8
Antrim	2,331,000	0.8	Livingston	9,105,000	0.4
Arenac	5,352,000	2.5	Luce	191,000	0.2
Baraga	64,000	0.1	Mackinac	618,000	0.3
Barry	7,414,000	0.9	Macomb	11,896,000	0.1
Bay	11,888,000	0.6	Manistee	8,432,000	2.5
Benzie	8,896,000	4.3	Marquette	1,124,000	0.1
Berrien	30,711,000	1.1	Mason	5,284,000	1.3
Branch	20,777,000	3.3	Mecosta	4,951,000	1.0
Calhoun	13,753,000	0.6	Menominee	5,028,000	1.3
Cass	24,956,000	3.2	Midland	1,292,000	0.1
Charlevoix	1,470,000	0.4	Missaukee	11,863,000	6.9
Cheboygan	714,000	0.2	Monroe	19,399,000	0.8
Chippewa	1,346,000	0.3	Montcalm	19,237,000	2.6
Clare	510,000	0.1	Montmorency	631,000	0.5
Clinton	14,601,000	1.4	Muskegon	9,616,000	0.4
Crawford	0	0.0	Newaygo	6,308,000	1.1
Delta	2,179,000	0.4	Oakland	7,849,000	0.0
Dickinson	2,523,000	0.5	Oceana	17,524,000	5.0
Eaton	9,326,000	0.5	Ogemaw	1,594,000	0.7
Emmet	1,638,000	0.3	Ontonagon	799,000	0.6
Genesee	4,382,000	0.1	Osceola	3,869,000	1.4
Gladwin	1,394,000	0.5	Oscoda	937,000	1.0
Gogebic	N.A.	0.0	Otsego	849,000	0.3
Grand Traverse	2,660,000	0.2	Ottawa	61,613,000	1.6
Gratiot	17,494,000	2.9	Presque Isle	3,195,000	1.6
Hillsdale	13,876,000	2.1	Roscommon	168,000	0.1
Houghton	741,000	0.1	Saginaw	12,303,000	0.3
Huron	24,505,000	4.1	St. Clair	6,682,000	0.2
Ingham	10,915,000	0.2	St. Joseph	9,153,000	0.9
Ionia	13,264,000	1.6	Sanilac	25,317,000	4.1
Iosco	259,000	0.1	Schoolcraft	N.A.	N.A.
Iron	659,000	0.4	Shiawassee	3,480,000	0.3
Isabella	5,427,000	0.7	Tuscola	16,224,000	1.9
Jackson	8,556,000	0.3	Van Buren	31,185,000	2.8
Kalamazoo	24,068,000	0.5	Washtenaw	7,813,000	0.1
Kalkaska	590,000	0.3	Wayne	8,299,000	0.0
Kent	36,757,000	0.4	Wexford	99,000	0.0
Keweenaw	N.A.	0.0	**Michigan**	**741,630,000**	**0.4**

Source: Bureau of Economic Analysis, Regional Economic Measurement Division (Washington, D.C.). N.A. Data not available.

Table XI-6. Cash Receipts from Farming in Michigan, by County: 1992

County	Cash Receipts (Millions of Dollars)			County	Cash Receipts (Millions of Dollars)		
	Crops	Livestock/Prod	Total		Crops	Livestock/Prod	Total
Alcona	$654	$4,003	$4,657	Lake	$202	$1,293	$1,495
Alger	197	1,800	1,997	Lapeer	47,716	29,085	76,801
Allegan	76,250	86,577	162,827	Leelanau	14,896	4,373	19,269
Alpena	4,323	8,076	12,399	Lenawee	69,067	36,919	105,986
Antrim	7,392	6,127	13,519	Livingston	20,228	19,127	39,355
Arenac	16,098	7,641	23,739	Luce	591	313	904
Baraga	96	827	923	Mackinac	292	2,991	3,283
Barry	12,926	26,340	39,266	Macomb	38,555	6,277	44,832
Bay	61,947	4,142	66,089	Manistee	11,186	1,256	12,442
Benzie	3,673	1,071	4,744	Marquette	1,512	1,045	2,557
Berrien	76,122	12,060	88,182	Mason	11,689	8,788	20,477
Branch	45,701	32,400	78,101	Mecosta	6,521	17,238	23,759
Calhoun	35,143	28,108	63,251	Menominee	1,161	19,375	20,536
Cass	29,804	53,118	82,922	Midland	12,892	5,904	18,796
Charlevoix	1,122	3,730	4,852	Missaukee	2,233	26,386	28,619
Cheboygan	1,012	4,525	5,537	Monroe	70,109	14,484	84,593
Chippewa	1,966	6,068	8,034	Montcalm	475,710	25,407	72,978
Clare	934	10,124	11,058	Montmorency	706	2,285	2,991
Clinton	34,053	49,060	83,113	Muskegon	21,363	14,072	35,435
Crawford	0	0	0	Newaygo	16,528	22,428	38,956
Delta	2,665	7,229	9,894	Oakland	31,438	3,471	34,909
Dickinson	3,169	2,693	5,862	Oceana	31,065	13,952	45,017
Eaton	38,043	19,146	57,189	Ogemaw	2,774	12,499	15,273
Emmet	2,091	3,878	5,969	Ontonagon	773	2,078	2,851
Genesee	22,929	15,928	38,857	Osceola	2,057	18,034	20,091
Gladwin	3,023	5,953	8,976	Oscoda	181	2,718	2,899
Gogebic	174	674	848	Otsego	1,463	2,232	3,695
Grand Traverse	12,370	4,859	17,229	Ottawa	129,211	111,792	241,003
Gratiot	58,520	32,925	91,445	Presque Isle	8,612	6,589	15,201
Hillsdale	35,522	37,264	72,786	Roscommon	135	126	261
Houghton	1,005	1,853	2,858	Saginaw	73,274	16,098	89,372
Huron	87,780	113,087	200,867	St. Clair	25,995	19,776	45,771
Ingham	34,932	30,934	65,866	St. Joseph	43,952	23,032	66,984
Ionia	29,393	56,424	85,817	Sanilac	62,208	69,444	131,652
Iosco	1,144	7,385	8,529	Schoolcraft	348	719	1,067
Iron	1,001	1,190	2,191	Shiawassee	28,761	21,996	50,757
Isabella	14,705	34,811	49,516	Tuscola	83,555	25,932	109,487
Jackson	28,186	33,880	62,066	Van Buren	72,533	20,084	92,617
Kalamazoo	60,159	27,776	87,935	Washtenaw	34,173	32,259	66,432
Kalkaska	1,576	1,270	2,846	Wayne	28,221	390	28,611
Kent	74,651	38,781	113,432	Wexford	861	2,776	3,637
Keweenaw	0	0	0	**Michigan**	**1,979,059**	**1,488,780**	**3,467,839**

Source: Bureau of Economic Analysis, Regional Economic Measurement Division (Washington, D.C.)

Table XI-7. Total Employment in Farm Production, Agricultural Services, Forestry, and Fishing in Michigan, by County: 1992

County	Farm	Agricult Serv/Forest/Fish	County	Farm	Agricult Serv/Forest/Fish
Alcona	282	43	Lake	127	30
Alger	88	38	Lapeer	1,864	367
Allegan	2,915	452	Leelanau	631	230
Alpena	548	N.A.	Lenawee	1,939	457
Antrim	383	N.A.	Livingston	1,175	562
Arenac	472	85	Luce	40	N.A.
Baraga	77	67	Mackinac	112	N.A.
Barry	1,221	183	Macomb	1,185	2,682
Bay	1,260	401	Manistee	459	N.A.
Benzie	210	63	Marquette	132	137
Berrien	2,777	657	Mason	596	156
Branch	1,377	N.A.	Mecosta	844	140
Calhoun	1,671	410	Menominee	633	163
Cass	1,215	256	Midland	566	229
Charlevoix	349	119	Missaukee	482	113
Cheboygan	219	86	Monroe	1,853	520
Chippewa	471	N.A.	Montcalm	1,492	356
Clare	392	N.A.	Montmorency	141	33
Clinton	1,974	N.A.	Muskegon	782	N.A.
Crawford	0	N.A.	Newaygo	1,011	N.A.
Delta	378	213	Oakland	869	5,164
Dickinson	196	80	Oceana	1,127	466
Eaton	1,574	341	Ogemaw	384	64
Emmet	244	221	Ontonagon	146	28
Genesee	1,234	1,045	Osceola	695	110
Gladwin	488	52	Oscoda	143	39
Gogebic	77	71	Otsego	177	60
Grand Traverse	646	389	Ottawa	3,311	1,683
Gratiot	1,443	195	Presque Isle	398	119
Hillsdale	1,593	160	Roscommon	34	N.A.
Houghton	199	N.A.	Saginaw	1,858	701
Huron	2,259	255	St. Clair	1,532	458
Ingham	1,430	1,348	St. Joseph	1,216	645
Ionia	1,719	153	Sanilac	2,572	206
Iosco	298	63	Schoolcraft	56	36
Iron	122	35	Shiawassee	1,563	232
Isabella	1,311	122	Tuscola	1,746	211
Jackson	1,624	461	Van Buren	2,414	822
Kalamazoo	1,315	1,057	Washtenaw	1,685	1,253
Kalkaska	110	68	Wayne	578	3,664
Kent	2,392	1,893	Wexford	211	N.A.
Keweenaw	0	0	**Michigan**	**77,332**	**35,495**

Source: Bureau of Economic Analysis, Regional Economic Measurement Division (Washington, D.C.). N.A. Data not available.

Table XI-8. Michigan Tree Volumes, by Species Group: 1993

Species Group	Inventory Volume	Net Annual Growth	Annual Mortality	Annual Harvests
Softwoods	Millions of Cubic Feet			
Jack pine	603	11	13	25
Red pine	1,627	82	1	23
White pine	870	38	2	5
Spruce	859	30	13	6
Balsam fir	823	18	23	7
Hemlock	871	18	4	3
Tamarack	181	5	2	1
Northern white-cedar	1,832	45	5	6
Other softwoods	116	8	0	0
Total Softwoods	**7,781**	**254**	**62**	**75**
Hardwoods				
White oak	821	21	0	6
Red oak	2,004	54	11	27
Hickory	158	4	1	0
Basswood	903	20	5	8
Beech	476	14	1	5
Yellow birch	498	5	7	3
Hard maple	4,034	117	14	40
Soft maple	3,454	115	14	31
Elm	282	17	6	1
Ash	1,152	48	7	6
Cottonwood	132	5	1	1
Balsam poplar	347	8	8	6
Aspen	3,209	112	54	104
Paper birch	845	14	10	13
Black cherry	497	15	2	3
Black walnut	54	2	0	0
Other hardwoods	205	8	1	1
Total Hardwoods	**19,070**	**576**	**142**	**254**
TOTAL ALL SPECIES	**26,851**	**830**	**204**	**329**

Source: Michigan Department of Natural Resources, Forest Management Division (Lansing, Michigan).

Table XI-9. Michigan Timberland Acreage, by Forest Type and Ownership Group: 1993

Forest Type	Acreage By Ownership Class (Data in Thousands)				
	National Forest	State/Other Public	Forest Industry	Other Private	Total
TOTAL	**2,513**	**4,057**	**1,514**	**10,518**	**18,603**
Jack Pine	207	361	7	160	735
Red Pine	313	258	22	291	884
White Pine	42	63	5	123	232
Balsam Fir	91	124	91	256	563
Black Spruce	90	146	67	158	460
White Spruce	40	26	10	72	147
Tamarack	19	46	13	70	149
No.White Cedar	141	381	196	627	1,345
Other Softwoods	0	5	1	103	109
Oak-Hickory	263	450	10	1,242	1,965
Elm-Ash-Soft Maple	107	250	55	1,208	1,620
Maple-Beech-Birch	826	1,098	868	4,355	7,146
Aspen	353	733	145	1,642	2,873
Paper Birch	19	77	25	170	291
Nonstocked	2	39	0	43	85

Source: Michigan Department of Natural Resources, Forest Management Division (Lansing, Michigan).

Table XI-10. Nonfuel Mineral Production in Michigan: 1990-1992

Mineral	1990		1991		1992	
	Quantity	Value (Thousands)	Quantity	Value (Thousands)	Quantity	Value (Thousands)
TOTAL	XX	**$1,440,463**	XX	**$1,503,268**	XX	**$1,586,977**
Cement:						
Masonry (Thousands of Short Tons)	272	23,880	225	22,440	234	20,381
Portland (Do.)	5,906	263,607	4,935	222,075	5,909	262,063
Clays (Metric Tons)	1,201,542	4,094	2,061,861	8,770	1,264,692	4,345
Gemstones	N.A.	11	N.A.	10	N.A.	1
Gypsum-Crude (Thousands of Short Tons)	2,000	11,511	1,721	13,052	1,770	13,889
Iron Ore-Usable (Thousands of Metric	10,034	W	12,741	W	12,881	W
Lime (Thousands of Short Tons)	622	30,898	613	30,959	636	31,253
Peat (Do.)	280	6,264	249	6,442	199	5,894
Sand And Gravel						
Construction (Do.)	51,761	155,559	44,800	132,200	47,994	143,107
Industrial (Do.)	2,310	19,285	2,093	18,464	1,897	19,506
Stone-Crushed (Do.)	43,100	129,000	40,989	129,490	38,600	125,500
Combined value of calcium	XX	796,354	XX	919,366	XX	961,038

Source: Robert H. Wood, II, and Milton A. Gere, Jr., "The Mineral Industry in Michigan" (Washington, D.C.: The Bureau of Mines, 1993).
N.A. not available, W Withheld to avoid disclosing company data, XX Not applicable.

Table XI-11. Number of Mining Establishments, Employment, and Average Weekly Wage in Michigan and the United States: 1970-1994

Year	Michigan			United States		
	Number of Units	Employment (Data in Thousands)	Average Weekly Wage	Number of Units	Employment (Data in Thousands)	Average Weekly Wage
1970	---	12	$---	---	623	$---
1971	---	11	---	---	609	---
1972	---	12	---	---	628	---
1973	---	13	---	---	642	---
1974	---	13	---	---	697	---
1975	---	14	---	---	752	---
1976	374	13	300	26,516	779	301
1977	396	12	316	27,565	813	327
1978	384	13	360	28,892	851	359
1979	380	13	406	30,259	958	396
1980	378	13	437	33,371	1,027	443
1981	392	13	468	38,494	1,139	494
1982	403	10	478	43,825	1,128	531
1983	423	9	503	43,632	952	554
1984	389	10	506	43,465	966	580
1985	479	10	468	42,229	927	602
1986	493	10	523	40,011	777	626
1987	466	10	533	37,472	717	634
1988	488	11	562	36,302	713	660
1989	470	10	597	33,713	692	688
1990	460	9	597	33,568	709	714
1991	456	9	665	33,107	689	747
1992	455	9	672	31,672	631	799
1993	461	9	702	30,750	599	816
1994	466	9	713	N.A.	N.A.	N.A.

Source: U.S. Bureau of Labor Statistics (Washington, D.C.: annually) and Michigan Employment Security Commission, Research and Statistics (Detroit, Michigan: annually). --- No data. N.A. data not available.

Table XI-12. Number of Mining Establishments, Employment, and Average Weekly Wage in Michigan, by County: 1992

County	Units	Employment	A.W.W.	County	Units	Employment	A.W.W.
Alcona	C	C	$C	Lake	0	0	$0.00
Alger	0	0	0.00	Lapeer	6	88	485.99
Allegan	8	84	584.21	Leelanau	0	0	0.00
Alpena	5	192	743.85	Lenawee	C	C	C
Antrim	4	9	436.49	Livingston	6	44	627.73
Arenac	C	C	C	Luce	C	C	C
Baraga	0	0	0.00	Mackinac	C	C	C
Barry	C	C	C	Macomb	6	32	653.87
Bay	5	26	542.86	Manistee	7	124	779.65
Benzie	C	C	C	Marquette	8	2,266	790.40
Berrien	10	117	586.16	Mason	C	C	C
Branch	C	C	C	Mecosta	C	C	C
Calhoun	7	103	566.70	Menominee	0	0	0.00
Cass	0	0	0.00	Midland	C	C	C
Charlevoix	C	C	C	Missaukee	C	C	C
Cheboygan	C	C	C	Monroe	5	80	597.27
Chippewa	C	C	C	Montcalm	3	28	413.24
Clare	C	C	C	Montmorency	C	C	C
Clinton	C	C	C	Muskegon	C	C	C
Crawford	C	C	C	Newaygo	C	C	C
Delta	C	C	C	Oakland	26	363	746.94
Dickinson	0	0	0.00	Oceana	6	79	544.89
Eaton	7	59	538.05	Ogemaw	5	32	376.82
Emmet	0	0	0.00	Ontonagon	C	C	C
Genesee	5	9	732.09	Osceola	C	C	C
Gladwin	C	C	C	Oscoda	0	0	0.00
Gogebic	0	0	0.00	Otsego	20	213	612.62
Grand Traverse	51	375	575.44	Ottawa	6	17	378.33
Gratiot	5	21	590.42	Presque Isle	4	386	606.40
Hillsdale	12	50	391.26	Roscommon	C	C	C
Houghton	C	C	C	Saginaw	6	55	483.61
Huron	0	0	0.00	St. Clair	6	20	636.28
Ingham	15	128	685.67	St. Joseph	C	C	C
Ionia	C	C	C	Sanilac	6	113	401.52
Iosco	4	126	568.55	Schoolcraft	C	C	C
Iron	C	C	C	Shiawassee	3	56	352.74
Isabella	31	658	558.63	Tuscola	6	12	464.36
Jackson	6	143	1,068.71	Van Buren	C	C	C
Kalamazoo	5	60	753.11	Washtenaw	7	46	1,229.26
Kalkaska	26	639	640.40	Wayne	20	275	909.95
Kent	17	123	603.92	Wexford	C	C	C
Keweenaw	0	0	0.00	**Michigan**	**455**	**9,000**	**672.00**

Source: Michigan Employment Security Commission, Research and Statistics (Detroit, Michigan). C Data not released due to confidentiality.

Table XI-13. Number and Type of Petroleum Rigs Operating and Wells Drilled in Michigan and the United States: 1983-1992

Year	Total Rotary Rigs Operating		Number of Wells Drilled							
			Total Drilled		New-Field Wildcat		Exploratory		Developmental	
	Mich	U.S.	Mich	U.S.	Mich	U.S.	Mich	U.S.	Mich	U.S.
1983	29	2,232	791	77,050	304	6,241	306	113,943	471	61,060
1984	34	2,428	1,131	86,412	537	6,619	537	15,048	574	69,113
1985	34	1,980	863	71,108	445	5,630	454	12,026	394	57,402
1986	24	964	542	39,480	236	3,527	260	7,153	265	31,493
1987	22	936	538	36,184	241	3,559	274	6,790	253	28,504
1988	20	936	640	32,479	230	3,271	254	6,241	383	25,285
1989	17	869	850	28,046	150	2,644	185	5,231	663	22,123
1990	13	1,010	992	30,767	123	2,661	137	5,031	852	24,934
1991	8	862	691	29,084	75	2,173	87	4,351	597	23,593
1992	5	721	635	21,301	44	1,141	62	3,262	573	17,176

Source: Baker Hughs Inc., and American Petroleum Institute.

Table XI-14. Number of Producing Wells, by Type, in Michigan and the United States: 1983-1992

Year	Type of Producing Wells					
	Crude Oil		Natural Gas		Stripper Wells	
	Michigan	U.S.	Michigan	U.S.	Michigan	U.S.
1983	4,913	603,290	539	214,354	3,361	416,493
1984	4,881	620,807	749	226,077	3,367	441,501
1985	5,143	646,626	755	245,765	3,500	452,543
1986	4,885	628,690	740	250,510	3,475	458,447
1987	4,996	620,181	670	253,856	3,285	460,429
1988	4,866	623,587	687	256,004	3,015	451,787
1989	5,557	603,356	1,265	261,225	3,040	454,150
1990	4,570	601,520	1,438	268,367	3,110	452,589
1991	4,508	613,810	1,984	272,541	3,967	463,854
1992	4,372	594,189	2,611	280,899	3,283	462,823

Source: World Oil, Energy Information Administration, (Washington, D.C.) Interstate Oil and Gas Commission, and National Stripper Well Association (Wichita Falls, Texas).

Table XI-15. Production from Oil and Gas Wells in Michigan and the United States: 1983-1992

Year	Well Production					
	Crude Oil (Thousands of Barrels)		Natural Gas (Million Cubic Feet)		Stripper (Thousands of Barrels)	
	Michigan	U.S.	Michigan	U.S.	Michigan	U.S.
1983	31,736	3,170,999	138,910	16,884,093	2,820	441,951
1984	30,554	3,249,696	144,537	18,304,339	3,145	462,013
1985	27,300	3,274,553	131,855	17,270,227	3,228	463,459
1986	25,688	3,168,252	127,287	16,858,675	3,272	455,882
1987	25,972	3,047,378	146,996	17,432,900	2,782	449,446
1988	23,250	2,983,172	146,145	17,918,465	2,674	446,837
1989	21,566	2,783,588	155,988	18,095,147	3,891	442,800
1990	19,675	2,684,687	172,151	18,561,596	3,136	386,916
1991	17,518	2,707,039	195,749	18,585,795	4,599	383,197
1992	15,579	2,624,632	189,250	18,616,969	3,403	377,288

Source: World Oil, Energy Information Administration (Washington, D.C.), Interstate Oil and Gas Commission, and National Stripper Well Association (Wichita Falls, Texas).

Table: XI-16. Cost of Drilling and Equipping Oil and Gas Wells in Michigan and the United States: 1991

Category	Michigan	United States
Number of Wells Drilled	650	27,194
Footage Drilled	1,551,377 (feet)	138,688,579 (feet)
Depth Per Well	2,387 (feet)	15,236 (feet)
Total Cost	$100,340,416	$11,461,003,397
Cost Per Well	$154,370	$421,453
Cost Per Foot	$64.68	$82.64

Source: Joint Association Survey on Drilling Costs, and Independent Petroleum Association of America (Washington, D.C.).

Table XI-17. Crude Oil and Natural Gas Revenues in Michigan and the United States: 1983-1992

Year	Crude Oil Revenue (Thousands of Dollars)		Natural Gas Revenue (Thousands of Dollars)	
	Michigan	U.S.	Michigan	U.S.
1983	$918,122	$83,048,464	$497,298	$43,577,527
1984	872,011	84,102,132	543,459	48,490,837
1985	714,168	78,883,982	474,678	43,166,977
1986	375,302	39,634,833	458,233	32,574,365
1987	457,886	46,960,095	476,267	28,972,057
1988	346,890	37,528,304	464,741	30,152,091
1989	389,482	44,119,870	492,922	30,495,203
1990	450,558	53,774,281	497,416	31,766,111
1991	348,258	44,248,412	331,818	28,383,253
1992	298,026	42,043,721	512,868	32,843,953

Source: Energy Information Administration (Washington, D.C.), and Independent Petroleum Association of America (Washington, D.C.).

CHAPTER XII
CONSTRUCTION

The Office of Management and Budget in the Executive Office of the President is responsible for maintaining the Standard Industrial Classification system. The SIC is used in all federal statistical programs and in most other programs where the focus is on economic activity.

According to the latest Standard Industrial Classification Manual,

> construction includes new work, additions, alterations, reconstruction, installations, and repairs.

> Three broad types of construction activity are covered: (1) building construction by general contractors or by operative builders; (2) heavy construction other than building by general contractors and special trade contractors; and (3) construction activity by other special trade contractors. Special trade contractors are primarily engaged in specialized construction activities, such as plumbing, painting, and electrical work, and work for general contractors under subcontract or directly for property owners.

The Bureau of the Census collects building permits data each month from the local units of government that issue such permits. The national data are published in Current Construction Reports. State and local data are released through various agencies in each state. For the residential construction component, the data for each state are published in Construction Reports, Series C-40.

In connection with its quinquennial Economic Censuses, the Census Bureau also conducts a Census of Construction Industries. The 1987 Census of Construction Industries has, for each state, and for Michigan's Ann Arbor, Detroit, and Grand Rapids Metropolitan Statistical Areas, data on establishments classified as being in the construction sector. A similar census is being prepared for 1992 and is not available at this writing.

Current data on employment, hours, and earnings are collected and disseminated by the Michigan Employment Security Commission in Detroit and by the Bureau of Labor Statistics in Washington, D.C.

For definitions on *Units, Establishments, Employment, and Average Weekly Wage* see the notes at the beginning of chapter XVI on Trade or chapter XVIII on Services.

LIST OF TABLES

Table   Page

XII-1. Number of Construction Establishments, Employment, and Average Weekly Wage in Michigan and the United States: 1956-1994 436

XII-2. Number of Residential and Non-residential Units Authorized in Michigan Permit Issuing Places, by Category, Selected Years: 1980, 1985, 1990, 1991, and 1992 437

XII-3. Valuation of Residential and Non-residential Units Authorized in Michigan Permit Issuing Places, by Category, Selected Years: 1980, 1985, 1990, 1991, and 1992 438

LIST OF TABLES

Table   **Page**

XII-4. Number of Construction Establishments, Employment, and Average Weekly
Wage in Michigan, by County: 1992 439

XII-5. Total Construction Wages and Total Construction Wages as a Percentage of Total
Wages in Michigan, by County: 1992 440

XII-6. Residential Construction Authorized by Building Permits and Public Contracts
in Michigan, by County: 1992 441

XII-7. Non-Residential Construction Authorized by Building Permits and Public
Contracts in Michigan, by County: 1992 442

Table XII-1. Number of Construction Establishments, Employment, and Average Weekly Wage in Michigan and the United States: 1956-1994

Year	Michigan			United States		
	Number of Units	Employment (Data in Thousands)	Average Weekly Wage	Number of Units	Employment (Data in Thousands)	Average Weekly Wage
1956	---	116	---	---	3,039	---
1957	---	109	---	---	2,962	---
1958	---	95	---	---	2,817	---
1959	---	98	---	---	3,004	---
1960	---	99	---	---	2,926	---
1961	---	93	---	---	2,859	---
1962	---	89	---	---	2,948	---
1963	---	95	---	---	3,010	---
1964	---	101	---	---	3,097	---
1965	---	113	---	---	3,232	---
1966	---	117	---	---	3,317	---
1967	---	122	---	---	3,248	---
1968	---	109	---	---	3,350	---
1969	---	131	---	---	3,575	---
1970	---	119	---	---	3,588	---
1971	---	121	---	---	3,704	---
1972	---	128	---	---	3,889	---
1973	---	131	---	---	4,097	---
1974	---	126	---	---	4,020	---
1975	---	106	---	---	3,525	---
1976	13,804	110	289	461,157	3,576	256
1977	14,334	123	309	482,616	3,851	264
1978	15,596	139	335	516,260	4,229	279
1979	15,826	140	367	535,508	4,463	304
1980	14,481	117	389	529,905	4,346	335
1981	13,347	107	415	512,506	4,188	366
1982	11,997	90	435	494,234	3,904	390
1983	12,003	87	425	498,186	3,946	393
1984	11,312	93	435	520,373	4,380	399
1985	15,186	108	437	547,666	4,668	411
1986	15,803	115	481	566,767	4,810	427
1987	16,784	123	500	600,540	4,958	445
1988	18,034	132	534	623,579	5,098	470
1989	19,604	140	544	628,455	5,171	485
1990	20,727	142	553	640,663	5,120	503
1991	20,769	129	552	642,972	4,650	514
1992	20,925	128	562	632,638	4,471	527
1993	21,749	133	574	636,516	4,574	530
1994	22,531	143	590	N.A.	N.A.	N.A.

Source: U.S. Bureau of Labor Statistics (Washington, D.C.) and Michigan Employment Security Commission, Research and Statistics (Detroit, Michigan). --- No data. N.A. data not available.

Table XII-2. Number of Residential and Non-residential Units Units Authorized in Michigan Permit Issuing Places, by Category, Selected Years: 1980, 1985, 1990, 1991, and 1992

Category	Number of Units				
	1980	1985	1990	1991	1992
TOTAL RESIDENTIAL	**28,976**	**37,675**	**38,945**	**34,070**	**37,296**
One-Family Houses	17,870	21,854	28,372	28,416	31,735
Two-Family Buildings	780	422	640	492	510
Three & Four Family Bldg.	999	1,655	924	570	489
Five or More Family Bldg.	9,327	13,744	9,009	4,592	4,562
TOTAL NON-RESIDENTIAL	**N.A.**	**N.A.**	**15,401**	**14,489**	**14,877**
Mobil Homes (House Trailers)	4,768	6,177	N.A.	N.A.	N.A.
Hotel/Motels/Tourist Courts/Cabins	1,629	5,149	1,610	823	716
Other Non-Housekeeping Shelters	123	157	162	136	104
Amusement & Recreational Buildings	125	165	164	172	151
Churches & Religious Buildings	142	117	103	137	115
Industrial Buildings	789	1,149	667	497	451
Public Parking Garages	320	27	24	22	25
Service Stations & Repair Garages	118	164	17,152	17,254	18,319
Hospitals & Institutional Buildings	42	47	175	163	128
Office/Bank/Professional Buildings	542	627	46	39	53
Public Works & Utility Buildings	83	126	617	472	409
Schools & Educational Buildings	42	33	118	109	114
Stores & Mercantile Buildings	934	1,211	55	32	36
Other Non-residential Buildings	5,734	7,048	1,025	851	874
Structures Other Than Buildings	5,149	5,308	9,493	9,109	9,654
ADDITIONS/ALTERATIONS/CONVERSIONS					
Housekeeping Residential Buildings	50,793	48,387	2,914	2,886	2,867
All Other Buildings & Structures	12,714	15,088	57,432	58,558	56,382
Residential Garages & Carports	13,241	16,665	12,262	12,096	11,548

Source: U.S. Bureau of the Census (Washington, D.C.). N.A. Data not available.

Table XII-3. Valuation of Residential and Non-residential Units Authorized in Michigan Permit Issuing Places, by Category, Selected Years: 1980, 1985, 1990, 1991, and 1992

Category	Valuation of Units (Data in Millions of Dollars)				
	1980	1985	1990	1991	1992
TOTAL RESIDENTIAL	**$1,164.1**	**$1,833.7**	**$2,751.7**	**$2,614.8**	**$3,022.1**
One-Family Houses	873.8	1,351.3	2,340.7	2,374.9	2,809.1
Two-Family Buildings	25.1	18.3	33.3	26.2	27.5
Three & Four Family Bldg.	31.1	67.6	51.8	34.9	29.9
Five or More Family Bldg.	281.0	396.5	325.9	178.8	155.6
TOTAL NON-RESIDENTIAL	N.A.	N.A.	1,475.3	1,082.1	1,002.4
Mobil Homes (House Trailers)	29.8	73.9	N.A.	N.A.	N.A.
Hotel/Motels/Tourist Courts/Cabins	51.8	130.9	47.3	19.8	23.2
Other Non-Housekeeping Shelters	0.9	0.9	4.1	2.6	2.3
Amusement & Recreational Buildings	11.9	17.8	26.9	40.0	20.1
Churches & Religious Buildings	30.1	26.0	30.6	44.4	41.5
Industrial Buildings	322.1	555.5	302.0	232.7	184.5
Public Parking Garages	15.3	40.0	64.9	20.2	10.9
Service Stations & Repair Garages	4.8	13.2	26.6	22.2	15.1
Hospitals & Institutional Buildings	51.9	69.9	35.4	29.3	80.3
Office/Bank/Professional Buildings	260.8	408.0	429.9	255.7	161.9
Public Works & Utility Buildings	74.0	9.5	19.1	13.4	14.2
Schools & Educational Buildings	37.9	12.0	37.5	14.4	12.8
Stores & Mercantile Buildings	158.1	250.1	368.5	289.0	332.5
Other Non-residential Buildings	51.3	62.2	105.8	99.1	109.5
Structures Other Than Buildings	23.9	43.5	28.2	21.5	19.2
ADDITIONS/ALTERATIONS/CONVERSIONS					
Housekeeping Residential Buildings	240.9	296.2	439.9	460.5	485.5
All Other Buildings & Structures	537.3	702.9	835.0	809.2	850.2
Residential Garages & Carports	53.0	83.6	102.7	110.5	119.7

Source: U.S. Bureau of the Census (Washington, D.C.). N.A. Data not available.

Table XII-4. Number of Construction Establishments, Employment, and Average Weekly Wage in Michigan, by County: 1992

County	Units	Employment	A.W.W.	County	Units	Employment	A.W.W.
Alcona	31	67	$279.42	Lake	15	24	$324.62
Alger	29	78	361.83	Lapeer	172	578	414.90
Allegan	184	774	471.50	Leelanau	91	414	350.79
Alpena	105	516	467.90	Lenawee	183	739	444.22
Antrim	76	227	336.15	Livingston	438	1,793	509.35
Arenac	42	144	284.77	Luce	13	88	206.50
Baraga	17	62	368.53	Mackinac	64	209	321.60
Barry	101	496	400.02	Macomb	2,032	11,160	583.20
Bay	231	1,383	424.24	Manistee	80	244	366.14
Benzie	58	222	492.21	Marquette	182	1,198	462.01
Berrien	332	1,733	436.99	Mason	69	320	433.46
Branch	63	326	430.32	Mecosta	72	208	284.05
Calhoun	194	1,910	586.09	Menominee	44	182	414.00
Cass	68	230	376.52	Midland	210	2,645	476.43
Charlevoix	125	442	383.39	Missaukee	31	165	508.59
Cheboygan	146	458	421.67	Monroe	271	1,018	508.73
Chippewa	110	408	391.84	Montcalm	100	520	446.81
Clare	76	251	317.39	Montmorency	55	181	319.99
Clinton	121	499	433.90	Muskegon	296	2,087	490.45
Crawford	36	112	297.21	Newaygo	60	186	350.10
Delta	98	477	480.46	Oakland	3,211	21,318	678.14
Dickinson	96	1,083	543.96	Oceana	71	310	366.40
Eaton	155	989	490.57	Ogemaw	57	158	294.73
Emmet	180	859	409.22	Ontonagon	26	102	338.95
Genesee	730	4,814	529.14	Osceola	46	325	671.67
Gladwin	44	228	387.16	Oscoda	19	78	345.24
Gogebic	34	131	354.79	Otsego	92	555	515.93
Grand Traverse	327	2,414	470.96	Ottawa	632	3,664	513.91
Gratiot	79	287	368.20	Presque Isle	56	125	292.04
Hillsdale	81	308	375.30	Roscommon	91	261	347.08
Houghton	85	542	426.81	Saginaw	421	3,038	510.03
Huron	108	359	329.22	St. Clair	349	1,772	541.10
Ingham	533	4,299	571.65	St. Joseph	95	517	499.12
Ionia	94	392	400.17	Sanilac	118	322	344.83
Iosco	95	279	348.74	Schoolcraft	19	62	331.36
Iron	39	131	420.25	Shiawassee	127	566	405.91
Isabella	117	677	591.09	Tuscola	125	446	317.28
Jackson	270	1,527	515.73	Van Buren	130	588	528.15
Kalamazoo	480	3,779	547.35	Washtenaw	588	3,314	600.76
Kalkaska	43	214	535.69	Wayne	2,566	17,689	637.13
Kent	1,226	11,122	548.70	Wexford	72	231	341.82
Keweenaw	2	6	197.79	**Michigan**	**21,749**	**132,500**	**574.00**

Source: Michigan Employment Security Commission, Research and Statistics (Detroit, Michigan).

Table XII-5. Total Construction Wages and Total Construction Wages as a Percentage of Total Wages in Michigan, by County: 1992

County	Total Construction Wages	Percent(%) of County Wages	County	Total Construction Wages	Percent(%) of County Wages
Alcona	$250,356	6.9	Lake	$100,373	3.2
Alger	386,643	4.0	Lapeer	3,124,603	5.0
Allegan	4,835,822	3.3	Leelanau	1,888,459	16.3
Alpena	3,169,799	6.9	Lenawee	4,297,877	3.1
Antrim	997,957	6.8	Livingston	11,977,732	8.9
Arenac	543,268	5.1	Luce	235,699	4.6
Baraga	300,374	4.2	Mackinac	905,993	8.3
Barry	2,603,857	6.8	Macomb	85,286,750	4.5
Bay	7,685,600	4.4	Manistee	1,169,571	4.4
Benzie	1,459,993	16.0	Marquette	7,292,220	7.3
Berrien	9,910,425	3.1	Mason	1,825,911	5.0
Branch	1,827,414	4.6	Mecosta	782,664	3.3
Calhoun	14,547,033	4.6	Menominee	977,101	3.0
Cass	1,133,588	3.1	Midland	16,418,475	6.7
Charlevoix	2,254,875	6.1	Missaukee	1,096,075	17.1
Cheboygan	2,568,367	12.6	Monroe	6,766,412	3.4
Chippewa	2,104,826	7.6	Montcalm	3,050,453	4.6
Clare	1,048,533	5.0	Montmorency	793,120	17.9
Clinton	2,834,141	7.2	Muskegon	13,361,298	4.9
Crawford	442,233	3.5	Newaygo	852,353	2.4
Delta	3,024,973	5.3	Oakland	188,536,385	4.5
Dickinson	7,720,068	15.2	Oceana	1,492,411	9.9
Eaton	6,342,867	7.1	Ogemaw	628,929	4.4
Emmet	4,625,286	8.4	Ontonagon	448,549	2.9
Genesee	33,219,489	3.3	Osceola	2,747,305	10.3
Gladwin	1,163,620	8.4	Oscoda	377,366	7.6
Gogebic	605,749	3.8	Otsego	3,744,660	11.0
Grand Traverse	14,862,026	9.0	Ottawa	24,586,846	5.5
Gratiot	1,383,764	2.7	Presque Isle	487,523	4.4
Hillsdale	1,499,427	2.6	Roscommon	1,205,070	9.5
Houghton	3,043,167	10.2	Saginaw	20,240,707	4.0
Huron	1,546,682	3.7	St. Clair	12,780,240	6.5
Ingham	32,004,886	4.3	St. Joseph	3,416,993	3.4
Ionia	2,064,530	4.5	Sanilac	1,461,596	4.0
Iosco	1,301,239	5.2	Schoolcraft	270,093	4.0
Iron	716,415	8.4	Shiawassee	2,995,495	4.7
Isabella	5,366,035	8.3	Tuscola	1,857,417	4.3
Jackson	10,330,615	4.1	Van Buren	4,072,943	5.6
Kalamazoo	26,915,928	4.3	Washtenaw	25,882,055	3.1
Kalkaska	1,474,346	7.4	Wayne	146,927,305	2.7
Kent	79,652,779	5.1	Wexford	1,038,984	2.1
Keweenaw	20,568	3.2	**Michigan**	**907,915,712**	**4.2**

Source: Michigan Employment Security Commission, Research and Statistics (Detroit, Michigan).

Table XII-6. Residential Construction Authorized by Building Permits and Public Contracts in Michigan, by County: 1992

County	Units	Cost	County	Units	Cost
Alcona	81	$4,613,096	Lake	90	$5,285,932
Alger	0	0	Lapeer	493	36,051,357
Allegan	569	44,462,013	Leelanau	255	26,343,116
Alpena	122	7,895,313	Lenawee	305	18,051,461
Antrim	157	12,231,800	Livingston	1,311	110,363,696
Arenac	50	2,746,021	Luce	34	1,966,800
Baraga	16	363,900	Mackinac	103	5,693,865
Barry	228	17,132,805	Macomb	3,356	283,794,706
Bay	242	19,520,053	Manistee	135	9,356,097
Benzie	171	12,021,789	Marquette	332	17,695,165
Berrien	496	51,132,402	Mason	178	10,440,030
Branch	113	6,571,074	Mecosta	215	13,616,352
Calhoun	422	20,911,182	Menominee	85	3,297,000
Cass	193	10,131,263	Midland	395	41,379,112
Charlevoix	205	16,814,046	Missaukee	53	3,467,816
Cheboygan	161	11,085,821	Monroe	760	55,246,888
Chippewa	167	8,895,650	Montcalm	243	13,369,320
Clare	152	7,497,159	Montmorency	83	2,905,000
Clinton	327	27,493,569	Muskegon	541	45,037,805
Crawford	108	6,132,700	Newaygo	178	9,195,086
Delta	194	8,688,594	Oakland	5,538	569,642,375
Dickinson	128	7,304,040	Oceana	91	6,814,000
Eaton	528	37,160,895	Ogemaw	105	4,061,163
Emmet	217	19,245,158	Ontonagon	39	1,292,425
Genesee	1,135	94,726,369	Osceola	98	4,109,519
Gladwin	224	15,278,447	Oscoda	69	4,763,139
Gogebic	75	2,570,029	Otsego	181	12,607,511
Grand Traverse	459	37,006,437	Ottawa	1,587	123,693,036
Gratiot	60	5,089,627	Presque Isle	94	4,719,681
Hillsdale	299	12,873,097	Roscommon	289	14,659,234
Houghton	67	4,489,062	Saginaw	553	46,058,224
Huron	130	7,588,318	St. Clair	888	65,941,069
Ingham	725	65,373,780	St. Joseph	152	11,965,410
Ionia	205	12,443,950	Sanilac	221	14,354,222
Iosco	127	6,846,660	Schoolcraft	51	2,083,396
Iron	75	3,446,700	Shiawassee	234	19,530,865
Isabella	163	11,801,298	Tuscola	178	10,790,246
Jackson	585	41,672,550	Van Buren	316	21,841,407
Kalamazoo	810	86,404,015	Washtenaw	1,156	130,912,430
Kalkaska	134	5,537,301	Wayne	3,184	237,957,054
Kent	2,581	216,575,548	Wexford	133	7,073,549
Keweenaw	30	1,395,004			

Source: U.S. Bureau of the Census (Washington, D.C.).

Table XII-7. Non-Residential Construction Authorized by Building Permits and Public Contracts in Michigan, by County: 1992

County	Units	Cost	County	Units	Cost
Alcona	214	$1,162,759	Lake	105	$997,026
Alger	0	0	Lapeer	511	6,550,095
Allegan	280	12,322,860	Leelanau	18	3,229,355
Alpena	129	3,341,555	Lenawee	167	9,679,251
Antrim	25	613,172	Livingston	152	17,653,261
Arenac	36	265,456	Luce	46	791,843
Baraga	9	38,750	Mackinac	39	991,189
Barry	185	2,945,405	Macomb	938	81,254,844
Bay	209	6,980,222	Manistee	16	1,128,213
Benzie	16	1,152,000	Marquette	105	5,475,708
Berrien	409	17,256,491	Mason	103	1,418,525
Branch	79	2,096,043	Mecosta	333	2,787,625
Calhoun	237	11,762,817	Menominee	31	1,072,310
Cass	158	2,286,007	Midland	208	10,964,648
Charlevoix	103	6,070,479	Missaukee	11	1,148,596
Cheboygan	117	2,274,889	Monroe	330	14,979,496
Chippewa	44	7,597,697	Montcalm	309	9,762,127
Clare	54	772,738	Montmorency	0	0
Clinton	233	11,862,214	Muskegon	270	14,391,360
Crawford	47	1,937,135	Newaygo	59	1,265,447
Delta	30	2,311,000	Oakland	1185	81,632,040
Dickinson	46	1,301,493	Oceana	98	3,351,900
Eaton	180	15,711,022	Ogemaw	7	803,000
Emmet	23	1,247,720	Ontonagon	16	338,159
Genesee	511	45,645,474	Osceola	50	979,165
Gladwin	16	1,116,289	Oscoda	53	673,418
Gogebic	55	927,747	Otsego	42	4,642,220
Grand Traverse	114	13,235,904	Ottawa	481	38,765,586
Gratiot	215	6,592,776	Presque Isle	89	1,182,371
Hillsdale	88	3,430,854	Roscommon	122	4,718,972
Houghton	40	4,010,026	Saginaw	244	24,346,676
Huron	137	7,431,460	St. Clair	264	21,185,127
Ingham	249	30,518,407	St. Joseph	205	7,728,738
Ionia	114	3,301,579	Sanilac	37	1,562,280
Iosco	113	2,016,421	Schoolcraft	41	446,052
Iron	40	733,600	Shiawassee	221	2,935,656
Isabella	65	4,144,137	Tuscola	220	5,630,925
Jackson	368	9,577,879	Van Buren	136	8,735,965
Kalamazoo	300	48,288,975	Washtenaw	291	15,485,965
Kalkaska	22	3,395,012	Wayne	1103	152,522,855
Kent	683	124,575,543	Wexford	195	6,876,616
Keweenaw	10	31,450			

Source: U.S. Bureau of the Census (Washington, D.C.).

CHAPTER XIII
MANUFACTURING

The Office of Management and Budget in the Executive Office of the President is responsible for maintaining the Standard Industrial Classification System. The SIC is used in all federal statistical programs and in most other programs where the focus is on economic activity.

According to the latest Standard Industrial Classification Manual

> manufacturing includes establishments engaged in the mechanical or chemical transformation of materials or substances into new products. These establishments are usually described as plants, factories, or mills and characteristically use power driven machines and materials handling equipment. Establishments engaged in assembling component parts of manufactured products are also considered manufacturing if the new product is neither a structure nor a fixed improvement. Also included is the blending of materials, such as lubricating oils, plastic resins, or liquors.

Although manufacturing includes the production of components for and the assembly of motor vehicles, a separate chapter, XIV is devoted to motor vehicles because of the importance of these activities in this state.

The Bureau of the Census conducts economic censuses for years ending in 2 and 7. The 1987 Census of Manufactures is the most recent available at this writing. The Michigan section has summary data for counties and places with 450 or more manufacturing employees and more detailed information for the state, large counties and places, and metropolitan statistical areas.

An Annual Survey of Manufactures (ASM) is taken for off-census years. The most recent of these is the 1991 Annual Survey of Manufactures. The ASM is a sample of approximately 55,000 establishments from a universe of about 200,000 establishments, nationwide. Inasmuch as the ASM is based on a sample, the amount of detail provided is far less than that from the Census.

Another Census Bureau program, Current Industrial Reports, provides current information for certain industries considered to be important. Some of these reports, the ones pertaining to steel production, for example, give data for individual states.

Manufacturers have formed a number of professional associations. One such, the American Iron and Steel Institute, monitors monthly steel production in the U.S. and in various centers, including Detroit. Its Annual Statistics Report, and Iron and Steel Works Directory for the United States and Canada provide information about the steel industry.

Together the Bureau of Economic Analysis and the Bureau of the Census publish a document entitled Foreign Direct Investment in the United States.

Current data on employment, hours, and earnings are collected and disseminated by the Michigan Employment Security Commission in Detroit and the Bureau of Labor Statistics in Washington, D.C.

For definitions on *Units, Establishments, Employment, and Average Weekly Wage* see the notes at the beginning of chapter XVI on Trade or chapter XVIII on Services.

LIST OF TABLES

Table   **Page**

XIII-1.   Manufacturing Employment and Number of Units in Michigan and the United
          States: 1956-1994 445

XIII-2.   Durable Goods Manufacturing Employment in Michigan, by Major Group:
          1970-1994 446

XIII-3.   Nondurable Goods Manufacturing Employment in Michigan, by Major Group:
          1970-1994 447

XIII-4.   Average Weekly Earnings in Manufacturing, by Industry Group, Michigan and
          the United States: 1970, 1980, 1985, 1990, and 1994 448

XIII-5.   Annual Payroll and Value Added in Michigan and United States Manufacturing:
          1955-1991 449

XIII-6.   Annual Hours and Earnings of Manufacturing Production Workers in Michigan:
          1956-1993 450

XIII-7.   Manufacturers' Expenditures for New Plant and Equipment in Michigan and the
          United States: 1955-1991 451

XIII-8.   Raw Steel Production in Michigan and the United States: 1951-1992 452

XIII-9.   Number of Manufacturing Establishments, Employment, and Average Weekly
          Wage in Michigan, by County: 1992 453

XIII-10. Total Wages in Manufacturing and Total Manufacturing Wages as a Percent
          of Total Wages in Michigan, by County: 1992 454

XIII-11. Value Added, Value of Shipments, and New Capital Expenditures by the
          Manufacturing Sector in Michigan, by County: 1987 455

XIII-12. Employment Levels in Foreign-Owned Manufacturing Establishments and as
          a Percentage of Total Manufacturing Employment in Michigan, by Industry
          Group: 1990 457

XIII-13. Employment in and Number of Foreign-Owned Manufacturing Establishments
          in Michigan, by Industry Group and Employment Size Class: 1990 458

Table XIII-1. Manufacturing Employment and Number of Units in Michigan and the United States: 1956-1994

Year	Michigan		United States	
	Number of Units	Employment (Data In Thousands)	Number of Units	Employment (Data in Thousands)
1956	---	1,109	---	17,243
1957	---	1,084	---	17,174
1958	---	895	---	15,945
1959	---	961	---	16,675
1960	---	976	---	16,796
1961	---	887	---	16,326
1962	---	952	---	16,853
1963	---	990	---	16,995
1964	---	1,032	---	17,274
1965	---	1,112	---	18,062
1966	---	1,180	---	19,214
1967	---	1,149	---	19,447
1968	---	1,173	---	19,781
1969	---	1,204	---	20,167
1970	---	1,081	---	19,367
1971	---	1,059	---	18,623
1972	---	1,097	---	19,151
1973	---	1,179	---	20,154
1974	---	1,114	---	20,077
1975	---	984	---	18,323
1976	12,561	1,062	314,544	18,997
1977	12,835	1,128	319,984	19,682
1978	12,948	1,180	327,441	20,505
1979	13,229	1,160	332,032	21,040
1980	13,051	999	337,237	20,285
1981	12,822	979	339,183	20,170
1982	12,904	877	342,573	18,780
1983	12,900	881	343,785	18,432
1984	12,480	963	345,872	19,372
1985	14,141	1,002	352,371	19,248
1986	14,459	1,000	355,045	18,947
1987	14,441	973	364,464	18,999
1988	15,009	955	371,776	19,314
1989	15,574	971	369,219	19,391
1990	16,041	944	378,536	19,076
1991	16,154	899	389,388	18,406
1992	16,087	901	385,766	18,040
1993	16,322	904	390,578	17,802
1994	16,653	952	N.A.	N.A.

Source: U.S. Bureau of Labor Statistics (Washington, D.C.: annually) and Michigan Employment Security Commission, Research and Statistics (Detroit, Michigan). --- No data. N.A. data not available.

Table XIII-2. Durable Goods Manufacturing Employment in Michigan, by Major Group: 1970-1994
(Data in Thousands)

Year	Total Manufacturing	Durable Goods	Lumber and Wood	Furniture and Fixtures	Stone/Clay /Glass	Primary Metals	Fabricated Metals	Machinery, except Electrical	Electrical and Electronic	Transportation	Instruments and Related	Misc. Manufact.
1970	1,081	863	14	21	21	89	142	164	43	351	9	9
1971	1,059	847	14	20	21	87	141	137	41	368	9	9
1972	1,097	880	15	21	23	88	147	140	42	384	10	10
1973	1,179	953	16	23	24	96	157	156	47	416	10	10
1974	1,114	897	16	22	23	94	142	158	45	378	11	10
1975	984	778	13	19	20	80	120	137	38	333	11	9
1976	1,062	845	14	20	20	86	137	138	40	371	11	9
1977	1,128	906	14	20	22	92	146	151	41	400	11	10
1978	1,180	953	14	22	22	92	156	160	43	424	12	9
1979	1,160	935	14	23	22	88	151	167	42	406	14	9
1980	999	795	12	23	19	67	118	158	35	340	14	9
1981	979	778	11	23	18	65	118	155	33	335	14	8
1982	877	685	10	22	15	51	102	132	30	303	13	7
1983	881	686	11	22	16	50	103	117	31	318	13	7
1984	963	755	12	25	17	54	119	129	34	344	14	8
1985	1,002	787	13	27	17	52	125	134	36	361	15	7
1986	1,000	783	13	28	18	50	123	133	38	360	15	7
1987	973	752	14	31	18	49	119	123	37	338	15	7
1988	955	727	16	34	17	47	120	122	34	314	17	7
1989	971	734	16	35	17	45	126	129	35	307	18	7
1990	944	710	15	36	16	42	121	127	32	295	18	8
1991	897	670	14	34	17	38	112	120	30	282	18	7
1992	901	671	15	34	17	37	114	115	30	286	17	7
1993	902	668	15	34	16	36	116	117	30	279	17	8
1994	949	707	17	37	17	37	126	126	32	289	18	8

Source: Michigan Employment Security Commission, Research and Statistics (Detroit, Michigan: monthly/annually).

446

Table XIII-3. Nondurable Goods Manufacturing Employment in Michigan, by Major Group: 1970-1994
(Data in Thousands)

Year	Total Manufacturing	Nondurable Goods	Food and Kindred	Textile Mill Products	Apparel and Other Textile	Paper and Allied Product	Printing and Publishing	Chemicals and Related	Petroleum and Coal	Rubber and Plastic	Leather Product
1970	1,081	218	55	4	19	29	35	45	3	26	4
1971	1,059	212	53	3	20	27	34	42	3	25	4
1972	1,097	218	52	3	22	27	37	42	3	29	4
1973	1,179	226	52	3	24	27	37	43	2	33	4
1974	1,114	217	52	3	22	26	36	42	3	31	4
1975	984	206	52	3	20	24	35	44	2	25	3
1976	1,062	216	51	3	23	25	34	46	3	29	4
1977	1,128	223	52	3	25	24	32	47	3	33	4
1978	1,180	227	52	2	26	24	34	46	3	37	4
1979	1,160	225	52	2	24	24	34	45	3	38	4
1980	999	204	49	2	18	22	33	44	3	30	3
1981	979	201	47	2	18	22	33	43	3	30	4
1982	877	192	46	1	16	20	33	42	3	28	3
1983	881	195	45	1	17	20	34	40	3	31	3
1984	963	208	46	1	19	21	37	41	2	37	3
1985	1,002	215	46	1	21	21	38	41	3	42	3
1986	1,000	217	46	1	22	21	39	40	2	44	2
1987	973	221	45	1	21	21	40	41	2	47	2
1988	955	229	45	1	21	21	43	43	2	51	2
1989	971	237	45	2	21	21	44	44	2	55	3
1990	944	234	45	1	20	21	45	45	2	53	3
1991	897	227	44	1	16	21	45	45	2	50	3
1992	901	230	44	2	17	21	45	44	2	52	3
1993	902	233	44	2	17	21	45	45	2	55	3
1994	949	243	44	2	19	21	45	45	2	61	3

Source: Michigan Employment Security Commission, Research and Statistics (Detroit, Michigan: monthly/annually).

Table XIII-4. Average Weekly Earnings in Manufacturing, by Industry Group, Michigan and the United States: 1970, 1980, 1985, 1990, and 1994

Industry	Michigan					United States				
	1970	1980	1985	1990	1994	1970	1980	1985	1990	1994
TOTAL MANUFACTURING	$168.33	$381.87	$544.78	$579.35	$724.24	$133.33	$288.62	$350.87	$331.98	$506.52
Durable Goods	171.45	396.02	574.2	612.36	785.13	143.07	310.78	415.71	468.76	543.54
Lumber & Wood Products	105.61	224.36	299.25	368.14	403.52	117.34	253.32	329.18	365.02	405.41
Furniture & Fixtures	135.32	268.15	396.07	420.25	456.23	108.58	209.17	282.50	333.13	386.22
Stone/Clay/Glass/Concrete	161.3	343.68	507.04	555.27	670.20	140.22	305.74	412.30	467.04	527.22
Primary Metals	170.55	418.3	511.89	633.63	728.84	158.77	391.78	484.31	561.68	640.10
Fabricated Metals	174.07	360.45	538.82	574.03	707.62	143.70	300.91	401.02	447.28	511.80
Industrial/Commercial/Computer Equipment	178.31	403.45	545.15	584.44	709.90	154.83	328.00	427.45	493.16	567.23
Electronic/Electrical Equipment ex computer	150.27	320.83	434.36	474.55	596.30	130.75	276.34	0.00	420.24	485.72
Transportation Equipment	177.84	436.14	663.49	711.78	990.46	163.62	379.34	541.45	591.36	730.95
Motor Vehicles & Equipment	179.01	438.23	673.95	725.16	1,002.51	170.07	394.00	582.47	617.34	780.62
Instruments & Related Products	135.99	265.83	340	404.07	488.37	132.93	275.31	0.00	464.02	520.00
Miscellaneous Manufacturing	N.A.	N.A.	N.A.	407.42	439.96	109.52	211.30	287.62	340.10	386.00
Non Durables	152.41	321.88	433.47	473.47	540.60	120.43	255.45	345.31	404.80	460.13
Food & Kindred Products	151.21	331.75	420.25	460.49	550.39	127.98	271.95	342.80	392.50	440.67
Tobacco Products	N.A.	N.A.	N.A.	N.A.	N.A.	110.00	294.89	444.91	636.22	738.84
Textile Mill Products*	138.49	340.2	569.38	575.5	632.90	97.76	203.31	265.99	320.00	380.72
Apparel and Other Textile Products*	N.A.	N.A.	N.A.	N.A.	N.A.	84.37	161.42	208.57	239.15	275.25
Paper & Allied Products	153.52	350.75	513.35	575.5	632.90	144.07	331.25	466.77	533.02	604.06
Printing & Publishing	163.54	298.57	360.96	392.46	467.06	147.78	279.36	367.04	426.00	468.60
Chemicals & Allied Products	166.92	362.11	514.11	614.88	707.63	153.50	344.45	484.36	576.80	655.78
Petroleum Products	N.A.	N.A.	N.A.	663.28	712.05	183.10	422.10	604.58	724.30	850.84
Rubber & Plastics	N.A.	N.A.	N.A.	364.73	408.51	129.40	263.42	353.46	401.14	451.54
Leather & Leather Products	N.A.	N.A.	N.A.	353.93	507.13	92.63	168.09	216.88	258.43	306.85

Source: U.S. Bureau of Labor Statistics (Washington, D.C.) and Michigan Employment Security Commission, Research and Statistics (Detroit, Michigan). *Michigan data combined for these two industries. N.A. Data not available.

Table XIII-5. Annual Payroll and Value Added in Michigan and United States Manufacturing: 1955-1991

Year	Yearly Payroll (In Millions)		Value Added by Manufacture (In Millions)	
	Michigan	United States	Michigan	United States
1955	$6,084	$69,097	$10,691	$135,023
1956	5,828	74,015	10,202	144,909
1957	5,836	76,315	10,375	147,838
1958	5,161	73,875	8,364	141,541
1959	5,855	81,204	10,535	161,536
1960	6,107	83,673	10,858	163,999
1961	5,678	83,677	10,192	164,281
1962	6,281	89,819	11,969	179,071
1963	6,951	99,899	13,090	192,083
1964	7,605	106,058	14,359	206,194
1965	8,586	113,972	16,886	226,940
1966	9,221	125,350	17,629	250,880
1967	9,357	132,208	17,242	261,984
1968	10,350	141,823	19,266	285,059
1969	11,042	152,765	20,523	304,441
1970	10,233	153,080	17,959	300,228
1971	11,129	156,203	20,271	314,138
1972	12,741	174,206	23,376	353,984
1973	14,768	193,325	27,170	405,584
1974	14,808	208,367	26,333	452,478
1975	14,100	209,519	25,084	442,485
1976	17,322	233,389	32,390	511,471
1977	20,054	264,013	37,566	585,166
1978	22,893	299,143	41,805	657,246
1979	N.A.	N.A.	N.A.	N.A.
1980	N.A.	N.A.	N.A.	N.A.
1981	N.A.	N.A.	N.A.	N.A.
1982	22,223	379,627	39,118	824,118
1983	23,950	394,829	48,206	882,139
1984	27,403	428,365	53,069	982,560
1985	29,051	442,954	53,662	999,137
1986	29,582	450,806	56,879	1,035,821
1987	30,628	475,651	60,259	1,165,747
1988	31,314	502,785	63,873	1,264,407
1989	31,437	519,292	66,131	1,308,103
1990	31,699	532,317	64,799	1,326,362
1991	30,757	529,019	63,351	1,313,829

Source: Bureau of the Census, Annual Survey of Manufactures (Washington, D.C.: annually); and Census of Manufactures (Washington, D.C.: quinquennially). N.A. not available.

Table XIII-6. Annual Hours and Earnings of Manufacturing Production Workers in Michigan: 1956-1993

Year	Hours	Average Weekly Earnings
1956	40.8	$94.98
1957	40.0	97.64
1958	39.5	99.70
1959	40.9	108.71
1960	40.8	112.00
1961	40.9	112.32
1962	41.8	121.43
1963	42.5	128.27
1964	43.5	135.11
1965	44.6	143.79
1966	43.3	145.10
1967	42.0	145.78
1968	43.3	164.15
1969	42.0	166.78
1970	40.6	168.33
1971	41.0	188.19
1972	42.8	211.52
1973	43.4	228.63
1974	41.3	232.35
1975	40.8	250.76
1976	42.7	290.97
1977	43.3	326.79
1978	42.9	346.20
1979	41.2	360.25
1980	40.1	381.87
1981	40.5	426.27
1982	40.2	449.33
1983	42.5	494.02
1984	43.2	526.18
1985	43.1	544.78
1986	42.6	545.28
1987	42.2	547.33
1988	43.3	581.52
1989	43.1	587.45
1990	41.8	579.35
1991	41.5	602.58
1992	41.8	619.06
1993	43.1	662.02

Source: U.S. Bureau of Labor Statistics (Washington, D.C.) and Michigan Employment Security Commission, Research and Statistics (Detroit, Michigan).

Table XIII-7. Manufacturers' Expenditures for New Plant and Equipment in Michigan and the United States: 1955-1991

Year	Michigan (Millions of Dollars)			United States (Millions of Dollars)		
	Total	New Machinery and Equipment	New Structures and Additions to Plant	Total	New Machinery and Equipment	New Structures and Additions to Plant
1955	$806	$609	$197	$8,233	$5,808	$2,426
1956	1,015	783	232	11,233	7,762	3,472
1957	695	566	129	12,144	8,279	3,865
1958	465	354	111	9,544	6,308	3,235
1959	531	430	102	9,140	6,558	2,582
1960	656	522	134	10,098	7,279	2,818
1961	562	453	110	9,780	7,031	2,749
1962	556	441	115	10,436	7,705	2,731
1963	762	591	171	11,370	8,404	2,966
1964	1,031	807	224	13,294	10,025	3,269
1965	1,453	N.A.	N.A.	16,615	12,429	4,186
1966	1,489	N.A.	N.A.	20,236	15,006	5,230
1967	1,360	1,024	336	21,503	15,789	5,714
1968	1,170	N.A.	N.A.	20,613	15,319	5,294
1969	1,372	N.A.	N.A.	22,291	16,485	5,806
1970	1,301	N.A.	N.A.	22,164	16,409	5,756
1971	1,202	N.A.	N.A.	20,941	15,599	5,342
1972	2,071	N.A.	N.A.	24,078	18,707	5,370
1973	1,998	N.A.	N.A.	26,973	20,958	6,016
1974	2,851	2,524	326	35,546	27,337	8,209
1975	2,263	1,956	307	37,262	29,828	7,434
1976	2,636	2,335	301	40,545	32,651	7,894
1977	3,739	3,364	475	48,641	40,036	8,604
1978	4,743	4,117	626	55,244	44,659	10,186
1979	N.A.	N.A.	N.A.	N.A.	56,746	14,034
1980	N.A.	N.A.	N.A.	N.A.	50,352	11,568
1981	N.A.	N.A.	N.A.	N.A.	61,619	13,622
1982	3,503	2,994	519	70,780	0	0
1983	2,547	2,086	461	61,920	0	0
1984	4,239	3,624	616	75,242	0	0
1985	5,719	4,931	788	83,132	67,992	15,139
1986	5,621	4,598	1,023	76,331	62,860	13,471
1987	4,794	3,989	805	78,648	65,734	12,914
1988	4,074	N.A.	N.A.	80,542	N.A.	N.A.
1989	5,939	5,081	858	97,187	80,524	16,663
1990	5,605	4,992	613	101,953	85,668	16,285
1991	5,268	4,689	579	98,916	84,038	14,879

Source: Bureau of the Census, <u>Annual Survey of Manufactures</u> (Washington, D.C.: annually); and <u>Census of Manufactures</u> (Washington, D.C.: quinquennially). N.A. Data not available.

Table XIII-8. Raw Steel Production in Michigan and the United States: 1951-1992

Year	Production (Thousands of Short Tons)		
	Michigan	United States	Michigan Percent(%) of U.S.
1951	4,829	105,200	4.6
1952	4,552	93,200	4.9
1953	5,142	111,482	4.6
1954	4,224	88,316	4.8
1955	5,999	116,858	5.1
1956	6,231	114,999	5.4
1957	6,220	112,630	5.5
1958	4,567	85,149	5.4
1959	5,634	95,361	6.0
1960	6,529	98,812	6.6
1961	6,644	97,417	6.8
1962	7,126	98,221	7.3
1963	8,447	109,011	7.7
1964	9,435	126,460	7.5
1965	8,990	131,237	6.9
1966	10,004	132,902	7.5
1967	9,247	126,323	7.3
1968	9,220	127,509	7.2
1969	10,039	141,008	7.1
1970	9,581	130,940	7.3
1971	9,069	120,443	7.5

Year	Production (Thousands of Short Tons)		
	Michigan	United States	Michigan Percent(%) of U.S.
1972	9,380	133,241	7.0
1973	10,945	150,799	7.3
1974	10,459	145,720	7.2
1975	9,093	116,642	7.8
1976	10,382	128,000	8.1
1977	10,051	125,333	8.0
1978	10,789	137,031	7.9
1979	10,922	136,341	8.0
1980	7,877	111,835	7.0
1981	8,943	120,828	7.4
1982	6,075	74,577	8.1
1983	7,262	84,615	8.6
1984	7,754	92,528	8.4
1985	7,297	88,259	8.3
1986	7,475	81,694	9.1
1987	7,699	88,118	8.7
1988	8,194	100,856	8.1
1989	8,172	99,195*	8.2
1990	8,104	87,325*	9.3
1991	7,002	79,809*	8.8
1992	7,834	83,733*	9.4

Source: U.S. Bureau of the Census (Washington D.C.), and the Michigan Information Center (Lansing, Michigan). *Metric Tons

Table XIII-9. Number of Manufacturing Establishments, Employment, and Average Weekly Wage in Michigan, by County: 1992

County	Units	Employment	A.W.W.	County	Units	Employment	A.W.W.
Alcona	30	208	$449.49	Lake	10	103	$331.43
Alger	20	767	618.07	Lapeer	111	4,566	490.93
Allegan	159	14,137	575.55	Leelanau	27	228	344.25
Alpena	57	2,193	630.32	Lenawee	153	9,441	612.07
Antrim	57	1,153	463.88	Livingston	172	5,807	571.47
Arenac	29	533	420.78	Luce	16	372	491.29
Baraga	44	503	447.20	Mackinac	18	80	319.25
Barry	56	2,381	597.13	Macomb	2,050	101,134	810.70
Bay	147	7,430	736.38	Manistee	42	1,467	655.15
Benzie	22	542	331.18	Marquette	55	719	387.41
Berrien	405	20,087	607.12	Mason	50	2,650	538.42
Branch	93	3,169	481.01	Mecosta	33	1,320	480.28
Calhoun	200	16,543	734.85	Menominee	81	2,958	454.96
Cass	76	3,133	516.81	Midland	66	12,784	906.73
Charlevoix	62	2,588	580.01	Missaukee	25	413	406.80
Cheboygan	43	556	480.68	Monroe	123	8,773	799.10
Chippewa	38	635	343.62	Montcalm	70	5,408	536.68
Clare	32	1,010	405.74	Montmorency	21	309	334.88
Clinton	42	1,598	588.25	Muskegon	306	15,377	643.12
Crawford	26	657	494.89	Newaygo	30	2,007	676.95
Delta	114	2,960	679.99	Oakland	2,463	102,824	812.18
Dickinson	57	2,484	595.99	Oceana	46	1,011	383.61
Eaton	90	2,888	519.37	Ogemaw	33	663	384.86
Emmet	62	1,471	457.80	Ontonagon	20	525	636.35
Genesee	342	47,352	885.19	Osceola	47	2,696	459.46
Gladwin	32	705	591.83	Oscoda	22	403	377.48
Gogebic	47	985	357.76	Otsego	37	1,239	484.53
Grand Traverse	171	5,204	470.63	Ottawa	498	31,045	591.21
Gratiot	47	2,664	555.43	Presque Isle	31	212	294.26
Hillsdale	98	5,745	504.54	Roscommon	24	376	379.63
Houghton	50	734	372.20	Saginaw	235	22,150	819.29
Huron	69	2,746	488.84	St. Clair	251	9,250	560.31
Ingham	279	26,420	781.47	St. Joseph	176	8,284	586.28
Ionia	74	3,806	484.03	Sanilac	78	3,622	418.40
Iosco	45	1,763	372.92	Schoolcraft	25	407	514.17
Iron	47	383	378.52	Shiawassee	91	4,036	481.19
Isabella	52	1,854	524.36	Tuscola	59	2,706	493.39
Jackson	301	11,493	597.43	Van Buren	119	4,489	525.58
Kalamazoo	364	28,431	759.28	Washtenaw	442	37,553	782.23
Kalkaska	18	845	445.94	Wayne	2,716	183,613	902.72
Kent	1,090	71,300	642.21	Wexford	76	3,533	483.74
Keweenaw	5	52	256.31	**Michigan**	**16,029**	**898,650**	**506.08**

Source: Michigan Employment Security Commission, Research and Statistics (Detroit, Michigan).

453

Table XIII-10. Total Wages in Manufacturing and Total Manufacturing Wages as a Percent of Total Wages in Michigan, by County: 1992

County	Total Manufacturing Wages	Percent(%) of County Wages	County	Total Manufacturing Wages	Percent(%) of County Wages
Alcona	$1,214,926	33.5	Lake	$449,116	14.2
Alger	6,167,597	63.6	Lapeer	29,083,872	46.9
Allegan	105,814,696	71.4	Leelanau	1,020,468	8.8
Alpena	17,958,543	38.9	Lenawee	75,104,041	54.3
Antrim	6,925,382	47.2	Livingston	43,156,245	32.2
Arenac	2,914,097	27.3	Luce	2,376,048	46.2
Baraga	2,925,157	40.8	Mackinac	331,965	3.0
Barry	18,476,582	48.0	Macomb	1,066,499,619	56.1
Bay	71,227,497	40.4	Manistee	12,491,352	47.1
Benzie	2,335,829	25.7	Marquette	3,622,668	3.6
Berrien	158,506,081	49.4	Mason	18,228,790	49.7
Branch	19,584,466	49.3	Mecosta	8,307,323	35.2
Calhoun	158,050,702	50.4	Menominee	17,498,566	54.2
Cass	21,047,937	57.1	Midland	150,565,719	61.1
Charlevoix	19,489,500	52.7	Missaukee	2,184,559	34.1
Cheboygan	3,465,277	17.0	Monroe	91,227,752	45.5
Chippewa	2,824,216	10.2	Montcalm	37,692,576	56.3
Clare	5,327,854	25.5	Montmorency	1,345,856	30.4
Clinton	12,236,576	31.2	Muskegon	128,545,227	47.1
Crawford	4,223,375	33.3	Newaygo	17,685,452	50.1
Delta	26,152,774	46.0	Oakland	1,087,434,661	25.8
Dickinson	19,256,709	37.9	Oceana	5,080,422	33.7
Eaton	19,489,186	21.8	Ogemaw	3,325,491	23.1
Emmet	8,759,883	15.9	Ontonagon	4,332,445	28.4
Genesee	545,471,564	53.9	Osceola	16,139,696	60.4
Gladwin	5,434,096	39.4	Oscoda	1,983,522	39.9
Gogebic	4,574,705	28.6	Otsego	7,809,077	23.0
Grand Traverse	31,924,045	19.4	Ottawa	238,812,791	53.7
Gratiot	19,222,203	37.7	Presque Isle	808,970	7.3
Hillsdale	37,702,245	64.3	Roscommon	1,859,799	14.7
Houghton	3,551,195	11.9	Saginaw	235,958,992	46.7
Huron	17,481,395	41.3	St. Clair	67,376,945	34.4
Ingham	268,272,845	36.0	St. Joseph	63,211,829	63.3
Ionia	23,930,189	51.8	Sanilac	19,732,158	54.2
Iosco	8,548,011	34.2	Schoolcraft	2,713,404	40.7
Iron	1,882,825	22.1	Shiawassee	25,261,848	39.9
Isabella	12,640,202	19.6	Tuscola	17,349,447	40.4
Jackson	89,289,654	35.4	Van Buren	30,667,589	42.4
Kalamazoo	280,588,137	45.2	Washtenaw	382,091,010	45.1
Kalkaska	4,899,807	24.6	Wayne	2,153,750,847	39.3
Kent	595,401,651	37.8	Wexford	22,251,595	45.3
Keweenaw	174,724	27.4	**Michigan**	**8,760,734,089**	**40.1**

Source: Michigan Employment Security Commission, Research and Statistics (Detroit, Michigan).

454

Table XIII-11. Value Added, Value of Shipments, and New Capital Expenditures by the Manufacturing Sector in Michigan, by County: 1987
(Data in Millions of Dollars)

County	Value Added By Manufacture	Value of Shipments	New Capital Expenditures	County	Value Added By Manufacture	Value of Shipments	New Capital Expenditures
Alcona	$9.8	$18.3	$0.5	Gogebic	$21.2	$36.0	$1.9
Alger	N.A.	N.A.	N.A.	Grand Traverse	228.7	467.8	10.5
Allegan	870.5	1,632.5	65.2	Gratiot	117.8	530.5	N.A.
Alpena	136.5	259.9	23.6	Hillsdale	300.9	598.9	18.1
Antrim	53.4	97.8	N.A.	Houghton	31.4	64.0	2.0
Arenac	26.5	51.1	0.9	Huron	137.3	228.8	N.A.
Baraga	23.8	65.0	0.9	Ingham	1,641.6	6,716.7	132.4
Barry	165.7	368.2	6.8	Ionia	198.6	388.9	10.3
Bay	N.A.	N.A.	N.A.	Iosco	49.9	87.0	1.3
Benzie	N.A.	N.A.	N.A.	Iron	14.2	29.9	1.4
Berrien	970.9	2,545.7	66.6	Isabella	80.6	144.6	2.7
Branch	162.6	426.7	11.7	Jackson	627.9	1,406.8	37.4
Calhoun	1,632.4	2,544.3	236.4	Kalamazoo	2,307.7	3,970.6	206.7
Cass	218.8	470.3	10.4	Kalkaska	53.2	110.9	5.6
Charlevoix	139.4	233.7	6.8	Kent	4,379.0	8,056.8	509.0
Cheboygan	76.6	142.8	4.0	Keweenaw	0.7	1.2	N.A.
Chippewa	21.4	41.0	0.9	Lake	3.8	7.4	0.1
Clare	43.2	93.6	1.9	Lapeer	223.1	434.2	N.A.
Clinton	131.8	322.3	N.A.	Leelanau	10.6	21.8	0.4
Crawford	6.8	14.8	N.A.	Lenawee	603.0	1,294.5	37.5
Delta	266.5	505.0	N.A.	Livingston	268.4	587.2	26.0
Dickinson	176.9	305.5	N.A.	Luce	12.9	28.6	1.0
Eaton	N.A.	N.A.	N.A.	Mackinac	5.2	9.4	0.1
Emmet	58.1	115.8	3.6	Macomb	5,753.9	15,626.6	351.1
Genesee	N.A.	N.A.	N.A.	Manistee	134.5	233.4	6.7
Gladwin	35.9	79.9	2.5	Marquette	36.4	68.2	2.0

Table XIII-11. Value Added, Value of Shipments, and New Capital Expenditures by the Manufacturing Sector in Michigan, by County: 1987 Continued
(Data in Millions of Dollars)

County	Value Added By Manufacture	Value of Shipments	New Capital Expenditures
Mason	$130.1	$227.9	$5.1
Mecosta	55.8	129.1	3.7
Menominee	136.4	287.4	5.3
Midland	N.A.	N.A.	N.A.
Missaukee	19.0	38.6	0.7
Monroe	635.1	1,400.4	N.A.
Montcalm	345.4	786.8	17.9
Montmorency	9.1	14.5	0.6
Muskegon	1,151.6	1,999.1	121.4
Newaygo	162.8	314.7	10.3
Oakland	8,437.0	22,001.9	408.9
Oceana	53.4	103.5	9.1
Ogemaw	50.1	97.9	2.3
Ontonagon	N.A.	N.A.	N.A.
Osceola	39.6	175.9	14.1
Oscoda	17.2	44.7	N.A.
Otsego	66.9	129.7	2.5
Ottawa	1,588.7	3,078.7	100.8
Presque Isle	6.9	18.8	0.5
Roscommon	9.5	26.9	1.0
Saginaw	1,789.1	3,507.4	193.5
St. Clair	490.1	1,069.5	39.2
St. Joseph	768.0	1,373.2	30.1
Sanilac	161.0	342.2	6.8
Schoolcraft	26.2	42.7	1.3
Shiawassee	181.9	346.7	15.9
Tuscola	$108.4	$258.3	$11.9
Van Buren	248.1	517.2	17.5
Washtenaw	2,901.2	7,348.1	227.1
Wayne	12,335.3	33,860.8	1,147.2
Wexford	148.4	327.5	9.5
Michigan	**60,258.6**	**146,338.8**	**4,793.5**

Source: U.S. Bureau of the Census, 1987 Census of Manufactures, Geographic Area Series, Michigan (Washington, D.C.: 1990). N.A. data not available.

Table XIII-12. Employment Levels in Foreign-Owned Manufacturing Establishments and as a Percentage of Total Manufacturing Employment in Michigan, by Industry Group: 1990

Industry	SIC	Employed in Foreign-Owned Establishments	Total Employment	Foreign-Owned as Percent(%) of Total
Total Manufacturing		**70,914**	**913,100**	**7.8**
Food and Kindred Products	20	3,034	36,900	8.2
Apparel and Other Textile Products	23	0 to 19	15,800	N.A.
Lumber and Wood Products	24	854	15,300	5.6
Furniture and Fixtures	25	100 to 249	32,800	N.A.
Paper and Allied Products	26	1,281	19,500	6.6
Printing and Publishing	27	2,799	49,000	5.7
Chemicals and Allied Products	28	7,039	30,600	23.0
Petroleum and Coal Products	29	250 to 499	1,800	N.A.
Rubber and Miscellaneous Products	30	3,810	52,600	7.2
Stone/Clay/Glass Products	32	2,316	15,200	15.2
Primary Metals Industries	33	9,913	43,500	22.8
Fabricated Metals Industries	34	6,384	113,300	5.6
Industrial Machinery and Equipment	35	8,892	116,900	7.6
Electronic and Other Electric Equipment	36	3,665	22,100	16.6
Transportation Equipment	37	9,192	206,200	4.5
Instruments and Related	38	2,750	15,300	18.0
Miscellaneous Manufacturing Industries	39	250 - 499	8,200	N.A.
Administrative and Auxiliary		8,300	114,800	7.2

N.A. Data not available.
Source: Bureau of Economic Analysis, and Bureau of Census, Foreign Direct Investment in The United States (Washington, D.C.: 1993).

Table XIII-13. Employment in and Number of Foreign-Owned Manufacturing Establishments in Michigan, by Industry Group and Employment Size Class: 1990

Industry	SIC	Number of Employees	Employment Size Class						Number of Establishments
			0-19	20-49	50-99	100-249	250-999	1,000 and Over	
Total Manufacturing		**70,914**	69	66	82	110	60	9	396
Food and Kindred Products	20	3,034	3	2	5	4	4	0	18
Apparel and Other Textile Products	23	0 to 19	1	0	0	0	0	0	1
Lumber and Wood Products	24	854	2	4	1	2	1	0	10
Furniture and Fixtures	25	100 to 249	0	0	0	1	0	0	1
Paper and Allied Products	26	1,281	2	1	1	3	2	0	9
Printing and Publishing	27	2,799	4	6	7	5	3	0	25
Chemicals and Allied Products	28	7,039	9	8	11	15	8	0	51
Petroleum and Coal Products	29	250 to 499	10	0	0	1	0	0	11
Rubber and Miscellaneous Products	30	3,810	3	3	8	10	5	0	29
Stone/Clay/Glass Products	32	2,316	0	2	3	5	3	0	13
Primary Metals Industries	33	9,913	1	5	4	9	4	2	25
Fabricated Metals Industries	34	6,384	3	2	6	6	8	1	26
Industrial Machinery and Equipment	35	8,892	8	16	13	18	7	1	63
Electronic and Other Electric Equipment	36	3,665	1	3	3	3	2	1	13
Transportation Equipment	37	9,192	0	1	1	11	6	2	21
Instruments and Related	38	2,750	1	0	3	2	1	1	8
Miscellaneous Manufacturing Industries	39	250 to 499	0	0	0	2	0	0	2
Administrative and Auxiliary		8,300	21	13	16	13	6	1	70

Source: Bureau of Economic Analysis, and Bureau of Census, Foreign Direct Investment in The United States (Washington, D.C.: 1993).

CHAPTER XIV
THE AUTOMOTIVE ECONOMY

Automotive production is part of the manufacturing sector. According to the Standard Industrial Classification Manual, this industry includes:

> establishments primarily engaged in manufacturing or assembling complete passenger automobiles, trucks, commercial cars, and buses, and special purpose vehicles which are for highway use;... establishments engaged primarily in manufacturing truck and bus bodies;...establishments primarily engaged in manufacturing motor vehicle parts and accessories;...establishments engaged primarily in manufacturing truck trailers;...and establishments primarily engaged in manufacturing self-contained motor homes on a purchased chassis.

The American Automobile Manufacturers Association collects a wide range of information on the automotive industry. The AAMA issues two annual compendia, Facts and Figures and World Motor Vehicle Data, as well as a variety of monthly statistical releases.

Two publishers, Crain Communications and Ward's Communications, also track the performance of the automotive industry, on a weekly basis. Crain publishes Automotive News and Ward's Communications publishes Automotive Reports and Ward's Auto World. Each also publishes an annual summary of the information it publishes in its weekly publications.

R.L. Polk & Company compiles monthly data on new car and truck sales, by make and model, by county.

The Bureau of the Census provides data on the automotive industry in its quinquennial Census of Manufactures and Annual Survey of Manufactures. (See chapter XII for discussion of the Census and Survey). The Bureau of Economic Analysis develops quarterly estimates of auto and truck output in its national income and product accounts. BEA estimates of new plant and equipment expenditures by vehicle and parts manufacturers also are available. Capacity utilization data are prepared by the Board of Governors of the Federal Reserve System. Materials consumption estimates are compiled by American Metal Market.

Current data on employment, hours, and earnings are collected and disseminated by the Michigan Employment Security Commission in Detroit and by the Bureau of Labor Statistics in Washington, D.C.

LIST OF TABLES

Table	Page
XIV-1. World Production of Motor Vehicles, by Selected Country: 1959-1994	461
XIV-2. Motor Vehicle Production in Michigan, the United States, and Michigan's Share of U.S. Production: 1957-1994	463
XIV-3. Total Factory Sales of Motor Vehicles from Canadian and U.S. Plants, by Canadian and U.S. Destinations: 1970-1994	464

LIST OF TABLES

Table		Page
XIV-4.	Factory Sales of Passenger Cars from Canadian and U.S. Plants, by Canadian and U.S. Destination: 1970-1994	465
XIV-5.	Factory Sales of Trucks and Buses from Canadian and U.S. Plants, by Canadian and U.S. Destinations: 1970-1994	466
XIV-6.	Transplant Light Vehicle Production in the United States: 1980-1994	467
XIV-7.	Motor Vehicle Employment in Michigan and the United States: 1970-1995	468
XIV-8.	Motor Vehicle and Supplier Employment in Michigan: 1970-1995	468
XIV-9.	Automaker Employment in Michigan: 1973-1995	469
XIV-10.	Michigan Motor Vehicle Production, by Location: 1993-1994	470
XIV-11.	Annual U.S. Motor Vehicle Retail Sales: 1956-1994	471
XIV-12.	New Passenger Car and Truck Registrations in Michigan and the United States, by Name Plate: 1993 and 1994	472
XIV-13.	New Plant and Equipment Expenditures in the United States, by Motor Vehicle and Parts Manufacturers: 1970-1993	473
XIV-14.	Percentage of Capacity Utilization in United States Manufacturing: 1970-1993	473
XIV-15.	Estimated Average Material Consumption in U.S.-Built Passenger Cars: Selected Years 1980, 1982, 1984, 1986, 1988, 1990, 1992, and 1993	474
XIV-16.	Auto Supplier Research and Development and Technical Centers in Michigan: 1994	475
XIV-17.	Research and Development Expenditures by Manufacturer: 1975-1994	478

Table XIV-1. World Production of Motor Vehicles, by Selected Country: 1959-1994

Year	United States	Canada	Mexico	Germany	France	Russia	Italy	United Kingdom	Japan	Total World Production
1959	6,723,588	367,939	51,118	1,785,885	1,283,159	494,994	500,784	1,560,427	262,814	13,870,355
1960	7,905,117	397,739	49,807	2,131,127	1,369,210	523,591	644,633	1,810,700	481,551	16,376,865
1961	6,652,938	386,923	62,563	2,232,025	1,244,223	555,330	759,140	1,464,134	813,879	15,209,431
1962	8,197,311	505,187	66,637	2,444,594	1,536,133	577,500	946,793	1,674,530	990,706	18,202,770
1963	9,108,776	631,356	69,135	2,761,896	1,736,977	587,012	1,180,536	2,011,720	1,283,531	20,720,346
1964	9,307,860	670,990	90,752	3,011,657	1,615,896	603,100	1,090,078	2,332,376	1,702,475	22,020,434
1965	11,137,830	846,609	96,654	3,094,533	1,641,696	634,312	1,175,548	2,177,261	1,875,614	24,567,935
1966	10,396,299	872,214	113,807	3,177,334	2,024,552	675,300	1,365,898	2,042,354	2,286,399	24,980,754
1967	9,023,736	919,508	126,365	2,616,420	2,009,672	728,800	1,542,669	1,937,119	3,146,486	24,183,537
1968	10,820,410	1,150,218	143,478	3,246,074	2,075,617	800,700	1,660,370	2,225,122	4,085,826	28,611,717
1969	10,205,911	1,326,478	165,164	3,752,247	2,459,072	844,300	1,595,951	2,182,793	4,674,923	30,083,671
1970	8,283,949	1,159,504	192,841	3,995,625	2,750,086	916,118	1,854,252	2,098,498	5,289,147	29,707,707
1971	10,671,654	1,346,765	210,840	4,043,484	3,010,294	1,142,700	1,817,019	2,198,146	5,810,774	33,728,068
1972	11,310,708	1,430,084	229,766	3,885,598	3,328,320	1,379,000	1,839,793	2,329,430	6,294,438	35,845,958
1973	12,681,513	1,574,820	285,513	4,029,268	3,596,179	1,602,000	1,957,994	2,163,941	7,082,757	39,236,122
1974	10,072,662	1,524,874	350,755	3,188,707	3,462,847	1,846,000	1,772,515	1,936,685	6,551,840	35,108,355
1975	8,986,605	1,424,006	360,678	3,383,665	2,861,305	1,964,056	1,458,629	1,648,399	6,941,591	33,322,385
1976	11,497,391	1,640,112	324,979	4,070,460	3,402,715	2,024,660	1,590,677	1,705,506	7,841,447	38,619,510
1977	12,702,782	1,775,445	280,813	4,308,610	3,507,881	2,088,369	1,583,917	1,714,240	8,514,522	41,240,509
1978	12,899,202	1,817,457	384,128	4,396,850	3,507,930	2,150,984	1,656,115	1,607,467	9,269,153	42,611,416
1979	11,479,993	1,631,661	444,426	4,469,743	3,613,458	2,173,200	1,632,289	1,478,512	9,635,546	41,978,835

Table XIV-1. World Production of Motor Vehicles, by Selected Country: 1959-1994 Continued

Year	United States	Canada	Mexico	Germany	France	Russia	Italy	United Kingdom	Japan	Total World Production
1980	8,009,841	1,374,359	490,006	4,095,138	3,378,433	2,199,200	1,610,287	1,312,914	11,042,884	38,837,509
1981	7,942,916	1,322,780	597,118	4,116,407	3,019,370	2,197,000	1,433,743	1,184,205	11,179,962	37,380,354
1982	6,985,595	1,276,452	472,637	4,284,465	3,148,807	2,172,700	1,453,043	1,156,477	10,731,794	36,418,953
1983	9,205,373	1,524,413	285,485	4,382,339	3,335,862	2,180,000	1,575,141	1,289,111	11,111,659	39,990,246
1984	10,939,048	1,829,283	343,698	4,290,562	3,062,157	2,209,400	1,601,177	1,133,731	11,464,920	42,141,483
1985	11,652,743	1,933,381	398,192	4,707,715	3,016,106	2,232,000	1,572,907	1,313,946	12,271,095	44,782,214
1986	11,334,775	1,854,125	272,168	4,861,407	3,194,615	2,226,000	1,831,700	11,334,775	12,259,817	45,233,421
1987	10,909,582	1,635,014	232,515	4,901,074	3,493,210	2,229,000	1,912,612	10,909,582	12,249,174	45,679,723
1988	11,214,000	1,949,000	512,776	4,894,484	3,698,465	2,080,255	2,111,019	1,544,848	12,700,000	48,210,000
1989	10,852,055	1,939,502	641,779	5,108,647	3,919,776	2,100,000	2,220,774	1,625,672	13,025,678	48,891,065
1990	9,780,236	1,896,106	820,558	5,163,442	3,768,993	2,040,000	2,120,850	1,565,744	13,486,796	48,112,643
1991	8,810,521	1,905,455	989,373	5,200,003	3,610,773	1,929,000	1,877,326	1,454,041	13,245,432	46,437,080
1992	9,731,478	1,970,649	1,080,863	5,193,942	3,767,824	2,465,605	1,686,487	1,540,333	12,499,284	49,799,548
1993	10,890,739	2,246,202	1,080,572	3,990,637	3,155,717	1,597,654	1,277,442	1,568,991	11,227,545	47,483,361
1994	12,249,990	2,321,811	1,106,176	4,356,138	3,558,438	1,011,552	1,534,469	1,694,638	10,554,119	49,967,594

Source: Americaan Automobile Manufacturers Association, Facts & Figures (Detroit, Michigan: annually).

Table XIV-2. Motor Vehicle Production in Michigan, the United States, and Michigan's Share of U.S. Production: 1957-1994

Year	Cars (Data in Thousands)			Trucks and Buses (Data in Thousands)		
	Michigan	U.S.	Mich % U.S.	Michigan	U.S.	Mich % U.S.
1957	2,118	6,120	35.0	180	1,100	16.0
1958	1,239	4,247	29.0	153	873	18.0
1959	1,658	5,599	30.0	184	1,124	16.0
1960	2,092	6,703	31.0	203	1,202	17.0
1961	1,774	5,522	32.0	171	1,130	15.0
1962	2,280	6,943	33.0	228	1,254	18.0
1963	2,590	7,644	34.0	265	1,464	18.0
1964	2,622	7,745	34.0	385	1,562	25.0
1965	3,255	9,335	35.0	495	1,802	27.0
1966	2,024	8,605	35.0	515	1,792	29.0
1967	2,600	7,413	35.0	459	1,611	28.0
1968	3,009	8,849	34.0	511	1,972	26.0
1969	2,873	8,224	35.0	533	1,982	27.0
1970	2,099	6,550	32.0	454	1,734	26.0
1971	2,836	8,584	33.0	587	2,088	28.0
1972	2,902	8,828	33.0	734	2,483	30.0
1973	3,268	9,667	34.0	1,012	3,015	34.0
1974	2,403	7,325	33.0	897	2,747	33.0
1975	2,249	6,717	33.0	757	2,270	33.0
1976	2,914	8,498	34.0	1,030	3,000	34.0
1977	2,852	8,214	31.0	1,077	2,489	31.0
1978	2,706	9,177	29.0	1,288	3,723	35.0
1979	2,582	8,434	31.0	996	3,046	33.0
1980	1,732	6,376	27.0	443	1,634	27.0
1981	2,040	6,253	33.0	460	1,690	27.0
1982	1,818	5,073	36.0	577	1,913	30.0
1983	2,077	6,781	31.0	697	2,421	29.0
1984	2,127	7,773	27.0	886	3,151	28.0
1985	2,400	8,186	29.0	898	3,466	26.0
1986	2,626	7,830	34.0	782	3,543	22.0
1987	2,560	7,095	36.0	842	3,880	22.0
1988	2,389	7,129	34.0	822	4,133	20.0
1989	2,124	6,830	31.0	925	4,295	22.0
1990	1,946	6,079	32.0	751	3,809	20.0
1991	1,567	5,439	29.0	593	3,444	17.0
1992	1,688	5,659	30.0	756	4,119	18.0
1993	1,798	5,963	30.0	1,013	4,891	21.0
1994	2,146	6,601	32.5	1,264	5,649	22.4

Source: Michigan Department of Treasury, Office of Revenue and Tax Analysis; and Automotive News Market Data Book (Detroit, Michigan, annually).

Table XIV-3. Total Factory Sales of Motor Vehicles from Canadian and U.S. Plants, by Canadian and U.S. Destinations: 1970-1994

Year	Plants In United States				Plants In Canada*			
	U.S. Total	U.S. Domestic	Exports To Canada	Other Exports	Canada Total	Canada Domestic	Exports To U.S.	Other Exports
1970	8,239,257	7,752,987	299,392	186,878	1,171,311	269,051	839,404	62,856
1971	10,637,738	10,036,022	421,156	180,560	1,354,795	341,141	946,076	67,578
1972	11,270,745	10,646,841	476,916	146,988	1,455,117	353,566	1,041,035	60,516
1973	12,637,335	11,865,662	596,562	175,111	1,581,566	435,480	1,077,667	68,419
1974	10,058,569	9,190,920	667,977	199,672	1,548,342	465,026	991,265	92,051
1975	8,985,012	8,076,058	683,054	225,900	1,433,310	432,847	894,572	105,891
1976	11,476,652	10,571,471	691,159	214,022	1,632,558	438,751	1,074,411	119,396
1977	12,642,370	11,691,488	721,151	229,731	1,761,185	447,173	1,179,586	134,426
1978	12,871,429	11,909,211	680,522	281,696	1,789,872	469,870	1,161,770	158,232
1979	11,455,932	10,419,219	740,491	296,222	1,606,249	539,043	930,617	136,589
1980	8,067,309	7,304,113	575,277	187,919	1,353,092	389,799	829,768	133,525
1981	7,955,792	7,262,515	543,597	149,680	1,286,663	305,925	820,076	160,662
1982	6,954,624	6,474,584	390,844	89,196	1,239,213	177,349	1,033,705	28,159
1983	9,153,120	8,461,570	611,499	80,051	1,491,302	245,972	1,215,548	29,782
1984	10,696,501	9,913,855	712,207	70,239	1,825,414	296,971	1,498,427	30,016
1985	11,359,164	10,629,909	833,449	62,806	1,922,394	352,760	1,556,050	13,584
1986	10,909,074	9,998,746	838,567	71,761	1,842,643	307,560	1,526,419	8,664
1987	10,906,557	9,995,675	814,476	96,406	1,608,133	285,926	1,313,730	8,477
1988	11,225,191	10,231,995	824,905	168,291	1,916,621	310,989	1,579,563	26,069
1989	10,869,366	9,933,004	747,425	188,937	1,829,387	271,617	1,525,529	32,241
1990	9,768,530	8,950,085	624,018	194,427	1,714,370	228,407	1,455,797	30,166
1991	8,782,542	7,912,022	616,996	253,524	1,570,539	214,290	1,319,799	36,450
1992	9,726,689	8,846,447	542,666	337,576	1,676,263	174,141	1,473,342	28,780
1993	10,855,551	9,942,888	567,748	344,915	1,900,473	203,404	1,670,120	26,949
1994	12,184,278	11,097,641	684,155	402,482	1,958,310	205,383	1,715,372	37,555

Source: American Automobile Manufacturing Association, Facts & Figures (Detroit, Michigan, annually). * Incomplete, reporting firms do not represent entire industry.

Table XIV-4. Factory Sales of Passenger Cars from Canadian and U.S. Plants, by Canadian and U.S. Destinations: 1970-1994

Year	Plants In United States				Plants In Canada*			
	U.S. Total	U.S. Domestic	Exports To Canada	Other Exports	Canada Total	Canada Domestic	Exports To U.S.	Other Exports
1970	6,546,817	6,187,318	245,746	113,753	919,232	206,933	681,872	30,427
1971	8,584,592	8,121,714	352,130	110,748	1,075,457	258,034	779,769	37,654
1972	8,823,928	8,352,470	382,463	89,005	1,136,894	262,971	836,630	37,293
1973	9,657,647	9,078,849	476,099	102,699	1,226,039	322,506	862,407	41,126
1974	7,331,256	6,721,294	500,463	109,499	1,171,843	316,978	802,370	52,495
1975	6,712,852	6,073,300	549,353	90,199	1,043,245	271,689	713,407	58,149
1976	8,497,603	7,837,801	562,635	97,167	1,134,644	250,525	808,788	75,331
1977	9,200,849	8,512,468	586,073	102,308	1,155,701	236,559	831,994	87,148
1978	9,165,190	8,493,563	541,552	130,075	1,127,573	155,701	764,835	107,037
1979	8,419,226	7,678,138	582,097	158,991	973,174	298,060	582,386	92,728
1980	6,400,026	5,840,305	488,857	70,864	827,124	201,588	539,239	86,297
1981	6,255,340	5,749,375	454,567	51,398	772,137	153,612	516,430	102,095
1982	5,049,184	4,696,403	320,292	32,489	782,489	107,846	662,014	12,629
1983	6,739,223	6,201,384	505,262	32,577	945,757	152,972	773,381	19,394
1984	7,621,176	7,029,722	561,894	29,560	1,015,202	163,065	830,447	21,690
1985	8,002,259	7,336,735	635,546	29,978	1,068,420	184,490	878,052	5,878
1986	7,516,189	6,868,529	610,281	37,379	1,051,342	157,595	889,553	4,194
1987	7,085,147	6,486,584	547,211	51,352	785,215	128,136	654,585	2,494
1988	7,104,617	6,436,681	565,741	102,195	970,903	118,367	844,744	7,792
1989	6,807,416	6,181,094	501,250	125,072	882,432	96,451	780,800	5,181
1990	6,049,749	5,501,871	416,459	131,419	901,903	102,557	795,621	3,725
1991	5,407,120	4,874,218	381,564	151,338	780,054	106,399	670,826	2,829
1992	5,684,221	5,163,935	299,722	220,564	768,917	71,344	693,518	4,055
1993	5,960,327	5,471,395	281,400	207,532	1,058,005	98,422	937,931	21,652
1994	6,551,613	5,966,570	343,549	241,494	926,515	75,604	818,764	32,147

Source: American Automobile Manufacturing Association, <u>Facts & Figures</u> (Detroit, Michigan, annually). * Incomplete, reporting firms do not represent entire industry.

Table XIV-5. Factory Sales of Trucks and Buses from Canadian and U.S. Plants, by Canadian and U.S. Destinations: 1970-1994

Year	Plants In United States				Plants In Canada*			
	U.S. Total	U.S. Domestic	Exports To Canada	Other Exports	Canada Total	Canada Domestic	Exports To U.S.	Other Exports
1970	1,692,440	1,565,669	53,646	73,125	252,079	62,118	157,532	32,429
1971	2,053,146	1,914,308	69,026	69,812	279,338	83,107	166,307	29,924
1972	2,446,807	2,294,371	94,453	57,983	318,223	90,595	204,405	23,223
1973	2,979,688	1,786,813	120,463	72,412	355,527	112,974	215,260	27,293
1974	2,727,313	2,469,626	167,514	90,173	376,499	148,048	188,895	39,556
1975	2,272,160	2,002,758	133,701	135,701	390,065	161,158	181,165	47,742
1976	2,979,049	2,733,670	128,524	116,855	497,914	188,226	265,623	44,065
1977	3,441,521	3,179,020	135,078	127,423	605,484	210,614	347,592	47,278
1978	3,706,239	3,415,648	138,970	151,621	662,299	214,169	396,935	51,195
1979	3,036,706	2,741,081	158,394	137,231	633,075	240,983	348,231	43,861
1980	1,667,283	1,463,808	86,420	117,055	525,968	188,211	290,529	47,228
1981	1,700,452	1,513,140	89,030	98,282	514,526	152,313	303,646	58,567
1982	1,905,440	1,778,181	70,552	56,707	456,724	69,503	371,691	15,530
1983	2,413,897	2,260,186	106,237	47,474	545,555	93,000	442,167	10,388
1984	3,075,325	2,884,133	150,313	40,679	810,212	133,906	667,980	8,326
1985	3,356,905	3,126,174	197,903	32,828	853,974	168,270	677,998	7,706
1986	3,392,885	3,130,217	228,286	34,382	791,301	149,965	636,866	4,470
1987	3,821,410	3,509,091	267,265	45,054	822,918	157,790	659,145	5,983
1988	4,120,574	3,795,314	259,164	66,096	945,718	192,622	734,819	18,277
1989	4,061,950	3,751,910	246,175	63,865	946,955	175,166	744,729	27,060
1990	3,718,781	3,448,214	207,559	63,008	812,467	125,850	660,176	26,441
1991	3,375,422	3,037,804	235,432	102,186	790,485	107,891	648,973	33,621
1992	4,042,468	3,682,512	242,944	117,012	907,346	102,797	779,824	24,725
1993	4,895,224	4,471,493	286,348	137,383	842,468	104,982	732,189	5,297
1994	5,632,665	5,131,071	340,606	160,988	1,031,795	129,779	896,608	5,408

Source: American Automobile Manufacturing Association, Facts & Figures (Detroit, Michigan, annually). * Incomplete, reporting firms do not represent entire industry.

Table XIV-6. Transplant Light Vehicle Production in the United States: 1980-1994
(Data in Thousands)

Auto Company	1980	1981	1982	1983	1984	1985	1986	1987	1988	1989	1990	1991	1992	1993	1994
Honda	-	-	-	55	139	145	234	324	366	362	465	451	458	404	499
Nissan	-	-	2	-	-	-	43	65	117	110	96	134	171	293	313
Toyota	-	-	-	-	-	-	-	-	19	151	218	188	240	234	276
AutoAlliance/1	-	-	-	-	-	-	-	4	167	216	184	165	169	219	247
Diamond-Star	-	-	-	-	-	-	-	-	2	91	143	164	140	136	170
NUMMI/2	-	-	-	-	-	65	206	187	130	192	205	20	181	207	229
SIA	-	-	-	-	-	-	-	-	-	3	32	58	58	47	54
BMW	-	-	-	-	-	-	-	-	-	-	-	-	-	-	0.4
Volkswagen	197	168	84	98	75	96	84	67	36	-	-	-	-	-	-
TOTAL CARS	197	168	86	153	214	306	567	647	837	1,125	1,343	1,180	1,417	1,540	1,788
Nissan	-	-	-	-	101	107	108	103	96	123	139	132	129	94	132
NUMMI	-	-	-	-	-	-	-	-	-	-	-	3	75	114	134
SIA/3	-	-	-	-	-	-	-	-	-	-	34	58	66	79	100
TOTAL LIGHT TRUCK	-	-	-	-	101	107	108	103	96	123	173	193	270	287	366
TOTAL LIGHT VEHICLES	197	168	86	153	315	413	675	750	933	1,248	1,516	1,373	1,687	1,827	2,154

/1 AutoAlliance is a joint venture of Mazda and Ford and the only transplant located in Michigan.
/2 NUMMI is the New United Motor Mfg. Inc. The company is jointly owned by Toyota and GM.
/3 SIA is Subaru-Isuzu Automotive Inc. The company is 51% owned by Fuji Industries and 49% by Isuzu.
- No data.
Source: Ward's Communications, Inc., Wards Automotive Yearbook (Detroit, Michigan: annually).

Table XIV-7. Motor Vehicle Employment in Michigan and the United States: 1970-1995
(Data in Thousands)

Year	Michigan	U.S.	Mich as a Percent(%) of U.S.	Year	Michigan	U.S.	Mich as a Percent(%) of U.S.
1970	335	799	42.0	1983	300	754	39.8
1971	354	849	41.7	1984	325	862	37.7
1972	370	875	42.2	1985	341	883	38.6
1973	401	977	41.1	1986	339	872	38.8
1974	366	908	40.3	1987	317	866	36.6
1975	321	792	40.5	1988	295	856	34.4
1976	358	881	40.6	1989	290	859	33.7
1977	387	947	40.8	1990	279	812	34.3
1978	410	1005	40.8	1991	267	789	33.8
1979	393	990	39.7	1992	272	809	33.7
1980	326	789	41.4	1993	267	837	31.2
1981	324	789	41.1	1994	278	886	31.4
1982	286	699	41.0	1995	283	933	30.4

Source: Michigan Employment Security Commission, Research and Statistics (Detroit, Michigan: special release).

Table XIV-8. Motor Vehicle and Supplier Employment in Michigan: 1970-1995
(Employment Data in Thousands)

Year	Employment	Percent(%) of Michigan Manufacturing	Year	Employment	Percent(%) of Michigan Manufacturing
1970	549	50.8	1983	452	51.3
1971	563	53.1	1984	497	51.7
1972	588	53.6	1985	519	51.7
1973	638	54.2	1986	514	51.4
1974	591	53.0	1987	483	49.7
1975	513	52.2	1988	471	49.3
1976	572	53.9	1989	474	48.8
1977	613	54.4	1990	456	48.3
1978	647	54.9	1991	431	48.1
1979	622	53.6	1992	439	48.7
1980	507	50.8	1993	438	48.2
1981	499	50.9	1994	463	48.7
1982	437	49.9	1995	475	48.8

Source: Michigan Employment Security Commission, Research and Statistics (Detroit, Michigan: special release).

Table XIV-9. Automaker Employment in Michigan: 1973-1994
(Data in Thousands)

Year	General Motors	Ford	Chrysler	AutoAlliance International	Total
1973	261	122	93	---	476
1974	227	118	82	---	427
1975	214	104	62	---	380
1976	239	111	79	---	429
1977	260	119	82	---	461
1978	274	128	80	---	482
1979	292	123	65	---	480
1980	244	96	44	---	384
1981	246	90	38	---	374
1982	179	82	32	---	293
1983	202	83	38	---	323
1984	227	87	43	---	357
1985	244	84	46	---	374
1986	245	83	47	1	376
1987	235	81	47	2	366
1988	201	85	44	3	333
1989	197	86	40	3	327
1990	179	80	38	3	301
1991	179	82	38	3	302
1992	154	80	38	4	276
1993	145	82	40	4	271
1994	159	85	44	4	292

Source: The Auto Companies (Detroit, Michigan).

Table XIV-10. Michigan Motor Vehicle Production, by Location: 1993-1994

Location	1993			1994		
	Total Cars	Total Trucks	Total Vehicles	Total Cars	Total Trucks	Total Vehicles
Chrysler-Total	**231,478**	**401,683**	**633,161**	**87,660**	**533,414**	**621,074**
Mack Avenue-Vipers	1,944	-	1,944	2,810	-	2,810
Sterling Heights	229,534	-	229,534	84,850	-	84,850
Dodge City	-	172,253	172,253	-	275,862	275,862
Jefferson Ave.	-	229,430	229,430	-	257,552	257,552
Ford-Total	**498,904**	**133,707**	**632,611**	**691,826**	**200,582**	**892,408**
Dearborn	106,238	-	106,238	199,048	-	199,048
Wayne Car	208,263	-	208,263	312,191	-	312,191
Wayne Truck	-	133,707	133,707	-	200,582	200,582
Wixom	184,403	-	184,403	180,587	-	180,587
Mazda-Total	219,076	-	219,076	247,004	-	247,004
Flatrock	219,076	-	219,076	247,004	-	247,004
General Motors-Total	**848,422**	**477,468**	**1,325,890**	**1,119,428**	**530,402**	**1,649,830**
Lake Orion	128,967	-	128,967	208,250	-	208,250
Hamtramck	117,080	-	117,080	222,844	-	222,844
Pontiac-West	-	95,976	95,976	-	116,301	116,301
Pontiac-East	-	234,778	234,778	-	237,918	237,918
Detroit	-	28,674	28,674	-	32,783	32,783
Flint-Buick City	221,816	-	221,816	268,749	-	268,749
Flint Truck	-	118,040	118,040	-	143,400	143,400
Lansing	335,428	-	335,428	419,585	-	419,585
Willow Run	45,131	-	45,131	0	-	0
TOTAL	**1,797,880**	**1,012,858**	**2,810,738**	**2,145,918**	**1,264,398**	**3,410,316**

- No data available.
Source: Ward's Communications, Inc., Ward's Automotive Yearbook (Detroit, Michigan: annually).

Table XIV-11. Annual U.S. Motor Vehicle Retail Sales: 1956-1994
(Data in Thousands)

Year	Total New Motor Vehicle Sales			New Passenger Car Sales			New Truck Sales		
	Domestic	Import	Total	Domestic	Import	Total	Domestic	Import	Total
1956	6,747	105	6,852	5,844	98	5,942	903	7	910
1957	6,704	223	6,927	5,826	207	6,033	878	16	894
1958	5,020	408	5,428	4,289	379	4,668	731	29	760
1959	6,414	651	7,065	5,486	614	6,100	928	37	965
1960	7,068	536	7,604	6,142	499	6,641	926	37	963
1961	6,464	408	6,872	5,556	379	5,935	908	29	937
1962	7,821	371	8,192	6,753	339	7,092	1,068	32	1,100
1963	8,564	426	8,990	7,334	386	7,720	1,230	40	1,270
1964	8,968	526	9,494	7,617	484	8,101	1,351	42	1,393
1965	10,302	583	10,885	8,763	569	9,332	1,539	14	1,553
1966	9,996	668	10,664	8,377	651	9,028	1,619	17	1,636
1967	9,092	790	9,882	7,568	769	8,337	1,524	21	1,545
1968	10,432	1,055	11,487	8,625	1,031	9,656	1,807	24	1,831
1969	10,400	1,152	11,552	8,464	1,118	9,582	1,936	34	1,970
1970	8,865	1,346	10,211	7,119	1,280	8,400	1,746	65	1,811
1971	10,693	1,646	12,338	8,681	1,561	10,242	2,011	85	2,096
1972	11,813	1,757	13,569	9,327	1,614	10,940	2,486	143	2,629
1973	12,591	1,981	14,572	9,676	1,748	11,424	2,916	233	3,148
1974	9,966	1,575	11,541	7,454	1,399	8,853	2,512	176	2,688
1975	9,302	1,801	11,103	7,053	1,571	8,624	2,249	229	2,478
1976	11,555	1,736	13,291	8,611	1,499	10,110	2,944	237	3,181
1977	12,461	2,398	14,859	9,109	2,074	11,183	3,352	323	3,675
1978	13,085	2,338	15,423	9,312	2,002	11,314	3,773	336	4,109
1979	11,351	2,802	14,153	8,341	2,332	10,673	3,010	470	3,480
1980	8,582	2,884	11,466	6,581	2,398	8,979	2,001	487	2,487
1981	8,018	2,778	10,796	6,209	2,327	8,536	1,809	451	2,260
1982	7,905	2,637	10,542	5,759	2,224	7,982	2,146	414	2,560
1983	9,454	2,858	12,312	6,795	2,387	9,182	2,658	471	3,129
1984	11,427	3,057	14,484	7,952	2,439	10,390	3,475	618	4,093
1985	12,107	3,617	15,724	8,205	2,838	11,042	3,902	779	4,682
1986	12,136	4,186	16,322	8,215	3,245	11,460	3,921	941	4,863
1987	11,136	4,053	15,189	7,081	3,196	10,277	4,055	858	4,912
1988	12,034	3,645	15,679	7,526	3,004	10,530	4,508	641	5,149
1989	11,476	3,237	14,713	7,073	2,699	9,772	4,403	538	4,941
1990	11,112	3,034	14,146	6,897	2,403	9,300	4,215	631	4,846
1991	9,950	2,589	12,539	6,137	2,038	8,175	3,813	551	4,365
1992	10,758	2,360	13,117	6,277	1,938	8,214	4,481	422	4,903
1993	12,022	2,177	14,199	6,734	1,783	8,518	5,287	394	5,681
1994	13,251	2,160	15,411	7,255	1,735	8,990	5,996	425	6,421

Source: Americaan Automobile Manufacturers Association, Facts & Figures (Detroit, Michigan: annually).

Table XIV-12. New Passenger Car and Truck Registrations in Michigan and the United States, by Name Plate: 1993 and 1994

Name Plate	1993		1994	
	Michigan	United States	Michigan	United States
TOTAL VEHICLES	**644,440**	**13,940,626**	**731,748**	**15,257,126**
Passenger Cars	**388,510**	**8,406,237**	**422,179**	**8,903,064**
Chrysler	15,688	194,600	14,599	196,266
Dodge	25,801	363,452	26,846	351,788
Plymouth	13,599	197,814	16,034	197,505
Ford	78,891	1,286,909	84,946	1,354,594
Lincoln	18,443	172,047	16,926	173,982
Mercury	22,702	406,793	24,135	387,120
Cadillac	13,134	196,712	16,000	206,022
Chevrolet	50,912	1,040,919	51,321	993,236
Oldsmobile	23,759	368,677	26,523	428,885
Pontiac	41,193	538,591	46,010	587,839
Other	13,924	918,502	10,041	619,899
Trucks	**388,510**	**5,534,389**	**309,569**	**6,354,062**
Chrysler	40,632	791,764	52,490	956,712
Ford	82,563	1,617,207	102,635	1,910,252
Chevrolet	61,222	1,278,268	73,259	1,442,385
G.M.C.	28,990	401,691	37,683	453,899
International	N.A.	N.A.	N.A.	N.A.
Jeep	18,051	391,410	21,664	433,375
PACCAR	971	34,000	1,027	41,824
Mack	260	17,336	253	21,296
Volvo-White	389	18,496	775	23,616
Other	3,447	270,449	3,944	331,352

N.A. Data not available.
Source: R.L. Polk & Company.

Table XIV-13. New Plant and Equipment Expenditures in the United States, by Motor Vehicle and Parts Manufacturers: 1970-1993*

Year	Expenditures on Motor Vehicle & Parts Manufacture (Data in Billions)	Percent (%) of Total Manufacturing Expenditures	Year	Expenditures on Motor Vehicle & Parts Manufacture (Data in Billions)	Percent (%) of Total Manufacturing Expenditures
1970	$8.36	3.3	1982	$7.48	2.2
1971	6.35	2.6	1983	6.90	2.0
1972	7.43	2.9	1984	10.63	2.7
1973	9.14	3.2	1985	13.86	3.3
1974	9.24	3.1	1986	13.00	3.2
1975	6.26	2.3	1987	10.88	2.7
1976	6.34	2.3	1988	9.49	2.1
1977	9.52	3.1	1989	10.92	2.3
1978	10.69	3.3	1990	10.51	2.1
1979	11.08	3.2	1991	9.44	1.9
1980	10.57	3.0	1992	8.11	1.6
1981	10.11	2.8	1993	11.63	2.1

Source: U.S. Department of Commerce, Bureau of Economic Analysis (Washington, D.C.). *Data adjusted for inflation.

Table XIV-14. Percentage of Capacity Utilization in United States Manufacturing: 1970-1993

Year	Percentage(%) All Manufacturing	Percentage(%) Motor Vehicle & Parts Manufacture	Year	Percentage(%) All Manufacturing	Percentage(%) Motor Vehicle & Parts Manufacture
1970	79.7	66.7	1982	72.8	52.5
1971	78.2	79.6	1983	74.9	65.4
1972	83.7	82.6	1984	80.4	78.6
1973	88.1	91.5	1985	79.5	83.4
1974	83.8	76.2	1986	79.0	79.5
1975	73.2	62.8	1987	81.4	78.1
1976	78.5	79.6	1988	83.9	80.5
1977	82.8	88.9	1989	83.9	79.2
1978	85.1	89.6	1990	82.3	72.6
1979	85.4	79.2	1991	78.2	67.5
1980	80.2	57.8	1992	77.8	71.9
1981	78.8	56.5	1993	80.9	78.8

Source: Board of Governors of the Federal Reserve System (Washington, D.C.).

Table XIV-15. Estimated Average Material Consumption in U.S.-Built Passenger Cars: Selected Years 1980, 1982, 1984, 1986, 1988, 1990, 1992, and 1993

Material	Calendar Year (Data in Pounds)							
	1980	1982	1984	1986	1988	1990	1992	1993
Conventional Steel	1,737	1,479	1,488	1,446	1,337	1,247	1,379	1,376
High Strength Steel	175	199	214	221	228	233	247	259
Stainless Steel	28	29	29	30	31	32	42	44
Other Steels	54	46	45	47	47	53	42	48
Iron	484	452	455	447	427	398	430	412
Aluminum	130	136	137	142	150	159	174	177
Rubber	131	132	134	132	130	128	133	135
Plastics and Plastic Composites	195	203	207	216	220	222	243	245
Glass	84	86	87	87	86	83	88	89
Copper and Brass	35	39	44	43	50	46	45	44
Zinc Die Castings	20	15	17	17	20	19	16	16
Powder Metal Parts	17	18	19	20	22	23	25	26
Fluids and Lubricants	178	180	180	183	177	167	177	189
Other Materials	96	91	88	90	89	88	96	93
Total	3,363	3,102	3,142	3,118	3,010	2,896	3,136	3,150

Source: American Metal Market.

Table XIV-16. Auto Supplier Research and Development and Technical Centers in Michigan: 1994

Company	Location	Employment	Products
A.A. Gage	Ferndale	40	gauges, position and test equip
Acco Controls Group	Wixom	60	control systems
Aero Detroit Inc	Madison Hts	1,000	prototyping
Aisin World Corp of America	Plymouth	17	powertrain, body, brake comp
Akebono America Inc	Farmington Hills	7	brake comp
Alco Fujikura Inc	Dearborn	66	wire harnesses
Allied Signal Inc	Southfield	1,200	brakes, safety restraints
Alps Automotive	Auburn Hills	80	elec systems and comp
American Standox Inc	Plymouth	16	aftermarket finishes
Applied Dynamics	Ann Arbor	58	simulation computers
Arco Chemical Co	Southfield	25	plastic resins, polyols
ASC Inc	Southgate	290	sunroofs, exterior/interior
Atoma International Inc	Livonia	200	seats, electronics, mirrors
BASF Corp	Southfield	300	paints, coatings
Balance Engineering	Troy	80	machine tools
Bertrand Faure Inc	Troy	50	seat components
Budd Co	Troy	70	stampings, wheel/brake, composites
Clark Laboratory	Buchanan	40	testing lab
Cloyes-Renold Automotive	Troy	8	CAM drive systems
C.T. Charton	St. Clair Shrores	24	shock absorbers
D&S Plastics International	Auburn Hills	50	plastic resins
Dana Corp	Ottawa Lake	100	transmission equipment
Donnelly Corp	Holland	N.A.	mirror systems/window systems
Dow Chemical Automotive	Southfield	50	plastics, fluids, magnesium
Dow Corning Corp	Plymouth	50	silicones, adhesives, lubricants
Du Pont Automotive	Troy	650	polymers, finishes, fibers
Dura Mechanical	Troy	90	window regulators, hood hinges
Eaton Corp	Southfield	270	powertrain
EG & G Kinematics	Troy	85	road simulation
Electro-Voice Inc	Buchanan	50	sound systems
Environmental Research	Ann Arbor	520	sensors, imaging
EPA Emissions Lab	Ann Arbor	316	emissions testing

Table XIV-16. Auto Supplier Research and Development and Technical Centers in Michigan: 1994 Continued

Company	Location	Employment	Products
Essex Specialty	Auburn Hills	200	adhesives, sealants
Fayette Tubular Products	Troy	80	AC hose accessories
Federal Mogul Corp	Ann Arbor	76	drivetrain comp
Fanuc Robotics N. America	Auburn Hills	550	robot systems
Fiberoptic Sensor	Ann Arbor	47	fiber-optic pressure monitoring
Findlay Industries Inc	Troy	110	seats, trim panels, headliners
Freudenberg-NOK	Plymouth	100	seals, gaskets, plastic comp
GE Plastics	Southfield	140	plastics, lighting systems
GMI Engineering	Flint	10	material research
Haden-Schweitzer Corp	Madison Heights	150	paint finishing systems
Handy & Harman	Auburn Hills	N.A.	fuel lines, controls, plastic
Hi-Lex Corp	Bloomfield Hills	34	window regulators, cable testing
Himont Inc	Lansing	80	composites
Hoechst Celanese	Auburn Hills	35	plastics, fibers, chemicals
Hughes Electronics	Livonia	25	electronics
Ichikoh America Inc	Ann Arbor	10	automotive exterior mirrors
Ikeda Engineering Inc	Farmington Hills	20	seats, trim
ICI America's Inc	Sterling Heights	80	polyurethane
ITT Automotive	Auburn Hills	600	ABS/traction control, wiper sys
Johnson Controls	Plymouth	600	seats, interiors
Kantus Engineering	Southfield	8	electronics
Kelsey-Hayes Co	Livonia	470	antilock brakes and controls
LDM Industries	Troy	50	plastic/molded trim
Lear Seating Corp	Southfield	200	seats
Litton Automated	Holland	54	computer controls, AGVs
Loctite Corp	Troy	28	sealants
LOF Automotive	Sterling Heights	27	glass
3M Co	Southfield	150	attachment systems
Mabuchi Motor	Auburn Hills	10	DC motors
Masco Corp	Taylor	100	interior/exterior systems
Masco Tech Inc	Auburn Hills	623	stamping, engineering services
McLaren Engines Inc	Livonia	100	engine testing and design

Table XIV-16. Auto Supplier Research and Development and Technical Centers in Michigan: 1994 Continued

Company	Location	Employment	Products
Medsker Electric Inc	Farmington Hills	6	dynamometers, testing equip
Michelin Automotive	Troy	100	tires
Michigan Auto Research	Ann Arbor	46	powertrains
Morton International	Rochester Hills	75	coatings, air bags
MSU Composite Center	East Lansing	112	composites
NGK Spark Plugs USA Inc	Farmington Hills	20	sensors, rotors
Nippondenso Tech Ctr Inc	Southfield	100	automotive parts, systems
North American Lighting	Farmington Hills	50	lighting systems
NSK Corp	Ann Arbor	19	bearings
NTN Bearing Corp	Ann Arbor	20	bearings
Parker Amchem	Madison Heights	350	conversion coating systems
PPG Industries Inc	Troy	N.A.	glass, coatings
Robert Bosch Corp	Farmington Hills	240	electrical/electronic comp
Rockwell International	Troy	150	plastics, component systems
Savant Inc	Midland	20	lubricant testing and research
SDRC	Madison Heights	26	CAD/CAM
Sensors Inc	Saline	72	gas analyzing
SI Systems	Rochester Hills	40	AGVs, AS/RS
Siemens Automotive	Auburn Hills	150	electronic systems
Tachi-S Engineering	Farmington Hills	26	seating systems
Thermotron Industries	Holland	6	environmental testing equip
Tri-Con Industries LTD	Auburn Hills	31	seating, trim
TRW Transport Electronics	Farmington Hills	300	electrical/electronic products
United Globe Nippon	Troy	28	sound dampening
Usui International Corp	Farmington Hills	10	fans
Vdo-Yazaki Corp	Rochester Hills	7	instrumentation
Woodbridge Group	Troy	7	seat testing
Yazaki EDS	Canton	123	research
TOTAL FIRMS - 92	---	**12,763**	---

Source: Wards AutoWorld.

Table XIV-17. Research and Development Expenditures by Manufacturer: 1975-1994
(Data in Millions)

Year	Total	General Motors	Ford	Chrysler
1975	$2,023	$1,114	$748	$161
1976	2,419	1,257	925	237
1977	2,907	1,451	1,170	286
1978	3,441	1,633	1,464	344
1979	4,028	1,950	1,720	358
1980	4,178	2,225	1,675	278
1981	4,218	2,250	1,718	250
1982	4,246	2,175	1,764	307
1983	4,718	2,602	1,751	365
1984	5,443	3,076	1,915	452
1985	6,252	3,625	2,018	609
1986	7,195	4,158	2,305	732
1987	7,648	4,361	2,514	773
1988	8,550	4,754	2,930	866
1989	9,373	5,248	3,167	958
1990	9,808	5,342	3,558	908
1991	10,570	5,887	3,728	955
1992	11,302	5,917	4,332	1,053
1993	12,281	6,030	5,021	1,230
1994	13,553	7,036	5,214	1,303

Source: Compiled by the American Automobile Manufacturers Association from annual reports of individual manufacturers.

Chapter XV
Transportation / Communication / Energy

The Office of Management and Budget in the Executive Office of the President is responsible for maintaining the Standard Industrial Classification system. The SIC is the system utilized in all federal statistical programs and in other programs where the focus is on economic activity.

According to the latest Standard Industrial Classification Manual,

> this division includes establishments providing, to the general public or to other business enterprises, passenger and freight transportation, communications services, or electricity, gas, steam, water or sanitary services, and all establishments of the United States Postal Service.

The Michigan Transportation Commission and the Michigan Department of Transportation provide a wide variety of data on transportation in this state in both their annual reports and by special release. At the national level, the Federal Highway Administration, the Federal Aviation Administration, and the Corps of Engineers publish data on highways, aviation, and waterways. The Interstate Commerce Commission publishes data on railroads.

The Michigan Department of State is the information source for motor vehicle registration. The Michigan Department of State Police compiles data on motor vehicle accidents.

The Michigan Press Association publishes an annual Michigan Newspaper Directory and Rate Book which gives circulation data for daily, semiweekly, and weekly newspapers. Editor and Publisher Company, in New York, is a source of national data.

The Federal Communications Commission publishes an annual Statistics of Communications Common Carriers which contains information on telephones.

The Michigan Public Service Commission regulates utilities in this state. Data on telephone companies and gas and electric utilities are maintained in the files of the PSC.

In Washington, D.C., the Energy Information Administration of the U.S. Department of Energy is a source of data on energy consumption in the various states. The Michigan Department of Commerce also has an Energy Administration agency.

Current data on employment, hours, and earnings are collected and disseminated by the Michigan Employment Security Commission in Detroit and by the Bureau of Labor Statistics in Washington, D.C.

LIST OF TABLES

Table	Page
XV-1. Distribution of the Michigan Transportation Fund, Fiscal Years: 1966-1995 . . .	482
XV-2. Transportation Employment, by Industry: 1970-1993	483

479

Chapter XV
Transportation / Communication / Energy

LIST OF TABLES

Table | **Page**

XV-3. Motor Vehicle Registrations in Michigan, by Type and by County: Fiscal Year 1993 484

XV-4. Motor Vehicle Accidents, Mileage, and Death Rates in Michigan: 1955-1992 486

XV-5. Number of Motor Vehicle Traffic Accidents, Persons Killed, and Injured in Michigan, by County: 1992 487

XV-6. Passengers, Mail, and Cargo for Air Carrier Airports: 1992 490

XV-7. Michigan Scheduled Air Carrier Airport Service Supply Indicators: 1993 492

XV-8. Annual Rail Transit Ridership: 1987-1993 492

XV-9. Annual Railroad Carloads and Tonnage in Michigan: 1985-1992 492

XV-10. Annual Ridership and Vehicle Hours for Each Local Public Transportation System in Michigan: 1992-1993 493

XV-11. Number and Circulation of Daily and Sunday Newspapers in Michigan: 1966-1992 495

XV-12. Michigan Daily Newspapers: 1992 496

XV-13. Number of Newspapers in Michigan, by Type: 1987-1994 497

XV-14. Number of Non-Newspaper Periodicals in Michigan, by Type: 1987-1994 . . . 497

XV-15. Total and Per Capita Energy Consumption in Michigan and the United States, Selected Years: 1960-1994 498

XV-16. Energy Consumption by Energy Type Measured in Trillions of British Thermal Units (BTUs) in Michigan, Selected Years: 1960-1992 499

XV-17. Per Capita Energy Consumption in Michigan and the United States in Trillions of British Thermal Units (BTUs), Selected Years: 1960-1991 499

XV-18. Residential Energy Consumption by Energy Type Measured in Trillions of British Thermal Units(BTUs) in Michigan, Selected Years: 1960-1992 500

Chapter XV
Transportation / Communication / Energy

List of Tables

Table		Page

XV-19. Commercial Energy Consumption by Energy Type Measured in Trillions of British Thermal Units (BTUs)in Michigan, Selected Years: 1960-1992 500

XV-20. Industrial Energy Consumption by Energy Type Measured in Trillions of British Thermal Units (BTUs) in Michigan, Selected Years: 1960-1992 500

XV-21. Transportation Energy Consumption by Energy Type Measured in Trillions of British Thermal Units (BTUs) in Michigan, Selected Years: 1960-1992 . . . 501

XV-22. Estimates of Energy Input at Electric Utilities by Energy Type Measured in Trillions of British Thermal Units (BTUs) in Michigan, Selected Years: 1960-1992 501

XV-23. Energy Price Estimates by Sector in Michigan, Selected Years: 1970-1992 . . . 502

XV-24. Energy Price Estimates by Source in Michigan, Selected Years: 1970-1991 . . . 503

XV-25. Energy Expenditure Estimates by Source in Michigan, Selected Years: 1970-1991 503

Table XV-1. Distribution of the Michigan Transportation Fund, Fiscal Years: 1966 - 1995
(Data in Millions)

Fiscal Years	Total	State Trunkline Fund	Comprehensive Transportation Fund	Counties	Municipalities
1966	266	125	0	93	48
1967	309	129	0	96	50
1968	309	148	0	104	57
1969	357	164	0	122	71
1970	380	175	0	129	76
1971	394	181	0	134	79
1972	420	193	0	143	84
1973	491	215	18	164	94
1974	540	231	21	185	103
1975	537	228	22	183	102
1976	652	277	27	223	125
1977	578	246	23	198	110
1978	586	249	24	201	112
1979	712	272	59	245	136
1980	684	260	56	236	131
1981	628	239	52	217	121
1982	608	231	50	210	117
1983	667	247	65	231	124
1984	794	278	79	280	157
1985	865	301	87	301	169
1986	900	316	91	315	178
1987	929	326	93	326	184
1988	984	345	99	345	195
1989	1,027	358	109	358	202
1990	1,033	361	107	361	204
1991	1,023	357	107	357	202
1992	1,061	371	110	370	209
1993	1,100	384	117	383	217
1994	1,127	392	120	392	222
1995	1,182	412	126	411	233

Source: Michigan Transportation Commission, Annual Report, Michigan Transportation Fund (Lansing, Michigan: annually).

Table XV-2. Transportation Employment, by Industry: 1970-1993

Year	Transportation Industry (Data in Thousands)					
	Railroad	Local/Suburban Passenger	Motor Freight/ Warehousing	U.S. Post Office	Air	Transport Services
1970	19.9	6.3	37.6	N.A.	5.7	N.A.
1971	19.0	5.8	37.8	N.A.	5.1	N.A.
1972	18.1	5.5	38.9	N.A.	5.2	N.A.
1973	17.6	5.6	42.4	N.A.	5.9	N.A.
1974	17.1	5.4	41.6	N.A.	6.0	N.A.
1975	17.0	4.8	37.4	N.A.	5.3	N.A.
1976	16.8	4.7	39.6	24.1	5.2	N.A.
1977	17.0	4.5	43.6	23.5	5.7	N.A.
1978	15.5	4.3	46.7	23.3	6.6	N.A.
1979	16.2	4.4	47.2	24.5	7.3	N.A.
1980	14.8	4.4	39.6	24.1	6.9	N.A.
1981	13.2	4.2	37.7	23.9	6.5	N.A.
1982	12.4	3.9	35.7	23.8	6.4	N.A.
1983	10.5	4.0	36.0	23.4	6.8	N.A.
1984	10.2	3.7	39.1	23.9	7.9	N.A.
1985	9.5	4.1	42.1	25.2	9.5	N.A.
1986	9.0	4.4	43.4	27.0	11.9	N.A.
1987	8.2	4.7	44.0	27.3	14.6	N.A.
1988	8.0	5.1	45.3	27.9	15.6	8.9
1989	7.7	5.7	45.6	27.9	16.4	9.8
1990	7.7	6.0	46.7	27.6	17.7	10.7
1991	7.4	6.0	46.3	27.2	17.6	10.9
1992	7.0	6.3	45.4	26.8	16.7	11.2
1993	7.0	6.4	47.4	26.7	16.3	11.8
1994	6.7	7.2	50.2	28.5	17.5	13.4

Source: Michigan Employment Security Commission, Research and Statistics (Detroit, Michigan). N.A. Data not available.

Table XV-3. Motor Vehicle Registrations in Michigan, by Type and by County: Fiscal Year 1993

County	Total	Passenger	Commercial	Trailer	Motorcycle
Alcona	6,046	2,702	1,915	110	262
Alger	4,282	2,366	1,074	161	141
Allegan	47,386	18,729	12,323	1,426	1,249
Alpena	16,551	7,634	4,692	383	509
Antrim	11,292	4,401	3,200	305	248
Arenac	8,329	3,803	2,446	213	264
Baraga	3,514	1,968	925	108	77
Barry	26,209	10,742	6,767	907	782
Bay	63,569	18,936	14,795	1,529	1,375
Benzie	7,711	3,111	2,083	236	195
Berrien	91,398	27,374	15,020	2,331	2,600
Branch	21,097	9,014	5,566	627	615
Calhoun	75,130	21,474	12,462	1,903	2,599
Cass	24,181	10,076	5,750	715	637
Charlevoix	13,349	5,314	3,334	424	380
Cheboygan	12,352	5,614	3,601	343	366
Chippewa	15,111	7,275	4,196	402	397
Clare	14,066	6,271	4,141	349	683
Clinton	31,220	11,512	7,645	801	983
Crawford	5,983	2,725	1,863	157	390
Delta	20,511	9,590	5,906	588	447
Dickinson	14,260	6,858	4,115	540	525
Eaton	49,589	15,975	10,436	1,304	2,522
Emmet	16,270	5,983	3,685	439	451
Genesee	236,511	59,245	36,328	5,107	5,590
Gladwin	12,516	5,602	3,838	375	438
Gogebic	8,267	3,964	1,728	208	487
Grand Traverse	42,540	13,291	10,104	1,002	829
Gratiot	20,258	8,134	5,462	579	648
Hillsdale	21,950	9,695	5,475	678	565
Houghton	16,024	5,910	2,650	432	349
Huron	20,547	9,200	5,323	488	525
Ingham	158,534	33,962	20,952	3,197	5,618
Ionia	27,151	10,741	6,265	754	670
Iosco	15,081	6,024	4,424	359	439
Iron	6,518	3,547	1,926	182	351
Isabella	23,774	9,081	5,505	600	566
Jackson	80,653	25,218	14,970	2,243	2,164
Kalamazoo	129,690	30,370	19,485	2,981	3,267
Kalkaska	7,275	4,351	2,643	229	194
Kent	301,188	74,037	53,003	6,357	6,138
Keweenaw	809	347	179	18	22
Lake	4,454	2,209	1,289	122	200

Table XV-3. Motor Vehicle Registrations in Michigan, by Type and by County: Fiscal Year 1993 Continued

County	Total	Passenger	Commercial	Trailer	Motorcycle
Lapeer	41,985	17,137	9,412	1,322	1,098
Leelanau	10,245	3,754	2,834	231	249
Lenawee	50,174	18,284	10,395	1,525	1,196
Livingston	75,522	23,628	15,170	2,161	1,783
Luce	2,659	1,649	1,113	66	99
Mackinac	5,412	2,813	1,628	144	168
Macomb	459,315	85,347	48,283	7,983	10,721
Manistee	12,595	5,359	3,280	341	445
Marquette	34,325	14,075	7,002	1,158	1,025
Mason	14,122	5,792	3,587	392	461
Mecosta	16,695	6,728	4,053	400	519
Menominee	12,164	5,367	3,500	380	437
Midland	48,094	12,819	10,348	1,266	963
Missaukee	5,872	3,433	2,042	144	212
Monroe	75,073	25,402	13,568	2,183	1,896
Montcalm	27,400	11,892	7,327	711	726
Montmorency	4,864	2,596	1,639	120	233
Muskegon	87,450	24,527	16,947	2,556	2,797
Newaygo	20,646	9,093	5,942	613	775
Oakland	704,167	118,809	71,370	12,382	14,605
Oceana	11,816	5,563	2,843	332	442
Ogemaw	10,234	5,073	3,294	259	356
Ontonagon	4,257	2,314	1,275	121	106
Osceola	10,583	5,232	2,874	276	378
Oscoda	4,368	2,292	1,420	122	193
Otsego	10,694	4,836	2,934	276	327
Ottawa	111,996	30,227	25,645	2,577	2,443
Presque Isle	7,632	4,031	2,333	159	274
Roscommon	12,977	4,972	3,890	278	621
Saginaw	119,622	30,376	22,131	2,024	2,744
St. Clair	85,738	26,719	14,505	2,242	2,828
St. Joseph	31,185	11,983	7,342	1,150	911
Sanilac	22,086	9,552	4,888	636	699
Schoolcraft	4,087	2,307	1,408	111	143
Shiawassee	37,994	14,454	8,679	1,173	1,210
Tuscola	29,723	12,788	8,186	864	762
Van Buren	35,704	13,859	7,174	1,022	1,145
Washtenaw	157,406	32,543	16,329	3,512	3,587
Wayne	1,091,558	173,476	86,132	15,901	23,842
Wexford	14,965	5,852	3,869	410	476
Michigan	**5,310,385**	**1,347,145**	**822,181**	**111,992**	**132,632**

Source: Michigan Secretary of State (Lansing, Michigan).

Table XV-4. Motor Vehicle Accidents, Mileage, and Death Rates in Michigan: 1955-1992

Years	Deaths	Injuries	Accidents	Estimated Mileage (Millions)	Death Rate
1955	2,016	62,234	196,812	28,283	7.1
1956	1,746	61,158	197,995	28,429	6.1
1957	1,548	60,067	191,915	29,252	5.3
1958	1,382	57,767	177,934	29,411	4.7
1959	1,473	64,873	198,771	30,679	4.8
1960	1,604	91,026	209,724	31,842	5.0
1961	1,567	93,350	199,973	32,102	4.9
1962	1,574	108,143	233,078	34,498	4.6
1963	1,887	126,896	261,794	36,452	5.2
1964	2,122	144,623	284,444	38,618	5.5
1965	2,136	155,258	310,598	40,857	5.2
1966	2,298	156,694	302,880	43,940	5.2
1967	2,137	151,297	299,004	45,054	4.7
1968	2,392	160,413	305,495	48,047	5.0
1969	2,487	175,400	331,223	50,905	4.9
1970	2,177	161,719	313,715	53,148	4.1
1971	2,152	157,664	314,015	55,540	3.9
1972	2,258	178,929	359,745	57,817	3.9
1973	2,213	169,485	350,864	58,478	3.8
1974	1,825	141,132	324,763	55,749	3.4
1975	1,811	147,299	333,560	56,261	3.2
1976	1,955	162,894	365,600	61,827	3.2
1977	1,950	166,389	374,751	64,800	3.0
1978	2,076	169,202	389,193	67,375	3.1
1979	1,849	162,571	366,435	64,882	2.9
1980	1,774	144,972	315,594	61,190	2.9
1981	1,589	136,455	302,831	62,000	2.6
1982	1,417	130,061	294,971	61,322	2.3
1983	1,331	135,811	300,797	63,560	2.1
1984	1,556	150,740	335,193	65,730	2.4
1985	1,569	157,417	386,904	68,413	2.3
1986	1,632	158,032	400,694	70,622	2.3
1987	1,632	156,318	397,224	75,715	2.2
1988	1,704	155,713	410,437	77,700	2.2
1989	1,630	154,537	417,252	79,900	2.0
1990	1,563	145,179	387,180	81,200	1.9
1991	1,425	135,830	364,847	81,900	1.7
1992	1,300	118,999	345,526	84,000	1.5

Source: Michigan Department of State Police, Michigan Traffic Accident Facts (Lansing, Michigan: annually).

Table XV-5. Number of Motor Vehicle Traffic Accidents, Persons Killed, and Injured in Michigan, by County: 1992

County	Accidents							Persons	
	Total	Fatal	Injury	Property Damage	Interstate	Local Street	State Route	Total Killed	Total Injured
Alcona	795	5	79	711	0	500	192	5	138
Alger	434	0	94	340	0	176	215	0	141
Allegan	3,182	21	701	2,460	212	2,036	652	24	1,116
Alpena	1,276	2	242	1,034	0	746	213	2	363
Antrim	861	8	146	707	0	505	156	10	199
Arenac	872	2	162	705	71	440	84	6	237
Baraga	460	4	47	409	0	206	51	6	82
Barry	2,119	5	399	1,715	0	1,507	612	5	574
Bay	3,679	17	930	2,732	148	2,294	1,118	20	1,351
Benzie	574	2	114	458	0	355	109	2	143
Berrien	5,540	12	1,379	4,149	795	3,258	666	13	2,032
Branch	1,784	7	346	1,431	151	1,143	60	8	485
Calhoun	5,776	36	1,123	4,622	993	3,892	845	29	1,651
Cass	1,801	19	356	1,426	3	1,128	535	24	514
Charlevoix	1,062	6	151	905	0	592	183	6	211
Cheboygan	917	3	255	659	169	475	204	3	387
Chippewa	1,401	8	241	1,152	327	794	280	9	346
Clare	1,380	3	280	1,097	0	781	154	3	390
Clinton	2,024	12	360	1,652	264	1,260	130	12	554
Crawford	860	4	135	721	217	446	179	4	219
Delta	2,191	3	323	1,865	1	1,285	337	3	466
Dickinson	1,351	4	214	1,133	0	614	323	4	331
Eaton	3,508	13	759	2,736	446	1,797	1,034	15	1,089
Emmet	1,432	3	283	1,146	6	736	126	3	412
Genesee	13,740	47	3,580	10,113	1,232	9,900	2,274	54	5,410
Gladwin	920	1	176	743	0	517	403	3	252
Gogebic	581	1	85	495	0	288	36	1	146
Grand Traverse	2,994	16	644	2,334	0	1,890	308	16	960

Table XV-5. Number of Motor Vehicle Traffic Accidents, Persons Killed, and Injured in Michigan, by County: 1992 Continued

County	Accidents							Persons	
	Total	Fatal	Injury	Property Damage	Interstate	Local Street	State Route	Total Killed	Total Injured
Gratiot	1,347	8	282	1,057	0	791	224	10	430
Hillsdale	1,656	13	313	1,330	0	1,071	436	16	446
Houghton	1,354	8	227	1,119	0	574	368	9	321
Huron	1,494	14	248	1,232	0	814	680	18	375
Ingham	11,122	21	2,527	8,574	1,523	7,030	2,195	25	3,513
Ionia	2,177	9	433	1,735	200	1,321	656	9	631
Iosco	1,226	7	203	1,016	0	696	235	7	300
Iron	767	1	94	672	0	404	210	1	128
Isabella	2,154	12	390	1,752	0	1,444	243	14	555
Jackson	5,767	30	1,225	4,512	823	3,772	926	35	1,828
Kalamazoo	9,739	30	1,963	7,744	739	7,110	1,338	31	2,774
Kalkaska	680	3	121	556	0	390	159	4	194
Kent	19,829	51	4,703	15,075	1,157	13,667	3,595	61	6,649
Keweenaw	69	0	14	55	0	34	5	0	16
Lake	517	2	103	412	0	332	91	3	143
Lapeer	2,763	15	574	2,174	146	1,671	946	15	843
Leelanau	586	3	112	471	0	325	261	3	188
Lenawee	2,930	24	705	2,201	0	1,690	535	29	1,060
Livingston	4,365	16	1,102	3,247	833	2,733	503	16	1,637
Luce	254	0	60	194	0	115	139	0	75
Mackinac	765	2	124	639	148	267	179	3	181
Macomb	22,914	56	6,318	16,540	1,261	15,208	6,445	59	9,306
Manistee	806	1	148	657	0	471	114	1	231
Marquette	2,781	7	500	2,274	0	1,636	316	7	726
Mason	1,156	8	221	927	0	738	24	9	327
Mecosta	2,023	5	320	1,698	0	1,108	372	5	467
Menominee	1,673	5	218	1,450	0	971	141	6	328
Midland	2,761	5	573	2,183	0	1,996	442	5	790

Table XV-5. Number of Motor Vehicle Traffic Accidents, Persons Killed, and Injured in Michigan, by County: 1992 Continued

County	Accidents							Persons	
	Total	Fatal	Injury	Property Damage	Interstate	Local Street	State Route	Total Killed	Total Injured
Missaukee	564	4	95	465	0	347	217	4	147
Monroe	3,875	17	1,053	2,805	322	2,316	569	20	1,585
Montcalm	2,561	10	487	2,064	0	1,554	933	12	744
Montmorency	434	1	79	354	0	275	159	1	108
Muskegon	5,558	16	1,308	4,234	71	3,883	683	17	1,929
Newaygo	1,630	10	372	1,248	0	1,072	558	13	583
Oakland	38,794	81	10,189	28,524	4,200	26,011	6,152	86	14,668
Oceana	856	3	217	636	0	603	49	3	326
Ogemaw	1,140	10	176	954	194	674	272	13	255
Ontonagon	527	3	61	463	0	150	253	3	94
Osceola	1,047	5	208	834	0	567	178	5	336
Oscoda	540	1	71	468	0	294	246	1	92
Otsego	931	6	203	722	208	511	212	6	282
Ottawa	5,941	27	1,447	4,467	334	4,148	558	27	2,115
Presque Isle	595	2	84	509	0	305	129	2	149
Roscommon	1,048	2	221	324	113	540	295	2	337
Saginaw	7,994	27	1,832	6,135	409	5,305	2,280	27	2,707
St. Clair	1,463	14	284	1,165	0	817	646	15	453
St. Joseph	472	1	77	394	0	195	152	2	114
Sanilac	1,800	14	459	1,327	135	1,052	613	15	681
Schoolcraft	4,866	17	1,159	3,690	718	3,032	1,115	21	1,785
Shiawassee	2,181	13	542	1,626	0	1,307	309	13	850
Tuscola	1,796	15	404	1,377	0	1,131	665	17	612
Van Buren	2,544	15	612	1,917	411	1,585	548	17	924
Washtenaw	10,181	32	2,284	7,865	1,115	6,829	935	32	3,210
Wayne	75,012	210	19,488	55,314	7,296	52,578	9,926	224	28,626
Wexford	1,420	10	327	1,083	0	569	387	11	492
Michigan	344,951	1,179	81,169	262,611	27,381	225,588	62,296	1,300	118,869

Source: Michigan Department of State Police, Michigan Traffic Accident Facts, 1992 (Lansing, Michigan: annually).

Table XV-6. Passengers, Mail, and Cargo for Air Carrier Airports: 1992

Airport Name	Passengers			Cargo (Tons)			Mail (Pounds)		
	Total	Enplaned	Deplaned	Total	Inbound	Outbound	Total	Inbound	Outbound
Alpena County Regional Airport	13,280	6,570	6,710	391,888	253,452	138,436	0	0	0
Detroit City Airport	561,962	285,011	276,951	2,898,892	2,049,144	849,748	0	0	0
Detroit Metropolitan Airport	22,914,828	11,472,424	11,442,404	401,147,270	208,780,692	192,366,578	192,965,971	99,014,259	93,951,712
Escanaba, Delta County Airport	29,986	14,823	15,163	1,542,412	771,787	770,625	3,547	0	3,547
Flint, Bishop Airport	281,910	140,678	141,232	23,198,731	13,081,811	10,116,920	171,606	4,064	167,542
Grand Rapids, Kent County International	1,444,052	722,855	721,197	40,525,421	19,056,111	21,469,310	22,889,921	13,605,514	9,284,407
Houghton County Memorial Airport	37,888	18,971	18,917	328,483	208,662	119,821	2,416	66	2,350
Iron Mountain/Kingsford, Ford Airport	23,396	11,672	11,724	1,621,985	1,046,571	575,414	0	0	0
Ironwood, Gogebic County Airport	9,727	4,857	4,870	189,522	110,899	78,623	671	37	634
Kalamazoo/Battle Creek International	546,916	272,804	274,112	825,541	523,351	302,190	298,862	96,310	202,552
Lansing, Capital City Airport	552,826	272,297	280,529	40,438,168	20,154,321	20,283,847	2,600,964	711,867	1,889,097
Manistee, Blacker Airport	3,609	1,794	1,815	536	312	224	0	0	0
Marquette County Airport	104,537	52,037	52,500	61,128	39,805	21,323	2,995	4	2,991
Menominee/Marinette Twin County Airport	2,999	1,508	1,491	372,002	180,529	191,473	0	0	0

Table XV-6. Passengers, Mail, and Cargo for Air Carrier Airport: 1992 Continued

Airport Name	Passengers			Cargo (Tons)			Mail (Pounds)		
	Total	Enplaned	Deplaned	Total	Inbound	Outbound	Total	Inbound	Outbound
Muskegon County Airport	101,801	50,769	51,032	84,351	42,596	41,755	0	0	0
Pellston Regional Airport	53,436	26,335	27,101	471,696	363,031	108,665	0	0	0
Saginaw/Midland/Bay City, Tri-City-Intl.	510,767	254,296	256,471	5,132,881	1,989,872	3,143,009	1,169,517	37,328	1,132,189
Sault Ste. Marie, Chippewa County Intl.	18,099	8,960	9,139	4,731	3,657	1,074	0	0	0
Traverse City, Cherry Capital Airport	293,999	146,095	147,904	2,483,620	1,700,364	783,256	622,148	4,816	617,332

Source: Michigan Department of Transportation (Lansing, Michigan).

Table XV-7. Michigan Scheduled Air Carrier Airport Service Supply Indicators: 1993

Community	Carriers Serving	Weekly Nonstop Arrivals			Weekly Nonstop Arriving Seats		
		Total	Jet Aircraft	Propeller Aircraft	Total	Jet Aircraft	Propeller Aircraft
Alpena	1	1,755	0	45	855	0	855
Detroit City	1	390	0	10	190	0	190
Detroit Metro	22	912,320	2,855	771	454,347	428,883	25,464
Escanaba	2	4,671	0	81	2,295	0	2,295
Flint	6	15,149	14	165	7,485	1,729	5,756
Grand Rapids	11	55,687	190	167	27,665	23,892	3,773
Houghton/Hancock	2	3,979	0	43	1,968	0	1,968
Iron Mtn./Kingsford	1	2,301	0	59	1,121	0	1,121
Ironwood	1	1,326	0	34	646	0	646
Kalamazoo/BCreek	10	28,111	53	206	13,926	6,717	7,209
Lansing	11	31,427	54	285	15,544	6,870	8,674
Manistee	1	975	0	25	475	0	475
Marquette	4	7,514	0	88	3,713	0	3,713
Menominee	1	1,716	0	44	836	0	836
Muskegon	3	4,284	0	84	2,100	0	2,100
Pellston	2	2,535	0	47	1,244	0	1,244
Sag./Mid./B.City	5	24,122	75	69	11,989	9,991	1,998
Sault Ste. Marie	1	1,482	0	38	722	0	722
Traverse City	4	10,115	13	92	5,005	1,625	3,380

Source: Michigan Department of Transportation, Bureau of Transportation Planning, Systems Monitoring Unit (Lansing, Michigan).

Table XV-8. Annual Rail Transit Ridership: 1987-1993

Year	Total Ridership	Detroit-Chicago	Port Huron-Chicago	Grand Rapids-Chicago
1987	477,919	305,208	110,734	61,977
1988	459,053	285,462	105,557	68,034
1989	461,394	296,398	98,952	66,044
1990	538,338	360,961	105,389	71,988
1991	564,441	390,145	104,129	70,167
1992	546,616	372,071	106,126	68,419
1993	572,566	391,386	114,886	66,294

Source: Michigan Department of Transportation, Bureau of Transportation Planning, Intermodal Section, Freight Planning Unit (Lansing, Mich).

Table XV-9. Annual Railroad Carloads and Tonnage in Michigan: 1985-1992

Year	Total Carloads	Total Tonnage	Michigan Originating Carloads	Michigan Terminating Carloads
1985	1,354,000	75,962,000	716,000	638,000
1986	1,320,000	75,012,000	675,000	645,000
1987	1,357,000	78,008,000	674,000	683,000
1988	1,464,000	84,589,000	703,000	761,000
1989	1,463,000	84,621,000	719,000	744,000
1990	1,377,000	87,049,000	684,000	693,000
1991	1,289,962	76,216,889	628,762	661,200
1992	1,348,424	76,018,527	674,486	673,938

Source: Michigan Department of Transportation, Bureau of Transportation Planning, Intermodal Section, Freight Planning Unit (Lansing, Mich).

Table XV-10. Annual Ridership and Vehicle Hours for Each Local Public Transportation System in Michigan: 1992-1993

Planning Area	Annual Ridership		Annual Vehicle Hours	
	1992	1993	1992	1993
Urban Systems	90,131,353	90,382,423	3,721,701	3,699,896
Ann Arbor Transp. Auth.	4,112,320	4,054,023	278,561	273,526
Battle Creek	754,105	777,909	47,585	47,863
Bay Co. Metro Ttrans Auth.	502,519	519,954	53,077	57,389
Benton Harbor Area/TCATA	165,931	162,473	31,202	31,923
DDOT	58,950,856	57,445,323	1,653,183	1,543,680
SMART	8,931,089	8,534,490	818,877	765,717
Flint Area/MTA	4,365,099	6,671,997	194,804	333,700
Grand Rapids Area/GRATA	3,618,962	3,898,842	158,314	161,329
Holland	140,793	150,122	21,795	22,543
Jackson Trans. Auth.	521,933	573,063	44,256	45,410
Kalamazoo Metro Transit	1,540,805	1,517,599	78,164	75,599
C.A.T.A.	4,448,047	4,112,058	209,634	206,033
Muskegon Area Trans. Auth	617,777	635,804	36,861	36,720
Niles Dial-a-Ride	97,243	109,549	17,347	17,335
Saginaw Transit System	1,363,874	1,219,217	78,041	81,129
Non-Urban Systems	5,731,649	5,674,745	1,089,033	961,617
Adrian	95,106	98,688	11,828	11,524
Altran	46,700	43,420	12,241	9,679
Alma	67,538	59,663	6,738	5,935
Alpena/Prell Services	82,948	83,976	12,542	12,555
Antrim Co.	83,748	75,373	19,144	17,403
Barry County Transit	76,476	79,438	10,113	10,472
Bay Metro Non-Urban	106,357	112,642	20,232	20,340
Belding	41,246	41,791	5,208	5,066
Berrien Co. Pub. Trans.	166,921	175,113	26,731	25,875
Big Rapids	102,124	116,433	12,246	12,488
Branch Area Trans. Auth.	83,257	88,824	15,827	18,006
Buchanan	13,416	17,331	3,644	3,692
Cadillac/Wexford	121,373	100,757	23,956	21,528
Caro Transit Authority	43,392	46,862	123,885	8,596
Charlevoix Co. Pub. Trans.	90,920	92,392	13,181	18,280
Clare Co. Pub. Trans Corp.	64,319	73,049	17,211	18,305
Crawford Co.	96,766	97,944	16,060	16,693
Smart/Lake Erie/Monroe	472,469	393,703	67,810	45,391
Dowagiac	30,280	26,909	4,978	4,798
Eaton Co. Eatran	155,522	141,362	32,739	25,153
EUPTA	80,726	74,886	13,426	13,341
Gladwin Co.	123,749	118,745	25,779	27,132
Gogebic Co. Public Trans.	38,323	35,747	7,084	7,056
Harbor Transit	168,647	173,320	22,152	22,279
Traverse City	303,255	325,023	52,420	57,999

Table XV-10. Annual Ridership and Vehicle Hours for Each Local Public Transportation System in Michigan: 1992-1993 Continued

Planning Area	Annual Ridership		Annual Vehicle Hours	
	1992	1993	1992	1993
Greenville	39,717	32,007	6,615	6,595
Hillsdale Dial-a-Ride	90,424	81,395	9,276	8,344
Houghton Co.	52,548	58,693	12,800	13,223
Huron Transit Corp.	163,896	172,715	38,932	40,772
Ionia Dial-a-Ride	92,673	84,079	7,713	8,041
Iosco Transit Corp.	19,061	26,013	6,553	6,510
Isabella Co. Trans Comm.	303,132	264,665	53,550	50,197
Jackson Non-Urban	44,377	46,973	9,834	11,930
Kalamazoo/Non-Urban	74,453	88,386	20,303	27,148
Kalkaska Pub. Trans Auth.	71,642	69,604	10,153	10,185
C.A.T.A./Non-Urban	54,936	63,436	16,095	15,154
Lapeer	56,447	93,040	9,877	15,933
Lenawee Co.	80,312	84,273	12,472	12,055
Livingston Co.	15,084	57,962	3,737	13,945
Ludington MTA	155,885	163,507	18,188	19,216
Manistee Co.	272,773	214,246	32,255	20,082
Marquette/Marqtran	330,775	322,988	49,655	46,728
Marshall	50,887	53,792	5,976	5,677
Mecosta Co.	76,206	65,665	10,492	9,789
Midland	157,486	160,867	28,272	29,092
Ogemaw Co. Pub. Transit	66,676	69,151	11,291	11,376
Ontonagon	45,280	43,622	8,823	9,191
Osceola Co.	41,363	41,595	6,700	6,772
Oscoda Co. Pub. Transit	33,732	38,098	8,972	8,537
Otsego Co. Pub. Transit	97,144	101,675	18,746	19,128
Roscommon Mini Bus Sys.	166,062	165,701	27,876	29,719
Sanilac Trans. Corp.	68,575	63,065	16,347	14,155
Saugatuck/Interurban	38,024	39,992	7,439	7,856
Sault Ste. Marie	60,049	52,715	8,716	8,642
Schoolcraft	39,756	37,582	4,282	4,866
Van Buren Co.	81,430	89,223	16,874	16,673
Yates Township	35,266	30,389	13,044	12,900

Source: Michigan Department of Transportation, Operational Data, Bus Passenger Transportation Program (Lansing, Michigan).

Table XV-11. Number and Circulation of Daily and Sunday Newspapers in Michigan: 1966-1992

Year	Daily Circulation		Sunday Newspapers	
	Number	Paid Circulation (In Thousands)	Number	Paid Circulation (In Thousands)
1966	54	2,410	11	2,093
1967	54	2,492	11	2,167
1968	54	2,435	12	2,085
1969	55	2,415	12	2,080
1970	56	2,512	13	2,189
1971	55	2,447	13	2,187
1972	55	2,510	14	2,245
1973	55	2,569	14	2,276
1974	55	2,527	14	2,269
1975	52	2,448	15	2,361
1976	53	2,453	14	2,225
1977	52	2,457	14	2,237
1978	52	2,458	17	2,366
1979	52	2,458	17	2,363
1980	52	2,448	15	2,361
1981	52	2,463	15	2,400
1982	52	2,492	15	2,447
1983	52	2,507	15	2,498
1984	52	2,524	15	2,533
1985	52	2,495	15	2,468
1986	52	2,549	15	2,468
1987	52	2,565	15	2,470
1988	52	2,532	16	2,455
1989	52	2,541	21	2,562
1990	52	2,373	23	2,431
1991	52	2,262	24	2,405
1992	52	2,373	23	2,431

Source: Editor & Publisher Co., Editor & Publisher International Year Book, (New York, New York: annually).

Table XV-12. Michigan Daily Newspapers: 1992

Paper Name	Circulation		Paper Name	Circulation	
	Daily	Sunday		Daily	Sunday
Adrian Daily Telegram	18,000	N.A.	Jackson Citizen Patriot	36,171	43,999
Albion Recorder	1,927	N.A.	Kalamazoo Gazette	65,836	82,195
Alpena News	13,200	N.A.	Lansing State Journal	71,425	94,217
Ann Arbor News	51,578	68,540	Ludington Daily News	8,087	N.A.
Bad Axe Huron Daily Tribune	8,899	N.A.	Manistee News Advocate	5,239	N.A.
Battle Creek Enquirer	28,432	38,444	Marquette Mining Journal	19,030	20,421
Bay City Times	40,193	52,468	Marshall Chronicle	2,011	N.A.
Big Rapids Pioneer	5,978	N.A.	Menominee Herald - Leader	4,600	N.A.
Cadillac News	9,748	N.A.	Midland Daily News	17,089	N.A.
Cheboygan Daily Tribune	4,122	N.A.	Monroe Evening News	24,076	N.A.
Coldwater Daily Reporter	7,448	N.A.	Mt Clemens Macomb Daily	47,859	N.A.
Detroit Free Press	623,408	1,191,790	Mt Pleasant Morning Sun	10,156	N.A.
Detroit Legal News	2,016	N.A.	Muskegon Chronicle	46,896	51,564
Detroit News	421,005	1,191,790	Niles Daily Star	3,603	N.A.
Dowagiac Daily News	2,808	N.A.	Owosso Argus - Press	11,830	N.A.
Escanaba Daily Press	11,281	N.A.	Petoskey News - Review	11,451	N.A.
Fenton Tri-County News	8,640	N.A.	Pontiac Oakland Press	73,469	81,434
Flint Journal	102,226	122,095	Port Huron Times Herald	30,678	39,023
Grand Haven Tribune	10,808	N.A.	Royal Oak Daily Tribune	26,486	N.A.
Grand Rapids Press	149,452	196,200	Saginaw News	56,577	66,475
Greenville Daily News	8,862	N.A.	Sault Ste Marie Evening News	7,734	8,600
Hillsdale Daily News	8,254	N.A.	South Haven Daily Tribune	4,178	N.A.
Holland Sentinel	19,769	19,855	St Joseph Herald Palladium	35,500	N.A.
Houghton Daily Mining Gazette	12,638	N.A.	Sturgis Journal	7,575	N.A.
Ionia Sentinel Standard	5,935	N.A.	Three Rivers Commercial News	3,901	N.A.
Iron Mountain Daily News	11,434	N.A.	Traverse City Record Eagle	26,485	37,546
Ironwood Daily Globe	8,108	N.A.	Ypsilanti Press	14,704	N.A.

Source: Michigan Press Association, 1992 Michigan Newspaper Directory (Lansing, Michigan: 1993). N.A. Data not available.

Table XV-13. Number of Newspapers in Michigan, by Type: 1987-1994

Newspaper Type	1987	1988	1989	1990	1991	1992	1993	1994
Daily	48	52	53	54	54	55	55	55
Evening Daily	38	39	39	40	40	40	39	39
Morning Daily	9	9	9	10	13	11	12	12
All Day Daily	1	1	1	1	0	0	0	0
Foreign Language Daily	0	0	0	0	0	0	0	0
Daily With Sunday Edition	15	15	16	16	18	24	24	25
Daily With Weekend Edition	0	0	0	0	0	0	0	0
Triweekly	0	2	2	2	0	2	3	3
Semiweekly	17	19	17	17	17	19	19	18
Weekly	234	279	284	303	311	305	307	316
Biweekly	0	1	1	2	3	2	2	2
Semimonthly	0	0	1	1	1	1	2	1
Monthly	0	2	3	5	9	7	10	11
Bimonthly	0	0	0	2	1	1	1	1
Variant	0	0	1	1	2	2	2	2
Total	**299**	**355**	**362**	**387**	**400**	**394**	**401**	**409**

Source: Gale Research, Incorporated, Gale Directory of Publications and Broadcast Media (Detroit, Michigan: annually).

Table XV-14. Number of Non-Newspaper Periodicals in Michigan, by Type: 1987-1994

Periodical Type	1987	1988	1989	1990	1991	1992	1993	1994
Daily	4	0	0	0	0	0	0	0
Triweekly	3	0	0	0	0	0	0	0
Semiweekly	1	0	0	0	0	0	0	0
Weekly	32	18	21	19	18	21	17	15
Biweekly	5	5	5	5	5	5	6	7
Semimonthly	2	3	3	3	2	2	3	4
Monthly	60	62	68	71	78	81	80	80
Bimonthly	27	30	36	44	42	41	40	39
Quarterly	31	38	42	49	50	44	48	48
Variant	23	30	27	22	17	15	19	19
Total	**188**	**187**	**203**	**213**	**212**	**209**	**213**	**212**

Source: Gale Research, Incorporated, Gale Directory of Publications and Broadcast Media (Detroit, Michigan: annually).

Table XV-15. Total and Per Capita Energy Consumption in Michigan and the United States, Selected Years: 1960-1994

Year	Michigan		United States		Michigan as a Percentage of the United States	
	Total Consumption (Trillions of BTUs)*	Per Capita Consumption (Millions of BTUs)	Total Consumption (Quatrillions of BTUs)*	Per Capita Consumption (Millions of BTUs)	Percentage(%) Total Consumption	Percentage(%) Per Capita Consumption
1960	1,819	233	43,795	244	4.2	95.2
1965	2,258	254	52,697	259	4.3	98.1
1970	2,693	300	66,334	321	4.1	93.6
1971	2,784	308	67,789	324	4.1	95.2
1972	2,959	326	71,275	337	4.2	96.7
1973	3,058	335	74,352	349	4.1	96.2
1974	2,910	319	72,528	337	4.0	94.8
1975	2,856	313	70,569	324	4.0	96.5
1976	2,976	325	74,392	339	4.0	95.9
1977	2,871	311	76,317	344	3.8	90.6
1978	2,936	317	78,158	348	3.8	91.0
1979	2,923	316	78,920	348	3.7	90.6
1980	2,796	304	75,985	331	3.7	91.7
1981	2,623	288	74,022	320	3.5	90.1
1982	2,484	275	70,806	303	3.5	90.6
1983	2,445	270	70,486	299	3.5	90.4
1984	2,626	289	74,085	311	3.5	92.9
1985	2,569	281	74,054	308	3.5	91.3
1986	2,688	293	74,290	307	3.6	95.4
1987	2,690	292	76,640	313	3.5	93.1
1988	2,737	296	80,269	325	3.4	91.0
1989	2,748	296	81,317	327	3.4	90.4
1990	2,735	292	81,143	322	3.4	90.7
1991	2,748	293	81,099	321	3.4	91.3
1992	2,784	295	82,144	321	3.4	91.9
1993	2,894	295	83,877	322	3.5	91.6
1994	N.A.	N.A.	85,595	322	N.A.	N.A.

*British Thermal Units. N.A. data not available for this printing.
Source: U.S. Department of Energy, Energy Information Administration (Washington, D.C.).

Table XV-16. Energy Consumption by Energy Type Measured in Trillions of British Thermal Units (BTUs) in Michigan, Selected Years: 1960-1992

Type	1960	1965	1970	1975	1980	1985	1990	1991	1992
Total Energy Consumed	**1,820**	**2,259**	**2,693**	**2,856**	**2,799**	**2,569**	**2,734**	**2,748**	**2,784**
Coal	653	830	829	751	759	782	786	760	702
Natural Gas (Dry)	383	564	821	895	875	720	835	844	909
Petroleum	717	809	982	1,100	965	833	893	905	914
Asphalt	20	15	26	26	23	18	26	23	24
Aviation Gasoline	7	13	4	2	3	1	1	1	1
Distillate Fuel	176	176	222	246	161	148	136	146	147
Jet Fuel	18	24	41	32	37	37	57	58	57
Kerosene	23	33	18	8	7	3	2	2	1
LPG	11	15	23	28	25	51	54	58	60
Lubricants	15	18	19	17	20	18	20	18	19
Motor Gasoline	346	410	509	569	510	491	522	532	533
Residual Fuel	74	54	63	115	84	20	17	11	11
Other Petroleum	27	49	58	59	96	46	58	57	61
Nuclear Power	0	2	4	79	173	146	231	290	201
Hydroelectric Power	35	15	14	15	72	15	-103	6	8
Geothermal Power	0	0	0	0	0	0	0	0	0
Net Interstate Sales of Electricity	31	39	43	17	-44	74	93	-57	50

Source: U.S. Department of Energy, Energy Information Administration (Washington, D.C.).

Table XV-17. Per Capita Energy Consumption in Michigan and the United States in Trillions of British Thermal Units (BTUs), Selected Years: 1960-1991

Type	1960	1965	1970	1975	1980	1985	1990	1991
Total Energy Consumed								
Michigan	1,819	2,258	2,693	2,856	2,796	2,569	2,735	2,748
United States	43,795	52,697	66,334	70,569	75,985	74,054	81,143	81,099
Residential								
Michigan	447	533	682	724	725	659	669	897
United States	8,284	10,119	13,310	14,454	15,069	15,193	16,889	16,377
Commercial								
Michigan	191	252	333	395	421	398	429	442
United States	4,749	5,900	8,344	9,443	10,586	11,531	12,616	13,020
Industrial								
Michigan	794	1,006	1,085	1,077	1,033	902	958	927
United States	20,163	24,244	28,593	28,429	30,635	27,281	29,902	29,601
Transportation								
Michigan	387	487	594	681	620	610	680	689
United States	10,599	12,434	16,087	18,244	19,695	20,068	22,537	22,121

Source: U.S. Department of Energy, Energy Information Administration (Washington, D.C.).

Table XV-18. Residential Energy Consumption by Energy Type Measured in Trillions of British Thermal Units (BTUs) in Michigan, Selected Years: 1960-1992

Type	1960	1965	1970	1975	1980	1985	1990	1991	1992
Total Residential Energy Consumption	**447**	**533**	**682**	**724**	**725**	**659**	**669**	**697**	**700**
Coal	20.8	15.3	7.2	3.3	2.6	2.2	2.3	2.3	1.7
Natural Gas	209	275	345	343	395	349	342	350	372
Petroleum	113	112	130	134	66	53	49	54	52
Electricity	30	39	58	70	76	76	86	91	88
Net Energy	373	441	541	552	540	480	480	498	513
Electrical System Energy Losses	74	92	141	172	185	179	189	198	187

Source: U.S. Department of Energy, Energy Information Administration (Washington, D.C.).

Table XV-19. Commercial Energy Consumption by Energy Type Measured in Trillions of British Thermal Units (BTUs) in Michigan, Selected Years: 1960-1992

Type	1960	1965	1970	1975	1980	1985	1990	1991	1992
Total Commercial Energy Consumption	**191**	**252**	**333**	**395**	**421**	**398**	**429**	**442**	**442**
Coal	39	28	13	6	5	4	4	4	3
Natural Gas	45	86	135	186	194	161	167	172	180
Petroleum	32	33	33	33	26	22	19	19	18
Electricity	22	31	44	50	57	63	75	78	77
Net Energy	137	178	226	275	282	250	265	273	278
Electrical System Energy Losses	54	74	108	120	139	148	164	169	164

Source: U.S. Department of Energy, Energy Information Administration (Washington, D.C.).

Table XV-20. Industrial Energy Consumption by Energy Type Measured in Trillions of British Thermal Units (BTUs) in Michigan, Selected Years: 1960-1992

Type	1960	1965	1970	1975	1980	1985	1990	1991	1992
Total Industrial Energy Consumption	**794**	**1006**	**1064**	**1076**	**1032**	**902**	**957**	**919**	**943**
Coal	329	383	320	246	219	170	118	93	76
Natural Gas	121	195	266	308	254	194	303	293	324
Petroleum	190	200	203	185	199	151	155	154	160
Hydroelectric	2	2	1	1	1	1	1	1	1
Electricity	43	66	86	99	105	115	120	119	122
Net Energy	688	848	877	839	778	631	696	659	684
Electrical System Energy Losses	106	158	208	238	254	270	261	260	260

Source: U.S. Department of Energy, Energy Information Administration (Washington, D.C.).

Table XV-21. Transportation Energy Consumption by Energy Type Measured in Trillions of British Thermal Units (BTUs) in Michigan, Selected Years: 1960-1992

Type	1960	1965	1970	1975	1980	1985	1990	1991	1992
Total Commercial Energy Consumption	**387**	**467**	**594**	**661**	**620**	**610**	**680**	**691**	**699**
Coal	5.6	1.2	0.5	0	0	0	0	0	0
Natural Gas	3	5	11	11	13	11	19	20	23
Petroleum	379	462	583	650	608	599	661	671	676
Moto Gasoline	327	393	490	554	500	481	513	523	525
Distillate Fuel	14	20	37	52	57	71	80	79	84
Electricity	---	0	0	0	0	0	0	---	---
Net Energy	387	467	594	661	620	610	680	691	699
Electrical System Energy Losses	0.1	0	0	0	0	0	0	---	---

Source: U.S. Department of Energy, Energy Information Administration (Washington, D.C.). --- BTU value less than 0.05.

Table XV-22. Estimates of Energy Input at Electric Utilities by Energy Type Measured in Trillions of British Thermal Units (BTUs) in Michigan, Selected Years: 1960-1992

Type	1960	1965	1970	1975	1980	1985	1990	1991	1992
Total Energy Input	**297**	**421**	**603**	**733**	**860**	**776**	**802**	**972**	**847**
Coal	256	400	487	495	532	606	662	661	621
Natural Gas	5	3	65	47	19	5	5	9	10
Petroleum	3	2	34	98	65	7	9	8	7
Nuclear Electricity	0	2	4	79	173	146	231	290	201
Hydroelectric	33	13	12	14	70	13	-105	4	7
Geothermal	0	0	0	0	0	0	0	0	0
Other	0	0	0	0	0	0	0	0	0

Source: U.S. Department of Energy, Energy Information Administration (Washington, D.C.).

Table XV-23. Energy Price Estimates by Sector in Michigan, Selected Years: 1970-1992

Type	Dollars per Million BTU							
	1970	1975	1980	1985	1988	1990	1991	1992
Total Energy Consumed	$1.70	$3.33	$6.61	$8.48	$7.44	$8.07	$8.14	$7.96
Residential	1.74	3.14	5.56	8.82	8.11	8.53	8.71	8.40
Primary Energy	1.10	1.93	3.72	6.41	5.34	5.37	5.36	5.24
Coal	1.42	3.06	3.70	3.86	3.45	3.39	3.15	3.18
Natural Gas	1.00	1.58	3.13	6.14	5.14	4.80	4.88	4.88
Petroleum	1.35	2.78	7.25	8.30	6.61	9.43	8.56	7.89
Electricity	6.99	11.32	16.76	21.62	21.68	22.94	23.64	23.77
Commercial Sector	2.11	3.40	6.38	10.12	9.43	10.17	10.22	10.09
Primary Energy	0.88	1.63	3.53	5.68	4.81	4.62	4.67	4.62
Coal	0.53	1.49	1.82	1.99	1.73	1.77	1.80	1.73
Natural Gas	0.83	1.45	3.13	5.61	4.81	4.43	4.53	4.48
Petroleum	1.23	2.69	6.86	6.84	5.17	6.93	6.63	6.48
Electricity	7.12	11.41	17.60	23.36	22.48	24.21	24.16	24.44
Industrial Sector	1.01	2.54	5.00	7.02	6.53	6.43	6.79	6.72
Primary Energy	0.71	1.81	3.68	4.75	4.10	4.07	4.37	4.29
Coal	0.54	1.82	2.04	2.03	1.73	1.78	1.78	1.73
Natural Gas	0.53	1.22	2.87	4.95	4.19	3.72	3.85	3.78
Petroleum	1.27	2.83	6.78	8.01	6.11	6.83	7.03	6.84
Electricity	3.74	7.83	13.18	16.75	15.94	17.14	17.25	17.29
Transportation Sector	2.50	4.46	9.63	8.96	6.93	8.51	8.12	7.92
Primary Energy	2.50	4.46	9.63	8.96	6.93	8.51	8.12	7.92
Coal	0.53	1.49	---	---	---	---	---	---
Petroleum	2.50	4.46	9.63	8.96	6.93	8.51	8.12	7.92
Motor Gasoline	2.71	4.72	10.09	9.10	7.15	8.78	8.37	8.16
Electricity	---	---	---	---	---	---	---	27.20
Electric Utility Sector	0.38	1.02	1.58	1.72	1.60	1.41	1.32	1.36
Coal	0.36	0.92	1.56	1.88	1.76	1.60	1.59	1.56
Natural Gas	0.42	1.28	2.74	4.43	2.56	2.11	1.96	1.95
Petroleum	0.63	1.98	4.24	5.15	2.79	3.26	2.89	2.92
Nuclear Fuel	0.36	0.28	0.49	0.80	0.88	0.79	0.65	.67
Biomass Fuels	---	---	---	---	---	---	---	---
Primary Energy-5 Sectors	1.12	2.23	4.39	5.18	4.21	4.49	4.38	4.47

Source: U.S. Department of Energy, Energy Information Administration (Washington, D.C.). --- No data.

Table XV-24. Energy Price Estimates by Source in Michigan, Selected Years: 1970-1991

Energy Source	Price in Dollars per Million of BTUs						
	1970	1975	1980	1985	1988	1990	1991
Total Energy	**$1.70**	**$3.33**	**$6.61**	**$8.48**	**$7.44**	**$8.07**	**$8.14**
Coal	0.44	1.23	1.71	1.92	1.76	1.63	1.62
Natural Gas (Dry)	0.77	1.42	3.05	5.70	4.80	4.33	4.43
Petroleum	2.00	3.72	8.48	8.67	6.65	8.21	7.89
Asphalt	0.84	2.12	4.04	5.00	3.21	3.06	2.87
Aviation Gasoline	2.17	3.45	9.02	9.99	7.41	9.32	8.71
Distillate Fuel	1.09	2.49	6.76	7.71	5.74	7.53	6.98
Jet Fuel	0.74	2.08	6.38	6.09	3.85	5.65	4.94
Kerosene	0.89	2.60	6.29	8.52	6.41	8.28	7.60
LPG	1.89	3.76	6.62	8.74	7.73	10.26	10.13
Lubricants	5.08	7.48	14.36	17.61	14.61	13.40	15.42
Motor Gasoline	2.71	4.72	10.09	9.10	7.15	8.78	8.37
Residual Fuel	0.59	1.96	3.90	4.45	2.86	3.00	2.54
Other Petroleum	1.25	2.92	7.80	8.21	5.50	6.69	5.95
Nuclear Power	0.36	0.28	0.49	0.80	0.88	0.79	0.65
Primary Energy	1.12	2.23	4.39	5.18	4.21	4.49	4.38

Source: U.S. Department of Energy, Energy Information Administration (Washington, D.C.).

Table XV-25. Energy Expenditure Estimates by Source in Michigan, Selected Years: 1970-1991

Energy Source	Expenditures in Millions of Dollars						
	1970	1975	1980	1985	1988	1990	1991
Total Energy	**$3,729.2**	**$7,609.8**	**$14,389.5**	**$16,295.4**	**$15,171.4**	**$16,571.4**	**$16,753.8**
Coal	363.6	925.0	1,299.2	1,499.0	1,458.6	1,283.4	1,231.9
Natural Gas (Dry)	620.2	1,235.6	2,596.2	3,954.1	3,507.2	3,433.8	3,538.2
Petroleum	1,925.7	4,020.3	8,007.8	7,044.2	6,087.6	7,156.4	7,034.3
Asphalt	21.5	54.6	94.0	92.2	61.2	80.1	66.0
Aviation Gasoline	7.9	6.0	22.2	10.1	9.0	10.1	9.0
Distillate Fuel	240.6	610.6	1,087.9	1,140.8	923.9	1,022.2	1,015.5
Jet Fuel	30.4	66.8	236.9	223.6	185.4	319.7	272.0
Kerosene	15.7	19.9	44.0	24.5	17.2	12.7	15.5
LPG	43.9	103.9	163.6	440.4	482.0	545.0	660.7
Lubricants	97.3	124.9	285.1	318.2	281.5	272.5	280.5
Motor Gasoline	1,378.2	2,686.4	5,144.7	4,465.3	3,848.7	4,581.8	4,456.4
Residual Fuel	33.7	217.0	315.1	56.0	51.2	44.2	23.2
Other Petroleum	56.4	130.2	614.4	273.2	243.2	268.1	235.5
Nuclear Power	1.5	22.2	85.1	117.0	119.2	181.4	189.1
Primary Energy	2,911.0	6,203.2	11,988.3	12,614.4	10,733.3	12,055.0	11,993.5

Source: U.S. Department of Energy, Energy Information Administration (Washington, D.C.).

CHAPTER XVI
TRADE

The Office of Management and Budget in the Executive Office of the President is responsible for maintaining the Standard Industrial Classification system. The SIC is used in all federal statistical programs and in most other programs where the focus is on economic activity.

According to the latest <u>Standard Industrial Classification Manual</u>,

> wholesale trade includes establishments or places of business primarily engaged in selling merchandise to retailers; to industrial, commercial, institutional, farm, construction contractors, or professional business users; or to other wholesalers; or acting as agents or brokers in buying or selling merchandise to such persons or companies.

> retail trade includes establishments engaged in selling merchandise for personal or household consumption and rendering services incidental to the sale of the goods.

It seems worth mentioning here that gasoline service stations and eating and drinking places are classified as retail trade and not as services.

This chapter also includes international trade which is comprised of merchandise that crosses international boundaries.

The Bureau of the Census conducts economic censuses for years ending in 2 and 7. The 1992 <u>Census of Wholesale Trade</u> and <u>Census of Retail Trade</u> are the latest such undertakings at this writing. The other 1992 economic censuses are being tabulated. These censuses are the source of detailed data for the state as well as summary data for counties and places.

For retail trade, monthly data for Michigan and the Detroit area are published in the Census Bureau's <u>Monthly Retail Trade</u>. This report is based on a sample of retail establishments.

The Census Bureau also prepares estimates of state of origin of manufactured exports from time to time in connection with its <u>Census of Manufactures</u> and <u>Annual Survey of Manufactures</u> (see Chapter XIII). Estimates of imports and exports that pass through the Detroit Customs District are published in <u>Highlights of U.S. Export and Import Trade</u> and in <u>Waterborne Exports and General Imports</u>, also published by the Bureau of the Census.

Current data on employment, hours, and earnings are collected and disseminated by the Michigan Employment Security Commission in Detroit and by the Bureau of Labor Statistics in Washington, D.C.

Some terms found in this chapter include:

Establishments: a single physical location at which business is conducted. It is not necessarily identical with a company or enterprise, which may consist of one establishment or more.

Units: Refer to the definition of establishments.

Employment: Includes both full-time and part-time workers.

Average Weekly Wage (AWW): AWW = ((Total wages/Employment)/Number of weeks).

Operating Expenses: Include payroll and overhead expenses.

Merchant Wholesalers: Establishments primarily engaged in buying and selling merchandise on their own account.

Manufacturer's Sales Branches and Offices: Establishments maintained by manufacturing, refining, and mining companies apart from their plants or mines for marketing their products at wholesale.

Agents, Brokers, and Commission Merchants: Establishments whose operators are in business for themselves and are primarily engaged in selling or buying goods for others.

List of Tables

Table		Page
XVI-1.	Wholesale Trade Establishments, Employment, and Average Weekly Wage in Michigan and the United States: 1970-1994	507
XVI-2.	Retail Trade Establishments, Employment, and Average Weekly Wage in Michigan and the United States: 1970-1994	508
XVI-3.	Wholesale and Retail Trade Sales in Michigan and the United States, Selected Years: 1947-1992	509
XVI-4.	Sales Figures for Wholesale Trade Establishments in Michigan, by Type of Operation: 1992	509
XVI-5.	Wholesale Trade Sales Figures in Michigan, by County: 1992	510
XVI-6.	Wholesale Trade Sales Figures in Michigan, by Type of Industry and Type of Operation: 1992	511
XVI-7.	Wholesale Trade Sales per Establishment in Michigan, by Type of Business and Operation: 1992	514
XVI-8.	Wholesale Trade Sales per Employee in Michigan, by Type of Business and Operation: 1992	515
XVI-9.	Wholesale Trade Operating Expenses as a Percent of Sales in Michigan, by Type of Business and Operation: 1992	516
XVI-10.	Wholesale Trade Total Wages and Wholesale Trade Total Wages as a Percentage of Total County Wages: 1992	517
XVI-11.	Retail Trade Total Wages and Retail Trade Total Wages as a Percentage of Total County Wages: 1992	518

List of Tables

Table   **Page**

XVI-12. Retail Trade Sales and Selected Ratios in Michigan, by Industry: 1992 519

XVI-13. Selected Retail Trade Statistics in Michigan, by County: 1992 522

XVI-14. Estimated Annual Sales of Retail Stores in the Detroit Metropolitan Statistical Area, Michigan, and the United States: 1978-1993 524

XVI-15. Number of Wholesale Trade Establishments, Employment, and Average Weekly Wage in Michigan, by County: 1992 525

XVI-16. Number of Retail Trade Establishments, Employment, and Average Weekly Wage in Michigan, by County: 1992 526

XVI-17. Value of Export Shipments by Manufacturing Plants in Michigan and the United States, by Industry Group: 1972, 1977, 1981, 1983, and 1993 527

XVI-18. Factory Shipments and Employment Related to Manufactured Exports by Major Industry Group, Michigan and the United States: 1989 528

XVI-19. Exports from Michigan to Other Countries, Value Greater Than 1 Million Dollars: 1988, 1992, and 1993 529

Table XVI-1. Wholesale Trade Establishments, Employment, and Average Weekly Wage in Michigan and the United States: 1970-1994

Year	Michigan			United States		
	Number of Units	Employment (Data in Thousands)	Average Weekly Wage	Number of Units	Employment (Data in Thousands)	Average Weekly Wage
1970	---	145	$---	---	4,006	$---
1971	---	145	---	---	4,014	---
1972	---	146	---	---	4,127	---
1973	, ---	151	---	---	4,291	---
1974	---	154	---	---	4,447	---
1975	---	147	---	---	4,430	---
1976	11,074	149	274	374,657	4,562	251
1977	11,310	152	297	387,052	4,723	268
1978	11,757	164	321	401,622	4,985	288
1979	12,016	170	352	416,951	5,221	314
1980	12,215	162	380	432,404	5,292	346
1981	12,394	158	406	449,169	5,375	374
1982	12,289	151	425	463,544	5,295	397
1983	12,231	155	441	472,655	5,283	413
1984	11,642	166	468	483,825	5,568	437
1985	13,295	175	487	497,339	5,727	457
1986	13,590	181	519	507,217	5,761	477
1987	14,606	186	542	524,547	5,848	501
1988	15,078	191	585	537,295	6,030	535
1989	16,405	196	605	552,327	6,187	551
1990	16,822	202	620	561,069	6,173	578
1991	17,450	198	641	586,565	6,081	601
1992	18,086	197	681	599,235	6,045	633
1993	18,293	197	707	599,677	6,113	648
1994	18,770	206	738	N.A.	N.A.	N.A.

--- No data. N.A. data not available.
Source: Michigan Employment Security Commission, Research and Statistics (Detroit, Michigan: annually).

Table XVI-2. Retail Trade Establishments, Employment, and Average Weekly Wage in Michigan and the United States: 1970-1994

Year	Michigan			United States		
	Number of Units	Employment (Data in Thousands)	Average Weekly Wage	Number of Units	Employment (Data in Thousands)	Average Weekly Wage
1970	---	458	$---	---	11,034	$---
1971	---	461	---	---	11,338	---
1972	---	479	---	---	11,822	---
1973	---	503	---	---	12,315	---
1974	---	511	---	---	12,539	---
1975	---	510	---	---	12,630	---
1976	37,173	531	135	1,103,081	13,193	128
1977	37,127	557	142	1,112,001	13,792	135
1978	36,937	585	151	1,126,287	14,556	143
1979	36,483	591	161	1,136,611	14,972	153
1980	35,876	572	170	1,144,275	15,018	164
1981	35,072	557	180	1,140,699	15,171	175
1982	34,449	543	184	1,145,201	15,158	184
1983	34,475	557	190	1,159,464	15,587	192
1984	32,867	580	199	1,164,104	16,512	200
1985	35,482	617	196	1,181,582	17,315	206
1986	35,464	639	211	1,190,304	17,880	214
1987	37,102	674	215	1,218,124	18,422	221
1988	37,795	703	221	1,223,066	19,023	230
1989	40,422	727	224	1,235,860	19,475	236
1990	40,924	748	229	1,254,735	19,601	244
1991	43,478	729	237	1,343,324	19,284	254
1992	44,507	728	249	1,378,793	19,346	266
1993	45,042	738	253	1,397,299	19,743	269
1994	45,664	764	262	N.A.	N.A.	N.A.

--- No data. N.A. data not available.

Source: Michigan Employment Security Commission, Research and Statistics (Detroit, Michigan: annually).

Table XVI-3. Wholesale and Retail Trade Sales in Michigan and the United States, Selected Years: 1947-1992

Year	Wholesale Trade Sales (Millions of Dollars)		Retail Trade Sales (Millions of Dollars)	
	Michigan	U.S.	Michigan	U.S.
1947	$ N.A.	$ N.A.	$5,854	$128,849
1954	10,087	233,976	8,168	169,968
1958	11,600	284,971	8,898	200,365
1963	14,055	358,386	10,855	244,202
1967	18,800	459,476	14,114	310,214
1972	26,546	695,224	20,546	457,405
1977	45,152	1,258,400	31,912	723,134
1982	59,806	1,997,895	39,216	1,065,917
1987	86,065	2,524,727	56,697	1,540,000
1992	125,671	3,249,874	71,523	1,894,880

N.A. data not available for this printing.
Source: Bureau of Census, 1992 Census of Wholesale Trade, Geographic Area Series, Michigan (Washington, D.C.: quinquennial), WC87-A-23; 1992 Census of Retail Trade, Geographic Area Series, Michigan Census of Retail Trade, Geographic Area Series, Michigan (Washington, D.C.: quinquennial), RC92-A-23; and similar documents for the U.S.

Table XVI-4. Sales Figures for Wholesale Trade Establishments in Michigan, by Type of Operation: 1992

Type of Operation	Sales ($ Thousands)	Type of Operation	Sales ($ Thousands)
TOTAL	$125,670,957	Merchandise Agents & Brokers	$20,745,183
Merchant Wholesalers	51,621,192	Auction Companies	1,007,734
Merchandise & Distribution	44,381,816	Brokers	3,117,980
Grain Elevators	631,763	Commission Merchants	1,376,727
Importers	4,677,492	Import Agents	(D)
Exporters	(D)	Export Agents	(D)
Manufactures Sales Branches & Offices	53,304,582	Manufacturers' Agents	11,511,228
Manufactures Sales Branches with Stock	18,992,550		
Manufactures Sales Branches without Stock	34,312,032		

(D) data withheld to avoid disclosure of individual firm data.
Source: Bureau of Census, 1992 Census of Wholesale Trade, Geographic Area Series, Michigan (Washington, D.C.: quinquennial), WC87-A-23; (Washington, D.C.: quinquennial).

Table XVI-5. Wholesale Trade Sales Figures in Michigan, by County: 1992

County	Sales (In Thousands $)	County	Sales (In Thousands $)	County	Sales (In Thousands $)	County	Sales (In Thousands $)
Alcona	$(D)	Gogebic	$38,093	Mason	$40,552	Tuscola	$277,754
Alger	5,769	Grand Traverse	657,278	Mecosta	45,840	Van Buren	215,722
Allegan	323,907	Gratiot	282,072	Menominee	148,358	Washtenaw	1,790,142
Alpena	139,626	Hillsdale	199,826	Midland	206,074	Wayne	29,862,912
Antrim	27,040	Houghton	61,272	Missaukee	23,974	Wexford	122,279
Arenac	73,374	Huron	202,082	Monroe	938,916	**Michigan**	**125,670,957**
Baraga	9,206	Ingham	2,538,126	Montcalm	76,217		
Barry	68,559	Ionia	124,213	Montmorency	5,827		
Bay	861,893	Iosco	22,890	Muskegon	754,464		
Benzie	(D)	Iron	21,727	Newaygo	59,921		
Berrien	1,313,135	Isabella	368,330	Oakland	54,415,337		
Branch	629,336	Jackson	939,223	Oceana	36,656		
Calhoun	530,494	Kalamazoo	1,485,457	Ogemaw	48,130		
Cass	231,051	Kalkaska	61,819	Ontonagon	(D)		
Charlevoix	(D)	Kent	10,676,977	Osceola	57,771		
Cheboygan	96,528	Keweenaw	(D)	Oscoda	(D)		
Chippewa	57,503	Lake	7,624	Otsego	201,476		
Clare	40,526	Lapeer	116,901	Ottawa	1,028,971		
Clinton	486,880	Leelanau	25,351	Presque Isle	17,256		
Crawford	40,699	Lenawee	239,339	Roscommon	10,571		
Delta	144,575	Livingston	468,673	Saginaw	1,529,243		
Dickinson	205,437	Luce	14,104	St. Clair	589,988		
Eaton	638,629	Mackinac	22,618	St. Joseph	573,232		
Emmet	114,428	Macomb	5,089,755	Sanilac	116,254		
Genesee	2,235,483	Manistee	123,419	Schoolcraft	12,993		
Gladwin	33,094	Marquette	158,300	Shiawassee	183,709		

Source: Bureau of Census, Michigan Information Center (Lansing, Michigan). (D) Data withheld to avoid disclosure of individual firm data.

Table XVI-6. Wholesale Trade Sales Figures in Michigan, by Type of Industry and Type of Operation: 1992
(Data in Thousands)

Type of Operation	Total Sales	Merchant Sales	Manufacturers Sales	Agents/Brokers/ Commission Merchants
WHOLESALE, TOTAL	$125,670,957	$51,621,192	$53,304,582	$20,745,183
DURABLES	84,614,339	28,198,404	40,035,372	16,380,563
Motor Vehicles & Parts	44,702,617	7,250,810	25,713,764	11,738,043
Motor Vehicles	20,282,754	3,389,010	(D)	(D)
Motor Vehicle Parts (New)	23,724,903	3,424,928	9,420,110	10,429,865
Tires & Tubes	1,003,254	295,166	(D)	(D)
Motor Vehicle Parts (Used)	141,706	141,706	---	---
Furniture & Home Furnishings	1,398,793	681,610	436,886	280,297
Furniture	678,801	419,635	127,366	131,800
Household Furniture	146,471	83,371	(D)	(D)
Office Furniture	532,330	336,264	(D)	(D)
Home Furnishings	719,992	261,975	309,520	148,497
Lumber & Const. Materials	2,923,681	2,241,362	485,951	196,368
Professional & Commercial Eqpt.	5,756,027	2,679,474	2,754,211	322,342
Photo Equipment	197,736	(D)	(D)	(D)
Office Equipment	627,302	275,980	327,614	23,708
Computers & Software	2,939,578	(D)	1,840,582	(D)
Hotel, Restaurant & Store Eqpt.	314,807	229,423	5,584	79,800
Medical Equipt. & Supplies	1,435,228	836,336	426,703	172,189
Ophthalmic Goods	89,479	79,680	(D)	(D)
Other Professional Eqpt.	151,897	(D)	(D)	(D)
Metals & Minerals exc. Petro	10,461,206	4,279,174	5,388,814	793,218
Metal Service Centers & Offices	10,180,402	(D)	(D)	770,080
Ferrous Metals	8,886,681	3,661,052	(D)	(D)
Nonferrous Metals	1,293,721	(D)	(D)	(D)
Coal & Other Minerals	280,804	(D)	(D)	23,138
Electrical Goods	5,455,905	2,228,611	2,169,468	1,057,808
Electrical Eqpt. incl. Construction	2,574,499	1,506,734	657,520	410,245
Electrical Appliances	941,882	198,340	602,673	140,869
Misc. Electronic Parts & Eqpt.	1,939,524	523,537	909,293	506,694

Table XVI-6. Wholesale Trade Sales Figures in Michigan, by Type of Industry and Type of Operation: 1992 Continued
(Data in Thousands)

Type of Operation	Total Sales	Merchant Sales	Manufacturers Sales	Agents/Brokers/ Commission Merchants
Communications Eqpt.	$865,531	$181,512	$(D)	$(D)
Other Electronic Parts & Eqpt.	1,073,993	342,025	(D)	(D)
Hardware, Plumbing, Heating	2,710,953	1,704,002	487,314	519,637
Hardware	1,260,576	707,559	300,322	252,695
Plumbing	884,342	578,176	125,744	180,422
Heating & Air Conditioning	502,690	381,110	(D)	(D)
Refrigeration Eqpt.	63,345	37,157	(D)	(D)
Machinery, Eqpt. & Supplies	8,696,420	5,307,309	2,471,574	917,537
Construct. & Mining exc. Oil, Eqpt.	474,817	437,320	24,341	13,156
Farm & Garden Mach. & Eqpt.	677,072	573,570	85,927	17,575
Farm Machinery & Eqpt.	579,329	475,827	(D)	(D)
Lawn & Garden Mach. & Supplies	97,743	97,743	(D)	(D)
Industrial Machinery & Eqpt.	3,993,068	2,530,271	843,927	618,870
Food Processing Mach. & Eqpt.	87,031	76,922	(D)	(D)
General Industrial Mach. & Parts	1,266,211	821,731	(D)	(D)
Metalworking Machinery	1,076,964	569,579	(D)	(D)
Materials Handling Eqpt.	545,307	410,272	(D)	(D)
Oil Well, Refinery Machinery	98,324	81,334	(D)	(D)
Other Indust. Mach. & Eqpt.	919,231	570,433	(D)	(D)
Industrial Supplies	3,047,451	1,350,101	1,474,338	223,012
Service Estab. Eqpt. & Supplies	360,722	(D)	(D)	12,772
Transport Eqpt. exc. Motor Veh.	143,290	(D)	(D)	32,152
Miscellaneous Durable Goods	2,508,737	1,826,052	127,372	555,313
NONDURABLE GOODS	**41,056,618**	**23,422,788**	**13,269,210**	**4,364,620**
Paper & Paper Products	2,289,400	1,432,200	641,568	215,632
Drugs & Druggist Sundries	2,615,218	1,915,703	616,755	82,760
Apparel & Piece Goods	1,061,997	486,211	379,948	195,838
Groceries & Related Products	17,011,972	10,085,894	4,285,743	2,640,335
Groceries, General	4,216,128	2,951,702	---	1,264,426
Packaged Frozen Foods	1,513,985	800,881	227,296	485,808

Table XVI-6. Wholesale Trade Sales Figures in Michigan, by Type of Industry and Type of Operation: 1992 Continued
(Data in Thousands)

Type of Operation	Total Sales	Merchant Sales	Manufacturers Sales	Agents/Brokers/ Commission Merchants
Dairy Products	$1,347,255	$918,625	$377,153	$51,477
Poultry & Poultry Products	137,411	(D)	(D)	(D)
Confectionery	597,236	175,531	323,948	97,757
Fish & Seafoods	82,699	82,699	---	---
Meats & Meat Products	1,705,393	1,169,683	(D)	(D)
Fresh Fruits & Vegetables	1,009,438	896,208	---	113,230
Misc. Groceries & Related	6,402,427	(D)	(D)	515,710
Coffee,Tea & Spices	300,586	49,162	(D)	(D)
Bread & Baked Goods	605,042	199,054	(D)	(D)
Soft Drinks	1,070,501	93,195	(D)	(D)
Canned Foods	2,539,428	(D)	(D)	(D)
Food & Bev. Basic Materials	233,741	(D)	(D)	(D)
Other Groceries	1,653,129	(D)	(D)	(D)
Farm Products-Raw Materials	1,656,118	1,536,885	---	119,233
Chemicals & Allied Prod.	4,739,467	1,132,859	3,141,793	464,815
Plastic Materials	2,356,766	469,135	1,519,015	368,616
Other Chemical Prod.	2,382,701	663,724	1,622,778	96,199
Petroleum & Petro. Products	5,821,106	2,204,017	3,591,782	25,307
Beer, Wine, Alcoholic Beverages	2,021,958	1,835,965	(D)	(D)
Misc. Nondurable Goods	3,839,382	2,793,054	(D)	(D)
Farm Supplies	806,749	661,341	(D)	(D)
Books, Periodicals & Newspapers	659,545	378,349	245,537	35,659
Flowers & Florist Supplies	150,749	142,398	---	8,351
Tobacco & Products	1,282,436	(D)	(D)	---
Paints, Varnishes & Supplies	322,219	107,814	136,751	77,654
Other Nondurable Goods	617,684	(D)	(D)	(D)

(D) data withheld to avoid disclosure of individual firm data. ---No data.
Source: Bureau of Census, 1992 Census of Wholesale Trade, Geographic Area Series, Michigan (Washington, D.C.: quinquennial).

Table XVI-7. Wholesale Trade Sales per Establishment in Michigan, by Type of Business and Operation: 1992

Industry Group	Type of Operation			
	Total Sales per Establishment	Merchant Wholesalers	Manufactures' Sales Branches and Offices	Agents, Brokers, and Commission Merchants
WHOLESALE, TOTAL	$8,098,921	$4,168,041	$42,541,566	$11,040,544
DURABLES	7,878,430	3,293,052	53,956,027	11,415,026
Motor Vehicles & Parts	22,497,543	4,850,040	172,575,597	34,221,700
Furniture & Home Furnishings	3,445,303	2,170,732	25,699,176	3,737,293
Lumber & Const. Materials	4,370,226	3,904,812	9,917,367	4,268,870
Professional & Commercial Eqpt.	4,260,568	2,348,356	22,762,074	3,621,820
Metals & Minerals exc. Petro	17,552,359	9,747,549	85,536,730	8,438,489
Electrical Goods	5,005,417	2,879,342	15,065,875	6,150,047
Hardware, Plumbing, Heating	3,178,140	2,434,289	16,243,800	4,224,691
Machinery, Eqpt. & Supplies	3,140,636	2,330,834	15,070,573	2,797,369
Miscellaneous Durable Goods	2,461,960	2,150,827	25,474,400	3,365,533
NONDURABLE GOODS	8,594,645	6,128,411	25,967,143	9,830,225
Paper & Paper Products	3,663,040	2,802,740	9,036,169	5,014,698
Drugs & Druggist Sundries	22,162,864	18,781,402	154,188,750	6,896,667
Apparel & Piece Goods	4,657,882	2,656,891	37,994,800	5,595,371
Groceries & Related Products	13,353,196	10,627,918	23,942,698	18,084,486
Farm Products-Raw Materials	7,962,106	8,046,518	---	7,013,706
Chemicals & Allied Prod.	9,010,394	3,120,824	34,149,924	6,546,690
Petroleum & Petro. Products	13,959,487	6,208,499	66,514,481	3,163,375
Beer, Wine, Alcoholic Beverages	8,677,931	8,196,272	(D)	(D)
Misc. Nondurable Goods	3,344,409	2,958,744	(D)	(D)

(D) data withheld to avoid disclosure of individual firm data. --- No data.
Source: Bureau of Census, 1992 Census of Wholesale Trade, Geographic Area Series, Michigan (Washington, D.C.: quinquennial).

Table XVI-8. Wholesale Trade Sales per Employee in Michigan, by Type of Business and Operation: 1992

Industry Group	Type of Operation			
	Total Employees per Establishment	Merchant Wholesalers	Manufactures' Sales Branches and Offices	Agents, Brokers, and Commission Merchants
WHOLESALE, TOTAL	678,551	$366,251	$1,529,499	$2,204,823
DURABLES	725,923	321,922	1,770,302	2,578,804
Motor Vehicles & Parts	1,732,794	479,900	3,050,992	5,191,527
Furniture & Home Furnishings	359,218	217,350	835,346	1,192,753
Lumber & Const. Materials	462,681	400,315	818,099	1,558,476
Professional & Commercial Eqpt.	298,611	212,623	435,311	928,939
Metals & Minerals exc. Petro	1,321,360	665,398	4,399,032	3,039,149
Electrical Goods	476,873	272,546	869,185	1,377,354
Hardware, Plumbing, Heating	322,694	235,002	727,334	1,082,577
Machinery, Eqpt. & Supplies	351,342	249,275	1,083,074	778,233
Miscellaneous Durable Goods	286,287	228,314	1,819,600	799,012
NONDURABLE GOODS	598,109	439,032	1,084,440	1,427,746
Paper & Paper Products	309,881	220,712	871,696	1,322,896
Drugs & Druggist Sundries	1,137,546	904,060	4,437,086	2,018,537
Apparel & Piece Goods	506,436	276,099	1,644,797	1,865,124
Groceries & Related Products	575,001	498,758	576,971	1,363,809
Farm Products-Raw Materials	861,664	899,289	---	559,779
Chemicals & Allied Prod.	969,414	395,828	1,719,646	2,324,075
Petroleum & Petro. Products	1,248,896	529,303	7,529,941	1,265,350
Beer, Wine, Alcoholic Beverages	381,070	354,160	(D)	(D)
Misc. Nondurable Goods	365,795	315,921	(D)	(D)

(D) data withheld to avoid disclosure of individual firm data. --- No data.

Source: Bureau of Census, 1992 Census of Wholesale Trade, Geographic Area Series, Michigan (Washington, D.C.: quinquennial).

Table XVI-9. Wholesale Trade Operating Expenses as a Percent of Sales in Michigan, by Type of Business and Operation: 1992

Industry Group	Type of Operation			
	Total (Percent)	Merchant Wholesalers (Percent)	Manufactures' Sales Branches and Offices (Percent)	Agents, Brokers, and Commission Merchants (Percent)
WHOLESALE, TOTAL	9.3	15.7	5.3	3.6
DURABLES	9.0	18.3	4.8	3.5
Motor Vehicles & Parts	3.9	11.3	2.6	2.1
Furniture & Home Furnishings	16.7	25.0	10.1	6.9
Lumber & Const. Materials	13.6	15.3	8.4	6.3
Professional & Commercial Eqpt.	24.0	26.9	22.8	9.8
Metals & Minerals exc. Petro	6.0	11.5	1.9	4.2
Electrical Goods	13.4	21.0	9.3	5.8
Hardware, Plumbing, Heating	18.3	24.7	7.4	7.6
Machinery, Eqpt. & Supplies	20.2	20.9	7.6	9.2
Miscellaneous Durable Goods	19.4	24.3	4.3	7.0
NONDURABLE GOODS	9.8	12.5	6.9	4.4
Paper & Paper Products	15.8	21.2	7.0	6.0
Drugs & Druggist Sundries	5.3	6.2	2.3	5.5
Apparel & Piece Goods	12.6	18.6	8.4	5.6
Groceries & Related Products	9.5	10.7	10.5	3.7
Farm Products-Raw Materials	6.7	7.1	---	2.7
Chemicals & Allied Prod.	8.7	18.6	5.7	4.7
Petroleum & Petro. Products	5.6	11.6	1.9	5.0
Beer, Wine, Alcoholic Beverages	16.9	17.7	(D)	(D)
Misc. Nondurable Goods	15.2	15.8	(D)	(D)

(D) data withheld to avoid disclosure of individual firm data. --- No data.

Source: Bureau of Census, 1992 Census of Wholesale Trade, Geographic Area Series, Michigan (Washington, D.C.: quinquennial).

Table XVI-10. Wholesale Trade Total Wages and Wholesale Trade Total Wages as a Percentage of Total County Wages: 1992

County	Total Wholesale Wages	Percent of Total County Wages	County	Total Wholesale Wages	Percent of Total County Wages
Alcona	$40,730	1.1	Lake	$417,423	13.2
Alger	142,670	1.5	Lapeer	2,528,649	4.1
Allegan	4,435,113	3.0	Leelanau	679,002	5.9
Alpena	3,207,673	6.9	Lenawee	4,083,168	3.0
Antrim	673,548	4.6	Livingston	6,403,011	4.8
Arenac	463,582	4.4	Luce	302,648	5.9
Baraga	32,663	0.5	Mackinac	409,306	3.7
Barry	1,198,906	3.1	Macomb	106,252,736	5.6
Bay	10,554,957	6.0	Manistee	1,628,493	6.1
Benzie	N.A.	0.0	Marquette	3,627,286	3.7
Berrien	12,164,325	3.8	Mason	812,477	2.2
Branch	2,221,571	5.6	Mecosta	616,815	2.6
Calhoun	10,680,647	3.4	Menominee	2,303,265	7.1
Cass	2,409,148	6.5	Midland	3,221,075	1.3
Charlevoix	380,317	1.0	Missaukee	212,400	3.3
Cheboygan	370,223	1.8	Monroe	8,275,050	4.1
Chippewa	788,459	2.9	Montcalm	1,735,742	2.6
Clare	546,167	2.6	Montmorency	118,755	2.7
Clinton	5,142,336	13.1	Muskegon	13,449,740	4.9
Crawford	343,188	2.7	Newaygo	2,005,237	5.7
Delta	1,924,260	3.4	Oakland	500,650,515	11.9
Dickinson	3,644,121	7.2	Oceana	487,829	3.2
Eaton	16,277,464	18.2	Ogemaw	1,147,052	8.0
Emmet	2,414,419	4.4	Ontonagon	N.A.	0.0
Genesee	56,014,381	5.5	Osceola	723,209	2.7
Gladwin	238,294	1.7	Oscoda	N.A.	0.0
Gogebic	447,721	2.8	Otsego	1,924,105	5.7
Grand Traverse	8,796,037	5.4	Ottawa	25,941,397	5.8
Gratiot	3,456,406	6.8	Presque Isle	380,175	3.5
Hillsdale	3,107,276	5.3	Roscommon	302,594	2.4
Houghton	1,219,085	4.1	Saginaw	23,836,079	4.7
Huron	3,487,137	8.2	St. Clair	10,222,649	5.2
Ingham	40,787,818	5.5	St. Joseph	4,666,701	4.7
Ionia	2,414,503	5.2	Sanilac	1,537,264	4.2
Iosco	379,748	1.5	Schoolcraft	66,798	1.0
Iron	435,112	5.1	Shiawassee	4,274,759	6.8
Isabella	6,025,465	9.3	Tuscola	3,162,504	7.4
Jackson	15,722,023	6.2	Van Buren	2,285,736	3.2
Kalamazoo	28,892,137	4.7	Washtenaw	39,587,081	4.7
Kalkaska	1,276,495	6.4	Wayne	412,465,004	7.5
Kent	179,483,584	11.4	Wexford	1,510,551	3.1
Keweenaw	N.A.	0.0	**Michigan**	**1,771,336,401**	**7.4**

Source: Michigan Employment Security Commission, Research and Statistics (Detroit, Michigan: annually). N.A. data not available.

Table XVI-11. Retail Trade Total Wages and Retail Trade Total Wages as a Percentage of Total County Wages: 1992

County	Total Retail Wages	Percent(%) Total County Wages	County	Total Retail Wages	Percent(%) Total County Wages
Alcona	$1,053,577	29.1	Lake	$843,576	26.7
Alger	889,971	9.2	Lapeer	10,768,489	17.4
Allegan	11,672,590	7.9	Leelanau	2,427,170	21.0
Alpena	6,211,310	13.4	Lenawee	16,049,516	11.6
Antrim	1,928,668	13.1	Livingston	20,472,149	15.3
Arenac	2,923,324	27.4	Luce	1,022,510	19.9
Baraga	887,932	12.4	Mackinac	3,054,242	27.8
Barry	4,410,849	11.5	Macomb	191,818,082	10.1
Bay	24,575,908	13.9	Manistee	3,498,933	13.2
Benzie	2,012,185	22.1	Marquette	13,028,546	13.1
Berrien	31,706,176	9.9	Mason	4,320,616	11.8
Branch	5,864,984	14.8	Mecosta	5,348,454	22.7
Calhoun	34,589,741	11.0	Menominee	3,094,692	9.6
Cass	3,429,341	9.3	Midland	14,032,875	5.7
Charlevoix	4,513,973	12.2	Missaukee	1,465,290	22.9
Cheboygan	5,484,516	26.9	Monroe	20,998,240	10.5
Chippewa	7,287,550	26.4	Montcalm	8,603,685	12.8
Clare	5,380,985	25.8	Montmorency	805,113	18.2
Clinton	7,092,148	18.1	Muskegon	32,753,776	12.0
Crawford	2,557,862	20.2	Newaygo	4,167,630	11.8
Delta	8,569,382	15.1	Oakland	457,063,177	10.9
Dickinson	6,158,044	12.1	Oceana	2,374,741	15.8
Eaton	13,603,310	15.2	Ogemaw	3,649,670	25.4
Emmet	9,555,138	17.4	Ontonagon	1,373,635	9.0
Genesee	98,418,445	9.7	Osceola	2,048,833	7.7
Gladwin	2,553,520	18.5	Oscoda	788,254	15.9
Gogebic	3,111,692	19.5	Otsego	5,984,702	17.6
Grand Traverse	26,936,734	16.4	Ottawa	38,709,175	8.7
Gratiot	6,373,745	12.5	Presque Isle	1,903,923	17.3
Hillsdale	5,144,757	8.8	Roscommon	4,803,890	38.0
Houghton	5,764,555	19.3	Saginaw	57,874,077	11.5
Huron	6,114,372	14.5	St. Clair	27,964,446	14.3
Ingham	86,943,707	11.7	St. Joseph	9,070,338	9.1
Ionia	7,403,040	16.0	Sanilac	4,457,863	12.2
Iosco	4,799,134	19.2	Schoolcraft	1,449,636	21.7
Iron	2,146,715	25.2	Shiawassee	10,385,428	16.4
Isabella	12,304,921	19.1	Tuscola	6,048,895	14.1
Jackson	34,498,682	13.7	Van Buren	10,238,673	14.2
Kalamazoo	57,414,040	9.3	Washtenaw	83,246,089	9.8
Kalkaska	2,299,179	11.5	Wayne	455,553,708	8.3
Kent	186,933,634	11.9	Wexford	6,650,710	13.5
Keweenaw	111,682	17.5	**Michigan**	**2,358,028,565**	**10.4**

Source: Michigan Employment Security Commission, Research and Statistics (Detroit, Michigan: annually).

Table XVI-12. Retail Trade Sales and Selected Ratios in Michigan, by Industry: 1992

Industry	Sales (Data in Thousands)	Sales per Unit	Sales per Employee
Total Retail Trade	**$71,523,046**	**$1,311,892**	**$101,192**
Building materials and garden supplies stores	4,053,009	1,392,308	150,871
Building materials and supply stores	2,792,229	2,051,601	179,935
Lumber and other building materials dealers	2,587,671	2,507,433	187,336
Paint, glass, and wallpaper stores	204,558	621,757	119,975
Hardware stores	599,687	656,831	87,571
Retail nurseries, lawn and garden supply stores	386,461	832,890	109,077
Manufactured (mobile) home dealers	274,632	1,587,468	287,573
General merchandise stores	11,775,693	10,430,198	119,020
Department stores (incl. leased depts.)	10,343,997	24,865,377	N.A.
Department stores (excl. leased depts.)	10,163,285	24,430,974	115,547
Conventional	1,551,107	21,248,041	114,245
Discount or mass merchandising	7,121,898	25,526,516	117,411
National chain	1,490,280	23,285,625	108,597
Variety stores	322,979	768,998	72,174
Miscellaneous general merchandise stores	1,289,429	4,400,782	198,191
Food stores	11,167,907	1,560,854	113,223
Grocery stores	10,433,221	1,986,902	121,090
Supermarkets and other general-line grocery stores	9,149,108	3,050,720	123,693
Convenience food stores	999,168	555,402	108,700
Convenience food/gasoline stores	220,942	780,714	123,087
Delicatessens	64,003	376,488	52,983
Meat and fish (seafood) markets	180,220	577,628	106,639
Retail bakeries	207,542	229,075	31,989
Retail bakeries-baking and selling	182,481	231,869	30,267
Retail bakeries-selling only	25,061	210,597	54,599
Other food stores	346,924	505,720	80,736
Fruit and vegetable markets	184,257	1,173,611	102,593
Candy, nut, and confectionery stores	59,936	271,204	49,168
Dairy products stores	9,802	116,690	60,882
Miscellaneous food stores	92,929	414,862	82,898
Automotive dealers	16,587,856	5,028,147	347,361
New and used car dealers	14,250,202	16,083,749	427,459
Used car dealers	451,015	898,436	283,479
Auto and home supply stores	1,035,839	740,943	109,462
Auto parts, tires, and accessories stores	910,098	694,201	106,258
Home and auto supply stores	125,741	1,445,299	140,023
Miscellaneous automotive dealers	850,800	1,658,480	252,988
Boat dealers	389,137	1,662,979	239,616
Recreational vehicle dealers	281,554	2,101,149	313,884
Motorcycle dealers	136,510	1,263,981	208,731

Table XVI-12. Retail Trade Sales and Selected Ratios in Michigan, by Industry: 1992 Continued

Industry	Sales (Data in Thousands)	Sales per Unit	Sales per Employee
Automotive dealers, n.e.c.	$43,599	$1,178,351	$231,910
Gasoline service stations	5,411,301	1,354,858	187,567
Gasoline/convenience food stores	2,197,274	1,599,180	185,018
Other gasoline service stations and truck stops	3,214,027	1,226,728	189,350
Apparel and accessory stores	3,534,404	705,329	86,117
Men's and boys' clothing and accessory stores	367,127	672,394	99,682
Women's clothing and specialty stores	1,428,388	689,044	76,503
Women's clothing stores	1,306,862	740,851	76,924
Women's accessory and specialty stores	121,526	393,288	72,251
Family clothing stores	893,223	1,433,745	94,842
Shoe stores	658,450	489,918	97,765
Men's shoe stores	55,975	528,066	110,842
Women's shoe stores	107,437	411,636	85,471
Children's and juveniles' shoe stores	13,699	318,581	75,269
Family shoe stores	342,527	437,455	93,382
Athletic footwear stores	138,812	919,285	123,608
Other apparel and accessory stores	187,216	440,508	73,852
Children's and infants' wear stores	105,578	647,718	77,460
Miscellaneous apparel and accessory stores	81,638	311,595	69,657
Furniture and homefurnishings stores	3,417,719	859,418	132,727
Furniture stores	1,083,491	1,166,298	130,384
Homefurnishings stores	796,906	694,169	111,331
Floor covering stores	482,656	967,246	141,417
Drapery, curtain, and upholstery stores	28,769	282,049	71,035
Miscellaneous homefurnishings stores	285,481	521,903	85,473
Household appliance stores	260,727	863,334	141,010
Radio, television, computer, and music stores	1,276,595	1,075,480	151,381
Radio, television, and electronics stores	779,087	1,281,393	166,223
Computer and software stores	223,441	1,276,806	207,659
Record and Prerecorded tape stores	184,111	664,661	103,842
Musical instrument stores	89,956	708,315	100,285
Eating and drinking places	6,953,991	444,401	27,279
Eating places	6,457,702	491,903	26,811
Restaurants	2,983,564	503,385	25,158
Cafeterias	115,785	661,629	29,121
Refreshment places	2,814,184	502,353	27,376
Other eating places	544,169	382,141	35,130
Drinking places	496,289	196,940	35,288
Drug and proprietary stores	3,054,333	1,742,346	130,005
Drug stores	2,928,357	1,767,264	129,384
Proprietary stores	125,976	1,312,250	146,314

Table XVI-12. Retail Trade Sales and Selected Ratios in Michigan, by Industry: 1992 Continued

Industry	Sales (Data in Thousands)	Sales per Unit	Sales per Employee
Miscellaneous retail stores	$5,566,833	$553,748	$91,930
Liquor stores	537,810	600,905	141,454
Used merchandise stores	149,754	278,872	49,164
Miscellaneous shopping goods stores	2,391,975	540,071	85,866
Sporting goods stores and bicycle shops	634,315	666,998	109,064
General line sporting goods stores	313,313	940,880	118,053
Specialty line sporting goods stores	321,002	519,421	101,519
Book stores	285,326	708,005	80,013
Jewelry stores	473,286	537,825	99,284
Other miscellaneous shopping goods stores	999,048	455,147	72,881
Stationery stores	51,303	442,267	82,880
Hobby, toy, and game shops	337,427	883,317	107,977
Camera and photographic supply stores	52,158	628,410	115,650
Gift, novelty, and souvenir shops	384,780	308,070	59,179
Luggage and leather goods stores	25,889	392,258	69,408
Sewing, needlework, and piece goods stores	147,491	493,281	55,910
Nonstore retailers	997,636	1,152,005	108,746
Catalog and mail-order houses	338,427	1,658,956	141,542
Automatic merchandising machine operators	255,870	1,173,716	98,753
Direct selling establishments	403,339	908,421	96,216
Fuel dealers	447,485	1,239,571	203,866
Fuel oil dealers	(D)	(D)	(D)
Liquefied petroleum gas (bottled gas) dealers	297,082	1,248,244	183,724
Fuel dealers, n.e.c.	(D)	(D)	(D)
Florists	222,961	234,203	44,699
Tobacco stores and stands	21,887	486,378	130,280
News dealers and newsstands	15,259	423,861	105,234
Optical goods stores	224,346	420,912	89,595
Miscellaneous retail stores, n.e.c.	557,720	398,656	83,541
Pet shops	127,220	447,958	72,947
Art dealers	61,031	406,873	110,764
Other miscellaneous retail stores, n.e.c.	369,469	382,869	84,334

(D) Withheld to avoid disclosing data on individual companies; data are included in broader kind-of-business totals. N.A. data not available. n.e.c. stands for not elswhere classified. Source: Bureau of Census, 1992 Census of Retail Trade, Geographic Area Series, Michigan (Washington, D.C.: quinquennial).

Table XVI-13. Selected Retail Trade Statistics in Michigan, by County: 1992

County	Sales (Thousands)	Sales per Unit	Sales per Employee	County	Sales (Thousands)	Sales per Unit	Sales per Employee
Alcona	$40,901	$629	$124	Gratiot	$213,832	$918	$87
Alger	36,382	433	89	Hillsdale	193,259	874	104
Allegan	473,348	1,001	100	Houghton	221,368	851	82
Alpena	237,518	935	98	Huron	250,248	854	96
Antrim	83,466	614	98	Ingham	2,482,821	1,424	90
Arenac	92,141	801	78	Ionia	249,232	985	99
Baraga	39,641	639	87	Iosco	204,367	841	98
Barry	187,343	961	89	Iron	84,579	723	90
Bay	828,085	1,149	97	Isabella	399,193	1,244	82
Benzie	66,793	618	113	Jackson	1,007,492	1,285	95
Berrien	1,036,884	1,093	90	Kalamazoo	1,924,253	1,429	93
Branch	209,372	956	97	Kalkaska	92,283	1,300	128
Calhoun	1,022,346	1,181	92	Kent	4,517,123	1,589	99
Cass	188,966	964	106	Keweenaw	4,068	194	68
Charlevoix	150,603	697	87	Lake	36,214	575	100
Cheboygan	205,231	626	104	Lapeer	454,562	1,306	118
Chippewa	263,271	860	97	Leelanau	81,389	546	94
Clare	172,568	890	94	Lenawee	578,695	1,058	102
Clinton	309,580	1,279	110	Livingston	778,715	1,524	108
Crawford	93,223	1,002	92	Luce	45,336	824	105
Delta	281,577	926	92	Mackinac	86,197	449	117
Dickinson	224,183	1,104	94	Macomb	6,865,635	1,648	107
Eaton	677,943	1,808	110	Manistee	156,284	868	114
Emmet	317,909	924	104	Marquette	499,381	1,032	90
Genesee	3,545,014	1,398	104	Mason	179,748	917	101
Gladwin	113,976	991	103	Mecosta	223,797	956	85
Gogebic	125,832	807	91	Menominee	106,400	812	76
Grand Traverse	885,612	1,207	103	Midland	501,077	1,207	95

Table XVI-13. Selected Retail Trade Statistics in Michigan, by County: 1992 Continued

County	Sales (Thousands)	Sales per Unit	Sales per Employee	County	Sales (Thousands)	Sales per Unit	Sales per Employee
Missaukee	$52,785	$1,035	$141	Presque Isle	$75,005	$647	$102
Monroe	772,559	1,219	106	Roscommon	184,002	840	109
Montcalm	314,759	1,022	102	Saginaw	1,917,128	1,351	94
Montmorency	46,037	590	101	St. Clair	1,047,317	1,170	98
Muskegon	1,023,935	1,235	95	St. Joseph	335,054	991	98
Newaygo	174,292	889	99	Sanilac	189,561	780	110
Oakland	12,035,247	1,599	111	Schoolcraft	69,557	748	117
Oceana	94,679	667	111	Shiawassee	456,765	1,298	113
Ogemaw	164,887	896	101	Tuscola	256,601	904	114
Ontonagon	59,826	748	95	Van Buren	373,427	996	101
Osceola	118,508	878	104	Washtenaw	2,857,974	1,666	104
Oscoda	33,056	601	88	Wayne	12,700,499	1,293	99
Otsego	237,124	1,355	120	Wexford	274,263	1,192	105
Ottawa	1,310,943	1,284	95	**Michigan**	**71,523,046**	**1,312**	**101**

Source: Bureau of Census, <u>1992 Census of Retail Trade, Geographic Area Series, Michigan</u> (Washington, D.C.: quinquennial).

Table XVI-14. Estimated Annual Sales of Retail Stores in the Detroit Metropolitan Statistical Area, Michigan and the United States: 1978-1993

Year	Detroit MSA (Millions of Dollars)		Michigan (Millions of Dollars)		United States (Millions of Dollars)	
	Total Store Sales	Nondurable Sales	Total Store Sales	Nondurable Sales	Total Store Sales	Nondurable Sales
1978	$16,555	$11,251	$33,865	$20,996	$804,019	$523,120
1979	18,224	12,497	37,220	23,588	896,561	590,120
1980	19,193	13,589	37,623	25,436	956,921	658,303
1981	20,109	13,941	39,411	26,569	1,038,163	713,952
1982	18,733	12,387	38,625	24,911	1,068,747	733,160
1983	20,765	13,412	42,376	26,456	1,170,163	779,314
1984	22,477	14,205	46,988	28,027	1,286,914	832,433
1985	24,363	14,742	52,293	29,966	1,375,027	876,902
1986	26,440	16,043	56,083	31,797	1,449,636	908,948
1987	28,265	16,867	58,552	33,226	1,541,299	965,436
1988	29,838	18,262	62,018	35,582	1,657,300	1,027,514
1989	31,502	19,046	66,894	37,863	1,761,381	1,102,655
1990	32,371	20,298	69,675	40,648	1,848,375	1,177,052
1991	32,725	20,650	69,582	41,662	1,862,951	1,209,479
1992	35,670	22,826	74,002	44,054	1,959,091	1,251,789
1993	38,381	24,573	79,236	46,114	2,081,611	1,297,021

Source: Bureau of the Census, Combined Annual and Revised Monthly Retail Trade, January 1984 through December 1993 (Washington, D.C.: annual).

Table XVI-15. Number of Wholesale Trade Establishments, Employment, and Average Weekly Wage in Michigan, by County: 1992

County	Units	Employment	A.W.W.	County	Units	Employment	A.W.W.
Alcona	5	17	$183.33	Lake	8	56	$572.35
Alger	9	38	296.00	Lapeer	79	472	411.78
Allegan	96	807	423.02	Leelanau	17	137	370.30
Alpena	55	598	412.78	Lenawee	125	692	454.51
Antrim	18	110	471.29	Livingston	196	740	665.05
Arenac	21	103	342.37	Luce	12	44	532.77
Baraga	5	6	435.26	Mackinac	21	96	326.99
Barry	37	180	516.70	Macomb	1,041	10,975	743.98
Bay	134	1,589	511.99	Manistee	21	504	251.00
Benzie	N.A.	N.A.	N.A.	Marquette	84	705	395.51
Berrien	229	2,002	468.26	Mason	30	138	453.80
Branch	58	381	449.41	Mecosta	21	125	378.51
Calhoun	153	1,592	515.93	Menominee	34	391	453.07
Cass	44	404	457.94	Midland	69	482	514.14
Charlevoix	23	78	377.00	Missaukee	10	45	360.00
Cheboygan	16	114	251.79	Monroe	132	1,140	558.39
Chippewa	29	168	361.07	Montcalm	65	383	348.03
Clare	28	134	313.86	Montmorency	9	37	243.48
Clinton	50	831	475.20	Muskegon	184	2,031	508.87
Crawford	10	83	317.58	Newaygo	41	418	368.54
Delta	60	366	403.79	Oakland	4,235	44,776	859.52
Dickinson	53	607	461.60	Oceana	18	93	413.41
Eaton	69	1,996	630.49	Ogemaw	14	180	491.16
Emmet	47	394	470.32	Ontonagon	N.A.	N.A.	N.A.
Genesee	473	6,821	632.19	Osceola	21	100	558.37
Gladwin	12	49	370.45	Oscoda	N.A.	N.A.	N.A.
Gogebic	21	101	333.97	Otsego	41	363	408.32
Grand Traverse	173	1,290	523.88	Ottawa	345	3,372	590.63
Gratiot	50	574	464.04	Presque Isle	19	82	355.89
Hillsdale	56	529	452.70	Roscommon	19	66	352.81
Houghton	42	266	351.61	Saginaw	281	3,612	507.92
Huron	54	601	446.54	St. Clair	141	1,330	591.63
Ingham	444	5,275	595.42	St. Joseph	61	1,007	384.63
Ionia	44	421	440.79	Sanilac	64	336	351.76
Iosco	28	99	295.83	Schoolcraft	9	17	314.39
Iron	21	120	277.98	Shiawassee	77	608	540.98
Isabella	80	952	486.18	Tuscola	58	579	420.68
Jackson	219	2,204	548.31	Van Buren	66	426	413.48
Kalamazoo	373	4,113	540.02	Washtenaw	493	4,921	618.87
Kalkaska	24	168	585.33	Wayne	3,117	45,009	704.43
Kent	1,265	22,525	612.65	Wexford	36	266	436.42
Keweenaw	N.A.	N.A.	N.A.	**Michigan**	**18,086**	**200,090**	**680.72**

Source: Michigan Employment Security Commission, Research and Statistics (Detroit, Michigan: annually). N.A. Data not available.

Table XVI-16. Number of Retail Trade Establishments, Employment, and Average Weekly Wage in Michigan, by County: 1992

County	Units	Employment	A.W.W.	County	Units	Employment	A.W.W.
Alcona	65	394	$206.25	Lake	57	393	$165.06
Alger	79	421	162.56	Lapeer	283	3,679	225.18
Allegan	377	4,170	214.80	Leelanau	133	905	207.56
Alpena	214	2,356	202.62	Lenawee	477	5,729	215.28
Antrim	122	780	189.45	Livingston	390	6,499	242.15
Arenac	97	1,242	180.60	Luce	53	401	195.79
Baraga	56	413	165.70	Mackinac	180	1,118	209.30
Barry	152	1,605	211.26	Macomb	3,231	58,291	252.84
Bay	619	9,003	209.87	Manistee	161	1,356	198.44
Benzie	90	695	222.44	Marquette	412	5,191	192.91
Berrien	819	11,312	215.43	Mason	170	1,669	199.25
Branch	198	2,204	204.59	Mecosta	184	2,324	177.03
Calhoun	678	13,084	203.25	Menominee	127	1,338	178.04
Cass	155	1,198	220.22	Midland	350	4,969	216.93
Charlevoix	170	1,705	203.52	Missaukee	45	452	249.49
Cheboygan	254	1,965	213.72	Monroe	509	6,901	233.61
Chippewa	251	2,800	199.57	Montcalm	250	3,096	213.60
Clare	145	2,002	207.00	Montmorency	66	400	154.60
Clinton	189	2,491	219.07	Muskegon	719	10,768	233.80
Crawford	77	1,037	189.71	Newaygo	160	1,569	203.86
Delta	269	3,423	192.26	Oakland	5,883	115,833	303.06
Dickinson	178	2,251	210.25	Oceana	141	1,047	173.70
Eaton	277	4,567	228.91	Ogemaw	142	1,373	203.84
Emmet	293	3,183	230.73	Ontonagon	74	584	180.67
Genesee	1,974	32,105	235.64	Osceola	113	795	198.55
Gladwin	99	1,115	175.98	Oscoda	43	364	166.68
Gogebic	140	1,366	175.11	Otsego	137	1,706	270.16
Grand Traverse	567	8,774	235.47	Ottawa	825	13,442	221.30
Gratiot	187	2,202	222.69	Presque Isle	105	741	197.34
Hillsdale	193	1,837	214.75	Roscommon	185	1,943	189.86
Houghton	229	2,489	178.17	Saginaw	1,101	19,764	224.99
Huron	244	2,518	186.97	St. Clair	633	9,444	227.48
Ingham	1,435	29,055	229.97	St. Joseph	296	3,634	191.86
Ionia	228	2,563	222.10	Sanilac	199	1,531	223.91
Iosco	199	1,867	198.12	Schoolcraft	82	565	197.69
Iron	100	813	203.34	Shiawassee	288	3,940	202.30
Isabella	260	4,666	202.76	Tuscola	226	2,283	203.64
Jackson	649	10,865	244.04	Van Buren	314	3,535	222.47
Kalamazoo	1,089	19,987	220.82	Washtenaw	1,266	24,413	261.98
Kalkaska	57	808	218.36	Wayne	8,319	133,713	261.83
Kent	2,220	55,374	259.48	Wexford	181	2,491	205.20
Keweenaw	21	69	117.21	**Michigan**	**44,507**	**729,413**	**248.41**

Source: Michigan Employment Security Commission, Research and Statistics (Detroit, Michigan: annually).

Table XVI-17. Value of Export Shipments by Manufacturing Plants in Michigan and the United States, by Industry Group: 1972. 1977, 1981, 1983, 1993

Manufacturing Industry	Michigan (In Millions of Dollars)					United States (In Millions of Dollars)				
	1972	1977	1981	1983	1993	1972	1977	1981	1983	1993
Total Manufacturing	$3,522	$6,937	$10,275	$10,391	$24,776	$36,608	$85,796	$164,283	$142,307	$423,238
Food & Kindred Products	61	153	174	184	294	3,046	6,782	12,142	10,471	20,847
Tobacco Products	N.A.	N.A.	N.A.	N.A.	2	N.A.	N.A.	N.A.	N.A.	4,262
Textile Mill Products	N.A.	N.A.	N.A.	N.A.	84	N.A.	N.A.	N.A.	N.A.	4,809
Apparel & Other Textiles	N.A.	79	212	198	67	N.A.	757	1,340	887	5,603
Lumber & Wood Products	N.A.	N.A.	N.A.	N.A.	74	N.A.	N.A.	N.A.	N.A.	7,420
Furniture & Fixtures	N.A.	N.A.	N.A.	N.A.	755	N.A.	N.A.	N.A.	N.A.	2,901
Paper & Allied Products	N.A.	N.A.	N.A.	N.A.	127	N.A.	N.A.	N.A.	N.A.	9,533
Printing & Publishing	17	29	16	64	79	988	2,100	4,108	3,572	4,192
Chemicals & Allied Products	N.A.	N.A.	N.A.	N.A.	990	N.A.	N.A.	N.A.	N.A.	43,493
Petroleum & Related Products	180	405	577	528	59	3,757	9,466	19,332	17,400	6,239
Rubber & Plastics	N.A.	N.A.	N.A.	N.A.	505	N.A.	N.A.	N.A.	N.A.	8,722
Leather & Leather Products	35	62	81	93	147	519	1,411	2,678	2,360	1,664
Stone/Clay/Glass/Concrete Products	N.A.	N.A.	N.A.	N.A.	322	N.A.	N.A.	N.A.	N.A.	3,978
Primary Metals	49	76	99	106	611	409	997	1,806	1,556	18,981
Fabricated Metals	126	196	177	122	2,048	1,490	2,792	6,163	3,713	13,867
Industrial Machinery & Computer Equipment	312	514	837	885	2,885	1,429	4,125	7,058	6,032	77,828
Electronic & Electrical Equipment ex Computers	464	986	1,832	1,206	1,673	7,824	19,142	38,430	29,040	60,831
Transportation Equipment	131	188	326	280	13,400	3,296	8,061	16,494	15,842	82,492
Instruments & Related Products	1,736	4,107	5,625	6,429	481	7,842	17,712	31,166	28,187	26,135
Miscellaneous Manufacturing	28	63	122	121	127	1,531	4,235	8,004	7,810	7,642

N.A. Data not available.
Source: U.S. Department of Commerce, State Export Zip Code Data Base (Washington, D.C.).

Table XVI-18. Factory Shipments and Employment Related to Manufactured Exports by Major Industry Group, Michigan and the United States: 1989

Manufacturing Industry	Value of Michigan Manufacturing Shipments (In Millions of Dollars)			Michigan as a Percent(%) of U.S.	Michigan Manufacturing Employment (Data in Thousands)			Michigan as a Percent(%) of U.S.
	Total Exports	Direct Exports	Supporting Exports		Total Exports	Direct Exports	Supporting Exports	
Total Manufacturing	**$23,667**	**$15,066**	**$8,602**	**5.1**	**$155**	**$77**	**$78**	**5.2**
Food & Kindred Products	332	176	154	1.4	1	0.5	0.5	1.4
Tobacco Products	N.A.	N.A.	N.A.	N.A.	N.A.	N.A.	N.A.	N.A.
Textile Mill Products	(D)	(D)	(D)	(D)	(D)	(D)	(D)	(D)
Apparel & Other Textiles	370	292	78	9.9	2	1	1	4.3
Lumber & Wood Products	194	95	98	1.6	2	1	1	2.4
Furniture & Fixtures	170	117	53	11.0	1	0.7	0.3	7.3
Paper & Allied Products	597	245	352	3.4	3	1	2	3.8
Printing & Publishing	357	113	244	3.2	5	2	3	4.0
Chemicals & Allied Products	1,676	1,185	490	2.9	7	5	2	3.8
Petroleum & Related Products	175	78	96	1.2	0.3	0.2	0.1	2.9
Rubber & Plastics	965	381	584	6.4	9	4	5	7.0
Leather & Leather Products	(D)	(D)	(D)	(D)	(D)	(D)	(D)	(D)
Stone/Clay/Glass/Concrete Products	281	154	126	5.4	2	1	1	4.6
Primary Metals	1,775	306	1,469	4.6	11	9	2	6.0
Fabricated Metals	2,759	1,081	1,678	12.1	23	8	15	10.9
Industrial Machinery	2,864	1,681	1,183	4.2	21	11	10	4.5
Computer and Office Equipment	347	238	109	1.3	1	0.5	0.5	0.7
Electronic & Electrical Equipment ex Computers	751	547	203	1.4	7	5	2	1.6
Transportation Equipment	9,773	8,115	1,658	13.1	38	33	5	10.5
Motor Vehicles and Equipment	9,518	7,920	1,598	28.0	36	31	5	30.6
Instruments & Related Products	407	327	80	1.9	3	2	1	1.5
Miscellaneous Manufacturing	91	75	16	1.9	0.4	0.2	0.2	0.9

(D) data withheld to avoid disclosure of individual firm information.

Source: Bureau of the Census, Manufacturing Analytical Reports, Exports from Manufacturing Establishments (Washington, D.C.: occasional). N.A. Data not available.

Table XVI-19. Exports from Michigan to Other Countries, Value Greater Than 1 Million Dollars: 1988, 1992, and 1993

Country	1993 Rank	1988 Export Value	1992 Export Value	1993 Export Value	Country	1993 Rank	1988 Export Value	1992 Export Value	1993 Export Value
Canada	1	$9,453,015,974	$14,165,457,132	$11,434,093,435	Argentina	29	$26,458,855	$48,302,409	$44,703,914
Mexico	2	1,249,939,425	1,397,472,658	5,630,458,341	Qatar	30	10,755,277	13,548,422	40,370,283
Japan	3	439,878,972	746,828,174	1,064,206,451	Norway	31	22,969,344	12,091,344	38,762,257
Saudi Arabia	4	191,373,566	330,195,610	976,550,824	Portugal	32	14,879,544	10,788,242	35,914,611
Germany	5	381,502,851	562,827,741	911,830,241	Malaysia	33	9,955,413	20,770,049	35,818,912
United Kingdom	6	358,722,222	467,800,578	473,551,889	Columbia	34	18,005,911	17,138,280	35,810,765
Belgium	7	249,135,944	285,492,296	404,631,816	Russia	35	N.A.	6,338,679	33,344,161
Austria	8	44,868,832	230,731,189	387,377,554	South Africa	36	22,703,347	29,225,291	32,894,200
France	9	219,322,864	281,702,005	361,653,889	Turkey	37	12,800,117	13,665,052	31,044,217
Taiwan	10	125,092,840	231,524,295	337,784,135	India	38	18,879,905	16,543,861	26,674,562
Australia	11	132,324,927	174,722,220	280,627,825	Hungary	39	1,087,481	9,965,800	24,319,089
China	12	36,992,843	63,972,479	211,329,538	Finland	40	17,033,169	15,748,971	23,489,169
Venezuela	13	143,312,909	210,409,847	199,137,592	Poland	41	485,471	10,859,833	23,478,532
Brazil	14	104,879,789	109,201,753	187,386,075	Dominican Republic	42	8,926,223	9,657,798	20,409,764
Hong Kong	15	53,209,165	88,433,463	179,088,206	Bahrain	43	1,843,988	4,128,856	18,632,287
South Korea	16	96,686,435	132,132,334	175,861,685	Oman	44	1,554,186	5,688,326	17,919,095
Kuwait	17	43,626,996	110,087,249	165,946,017	New Zealand	45	22,411,841	18,990,631	16,390,195
Spain	18	56,862,425	91,214,111	165,933,606	Panama	46	1,665,459	4,649,207	15,849,601
United Arab Emirates	19	12,187,678	56,052,344	150,148,215	Ireland	47	76,416,469	20,453,317	15,658,185
Israel	20	0	33,309,621	129,444,744	Costa Rica	48	4,644,678	5,057,058	14,248,545
Italy	21	82,737,161	124,382,999	125,454,746	Lebanon	49	959,440	4,785,106	14,185,752
Netherlands	22	150,513,457	141,692,190	120,262,374	Ecuador	50	6,813,445	5,781,992	14,145,209
Thailand	23	34,510,402	69,246,390	101,592,309	Nigeria	51	712,190	5,385,391	13,889,310
Sweden	24	46,564,831	73,369,931	81,642,559	Egypt	52	43,004,830	24,773,223	13,152,715
Singapore	25	40,091,493	55,602,504	81,493,800	Luxembourg	53	1,905,284	5,927,601	12,652,425
Switzerland	26	44,954,251	76,031,609	79,381,613	Guatemala	54	2,767,663	4,779,503	12,211,508
Philippines	27	14,284,920	29,823,109	74,201,225	Peru	55	3,919,172	2,945,665	12,004,555
Chile	28	9,066,945	18,378,370	62,406,499	Denmark	56	5,014,888	8,530,872	11,087,390

Table XVI-19. Exports from Michigan to Other Countries, Value Greater Than 1 Million Dollars: 1988, 1992, and 1993 Continued

Country	1993 Rank	1988 Export Value	1992 Export Value	1993 Export Value	Country	1993 Rank	1988 Export Value	1992 Export Value	1993 Export Value
Indonesia	57	$4,738,743	$12,638,308	$10,495,033	Uruguay	71	$559,612	$859,012	$2,397,629
Greece	58	17,681,927	6,022,411	8,722,708	Latvia	72	N.A.	510,982	1,959,976
Bahamas	59	6,077,107	6,810,254	8,351,547	Syria	73	126,730	2,605,273	1,788,433
Netherlands Antilles	60	1,069,173	2,024,520	8,077,823	Lithuania	74	N.A.	85,658	1,513,796
Pakistan	61	3,242,766	2,482,419	5,457,210	Cayman Islands	75	491,689	210,093	1,469,407
El Salvador	62	1,705,094	6,560,164	5,295,705	Morocco	76	34,124	2,223,558	1,435,794
Jamaica	63	1,163,459	2,090,859	5,076,052	Romania	77	117,586	1,130,573	1,399,850
Haiti	64	972,775	585,647	4,952,910	Ghana	78	42,217	187,425	1,391,063
Jordan	65	11,844,180	2,140,945	4,844,791	Barbados	79	565,496	376,089	1,182,535
Bermuda	66	541,756	1,702,325	4,743,602	French Polynesia	80	1,048,713	216,312	1,146,123
The Czech Republic	67	351,228	0	4,001,383	Trinidad and Tobago	81	864,628	1,803,369	1,128,660
Honduras	68	665,183	1,029,392	3,486,295	Iceland	82	2,773,849	1,338,021	1,094,741
Republic of Yemen	69	170,072	368,085	3,039,050	Total		14,258,296,200	20,789,471,208	25,322,489,871
Iran	70	0	2,746,731	2,897,472					

N.A. indicates data not available.

Source: U.S. Department of Commerce, State Export Zip Code Data Base (Washington, D.C.).

CHAPTER XVII
FINANCE / INSURANCE / REAL ESTATE

The Office of Management and Budget in the Executive Office of the President is responsible for maintaining the Standard Industrial Classification system. The SIC is used in all federal statistical programs and in most other programs where the focus is on economic activity.

According to the latest Standard Industrial Classification Manual,

> this division includes establishments operating primarily in the fields of finance, insurance, and real estate. Finance includes depository institutions, nondepository credit institutions, holding (but not primarily operating) companies, other investment companies, brokers and dealers in securities and commodity contracts, and security and commodity exchanges. Insurance covers carriers of all types of insurance, and insurance agents and brokers. Real estate includes owners, lessors, lessees, buyers, sellers, agents, and developers of real estate.

Statistics on Michigan financial institutions are published annually by the Michigan Financial Institutions Bureau in its Annual Report. County data on banking are available from the Federal Deposit Insurance Corporation data books.

The American Council of Life Insurance publishes an annual Life Insurance Fact Book.

The Michigan Association of Realtors compiles data on home sales by its various boards. The Federal Home Loan Bank of Indianapolis prepares statistics on mortgage terms.

Current data on employment, hours, and earnings are collected and disseminated by the Michigan Employment Security Commission in Detroit and by the Bureau of Labor statistics in Washington, D.C.

Some terms found in this chapter include:

Establishments: a single physical location at which business is conducted. It is not necessarily identical with a company or enterprise, which may consist of one establishment or more.

Units: Refer to the definition of establishments.

Employment: Includes both full-time and part-time workers.

Average Weekly Wage (AWW): AWW = ((Total wages/Employment)/Number of weeks).

List of Tables

Table   **Page**

XVII-1. Number of Finance, Insurance, and Real Estate Units, Employment, and
Average Weekly Wage in Michigan and the United States: 1970-1994 533

XVII-2. Number of Banks, Savings and Loan, and Credit Union Offices and Branches
in Michigan: 1970-1992 534

CHAPTER XVII
FINANCE / INSURANCE / REAL ESTATE

List of Tables

Table   **Page**

XVII-3. Number of Finance, Insurance, and Real Estate Units, Employment, and Average Weekly Wages in Michigan, by County: 1992 535

XVII-4. Total Wages in Finance, Insurance, and Real Estate and as a Percentage of Total Wages in Michigan, by County: 1992 536

XVII-5. Number of FDIC Member Banks and Branches and Total Deposits in Michigan, by County: 1992 537

XVII-6. Summary Ratios for Commercial Banks in Michigan: 1988-1992 539

XVII-7. Purchases of Life Insurance in Michigan and the United States: 1985-1992 . . . 541

XVII-8. Total Amount of Life Insurance In-Force in Michigan and the United States: 1991-1992 541

XVII-9. Average Amount of Life Insurance In-Force per Household in Michigan and the United States: 1991-1992 541

XVII-10. Life Insurance and Annuity Benefit Payments in Michigan and the United States: 1991-1992 542

XVII-11. Premium Receipts of Life Insurance Companies in Michigan and the United States: 1991-1992 542

XVII-12. Mortgages Owned by Life Insurance Companies in Michigan and the United States: 1991-1992 542

XVII-13. Real Estate Owned by Life Insurance Companies in Michigan and the United States: 1991-1992 542

XVII-14. Average Selling Prices of Existing Residential Homes in Michigan, by Realtor board: 1986-1993 543

XVII-15. Terms on Conventional Single-Family Mortgages in Michigan: 1976-1993 . . . 544

Table XVII-1. Number of Finance, Insurance, and Real Estate Units, Employment, and Average Weekly Wage in Michigan and the United States: 1970-1994

Year	Michigan			United States		
	Number of Units	Employment (Data in Thousands)	Average Weekly Wage	Number of Units	Employment (Data in Thousands)	Average Weekly Wage
1970	---	120	$---	---	3,645	$---
1971	---	121	---	---	3,772	---
1972	---	128	---	---	3,908	---
1973	---	130	---	---	4,046	---
1974	---	134	---	---	4,148	---
1975	---	134	---	---	4,165	---
1976	9,060	137	204	351,355	4,271	206
1977	9,278	142	217	357,806	4,467	220
1978	9,555	147	237	370,585	4,724	239
1979	9,694	155	258	381,723	4,975	259
1980	9,695	157	282	391,329	5,160	287
1981	9,587	155	300	396,688	5,298	314
1982	9,274	152	322	400,565	5,340	343
1983	9,193	151	345	407,296	5,466	376
1984	8,734	154	359	415,478	5,684	398
1985	10,068	163	381	428,476	5,948	429
1986	10,239	171	412	438,575	6,273	466
1987	10,604	180	439	457,696	6,533	500
1988	11,018	186	461	469,989	6,630	533
1989	11,495	187	471	472,651	6,668	544
1990	12,095	191	497	491,100	6,709	571
1991	12,514	189	516	526,377	6,646	596
1992	13,961	191	567	543,578	6,571	670
1993	14,434	192	581	558,028	6,604	693
1994	15,977	196	593	N.A.	N.A.	N.A.

Source: U.S. Bureau of Labor Statistics (Washington, D.C.) and Michigan Employment Security Commission, Research and Statistics (Detroit, Michigan: annually). N.A. data not available.

Table XVII-2. Number of Banks, Savings and Loan, and Credit Union Offices and Branches in Michigan: 1970-1992

Year	Commercial Banks				Savings & Loan		Credit Unions		
	State Banks	State Branches	National Banks	National Branches	Total Offices	Associations	Total	State Charter	Federal Charter
1970	230	649	103	N.A.	248	68	1,159	787	372
1971	227	667	104	N.A.	390	65	1,118	754	364
1972	226	707	106	N.A.	307	65	1,092	724	368
1973	229	742	111	N.A.	326	65	1,069	706	363
1974	230	790	117	N.A.	360	66	1,044	679	365
1975	231	822	120	N.A.	400	67	1,023	656	367
1976	238	847	122	N.A.	434	66	988	630	358
1977	239	875	123	764	478	66	963	611	352
1978	240	929	125	815	526	65	937	597	350
1979	247	1,028	123	907	563	65	929	584	345
1980	250	1,095	126	971	608	63	924	572	340
1981	250	1,138	126	997	636	59	869	560	309
1982	251	1,156	125	1,009	635	53	823	531	292
1983	248	1,140	124	981	651	52	794	516	278
1984	248	1,142	119	972	643	53	764	500	264
1985	241	1,141	119	934	649	52	730	480	250
1986	238	1,165	109	N.A.	N.A.	50	708	465	243
1987	219	1,133	92	N.A.	N.A.	50	682	446	236
1988	204	1,129	83	N.A.	N.A.	46	661	433	228
1989	195	1,176	75	N.A.	N.A.	44	631	411	220
1990	171	1,085	65	N.A.	N.A.	42	601	386	215
1991	170	1,199	62	N.A.	N.A.	N.A.	583	373	210
1992	167	1,367	N.A.	N.A.	N.A.	N.A.	562	356	206

Source: Michigan Financial Institutions Bureau, Annual Report (Lansing, Michigan: annual). N.A. data not available.

Table XVII-3. Number of Finance, Insurance, and Real Estate Units, Employment, and Average Weekly Wages in Michigan, by County: 1992

County	Units	Employment	A.W.W.	County	Units	Employment	A.W.W.
Alcona	5	11	$284.73	Lake	9	54	$355.24
Alger	14	75	329.57	Lapeer	76	525	399.24
Allegan	86	382	368.79	Leelanau	31	97	402.04
Alpena	51	359	344.72	Lenawee	140	1,028	471.06
Antrim	33	108	366.94	Livingston	149	2,797	454.82
Arenac	16	141	330.77	Luce	10	73	365.47
Baraga	13	76	362.54	Mackinac	21	101	278.75
Barry	49	557	404.72	Macomb	984	8,477	497.10
Bay	153	1,377	419.83	Manistee	35	185	318.51
Benzie	23	130	363.25	Marquette	107	1,081	369.10
Berrien	280	2,466	486.14	Mason	42	226	386.41
Branch	56	369	393.31	Mecosta	49	290	283.07
Calhoun	190	2,707	546.03	Menominee	36	222	373.84
Cass	44	299	403.39	Midland	100	774	551.38
Charlevoix	55	290	355.88	Missaukee	14	79	398.28
Cheboygan	32	223	417.25	Monroe	152	1,009	395.14
Chippewa	52	302	301.44	Montcalm	70	392	360.52
Clare	40	198	304.96	Montmorency	12	47	223.13
Clinton	52	376	386.90	Muskegon	197	1,457	452.97
Crawford	16	139	331.08	Newaygo	36	417	399.81
Delta	72	579	370.64	Oakland	3,065	47,878	638.66
Dickinson	53	338	354.86	Oceana	27	150	356.44
Eaton	98	1,755	626.50	Ogemaw	22	91	431.59
Emmet	70	354	419.16	Ontonagon	11	89	378.38
Genesee	525	4,957	529.59	Osceola	22	96	310.99
Gladwin	18	109	384.00	Oscoda	10	33	246.90
Gogebic	38	233	399.65	Otsego	49	288	436.01
Grand Traverse	181	1,815	459.41	Ottawa	248	2,194	461.51
Gratiot	53	383	362.33	Presque Isle	21	111	318.09
Hillsdale	54	305	329.50	Roscommon	35	122	278.04
Houghton	62	573	424.64	Saginaw	300	3,276	465.66
Huron	63	349	361.69	St. Clair	157	1,147	424.38
Ingham	604	8,383	540.37	St. Joseph	81	533	355.21
Ionia	58	497	357.39	Sanilac	64	309	336.17
Iosco	41	367	318.86	Schoolcraft	12	98	386.96
Iron	25	169	320.26	Shiawassee	67	586	370.90
Isabella	71	462	410.07	Tuscola	63	350	340.02
Jackson	168	1,749	451.27	Van Buren	70	323	353.58
Kalamazoo	390	7,272	469.42	Washtenaw	463	4,721	530.09
Kalkaska	14	54	307.57	Wayne	1,868	51,110	625.12
Kent	952	13,067	584.29	Wexford	41	193	408.70
Keweenaw	2	7	160.83	**Michigan**	**13,833**	**189**	**566.90**

Source: U.S. Bureau of Labor Statistics (Washington, D.C.) and Michigan Employment Security Commission, Research and Stats (Detroit, MI).

Table XVII-4. Total Wages in Finance, Insurance, Real Estate and as Percent of Total Wages in Michigan, by County: 1992

County	Total F/I/RE Wages	Percent(%) of County Wages	County	Total F/I/RE Wages	Percent(%) of County Wages
Alcona	$38,916	1.1	Lake	$247,336	7.8
Alger	319,202	3.3	Lapeer	2,727,814	4.4
Allegan	1,821,642	1.2	Leelanau	506,372	4.4
Alpena	1,605,717	3.5	Lenawee	6,287,141	4.5
Antrim	513,142	3.5	Livingston	16,542,267	12.3
Arenac	604,962	5.7	Luce	348,154	6.8
Baraga	358,417	5.0	Mackinac	365,186	3.3
Barry	2,929,956	7.6	Macomb	54,758,470	2.9
Bay	7,520,804	4.3	Manistee	763,177	2.9
Benzie	615,890	6.8	Marquette	5,186,766	5.2
Berrien	15,574,443	4.9	Mason	1,135,637	3.1
Branch	1,886,388	4.7	Mecosta	1,063,158	4.5
Calhoun	19,215,039	6.1	Menominee	1,079,269	3.3
Cass	1,569,055	4.3	Midland	5,539,616	2.2
Charlevoix	1,337,580	3.6	Missaukee	407,819	6.4
Cheboygan	1,205,699	5.9	Monroe	5,172,053	2.6
Chippewa	1,182,270	4.3	Montcalm	1,836,720	2.7
Clare	784,851	3.8	Montmorency	135,990	3.1
Clinton	1,889,123	4.8	Muskegon	8,580,489	3.1
Crawford	599,054	4.7	Newaygo	2,167,311	6.1
Delta	2,789,245	4.9	Oakland	397,603,922	9.5
Dickinson	1,559,317	3.1	Oceana	693,240	4.6
Eaton	14,309,790	16.0	Ogemaw	514,693	3.6
Emmet	1,914,830	3.5	Ontonagon	438,079	2.9
Genesee	34,140,439	3.4	Osceola	386,190	1.4
Gladwin	541,208	3.9	Oscoda	103,812	2.1
Gogebic	1,207,268	7.6	Otsego	1,637,615	4.8
Grand Traverse	10,833,382	6.6	Ottawa	13,165,153	3.0
Gratiot	1,803,231	3.5	Presque Isle	459,736	4.2
Hillsdale	1,307,635	2.2	Roscommon	436,107	3.4
Houghton	3,160,206	10.6	Saginaw	19,824,516	3.9
Huron	1,638,308	3.9	St. Clair	6,328,618	3.2
Ingham	58,850,205	7.9	St. Joseph	2,458,522	2.5
Ionia	2,304,687	5.0	Sanilac	1,349,665	3.7
Iosco	1,521,862	6.1	Schoolcraft	491,665	7.4
Iron	703,563	8.3	Shiawassee	2,817,822	4.5
Isabella	2,466,890	3.8	Tuscola	1,546,005	3.6
Jackson	10,257,244	4.1	Van Buren	1,482,447	2.1
Kalamazoo	44,412,516	7.2	Washtenaw	32,572,967	3.8
Kalkaska	214,130	1.1	Wayne	415,249,199	7.6
Kent	99,275,478	6.3	Wexford	1,022,520	2.1
Keweenaw	18,814	3.0	**Michigan**	**5,581,365,760.08**	**6.3**

Source: Michigan Employment Security Commission, Research and Statistics (Detroit, Michigan).

Table XVII-5. Number of FDIC Member Banks and Branches and Total Deposits in Michigan, by County: 1992
(Deposit Data in Thousands)

County	Number of Banks	Number of Branches	Total Deposits	Individuals/Partnerships/ Corporations Deposits	All Other Deposits
Alcona	2	3	$33,165	$31,976	$1,189
Alger	4	8	74,070	67,906	6,164
Allegan	10	26	449,517	428,393	21,124
Alpena	3	11	196,174	172,676	23,498
Antrim	6	12	167,834	151,127	16,707
Arenac	4	9	117,149	107,216	9,933
Baraga	3	4	60,990	55,622	5,368
Barry	5	7	177,298	160,656	16,642
Bay	8	33	693,888	661,249	32,639
Benzie	5	7	123,093	114,809	8,284
Berrien	11	58	1,242,543	1,144,919	97,624
Branch	4	15	260,823	245,471	15,352
Calhoun	9	32	698,576	681,907	16,669
Cass	5	13	199,220	184,501	14,719
Charlevoix	6	14	197,133	178,773	18,360
Cheboygan	2	11	181,139	162,994	18,145
Chippewa	5	12	233,492	208,265	25,227
Clare	4	10	183,143	168,442	14,701
Clinton	5	14	235,106	215,945	19,161
Crawford	4	6	87,868	77,719	10,149
Delta	6	15	305,336	282,813	22,523
Dickinson	6	12	241,232	223,162	18,070
Eaton	10	25	410,593	395,699	14,895
Emmet	6	16	325,577	305,391	20,186
Genesee	10	90	2,726,269	2,549,718	176,551
Gladwin	3	7	124,770	116,239	8,531
Gogebic	4	7	164,357	157,021	7,336
Grand Traverse	6	30	663,924	643,338	20,586
Gratiot	4	17	326,125	298,287	27,838
Hillsdale	7	14	260,626	248,481	12,145
Houghton	5	13	232,763	222,943	9,820
Huron	8	20	370,309	344,504	25,805
Ingham	17	70	2,040,851	1,920,705	120,145
Ionia	7	19	329,868	301,951	27,917
Iosco	3	10	160,070	144,570	15,500
Iron	4	7	133,847	119,711	14,136
Isabella	4	19	321,111	302,407	18,704
Jackson	6	42	752,021	732,196	19,825
Kalamazoo	9	56	1,438,838	1,394,745	44,093
Kalkaska	2	3	54,754	49,199	5,555
Kent	20	166	5,253,881	4,911,617	342,266
Keweenaw	1	1	9,022	7,579	1,443

Table XVII-5. Number of FDIC Member Banks and Branches, and Total Deposits in Michigan, by County: 1992 Continued
(Deposit Data in Thousands)

County	Number of Banks	Number of Branches	Total Deposits	Individuals/Partnerships/ Corporations Deposits	All Other Deposits
Lake	1	2	$27,569	$22,337	$5,232
Lapeer	8	22	381,935	359,372	22,563
Leelanau	3	7	101,120	96,965	4,156
Lenawee	9	38	767,847	720,329	47,518
Livingston	9	28	600,740	573,368	27,372
Luce	2	2	51,608	45,216	6,392
Mackinac	3	9	95,565	82,330	13,235
Macomb	10	151	6,380,492	6,183,174	197,318
Manistee	4	13	180,032	164,013	16,019
Marquette	6	29	464,010	419,754	44,256
Mason	4	9	205,380	189,062	16,318
Mecosta	4	14	191,077	174,040	17,037
Menominee	4	9	175,504	161,934	13,570
Midland	6	21	497,153	435,096	62,057
Missaukee	3	4	68,982	63,930	5,052
Monroe	5	37	1,015,081	852,373	162,708
Montcalm	9	23	345,321	315,880	29,441
Montmorency	2	3	76,584	72,398	4,186
Muskegon	6	33	919,008	868,949	50,059
Newaygo	5	11	201,924	186,260	15,664
Oakland	23	284	11,763,676	11,484,743	278,934
Oceana	4	7	135,751	120,798	14,953
Ogemaw	5	7	135,666	128,070	7,596
Ontonagon	3	6	75,914	68,274	7,640
Osceola	5	7	135,602	125,105	10,497
Oscoda	1	2	38,453	37,761	692
Otsego	3	9	190,116	185,311	4,805
Ottawa	15	63	1,663,153	1,423,385	239,766
Presque Isle	4	4	91,318	87,612	3,706
Roscommon	2	8	163,106	157,352	5,754
Saginaw	8	53	1,262,082	1,184,780	77,302
St. Clair	7	21	313,417	298,639	14,778
St. Joseph	2	4	80,263	72,575	7,688
Sanilac	7	19	434,586	410,713	23,873
Schoolcraft	7	39	977,541	935,204	42,337
Shiawassee	7	26	403,902	384,953	18,949
Tuscola	10	23	353,384	325,333	28,051
Van Buren	7	19	375,797	337,786	38,011
Washtenaw	12	73	2,062,058	1,949,046	113,011
Wayne	23	365	20,018,591	18,205,032	1,813,558
Wexford	3	14	242,409	221,186	21,223
Michigan	**222**	**2,482**	**75,922,082**	**71,023,280**	**4,898,801**

Source: Federal Deposit Insurance Corporation, FDIC Data Book-Operating Banks and Branches (Washington, D.C.: 1993).

Table XVII-6. Summary Ratios(%) for Commercial Banks in Michigan: 1988-1992

Earnings and Profitability	12/31/88	12/31/89	12/31/90	12/31/91	12/31/92
PERCENT(%) OF AVERAGE ASSETS					
Interest Income (TE)	9.30	9.95	9.86	9.33	8.22
-Interest Expense	4.05	5.55	5.50	4.92	3.62
Net Interest Income (TE)	4.35	4.41	4.39	4.42	4.57
+Noninterest Income	0.56	0.56	0.56	0.61	0.66
Memo Fee Income	N/A	N/A	N/A	0.15	0.18
-Overhead Expense	3.14	3.11	3.17	3.30	3.36
-Provision Loan & Lease Losses	0.20	0.21	0.23	0.25	0.24
=Pretax Operating Income (TE)	1.62	1.67	1.58	1.52	1.70
=Securities Gains (Losses)	0.00	0.00	0.00	0.01	0.02
-Pretax Net Operating Inc (TE)	1.61	1.68	1.58	1.56	1.74
Net Operating Income	1.05	1.10	1.04	1.02	1.14
Adjusted Net Operating Income	1.11	1.17	1.11	1.08	1.24
Adjusted Net Income	1.13	1.18	1.12	1.09	1.23
Net Income	1.06	1.11	1.04	1.02	1.14
Margin Analysis					
Avg Earning Assets to Avg Assets	0.24	0.23	0.25	0.29	0.23
Avg Int-Bearing Funds to Avg Ast	12.45	12.72	11.24	10.20	13.75
Int Inc (TE) to Avg Earn Assets	5.90	5.73	5.41	5.07	6.89
Int Expense to Avg Earn Assets	1.25	1.24	1.25	1.32	1.38
Net Int Inc - TE to Avg Earn Asset	4.68	4.72	4.70	4.73	4.91
Loan & Lease Analysis					
Net Loss to Average Total Ln&LS	0.24	0.23	0.25	0.29	0.23
Earnings Coverage of Net Loss(x)	12.45	12.72	11.24	10.2	13.75
LN&LS Allowance to Net Losses (x)	5.90	5.73	5.41	5.07	6.89
LN&LS Allowance to Total Ln&Ls	1.25	1.24	1.25	1.32	1.38
Liquidity					
Volatile Liability Dependence	-12.44	-9.03	-6.13	-7.19	-5.56
Net Loans & Leases to Assets	59.08	60.11	61.08	60.12	59.75
Capitalization					
Member Tier One Leverage Capital	N/A	N/A	7.83	7.92	8.26
National Tier One Leverage Cap	N/A	N/A	7.81	7.89	8.22
Nonmember Tier One Leverage Cap	N/A	N/A	7.81	7.89	8.22
Cash Dividends to Net Income	40.28	46.74	44.9	41.68	38.94
Retain Earns to Avg Total Equity	7.06	6.32	6.31	6.74	7.06

Table XVII-6. Summary Ratios(%) for Commercial Banks in Michigan: 1988-1992 Continued

Earnings and Profitability	12/31/88	12/31/89	12/31/90	12/31/91	12/31/92
PERCENT(%) OF AVERAGE ASSETS (continued)					
Growth Rates					
Assets	6.27	6.53	6.15	5.44	5.12
Member Tier One Capital	N.A.	N.A.	N.A.	7.59	8.09
National Tier One Capital	N.A.	N.A.	N.A.	7.57	7.76
Nonmember Tier One Capital	N.A.	N.A.	N.A.	7.58	8.06
Net Loans & Leases	10.31	9.64	6.9	3.89	5.2
Temporary Investments	5.46	-3.07	-6.05	7.14	-12.51
Volatile Liabilities	29.25	16.62	9.99	-2.66	-8.18
% Non Current Loans & Leases					
Total LN&LS-90+ Days Past Due	0.32	0.34	0.34	0.37	0.25
-Nonaccrual	0.53	0.5	0.57	0.64	0.53
-Total	0.99	0.96	1.09	1.18	0.94
Total Assets ($millions)	**85,059**	**91,112**	**93,802**	**98,773**	**100,288**
Equity Capital ($millions)	**5,462**	**5,849**	**6,204**	**6,742**	**7,275**

N.A. Data not available.
Source: Federal Deposit Insurance Corps Disclosure Group, <u>Uniform Bank Performance Report, State Averages</u> (Washington, D.C.: annually).

Table XVII-7. Purchases of Life Insurance in Michigan and the United States 1985-1992

Year	Michigan	U.S.	Year	Michigan	U.S.
1985	$26,850,000,000	$910,944,000,000	1989	$27,681,000,000	$1,020,719,000,000
1986	27,541,000,000	933,592,000,000	1990	28,094,000,000	1,069,660,000,000
1987	27,802,000,000	986,660,000,000	1991	27,809,000,000	1,041,508,000,000
1988	28,515,000,000	995,686,000,000	1992	27,692,000,000	1,048,135,000,000

Source: American Council of Life Insurance, Life Insurance Fact Book (Washington, D.C.: annually).

Table XVII-8. Total Amount of Life Insurance In-Force in Michigan and the United States: 1991-1992

Type of Insurance	Michigan		United States	
	1991	1992	1991	1992
Total				
Number of Policies	13,494,000	13,921,000	374,849,000	366,025,000
Amount in Dollars($)	$361,165,000,000	$354,429,000,000	$9,986,336,000,000	$10,405,792,000,000
Ordinary				
Number of Policies	4,607,000	4,562,000	136,984,000	138,304,000
Amount in Dollars($)	$169,942,000,000	$168,385,000,000	$5,677,777,000,000	$5,941,810,000,000
Group				
Number of Policies	5,494,000	6,243,000	141,086,000	141,696,000
Amount in Dollars($)	$179,438,000,000	$176,147,000,000	$4,057,606,000,000	$4,240,919,000,000
Industrial				
Number of Policies	841,000	728,000	33,025,000	30,069,000
Amount in Dollars($)	$724,000,000	$641,000,000	$22,475,000,000	$20,973,000,000
Credit				
Number of Policies	2,552,000	2,388,000	63,754,000	55,956,000
Amount in Dollars($)	$11,061,000,000	$9,256,000,000	$228,478,000,000	$202,090,000,000

Source: American Council of Life Insurance, Life Insurance Fact Book (Washington, D.C.: annually).

Table XVII-9. Average Amount of Life Insurance In-Force per Household in Michigan and the United States: 1991-1992

Year	Michigan	United States
1991	$100,500	$102,700
1992	100,600	106,600

Source: American Council of Life Insurance, Life Insurance Fact Book (Washington, D.C.: annually), U.S. Bureau of Census.

Table XVII-10. Life Insurance and Annuity Benefit Payments in Michigan and the United States: 1991-1992

Type of Payment	Michigan		United States	
	1991	1992	1991	1992
Total Payments	**$4,088,500,000**	**$4,003,500,000**	**$91,585,400,000**	**$95,043,000,000**
Death Payments	1,027,600,000	993,800,000	25,406,700,000	27,234,600,000
Matured Endowments	22,700,000	20,900,000	668,500,000	649,400,000
Annuity Payments	1,906,200,000	1,825,900,000	33,257,500,000	34,402,100,000
Disability Payments	20,600,000	21,600,000	547,300,000	591,900,000
Surrender Values	531,800,000	559,400,000	16,281,800,000	16,813,800,000
Policy and Contract Dividends	579,600,000	581,900,000	15,423,600,000	15,351,200,000

Source: American Council of Life Insurance, Life Insurance Fact Book (Washington, D.C.: annually).

Table XVII-11. Premium Receipts of Life Insurance Companies in Michigan and the United States: 1991-1992

Type of Receipts	Michigan		United States	
	1991	1992	1991	1992
Total Receipts	**$9,080,000,000**	**$8,821,000,000**	**$248,600,000,000**	**$263,674,000,000**
Life	2,371,000,000	2,421,000,000	71,215,000,000	75,230,000,000
Annuity	1,841,000,000	1,880,000,000	43,427,000,000	45,209,000,000
Health	1,481,000,000	1,543,000,000	57,342,000,000	60,391,000,000
Deposit Administration Funds	3,387,000,000	2,977,000,000	76,616,000,000	82,844,000,000

Source: American Council of Life Insurance, Life Insurance Fact Book (Washington, D.C.: annually).

Table XVII-12. Mortgages Owned by Life Insurance Companies in Michigan and the United States: 1991-1992

Type of Mortgage	Michigan		United States	
	1991	1992	1991	1992
Total Mortgage	**$6,954,300,000**	**$6,650,500,000**	**$260,375,200,000**	**$241,997,000,000**
Farm	41,300,000	71,800,000	10,029,300,000	9,208,000,000
Nonfarm	6,913,000,000	6,578,700,000	250,345,900,000	232,789,000,000

Source: American Council of Life Insurance, Life Insurance Fact Book (Washington, D.C.: annually).

Table XVII-13. Real Estate Owned by Life Insurance Companies in Michigan and the United States: 1991-1992

Type of Real Estate	Michigan		United States	
	1991	1992	1991	1992
Total Real Estate	**$648,100,000**	**$668,948,000**	**$45,916,472,000**	**$49,886,338,000**
Farm	27,966,000	10,874,000	2,584,679,000	2,677,961,000
Nonfarm	620,134,000	658,074,000	43,331,793,000	47,208,377,000

Source: American Council of Life Insurance, Life Insurance Fact Book (Washington, D.C.: annually).

Table XVII-14. Average Selling Price of Existing Residential Homes in Michigan, by Realtor board: 1986-1993

Board	1986	1987	1988	1989	1990	1991	1992	1993
Alpena/Alcona/Presque Isle Board of REALTORS®	$N.A.	$N.A.	$N.A.	$N.A.	$49,064	$54,412	$57,163	$62,128
Ann Arbor Area Board of REALTORS®	73,433	88,729	105,870	116,088	122,319	129,718	130,021	134,794
Battle Creek Area Association of REALTORS®	N.A.	48,129	48,400	50,514	55,522	56,875	60,530	64,625
Down River Board of REALTORS®	51,788	53,481	57,286	62,986	67,861	66,249	73,610	75,580
Flint Area Association of REALTORS®	50,737	54,202	56,250	60,368	62,671	67,822	69,631	74,303
Grand Rapids Association of REALTORS®	54,127	62,911	69,014	73,822	77,882	80,714	83,349	88,377
Gratiot-Isabella Board of REALTORS®	N.A.	N.A.	N.A.	N.A.	N.A.	51,318	52,304	56,186
Greater Lansing Board of REALTORS®	58,451	61,602	64,308	69,074	72,051	75,933	78,456	82,189
Greater Kalamazoo Association of REALTORS®	56,409	56,466	59,178	66,925	70,876	76,231	79,004	84,432
Holland Board of REALTORS®	60,269	64,883	75,680	79,834	83,517	90,747	91,534	94,545
Jackson Area Association of REALTORS®	46,072	47,424	52,942	56,687	62,773	65,217	68,664	N.A.
Livingston County Association of REALTORS®	71,955	83,362	95,169	106,119	114,996	115,731	120,336	124,582
North Oakland County Board of REALTORS®	N.A.	N.A.	79,371	88,332	90,402	97,242	103,506	108,982
Rochester Area Association of REALTORS®	N.A.	N.A.	N.A.	N.A.	128,890	134,929	141,244	149,291
Saginaw Board of REALTORS®	49,515	50,679	51,957	56,319	58,492	62,960	67,189	69,651
Shiawassee County Board of REALTORS®	N.A.	N.A.	N.A.	N.A.	48,355	52,746	53,547	57,821
South Oakland County Board of REALTORS®	60,907	68,781	73,707	79,576	82,142	89,299	89,724	95,642
Southwestern Michigan Association of REALTORS®	49,925	56,876	62,881	69,745	75,704	78,303	82,902	85,228
St. Joseph County Association of REALTORS®	N.A.	N.A.	N.A.	N.A.	N.A.	46,563	47,235	55,333
West Central Board of REALTORS®	N.A.	N.A.	N.A.	N.A.	47,804	47,705	51,211	57,814
Western Wayne-Oakland Association of REALTORS®	72,202	76,538	86,232	92,522	95,671	96,742	96,571	N.A.
Macomb County Association of REALTORS®	61,583	68,483	77,071	79,891	82,596	90,316	91,535	N.A.
Total	**$61,370**	**$66,342**	**$73,692**	**$79,241**	**$83,652**	**$86,179**	**$76,625**	**$81,075**

Source: Michigan Association of Realtors (Lansing, Michigan). N.A. data not available.

Table XVII-15. Terms on Conventional Single-Family Mortgages in Michigan: 1976-1993

Year	Contract Interest Rate (%)	Initial Fees and Charges (%)	Effective Interest Rate (%)	Term to Maturity (Years)	Purchase Price (In Thousands)	Loan to Price Ratio (%)
1976	8.98	0.89	9.12	25.9	$39.3	74.1
1977	8.87	0.83	9.01	26.1	42.4	74.7
1978	9.41	0.87	9.56	27.8	51.0	74.9
1979	10.97	0.97	11.15	27.4	55.3	74.9
1980	12.68	1.35	12.98	27.6	62.7	73.4
1981	14.33	1.74	14.70	27.6	71.8	72.4
1982	14.22	2.07	14.66	27.2	73.0	72.7
1983	11.81	2.15	12.22	28.3	68.2	75.6
1984	11.50	2.48	11.97	27.0	68.3	77.2
1985	11.41	2.50	11.89	22.6	72.0	74.5
1986	10.08	2.36	10.51	21.8	77.8	72.8
1987	9.38	2.68	9.86	23.0	88.0	73.0
1988	9.19	2.58	9.64	25.0	93.9	73.0
1989	9.89	2.30	10.30	25.4	103.4	71.7
1990	9.92	2.05	10.28	25.6	106.3	72.3
1991	9.01	1.89	9.33	24.7	112.2	71.8
1992	7.92	1.92	8.28	20.9	119.9	71.6
1993	6.99	1.96	7.33	23.0	112.3	75.1

Source: Federal Home Loan Bank of Indianapolis (Indianapolis, Indiana).

CHAPTER XVIII
SERVICES

The Office of Management and Budget in the Executive Office of the President is responsible for maintaining the Standard Industrial Classification system. The SIC is used in all federal statistical programs and in most other programs where the focus is on economic activity.

According to the latest Standard Industrial Classification Manual,

> services includes establishments primarily engaged providing a wide variety of services for individuals, businesses, and government establishments, and other organizations. Hotels and other lodging places; establishments providing personal, business, repair, and amusement services; health, legal, engineering, and other professional services; educational institutions; membership organizations, and other miscellaneous services are included.

It seems worth mentioning here that gasoline service stations and eating and drinking places are classified as retail trade and not as services.

The Bureau of the Census conducts economic censuses for the years ending in 2 and 7. The 1992 Census of Service Industries is the latest such undertaking at this writing. These censuses are the source of detailed statistics for the state as well as summary data for counties and places.

Current data on employment, hours, and earnings are collected and disseminated by the Michigan Employment Security Commission in Detroit and by the Bureau of Labor Statistics in Washington, D.C.

Some terms found in this chapter include:

Establishments: a single physical location at which business is conducted. It is not necessarily identical with a company or enterprise, which may consist of one establishment or more.

Receipts: Basic dollar volume measure for service establishments of firms subject to Federal income tax. It includes receipts from customers or clients for services rendered, from the use of facilities, and from merchandise sold during the reference year whether or not payment was received in the reference year, except for services reported on a cash basis. Receipts are net after deductions for refunds and allowances for merchandise returned by customers.

Revenue: Basic dollar volume measure for firms exempt from Federal income tax. It includes revenue from customers or clients for services rendered and merchandise sold during the reference year, whether or not payment was received in the reference year. Revenue does not include sales, admissions, or other taxes collected by the organization from customers or clients and paid directly to government entity.

Units: Refer to the definition of establishments.

Employment: Includes both full-time and part-time workers.

Average Weekly Wage (AWW): AWW = ((Total wages/Employment)/Number of weeks).

CHAPTER XVIII
SERVICES

List of Tables

Table   **Page**

XVIII-1.   Number of Private Service Units, Employment, and Average Weekly Wage
in Michigan and the United States: 1970-1994   547

XVIII-2.   Services Industry Units, Employment, Receipts*, and Average Weekly
Wage in Michigan, 2 Digit SIC Industry Group: 1992*, 1993   548

XVIII-3.   Number of Private Service Units, Employment, and Total Wages in
Michigan, by 3-Digit SIC Classification: 1993   549

XVIII-4.   Number of Private Service Units, Employment, and Average Weekly Wage
in Michigan, by County: 1992   551

XVIII-5.   Total Wages in Services and as a Percentage of Total Wages in Michigan,
by County: 1992   552

XVIII-6.   Service Industry Receipts and Revenues in Michigan, by Industry and
Profit/Nonprofit Classification: 1992   553

XVIII-7.   Service Industry Receipts per Establishment and per Employee in Michigan,
for Profit Establishments: 1992   557

XVIII-8.   Service Industry Receipts in Michigan, by County: for Profit Establishments
1992   562

XVIII-9.   Service Industry Receipts per Establishment and per Employee in Michigan,
by County: for Profit Establishments 1992   565

Table XVIII-1. Number of Private Service Units, Employment, and Average Weekly Wage in Michigan and the United States: 1970-1994

Year	Michigan			United States		
	Number of Units	Employment (Data in Thousands)	Average Weekly Wage	Number of Units	Employment (Data in Thousands)	Average Weekly Wage
1970	---	408	$---	---	11,548	$---
1971	---	420	---	---	11,797	---
1972	---	455	---	---	12,276	---
1973	---	489	---	---	12,857	---
1974	---	510	---	---	13,441	---
1975	---	514	---	---	13,892	---
1976	38,207	541	181	1,125,113	14,551	168
1977	39,398	580	194	1,155,726	15,302	180
1978	41,899	614	211	1,255,277	16,252	193
1979	43,410	627	231	1,327,279	17,112	210
1980	44,415	644	254	1,398,266	17,890	232
1981	45,002	650	275	1,445,113	18,615	256
1982	45,988	650	291	1,500,404	19,021	278
1983	47,249	675	305	1,567,743	19,664	295
1984	45,444	708	315	1,624,731	20,746	309
1985	52,324	760	329	1,696,870	21,927	324
1986	53,094	794	352	1,758,451	22,957	339
1987	55,858	826	370	1,876,703	24,110	364
1988	57,196	863	387	1,950,328	25,504	384
1989	61,923	912	399	2,009,401	26,907	399
1990	64,069	942	418	2,076,654	27,934	423
1991	64,057	934	435	2,182,664	28,336	443
1992	65,277	980	457	2,272,841	29,053	468
1993	67,967	1,016	463	2,359,423	30,192	475
1994	69,125	1,019	475	N.A.	N.A.	N.A.

Source: Michigan Employment Security Commission, Research and Statistics (Detroit, Michigan: annually). N.A. data not available.

Table XVIII-2. Services Industry Units, Employment, Receipts*, and Average Weekly Wage in Michigan, 2 Digit SIC Industry Group: 1992*, 1993

Industry	SIC	Number of Units	Employment	Receipts* (Data in Thousands)	Average Weekly Wage
Total Services		**67,967**	**974,966**	**$51,880,464**	**$463**
Hotels & Motels	70	1,648	33,583	1,249,238	215
Personal Services	72	5,486	41,640	1,469,981	257
Business Services	73	9,747	209,783	8,305,842	432
Automotive Repair/Services/Parking	75	5,680	33,588	2,482,856	380
Miscellaneous Repair Services	76	2,255	13,087	1,137,072	485
Motion Pictures	78	1,082	12,676	840,043	298
Amusement & Recreation Services	79	2,749	39,521	1,648,271	298
Health Services	80	15,057	331,400	21,891,285	540
Legal Services	81	4,415	25,767	2,561,360	876
Educational Services	82	840	28,317	345,082	402
Social Services	83	4,152	73,428	2,320,567	283
Museums/Galleries/Gardens	84	69	1,831	83,899	238
Membership Organizations	86	3,773	41,193	823,433	302
Engineering/Accounting/Management Services	87	7,868	82,648	6,500,628	716
Private Household Services	88	2,846	4,817	0	212
Miscellaneous Services	89	302	1,691	221,705	742

* Receipts figures are for 1992. All other data for this table is for 1993.
Source: Michigan Employment Security Commission, Research and Statistics (Detroit, Michigan: annually) and Bureau of Census, 1992 Census of Service Industries, Geographic Area Series, Michigan (Washington, D.C.: quinquennial).

Table XVIII-3. Number of Private Service Units, Employment, and Total Wages in Michigan, by 3-Digit SIC Classification: 1993

Industry	SIC	Units	Employment	Total Wages
Hotels and Motels	701	1,923	32,319	$ 362,261,193.57
Rooming and Boarding Homes	702	28	73	754,982.95
Camps and Recreational Vehicle Parks	703	262	1,022	10,799,236.48
Membership-Basis Organization Hotels	704	59	193	1,725,345.19
Laundry, Cleaning & Garment Services	721	2,252	15,198	209,321,532.34
Photographic Studios, Portrait	722	421	2,570	33,014,614.88
Beauty Shops	723	3,209	14,081	164,944,578.97
Barber Shops	724	96	349	5,614,722.16
Shoe Repair and Shoeshine Parlors	725	80	370	4,870,827.10
Funeral Service and Crematories	726	570	3,545	80,402,387.86
Miscellaneous Personal Services	729	981	5,618	57,986,694.87
Advertising	731	1,012	11,245	472,601,209.11
Credit Reporting and Collection	732	237	2,150	53,438,260.08
Mailing, Reproduction, Stenographic	733	1,219	8,061	203,093,635.52
Services to Buildings	734	2,533	25,278	284,403,738.62
Misc. Equipment Rental & Leasing	735	924	5,482	148,475,137.28
Personnel Supply Services	736	1,556	84,354	1,238,606,844.80
Computer and Data Processing Services	737	2,369	34,426	1,512,507,750.62
Miscellaneous Business Services	738	3,749	38,991	805,258,178.55
Automotive Rentals, No Drivers	751	445	4,502	104,973,992.58
Automobile Parking	752	58	1,261	17,996,575.90
Automotive Repair Shops	753	5,851	19,119	429,760,626.51
Automotive Services, Except Repair	754	1,487	8,798	110,978,717.12
Electrical Repair Shops	762	728	3,551	92,434,279.69
Watch, Clock and Jewelry Repair	763	76	224	4,211,085.61
Reupholstery and Furniture Repair	764	269	731	13,185,733.83
Miscellaneous Repair Shops	769	1,961	8,618	220,951,954.20
Motion Picture Production & Services	781	376	2,863	95,496,406.23
Motion Picture Distribution & Services	782	29	818	21,985,439.12
Motion Picture Theaters	783	212	4,121	36,118,190.18
Video Tape Rental	784	913	4,894	43,317,892.52
Dance Studios, Schools and Halls	791	208	673	4,504,981.41
Producers, Orchestras, Entertainers	792	346	2,327	48,795,357.66
Bowling Centers	793	509	5,944	56,586,632.09
Commercial Sports	794	197	3,772	179,843,747.01

Table XVIII-3. Number of Private Service Units, Employment, and Total Wages in Michigan, by 3-Digit SIC Classification: 1993 Continued

Industry	SIC	Units	Employment	Total Wages
Misc. Amusement, Recreation Services	799	2,413	26,840	$321,177,235.67
Offices & Clinics of Medical Doctors	801	7,469	50,970	2,414,844,193.03
Offices and Clinics of Dentists	802	5,217	25,698	639,728,627.81
Offices of Osteopathic Physicians	803	1,325	7,321	277,305,558.19
Offices of Other Health Practitioners	804	3,453	14,138	361,119,427.78
Nursing and Personal Care Facilities	805	536	46,413	650,967,350.21
Hospitals	806	221	158,251	4,353,957,458.52
Medical and Dental Laboratories	807	598	8,082	230,404,656.22
Home Health Care Services	808	391	15,615	265,832,343.97
Health and Allied Services, nec	809	351	5,153	116,189,117.29
Legal Services	811	6,053	25,853	1,174,862,547.03
Elementary and Secondary Schools	821	328	11,201	182,695,896.06
Colleges and Universities	822	92	13,310	320,241,981.98
Libraries	823	25	110	1,750,499.02
Vocational Schools	824	194	1,548	33,066,050.74
Schools & Educational Services, nec	829	395	2,160	53,759,813.09
Individual and Family Services	832	1,157	19,650	339,622,496.36
Job Training and Related Services	833	233	8,147	119,858,643.24
Child Day Care Services	835	1,834	9,719	93,132,309.08
Residential Care	836	1,845	29,870	409,728,780.78
Social Services, nec	839	423	6,108	120,838,134.41
Museums and Art Galleries	841	74	1,710	20,949,927.90
Botanical and Zoological Gardens	842	9	122	1,737,964.52
Business Associations	861	614	3,254	97,869,388.11
Professional Organizations	862	149	1,233	43,721,990.85
Labor Organizations	863	1,098	9,229	174,752,842.10
Civic and Social Associations	864	1,435	14,057	158,897,458.93
Political Organizations	865	75	278	3,507,801.32
Religious Organizations	866	897	11,615	142,282,144.11
Membership Organizations, nec	869	261	1,574	25,768,640.61
Engineering & Architectural Services	871	3,075	37,886	1,604,316,926.67
Accounting, Auditing & Bookkeeping	872	3,522	18,381	586,803,778.54
Research and Testing Services	873	716	11,322	337,359,482.89
Management and Public Relations	874	3,593	15,203	554,944,405.08
Private Households	881	4,536	4,921	53,274,752.27
Services, nec	899	432	1,697	65,524,609.30

Note: nec stands for note elsewhere classified

Source: Michigan Employment Security Commission, Research and Statistics (Detroit, Michigan: annually).

SERVICES

Table XVIII-4. Number of Private Service Units, Employment, and Average Weekly Wage in Michigan, by County: 1992

County	Units	Employment	A.W.W.	County	Units	Employment	A.W.W.
Alcona	39	276	$257.31	Lake	36	270	$299.05
Alger	48	328	235.49	Lapeer	341	2,152	319.51
Allegan	339	2,848	295.43	Leelanau	120	1,234	266.56
Alpena	248	1,973	264.74	Lenawee	579	5,754	349.63
Antrim	110	879	256.29	Livingston	670	6,231	359.66
Arenac	78	664	299.23	Luce	56	167	201.58
Baraga	44	614	235.22	Mackinac	143	1,216	273.28
Barry	200	1,593	341.43	Macomb	4,530	55,701	468.90
Bay	735	7,835	411.79	Manistee	166	1,004	268.35
Benzie	97	712	252.72	Marquette	539	6,064	412.32
Berrien	1,100	13,608	362.31	Mason	203	1,781	332.08
Branch	214	1,312	341.12	Mecosta	185	1,570	255.13
Calhoun	881	11,613	380.07	Menominee	106	1,341	251.07
Cass	177	1,315	293.68	Midland	582	9,383	414.28
Charlevoix	176	1,208	299.79	Missaukee	42	230	227.02
Cheboygan	254	1,549	297.12	Monroe	595	5,906	357.93
Chippewa	249	2,578	298.68	Montcalm	250	2,475	302.66
Clare	152	1,402	292.86	Montmorency	53	355	206.83
Clinton	214	1,654	341.17	Muskegon	954	11,780	375.83
Crawford	105	1,094	287.98	Newaygo	167	1,303	310.26
Delta	283	2,630	306.98	Oakland	12,844	193,576	564.89
Dickinson	251	1,930	324.56	Oceana	119	590	251.00
Eaton	346	3,500	357.90	Ogemaw	105	686	285.91
Emmet	327	4,748	402.80	Ontonagon	55	326	197.85
Genesee	2,767	35,451	460.71	Osceola	81	701	324.22
Gladwin	90	778	278.64	Oscoda	45	426	209.00
Gogebic	138	1,396	279.39	Otsego	190	1,967	330.80
Grand Traverse	895	11,148	397.98	Ottawa	1,159	15,944	349.68
Gratiot	219	2,956	347.30	Presque Isle	84	690	294.96
Hillsdale	196	1,625	347.04	Roscommon	130	736	285.55
Houghton	261	2,503	311.46	Saginaw	1,434	20,113	434.16
Huron	230	1,802	342.75	St. Clair	770	8,222	377.74
Ingham	2,640	38,236	428.40	St. Joseph	321	2,336	299.80
Ionia	228	1,519	288.51	Sanilac	169	1,453	295.71
Iosco	181	1,316	325.69	Schoolcraft	65	328	260.85
Iron	98	455	302.45	Shiawassee	336	2,889	363.45
Isabella	363	4,752	289.64	Tuscola	229	2,037	341.84
Jackson	897	10,747	392.88	Van Buren	324	2,172	306.27
Kalamazoo	1,701	28,256	416.49	Washtenaw	2,638	36,878	507.85
Kalkaska	72	303	417.00	Wayne	11,552	222,644	485.94
Kent	3,813	66,186	409.32	Wexford	213	2,647	352.90
Keweenaw	15	104	216.46	**Michigan**	**67,967**	**1,016,000**	**475.00**

Source: Michigan Employment Security Commission, Research and Statistics (Detroit, Michigan: annually).

551

Table XVIII-5. Total Wages in Services and as a Percentage of Total Wages in Michigan, by County: 1992

County	Total Services Wages	Percent of Total County Wages	County	Total Services Wages	Percent of Total County Wages
Alcona	$921,044	25.4	Lake	$1,050,013	33.3
Alger	996,098	10.3	Lapeer	8,964,198	14.5
Allegan	10,938,039	7.4	Leelanau	4,263,826	36.8
Alpena	6,800,660	14.7	Lenawee	26,178,191	18.9
Antrim	2,914,991	19.9	Livingston	29,180,751	21.8
Arenac	2,580,447	24.2	Luce	436,378	8.5
Baraga	1,876,749	26.2	Mackinac	4,202,312	38.3
Barry	7,060,700	18.3	Macomb	339,848,465	17.9
Bay	42,040,380	23.8	Manistee	3,504,161	13.2
Benzie	2,333,364	25.7	Marquette	32,539,819	32.8
Berrien	64,110,244	20.0	Mason	7,673,221	20.9
Branch	5,835,831	14.7	Mecosta	5,200,106	22.0
Calhoun	57,417,794	18.3	Menominee	4,389,770	13.6
Cass	5,013,197	13.6	Midland	50,623,356	20.5
Charlevoix	4,699,966	12.7	Missaukee	677,572	10.6
Cheboygan	5,943,065	29.1	Monroe	27,508,864	13.7
Chippewa	10,062,047	36.4	Montcalm	9,736,461	14.5
Clare	5,338,234	25.6	Montmorency	961,093	21.7
Clinton	7,348,159	18.7	Muskegon	57,566,986	21.1
Crawford	4,088,702	32.2	Newaygo	5,261,718	14.9
Delta	10,505,938	18.5	Oakland	1,423,817,518	33.8
Dickinson	8,162,232	16.1	Oceana	1,878,103	12.5
Eaton	16,289,524	18.2	Ogemaw	2,551,191	17.8
Emmet	24,826,783	45.1	Ontonagon	835,973	5.5
Genesee	212,534,659	21.0	Osceola	2,955,228	11.1
Gladwin	2,809,890	20.4	Oscoda	1,161,162	23.4
Gogebic	5,003,080	31.3	Otsego	8,451,960	24.8
Grand Traverse	57,675,388	35.1	Ottawa	72,788,034	16.4
Gratiot	13,357,541	26.2	Presque Isle	2,650,142	24.1
Hillsdale	7,361,216	12.6	Roscommon	2,730,771	21.6
Houghton	10,154,448	34.0	Saginaw	113,631,007	22.5
Huron	8,029,447	19.0	St. Clair	40,425,498	20.6
Ingham	213,359,025	28.6	St. Joseph	9,091,437	9.1
Ionia	5,665,566	12.3	Sanilac	5,590,662	15.4
Iosco	5,558,382	22.2	Schoolcraft	1,117,310	16.7
Iron	1,797,577	21.1	Shiawassee	13,692,512	21.7
Isabella	17,921,656	27.8	Tuscola	9,045,144	21.1
Jackson	54,968,111	21.8	Van Buren	8,644,814	12.0
Kalamazoo	153,149,450	24.7	Washtenaw	243,786,399	28.8
Kalkaska	1,647,882	8.3	Wayne	1,407,028,166	25.7
Kent	352,668,161	22.4	Wexford	12,160,320	24.7
Keweenaw	282,963	44.4	**Michigan**	**$5,524,622,055**	**24.9**

Source: Michigan Employment Security Commission, Research and Statistics (Detroit, Michigan: annually).

Table XVIII-6. Service Industry Receipts and Revenues in Michigan, by Industry and Profit/Nonprofit Classification: 1992

Industry	SIC	Receipts and Revenues (Millions of Dollars)		
		Total Receipts & Revenues	Profit Receipts	Nonprofit Revenues
Hotels and Motels	701	$1,172,109	$1,172,109	$---
Rooming and Boarding Homes	702	2,690	2,690	---
Camps and Recreational Vehicle Parks	703	62,363	37,597	24,766
Membership-Basis Organization Hotels	704	12,076	---	12,076
Laundry, Cleaning & Garment Services	721	572,634	572,634	---
Photographic Studios, Portrait	722	89,981	89,981	---
Beauty Shops	723	351,695	351,695	---
Barber Shops	724	10,734	10,734	---
Shoe Repair and Shoeshine Parlors	725	11,141	11,141	---
Funeral Service and Crematories	726	281,846	281,846	---
Miscellaneous Personal Services	729	151,950	151,950	---
Tax Return Prep. Services	7291	44,847	44,847	---
Misc. Personal Services	7299	107,103	107,103	---
Advertising	731	834,176	834,176	---
Credit Reporting and Collection	732	125,648	125,648	---
Collection Services	7322	82,910	82,910	---
Credit Reporting Services	7323	42,738	42,738	---
Mailing, Reproduction, Stenographic	733	577,649	577,649	---
Direct Mail Advertising	7331	151,983	151,983	---
Photocopying & Duplicating	7334	94,386	94,386	---
Commercial Photography	7335	44,341	44,341	---
Commercial Art & Design	7336	227,194	227,194	---
Secretarial & Court Reporting	7338	59,745	59,745	---
Services to Buildings	734	508,962	508,962	---
Pest Control	7342	58,325	58,325	---
Building Cleaning & Maintenance	7349	450,637	450,637	---
Misc. Equipment Rental & Leasing	735	600,119	600,119	---
Personnel Supply Services	736	1,403,047	1,403,047	---
Employment Agencies	7361	81,377	81,377	---
Help Supply Services	7363	1,321,670	1,321,670	---
Temporary Help Supply	part	1,069,039	1,069,039	---
Employee Leasing	part	200,265	200,265	---
Other Help Supply	part	52,366	52,366	---
Computer and Data Processing Services	737	2,510,189	2,510,189	---
Programming,Software,Systems	7371,2,3	1,261,169	1,261,169	---
Processing & Data Preparation Services	7374	788,292	788,292	---
Information Retrieval Services	7375	33,393	33,393	---
Computer Facilities Management	7376	75,839	75,839	---
Computer Rental & Leasing	7377	80,471	80,471	---
Computer Maintenance & Repair	7378	176,891	176,891	---

Table XVIII-6. Service Industry Receipts and Revenues in Michigan, by Industry and Profit/Nonprofit Classification: 1992 Continued

Industry	SIC	Receipts and Revenues (Millions of Dollars)		
		Total Receipts & Revenues	Profit Receipts	Nonprofit Revenues
Misc. Computer Services	7379	$94,134	$94,134	$---
Computer Consultants	part	81,761	81,761	---
Other Computer Services	part	12,373	12,373	---
Miscellaneous Business Services	738	1,746,052	1,746,052	---
Guard Services	7381	238,232	238,232	---
Security Systems Services	7382	94,016	94,016	---
News Syndicates	7383	11,606	11,606	---
Photofinishing Laboratories	7384	97,384	97,384	---
Photofinishing exc. "One-hour" Labs.	part	72,248	72,248	---
One-hour(mini) Photofinishing	part	25,136	25,136	---
Misc. Business Services	7389	1,304,814	1,304,814	---
Interior Designing	part	46,722	46,722	---
Water Softening Services	part	60,280	60,280	---
Packaging & Labeling Services	part	208,631	208,631	---
Convention & Trade Show Services	part	45,450	45,450	---
Other Business Services	part	943,731	943,731	---
Automotive Rentals, No Drivers	751	554,314	554,314	---
Truck Rental & Leasing	7513	300,342	300,342	---
Truck Rental	part	151,931	151,931	---
Truck Leasing exc. Finance Lease	part	148,411	148,411	---
Passenger Car Rental	7514	206,715	206,715	---
Passenger Car Leasing exc. Finance	7515	41,648	41,648	---
Trailer & Rec. Vehicle Rental	7519	5,609	5,609	---
Automobile Parking	752	57,160	57,160	---
Automotive Repair Shops	753	1,556,637	1,556,637	---
Top & Body Repair & Paint Shops	7532	554,884	554,884	---
Exhaust System Repair	7533	147,935	147,935	---
Tire Retreading & Repair	7534	36,815	36,815	---
Auto Glass Replacement	7536	105,351	105,351	---
Transmission Repair Shops	7537	56,328	56,328	---
General Automotive Repair Shops	7538	535,172	535,172	---
Misc. Auto Repair	7539	120,152	120,152	---
Radiator Repair	part	29,275	29,275	---
Brake, Front End, Wheel Alignment	part	58,189	58,189	---
Other Auto Repair	part	32,688	32,688	---
Automotive Services, Except Repair	754	314,745	314,745	---
Carwashes	7542	135,882	135,882	---
Misc. Auto Services	7549	178,863	178,863	---
Lubrication Shops	part	93,912	93,912	---
Towing Services	part	54,754	54,754	---

Table XVIII-6. Service Industry Receipts and Revenues in Michigan, by Industry and Profit/Nonprofit Classification: 1992 Continued

Industry	SIC	Receipts and Revenues (Millions of Dollars)		
		Total Receipts & Revenues	Profit Receipts	Nonprofit Revenues
Other Auto Services	part	$30,197	$30,197	$---
Electrical Repair Shops	762	339,877	339,877	---
Radio & TV Repair	7622	45,580	45,580	---
Refrigeration & Air Conditioning Repair	7623	62,361	62,361	---
Other Electrical & Electronic Repair	7629	231,936	231,936	---
Watch, Clock and Jewelry Repair	763	9,262	9,262	---
Reupholstery and Furniture Repair	764	31,286	31,286	---
Miscellaneous Repair Shops	769	756,617	756,617	---
Motion Picture Production & Services	781	395,703	395,703	---
Motion Picture Distribution & Services	782	37,780	37,780	---
Motion Picture Theaters	783	215,150	215,150	---
Video Tape Rental	784	191,410	191,410	---
Dance Studios, Schools and Halls	791	14,954	14,954	---
Producers, Orchestras, Entertainers	792	145,058	90,219	54,839
Bowling Centers	793	204,703	204,703	---
Commercial Sports	794	314,969	314,969	---
Professional Sports Clubs	7941	191,166	191,166	---
Racing inc. Track Operation	7948	123,803	123,803	---
Misc. Amusement, Recreation Services	799	967,792	735,693	232,099
Physical Fitness Facilities	7991	(D)	107,027	(D)
Public Golf Courses	7992	172,242	172,242	---
Coin Operated Games	7993	38,493	38,493	---
Amusement Parks	7996	21,284	21,284	---
Membership Sports & Recreation Clubs	7997	(D)	157,917	(D)
Other Amusement & Recreation Serv.	7999	254,799	238,730	16,069
Offices & Clinics of Medical Doctors	801	(D)	3,899,622	(D)
Offices of Medical Doctors	part	(D)	3,619,096	(D)
General Medical Clinics	part	(D)	280,526	(D)
Offices and Clinics of Dentists	802	(D)	1,475,023	(D)
Offices of Osteopathic Physicians	803	593,339	593,339	---
Offices of Other Health Practitioners	804	684,489	684,489	---
Offices & Clinics of Chiropractors	8041	155,693	155,693	---
Offices & Clinics of Optometrists	8042	203,832	203,832	---
Offices & Clinics of Podiatrists	8043	112,871	112,871	---
Offices & Clinics, Other	8049	212,093	212,093	---
Nursing and Personal Care Facilities	805	1,403,567	870,163	533,404
Skilled Nursing Care Facilities	8051	1,196,106	776,024	420,082
Intermediate Care Facilities	8052	161,772	77,045	84,727
Other Nursing & Personal Care	8059	45,689	17,094	28,595
Hospitals	806	11,444,321	79,682	11,364,639

Table XVIII-6. Service Industry Receipts and Revenues in Michigan, by Industry and Profit/Nonprofit Classification: 1992 Continued

Industry	SIC	Receipts and Revenues (Millions of Dollars)		
		Total Receipts & Revenues	Profit Receipts	Nonprofit Revenues
General Medical & Surgical	8062	$10,395,142	$---	$10,395,142
Psychiatric Hospitals	8063	596,292	49,969	546,323
Other Specialty Hospitals	8069	452,887	29,713	423,174
Medical and Dental Laboratories	807	544,231	544,231	---
Medical Laboratories	8071	464,351	464,351	---
Dental Laboratories	8072	79,880	79,880	---
Home Health Care Services	808	494,876	227,965	266,911
Health and Allied Services, nec	809	594,304	332,193	262,111
Legal Services	81	2,561,360	2,517,595	43,765
Elementary and Secondary Schools		NO SURVEY	NO SURVEY	NO SURVEY
Colleges and Universities		NO SURVEY	NO SURVEY	NO SURVEY
Libraries	823	(D)	(D)	3,378
Vocational Schools	824	(D)	143,750	(D)
Schools & Educational Services, nec	829	(D)	(D)	(D)
Individual and Family Services	832	604,529	46,399	558,130
Job Training and Related Services	833	339,902	56,658	283,244
Child Day Care Services	835	194,845	110,807	84,038
Residential Care	836	660,011	198,111	461,900
Social Services, nec	839	519,280	12,592	506,688
Museums and Art Galleries	841	(D)	(D)	76,579
Botanical and Zoological Gardens	842	(D)	(D)	6,525
Business Associations	861	228,317	---	228,317
Professional Organizations	862	127,159	---	127,159
Labor Organizations		NO SURVEY	NO SURVEY	NO SURVEY
Civic and Social Associations	864	384,409	---	384,409
Political Organizations		NO SURVEY	NO SURVEY	NO SURVEY
Religious Organizations		NO SURVEY	NO SURVEY	NO SURVEY
Membership Organizations, nec	869	83,548	---	83,548
Engineering & Architectural Services	871	3,028,212	3,028,212	---
Engineering Services	8711	2,686,699	2,686,699	---
Architectural Services	8712	279,232	279,232	---
Surveying Services	8713	62,281	62,281	---
Accounting, Auditing & Bookkeeping	872	1,060,391	1,060,391	---
Research and Testing Services	873	880,220	640,625	239,595
Commercial Physical & Biologic. Res.	8731	(D)	288,805	(D)
Commercial Physical Res.	part	(D)	244,785	(D)
Comm. Biologic. & Medical Res.	part	(D)	44,020	(D)
Comm. Econ.,Soc., Educ. Res.	8732	(D)	177,612	(D)
Noncommercial Research Orgs.	8733	183,338	---	183,338
Testing Laboratories	8734	192,545	174,208	18,337

Table XVIII-6. Service Industry Receipts and Revenues in Michigan, by Industry and Profit/Nonprofit Classification: 1992 Continued

Industry	SIC	Receipts and Revenues (Millions of Dollars)		
		Total Receipts & Revenues	Profit Receipts	Nonprofit Revenues
Management and Public Relations Services	874	$1,531,805	$1,497,571	$34,234
Management Services	8741	624,813	603,796	21,017
Management Consulting Services	8742	622,206	618,276	3,930
Public Relations Services	8743	(D)	(D)	505
Facilities Support Management Services	8744	(D)	(D)	---
Other Business Consulting Services	8748	115,735	106,953	8,782
Services, nec	899	221,705	221,705	---

Source: Bureau of Census, 1992 Census of Service Industries, Geographic Area Series, Michigan (Washington, D.C.: quinquennial). (D) data withheld to avoid disclosure of individual firm data. --- No data.

Table XVIII-7. Service Industry Receipts per Establishment and per Employee in Michigan, for Profit Establishments: 1992

Industry	SIC	Receipts per Establishment	Receipts per Employee
Hotels and Motels	701	$874,708	$37,720
Rooming and Boarding Homes	702	86,774	31,647
Camps and Recreational Vehicle Parks	703	214,840	73,146
Membership-Basis Organization Hotels	704	---	---
Laundry, Cleaning & Garment Services	721	294,413	38,273
Photographic Studios, Portrait	722	211,720	47,786
Beauty Shops	723	129,825	24,939
Barber Shops	724	111,813	30,067
Shoe Repair and Shoeshine Parlors	725	135,866	34,070
Funeral Service and Crematories	726	477,705	74,425
Miscellaneous Personal Services	729	160,794	18,878
Tax Return Prep. Services	7291	152,024	9,302
Misc. Personal Services	7299	164,774	33,179
Advertising	731	1,345,445	96,392
Credit Reporting and Collection	732	664,804	59,832
Collection Services	7322	579,790	52,375
Credit Reporting Services	7323	929,087	82,665
Mailing, Reproduction, Stenographic	733	598,600	78,560
Direct Mail Advertising	7331	1,746,931	87,296
Photocopying & Duplicating	7334	720,504	62,632
Commercial Photography	7335	354,728	105,323
Commercial Art & Design	7336	567,985	83,589
Secretarial & Court Reporting	7338	269,122	61,848
Services to Buildings	734	272,902	22,655
Pest Control	7342	339,099	51,252
Building Cleaning & Maintenance	7349	266,177	21,129

Table XVIII-7. Service Industry Receipts per Establishment and per Employee in Michigan, for Profit Establishments: 1992 Continued

Industry	SIC	Receipts per Establishment	Receipts per Employee
Misc. Equipment Rental & Leasing	735	$787,558	$104,569
Personnel Supply Services	736	1,278,985	19,867
Employment Agencies	7361	249,623	50,109
Help Supply Services	7363	1,714,228	19,155
Temporary Help Supply	part	1,755,401	17,833
Employee Leasing	part	1,655,083	26,745
Other Help Supply	part	1,277,220	33,504
Computer and Data Processing Services	737	1,501,309	86,861
Programming,Software,Systems	7371,2,3	1,267,507	116,916
Processing & Data Preparation Services	7374	2,616,831	58,074
Information Retrieval Services	7375	1,517,864	106,687
Computer Facilities Management	7376	2,808,852	78,427
Computer Rental & Leasing	7377	3,831,952	265,581
Computer Maintenance & Repair	7378	1,187,188	108,990
Misc. Computer Services	7379	567,072	87,976
Computer Consultants	part	605,637	87,821
Other Computer Services	part	399,129	89,014
Misc. Business Services	738	815,150	48,476
Guard Services	7381	692,535	16,789
Security Systems Services	7382	1,305,778	55,206
News Syndicates	7383	1,160,600	134,953
Photofinishing Laboratories	7384	586,651	58,454
Photofinishing exc. "One-hour" Labs.	part	976,324	59,414
One-hour(mini) Photofinishing	part	273,217	55,858
Other Business Services	7389	841,815	71,014
Interior Designing	part	324,458	104,993
Water Softening Services	part	558,148	77,881
Packaging & Labeling Services	part	2,128,888	82,626
Convention & Trade Show Services	part	710,156	69,495
Business Services,Not Classified	part	830,749	67,525
Automotive Rentals, No Drivers	751	1,674,665	150,752
Truck Rental & Leasing	7513	2,145,300	202,934
Truck Rental	part	1,999,092	209,271
Truck Leasing exc. Finance Lease	part	2,318,922	198,158
Passenger Car Rental	7514	1,531,222	103,358
Passenger Car Leasing exc. Finance	7515	1,224,941	308,504
Trailer & Rec. Vehicle Rental	7519	254,955	90,468
Automobile Parking	752	396,944	54,751
Automotive Repair Shops	753	333,256	76,287
Top & Body Repair & Paint Shops	7532	378,760	76,126
Exhaust System Repair	7533	380,296	82,923

Table XVIII-7. Service Industry Receipts per Establishment and per Employee in Michigan, for Profit Establishments: 1992 Continued

Industry	SIC	Receipts per Establishment	Receipts per Employee
Tire Retreading & Repair	7534	$856,163	$110,556
Auto Glass Replacement	7536	470,317	87,067
Transmission Repair Shops	7537	257,205	69,455
General Automotive Repair Shops	7538	275,011	72,783
Misc. Auto Repair	7539	312,083	73,940
Radiator Repair	part	281,490	78,696
Brake, Front End, Wheel Alignment	part	401,303	83,725
Other Auto Repair	part	240,353	58,581
Automotive Services, Except Repair	754	265,608	38,747
Carwashes	7542	219,874	31,201
Misc. Auto Services	7549	315,455	47,469
Lubrication Shops	part	312,000	42,785
Towing Services	part	337,988	50,004
Other Auto Services	part	290,356	63,174
Electrical Repair Shops	762	522,888	70,092
Radio & TV Repair	7622	238,639	60,132
Refrigeration & Air Conditioning Repair	7623	670,548	101,731
Other Electrical & Electronic Repair	7629	633,705	66,687
Watch, Clock and Jewelry Repair	763	127,288	44,248
Reupholstery and Furniture Repair	764	158,010	43,696
Miscellaneous Repair Shops	769	485,322	80,577
Motion Picture Production & Services	781	1,735,539	191,717
Motion Picture Distribution & Services	782	2,098,889	119,180
Motion Picture Theaters	783	986,927	55,223
Video Tape Rental	784	243,215	39,071
Dance Studios, Schools and Halls	791	95,248	21,062
Producers, Orchestras, Entertainers	792	533,840	100,579
Bowling Centers	793	514,329	29,445
Commercial Sports	794	3,181,505	100,022
Professional Sports Clubs	7941	5,310,167	98,947
Racing inc. Track Operation	7948	1,965,127	101,728
Misc. Amusement, Recreation Services	799	430,482	49,362
Physical Fitness Facilities	7991	348,622	33,731
Public Golf Courses	7992	545,070	89,245
Coin Operated Games	7993	331,836	55,465
Amusement Parks	7996	434,367	82,496
Membership Sports & Recreation Clubs	7997	591,449	42,715
Other Amusement & Recreation Serv.	7999	361,820	46,285
Offices & Clinics of Medical Doctors	801	657,055	95,934
Offices of Medical Doctors	part	624,197	94,213

Table XVIII-7. Service Industry Receipts per Establishment and per Employee in Michigan, for Profit Establishments: 1992 Continued

Industry	SIC	Receipts per Establishment	Receipts per Employee
General Medical Clinics	part	$2,047,635	$125,515
Offices and Clinics of Dentists	802	339,242	57,138
Offices of Osteopathic Physicians	803	494,037	74,130
Offices of Other Health Practitioners	804	261,855	64,794
Offices & Clinics of Chiropractors	8041	165,984	60,534
Offices & Clinics of Optometrists	8042	335,802	74,013
Offices & Clinics of Podiatrists	8043	282,178	67,185
Offices & Clinics, Other	8049	317,030	59,610
Nursing and Personal Care Facilities	805	2,061,998	26,591
Skilled Nursing Care Facilities	8051	2,648,546	26,883
Intermediate Care Facilities	8052	819,628	23,590
Other Nursing & Personal Care	8059	488,400	28,924
Hospitals	806	7,968,200	55,800
General Medical & Surgical	8062	---	---
Psychiatric Hospitals	8063	7,138,429	57,502
Other Specialty Hospitals	8069	9,904,333	53,154
Medical and Dental Laboratories	807	1,015,356	70,405
Medical Laboratories	8071	1,879,964	75,800
Dental Laboratories	8072	276,401	49,800
Home Health Care Services	808	844,315	25,477
Health and Allied Services, nec	809	843,129	65,638
Legal Services	81	543,405	97,491
Elementary and Secondary Schools	821	NO SURVEY	NO SURVEY
Colleges and Universities	822	NO SURVEY	NO SURVEY
Libraries	823	(D)	(D)
Vocational Schools	824	789,835	57,569
Schools & Educational Services, nec	829	(D)	(D)
Individual and Family Services	832	164,535	32,768
Job Training and Related Services	833	699,481	42,409
Child Day Care Services	835	104,240	16,670
Residential Care	836	231,980	27,094
Social Services, nec	839	273,739	45,789
Museums and Art Galleries	841	(D)	(D)
Botanical and Zoological Gardens	842	(D)	(D)
Business Associations	861	---	---
Professional Organizations	862	---	---
Labor Organizations	863	---	---
Civic and Social Associations	864	---	---
Political Organizations	865	---	---
Religious Organizations	866	---	---

Table XVIII-7. Service Industry Receipts per Establishment and per Employee in Michigan, for Profit Establishments: 1992 Continued

Industry	SIC	Receipts per Establishment	Receipts per Employee
Membership Organizations, nec	869	$---	$---
Engineering & Architectural Services	871	1,282,054	90,101
Engineering Services	8711	1,605,917	93,146
Architectural Services	8712	568,701	79,395
Surveying Services	8713	314,551	49,505
Accounting, Auditing & Bookkeeping	872	412,925	65,031
Research and Testing Services	873	1,835,602	65,739
Commercial Physical & Biologic. Res.	8731	3,040,053	105,403
Commercial Physical Res.	part	3,765,923	112,908
Comm. Biologic. & Medical Res.	part	1,467,333	76,958
Comm. Econ.,Soc., Educ. Res.	8732	1,505,186	35,867
Noncommercial Research Orgs.	8733	---	---
Testing Laboratories	8734	1,280,941	84,855
Management and Public Relations Services	874	704,077	72,113
Management Services	8741	981,782	48,744
Management Consulting Services	8742	599,105	104,386
Public Relations Services	8743	(D)	(D)
Facilities Support Management Services	8744	(D)	(D)
Other Business Consulting Services	8748	295,450	81,395
Services, nec	899	470,711	84,298

Source: Bureau of Census, 1992 Census of Service Industries, Geographic Area Series, Michigan (Washington, D.C.: quinquennial). (D) data withheld to avoid disclosure of individual firm data. --- No data.

Table XVIII-8. Service Industry Receipts in Michigan, by County: for Profit Establishments 1992

County	Total	Hotels and Motels	Personal Services	Business Services	Automotive Repair	Misc. Repair	Amusement/ Recreation	Health Services	Legal Services	Engineering/ Management
							Receipts (Data in Millions of Dollars)			
Alcona	$5,158	$(D)	$(D)	$(D)	$(D)	$(D)	$900	$2,217	$295	$(D)
Alger	11,628	1,958	(D)	(D)	821	(D)	776	4,034	409	(D)
Allegan	101,906	(D)	7,718	9,513	12,716	4,712	10,171	41,569	2,507	5,291
Alpena	57,420	5,287	3,744	6,161	8,221	1,964	2,720	22,191	2,273	3,488
Antrim	33,817	(D)	1,823	(D)	1,929	556	2,456	2,795	1,573	1,508
Arenac	15,717	895	1,018	(D)	1,969	(D)	(D)	(D)	612	347
Baraga	6,558	647	520	(D)	(D)	355	(D)	3,610	(D)	(D)
Barry	46,395	446	2,745	3,957	6,224	5,632	2,569	16,167	1,942	5,586
Bay	223,212	(D)	17,677	21,525	19,100	12,458	17,343	88,728	14,553	19,707
Benzie	22,541	12,060	895	1,160	429	(D)	1,837	3,865	566	516
Berrien	392,790	20,519	23,128	103,112	26,001	16,417	18,791	120,105	23,143	28,720
Branch	72,353	3,903	3,374	14,624	5,860	7,367	9,268	17,906	2,025	7,052
Calhoun	381,437	(D)	26,508	90,629	46,037	8,752	22,703	124,365	11,161	(D)
Cass	43,568	311	3,460	10,237	7,173	2,004	3,833	9,851	2,600	3,710
Charlevoix	38,371	(D)	2,303	3,744	1,290	(D)	2,968	5,993	2,311	4,197
Cheboygan	41,397	12,493	3,795	1,977	2,127	(D)	2,500	9,441	4,185	2,987
Chippewa	78,625	12,737	3,588	2,533	3,019	(D)	25,327	21,811	3,387	4,226
Clare	33,403	(D)	1,834	4,612	1,747	(D)	2,533	12,723	2,547	1,693
Clinton	74,862	(D)	3,947	15,628	8,478	1,111	6,753	25,131	3,384	7,432
Crawford	21,242	6,068	1,040	1,527	981	442	1,568	7,173	971	688
Delta	61,212	5,481	4,257	4,879	8,249	3,771	3,342	18,834	5,248	6,346
Dickinson	64,494	4,344	3,639	4,711	6,458	6,467	2,113	26,515	5,386	4,540
Eaton	217,752	(D)	6,997	117,939	18,015	5,075	4,532	38,161	5,403	10,984
Emmet	127,789	26,830	4,577	10,460	4,571	1,699	4,647	59,923	5,683	7,775
Genesee	1,232,973	17,090	58,999	294,327	98,367	32,209	60,987	459,804	64,804	115,029
Gladwin	15,967	(D)	1,406	1,324	2,072	(D)	610	6,322	657	2,423
Gogebic	33,079	9,112	1,736	919	1,691	(D)	6,058	9,080	2,222	1,775
Grand Traverse	378,155	64,490	16,121	40,164	28,254	11,622	17,867	107,283	25,241	58,289

Table XVIII-8. Service Industry Receipts in Michigan, by County: for Profit Establishments 1992 Continued

Receipts (Data in Millions of Dollars)

County	Total	Hotels and Motels	Personal Services	Business Services	Automotive Repair	Misc. Repair	Amusement/ Recreation	Health Services	Legal Services	Engineering/ Management
Gratiot	$51,630	$(D)	$2,921	$4,808	$5,191	$3,366	$2,482	$26,114	$1,565	$2,863
Hillsdale	45,828	(D)	3,302	12,558	3,185	2,431	2,318	11,638	2,090	5,959
Houghton	51,056	3,795	2,462	3,375	3,958	287	2,400	18,998	5,324	10,136
Huron	44,928	1,458	3,955	2,683	5,731	2,078	3,295	15,605	1,385	2
Ingham	1,201,443	(D)	52,003	200,866	74,701	27,340	72,146	336,981	125,042	229,603
Ionia	54,289	(D)	6,395	3,447	6,506	(D)	7,595	19,705	2,251	5,981
Iosco	38,379	4,693	3,105	2,081	3,583	1,803	2,864	16,127	(D)	2,148
Iron	17,766	562	1,157	574	(D)	---	3,970	5,796	3,307	1,084
Isabella	122,979	(D)	4,757	14,893	7,872	1,952	9,158	34,816	6,344	24,229
Jackson	328,711	8,551	19,970	49,317	24,842	16,806	27,316	115,475	15,234	41,668
Kalamazoo	879,467	(D)	49,528	193,540	61,658	39,142	44,692	292,785	66,369	76,406
Kalkaska	12,015	602	514	1,438	3,311	(D)	2,254	2,825	(D)	(D)
Kent	2,311,295	82,176	106,846	432,289	246,288	71,269	115,012	599,136	211,428	376,342
Keweenaw	828	(D)	---	---	---	(D)	---	(D)	---	---
Lake	6,245	1,205	(D)	(D)	(D)	(D)	802	(D)	(D)	490
Lapeer	84,660	2,892	5,675	8,215	10,768	1,733	5,936	32,871	4,470	8,570
Leelanau	42,463	10,793	1,214	2,369	1,621	712	(D)	6,265	654	4,058
Lenawee	143,617	(D)	10,792	18,983	19,091	6,072	10,713	51,877	8,514	8,147
Livingston	259,482	(D)	10,691	44,947	32,116	16,393	24,824	81,538	8,726	23,670
Luce	6,776	1,263	(D)	(D)	1,553	(D)	234	2,340	255	329
Mackinac	49,788	39,261	567	(D)	1,331	486	2,685	2,120	(D)	1,080
Macomb	2,783,729	36,110	101,597	506,787	224,129	132,745	135,652	733,375	82,603	789,233
Manistee	28,998	3,130	2,002	1,401	1,685	374	724	16,354	1,401	1,020
Marquette	152,568	10,210	6,708	15,711	12,093	(D)	6,713	72,999	9,076	13,647
Mason	54,157	4,799	2,638	4,578	4,214	(D)	3,305	16,193	1,910	9,720
Mecosta	59,501	(D)	3,436	13,062	6,082	965	2,941	19,892	2,029	3,923
Menominee	24,635	(D)	1,477	4,820	2,624	981	1,104	9,639	1,232	(D)
Midland	220,765	(D)	13,512	66,130	12,586	4,912	13,012	74,437	5,714	13,631

563

Table XVIII-8. Service Industry Receipts in Michigan, by County: for Profit Establishments 1992 Continued

County	Receipts (Data in Millions of Dollars)									
	Total	Hotels and Motels	Personal Services	Business Services	Automotive Repair	Misc. Repair	Amusement/ Recreation	Health Services	Legal Services	Engineering/ Management
Missaukee	$9,523	$(D)	$341	$(D)	$1,115	$262	$867	$3,771	$(D)	$(D)
Monroe	225,338	6,530	10,273	31,362	18,153	35,019	26,357	76,578	8,147	10,305
Montcalm	54,242	(D)	5,464	3,881	8,025	3,217	3,996	21,238	1,787	3,485
Montmorency	8,755	750	263	(D)	(D)	(D)	2,718	3,492	132	682
Muskegon	458,906	(D)	17,868	37,774	25,123	10,689	46,340	127,152	26,050	144,508
Newaygo	34,498	1,110	2,903	4,885	3,843	(D)	2,457	13,245	1,880	3,245
Oakland	10,543,155	191,540	260,801	3,502,846	394,277	228,866	561,881	1,987,738	812,749	2,355,166
Oceana	17,312	3,299	1,409	(D)	1,428	726	2,197	4,427	910	720
Ogemaw	29,961	2,261	2,343	3,484	2,062	0	2,036	13,576	1,202	2,395
Ontonagon	9,742	1,665	715	(D)	1,211	1,404	447	3,133	(D)	255
Osceola	15,342	(D)	896	1,601	3,246	2,054	(D)	3,848	651	668
Oscoda	5,390	(D)	887	(D)	1,008	(D)	529	(D)	(D)	(D)
Otsego	79,646	19,268	2,706	4,238	9,431	5,316	5,146	18,940	6,844	5,907
Ottawa	470,992	15,523	30,303	109,053	44,463	28,816	26,762	130,050	14,710	57,085
Presque Isle	10,773	785	890	(D)	1,645	(D)	807	2,679	576	776
Roscommon	25,047	2,540	1,365	656	5,192	855	2,606	9,547	916	1,136
Saginaw	602,093	(D)	34,938	97,659	51,551	14,382	29,777	219,391	50,534	60,738
St. Clair	259,018	19,746	16,283	25,797	21,719	15,955	18,366	95,674	15,461	23,827
St. Joseph	94,845	4,410	4,960	13,676	20,617	8,395	4,549	27,284	4,799	4,902
Sanilac	38,000	1,618	3,109	4,480	3,651	2,351	4,087	13,706	2,365	1,904
Schoolcraft	11,620	3,376	1,077	(D)	1,300	(D)	(D)	4,442	(D)	525
Shiawassee	101,530	456	5,094	15,942	9,210	7,669	7,200	41,153	3,612	7,906
Tuscola	42,419	(D)	3,366	1,433	6,428	836	4,714	20,441	1,868	2,000
Van Buren	90,781	(D)	6,116	10,467	7,472	2,313	7,179	18,365	3,180	(D)
Washtenaw	1,623,120	(D)	47,092	465,341	58,149	20,373	80,198	352,011	71,030	430,241
Wayne	7,271,882	230,113	378,323	1,565,559	673,322	282,488	597,250	1,580,737	719,543	1,075,324
Wexford	78,045	8,004	4,533	15,863	9,627	(D)	4,981	21,703	3,061	8,196
Michigan	**35,123,794**	**1,212,396**	**1,469,981**	**8,305,842**	**2,482,856**	**1,137,072**	**2,201,376**	**8,706,707**	**2,517,595**	**6,226,799**

Source: Bureau of Census, 1992 Census of Service Industries, Geographic Area Series, Michigan (Washington, D.C.: quinquennial). (D) data withheld to avoid disclosure of individual firm data. — No data.

Table XVIII-9. Service Industry Receipts per Establishment and per Employee in Michigan, by County: for Profit Establishments 1992

County	Receipts per Establishment	Receipts per Employee	County	Receipts per Establishment	Receipts per Employee
Alcona	$184,214	$36,324	Lake	$195,156	$31,070
Alger	270,419	51,680	Lapeer	247,544	47,966
Allegan	281,508	41,476	Leelanau	348,057	42,676
Alpena	270,849	42,502	Lenawee	270,465	43,219
Antrim	281,808	27,583	Livingston	369,107	45,467
Arenac	221,366	48,811	Luce	150,578	43,716
Baraga	187,371	44,013	Mackinac	440,602	71,948
Barry	250,784	49,462	Macomb	577,777	57,975
Bay	341,825	50,466	Manistee	210,130	34,895
Benzie	234,802	40,109	Marquette	340,554	46,486
Berrien	420,096	44,762	Mason	300,872	52,124
Branch	356,419	41,086	Mecosta	308,295	41,120
Calhoun	452,476	38,232	Menominee	270,714	34,455
Cass	239,385	42,176	Midland	454,249	44,572
Charlevoix	244,401	45,036	Missaukee	244,179	27,209
Cheboygan	183,173	51,746	Monroe	439,255	48,870
Chippewa	370,873	53,341	Montcalm	232,798	33,944
Clare	267,224	38,796	Montmorency	213,537	37,575
Clinton	321,296	49,381	Muskegon	522,672	69,133
Crawford	262,247	38,834	Newaygo	222,568	44,919
Delta	280,789	45,009	Oakland	805,744	65,786
Dickinson	305,659	46,667	Oceana	174,869	39,435
Eaton	598,220	68,713	Ogemaw	280,009	46,523
Emmet	456,389	53,558	Ontonagon	198,816	39,124
Genesee	462,828	50,519	Osceola	187,098	66,416
Gladwin	215,770	44,725	Oscoda	158,529	41,462
Gogebic	303,477	27,451	Otsego	442,478	51,853
Grand Traverse	415,555	58,592	Ottawa	416,439	40,550
Gratiot	205,697	41,271	Presque Isle	153,900	36,894
Hillsdale	303,497	36,228	Roscommon	195,680	46,298
Houghton	259,168	40,943	Saginaw	457,517	50,524
Huron	214,967	47,442	St. Clair	325,399	50,471
Ingham	539,732	57,003	St. Joseph	308,941	48,614
Ionia	266,123	42,380	Sanilac	242,038	51,913
Iosco	220,569	39,854	Schoolcraft	207,500	40,772
Iron	246,750	40,562	Shiawassee	290,086	51,987
Isabella	374,936	43,166	Tuscola	208,961	40,399
Jackson	399,406	50,323	Van Buren	297,643	46,867
Kalamazoo	540,213	45,549	Washtenaw	640,032	65,676
Kalkaska	190,714	55,115	Wayne	720,202	61,765
Kent	606,798	52,601	Wexford	396,168	41,691
Keweenaw	103,500	75,273	**Michigan**	**572,991**	**57,207**

Source: Bureau of Census, 1992 Census of Service Industries, Geographic Area Series, Michigan (Washington, D.C.).

This chapter provides information on Michigan enterprises (companies), and Michigan science and technology. It also includes economic multipliers for the state. Information on auto industry research and development, specifically, can be found in Chapter XIV and data on graduates in science and engineering is covered in Chapter III.

The data on Michigan's largest public companies are provided by the financial public relations consulting firm Durocher, Dixson, Werba located in Detroit. Public companies are those whose shares are listed on a national or regional stock exchange. The listing of Michigan's largest private for profit and nonprofit companies is based on information from <u>Ward's Business Directory of U.S. Private and Public Companies</u> published by Gale Research Inc., also located in Detroit. Private companies are those whose shares are "closely held" and not available for public purchase. Nonprofit companies can appear in any industry, but, the largest are typically found in the hospital and health sector.

Industrial research and development activity is tracked by the National Science Foundation in Washington, D.C. Data on employment of scientific workers in Michigan were drawn from the 1990 <u>Census of Population</u>. Patents and inventors are reported by the U.S. Patent and Trademark Office, also in Washington, D.C. "Utility" patents are defined as patents for inventions. Design patents and botanical patents are not included in this count because the standard series published by the U.S. Patent and Trademark Office tabulate presents data on utility patents only. Utility patents represent 93 percent of the Michigan total.

The output, earnings, and employment multipliers were prepared by the Bureau of Economic Analysis (BEA) of the U.S. Department of Commerce. The multipliers begin with BEA's 500 sector input/output model for the nation. These input/output relationships are extrapolated to regions based on detailed wage and salary data. These can be used to adjust the national pattern to show a region's industry structure and trading patterns.

The Michigan Employment Security Commission is the source of the summary statistics by size of establishment for units, employment, and wages. The information on *incorporated* business owners is drawn from the 1990 Census of Population. The data on the *unincorporated* self-employed (proprietors) is estimated by the Bureau of Economic Analysis as an input in the personal income tabulations.

LIST OF TABLES

Table		Page
XIX-1.	Michigan's Top Manufacturing Companies, Ranked by Sales: Fiscal Year 1992	568
XIX-2.	Michigan's Top Service Companies, Ranked by Revenues: Fiscal Year 1992	569
XIX-3.	Michigan's Top Retail Trade Companies, Ranked by Sales: Fiscal Year 1992	570
XIX-4.	Michigan's Top Utility Companies, Ranked by Assets: Fiscal Year 1992	570

LIST OF TABLES

Table		Page
XIX-5.	Michigan's Top Insurance Companies, Ranked by Revenues: Fiscal Year 1992	570
XIX-6.	Michigan's Top Financial Institutions, Ranked by Assets: Fiscal Year 1992	571
XIX-7.	Michigan's Largest Private and Nonprofit Companies, Ranked by Sales: 1992	572
XIX-8.	Industrial Research and Development Expenditures in Michigan and the United States, by Source of Funds: 1963-1993	582
XIX-9.	Research and Development Expenditures and Expenditures as a Percentage of Gross State Product, by State: 1993	582
XIX-10.	U.S. Utility Patents Issued to Residents of Michigan and the United States: 1966-1992	584
XIX-11.	U.S. Utility Patents, by Industry in Michigan: 1992	584
XIX-12.	Number of Inventors and Number of U.S. Utility Patents, Ranked by State: 1993	585
XIX-13.	Number of Utility Patents and Number of Inventors in Michigan, by County: 1992	587
XIX-14.	Number of Scientific Workers in Michigan, by County: 1990	588
XIX-15.	Output, Earnings, and Employment Multipliers for Michigan, by Industry: 1992 (See accompanying user notes)	590
XIX-16.	Units, Employment, and Wages by Size of Firm in Michigan, by Industry Group: 1st Qtr 1994	592
XIX-17.	Number of Units, Employment, and Average Weekly Wage by Size of Firm in Michigan, by County: 1st Qtr 1994	596
XIX-18.	Incorporated Business Owners in Michigan, by County: 1990	610
XIX-19.	Unincorporated Self Employed (Proprietors) in Michigan, by County: 1990	611

Table XIX-1. Michigan's Top Manufacturing Companies, Ranked by Sales: Fiscal Year 1992

1992 Rank	Company	Net Sales (Thousands of Dollars)	Assets (Thousands of Dollars)
1	General Motors (Detroit)	$132,429,400	$191,012,800
2	Ford Motor (Dearborn))	100,132,300	180,545,200
3	Chrysler (Highland Park)	36,897,000	40,653,000
4	Dow Chemical (Midland)	18,971,000	25,360,000
5	Whirlpool (Benton Harbor)	7,301,000	6,118,000
6	Kellogg (Battle Creek)	6,190,600	4,015,000
7	Upjohn (Kalamazoo)	3,668,866	4,604,923
8	Masco Corp. (Taylor)	3,525,000	3,986,560
9	Dow Corning (Midland)	1,955,700	2,190,700
10	Masco Tech (Taylor)	1,656,840	1,877,310
11	Lear Seating (Southfield)	1,422,700	799,900
12	Gerber Products (Fremont)	1,293,127	893,723
13	Federal- Mogul (Southfield)	1,264,000	1,099,500
14	Tecumseh Products (Tecumseh)	1,258,500	1,078,600
15	Holnam (Dundee)	946,176	1,353,132
16	Herman Miller (Zeeland)	804,675	471,268
17	SPX (Muskegon)	801,169	560,328
18	Thorn Apple Valley (Southfield)	739,733	132,600
19	International Controls (Kalamazoo)	716,733	476,397
20	Valassis Communications (Livonia)	684,029	292,718
21	La-Z-Boy Chair (Monroe)	619,471	376,722
22	Fruehauf Trailer (Southfield)	488,898	276,658
23	Stryker (Kalamazoo)	477,054	340,272
24	Perrigo (Allegan)	409,785	316,946
25	Hayes Wheels International (Romulus)	408,700	499,900
26	Douglas & Lomason (Farmington Hills)	391,178	156,351
27	Trimas (Ann Arbor)	388,230	466,620
28	R.P.Scherer (Troy)	337,786	541,950
29	Wolverine World Wide (Rockford)	293,136	204,011
30	Donnelly (Holland)	271,399	131,229
31	Champion Enterprise (Auburn Hills)	270,554	80,508
32	Kysor Industrial (Cadillac)	262,174	135,850
33	Sparton (Jackson)	245,380	98,571
34	Walbro (Cass City)	241,416	193,020
35	Simpson Industries (Bingham Farms)	222,825	169,971
36	National - Standard (Niles)	215,133	113,939
37	Core Industries (Bloomfield Hills)	183,734	156,583
38	Guardsman Products (Grand Rapids)	152,197	83,494
39	Knape & Vogt (Grand Rapids)	124,851	88,333
40	Spartan Motors (Charlotte)	124,031	56,381
41	Larizza Industries (Troy)	111,307	62,657
42	Detrex (Southfield)	96,754	59,662

Table XIX-1. Michigan's Top Manufacturing Companies, Ranked by Sales: Fiscal Year 1992 Continued

1992 Rank	Company	Net Sales (Thousands of Dollars)	Assets (Thousands of Dollars)
43	Maxco (Lansing)	$91,878	$38,227
44	Newcor (Bloomfield Hills)	90,564	75,702
45	Ameriwood Industries International (Grandville)	87,692	44,954
46	Durakon Industries (Lapeer)	86,961	47,415
47	Gelman Sciences (Ann Arbor)	81,460	61,530
48	Federal Screw Works (Detroit)	67,618	46,952
49	Hastings Manufacturing (Hastings)	64,967	41,313
50	Thermo Process Systems (Livonia)	47,235	88,582

Source: Durocher•Dixson•Werba, Incorporated 1993 Michigan Public 100 (Detroit, Michigan: 1993).

Table XIX-2. Michigan's Top Service Companies, Ranked by Revenues: Fiscal Year 1992
(Data in Thousands)

1992 Rank	Company	Revenues	Assets
1	Kelly Services (Troy)	$1,722,526	$496,075
2	Pulte (Bloomfield Hills)	1,369,944	3,705,544
3	Handleman (Troy)	1,020,237	655,075
4	ALC Communications (Birmingham)	376,064	143,266
5	Compuware (Farmington Hills)	175,025	135,490
6	Comshare (Ann Arbor)	119,174	107,963
7	First of Michigan (Detroit)	59,879	67,959
8	Universal Standard Medical Labs. (Southfield)	44,618	50,117
9	F.A. Tucker Group (Troy/Chicago)	43,509	25,748
10	Sandy (Troy)	37,768	15,548
11	United American Healthcare (Detroit)	34,871	23,644
12	International R & D (Mattawan)	34,385	47,627
13	Saga Communications (Grosse Pointe Farms)	31,010	54,933
14	Credit Acceptance (Southfield)	18,691	128,183
15	Thomas Edison Inn (St.Claire)	14,345	20,145
16	Associated Mariner Financial (Livonia)	11,524	2,095
17	Manatron (Kalamazoo)	10,084	11,866
18	Detriot & Canada Tunnel (Detroit)	8,409	16,608
19	Randers Group (Norton Shores)	6,822	7,605
20	Omega Healthcare Investors (Ann Arbor)	5,968	144,752
21	Metropolitan Realty (Detroit)	3,829	41,236
22	Inter - Active Services (Walled Lake)	3,411	10,632
23	M.S.E. Cable Systems (Rochester Hills)	2,405	2,817
24	Taubman Centers (Bloomfield Hills)	1,926	392,758
25	KMS Industries (Ann Arbor)	887	4,353

Source: Durocher•Dixson•Werba, Incorporated 1993 Michigan Public 100 (Detroit, Michigan: 1993).

Table XIX-3. Michigan's Top Retail Trade Companies, Ranked by Sales: Fiscal Year 1992
(Data in Thousands)

1992 Rank	Company	Sales	Assets
1	Kmart (Troy)	$37,724,000	$18,931,000
2	F & M Distributors (Warren)	736,925	315,828
3	Perry Drug Stores (Pontiac)	674,431	270,508
4	Arbor Drugs (Troy)	476,848	200,423
5	Jacobson Stores (Jackson)	411,631	250,395
6	Fretter (Livonia)	361,603	177,131
7	Wolohan Lumber (Saginaw)	343,938	155,963
8	Gantos (Grand Rapids)	265,918	113,575
9	Cattleman's (Detroit)	123,818	14,647
10	Crowley, Milner (Detroit)	106,349	N.A.
11	NuVision (Flint)	42,536	22,614
12	Tubby's (Fraser)	1,623	3,481

Source: Durocher•Dixson•Werba, Incorporated <u>1993 Michigan Public 100</u> (Detroit, Michigan: 1993).

Table XIX-4. Michigan's Top Utility Companies, Ranked by Assets: Fiscal Year 1992
(Data in Thousands)

1992 Rank	Company	Sales	Assets
1	Detroit Edison (Detroit)	$10,445,853	$3,558,143
2	CMS Energy (Dearborn)	6,848,000	3,073,000
3	MCN (Detroit)	1,648,989	1,438,280
4	S.E. Michigan Gas (Port Huron)	326,624	251,526
5	Upper Peninsula Energy (Houghton)	118,956	61,452
6	Eselco (Sault Ste. Marie)	46,592	30,292

Source: Durocher•Dixson•Werba, Incorporated <u>1993 Michigan Public 100</u> (Detroit, Michigan: 1993).

Table XIX-5. Michigan's Top Insurance Companies, Ranked by Revenues: Fiscal Year 1992
(Data in Thousands)

1992 Rank	Company	Sales	Assets
1	Citizens Corp. (Howell)	$761,285	$1,232,097
2	Foremost (Grand Rapids)	460,470	730,478
3	Physicians Insurance (Okemos)	71,250	249,339
4	H.W. Kaufman (Southfield)	39,131	35,305

Source: Durocher•Dixson•Werba, Incorporated <u>1993 Michigan Public 100</u> (Detroit, Michigan: 1993).

Table XIX-6. Michigan's Top Financial Institutions, Ranked by Assets: Fiscal Year 1992
(Data in Thousands)

1992 Rank	Company	Assets	Deposits	Loans
1	NBD Bancorp (Detroit)	$40,937,190	$31,000,751	$24,725,922
2	Comerica (Detroit)	26,586,814	20,394,709	17,509,629
3	First of America (Kalamazoo)	20,146,767	18,035,553	13,516,057
4	Michigan National (Farmington Hills)	10,634,931	8,975,293	6,555,577
5	Standard Federal (Troy)	9,544,731	6,527,603	4,883,887
6	FirstFed Michigan (Detroit)	9,399,351	3,445,222	3,661,233
7	Old Kent Financial (Grand Rapids)	8,698,574	7,253,540	4,786,839
8	Great Lakes Bancorp (Ann Arbor)	2,798,341	1,684,153	1,819,945
9	Citizens Banking (Flint)	2,498,834	2,086,144	1,535,036
10	First Michigan Bank (Holland)	2,161,097	1,852,975	1,297,132
11	Chemical Financial (Midland)	1,405,314	1,218,924	577,252
12	D & N Financial (Hancock)	1,212,196	881,424	687,758
13	Heritage Bankcorp (Taylor)	930,790	787,175	493,465
14	Mutual Savings Bank (Bay City)	754,628	501,889	235,513
15	Republic Bancorp (Owosso)	733,967	563,080	286,506
16	Michigan Financial (Marquette)	720,143	651,425	444,688
17	CB Financial (Jackson)	645,089	560,781	306,956
18	CFSB Bancorp (Lansing)	633,872	560,428	297,488
19	Shoreline Financial (Benton Harbor)	533,004	480,458	350,174
20	First National (Clinton Township)	453,622	410,936	312,631
21	Pinnacle Financial Services (St. Joseph)	394,880	352,319	256,742
22	Franklin Bank (Southfield)	391,029	340,910	327,313
23	Independent Bank Corp. (Ionia)	367,546	327,012	229,609
24	Central Holding (Clinton Township)	357,859	303,067	240,565
25	First State Financial (Eastpointe)	356,277	320,234	155,245
26	Empire Banc (Traverse City)	293,557	267,855	194,680
27	Security Savings (Jackson)	269,683	196,658	113,266
28	Firstbank Corporation (Alma)	242,105	213,847	141,037
29	Mackinac Financial (Detroit)	210,113	151,118	158,370
30	Interfirst Bankcorp (Ann Arbor)	201,699	112,141	35,333
31	Royal Bank Group (Royal Oak)	187,466	171,795	119,738
32	Charter National Bancorp (Taylor)	171,515	151,970	105,122
33	Fidelity Financial (Birmingham)	158,503	139,716	80,896
34	Oxford Bank (Oxford)	155,825	140,588	88,738
35	FNBH Bancorp (Howell)	154,703	140,925	106,913
36	County Bank Corp. (Lapeer)	154,159	139,937	90,680
37	Madison National Bank (Madison Heights)	114,377	103,479	82,565
38	Sturgis Federal Savings Bank (Sturgis)	102,965	85,065	63,329
39	First Independence (Detroit)	81,480	73,900	31,348
40	Capital Directions (Mason)	78,188	70,557	47,126
41	Midwest Guaranty Bancorp (Troy)	60,068	52,874	40,320

Source: Durocher•Dixson•Werba, Incorporated <u>1993 Michigan Public 100</u> (Detroit, Michigan: 1993).

Table XIX-7. Michigan's Largest Private and Nonprofit Companies, Ranked by Sales: 1992

Rank	Name	City	Line of Business	Sales	Revenue Year	U.S. Employment
1	Meijer Inc	Grand Rapids	Groceries and General Merchandise Store	$7,200,000,000	92	55,000
2	Amway Corp	Ada	Manufacturing Cosmetics, Toiletries, and Household Cleaners	3,900,000,000	92	10,000
3	Blue Cross and Blue Shield of Michigan	Detroit	Health Insurance and Health Maintenance Organization	2,488,600,000	92	8,500
4	Domino's Pizza Inc	Ann Arbor	Pizza	2,400,000,000	92	20,000
5	Steelcase Inc	Grand Rapids	Manufacturing Metal and Wood Office Furniture	2,400,000,000	92	19,000
6	Little Caesar Enterprises Inc	Detroit	Pizza	2,050,000,000	92	86,000
7	Spartan Stores Inc	Grand Rapids	Grocery Store	2,000,000,000	91	2,100
8	Mercy Health Services	Farmington Hills	General Hospitals/Health Maintenance Organization	1,500,000,000	91	24,000
9	Taubman Investment Company	Bloomfield Hills	Department Stores and Restaurants	1,500,000,000	92	18,000
10	Penske Corp	Detroit	Truck Rentals and Racetrack Operator, New and Used Automobile Dealers	1,420,000,000	92	10,000
11	Henry Ford Health System	Detroit	Hospital Care and Health Maintenance	1,260,000,000	92	15,962
12	Michigan Mutual Insurance Co	Detroit	Underwriter of Accident, Health, Property and Casualty Insurance	1,238,000,000	92	1,700
13	Guardian Industries Corp	Northville	Manufacturing Glass Products	1,070,000,000	92	8,000
14	Lear Holdings Corp	Southfield	Manufacturing Automotive Seats	1,000,000,000	92	10,500
15	Gordon Food Service Inc	Grand Rapids	Groceries and Food Service Equipment and Supplies	780,000,000	92	1,800
16	International Controls Corp	Kalamazoo	Manufacturing Truck Trailers and Automotive Stampings	716,000,000	92	4,197
17	Stroh Brewery Co	Detroit	Beer Manufacturing	680,000,000	92	2,682
18	Haworth Inc	Holland	Manufacturing Wooden and Metal Office and Store Fixtures	600,000,000	91	4,500

Table XIX-7. Michigan's Largest Private and Nonprofit Companies, Ranked by Sales: 1992 Continued

Rank	Name	City	Line of Business	Sales	Revenue Year	U.S. Employment
19	Barton Malow Enterprises Inc	Detroit	Constuction Management and Industrial Building Contractor	$590,000,000	91	800
20	Oakwood Health Services Corp	Dearborn	Operator of Hospitals	540,000,000	91	8,713
21	Rouge Steel Co	Dearborn	Manufacturing Steel Works and Rolled Steel	530,000,000	92	3,000
22	All-Phase Electric Supply Co	Benton Harbor	Wholesale of Electrical, Industrial, and Technical Supplies	510,000,000	91	1,850
23	Universal Companies Inc	Grand Rapids	Wholesale Lumber	475,000,000	92	2,500
24	J M B Properties Co	Farmington Hills	Developer of Commercial and Residential Real Estate	430,000,000	92	2,000
25	Walbridge Aldinger Co	Detroit	Industrial, Nonresidential and Commercial Building Contractor	420,000,000	92	1,200
26	D & W Food Centers Inc	Grand Rapids	Grocery Store	400,000,000	91	3,200
27	Prince Corp	Holland	Manufacturing Automotive Trimmings	400,000,000	92	2,500
28	W B Doner and Co	Southfield	Advertising Agency	395,300,000	91	560
29	Dart Container Corp	Mason	Manufacturing Disposable Food Containers	370,000,000	92	3,000
30	Murco Inc	Plainwell	Meat Packing Plant	350,000,000	92	750
31	Copper and Brass Sales Inc	East Detroit	Wholesale Metal Service Center	350,000,000	91	1,185
32	Foodland Distributors	Livonia	Grocery Distribution	350,000,000	91	982
33	Jervis B Webb Co Inc	Farmington Hills	Manufacturing Conveyors and Equipment	330,000,000	92	2,300
34	Country Fresh Inc	Grand Rapids	Manufacturing Dairy Products	330,000,000	92	1,170
35	Mclouth Steel	Trenton	Manufacturing Steel Coils	320,000,000	92	1,600
36	Flint Ink Corp	Detroit	Manufacturing Printing Ink	320,000,000	91	2,600
37	Erb Lumber Co	Birmingham	Retail Lumber and Building Materials, Apartment Operators	320,000,000	92	2,000
38	Bissell Inc	Grand Rapids	Manufacturing Carpet Sweepers and Vacuums	320,000,000	92	2,500
39	Sealed Power Technologies	Muskegon	Manufacturing Ring Piston Rings, Cylinder Sleeves, Filters, Die Casting	320,000,000	91	3,000

Table XIX-7. Michigan's Largest Private and Nonprofit Companies, Ranked by Sales: 1992 Continued

Rank	Name	City	Line of Business	Sales	Revenue Year	U.S. Employment
40	General Automotive Corp	Ann Arbor	Manufacturing Truck and Bus Bodies and Vehicle Parts	$320,000,000	92	1,300
41	City Management Corp	Detroit	Waste Hauling Services	310,000,000	92	2,000
42	Freudenberg-Nok	Plymouth	Manufacturing Rubber and Oil Seals, Vibration Control System	310,000,000	92	3,600
43	ABC Appliance Inc	Pontiac	Appliance Store	280,000,000	92	1,500
44	Takata Inc	Auburn Hills	Manufacturing Automobile Safety Devices and Trimmings	270,000,000	92	3,800
45	Booth Newspapers Inc	Grand Rapids	Newspaper Publishing and Printing	260,000,000	92	2,700
46	CMI International Inc	Southfield	Manufacturing Aluminum and Iron Foundry, Development of Dies	260,000,000	92	2,700
47	ASC Inc	Southgate	Sunroofs and Convertible Installation	260,000,000	92	3,000
48	JSJ Corp	Grand Haven	Manufacturing Metal Stampings and Plastic Products	260,000,000	92	2,500
49	First Security Savings Bank	Bloomfield Hills	Savings Bank	260,000,000	92	500
50	G & R Felpausch Co	Hastings	Grocery Store	260,000,000	92	2,000
51	Becker Group Inc	Warren	Manufacturing Automotive Plastics Products	250,000,000	92	2,400
52	R L Polk and Co	Detroit	Bank Directory Publishing and Information Retrieval Service	250,000,000	92	6,000
53	Bronson Healthcare Group	Kalamazoo	Hospitals	250,000,000	92	3,000
54	Sinai Health Care System	Detroit	General Hospitals	250,000,000	92	3,000
55	Auto Wares Inc	Grand Rapids	Wholesale Motor Vehicle Parts	240,000,000	91	450
56	Elias Brothers Restaurants Inc	Warren	Restaurants	220,000,000	92	6,000
57	Motor Wheel Corp	Lansing	Manufacturing Vehicle Parts and Metal Automotive Stampings	220,000,000	92	2,000
58	Invetech Co	Detroit	Wholesale Industrial Supplies and Power Transmissions	215,000,000	92	950
59	Quality Stores Inc	North Muskegon	Auto and Home Supply Store	200,000,000	91	1,500

Table XIX-7. Michigan's Largest Private and Nonprofit Companies, Ranked by Sales: 1992 Continued

Rank	Name	City	Line of Business	Sales	Revenue Year	U.S. Employment
60	Edward C Levy Co	Detroit	Manufacturing Line, Paving Mixtures, and Concrete	$200,000,000	92	2,000
61	Brooks Beverage Management Inc	Holland	Manufacturing Bottled and Canned Soft Drinks	200,000,000	91	1,400
62	Honigman Miller Schwartz and Cohn	Detroit	Law Firm	190,000,000	91	750
63	Progressive Tool and Industries Co	Southfield	Manufacturing Welding Equipment	190,000,000	92	1,700
64	Letica Corp	Rochester	Manufacturing Plastics Pails, Cups	190,000,000	92	1,500
65	Centra Inc	Sterling Heights	Long Distance Trucking	180,000,000	92	2,000
66	H Cutler Co	Grand Rapids	Manufacturing Childrens Clothes	175,000,000	92	1,500
67	Tyler Refrigeration	Niles	Manufacturing Commercial Refrigeration Equipment	160,000,000	92	1,250
68	Dickinson, Wright, Moon, Van Dusen and Freeman	Detroit	Law Firm	150,000,000	91	605
69	Hardings Markets West Inc	Plainwell	Grocery Store	150,000,000	91	1,200
70	Prestolite Wire Corp	Farmington Hills	Manufacturing Automotive Engine wiring	148,000,000	92	1,200
71	Commercial Contracting Corp	Troy	Installation of Heavy Industrial Machinery	140,000,000	92	1,500
72	Lobdell-Emery Manufacturing Co	Alma	Manufacturing Auto Stampings	140,000,000	91	1,500
73	Alro Steel Corp	Jackson	Steel Wholesale	140,000,000	92	850
74	Zantop International Airlines Inc	Ypsilanti	Freight Air Transportation	130,000,000	92	1,000
75	American Seating Co	Grand Rapids	Manufacturing Office and Motor Vehicle Equipment	130,000,000	92	1,000
76	Plastipak Packaging Inc	Plymouth	Manufacturing Plastic Containers and Bottles	130,000,000	92	1,500
77	Aetna Industries Inc	Center Line	Auto Body Material Shop	125,000,000	92	1,200
78	Lacks Enterprises Inc	Grand Rapids	Manufacturing Automotive Stampings	125,000,000	92	1,250
79	Gainey Transportation Services Inc	Grand Rapids	Long Distance Trucking	125,000,000	92	700
80	General Safety Corp	St Clair Shores	Manufacturing Automobile Seat Belts	120,000,000	92	1,200
81	Harlan Electric Co	Southfield	Electrical Contractor	120,000,000	92	2,500

Table XIX-7. Michigan's Largest Private and Nonprofit Companies, Ranked By Sales: 1992 Continued

Rank	Name	City	Line of Business	Sales	Revenue Year	U.S. Employment
82	American Tape Co	Marysville	Coated & Laminated Paper	$120,000,000	92	550
83	Munson Medical Center	Traverse City	General Medical Hospital	120,000,000	92	2,500
84	Holtzman and Silverman Cos	Farmington Hills	Developer of Residential Real Estate	120,000,000	92	600
85	Leslie Metal Arts Company Inc	Grand Rapids	Manufacturing Automotive Stampings	120,000,000	92	1,150
86	Williams International Corp	Walled Lake	Manufacturing Aircraft Engines and Engine Parts	120,000,000	92	1,000
87	Durametallic Corp	Kalamazoo	Metallic and Mechanical Seals	120,000,000	92	600
88	Harrow Industries Inc	Grand Rapids	Manufacturing Hardware	110,000,000	92	1,250
89	Bartech Inc	Ypsilanti	Temporary Help Employment Agency	110,000,000	92	950
90	Comprehensive Health Services Inc	Detroit	Health Maintenance Organization	110,000,000	92	500
91	Autostyle	Grand Rapids	Manufacturing Plastic Automotive Parts	107,100,000	92	1,000
92	Active Tool and Manufacturing Company Inc	Roseville	Manufacturing Automobile Stampings, Dies and Tools	100,000,000	91	1,400
93	Alma Piston Co	Alma	Manufacturing Motor Vehicle Parts and Air Compressors	100,000,000	92	750
94	S and H Fabricating and Engineering	Walled Lake	Manufacturing Hoses and Tubes Assembly	100,000,000	92	1,000
95	Leco Corp	St Joseph	Manufacturing Analytical Instruments	100,000,000	92	1,000
96	Dunham's Athleisure Corp	Waterford	Sporting Good Store	100,000,000	92	1,600
97	Dura Mechanical Components Inc	Troy	Manufacturing Parking Brake Systems, Windows	100,000,000	91	1,000
98	Ring Screw Works	Madison Heights	Manufacturing Automotive Fasteners	100,000,000	92	600
99	Acheson Industries Inc	Port Huron	Manufacturing Chemicals	100,000,000	92	1,100
100	HDS Services	Farmington Hills	Nutrition Management and Consulting	97,000,000	91	420
101	Miller, Canfield, Paddock, and Stone	Detroit	Law Firm	96,000,000	92	575
102	Allied Film and Video Inc	Detroit	Video Duplication	96,000,000	92	700
103	Carhartt Inc	Dearborn	Manufacturing Mens Work Clothes	95,000,000	92	1,500

Table XIX-7. Michigan's Largest Private and Nonprofit Companies, Ranked by Sales: 1992 Continued

Rank	Name	City	Line of Business	Sales	Revenue Year	U.S. Employment
104	Key Plastics Inc	Plymouth	Manufacturing Automotive Injection Molded Plastics	$92,000,000	92	1,000
105	Indian Head Industries Inc	Southfield	Manufacturing Gaskets, Truck Brakes, Automotive Trim	91,000,000	91	650
106	Aco Inc	Farmington Hills	Hardware Store	90,000,000	91	1,000
107	Inverness Castings Group Inc	Bangor	Manufacturing Zinc and Aluminum Die Castings	90,000,000	92	750
108	Dykema Gossett	Detroit	Law Firm	88,500,000	92	650
109	Thompson International	Troy	Manufacturing Wheel Covers	87,000,000	92	650
110	MNP Corp	Utica	Manufacturing Nails, Bolts, Screws, Rivets, Washers, etc, and Testing	87,000,000	92	450
111	Container Products Inc	Southfield	Manufacturing Carbon, Stainless Steel, and Plastic Pails	85,000,000	91	500
112	Church's Lumber Yards	Utica	Retail Lumber and Building Supplies	84,000,000	92	500
113	Environmental Research Institute of Michigan	Ann Arbor	Environmental Research	80,900,000	92	775
114	Batts Inc	Zeeland	Manufacturing Plastic and Wooden Hangers	80,000,000	92	500
115	Mitchell Corporation of Owosso	Owosso	Manufacturing Motor Vehicle Parts, Plastic Products, Apparel Findings	80,000,000	92	1,000
116	Delfield Co	Mount Pleasant	Manufacturing Commercial Freezers and Food Service Equipment	80,000,000	92	700
117	Sucre Holding Inc	Bay City	Leasing of Property	76,000,000	92	660
118	Unistrut International Corp	Ann Arbor	Manufacturing Steel for Industrial and Non-residential Use	75,000,000	91	590
119	Michigan Health Care Corp	Detroit	Mental Health, Medical, and Surgical Hospitals	75,000,000	92	2,500
120	Peterson American Corp	Southfield	Manufacturing Springs, Hose Clamps, and Wire Forms	75,000,000	92	645
121	L & W Engineering Company	Belleville	Manufacturing Automotive Stampings	75,000,000	92	425

Table XIX-7. Michigan's Largest Private and Nonprofit Companies, Ranked by Sales: 1992 Continued

Rank	Name	City	Line of Business	Sales	Revenue Year	U.S. Employment
122	ECS/Roush Co	Livonia	Manufacturing Automobiles Engines and Control Systems	$73,000,000	91	550
123	C A Muer Corp	Detroit	Restaurant	73,000,000	92	2,000
124	Lake Shore Inc	Iron Mountain	Manufacturing Industrial Trucks & Underground Mining Equipment	73,000,000	91	600
125	Automotive Moulding Co	Warren	Manufacturing Metal Automotive Stampings, Rubber, Plastic Products	70,000,000	92	625
126	Yale-South Haven Inc	South Haven	Manufacturing Rubber Goods, Gaskets, Packing, and Sealing Devices	70,000,000	92	450
127	Union Pump Co	Battle Creek	Manufacturing Industrial, Chemical, Nuclear, and Petroleum Pumps	67,000,000	92	500
128	Bill Knapps Michigan Inc	Battle Creek	Restaurant	66,000,000	91	4,000
129	ISI Robotics Inc	Fraser	Manufacturing Robots	65,000,000	92	600
130	Summit Polymers Inc	Kalamazoo	Manufacturing Plastic Products	65,000,000	91	895
131	Booth American Co	Detroit	Radio and Cable Television Services	62,000,000	91	600
132	Fourmidable Group	Farmington Hills	Property Management	61,000,000	92	600
133	Daane's Food Market	Grandville	Supermarket	60,000,000	92	600
134	Real Estate One Inc	Farmington Hills	Real Estate Agency	60,000,000	91	800
135	Pioneer Engineering and Manufacturing	Warren	Engineering	60,000,000	92	800
136	R J Tower Holding Co	Greenville	Manufacturing Automotive Stampings	60,000,000	92	560
137	U S Manufacturing Corp	Roseville	Manufacturing Motor Vehicle Parts, Iron and Steel Forgings	60,000,000	91	600
138	Chivas Products Ltd	Sterling Heights	Manufacturing Car Interior Parts	60,000,000	92	600
139	Melling Tool Co	Jackson	Manufacturing Vehicle Parts, Dies, Tools	60,000,000	92	500
140	Evans Industries Inc	Detroit	Manufacturing Laminated Plastics and Adhesives	60,000,000	92	600
141	Macdonald's Industrial Products	Grand Rapids	Manufacturing Zinc and Aluminum	58,000,000	92	500
142	Edwards Brothers Inc	Ann Arbor	Manufacturing Books and Periodicals	56,000,000	92	800

Table XIX-7. Michigan's Largest Private and Nonprofit Companies, Ranked by Sales: 1992 Continued

Rank	Name	City	Line of Business	Sales	Revenue Year	U.S. Employment
143	Voplex Corp	Lapeer	Manufacturing Plastic Automobile Products	$56,000,000	91	600
144	Irwin Seating Company Inc	Grand Rapids	Manufacturing Public Seating and Classroom Furniture	56,000,000	92	475
145	Fabex Inc	Novi	Manufacturing Motor Vehicle Parts	55,000,000	92	500
146	Lionel Trains Inc	Chesterfield	Manufacturing Toy Trains	55,000,000	92	600
147	O/E Automation Inc	Troy	School of Business, Vocations, and Computers	54,000,000	92	500
148	Ashcraft's Market Inc	Harrison	Supermarket	53,000,000	92	610
149	Livernois Group	Dearborn	Manufacturing Automotive Equipment and Automotive Engineering	53,000,000	92	600
150	Libralter Plastics Inc	Walled Lake	Manufacturing Plastic Injection Molding	51,000,000	92	500
151	Hawtal Whiting Inc	Troy	Automobile Design and Engineering	51,000,000	91	500
152	Metalloy Corp	Hudson	Manufacturing Aluminum Foundries and Metal Heat Treating	50,000,000	91	450
153	Wollin Products Inc	Stevensville	Manufacturing Custom Injection Molding	50,000,000	92	450
154	Armstrong International Inc	Three Rivers	Pipe Fittings & Refrigeration, Heating	50,000,000	92	600
155	TCH Industries Inc	Grand Rapids	Manufacturing Nonferrous Metal and Aluminum	50,000,000	92	550
156	Crown Group Inc	Warren	Application of Coating to Plastics and Metals	50,000,000	92	800
157	New York Carpet World	Southfield	Floor Covering Store	50,000,000	91	490
158	Awrey Bakeries Inc	Livonia	Manufacturing Bakery Products	50,000,000	91	450
159	Grocers Baking Co	Grand Rapids	Manufacturing Bread and Other Bakery Products	50,000,000	91	650
160	Besser Co	Alpena	Manufacturing Concrete Producing Machinery	50,000,000	92	550
161	Lectron Products Inc	Rochester Hills	Manufacturing Automotive Electronic Components	50,000,000	91	800
162	William Bolthouse Farms Inc	Grant	Vegetables, Melons and Crop Preparation	50,000,000	91	900
163	Holland Hitch Co	Holland	Manufacturing Truck Hitches	49,000,000	92	700
164	Smith Group Inc	Detroit	Architectural Engineering	47,600,000	92	430

Table XIX-7. Michigan's Largest Private and Nonprofit Companies, Ranked by Sales: 1992 Continued

Rank	Name	City	Line of Business	Sales	Revenue Year	U.S. Employment
165	Westdale-Better Homes and Gardens	Grand Rapids	Residential and Commercial Real Estate Broker	$46,000,000	91	450
166	Olsonite Corp	Detroit	Manufacturing Toilet and Wooden Toilet Seats	45,000,000	91	500
167	Boyne USA Resorts Inc	Boyne Falls	Hotels and Recreational Camps	45,000,000	92	1,200
168	Giffels Associates Inc	Southfield	Architectural and Engineering	44,500,000	92	503
169	Guardian Security Services Inc	Southfield	Security Guard Service	44,000,000	91	1,500
170	Schweizer Real Estate Inc	Sterling Heights	Residential Real Estate Brokerage Firm	44,000,000	91	430
171	John Henry Co	Lansing	Commercial Horticultural Industry Printing	42,000,000	92	445
172	Corrigan Mowing Systems Inc	Farmington	Long Distance Trucking	42,000,000	91	600
173	Childtime Children's Centers Inc	Brighton	Day Care Centers and Preschool and Kindergarten	41,000,000	91	2,300
174	Ace-Tex Corp	Detroit	Manufacturing, Repair, Rental of Garments	41,000,000	91	600
175	Numatics Inc	Highland	Manufacturing Pneumatic Valves	40,000,000	92	450
176	Gast Manufacturing Corp	Benton Harbor	Manufacturing Pumps and Equipment	40,000,000	92	600
177	Complete Business Solutions Inc	Farmington Hills	Computer Consultant and Developer of Software	40,000,000	92	650
178	Henderson Glass Inc	Troy	Replacement and Installation of Automobile Glass	38,000,000	91	500
179	Suburban Communications Corp	Livonia	Newspaper	37,000,000	92	700
180	Zelenka Nursery Inc	Grand Haven	Designer Ornamental Wood	35,300,000	92	900
181	Canteen Service Co	Grand Rapids	Restaurants and Automatic Merchandise Machines	35,000,000	92	675
182	Mexican Industries in Michigan Inc	Detroit	Manufacturing Leather Automotive Trimming	31,000,000	91	450
183	Mr Bulky Treats and Gifts	Troy	Specialty Food Gift Items	31,000,000	92	450
184	Howard Miller Clock Co	Zeeland	Manufacturing Wood Household Furniture, Marine	30,000,000	92	500

Table XIX-7. Michigan's Largest Private and Nonprofit Companies, Ranked by Sales: 1992 Continued

Rank	Name	City	Line of Business	Sales	Revenue Year	U.S. Employment
185	Roskam Baking Co	Grand Rapids	Manufacturing Breading, Pancake Mix, Stuffing, Croutons	$30,000,000	91	450
186	Trappers Alley	Detroit	Commercial and Nonresidential Developer	30,000,000	92	500
187	Realtron Corp	Redford	Computer Book Publishing, Multilisting	30,000,000	91	450
188	Rapid Design Service Inc	Grand Rapids	Industrial Design Engineering Firm	30,000,000	91	900
189	U S Maintenance Corp	Oak Park	Janitorial Services	29,000,000	92	1,700
190	Morbark Industries Inc	Winn	Manufacture Portable and Stationary Chippers	27,000,000	92	500
191	Homemaker Shops Inc	Southfield	Gift Items and Bath Accessory Store	26,000,000	92	460
192	Crotty Corp	Quincy	Motor Vehicle Parts/Packing/Sealing Devices	25,000,000	92	450
193	Modern Plastics Corp	Benton Harbor	Manufacture Custom Made Plastic Injection Molding	25,000,000	92	450
194	United Steel and Wire Co	Battle Creek	Manufacturing Wire Shopping Baskets	25,000,000	92	450
195	Zehnders of Frankenmuth Inc	Frankenmuth	Restaurant, Motel, Golf Course and Shop	25,000,000	91	618
196	Hope Network Inc	Grand Rapids	Job Training and Placement	24,000,000	92	858
197	Central Quality Services Corp	Detroit	Rental of Linen and Uniforms	22,000,000	91	450
198	Fables Innkeepers Management Inc	Kentwood	Restaurant	20,000,000	91	600
199	Matvest	Dearborn	Manufacturing Electromechanical Components, Utility Contract Service	19,000,000	92	500
200	Unique Restaurant Corp	Bingham Farms	Restaurant and Delicatessen	18,000,000	92	500
201	Holly's Inc	Grand Rapids	Restaurant and Hotel	15,000,000	92	1,000
202	Grand Hotel Inc	Mackinac Island	Hotel and Food Place	13,000,000	92	450
203	Unibar Maintenance Services Inc	Ann Arbor	Janitorial Services	12,000,000	92	700
204	Machus Enterprises Inc	Birmingham	Restaurant	10,000,000	92	450
205	Quality Awning and Construction Co	Dearborn	Residential and Commercial Real Estate, Restoration Insurance	5,000,000	92	450
206	Glen's Markets No 5 Inc	Gaylord	Grocery Store	5,000,000	91	2,000

Source: Ward's Business Directory of U.S. Private & Public Companies: Published by Gale Research Co. (Detroit, Michigan).

Table XIX-8. Industrial Research and Development Expenditures in Michigan and the United States, by Source of Funds: 1963-1993

Year	Federal Funds (In Millions of Dollars)			Company Funds (In Millions of Dollars)		
	Michigan	U.S.	Michigan as a Percent(%) of U.S.	Michigan	U.S.	Michigan as a Percent(%) of U.S.
1963	65	7,270	0.89	797	5,360	14.87
1964	65	7,600	0.85	835	5,753	14.51
1965	67	7,740	0.86	895	6,445	13.89
1966	98	8,287	1.18	977	7,254	13.47
1967	115	8,388	1.39	952	8,032	11.85
1968	98	8,559	1.14	1,086	8,876	12.23
1969	83	8,619	0.96	1,228	9,856	12.46
1970	77	7,785	0.99	1,171	10,073	11.62
1971	78	7,671	1.02	1,338	10,643	12.57
1972	86	8,090	1.06	1,500	11,347	13.22
1973	56	8,222	0.68	1,832	12,699	14.43
1974	78	8,332	0.94	1,990	14,038	14.18
1975	114	8,765	1.3	1,858	14,776	12.57
1976	124	9,285	1.33	2,248	17,391	12.93
1977	144	10,545	1.37	2,614	19,362	13.50
1979	N.A.	12,460	N.A.	3,589	25,493	14.10
1981	N.A.	16,468	N.A.	4,272	35,362	12.10
1983	N.A.	20,215	N.A.	5,501	42,600	12.91
1985	85	26,830	0.32	5,890	51,439	11.45
1987	115	31,403	0.37	7,300	64,902	11.25
1989	99	31,366	0.32	8,369	70,233	11.92
1991	89	25,308	0.35	8,027	76,938	10.43
1993	153	22,813	0.67	9,771	95,521	10.23

Source: National Science Foundation, Research and Development in Industry (Washington, D.C.: annually). N.A. data not available.

Table XIX-9. Research and Development Expenditures and Expenditures as a Percentage of Gross State Product, by State: 1993

State	Total Research & Development Expenditures (In Millions of Dollars)	Research & Development Expenditures as a Percent(%) of Gross State Product
New Mexico	$2,752	7.7
Maryland	7,442	6.1
Massachusetts	9,468	5.5
Delaware	1,247	5.3
Michigan	10,778	5.2
Washington	5,422	4.1
California	33,721	4.1
New Jersey	9,182	3.9
Colorado	2,864	3.2
Pennsylvania	8,278	2.9
Vermont	343	2.7

Table XIX-9. Research and Development Expenditures and Expenditures as a Percentage of Gross State Product, by State: 1993 Continued

State	Total Research & Development Expenditures (In Millions of Dollars)	Research & Development Expenditures as a Percent(%) of Gross State Product
Connecticut	$2,809	2.7
Ohio	6,395	2.6
Minnesota	2,922	2.5
Alabama	1,967	2.3
Illinois	6,768	2.2
New York	10,975	2.1
Idaho	477	2.1
Rhode Island	484	2.1
Arizona	1,608	2.0
Indiana	2,560	2.0
Utah	753	1.9
Virginia	2,939	1.8
North Carolina	2,745	1.6
Wisconsin	1,851	1.6
Texas	6,966	1.6
New Hampshire	438	1.6
Missouri	1,789	1.5
Iowa	902	1.4
Florida	3,526	1.2
Oregon	774	1.2
Hawaii	380	1.1
Tennessee	1,214	1.0
South Carolina	713	0.9
Georgia	1,577	0.9
West Virginia	280	0.9
Oklahoma	533	0.8
Kansas	463	0.8
Nebraska	295	0.7
Mississippi	325	0.7
North Dakota	91	0.7
Arkansas	301	0.6
Nevada	218	0.6
Kentucky	429	0.5
Montana	85	0.5
Louisiana	470	0.5
Alaska	130	0.4
Maine	114	0.4
Wyoming	63	0.4
South Dakota	58	0.4

Source: National Science Foundation, Research and Development in Industry (Washington, D.C.: annually).

Table XIX-10. U.S. Utility Patents Issued to Residents of Michigan and the United States: 1966-1992

Year	Michigan	United States	Michigan as Percent(%) of U.S.	Year	Michigan	United States	Michigan as Percent(%) of U.S.
1966-1972	26,335	431,039	6.1	1982	1,741	33,896	5.1
1972	3,027	51,518	5.9	1983	1,677	32,871	5.1
1973	2,923	51,501	5.7	1984	2,058	38,367	5.4
1974	2,928	50,644	5.8	1985	2,066	39,555	5.2
1975	2,586	46,715	5.5	1986	2,080	38,126	5.5
1976	2,342	44,281	5.3	1987	2,211	43,518	5.1
1977	2,250	41,484	5.4	1988	2,196	40,496	5.4
1978	2,348	41,255	5.7	1989	2,619	50,185	5.2
1979	1,711	30,078	5.7	1990	2,529	47,393	5.3
1980	2,121	37,356	5.7	1991	2,812	51,183	5.5
1981	2,252	39,222	5.7	1992	2,833	52,252	5.4

Source: U.S. Patent and Trademark Office, Office of Information Systems/OEIPS, TAF Program: Patenting Trends in the United States-State/County Report: 1963-1992 (Washington, D.C.: 1993).

Table XIX-11. U.S. Utility Patents, by Industry in Michigan: 1992

Industry	Number of Patents	Industry	Number of Patents
Total, All Industries	**2,833**	Fabricated Metals	361
Food and Kindred Products	6	Machinery, Except Electrical	650
Textile Mill Products	11	Electrical/Electronic Machinery	303
Chemicals and Allied Products	375	Transportation Equipment	329
Petroleum and Natural Gas Extracting and Refining	12	Motor Vehicles and Equipment	186
Rubber and Miscellaneous Plastics Products	163	Professional & Scientific Instruments	237
Stone/Clay/Glass/Concrete Products	70	All Other Industries	290
Primary Metals	28		

Source: U.S. Patent and Trademark Office, Office of Information Systems/OEIPS,TAF Program: Patenting Trends in the United States-State/County Report: 1963-1992 (Washington, D.C.: 1993).

Table XIX-12. Number of Inventors and Number of U.S. Utility Patents, Ranked by State: 1993

Rank	State	Number of Inventors	Rank	State	Number of Patents
1	California	2,882	1	California	8,170
2	New York	1,148	2	New York	4,691
3	Florida	918	3	Texas	3,390
4	Texas	908	4	New Jersey	2,913
5	Illinois	706	5	**Michigan**	**2,875**
6	**Michigan**	**647**	6	Illinois	2,846
7	New Jersey	605	7	Pennsylvania	2,677
8	Pennsylvania	590	8	Ohio	2,529
9	Ohio	519	9	Massachusetts	2,210
10	Massachusetts	473	10	Florida	1,777
11	Washington	365	11	Minnesota	1,544
12	Colorado	363	12	Connecticut	1,544
13	Minnesota	334	13	Wisconsin	1,139
14	Connecticut	325	14	Maryland	999
15	Maryland	324	15	Indiana	972
16	Arizona	308	16	Colorado	910
17	Virginia	291	17	North Carolina	908
18	North Carolina	278	18	Washington	900
19	Georgia	260	19	Virginia	875
20	Wisconsin	253	20	Arizona	848
21	Louisiana	233	21	Georgia	705
22	Oregon	232	22	Missouri	632
23	Utah	213	23	Oklahoma	595
24	Indiana	199	24	Oregon	588
25	Missouri	191	25	Tennessee	554
26	Oklahoma	191	26	Delaware	507
27	Tennessee	183	27	Louisiana	431
28	South Carolina	154	28	South Carolina	423
29	Nevada	114	29	Utah	419
30	Alabama	114	30	Iowa	366
31	New Mexico	112	31	New Hampshire	363
32	Nebraska	88	32	Idaho	332
33	Kansas	88	33	Kentucky	277
34	Idaho	83	34	Alabama	271
35	Kentucky	82	35	Kansas	242

Table XIX-12. Number of Inventors and Number of U.S. Utility Patents, Ranked by State: 1993 Continued

Rank	State	Number of Inventors		Rank	State	Number of Patents
36	New Hampshire	82		36	New Mexico	233
37	Montana	79		37	Rhode Island	219
38	Iowa	78		38	West Virginia	172
39	Mississippi	74		39	Nebraska	169
40	Rhode Island	64		40	Nevada	139
41	Hawaii	63		41	Vermont	131
42	Maine	61		42	Arkansas	114
43	Arkansas	55		43	Maine	114
44	Delaware	47		44	Mississippi	102
45	North Dakota	42		45	Montana	88
46	Alaska	38		46	Hawaii	80
47	Vermont	36		47	North Dakota	60
48	West Virginia	32		48	Alaska	50
49	South Dakota	31		49	Wyoming	35
50	Wyoming	21		50	South Dakota	32

Source: U.S. Patent and Trademark Office, Office of Information Systems/OEIPS, TAF Program, Independent Inventors by State by Year Utility Patents Report January 1975-December 1993 (Washington, D.C.: 1994).

Table XIX-13. Number of Utility Patents and Number of Inventors in Michigan, by County: 1992

County	Number of Patent Grants	Number of Inventors	County	Number of Patent Grants	Number of Inventors
Alger	1	1	Leelanau	1	3
Allegan	12	29	Lenawee	23	36
Alpena	1	2	Livingston	27	45
Antrim	1	3	Macomb	235	391
Arenac	4	7	Manistee	5	5
Barry	4	10	Marquette	2	3
Bay	18	39	Mason	1	---
Berrien	51	90	Mecosta	5	7
Branch	2	4	Menominee	1	1
Calhoun	25	39	Midland	277	394
Cass	13	14	Monroe	21	32
Charlevoix	3	6	Montcalm	8	9
Cheboygan	1	2	Montmorency	1	2
Chippewa	1	1	Muskegon	20	37
Clare	3	3	Newaygo	---	2
Clinton	4	5	Oakland	716	1,110
Crawford	1	1	Oceana	6	8
Delta	2	4	Ogemaw	1	1
Dickinson	1	3	Ontonagon	1	1
Eaton	13.5	22.5	Osceola	5	9
Emmet	2	2	Oscoda	1	1
Genesee	84	121	Otsego	1	1
Gladwin	8	11	Ottawa	122	237
Grand Traverse	11	19	Presque Isle	3	4
Gratiot	6	6	Saginaw	40	69
Hillsdale	6	7	St. Clair	27	43
Houghton	10	16	St. Joseph	14	13
Huron	1	3	Sanilac	7	9
Ingham	57.5	80.5	Shiawassee	9	12
Ionia	4	6	Tuscola	13	19
Iosco	2	2	Van Buren	8	12
Isabella	8	15	Washtenaw	172	333
Jackson	45	56	Wayne	416	606
Kalamazoo	90	107	Wexford	8	22
Kent	112	213	Counties Not Available	11	12
Lapeer	16	26			

Source: U.S. Patent and Trademark Office, Office of Information Systems (Washington, D.C.).

Table XIX-14. Number of Scientific Workers in Michigan, by County: 1990

County	Total Science Workers	Total Science Workers as (%) of Total Employment	Engineers	Scientists	Technicians exc. Health
Alcona	83	2.5	11	14	58
Alger	74	2.3	16	12	46
Allegan	1,218	2.9	348	209	661
Alpena	312	2.5	39	44	229
Antrim	130	1.8	38	19	73
Arenac	73	1.4	23	4	46
Baraga	63	2.3	9	16	38
Barry	719	3.2	178	100	441
Bay	1,740	3.6	544	249	947
Benzie	63	1.3	26	6	31
Berrien	3,136	4.3	979	640	1,517
Branch	317	1.8	95	47	175
Calhoun	2,144	3.7	616	469	1,059
Cass	626	2.7	171	84	371
Charlevoix	288	3.0	102	51	135
Cheboygan	152	1.9	36	19	97
Chippewa	221	1.8	41	30	150
Clare	206	2.6	42	23	141
Clinton	1,241	4.3	302	288	651
Crawford	123	2.6	20	20	83
Delta	372	2.5	100	66	206
Dickinson	366	3.2	179	15	172
Eaton	2,175	4.6	628	479	1,068
Emmet	218	1.8	53	34	131
Genesee	6,697	3.7	2,918	960	2,819
Gladwin	171	2.5	68	13	90
Gogebic	80	1.2	13	28	39
Grand Traverse	1,072	3.4	314	151	607
Gratiot	339	2.1	97	39	203
Hillsdale	405	2.2	151	28	226
Houghton	608	4.7	140	134	334
Huron	237	1.7	40	31	166
Ingham	7,961	5.7	1,428	2,140	4,393
Ionia	596	2.5	137	80	379
Iosco	211	2.2	42	24	145
Iron	128	2.8	21	42	65
Isabella	730	3.0	107	161	462
Jackson	2,373	3.7	991	296	1,086
Kalamazoo	5,889	5.3	1,276	1,791	2,822
Kalkaska	121	2.3	20	13	88
Kent	8,788	3.5	2,944	1,519	4,325
Keweenaw	19	3.8	4	0	15

Table XIX-14. Number of Scientific Workers in Michigan, by County: 1990 Continued

County	Total Science Workers	Total Science Workers as (%) of Total Employment	Engineers	Scientists	Technicians exc. Health
Lake	41	1.8	10	5	26
Lapeer	1,179	3.6	490	77	612
Leelanau	215	2.8	59	38	118
Lenawee	1,038	2.6	359	145	534
Livingston	3,855	6.6	1,600	678	1,577
Luce	45	2.2	5	23	17
Mackinac	48	1.2	12	13	23
Macomb	24,040	6.8	9,260	3,452	11,328
Manistee	168	2.1	42	37	89
Marquette	882	3.1	215	146	521
Mason	245	2.4	55	48	142
Mecosta	456	3.0	46	33	377
Menominee	240	2.2	90	30	120
Midland	4,104	11.9	1,453	1,395	1,256
Missaukee	108	2.3	43	16	49
Monroe	2,017	3.3	836	287	894
Montcalm	324	1.6	122	39	163
Montmorency	40	1.5	0	10	30
Muskegon	2,366	3.6	794	231	1,341
Newaygo	425	2.8	112	66	247
Oakland	42,377	7.6	18,879	8,398	15,100
Oceana	194	2.2	43	19	132
Ogemaw	94	1.6	31	3	60
Ontonagon	94	2.7	20	14	60
Osceola	167	2.2	56	31	80
Oscoda	51	2.0	0	17	34
Otsego	231	2.9	32	67	132
Ottawa	4,058	4.2	1,573	520	1,965
Presque Isle	112	2.3	33	25	54
Roscommon	118	1.9	15	30	73
Saginaw	3,189	3.7	1,353	513	1,323
St. Clair	2,136	3.3	788	252	1,096
St. Joseph	730	2.8	248	54	428
Sanilac	314	2.0	71	25	218
Schoolcraft	61	2.1	18	14	29
Shiawassee	923	2.9	358	88	477
Tuscola	430	1.9	171	53	206
Van Buren	1,072	3.6	273	132	667
Washtenaw	13,528	8.9	3,655	3,270	6,603
Wayne	38,596	4.6	13,716	7,461	17,419
Wexford	256	2.4	63	44	149
Michigan	**203,052**	**4.9**	**72,306**	**38,187**	**92,559**

Source: U.S. 1990 Census of Population, Social and Economic Characteristics, Michigan (Washington, D.C.: decennial).

NOTE: The multipliers presented in Table XIX-15 were generated to express firm/supplier relationships that exist at the statewide level. Successful application of the multipliers at the sub-state level involves two related issues. First, the geographic unit of analysis should be an economically cohesive area, such as a Metropolitan Statistical Area (MSA) or economic planning region. Applying the multipliers to a single county or city, rather than regionally, is likely to substantially *overstate* the impact of a project because of economic "leakages" to adjacent areas. In an area with extensive cross-county commuting and economic links, a sizable proportion of supply, materials, and worker requirements are likely to be met from neighboring counties.

Secondly, it is important for the user to judge, even in broad terms, whether a specific project will generate economic effects that are greatly different regionally and statewide. For example, the economic linkages involved in a public construction project may be roughly similar statewide and in a sub-state region. On the other hand, the effects of the opening or closing of a manufacturing facility may be very different statewide versus locally. The firm/supplier network may be much more extensive statewide than regionally. In Michigan, this is certainly true of the auto industry, where an assembly plant in one area will draw from suppliers throughout the state. In this case, application of the statewide multipliers to a sub-state area is inappropriate (the exception would be a very large economic region such as all of Southeast Michigan). The analyst should modify the statewide relationship based on knowledge of local conditions.

Another important caution involves the potential for overestimation of the effects of a plant or facility shutdown. The multipliers do not reflect the income maintenance programs that, at least in the short run, may mitigate the decline in household incomes. The analyst should adjust for the value of unemployment insurance, as well as severance pay and retirement benefits if these are made available to the displaced workers.

Users may wish to consult the publication from which this table is derived for an extensive set of practical examples of multiplier use. The source of this information is listed following the table. Users who wish to obtain multipliers specifically designed for a particular area should contact the Bureau of Economic Analysis in Washington, D.C. For a fee, the Bureau will develop sub-state multipliers down to the county level.

Table XIX-15. Output, Earnings, and Employment Multipliers for Michigan, by Industry: 1992

Industry	Final Demand Multipliers-1			Direct-Effect Multipliers-2	
	Output (Dollars)	Earnings (Dollars)	Employment (Number of Jobs)	Earnings (Dollars)	Employment (Number of Jobs)
Agriculture, Forestry, and Fisheries					
Agric. Products/Agric./Forestry/Fishery Services	1.7833	0.4433	35.1	2.0227	1.5571
Forestry and Fishery Products	1.3907	0.1655	9.7	4.3015	2.8744
Mining					
Coal mining	1.0000	0.0000	0.0	0.0000	0.0000
Crude petroleum and natural gas	1.4477	0.1922	7.4	1.9540	2.4041
Miscellaneous mining	2.1005	0.6123	23.1	2.0412	2.4836
Construction					
New construction	2.1913	0.7068	30.2	2.2622	2.4017
Maintenance and repair construction	2.1249	0.7839	31.7	1.8160	2.0795
Manufacturing					
Food and kindred products and tobacco	1.8095	0.3463	15.6	2.7893	3.5207
Textile mill products	1.8086	0.4338	17.2	2.1632	2.4775
Apparel	1.9003	0.5207	19.6	2.0166	2.5507
Paper and allied products	2.0237	0.4627	17.3	2.4461	2.9950
Printing and publishing	2.0789	0.6313	27.2	1.9957	2.1020
Chemicals and petroleum refining	1.8646	0.3814	13.5	2.6099	3.6920
Rubber and leather products	2.0897	0.5349	23.1	2.1968	2.1780
Lumber and wood products and furniture	2.1002	0.6155	25.1	2.2339	2.4543
Stone, clay, and glass products	2.0487	0.5704	21.4	2.1583	2.6170
Primary metal industries	2.1519	0.6099	21.7	2.3001	2.9811
Fabricated metal products	2.3508	0.7035	26.3	2.4326	2.8572
Machinery, except electrical	2.1657	0.7215	26.1	2.0200	2.5140
Electric and electronic equipment	2.1782	0.6437	24.7	2.2883	2.6706
Motor vehicles and equipment	2.4770	0.5631	19.3	3.8872	6.4247*
Transportation equipment, except motor vehicles	2.1356	0.6068	22.2	2.3016	2.8092

Table XIX-15. Output, Earnings, and Employment Multipliers for Michigan, by Industry: 1992 Continued

Industry	Final Demand Multipliers-1			Direct-Effect Multipliers-2	
	Output (Dollars)	Earnings (Dollars)	Employment (Number of Jobs)	Earnings (Dollars)	Employment (Number of Jobs)
Instruments and related products	1.9835	0.6288	25.1	1.9363	2.1917
Miscellaneous	2.0648	0.5597	24.5	2.3398	2.3571
**Transportation and public utilities **					
Transportation	1.8959	0.7181	28.8	1.6852	1.9438
Communication	1.5725	0.4777	18.1	1.6155	2.0005
Electric, gas, water, and sanitary services	1.5810	0.2116	7.5	2.5793	3.6638
Wholesale and retail trade					
Wholesale trade	1.7576	0.6537	24.2	1.5886	2.0117
Retail trade	1.9514	0.7817	48.7	1.6056	1.4420
Finance, Insurance, and Real Estate					
Finance	1.9620	0.7142	31.4	1.8422	2.0065
Insurance	2.2135	0.8286	33.8	2.0020	2.3495
Real estate	1.2046	0.0793	3.7	5.4688	4.6981
Services					
Hotels and lodging places and amusements	1.8605	0.5745	38.3	1.8490	1.5260
Personal services	1.8953	0.7571	50.0	1.5949	1.3903
Business services	1.9725	0.8518	36.5	1.6153	1.7696
Eating and drinking places	1.9395	0.5800	49.9	1.8537	1.3398
Health services	2.0127	0.9067	39.2	1.5110	1.6294
Miscellaneous services	2.0881	0.7281	42.0	1.8223	1.5856
Households	1.0659	0.3317	17.5	----	----

--- No data. * Reflects final assembly plants. Parts or office facility multiplier would resemble other manufacturing multipliers. **Includes Federal Government Enterprises. Source: Bureau of Economic Analysis, Regional Multipliers: A User Handbook for the Regional Input-Output Modeling System, RIMSII (Washington, D.C.).

The multipliers in this table are presented in two different formats because the starting data available to users for the multiplier analysis will vary.

1). **Final Demand Multipliers:** These are designed for users who know the dollar value of a new project or export contract. For example, a user may wish to analyze the effects of a $100 million new construction project in the state. The multiplier table shows the Output, Earnings and Employment multipliers for new construction. Applying these multipliers to the $100 million figure indicates that the project will: (A) Raise state output by a total of $219.1 million ($100 million x 2.1913), and (B) Increase household earnings by a total of $70.7 million ($100 million x 0.7068).

Computation of the employment effect is more complex. The Final Demand Employment multiplier is per $1 million dollars, whereas the Final Demand Output and Earnings multipliers apply to each dollar. Also the Employment multiplier is based on 1989 dollars, so to properly calculate the employment effect, the current value of the project needs to be inflation adjusted to a 1989 base. Using the Detroit area Consumer Price Index, $100 million in 1995 dollars translates into $82.3 million in 1989 dollars. Multiplying 82.3 times the new construction employment multiplier of 30.2 yields an employment figure of 2,485.

2). **Direct Effects Multipliers:** These are designed for cases where the initial number of jobs or amount of earnings is known. For example, the user may know that a new metal parts facility will employ 100 workers with an annual payroll of $3 million. Using the Direct Effect multipliers for Fabricated Metal Products, the total employment impact of the new facility is calculated at 243 jobs (100 x 2.4326) and the total earnings impact at $8.57 million ($3 million x 2.8572).

Table XIX-16. Units, Employment, and Wages by Size of Firm in Michigan, by Industry Group: 1st Qtr 1994

Industry/ Employment Range	Units	Employment	Total Wages	Average Weekly Wage (A.W.W.)
Total, All Industries				
0-4	109,505	182,348	$987,079,115	$416
5-9	38,440	251,252	1,267,408,605	388
10-19	24,697	328,403	1,784,789,952	418
20-49	16,769	503,167	2,870,564,139	439
50-99	5,901	402,314	2,417,127,545	462
100-249	3,434	511,582	3,245,924,159	488
250-499	933	315,409	2,305,849,032	562
500-999	394	263,649	2,086,139,477	609
1000+	255	587,923	7,087,126,293	927
Total	**200,328**	**3,346,048**	**24,052,008,312**	**553**
Agriculture/Forestry/Fishing				
0-4	3,100	3,720	11,783,829	244
5-9	743	4,737	16,027,685	260
10-19	455	5,680	20,669,259	280
20-49	226	5,934	22,755,542	295
50-99	53	3,353	12,885,889	296
100-249	7	651	2,254,612	266
250-499	4	1,271	8,687,986	526
500-999	C	C	C	C
1000+	0	0	0	0
Total	**4,589**	**25,644**	**96,459,028**	**289**
Mining				
0-4	266	389	2,748,895	544
5-9	69	469	2,843,051	466
10-19	61	804	6,057,862	580
20-49	53	1,663	12,493,417	578
50-99	16	1,183	10,477,983	681
100-249	3	456	4,970,836	839
250-499	C	C	C	C
500-999	C	C	C	C
1000+	C	C	C	C
Total	**472**	**8,087**	**70,997,818**	**675**

Table XIX-16. Units, Employment, and Wages by Size of Firm in Michigan, by Industry Group: 1st Qtr 1994 Continued

Industry/ Employment Range	Units	Employment	Total Wages	Average Weekly Wage (A.W.W.)
Construction				
0-4	15,594	20,951	$104,584,169	$384
5-9	3,394	21,537	118,407,425	423
10-19	1,873	24,418	160,872,853	507
20-49	870	24,637	190,473,220	595
50-99	216	14,253	126,405,497	682
100-249	68	8,837	79,150,977	689
250-499	7	2,198	26,027,173	911
500-999	C	C	C	C
1000+	0	0	0	0
Total	**22,023**	**117,585**	**807,578,087**	**528**
Manufacturing				
0-4	5,282	9,599	57,418,054	460
5-9	2,759	18,539	115,839,069	481
10-19	2,815	38,889	279,112,459	552
20-49	2,799	86,256	666,677,760	595
50-99	1,308	91,032	726,709,573	614
100-249	977	147,703	1,248,966,053	650
250-499	362	124,090	1,175,975,008	729
500-999	137	90,623	1,058,664,951	899
1000+	121	323,623	5,161,084,598	1,227
Total	**16,560**	**930,353**	**10,490,447,524**	**867**
Transportation/Communication/ Utilities				
0-4	266	389	2,748,895	544
5-9	69	469	2,843,051	466
10-19	61	804	6,057,862	580
20-49	53	1,663	12,493,417	578
50-99	16	1,183	10,477,983	681
100-249	3	456	4,970,836	839
250-499	C	C	C	C
500-999	C	C	C	C
1000+	C	C	C	C
Total	**472**	**8,087**	**70,997,818**	**675**

Table XIX-16. Units, Employment, and Wages by Size of Firm in Michigan, by Industry Group: 1st Qtr 1994 Continued

Industry/ Employment Range	Units	Employment	Total Wages	Average Weekly Wage (A.W.W.)
Wholesale Trade				
0-4	10,939	16,986	$167,140,892	$757
5-9	3,302	21,613	174,213,651	620
10-19	2,267	30,337	248,009,079	629
20-49	1,460	43,699	367,958,540	648
50-99	401	27,605	255,100,317	711
100-249	207	30,003	281,759,250	722
250-499	36	11,810	110,765,830	721
500-999	13	8,615	125,233,560	1,118
1000+	6	8,904	111,106,661	960
Total	**18,631**	**199,572**	**1,841,287,779**	**710**
Retail Trade				
0-4	19,390	38,145	110,433,775	223
5-9	10,462	69,582	196,580,435	217
10-19	7,177	95,383	277,672,295	224
20-49	5,363	163,095	479,684,322	226
50-99	1,873	125,736	428,199,356	262
100-249	784	113,376	396,148,219	269
250-499	129	44,807	145,909,087	250
500-999	91	60,550	200,059,824	254
1000+	11	22,702	68,383,403	232
Total	**45,280**	**733,375**	**2,303,070,716**	**242**
Finance/Insurance/ Real Estate				
0-4	9,355	16,268	107,862,453	510
5-9	2,989	19,395	115,643,045	459
10-19	1,773	23,539	154,862,032	506
20-49	994	29,876	227,965,651	587
50-99	311	21,103	165,493,637	603
100-249	160	24,823	195,529,217	606
250-499	48	16,471	152,319,685	711
500-999	21	13,931	122,021,418	674
1000+	12	29,153	238,262,946	629
Total	**15,663**	**194,558**	**1,479,960,084**	**585**

Table XIX-16. Units, Employment, and Wages by Size of Firm in Michigan, by Industry Group: 1st Qtr 1994 Continued

Industry/ Employment Range	Units	Employment	Total Wages	Average Weekly Wage (A.W.W.)
Services				
0-4	10,939	16,986	$167,140,892	$757
5-9	3,302	21,613	174,213,651	620
10-19	2,267	30,337	248,009,079	629
20-49	1,460	43,699	367,958,540	648
50-99	401	27,605	255,100,317	711
100-249	207	30,003	281,759,250	722
250-499	36	11,810	110,765,830	721
500-999	13	8,615	125,233,560	1,118
1000+	6	8,904	111,106,661	960
Total	**18,631**	**199,572**	**1,841,287,779**	**710**

Source: Michigan Employment Security Commission, Research and Statistics (Detroit, Michigan: quarterly).   C=data withheld due to confidentiality restrictions.

Table XIX-17. Number of Units, Employment, and Average Weekly Wage by Size of Firm in Michigan, by County: 1st Qtr 1994

County/ Employment Range	Units	Employment	A.W.W.	County/ Employment Range	Units	Employment	A.W.W.
Michigan				**Allegan**			
0	28,157	C	$C	0	199	C	$C
1-4	81,348	175,472	416.53	1-4	623	1,349	312.89
5-9	38,440	251,252	388.03	5-9	321	2,052	300.86
10-19	24,697	328,403	418.06	10-19	183	2,336	294.39
20-49	16,769	503,167	438.85	20-49	113	3,406	406.18
50-99	5,901	402,314	462.16	50-99	37	2,442	379.41
100-249	3,434	511,582	488.07	100-249	27	4,199	494.9
250-499	932	314,959	562.24	250-499	7	2,358	550.99
500-999	394	263,649	608.66	500-999	3	2,091	487.16
1000+	255	587,923	927.27	1000+	3	6,694	592.76
Total	**200,327**	**3,345,597**	**552.93**	**Total**	**1,516**	**26,953**	**460.44**
Alcona				**Alpena**			
0	60	C	C	0	116	C	C
1-4	84	181	220.79	1-4	347	770	251.04
5-9	26	156	226.35	5-9	160	1,053	249.27
10-19	17	225	283.71	10-19	109	1,458	311.69
20-49	10	331	377.76	20-49	52	1,584	358.89
50-99	0	0	0	50-99	19	1,225	364
100-249	0	0	0	100-249	8	1,273	400.59
250-499	0	0	0	250-499	4	1,588	710.69
500-999	0	0	0	500-999	0	0	0
1000+	0	0	0	1000+	0	0	0
Total	**197**	**900**	**294.14**	**Total**	**815**	**8,966**	**397.85**
Alger				**Antrim**			
0	59	C	C	0	100	C	C
1-4	96	177	235.89	1-4	233	495	263.09
5-9	36	258	190.97	5-9	76	483	256.58
10-19	21	281	319.14	10-19	33	418	279.58
20-49	12	317	210.31	20-49	20	569	332.89
50-99	C	C	C	50-99	3	216	307.31
100-249	C	C	C	100-249	4	519	544.99
250-499	C	C	C	250-499	C	C	C
500-999	0	0	0	500-999	0	0	0
1000+	0	0	0	1000+	0	0	0
Total	**228**	**1,871**	**412.03**	**Total**	**470**	**3,212**	**310.86**

Table XIX-17. Number of Units, Employment, and Average Weekly Wage by Size of Firm in Michigan, by County: 1st Qtr 1994 Continued

County/ Employment Range	Units	Employment	A.W.W.	County/ Employment Range	Units	Employment	A.W.W.
Arenac				Bay			
0	74	C	$C	0	268	C	$C
1-4	135	312	232.12	1-4	904	1,991	298.63
5-9	70	452	227.09	5-9	484	3,243	295.66
10-19	25	345	259.82	10-19	289	3,797	333.09
20-49	18	508	404.37	20-49	184	5,373	360.81
50-99	6	426	328.57	50-99	64	4,350	372.8
100-249	C	C	C	100-249	26	4,034	399.37
250-499	C	C	C	250-499	3	1,013	641.65
500-999	0	0	0	500-999	C	C	C
1000+	0	0	0	1000+	3	4,650	1026.59
Total	**331**	**2,850**	**288.21**	**Total**	**2,227**	**29,992**	**475.95**
Baraga				Benzie			
0	31	C	C	0	90	C	C
1-4	88	189	291.60	1-4	158	322	237.05
5-9	39	256	287.54	5-9	55	334	236.67
10-19	27	366	318.37	10-19	23	311	306.18
20-49	12	356	222.7	20-49	21	669	283.07
50-99	C	C	C	50-99	4	323	361.39
100-249	C	C	C	100-249	C	C	C
250-499	C	C	C	250-499	C	C	C
500-999	0	0	0	500-999	0	0	0
1000+	0	0	0	1000+	0	0	0
Total	**202**	**1,967**	**314.71**	**Total**	**353**	**2,390**	**278.58**
Barry				Berrien			
0	89	C	C	0	472	C	C
1-4	346	789	281.93	1-4	1,419	3,202	328.25
5-9	114	760	281.26	5-9	687	4,495	334.71
10-19	77	907	309.85	10-19	419	5,554	351.96
20-49	38	1,173	320.71	20-49	303	8,923	373.37
50-99	8	533	331.95	50-99	108	7,225	384.7
100-249	10	1,381	464.89	100-249	57	8,692	413.76
250-499	3	1,066	512.54	250-499	18	5,765	475.80
500-999	C	C	C	500-999	6	4,093	468.48
1000+	0	0	0	1000+	4	6,823	1192.73
Total	**687**	**7,774**	**393.69**	**Total**	**3,493**	**54,945**	**492.65**

Table XIX-17. Number of Units, Employment, and Average Weekly Wage by Size of Firm in Michigan, by County: 1st Qtr 1994 Continued

County/ Employment Range	Units	Employment	A.W.W.	County/ Employment Range	Units	Employment	A.W.W.
Branch				**Charlevoix**			
0	68	C	$C	0	134	C	$C
1-4	331	720	310.38	1-4	308	663	267.49
5-9	166	1,084	291.21	5-9	107	658	291.61
10-19	83	1,128	326.4	10-19	51	702	289.45
20-49	52	1,453	361.37	20-49	41	1,249	323.98
50-99	17	1,161	371.42	50-99	12	857	451.65
100-249	15	2,100	393.82	100-249	7	1,135	624.05
250-499	C	C	C	250-499	C	C	C
500-999	0	0	0	500-999	C	C	C
1000+	0	0	0	1000+	0	0	0
Total	**734**	**8,295**	**362.65**	**Total**	**663**	**6,812**	**417.37**
Calhoun				**Cheboygan**			
0	247	C	C	0	286	C	C
1-4	950	2,131	335.61	1-4	311	708	273.1
5-9	547	3,621	323.89	5-9	109	673	298.01
10-19	376	4,963	334.77	10-19	48	621	300.6
20-49	211	6,394	370.09	20-49	31	894	313.31
50-99	74	4,950	429.58	50-99	9	610	302.35
100-249	61	9,165	416.83	100-249	5	654	269.51
250-499	13	4,986	703.66	250-499	C	C	C
500-999	7	4,356	442.70	500-999	0	0	0
1000+	6	9,867	739.77	1000+	0	0	0
Total	**2,492**	**50,477**	**487.57**	**Total**	**800**	**4,515**	**304.77**
Cass				**Chippewa**			
0	102	C	C	0	178	C	C
1-4	288	643	284.30	1-4	344	738	281.65
5-9	137	889	284.16	5-9	138	902	265.49
10-19	66	827	318.3	10-19	72	943	294.06
20-49	37	1,088	389.48	20-49	57	1,714	271.67
50-99	18	1,200	405.07	50-99	21	1,393	323.60
100-249	9	1,315	496.21	100-249	8	1,135	221.96
250-499	3	1,164	606.98	250-499	C	C	C
500-999	0	0	0	500-999	0	0	0
1000+	0	0	0	1000+	C	C	C
Total	**660**	**7,136**	**416.29**	**Total**	**820**	**8,287**	**282.90**

Table XIX-17. Number of Units, Employment, and Average Weekly Wage by Size of Firm in Michigan, by County: 1st Qtr 1994 Continued

County/ Employment Range	Units	Employment	A.W.W.	County/ Employment Range	Units	Employment	A.W.W.
Clare				**Delta**			
0	87	C	$C	0	141	C	$C
1-4	230	502	242.89	1-4	428	973	250.07
5-9	113	749	213.50	5-9	196	1,294	269.64
10-19	48	663	286.17	10-19	123	1,627	305.01
20-49	34	1,030	330.52	20-49	78	2,310	312.71
50-99	15	969	281.54	50-99	12	737	321.98
100-249	5	828	314.21	100-249	12	1,496	320.17
250-499	C	C	C	250-499	3	1,284	315.23
500-999	C	C	C	500-999	0	0	0
1000+	0	0	0	1000+	C	C	C
Total	**534**	**5,748**	**283.94**	**Total**	**994**	**11,077**	**393.15**
Clinton				**Dickinson**			
0	94	C	C	0	90	C	C
1-4	340	724	316.80	1-4	326	741	280.97
5-9	182	1,183	321.34	5-9	156	1,019	316.24
10-19	105	1,359	327.35	10-19	94	1,260	335.24
20-49	57	1,711	325.01	20-49	69	2,027	344.36
50-99	15	1,040	320.17	50-99	23	1,450	394.13
100-249	8	1,207	357.77	100-249	11	1,380	309.91
250-499	C	C	C	250-499	C	C	C
500-999	C	C	C	500-999	C	C	C
1000+	0	0	0	1000+	0	0	0
Total	**805**	**9,226**	**400.51**	**Total**	**773**	**10,004**	**415.79**
Crawford				**Eaton**			
0	60	C	C	0	171	C	C
1-4	113	235	229.07	1-4	171	20	357.76
5-9	63	398	254.19	5-9	486	1,030	328.65
10-19	27	350	260.25	10-19	166	2,148	325.63
20-49	16	487	391.62	20-49	90	2,708	417.45
50-99	7	482	263.94	50-99	34	2,397	368.81
100-249	4	549	390.45	100-249	21	3,166	382.54
250-499	C	C	C	250-499	7	2,456	522.45
500-999	0	0	0	500-999	C	C	C
1000+	0	0	0	1000+	0	0	0
Total	**291**	**2,944**	**318.6**	**Total**	**1,228**	**17,121**	**446.31**

Table XIX-17. Number of Units, Employment, and Average Weekly Wage by Size of Firm in Michigan, by County: 1st Qtr 1994 Continued

County/ Employment Range	Units	Employment	A.W.W.	County/ Employment Range	Units	Employment	A.W.W.
Emmet				**Gogebic**			
0	164	C	$C	0	57	C	$ C
1-4	464	1,038	298.82	1-4	201	441	227.15
5-9	231	1,544	296.82	5-9	78	517	249.30
10-19	109	1,440	333.19	10-19	56	742	269.75
20-49	61	1,890	323.2	20-49	27	822	242.85
50-99	16	1,073	360.57	50-99	13	988	246.72
100-249	12	1,460	360.4	100-249	5	759	310.28
250-499	C	C	C	250-499	C	C	C
500-999	C	C	C	500-999	0	0	0
1000+	C	C	C	1000+	0	0	0
Total	**1,060**	**10,958**	**359.23**	**Total**	**439**	**4,816**	**270.33**
Genesee				**Grand Traverse**			
0	926	C	C	0	354	C	C
1-4	2,895	6,505	367.64	1-4	1,061	2,337	374.77
5-9	1,612	10,473	351.78	5-9	593	3,925	342.67
10-19	1,005	13,346	372.31	10-19	329	4,393	416.68
20-49	641	18,684	381.75	20-49	209	6,316	405.96
50-99	217	14,625	376.98	50-99	61	4,190	351.97
100-249	111	16,075	417.59	100-249	31	4,404	382.3
250-499	21	7,010	463.91	250-499	5	1,742	387.77
500-999	10	6,945	421.22	500-999	4	2,495	368.88
1000+	14	45,900	1198.87	1000+	C	C	C
Total	**7,452**	**139,768**	**656.03**	**Total**	**2,648**	**32,764**	**382.25**
Gladwin				**Gratiot**			
0	60	C	C	0	110	C	C
1-4	145	311	229.92	1-4	299	681	216.07
5-9	68	449	265.11	5-9	149	959	270.01
10-19	36	504	351.8	10-19	74	983	314.14
20-49	18	503	367.5	20-49	62	1,912	328.52
50-99	7	433	345	50-99	21	1,638	334.75
100-249	6	991	434.01	100-249	10	1,521	532.65
250-499	0	0	0	250-499	3	940	415.36
500-999	0	0	0	500-999	3	1,557	586.61
1000+	0	0	0	1000+	0	0	0
Total	**340**	**3,197**	**354.47**	**Total**	**731**	**10,199**	**393.2**

Table XIX-17. Number of Units, Employment, and Average Weekly Wage by Size of Firm in Michigan, by County: 1st Qtr 1994 Continued

County/ Employment Range	Units	Employment	A.W.W.	County/ Employment Range	Units	Employment	A.W.W.
Hillsdale				**Ingham**			
0	91	C	$C	0	775	C	C
1-4	334	717	294.87	1-4	2,521	5,638	444.5
5-9	176	1,122	302.68	5-9	1,351	8,897	405.92
10-19	93	1,242	357.11	10-19	847	11,393	422.96
20-49	47	1,416	378.75	20-49	598	17,767	390.26
50-99	13	910	418.29	50-99	215	14,565	384.24
100-249	14	2,212	497.12	100-249	110	17,073	419.87
250-499	8	2,782	455.84	250-499	30	9,278	478.47
500-999	C	C	C	500-999	11	7,433	421.56
1000+	0	0	0	1000+	7	25,269	868.82
Total	**777**	**10,989**	**423.67**	**Total**	**6,465**	**117,530**	**512.68**
Houghton				**Ionia**			
0	115	C	C	0	96	C	C
1-4	349	788	247.71	1-4	339	802	281.87
5-9	159	1,019	246.88	5-9	168	1,102	282.64
10-19	97	1,306	246.61	10-19	111	1,477	316.79
20-49	56	1,614	255.93	20-49	60	1,670	316.12
50-99	17	1,144	392.51	50-99	22	1,510	378.71
100-249	10	1,544	318.45	100-249	7	959	493.93
250-499	C	C	C	250-499	3	952	472.39
500-999	0	0	0	500-999	C	C	C
1000+	0	0	0	1000+	0	0	0
Total	**804**	**7,749**	**291.9**	**Total**	**808**	**9,520**	**371.32**
Huron				**Iosco**			
0	156	C	C	0	133	C	C
1-4	376	811	293.13	1-4	265	567	240.32
5-9	168	1,086	264.54	5-9	126	801	248.74
10-19	95	1,225	307.65	10-19	66	886	319.85
20-49	49	1,305	412.77	20-49	31	982	297.6
50-99	20	1,404	383.9	50-99	7	483	479.35
100-249	14	2,028	380.01	100-249	5	568	260.96
250-499	3	974	463.99	250-499	C	C	C
500-999	C	C	C	500-999	C	C	C
1000+	0	0	0	1000+	0	0	0
Total	**882**	**9,443**	**376.95**	**Total**	**636**	**5,730**	**324.39**

Table XIX-17. Number of Units, Employment, and Average Weekly Wage by Size of Firm in Michigan, by County: 1st Qtr 1994 Continued

County/ Employment Range	Units	Employment	A.W.W.	County/ Employment Range	Units	Employment	A.W.W.
Iron				**Kalamazoo**			
0	84	C	$C	0	489	C	$C
1-4	158	372	245.45	1-4	1,745	3,766	381.95
5-9	63	396	228.46	5-9	1,052	6,989	372.73
10-19	41	543	408.05	10-19	728	9,683	402.03
20-49	14	415	272.09	20-49	514	15,608	425.48
50-99	4	289	336.53	50-99	194	13,000	375.05
100-249	C	C	C	100-249	94	14,033	416.88
250-499	0	0	0	250-499	27	9,032	490.41
500-999	0	0	0	500-999	9	6,689	611.11
1000+	0	0	0	1000+	6	19,422	802.76
Total	**366**	**2,227**	**292.27**	**Total**	**4,858**	**98,354**	**503.01**
Isabella				**Kalkaska**			
0	148	C	C	0	50	C	C
1-4	420	928	327.41	1-4	116	252	366.67
5-9	229	1,541	309.06	5-9	61	388	379.11
10-19	150	1,964	292.88	10-19	31	407	494.71
20-49	86	2,553	335.19	20-49	21	686	605.09
50-99	31	2,173	309.65	50-99	11	728	485.01
100-249	14	1,990	310.6	100-249	5	668	390.54
250-499	C	C	C	250-499	C	C	C
500-999	3	1,735	416.83	500-999	0	0	0
1000+	C	C	C	1000+	0	0	0
Total	**1,084**	**14,859**	**328.1**	**Total**	**296**	**3,437**	**464.28**
Jackson				**Kent**			
0	335	C	C	0	1,215	C	C
1-4	1,056	2,373	350.29	1-4	4,492	9,744	423.88
5-9	552	3,571	354.63	5-9	2,355	15,480	412.45
10-19	402	5,262	415.26	10-19	1,620	21,755	434.34
20-49	251	7,289	412.08	20-49	1,248	37,863	469.44
50-99	86	6,025	433.92	50-99	515	35,204	458.21
100-249	53	8,251	480.72	100-249	295	43,624	460.17
250-499	12	3,755	582	250-499	74	24,885	442.74
500-999	3	1,886	310.31	500-999	36	23,947	457.84
1000+	C	C	C	1000+	24	50,409	665.71
Total	**2,752**	**42,445**	**472.98**	**Total**	**11,874**	**263,374**	**492.38**

Table XIX-17. Number of Units, Employment, and Average Weekly Wage by Size of Firm in Michigan, by County: 1st Qtr 1994 Continued

County/ Employment Range	Units	Employment	A.W.W.	County/ Employment Range	Units	Employment	A.W.W.
Keweenaw				**Leelanau**			
0	14	C	$C	0	128	C	$C
1-4	26	57	216.17	1-4	232	505	303.91
5-9	5	39	273.22	5-9	67	447	322.06
10-19	C	C	C	10-19	37	503	271.31
20-49	C	C	C	20-49	19	580	270.5
50-99	0	0	0	50-99	C	C	C
100-249	0	0	0	100-249	4	608	267.43
250-499	0	0	0	250-499	C	C	C
500-999	0	0	0	500-999	0	0	0
1000+	0	0	0	1000+	0	0	0
Total	**48**	**147**	**235.44**	**Total**	**490**	**3,105**	**290.46**
Lake				**Lenawee**			
0	29	C	C	0	259	C	C
1-4	67	149	189.93	1-4	757	1,716	300.93
5-9	23	145	203.16	5-9	398	2,581	290.45
10-19	18	216	232.61	10-19	206	2,684	320.41
20-49	10	280	365.1	20-49	130	3,788	336.14
50-99	C	C	C	50-99	46	3,009	397.61
100-249	0	0	0	100-249	23	3,649	456.33
250-499	0	0	0	250-499	15	5,025	561.03
500-999	0	0	0	500-999	C	C	C
1000+	0	0	0	1000+	C	C	C
Total	**149**	**959**	**285.96**	**Total**	**1,837**	**25,680**	**469.07**
Lapeer				**Livingston**			
0	184	C	C	0	353	C	C
1-4	545	1,204	301.32	1-4	1,030	2,136	437.74
5-9	233	1,535	332.01	5-9	464	2,990	353.27
10-19	123	1,635	372.32	10-19	263	3,478	386.67
20-49	88	2,557	320.62	20-49	159	4,894	393.49
50-99	24	1,601	336.19	50-99	48	3,137	464.55
100-249	18	2,768	449.32	100-249	33	4,908	481.06
250-499	5	1,552	424.36	250-499	7	2,330	597.04
500-999	C	C	C	500-999	6	3,836	533.33
1000+	0	0	0	1000+	0	0	0
Total	**1,221**	**13,420**	**370.1**	**Total**	**2,363**	**27,762**	**451.88**

Table XIX-17. Number of Units, Employment, and Average Weekly Wage by Size of Firm in Michigan, by County: 1st Qtr 1994 Continued

County/ Employment Range	Units	Employment	A.W.W.	County/ Employment Range	Units	Employment	A.W.W.
Luce				**Manistee**			
0	45	C	$C	0	120	C	$C
1-4	81	183	257.86	1-4	237	506	257.98
5-9	19	133	297.39	5-9	102	657	262.33
10-19	14	175	227.7	10-19	57	731	296.32
20-49	10	361	239.81	20-49	31	931	309.83
50-99	0	0	0	50-99	3	233	364.23
100-249	0	0	0	100-249	5	727	512.89
250-499	C	C	C	250-499	C	C	C
500-999	0	0	0	500-999	0	0	0
1000+	0	0	0	1000+	0	0	0
Total	**170**	**1,147**	**346.04**	**Total**	**557**	**4,451**	**417.18**
Mackinac				**Marquette**			
0	221	C	C	0	202	C	C
1-4	159	325	239.53	1-4	650	1,406	295.73
5-9	62	405	259.67	5-9	331	2,177	308.48
10-19	23	296	239.98	10-19	198	2,622	306.1
20-49	13	364	263.46	20-49	108	3,255	285.16
50-99	4	238	277.19	50-99	41	2,908	355.86
100-249	C	C	C	100-249	9	1,206	299.74
250-499	C	C	C	250-499	4	1,259	479.39
500-999	0	0	0	500-999	C	C	C
1000+	0	0	0	1000+	C	C	C
Total	**484**	**2,294**	**244.78**	**Total**	**1,546**	**18,536**	**402.62**
Macomb				**Mason**			
0	2,190	C	C	0	102	C	C
1-4	5,746	13,013	423.88	1-4	262	585	273.31
5-9	3,020	19,831	420.84	5-9	133	881	297.75
10-19	2,025	26,837	455	10-19	73	964	311.37
20-49	1,439	43,196	455.17	20-49	35	1,008	334.8
50-99	471	31,933	506.68	50-99	14	958	292.07
100-249	251	36,211	492.65	100-249	11	1,810	409.3
250-499	68	22,360	686.07	250-499	4	1,459	541.13
500-999	32	21,604	761.2	500-999	0	0	0
1000+	19	48,701	1163.47	1000+	0	0	0
Total	**15,261**	**264,344**	**637.27**	**Total**	**634**	**7,674**	**374.27**

Table XIX-17. Number of Units, Employment, and Average Weekly Wage by Size of Firm in Michigan, by County: 1st Qtr 1994 Continued

County/ Employment Range	Units	Employment	A.W.W.	County/ Employment Range	Units	Employment	A.W.W.
Mecosta				**Missaukee**			
0	101	C	$C	0	45	C	$C
1-4	260	578	262.76	1-4	84	175	255.61
5-9	105	684	272.63	5-9	43	283	265.79
10-19	76	983	241.83	10-19	21	275	306.43
20-49	43	1,257	306.99	20-49	11	408	382.62
50-99	14	888	274.96	50-99	C	C	C
100-249	11	1,592	319.69	100-249	C	C	C
250-499	C	C	C	250-499	0	0	0
500-999	0	0	0	500-999	0	0	0
1000+	0	0	0	1000+	0	0	0
Total	**611**	**6,362**	**287.45**	**Total**	**208**	**1,552**	**328.12**
Menominee				**Monroe**			
0	70	C	C	0	279	C	C
1-4	186	412	293.28	1-4	795	1,745	336.05
5-9	101	638	301.7	5-9	456	2,955	308.72
10-19	58	746	286.48	10-19	224	2,889	384.19
20-49	44	1,344	336.8	20-49	147	4,376	380.07
50-99	12	846	328.17	50-99	44	2,990	434.55
100-249	12	2,023	369.23	100-249	27	4,163	448.61
250-499	3	1,091	477.09	250-499	5	1,879	728.39
500-999	0	0	0	500-999	4	2,654	514.22
1000+	0	0	0	1000+	3	4,902	1362.31
Total	**486**	**7,109**	**355.51**	**Total**	**1,984**	**28,565**	**589.93**
Midland				**Montcalm**			
0	185	C	C	0	143	C	C
1-4	643	1,361	346.3	1-4	406	886	316.61
5-9	316	2,082	348.42	5-9	214	1,386	275.29
10-19	195	2,571	377.15	10-19	103	1,318	293.42
20-49	118	3,600	384.86	20-49	59	1,742	325.56
50-99	40	2,643	437.94	50-99	10	702	407.5
100-249	29	4,287	440.41	100-249	16	2,558	327.27
250-499	4	1,351	439.64	250-499	4	1,540	525.97
500-999	C	C	C	500-999	C	C	C
1000+	3	12,203	915.24	1000+	C	C	C
Total	**1,534**	**30,696**	**602.19**	**Total**	**958**	**13,345**	**392.6**

Table XIX-17. Number of Units, Employment, and Average Weekly Wage by Size of Firm in Michigan, by County: 1st Qtr 1994 Continued

County/ Employment Range	Units	Employment	A.W.W.	County/ Employment Range	Units	Employment	A.W.W.
Montmorency				**Oakland**			
0	61	C	$C	0	4,920	C	$C
1-4	103	224	229.33	1-4	14,650	30,349	576.89
5-9	30	195	200.28	5-9	6,212	40,549	510.74
10-19	22	272	203.43	10-19	4,250	57,162	528.57
20-49	12	306	310.72	20-49	3,001	90,991	541.35
50-99	C	C	C	50-99	1,113	76,240	562.43
100-249	C	C	C	100-249	633	95,599	575.67
250-499	0	0	0	250-499	154	51,507	631.93
500-999	0	0	0	500-999	70	47,563	636.43
1000+	0	0	0	1000+	36	83,122	908.07
Total	**230**	**1,277**	**252.42**	**Total**	**35,039**	**574,164**	**617.38**
Muskegon				**Oceana**			
0	349	C	C	0	122	C	C
1-4	1,109	2,538	327.11	1-4	234	485	242.38
5-9	579	3,852	320.02	5-9	110	719	245.76
10-19	420	5,508	363.31	10-19	53	645	264.36
20-49	258	7,901	389.72	20-49	28	814	387.63
50-99	91	6,360	406.77	50-99	10	644	390.16
100-249	50	7,463	478.11	100-249	C	C	C
250-499	12	3,777	588.25	250-499	0	0	0
500-999	6	4,060	741.7	500-999	0	0	0
1000+	3	3,725	741.7	1000+	0	0	0
Total	**2,877**	**45,233**	**471.04**	**Total**	**558**	**3,556**	**325.77**
Newaygo				**Ogemaw**			
0	86	C	C	0	85	C	C
1-4	288	637	254.58	1-4	182	382	217.93
5-9	129	850	266.68	5-9	89	581	268
10-19	66	891	258.4	10-19	49	612	283.69
20-49	37	1,057	357.78	20-49	32	986	320.57
50-99	8	576	440.59	50-99	10	750	367.08
100-249	4	611	257.96	100-249	C	C	C
250-499	C	C	C	250-499	C	C	C
500-999	0	0	0	500-999	0	0	0
1000+	C	C	C	1000+	0	0	0
Total	**620**	**6,487**	**399.04**	**Total**	**450**	**3,877**	**305.41**

Table XIX-17. Number of Units, Employment, and Average Weekly Wage by Size of Firm in Michigan, by County: 1st Qtr 1994 Continued

County/ Employment Range	Units	Employment	A.W.W.	County/ Employment Range	Units	Employment	A.W.W.
Ontonagon				**Otsego**			
0	31	C	$C	0	97	C	$C
1-4	103	244	237.91	1-4	255	561	304.29
5-9	27	187	359	5-9	151	973	362.73
10-19	24	305	260.75	10-19	64	821	371.54
20-49	13	425	221.98	20-49	53	1,559	409.89
50-99	C	C	C	50-99	23	1,622	377.85
100-249	C	C	C	100-249	8	1,320	329.88
250-499	C	C	C	250-499	C	C	C
500-999	C	C	C	500-999	0	0	0
1000+	0	0	0	1000+	0	0	0
Total	**203**	**2,618**	**420.25**	**Total**	**653**	**7,375**	**372.07**
Osceola				**Ottawa**			
0	63	C	$C	0	481	C	$C
1-4	146	316	215.96	1-4	1,718	3,796	397.28
5-9	80	505	275.77	5-9	843	5,440	344.26
10-19	42	541	471.2	10-19	586	7,755	381.08
20-49	17	502	397.55	20-49	417	12,498	391.8
50-99	C	C	C	50-99	121	8,236	384.91
100-249	8	1,364	530.2	100-249	88	13,826	435.91
250-499	C	C	C	250-499	21	6,661	632.9
500-999	0	0	0	500-999	16	9,865	548.72
1000+	C	C	C	1000+	5	11,382	547.2
Total	**361**	**5,407**	**433.11**	**Total**	**4,296**	**79,646**	**456.69**
Oscoda				**Presque Isle**			
0	36	C	$C	0	93	C	$C
1-4	76	160	203.77	1-4	166	367	208.71
5-9	28	180	202.93	5-9	69	425	244.73
10-19	16	217	198.58	10-19	26	343	206.72
20-49	10	302	254.03	20-49	15	493	232.76
50-99	3	217	339.86	50-99	C	C	C
100-249	0	0	0	100-249	C	C	C
250-499	C	C	C	250-499	C	C	C
500-999	0	0	0	500-999	0	0	0
1000+	0	0	0	1000+	0	0	0
Total	**171**	**1,709**	**263.28**	**Total**	**374**	**2,270**	**323.84**

Table XIX-17. Number of Units, Employment, and Average Weekly Wage by Size of Firm in Michigan, by County: 1st Qtr 1994 Continued

County/Employment Range	Units	Employment	A.W.W.	County/Employment Range	Units	Employment	A.W.W.
Roscommon				**St. Joseph**			
0	131	C	$C	0	133	C	$C
1-4	230	483	207.29	1-4	437	968	294.44
5-9	95	629	253.53	5-9	257	1,627	310.13
10-19	47	616	238.97	10-19	140	1,781	326.78
20-49	25	872	262.06	20-49	93	2,883	372.91
50-99	11	724	238.29	50-99	37	2,547	413.62
100-249	3	452	334.35	100-249	27	3,637	468.16
250-499	0	0	0	250-499	9	3,264	659.15
500-999	0	0	0	500-999	3	1,806	753.94
1000+	0	0	0	1000+	0	0	0
Total	**542**	**3,816**	**253.48**	**Total**	**1,136**	**18,544**	**470.76**
Saginaw				**Sanilac**			
0	472	C	C	0	139	C	C
1-4	1,528	3,401	324.17	1-4	374	869	277.47
5-9	945	6,183	331.68	5-9	149	941	278.93
10-19	618	8,006	352.18	10-19	72	926	313.64
20-49	341	10,251	378.13	20-49	45	1,229	305.1
50-99	148	9,734	381.93	50-99	18	1,350	451.19
100-249	72	10,705	429.39	100-249	11	1,731	455.1
250-499	17	6,052	497.1	250-499	4	1,290	371.51
500-999	3	1,683	380.13	500-999	0	0	0
1000+	8	19,579	1096.67	1000+	0	0	0
Total	**4,152**	**75,863**	**572.1**	**Total**	**812**	**8,372**	**365.14**
St. Clair				**Schoolcraft**			
0	399	C	C	0	55	C	C
1-4	1,095	2,449	350.36	1-4	87	180	194.49
5-9	533	3,469	333.24	5-9	40	244	277.61
10-19	328	4,349	354.58	10-19	25	333	307.66
20-49	203	5,945	376.04	20-49	11	342	355.19
50-99	68	4,781	382.69	50-99	3	189	255.6
100-249	54	8,398	391.64	100-249	C	C	C
250-499	12	3,665	686.88	250-499	0	0	0
500-999	C	C	C	500-999	0	0	0
1000+	C	C	C	1000+	0	0	0
Total	**2,696**	**36,622**	**433.86**	**Total**	**222**	**1,463**	**345.39**

Table XIX-17. Number of Units, Employment, and Average Weekly Wage by Size of Firm in Michigan, by County: 1st Qtr 1994 Continued

County/ Employment Range	Units	Employment	A.W.W.	County/ Employment Range	Units	Employment	A.W.W.
Shiawassee				**Washtenaw**			
0	153	C	$C	0	898	C	$C
1-4	424	935	298.3	1-4	2,722	5,657	469.3
5-9	239	1,556	285.33	5-9	1,262	8,288	424.89
10-19	125	1,668	348.31	10-19	806	10,977	399.6
20-49	79	2,327	328.36	20-49	586	17,278	464.17
50-99	35	2,272	378.99	50-99	196	13,216	490.01
100-249	13	1,861	428.01	100-249	120	18,101	535.77
250-499	6	2,104	428.71	250-499	37	12,344	577.88
500-999	C	C	C	500-999	16	9,848	542
1000+	0	0	0	1000+	8	21,047	1041.06
Total	**1,075**	**13,666**	**366.4**	**Total**	**6,651**	**117,171**	**591.53**
Tuscola				**Wayne**			
0	127	C	C	0	4,239	C	C
1-4	394	869	255.95	1-4	12,908	28,133	418.78
5-9	162	1,086	257.15	5-9	6,010	39,367	415.53
10-19	97	1,284	300.97	10-19	4,235	56,753	443.27
20-49	54	1,589	309.93	20-49	3,048	91,810	461.54
50-99	18	1,221	373.78	50-99	1,097	74,955	503.16
100-249	10	1,475	362.02	100-249	661	97,117	553.92
250-499	4	1,477	562.19	250-499	202	69,415	611.88
500-999	0	0	0	500-999	99	68,825	736.33
1000+	0	0	0	1000+	81	179,478	966.31
Total	**866**	**9,014**	**355.48**	**Total**	**32,580**	**706,990**	**642.52**
Van Buren				**Wexford**			
0	188	C	C	0	86	C	C
1-4	536	1,151	297.87	1-4	294	636	457
5-9	217	1,370	257.3	5-9	136	897	303.05
10-19	141	1,867	293.81	10-19	93	1,203	315.55
20-49	86	2,509	364.37	20-49	65	1,845	417.2
50-99	29	1,992	399.66	50-99	19	1,356	322.75
100-249	13	1,698	317.8	100-249	13	2,138	343.21
250-499	5	1,858	558.64	250-499	5	1,901	478.8
500-999	C	C	C	500-999	C	C	C
1000+	0	0	0	1000+	0	0	0
Total	**1,216**	**13,110**	**397.83**	**Total**	**713**	**11,262**	**384.97**

Source: Michigan Employment Security Commission. C=data withheld due to confidentiality restrictions.

Table XIX-18. Incorporated Business Owners in Michigan, by County: 1990

County	Incorporated Self Employed	Percent(%) of Employment	County	Incorporated Self Employed	Percent(%) of Employment
Alcona	114	3.5	Lake	50	2.2
Alger	57	1.7	Lapeer	849	2.6
Allegan	877	2.1	Leelanau	294	3.8
Alpena	220	1.8	Lenawee	1,088	2.7
Antrim	297	4.1	Livingston	2,329	4.0
Arenac	147	2.7	Luce	39	1.9
Baraga	85	3.1	Mackinac	160	4.1
Barry	428	1.9	Macomb	9,533	2.7
Bay	1,172	2.4	Manistee	198	2.5
Benzie	128	2.6	Marquette	696	2.4
Berrien	1,821	2.5	Mason	235	2.3
Branch	505	2.8	Mecosta	246	1.6
Calhoun	1,165	2.0	Menominee	253	2.4
Cass	594	2.6	Midland	613	1.8
Charlevoix	224	2.3	Missaukee	118	2.5
Cheboygan	326	4.0	Monroe	1,020	1.7
Chippewa	216	1.8	Montcalm	488	2.4
Clare	189	2.4	Montmorency	59	2.2
Clinton	663	2.3	Muskegon	1,411	2.2
Crawford	121	2.5	Newaygo	267	1.8
Delta	381	2.6	Oakland	24,119	4.3
Dickinson	393	3.5	Oceana	209	2.4
Eaton	1,043	2.2	Ogemaw	177	2.9
Emmet	570	4.8	Ontonagon	63	1.8
Genesee	3,804	2.1	Osceola	155	2.1
Gladwin	163	2.4	Oscoda	80	3.2
Gogebic	156	2.4	Otsego	346	4.3
Grand Traverse	1,093	3.5	Ottawa	2,736	2.8
Gratiot	422	2.6	Presque Isle	166	3.4
Hillsdale	447	2.4	Roscommon	152	2.5
Houghton	245	1.9	Saginaw	1,866	2.1
Huron	503	3.7	St. Clair	1,761	2.7
Ingham	3,020	2.2	St. Joseph	775	2.9
Ionia	343	1.5	Sanilac	384	2.4
Iosco	248	2.5	Schoolcraft	63	2.2
Iron	160	3.5	Shiawassee	680	2.2
Isabella	555	2.3	Tuscola	561	2.5
Jackson	1,337	2.1	Van Buren	800	2.7
Kalamazoo	2,572	2.3	Washtenaw	3,310	2.2
Kalkaska	119	2.3	Wayne	15,537	1.8
Kent	6,590	2.7	Wexford	203	1.9
Keweenaw	3	0.6	**Michigan**	**107,605**	**2.3**

Source: U.S. 1990 Census of Population, <u>Social and Economic Characteristics, Michigan</u> (Washington, D.C.: decennial).

Table XIX-19. Unincorporated Self-Employed (Proprietors) in Michigan, by County: 1990

County	Unincorporated Self Employed	Percent(%) of Employment	County	Unincorporated Self Employed	Percent(%) of Employment
Alcona	996	38.9	Lake	690	34.2
Alger	676	21.2	Lapeer	6,114	24.4
Allegan	8,101	21.6	Leelanau	2,369	37.3
Alpena	2,424	16.3	Lenawee	6,767	17.4
Antrim	1,869	26.8	Livingston	9,304	23.1
Arenac	1,347	23.5	Luce	527	18.6
Baraga	474	15.2	Mackinac	1,050	19.4
Barry	4,510	32.2	Macomb	43,686	12.5
Bay	6,666	14.6	Manistee	1,871	20.8
Benzie	1,282	27.8	Marquette	3,654	10.6
Berrien	11,608	14.2	Mason	2,269	20.1
Branch	3,413	20.7	Mecosta	3,192	22.7
Calhoun	6,937	10.1	Menominee	2,136	19.3
Cass	3,716	26.6	Midland	5,265	12.8
Charlevoix	2,442	22.8	Missaukee	1,225	35.8
Cheboygan	1,760	20.1	Monroe	8,429	18.8
Chippewa	2,204	15.6	Montcalm	3,827	18.4
Clare	2,007	22.2	Montmorency	666	26.2
Clinton	5,208	32.7	Muskegon	8,326	11.9
Crawford	871	17.4	Newaygo	2,690	23.0
Delta	2,518	14.8	Oakland	91,598	12.6
Dickinson	1,905	11.8	Oceana	2,744	31.9
Eaton	7,535	26.4	Ogemaw	1,727	26.8
Emmet	3,183	19.0	Ontonagon	747	17.3
Genesee	22,262	11.1	Osceola	2,169	27.5
Gladwin	1,727	28.5	Oscoda	734	29.1
Gogebic	1,085	15.7	Otsego	1,831	18.0
Grand Traverse	8,178	18.0	Ottawa	15,228	15.0
Gratiot	3,618	21.2	Presque Isle	1,199	23.4
Hillsdale	3,833	21.7	Roscommon	1,776	24.9
Houghton	1,854	13.0	Saginaw	12,581	11.8
Huron	4,047	25.0	St. Clair	10,287	19.0
Ingham	21,822	10.8	St. Joseph	4,621	17.3
Ionia	4,099	21.1	Sanilac	4,402	26.4
Iosco	2,303	15.3	Schoolcraft	630	21.0
Iron	882	18.2	Shiawassee	5,671	23.1
Isabella	4,491	15.8	Tuscola	4,193	24.1
Jackson	8,987	13.7	Van Buren	5,521	22.0
Kalamazoo	15,891	11.8	Washtenaw	23,654	11.1
Kalkaska	948	19.4	Wayne	74,490	7.2
Kent	35,219	10.6	Wexford	2,192	15.2
Keweenaw	118	26.5	**Michigan**	**607,068**	**12.8**

Source: Bureau of Economic Analysis, Regional Economic Measurement Division (Washington, D.C.).

APPENDIX A
MSA AND OTHER GEOGRAPHIC AREAS

The tables in the other sections of the Abstract mainly provide statewide and county data, or in a few cases sub-county information. There are users, however, who need information that has already been summarized by geographic region. The most common type of requests involve population and economic data for the state's Metropolitan Statistical Areas (MSAs). In addition to the metropolitan area summary, the tables in Appendix A have been compiled to help users who require summary data for regions that are broader than counties. Population data are often aggregated in a number of other formats for analysis purposes.

Metropolitan Statistical Areas are officially designated by the U.S. Office of Management and Budget based on criteria of population size, urbanization, presence of central city (or cities) and commuting patterns. MSAs may consist of one county or a combination of several adjacent counties. Typically, MSA boundaries are defined every decade, once the latest decennial census information becomes available. Currently there are nine metropolitan areas in Michigan. Six are multi-county regions and three are single county areas. The names of the Michigan MSAs and the counties that comprise them are:

MSA	**Counties**
Ann Arbor	Livingston, Washtenaw and Lenawee
Benton Harbor	Berrien
Detroit	Lapeer, St. Clair, Oakland, Macomb, Wayne and Monroe
Flint	Genesee
Grand Rapids-Muskegon-Holland	Muskegon, Ottawa, Kent and Allegan
Jackson	Jackson
Kalamazoo-Battle Creek	Kalamazoo, Calhoun and Van Buren
Lansing	Clinton, Eaton and Ingham
Saginaw-Bay-Midland	Bay, Midland and Saginaw

Since the data in this section is a geographic aggregation of topics presented in other sections of the book, users should consult the relevant chapter notes for background information concerning the data. The following table provides a crosswalk to these chapter notes.

Appendix A - Table Number	**Reference Chapter**	**Data Source**
A-1, A-2, A-3, A-7, A-8	Population & Housing (page 1)	U.S. Bureau of Census
A-4	Labor Market (page 140)	Michigan Employment Security Commission
A-5, A-6	Income/Output/Prices (page 233)	Bureau of Economic Analysis
A-9, A-11	Trade (page 504)	U.S. Bureau of Census
A-10	Services (page 545)	U.S. Bureau of Census

LIST OF TABLES

Table

Page

Table A-1.   Population Change and Distribution in Michigan, by Subcounty
Areas: 1960-1994 Selected Years 614

Table A-2.   Population in Michigan, by Subcounty Divisions in Metro and
Nonmetro Areas: 1960-1994 Selected Years 615

Table A-3.   Population in Michigan, by Metropolitan Statistical Area (MSA)
and Central City: 1960-1994 Selected Years 617

Table A-4.   Labor Force Statistics and Industry Employment in Michigan, by
Metropolitan Statistical Area (MSA) and the Upper Peninsula:
1990-1995 619

Table A-5.   Total Personal Income in Michigan, by Metropolitan Statistical
Area (MSA): 1969-1993 Selected Years 629

Table A-6.   Per Capita Income in Michigan, by Metropolitan Statistical Area
(MSA): 1969-1993 Selected Years 629

Table A-7.   Household, Family, and Non-Family Income in Michigan, by
Metropolitan Statistical Area (MSA): 1989 630

Table A-8.   Educational Attainment Distribution of Persons 25 Years of Age
and Older in Michigan, by Metropolitan Statistical Area (MSA):
1990 630

Table A-9.   Wholesale Trade Sales in Michigan, by Metropolitan Statistical
Area (MSA): 1992 631

Table A-10.   Service Industry Receipts in Michigan, by Metropolitan
Statistical Area (MSA): for Profit Establishments 1992 631

Table A-11.   Retail Trade Sales and Selected Ratios in Michigan, by
Metropolitan Statistical Area (MSA): 1992 632

613

Table A-1. Population Change and Distribution in Michigan, by Subcounty Areas: 1960-1994 Selected Years

Type of Area	1960	1970	1980	1990	1994	1960-1970	1970-1980	1980-1990	1990-1994
	Population					Numerical Change			
Michigan Total	**7,823,980**	**8,881,826**	**9,262,044**	**9,295,277**	**9,496,550**	**1,057,846**	**380,218**	**33,233**	**201,273**
All cities	4,871,945	5,623,972	5,332,303	5,183,548	5,175,926	752,027	-291,669	-148,755	-7,622
Detroit	1,670,144	1,514,063	1,203,369	1,027,974	992,038	-156,081	-310,694	-175,395	-35,936
Other cities	3,201,801	4,109,909	4,128,934	4,155,574	4,183,888	908,108	19,025	26,640	28,314
Townships	2,952,035	3,257,854	3,929,741	4,111,729	4,320,624	305,819	671,887	181,988	208,895
Villages	365,357	285,848	275,704	272,063	285,011	-79,509	-10,144	-3,641	12,948
Remainder	2,586,678	2,972,006	3,654,037	3,839,666	4,035,613	385,328	682,031	185,629	195,947
	Percent Distribution(%)					Percent Change(%)			
Michigan Total	**100.0**	**100.0**	**100.0**	**100.0**	**100.0**	**13.5**	**4.3**	**0.4**	**2.2**
All cities	62.3	63.3	57.6	55.8	54.5	15.4	-5.2	-2.8	-0.1
Detroit	21.3	17.0	13.0	11.1	10.4	-9.3	-20.5	-14.6	-3.5
Other cities	40.9	46.3	44.6	44.7	44.1	28.4	0.5	0.6	0.7
Townships	37.7	36.7	42.4	44.2	45.5	10.4	20.6	4.6	5.1
Villages	4.7	3.2	3.0	2.9	3.0	-21.8	-3.5	-1.3	4.8
Remainder	33.1	33.5	39.5	41.3	42.5	14.9	22.9	5.1	5.1

Source: U.S. Bureau of the Census, 1960, 1970, 1980, and 1990 Census. Population estimates for 1994 were developed through the Federal-State Cooperative Program for Population Estimates.

Table A-2. Population in Michigan, by Subcounty Divisions in Metro and Nonmetro Areas: 1960-1994 Selected Years

Area	Population					Percent Change(%)			
	1960	1970	1980	1990	1994	1960-1970	1970-1980	1980-1990	1990-1994
State Total									
Cities	4,871,945	5,623,972	5,332,303	5,183,548	5,175,926	15.4	-5.2	-2.8	-0.1
Villages	365,357	285,848	275,697	272,063	285,011	-21.8	-3.6	-1.3	4.8
Townships Adjacent to cities	1,683,216	1,705,870	1,983,333	2,048,446	2,143,088	1.3	16.3	3.3	4.6
Other townships	903,462	1,266,136	1,670,711	1,791,220	1,892,525	40.1	32.0	7.2	5.7
Total	**7,823,980**	**8,881,826**	**9,262,044**	**9,295,277**	**9,496,550**	**13.5**	**4.3**	**0.4**	**2.2**
Metropolitan Areas									
Cities	4,455,336	5,201,149	4,895,308	4,753,298	4,734,893	16.7	-5.9	-2.9	-0.4
Villages	244,339	159,390	157,911	155,413	162,631	-34.8	-0.9	-1.6	4.6
Townships Adjacent to cities	1,477,315	1,465,676	1,685,547	1,731,583	1,812,434	-0.8	15.0	2.7	4.7
Other townships	455,773	739,094	980,029	1,057,349	1,126,839	62.2	32.6	7.9	6.6
Total	**6,632,763**	**7,565,309**	**7,718,795**	**7,697,643**	**7,836,797**	**14.1**	**2.0**	**-0.3**	**1.8**
Nonmetropolitan Areas									
Cities	416,609	422,823	436,995	430,250	441,033	1.5	3.4	-1.5	2.5
Villages	121,018	126,458	117,786	116,650	122,380	4.5	-6.9	-1.0	4.9
Townships Adjacent to cities	205,901	240,194	297,786	316,863	330,654	16.7	24.0	6.4	4.4
Other townships	447,689	527,042	690,682	733,871	765,686	17.7	31.0	6.3	4.3
Total	**1,191,217**	**1,316,517**	**1,543,249**	**1,597,634**	**1,659,753**	**10.5**	**17.2**	**3.5**	**3.9**

Table A-2. Population in Michigan, by Subcounty Divisions in Metro and Nonmetro Areas: 1960-1994 Selected Years Continued

Area	Population					Percent Change(%)			
	1960	1970	1980	1990	1994	1960-1970	1970-1980	1980-1990	1990-1994
Nonmetro - Southern Lower Peninsula									
Cities	149,411	167,900	182,621	184,084	188,437	12.4	8.8	0.8	2.4
Villages	77,508	79,385	75,723	75,182	77,839	2.4	-4.6	-0.7	3.5
Townships Adjacent to cities	101,347	113,109	123,442	128,071	131,964	11.6	9.1	3.7	3.0
Other townships	228,497	267,811	344,993	357,848	372,955	17.2	28.8	3.7	4.2
Total	**556,763**	**628,205**	**726,779**	**745,185**	**771,195**	**12.8**	**15.7**	**2.5**	**3.5**
Northern Lower Peninsula									
Cities	118,239	116,874	114,457	112,611	118,331	-1.2	-2.1	-1.6	5.1
Villages	22,542	23,591	25,692	26,542	29,501	4.7	8.9	3.3	11.1
Townships Adjacent to cities	61,767	81,917	118,021	131,031	139,444	32.6	44.1	11.0	6.4
Other townships	125,954	161,583	238,543	268,350	282,772	28.3	47.6	12.5	5.4
Total	**328,502**	**383,965**	**496,713**	**538,534**	**570,048**	**16.9**	**29.4**	**8.4**	**5.9**
Upper Peninsula									
Cities	148,959	138,049	139,917	133,555	134,265	-7.3	1.4	-4.5	0.5
Villages	20,968	23,482	16,371	14,926	15,040	12.0	-30.3	-8.8	0.8
Townships Adjacent to cities	42,787	45,168	56,323	57,761	59,246	5.6	24.7	2.6	2.6
Other townships	93,238	97,648	107,146	107,673	109,959	4.7	9.7	0.5	2.1
Total	**305,952**	**304,347**	**319,757**	**313,915**	**318,510**	**-0.5**	**5.1**	**-1.8**	**1.5**

Source: U.S. Bureau of the Census, 1960, 1970, 1980, and 1990 Census. Population estimates for 1994 developed through the Federal-State Cooperative Program for Population Estimates.

Table A-3. Population in Michigan, by Metropolitan Statistical Area (MSA) and Central City: 1960-1994 Selected Years

MSA	Population						Percent Change(%)			
	1960	1970	1980	1990	1994	1960-1970	1970-1980	1980-1990	1990-1994
Ann Arbor	**288,462**	**375,021**	**454,977**	**490,058**	**515,298**	**30.0**	**21.3**	**7.7**	**5.2**
Ann Arbor city	67,340	100,035	107,969	109,608	108,817	48.6	7.9	1.5	-0.7
Remainder	221,122	274,986	347,008	380,450	406,481	24.4	26.2	9.6	6.8
Benton Harbor	**149,865**	**163,940**	**171,276**	**161,378**	**161,734**	**9.4**	**4.5**	**-5.8**	**0.2**
Benton Harbor city	19,136	16,481	14,707	12,818	13,186	-13.9	-10.8	-12.8	2.9
Remainder	130,729	147,459	156,569	148,560	148,548	12.8	6.2	-5.1	0.0
Detroit	**4,013,393**	**4,495,299**	**4,387,735**	**4,266,654**	**4,307,107**	**12.0**	**-2.4**	**-2.8**	**0.9**
Detroit city	1,670,144	1,514,063	1,203,369	1,027,974	992,038	-9.3	-20.5	-14.6	-3.5
Pontiac city	82,233	85,279	76,715	71,136	66,708	3.7	-10.0	-7.3	-6.2
Dearborn city	112,007	104,199	90,660	89,286	86,187	-7.0	-13.0	-1.5	-3.5
Port Huron city	36,084	35,794	33,981	33,694	33,374	-0.8	-5.1	-0.8	-0.9
Sum of central cities	1,900,468	1,739,335	1,404,725	1,222,090	1,178,307	-8.5	-19.2	-13.0	-3.6
Remainder	2,112,925	2,755,964	2,983,010	3,044,564	3,128,800	30.4	8.2	2.1	2.8
Flint	**374,313**	**445,589**	**450,449**	**430,459**	**433,297**	**19.0**	**1.1**	**-4.4**	**0.7**
Flint city	196,940	193,317	159,611	140,925	138,164	-1.8	-17.4	-11.7	-2.0
Remainder	177,373	252,272	290,838	289,534	295,133	42.2	15.3	-0.4	1.9
Grand Rapids-Muskegon-Holland	**669,578**	**763,226**	**840,824**	**937,891**	**984,990**	**14.0**	**10.2**	**11.5**	**5.0**
Grand Rapids city	177,313	197,649	181,843	189,126	190,395	11.5	-8.0	4.0	0.7
Muskegon city	46,485	44,631	40,823	39,809	40,639	-4.0	-8.5	-2.5	2.1
Holland city	24,777	26,479	26,281	30,745	31,558	6.9	-0.7	17.0	2.6
Sum of cities	248,575	268,759	248,947	259,680	262,592	8.1	-7.4	4.3	1.1
Remainder	421,003	494,467	591,877	678,211	722,398	17.4	19.7	14.6	6.5

Table A-3. Population in Michigan, by Metropolitan Statistical Area (MSA) and Central City: 1960-1994 Selected Years Continued

MSA	Population					Percent Change(%)			
	1960	1970	1980	1990	1994	1960-1970	1970-1980	1980-1990	1990-1994
Jackson	**131,994**	**143,274**	**151,495**	**149,756**	**153,289**	**8.5**	**5.7**	**-1.1**	**2.4**
Jackson city	50,720	45,484	39,739	37,425	38,303	-10.3	-12.6	-5.8	2.3
Remainder	81,274	97,790	111,756	112,331	114,986	20.3	14.3	0.5	2.4
Kalamazoo-Battle Creek	**356,965**	**399,686**	**420,771**	**429,453**	**442,637**	**12.0**	**5.3**	**2.1**	**3.1**
Kalamazoo city	82,089	85,555	79,722	80,277	81,644	4.2	-6.8	0.7	1.7
Battle Creek city	44,169	38,931	35,724	53,516	55,053	-11.9	-8.2	49.8	2.9
Sum of cities	126,258	124,486	115,446	133,793	136,697	-1.4	-7.3	15.9	2.2
Remainder	230,707	275,200	305,325	295,660	305,940	19.3	10.9	-3.2	3.5
Lansing	**298,949**	**378,423**	**419,750**	**432,674**	**436,130**	**26.6**	**10.9**	**3.1**	**0.8**
Lansing city	107,807	131,403	130,414	127,321	119,590	21.9	-0.8	-2.4	-6.1
East Lansing city	30,198	47,540	51,392	50,677	50,322	57.4	8.1	-1.4	-0.7
Sum of cities	138,005	178,943	181,806	177,998	169,912	29.7	1.6	-2.1	-4.5
Remainder	160,944	199,480	237,944	254,676	266,218	23.9	19.3	7.0	4.5
Saginaw-Bay-Midland	**349,244**	**400,851**	**421,518**	**399,320**	**402,307**	**14.8**	**5.2**	**-5.3**	**0.7**
Bay City	53,604	49,449	41,593	38,936	38,389	-7.8	-15.9	-6.4	-1.4
Midland city	27,779	35,176	37,269	38,053	39,568	26.6	6.0	2.1	4.0
Saginaw city	98,265	91,849	77,508	69,512	70,607	-6.5	-15.6	-10.3	1.6
Sum of cities	179,648	176,474	156,370	146,501	148,564	-1.8	-11.4	-6.3	1.4
Remainder	169,596	224,377	265,148	252,819	253,743	32.3	18.2	-4.6	0.4
Michigan	**7,823,980**	**8,881,826**	**9,262,044**	**9,295,277**	**9,496,539**	**13.5**	**4.3**	**0.4**	**2.2**

Source: U.S. Bureau of the Census, 1960, 1970, 1980, and 1990 Census. Population estimates for 1994 developed through the Federal-State Cooperative Program for Population Estimates.

Table A-4. Labor Force Statistics and Industry Employment in Michigan, by Metropolitan Statistical Area (MSA) and the Upper Peninsula: 1990-1995

Area/Industry	1990	1991	1992	1993	1994	1995
Ann Arbor MSA						
Labor Force	263,600	264,700	275,300	274,200	275,300	271,600
Employment	248,500	245,500	258,600	261,800	264,500	261,300
Unemployment	15,100	19,200	16,700	12,400	10,800	10,300
Rate(%)	5.7	7.3	6.1	4.5	3.9	3.8
Wage and Salary Employment	237,600	236,600	242,700	243,700	247,600	253,100
Goods Producing	62,700	59,000	60,700	58,300	59,100	60,300
Mining	100	100	100	100	100	100
Construction	6,900	6,000	6,000	6,400	6,900	7,100
Manufacturing	55,700	52,900	54,600	51,800	52,100	53,100
Durable Goods	43,000	40,400	41,800	38,500	38,900	39,700
Nondurable Goods	12,700	12,500	12,800	13,400	13,200	13,400
Service Producing	174,900	177,300	182,100	185,400	188,500	192,800
Private Service Producing	111,000	111,900	115,300	118,000	120,800	123,300
Transportation/Communication/Utilities	6,400	5,900	5,500	5,900	6,400	6,700
Wholesale Trade	7,400	7,200	7,300	7,000	7,200	7,300
Retail Trade	38,300	38,700	39,700	40,600	41,500	42,200
Finance/Insurance/Real Estate	8,800	8,800	9,000	9,500	9,600	9,600
Services	50,000	51,200	53,800	54,900	56,100	57,500
Government	63,900	65,400	66,700	67,400	67,700	69,500
Federal	3,400	3,200	3,400	3,400	3,500	3,400
State	40,700	41,600	41,800	42,400	43,000	45,100
Local	19,800	20,600	21,600	21,500	21,200	20,900

Source: Michigan Employment Security Commission, Research and Statistics (Detroit, Michigan).

Table A-4. Labor Force Statistics and Industry Employment in Michigan, by Metropolitan Statistical Area (MSA) and the Upper Peninsula: 1990-1995 Continued

Area/Industry	1990	1991	1992	1993	1994	1995
Benton Harbor MSA						
Labor Force	**80,800**	**80,000**	**81,100**	**82,000**	**82,600**	**81,300**
Employment	75,000	72,700	74,000	76,100	77,500	76,900
Unemployment	5,800	7,300	7,100	5,900	5,100	4,400
Rate(%)	7.2	9.1	8.8	7.2	6.1	5.5
Wage and Salary Employment	**67,800**	**66,000**	**66,600**	**67,600**	**69,200**	**70,800**
Goods Producing	**23,700**	**22,400**	**22,000**	**21,800**	**22,400**	**23,100**
Mining	X	X	X	100	100	100
Construction	X	X	X	1,700	1,700	1,800
Manufacturing	21,800	20,600	20,100	19,900	20,600	21,200
Durable Goods	15,800	14,900	14,500	14,500	15,000	15,700
Nondurable Goods	6,000	5,700	5,600	5,400	5,600	5,500
Service Producing	**44,100**	**43,600**	**44,500**	**45,800**	**46,700**	**47,600**
Private Service Producing	**35,200**	**34,700**	**35,500**	**36,800**	**37,800**	**38,800**
Transportation/Communication/Utilities	2,700	2,700	2,800	2,800	2,900	2,900
Wholesale Trade	2,400	2,300	2,200	2,300	2,200	2,300
Retail Trade	11,800	11,800	11,800	12,300	12,800	13,200
Finance/Insurance/Real Estate	2,700	2,600	2,600	2,600	2,700	2,600
Services	15,600	15,200	16,100	16,700	17,300	17,800
Government	8,800	8,900	9,100	9,100	8,900	8,800
Federal	500	400	500	400	500	500
State	600	600	500	500	500	600
Local	7,800	7,900	8,100	8,100	7,900	7,800

Source: Michigan Employment Security Commission, Research and Statistics (Detroit, Michigan). X = data included in total Goods Producing because of confidentiality.

Table A-4. Labor Force Statistics and Industry Employment in Michigan, by Metropolitan Statistical Area (MSA) and the Upper Peninsula: 1990-1995 Continued

Area/Industry	1990	1991	1992	1993	1994	1995
Detroit MSA						
Labor Force	**2,100,000**	**2,078,000**	**2,101,000**	**2,111,000**	**2,131,000**	**2,122,000**
Employment	1,943,000	1,886,000	1,912,000	1,960,000	2,010,000	2,015,000
Unemployment	156,000	192,000	189,000	151,000	121,000	106,000
Rate(%)	7.5	9.2	9.0	7.2	5.7	5.0
Wage and Salary Employment	**1,902,000**	**1,847,000**	**1,852,000**	**1,889,000**	**1,958,000**	**2,025,000**
Goods Producing	**501,000**	**468,000**	**465,000**	**473,000**	**500,000**	**513,000**
Mining	1,000	1,000	1,000	1,000	1,000	1,000
Construction	62,000	56,000	55,000	57,000	62,000	70,000
Manufacturing	437,000	411,000	409,000	416,000	437,000	442,000
Durable Goods	356,000	335,000	333,000	339,000	356,000	361,000
Nondurable Goods	82,000	76,000	77,000	77,000	81,000	81,000
Service Producing	**1,401,000**	**1,379,000**	**1,387,000**	**1,416,000**	**1,458,000**	**1,511,000**
Private Service Producing	**1,169,000**	**1,148,000**	**1,157,000**	**1,184,000**	**1,226,000**	**1,280,000**
Transportation/Communication/Utilities	88,000	84,000	84,000	85,000	87,000	89,000
Wholesale Trade	113,000	112,000	113,000	114,000	116,000	120,000
Retail Trade	350,000	339,000	334,000	338,000	347,000	362,000
Finance/Insurance/Real Estate	109,000	108,000	107,000	109,000	110,000	110,000
Services	508,000	506,000	519,000	539,000	565,000	598,000
Government	233,000	231,000	230,000	232,000	231,000	232,000
Federal	32,000	31,000	30,000	30,000	30,000	31,000
State	29,000	29,000	29,000	29,000	29,000	28,000
Local	171,000	170,000	171,000	173,000	173,000	173,000

Source: Michigan Employment Security Commission, Research and Statistics (Detroit, Michigan).

Table A-4. Labor Force Statistics and Industry Employment in Michigan, by Metropolitan Statistical Area (MSA) and the Upper Peninsula: 1990-1995 Continued

Area/Industry	1990	1991	1992	1993	1994	1995
Flint MSA						
Labor Force	**197,900**	**198,500**	**198,300**	**197,100**	**202,300**	**203,500**
Employment	179,400	174,600	175,400	178,900	186,700	190,400
Unemployment	18,500	2,390	22,900	18,200	15,600	13,100
Rate(%)	9.4	12.0	11.5	9.2	7.7	6.4
Wage and Salary Employment	**170,200**	**165,800**	**164,600**	**166,000**	**174,500**	**183,400**
Goods Producing	**56,400**	**53,200**	**52,300**	**50,700**	**52,900**	**54,200**
Mining	X	X	X	X	X	X
Construction	X	X	X	X	X	X
Manufacturing	51,000	48,300	47,300	45,700	47,400	48,700
Durable Goods	47,200	44,500	43,700	42,100	43,900	45,200
Nondurable Goods	3,800	3,800	3,700	3,600	3,400	3,400
Service Producing	**113,800**	**112,600**	**112,400**	**115,300**	**121,600**	**129,100**
Private Service Producing	**90,100**	**88,600**	**88,400**	**91,500**	**97,600**	**104,600**
Transportation/Communication/Utilities	4,500	4,800	4,500	4,800	5,100	5,400
Wholesale Trade	7,900	7,500	7,200	7,200	7,200	7,400
Retail Trade	34,600	32,800	32,300	33,100	35,000	36,700
Finance/Insurance/Real Estate	6,000	6,100	6,100	6,200	6,300	6,400
Services	37,100	37,400	38,300	40,300	43,900	48,700
Government	23,700	24,000	23,900	23,800	24,000	24,500
Federal	1,500	1,400	1,400	1,300	1,400	1,500
State	2,400	2,300	2,200	2,200	2,300	2,300
Local	19,800	20,300	20,300	20,200	20,300	20,700

Source: Michigan Employment Security Commission, Research and Statistics (Detroit, Michigan),   X = data included in total Goods Producing because of confidentiality.

Table A-4. Labor Force Statistics and Industry Employment in Michigan, by Metropolitan Statistical Area (MSA) and the Upper Peninsula: 1990-1995 Continued

Area/Industry	1990	1991	1992	1993	1994	1995
Grand Rapids-Muskegon-Holland MSA						
Labor Force	**491,000**	**492,700**	**504,400**	**518,100**	**528,700**	**525,700**
Employment	459,600	453,400	465,500	488,500	503,600	502,600
Unemployment	31,400	39,300	38,900	29,600	25,100	23,000
Rate(%)	6.4	8.0	7.7	5.7	4.7	4.4
Wage and Salary Employment	**450,300**	**445,800**	**453,700**	**471,500**	**490,900**	**505,600**
Goods Producing	**155,200**	**149,300**	**150,400**	**154,900**	**163,700**	**171,400**
Mining	300	300	300	300	300	300
Construction	20,300	17,900	18,000	19,000	20,500	21,900
Manufacturing	134,600	131,100	132,200	135,600	142,900	149,200
Durable Goods	91,600	88,100	87,100	87,900	93,100	97,600
Nondurable Goods	43,000	43,100	45,000	47,700	49,800	51,600
Service Producing	**295,100**	**296,500**	**303,300**	**316,700**	**327,200**	**334,200**
Private Service Producing	**247,000**	**247,500**	**253,100**	**266,100**	**276,000**	**282,500**
Transportation/Communication/Utilities	16,200	15,800	16,500	16,900	17,200	17,300
Wholesale Trade	29,600	29,500	28,600	29,700	30,800	31,400
Retail Trade	84,800	83,600	83,000	84,800	87,200	89,200
Finance/Insurance/Real Estate	17,700	18,300	18,900	19,800	20,200	20,800
Services	98,700	100,400	106,100	115,000	120,800	123,800
Government	48,100	49,000	50,100	50,500	51,200	51,700
Federal	3,700	3,500	3,600	3,600	3,700	3,900
State	6,300	6,000	5,800	5,800	6,000	6,100
Local	38,000	39,400	40,700	41,100	41,500	41,800

Source: Michigan Employment Security Commission, Research and Statistics (Detroit, Michigan).

Table A-4. Labor Force Statistics and Industry Employment in Michigan, by Metropolitan Statistical Area (MSA) and the Upper Peninsula: 1990-1995 Continued

Area/Industry	1990	1991	1992	1993	1994	1995
Jackson MSA						
Labor Force	**70,900**	**70,100**	**71,400**	**73,000**	**73,700**	**72,500**
Employment	65,800	63,600	64,800	67,600	69,100	68,600
Unemployment	5,200	6,400	6,600	5,400	4,700	3,900
Rate(%)	7.3	9.2	9.3	7.3	6.3	5.4
Wage and Salary Employment	**55,400**	**53,700**	**54,100**	**55,600**	**57,000**	**58,400**
Goods Producing	**14,900**	**13,600**	**13,700**	**14,000**	**14,500**	**14,900**
Mining	200	100	100	100	100	100
Construction	1,800	1,600	1,600	1,700	1,600	1,700
Manufacturing	13,000	11,900	11,900	12,200	12,700	13,100
Durable Goods	10,300	9,300	9,400	9,600	10,100	10,400
Nondurable Goods	2,700	2,600	2,600	2,600	2,700	2,700
Service Producing	**40,400**	**40,100**	**40,400**	**41,600**	**42,600**	**43,500**
Private Service Producing	**30,200**	**30,000**	**30,200**	**31,400**	**32,500**	**33,400**
Transportation/Communication/Utilities	4,000	3,800	3,500	3,600	3,600	3,600
Wholesale Trade	2,300	2,100	2,200	2,200	2,300	2,400
Retail Trade	11,100	11,300	11,000	11,300	11,700	11,900
Finance/Insurance/Real Estate	1,800	1,800	1,800	1,800	1,900	1,900
Services	11,100	11,000	11,800	12,500	13,100	13,700
Government	10,200	10,100	10,200	10,100	10,000	10,100
Federal	500	400	400	400	400	400
State	3,400	3,200	3,100	3,100	3,000	3,000
Local	6,400	6,500	6,700	6,700	6,600	6,600

Source: Michigan Employment Security Commission, Research and Statistics (Detroit, Michigan).

624

Table A-4. Labor Force Statistics and Industry Employment in Michigan, by Metropolitan Statistical Area (MSA) and the Upper Peninsula: 1990-1995 Continued

Area/Industry	1990	1991	1992	1993	1994	1995
Kalamazoo-Battle Creek MSA						
Labor Force	**217,500**	**216,600**	**219,800**	**223,300**	**225,300**	**221,600**
Employment	203,000	200,200	204,500	210,800	213,700	210,600
Unemployment	14,500	16,500	15,300	12,500	11,600	11,000
Rate(%)	6.7	7.6	6.9	5.6	5.1	5.0
Wage and Salary Employment	**192,700**	**190,500**	**193,000**	**196,200**	**199,900**	**203,300**
Goods Producing	**56,800**	**54,600**	**55,700**	**55,800**	**56,700**	**57,500**
Mining	200	200	200	200	200	200
Construction	6,600	6,200	6,400	6,400	6,700	6,800
Manufacturing	50,100	48,200	49,100	49,300	49,900	50,600
Durable Goods	22,100	20,600	21,000	21,100	21,700	22,300
Nondurable Goods	28,000	27,600	28,100	28,200	28,200	28,300
Service Producing	**135,800**	**135,900**	**137,300**	**140,400**	**143,200**	**145,800**
Private Service Producing	**102,100**	**102,000**	**103,700**	**106,700**	**109,600**	**111,900**
Transportation/Communication/Utilities	6,000	6,200	6,100	6,200	6,300	6,500
Wholesale Trade	6,800	6,700	6,600	6,600	6,700	6,800
Retail Trade	36,600	36,000	35,900	36,400	36,900	37,800
Finance/Insurance/Real Estate	9,400	9,500	9,800	10,400	10,600	10,800
Services	43,300	43,600	45,300	47,200	49,100	50,100
Government	33,700	33,900	33,600	33,700	33,600	33,900
Federal	5,700	5,600	5,600	5,200	5,300	5,300
State	8,500	8,400	8,100	8,400	8,300	8,200
Local	19,500	19,900	19,900	20,000	20,000	20,300

Source: Michigan Employment Security Commission, Research and Statistics (Detroit, Michigan).

Table A-4. Labor Force Statistics and Industry Employment in Michigan, by Metropolitan Statistical Area (MSA) and the Upper Peninsula: 1990-1995 Continued

Area/Industry	1990	1991	1992	1993	1994	1995
Lansing MSA						
Labor Force	**233,500**	**231,600**	**232,600**	**232,600**	**233,400**	**228,900**
Employment	217,900	213,900	218,700	220,400	223,400	219,700
Unemployment	15,600	17,700	14,000	12,200	10,100	9,200
Rate(%)	6.7	7.6	6.0	5.2	4.3	4.0
Wage and Salary Employment	**216,500**	**213,200**	**215,400**	**214,100**	**217,900**	**220,700**
Goods Producing	**38,000**	**34,600**	**36,200**	**33,900**	**36,000**	**37,300**
Mining	300	200	200	300	300	300
Construction	6,500	6,000	5,800	6,000	5,900	6,100
Manufacturing	31,300	28,400	30,100	27,600	29,800	31,000
Durable Goods	26,100	23,500	25,000	22,400	24,300	25,300
Nondurable Goods	5,200	4,900	5,100	5,200	5,500	5,700
Service Producing	**178,500**	**178,600**	**179,300**	**180,300**	**181,900**	**183,400**
Private Service Producing	**109,800**	**109,700**	**110,600**	**114,200**	**116,100**	**118,300**
Transportation/Communication/Utilities	6,200	6,500	6,200	6,200	6,000	6,100
Wholesale Trade	8,400	8,500	8,200	8,000	8,200	8,400
Retail Trade	40,100	38,600	38,500	39,200	39,600	40,100
Finance/Insurance/Real Estate	12,100	12,200	12,200	12,200	12,200	12,700
Services	43,100	43,900	45,400	48,500	50,000	51,000
Government	68,700	68,900	68,700	66,100	65,800	65,100
Federal	20,500	3,200	3,200	3,100	3,100	3,200
State	43,000	42,700	42,200	41,600	41,500	40,700
Local	22,400	23,100	23,300	21,400	21,100	21,200

Source: Michigan Employment Security Commission, Research and Statistics (Detroit, Michigan).

Table A-4. Labor Force Statistics and Industry Employment in Michigan, by Metropolitan Statistical Area (MSA) and the Upper Peninsula: 1990-1995 Continued

Area/Industry	1990	1991	1992	1993	1994	1995
Saginaw-Bay-Midland MSA						
Labor Force	**187,700**	**188,600**	**192,300**	**192,100**	**194,000**	**192,500**
Employment	173,500	172,400	176,200	178,900	181,600	181,500
Unemployment	14,200	16,200	16,100	13,200	12,400	10,900
Rate(%)	7.6	8.6	8.4	6.9	6.4	5.7
Wage and Salary Employment	**163,400**	**162,700**	**164,900**	**165,700**	**169,200**	**174,600**
Goods Producing	**51,700**	**50,400**	**49,800**	**48,700**	**48,600**	**49,300**
Mining	X	X	X	X	X	X
Construction	X	X	X	X	X	X
Manufacturing	43,400	42,700	42,400	41,200	41,000	41,300
Durable Goods	25,500	25,100	25,000	24,500	24,500	24,900
Nondurable Goods	17,900	17,600	17,400	16,700	16,500	16,400
Service Producing	**111,700**	**112,300**	**115,100**	**117,000**	**120,700**	**125,300**
Private Service Producing	**90,900**	**91,300**	**93,400**	**95,200**	**98,400**	**102,800**
Transportation/Communication/Utilities	6,300	6,500	6,500	6,600	6,900	7,300
Wholesale Trade	6,300	6,200	6,200	6,300	6,300	6,300
Retail Trade	34,300	34,100	34,900	35,300	36,600	38,700
Finance/Insurance/Real Estate	6,000	6,300	6,100	6,300	6,400	6,300
Services	37,900	38,400	39,700	40,800	42,200	44,200
Government	20,800	20,900	21,700	21,700	22,200	22,500
Federal	1,800	1,700	1,800	1,800	1,900	1,900
State	2,300	2,300	2,300	2,300	2,600	2,600
Local	16,700	17,000	17,600	17,600	17,800	17,900

Source: Michigan Employment Security Commission, Research and Statistics (Detroit, Michigan), X = data included in total Goods Producing because of confidentiality.

Table A-4. Labor Force Statistics and Industry Employment in Michigan, by Metropolitan Statistical Area (MSA) and the Upper Peninsula: 1990-1995 Continued

Area/Industry	1990	1991	1992	1993	1994	1995
Upper Peninsula						
Labor Force	**138,700**	**141,400**	**146,000**	**148,700**	**151,600**	**148,500**
Employment	126,300	126,800	130,500	135,700	138,600	136,200
Unemployment	12,400	14,600	15,500	13,000	12,900	12,200
Rate(%)	9.0	10.3	10.6	8.7	8.5	8.2
Wage and Salary Employment	**114,700**	**114,700**	**116,700**	**119,600**	**123,400**	**125,400**
Goods Producing	**25,400**	**23,600**	**23,200**	**23,400**	**24,000**	**24,000**
Mining	3,000	3,400	3,500	3,300	3,400	3,200
Construction	6,200	5,000	4,700	4,900	5,100	5,300
Manufacturing	16,200	15,200	15,000	15,200	15,500	15,500
Durable Goods	10,700	9,800	9,500	9,600	9,900	10,000
Nondurable Goods	5,500	5,400	5,500	5,600	5,600	5,600
Service Producing	**89,300**	**91,100**	**93,400**	**96,300**	**99,400**	**101,400**
Private Service Producing	**56,200**	**57,700**	**59,900**	**62,600**	**65,400**	**67,500**
Transportation/Communication/Utilities	5,400	5,400	5,600	5,600	5,600	5,500
Wholesale Trade	3,100	3,100	3,200	3,300	3,300	3,400
Retail Trade	23,400	23,500	23,800	24,400	25,400	26,100
Finance/Insurance/Real Estate	3,900	4,000	4,100	4,200	4,300	4,300
Services	20,500	21,700	23,300	25,000	26,700	28,300
Government	33,100	33,300	33,500	33,700	34,000	33,900
Federal	3,500	3,300	3,300	3,300	3,200	2,700
State	10,700	10,600	10,300	10,400	10,800	11,000
Local	18,900	19,400	19,900	20,000	20,100	20,200

Source: Michigan Employment Security Commission, Research and Statistics (Detroit, Michigan).

Table A-5. Total Personal Income in Michigan, by Metropolitan Statistical Area (MSA): 1969-1993 Selected Years

MSA	1969	1979	1983	1987	1990	1991	1992	1993
Michigan	**$35,620,151**	**$88,159,699**	**$108,026,458**	**$143,403,708**	**$169,808,350**	**$175,249,961**	**$185,702,201**	**$194,718,083**
Ann Arbor	1,577,162	4,628,196	5,934,925	8,203,093	10,064,185	10,462,037	11,271,463	11,906,626
Benton Harbor	632,110	1,429,490	1,735,941	2,234,579	2,579,301	2,673,346	2,849,652	3,017,919
Detroit	19,886,107	46,418,210	55,173,568	74,195,085	87,448,585	88,700,541	93,952,942	98,367,198
Flint	1,789,496	4,436,485	5,345,539	6,489,054	7,245,468	7,703,964	7,983,303	8,277,505
Grand Rapids/Muskegon/Holland	2,804,843	7,388,571	9,693,735	13,409,508	16,308,185	17,211,351	18,446,138	19,545,092
Jackson	558,539	1,344,767	1,595,896	2,023,312	2,339,680	2,405,729	2,529,655	2,646,793
Kalamazoo/Battle Creek	1,503,142	3,656,021	4,672,708	6,169,444	7,374,041	7,773,782	8,201,116	8,599,518
Lansing	1,413,266	3,715,581	4,820,656	6,175,040	7,321,044	7,678,429	8,135,267	8,343,512
Saginaw/Bay/Midland	1,485,861	3,878,548	4,691,667	5,816,570	6,823,690	7,102,799	7,495,183	7,819,878
Metro portion	31,650,526	76,895,869	93,664,635	124,715,685	147,504,179	151,711,978	160,864,719	168,524,041
Nonmetro portion	3,969,625	11,263,830	14,361,823	18,688,023	22,304,171	23,537,983	24,837,482	26,194,042

Source: U.S. Department of Commerce, Economics & Statistics Administration, Bureau of Economic Analysis, Regional Economic Measurement Division, R.E.I.S. May 1994 CD-ROM (Washington, D.C.: annually).

Table A-6. Per Capita Income in Michigan, by Metropolitan Statistical Area (MSA): 1969-1993 Selected Years

MSA	1969	1979	1983	1987	1990	1991	1992	1993
Michigan	**$4,057**	**$9,532**	**$11,939**	**$15,607**	**$18,237**	**$18,703**	**$19,707**	**$20,584**
Ann Arbor	4,392	10,282	13,180	17,455	20,451	20,987	22,349	23,378
Benton Harbor	3,862	8,233	10,761	13,882	15,985	16,566	17,639	18,660
Detroit	4,442	10,563	13,027	17,374	20,482	20,701	21,853	22,856
Flint	4,012	9,835	12,260	14,907	16,809	17,838	18,468	19,139
Grand Rapids/Muskegon/Holland	3,720	8,885	11,370	14,909	17,317	18,036	19,126	20,062
Jackson	3,912	8,859	10,936	13,768	15,585	15,921	16,687	17,349
Kalamazoo/Battle Creek	3,821	8,733	11,221	14,630	17,133	17,964	18,795	19,538
Lansing	3,805	8,982	11,673	14,526	16,887	17,630	18,666	19,140
Saginaw/Bay/Midland	3,735	9,213	11,475	14,542	17,066	17,721	18,631	19,400
Metro portion	4,217	9,979	12,456	16,346	19,132	19,573	20,655	21,569
Nonmetro portion	3,110	7,300	9,396	11,989	13,929	14,537	15,190	15,910

Source: U.S. Department of Commerce, Economics & Statistics Administration, Bureau of Economic Analysis, Regional Economic Measurement Division, R.E.I.S. May 1994 CD-ROM (Washington, D.C.: annually).

Table A-7. Household, Family, and Non-Family Income in Michigan, by Metropolitan Statistical Area (MSA): 1989

MSA	Total Households		Family Households		Non-Family Households	
	Number	Median Income	Number	Median Income	Number	Median Income
Michigan	**3,424,122**	**$31,020**	**2,458,481**	**$36,652**	**965,641**	**$16,506**
Ann Arbor*	175,674	37,400	120,463	45,600	55,211	21,400
Benton Harbor	61,390	27,245	44,392	32,219	16,998	14,176
Detroit*	1,541,853	34,000	1,092,562	40,500	444,291	18,600
Flint	161,501	31,030	116,872	36,760	44,629	16,424
Grand Rapids/Muskegon/Holland*	334,783	31,900	247,505	36,800	87,278	17,600
Jackson	53,891	29,156	39,211	33,967	14,680	15,502
Kalamazoo/Battle Creek*	161,344	29,000	112,195	34,900	49,149	16,100
Lansing	156,994	32,156	106,447	38,660	50,547	19,339
Saginaw/Bay/Midland	148,098	29,157	109,208	34,727	38,890	14,194

Source: U.S. Bureau of the Census, 1990 Census, Tape STF-3. * Median income for MSA is weighted average of component county medians.

Table A-8. Educational Attainment Distribution of Persons 25 Years of Age and Older in Michigan, by Metropolitan Statistical Area (MSA): 1990

Educational Attainment - Percent Distribution (%)

MSA	Total	Less Than High School	High School Graduate	College			
				Some College, No Degree	Associate's Degree	Bachelor's Degree	Graduate or Professional Degree
Michigan	**100.0**	**23.3**	**32.3**	**20.4**	**6.7**	**10.9**	**6.4**
Ann Arbor	100.0	15.3	26.2	21.1	6.6	16.7	14.2
Benton Harbor	100.0	25.3	31.9	19.1	7.0	10.4	6.3
Detroit	100.0	24.6	30.3	21.1	6.4	11.2	6.4
Flint	100.0	23.2	33.9	22.7	7.4	8.0	4.8
Grand Rapids/Muskegon/Holland	100.0	21.4	33.1	19.9	7.8	12.2	5.6
Jackson	100.0	22.3	34.1	22.4	8.3	8.8	4.1
Kalamazoo/Battle Creek	100.0	20.6	31.2	20.6	7.2	12.5	7.8
Lansing	100.0	15.8	27.6	24.1	7.9	14.5	10.2
Saginaw/Bay/Midland	100.0	23.8	34.7	19.2	7.1	9.6	5.5

Source: U.S. Bureau of the Census, 1990 Census, Tape STF-3.

Table A-9. Wholesale Trade Sales in Michigan, by Metropolitan Statistical Area (MSA): 1992
(Data in Thousands of Dollars)

MSA	Total			Merchant Wholesaler			Other Operating Type		
	Total Wholesale	Durable Goods	Nondurable Goods	Total Merchant Wholesale	Durable Goods	Nondurable Goods	Total Other Operating	Durable Goods	Nondurable Goods
Michigan	**$125,670,957**	**$84,614,339**	**$41,056,618**	**$51,621,192**	**$28,198,404**	**$23,422,788**	**$74,049,765**	**$56,415,935**	**$17,633,830**
Ann Arbor	2,498,154	1,488,325	1,009,829	1,702,889	938,147	764,742	795,265	550,178	245,087
Benton Harbor	1,313,135	833,105	480,030	400,803	185,378	215,425	912,332	647,727	264,605
Detroit	91,013,809	68,180,477	22,833,332	28,478,500	17,444,494	11,034,006	62,535,309	50,735,983	11,799,326
Flint	2,235,483	1,557,801	677,682	1,083,684	667,718	415,966	1,151,799	890,083	261,716
Grand Rapids/Muskegon/Holland	12,784,319	5,675,460	7,108,859	8,960,619	4,453,534	4,507,085	3,823,700	1,221,926	2,601,774
Jackson	939,223	516,484	422,739	426,322	268,072	158,250	512,901	248,412	264,489
Kalamazoo/Battle Creek	2,231,673	1,248,852	982,821	1,462,877	795,343	667,534	768,796	453,509	315,287
Lansing	3,663,635	1,850,590	1,813,045	2,319,218	833,380	1,485,838	1,344,417	1,017,210	327,207
Saginaw/Bay/Midland	2,597,210	955,815	1,641,395	1,879,313	757,524	1,121,789	717,897	198,291	519,606

Source: Bureau of Census, 1992 Census of Wholesale Trade, Geographic Area Series, Michigan (Washington, D.C.: quinquennial).

Table A-10. Service Industry Receipts in Michigan, by Metropolitan Statistical Area (MSA): for Profit Establishments 1992
(MSA Data in Thousands, Data for Michigan in Millions)

Receipts($) (Data in Millions of Dollars)

County	Total	Hotels and Motels	Personal Services	Business Services	Automotive Repair	Misc. Repair	Amusement/Recreation	Health Services	Legal Services	Engineering/Management
Michigan	**$35,123,794**	**$1,212,396**	**$1,469,981**	**$8,305,842**	**$2,482,856**	**$1,137,072**	**$2,201,376**	**$8,706,707**	**$2,517,595**	**$6,226,799**
Ann Arbor	2,026,219	64,331	68,575	529,271	109,356	42,838	15,735	485,426	88,270	462,058
Benton Harbor	392,790	20,519	23,128	103,112	26,001	16,417	18,791	120,105	23,143	28,720
Detroit	21,167,782	486,931	772,952	5,640,566	1,342,368	696,806	1,345,442	4,506,973	1,642,973	4,262,425
Flint	1,232,973	17,090	58,999	294,327	98,367	32,209	60,987	459,804	64,804	115,029
Grand Rapids/Muskegon/Holland	3,343,099	116,737	162,735	588,629	328,590	115,486	198,285	897,907	254,695	583,226
Jackson	328,711	8,551	19,970	49,317	24,842	16,806	27,316	115,475	15,234	41,668
Kalamazoo/Battle Creek	1,351,685	54,144	82,152	294,636	115,167	50,207	74,574	435,515	80,710	131,098
Lansing	1,494,057	50,860	62,947	334,433	101,194	33,526	83,431	406,273	133,829	284,019
Saginaw/Bay/Midland	1,046,070	47,482	66,127	185,314	83,237	31,752	60,132	382,556	70,801	94,076

Source: Bureau of Census, 1992 Census of Service Industries, Geographic Area Series, Michigan (Washington, D.C.: quinquennial).

Table A-11. Retail Trade Sales and Selected Ratios in Michigan, by Metropolitan Statistical Area (MSA): 1992

MSA	Sales($) (In Thousands)	Sales($) per Unit	Sales($) per Employee
Michigan	**$71,523,046**	**$1,312**	**$101**
Ann Arbor	4,215,384	1,520	104
Benton Harbor	1,036,884	1,093	90
Detroit	33,875,819	1,448	105
Flint	3,545,014	1,398	104
Grand Rapids/Muskegon/Holland	7,325,349	1,418	98
Jackson	1,007,492	1,285	95
Kalamazoo/Battle Creek	3,320,026	1,283	94
Lansing	3,470,344	1,470	95
Saginaw/Bay/Midland	3,346,290	1,271	95

Source: Bureau of Census, 1992 Census of Retail Trade, Geographic Area Series, Michigan (Washington, D.C.: quinquennial).

APPENDIX B

DATA SOURCE CONTACT LIST
STATE OF MICHIGAN

Michigan Employment Security Commission
7310 Woodward Avenue
Labor Market Information - Room 520
Detroit, Michigan 48202
Employment/Hours/Earnings: (313) 876-5480
Unemployment Statistics: (313) 876-5427
Occupation/Industry Forecasts: (313) 876-5439
Wages: (313) 876-5372

Michigan Information Center
Demographic Research and Statistics
Department of Management and Budget
P.O. Box 30026
Lansing, Michigan 48909
Contact Person: Carolyn Lauer
Telephone: (517) 373-7910
Fax: (517) 335-1521

Michigan Department of Aging
611 W. Ottawa Street - Third Floor
P.O. Box 30026
Lansing, Michigan 48909
General Information - (517) 373-8230
Fax: (517) 373-4092
TDD: (517) 373-4096

Michigan Department of Agriculture
Michigan Agricultural Statistics Service
201 Federal Building
P.O. Box 20008
Lansing, Michigan 48901-0608
Statistics Services - (517) 377-1831
Fax: Statistics Services - (517) 377-1829
General Information - (517) 373-1104

Michigan Department of Civil Rights
Executive Office
Ingham County Building - Fourth Floor
303 W. Kalamazoo
Lansing, Michigan 48913
Telephone: (517) 335-3164
Fax: (517) 335-6513

Michigan Department of Corrections
Administration and Programs Administration
Grandview Plaza
P.O. Box 30003
Lansing, Michigan 48909
Statistical Information: (517) 373-6850
General Information (517) 335-1426

Michigan Department of Education
Hannah Building
P.O. Box 30008
Lansing, Michigan 48909
Instructional Services: (517) 373-4595
Postsecondary Education: (517) 335-4933

Michigan Department of Management & Budget
Office of Financial Management
Steven T. Mason Building - Third Floor
530 W. Allegan
P.O. Box 30026
Lansing, Michigan 48909
Telephone: (517) 373-3029

Michigan Department of Mental Health
Lewis Cass Building
Basement
Lansing, Michigan 48913
Telephone: (517) 373-3740
TTY (517) 373-3573

Michigan Department of Natural Resources
Air Quality Division
Mason Building - Fourth Floor
530 W. Allegan
P.O. Box 30028
Lansing, Michigan 48909
Telephone: (517) 373-7069

APPENDIX B

DATA SOURCE CONTACT LIST
STATE OF MICHIGAN - CONTINUED

Michigan Department of Natural Resources
Environmental Response Division
Knapps Centre
309 S. Washington
P.O. Box 30028
Lansing, Michigan 48909
Telephone: (517) 373-9837

Surface Water Quality Division
Knapps Centre - Second Floor
309 S. Washington
P.O. Box 30028
Lansing, Michigan 48909
Telephone: (517) 373-1949

Michigan Department of Public Health
Office of the State Registrar
Statistical Services Section
3423 N. Martin L. King Jr. Blvd.
P.O. Box 30195
Lansing, Michigan 48909
Statistical Information: (517) 335-8705
General Information: (517) 335-8000

Bureau of Safety and Regulation
MIOSHA Division
State Secondary Complex - First Floor
7150 Harris Drive
Box 30015
Lansing, Michigan 48909
Telephone: (517) 322-1845

Michigan Department of Social Services
Policy Analysis Division
Data Reporting Unit
Grand Tower - Suite 1503
235 S. Grand Avenue/Cesar Chaves Avenue
P.O. Box 30037
Lansing, Michigan 48909
Telephone: (517) 373-6830

Michigan Department of State
Treasury Building
430 W. Allegan Street
Lansing, Michigan 48918
Information-Detroit: (313) 256-1180
Public Information: (517) 2520

Michigan Department of State Police
Support Services Bureau
Central Records Division
Uniform Crime Reporting Section
7150 Harris Drive
Lansing, Michigan 48913
Telephone: (517) 322-1150

Michigan Supreme Court
State Court Administrative Office
611 West Ottawa Street
P.O. Box 30048
Lansing, Michigan 48909
Telephone: (517) 373-0130

Michigan Travel Bureau
Travel Information Division
Town Center Building - Suite F
333 S. Capitol Avenue, P.O. Box 30226
Lansing, Michigan 48909
Telephone: (517) 335-1863

Michigan Department of Transportation
Transportation Building
425 W. Ottawa, P.O. Box 30050
Lansing, Michigan 48909
Telephone: (517) 373-2090

Bureau of Workers Disability Compensation
Victor Office Center - Second Floor
201 N. Washington Square
Box 30016, Lansing, Michigan 40909
Telephone: (517) 373-3480

APPENDIX B

DATA SOURCE CONTACT LIST
FEDERAL GOVERNMENT

U.S. Department of Energy
Energy Information Division
Office of Energy Information Services
Energy Information Administration
Washington, D.C. 20585
Telephone: (202) 586-8800

Bureau of Economic Analysis
Economics and Statistics Administration
Regional Economic Measurement Division
U.S. Department of Commerce
Washington, D.C. 20230
Telephone: (202) 606-5360

National Oceanic and Atmospheric Administration
National Climatic Data Center
Federal Building, 37 Battery Park Avenue
Asheville, North Carolina 28801-2733
Telephone: (704) 271-4800

U.S. Patent and Trademark Office
Technology Assessment and Forecast Program
CP2-9D30, Washington, D.C. 20234
Telephone: (703) 308-0322
Fax: (703) 308-0493

Social Security Administration
Office of Research and Statistics
U.S. Department of Health & Human Services
Van Ness Centre - Room 209
4301 Connecticut Avenue, N.W.
Washington, D.C. 20008
Telephone: (202) 2827138

U.S. Department of Treasury
Internal Revenue Service
Statistics of Income Division
P.O. Box 2608, Washington, D.C. 20013
Telephone: (202) 874-0410

National Center for Health Statistics
Scientific and Technical Information Branch
U.S. Department of Health and Human Services
6525 Belcrest Road - Room 1064
Hyattsville, MD 20782
Telephone: (301) 436-8500

OTHER AGENCIES

Federal Deposit Insurance Corp
Office of Corporate Communications
FDIC, 550 17th Street, N.W.
Washington, D.C. 20429

Federal Home Loan Bank of Indianapolis
8250 Woodfield Crossing Blvd.
Indianapolis, Indiana 46240
Telephone: (317) 465-0200

Federal Reserve Board
Division of Research and Statistics
Washington, D.C. 20551
Telephone: (202) 452-3301

National Science Foundation
Office of Public Information
1800 G Street, N.W.
Washington, D.C. 20550
Telephone: (202) 357-1110

Southeast Michigan Council of Governments
660 Plaza Drive - Suite 1900
Detroit, Michigan 48226
Telephone: (313) 961-4266

APPENDIX B

DATA SOURCE CONTACT LIST
PRIVATE INDUSTRY

American Automobile Manufacturers Association
Detroit Office
7430 Second Avenue - Suite 300
Detroit, Michigan 48202
Telephone: (313) 872-4311
Fax: (313) 872-5400

American Council of Life Insurance
1001 Pennsylvania Avenue, N.W.
Washington, D.C. 20004-2599

Durocher, Dixson, Werba
Public & Financial Relations
Suite 2250
400 Renaissance Center
Detroit, Michigan 48243-1605
Telephone: (313) 259-7414

Gale Research Inc.
835 Penobscot Building
Detroit, Michigan 48226-4094

Independent Petroleum Association of America
Petroleum Information Services Department
1101 16th Street, N.W.
Washington, D.C. 20036
Telephone: (202) 857-4760
Fax: (202) 857-4799

Michigan Association of Realtors
Communications and Public Relations
P.O. Box 40725
Lansing, Michigan 48901
Telephone: (517) 372-8890

Michigan Hospital Association
6215 West St. Joseph Highway
Lansing, Michigan 48917
Telephone: (517) 323-3443

National Sporting Goods Association
International Headquarters
1699 Wall Street
Mt Prospect, Illinois 60056-5780
(708) 439-4000

Tax Foundation
1250 H Street, N.W.
Suite 750
Washington, D.C. 20005-3908
Telephone: (202) 783-2760
Fax: (202) 942-7675

Glenmary Research Center
750 Piedmont Avenue, N.E.
Atlanta, Georgia 30308

INDEX

A

Abortions
County 71
Michigan 70
Accidents, Motor Vehicle
Death Rates 486
Mileage 486
Persons Killed and Injured 487
Traffic 487
AFDC
see Child Support, Income Maintenance
Programs
Agriculture; see also Crops, Farm
Employment 427
Rank 422
Air Carrier
Passengers, Mail, and Cargo 490
Service 492
Air Quality
Carbon Monoxide 409
Emission Trends 407
Lead 410
Nitrogen Dioxide 409
Ozone 408
Particle Matter 409
Sulfur Dioxide 410
Aircraft
see Air Carrier
Airports
see Air Carrier
American Indian
see table I-5
Ancestry
County 38
Athletics
see Sports
Automobiles
see Motor Vehicles

B

Banks 534, 539
Banks and Branches 537
Births
County 68
Infant 68
Live Birth Rates 57
Live Births 57
Michigan 57
Rates by Age of Mother 59
United States 57
Building Permits
see Construction

C

Camping
see State Parks
Cancer
Age, Race, Sex 74-77
Age-Adjusted Incidence 83
Age-Specific/Adjusted Incidence 82
Cases 83
County 83
Death Rates 77
Deaths 76, 83
Final Death Rates 83
Incidence Rates 75
Primary Site 78, 80
Survival Rates 85
Cars
see Motor Vehicles, Factory Sales
Central City
Population 617
Child Abuse
see Protective Services
Child Support
AFDC and Non-AFDC Case 264
Community Colleges
see Education, Colleges and Universities
Commuting
County 204
Companies
Largest Private and Nonprofit 572
Retail Trade 570
Top Financial 571
Top Insurance 570
Top Manufacturing 568
Top Service 569
Top Utility 570

INDEX

Companies by Size Class
see Size of Firm

Construction
Average Weekly Wage 436, 439
Building Permits, Nonresidential . . . 442
Building Permits, Residential 441
Employment 436, 439
Establishments 436, 439
Public Contracts, Nonresidential . . . 442
Public Contracts, Residential 441
Residential and Nonresidential . 437, 438
Wages 440

Consumer Price Index
Detroit Area and United States 241
Percentage Change 243

Correctional Institutions
see Prison

County
see Specific Topics

Court of Appeals
Filings per Judge 319
Trends in Dispositions 319

Court of Claims
Cases Referred to Mediation 320
Summary Report 320

Court, Circuit
Cases Pending 324
Filings per Judge 325
Summary Report 329
Trends in Filings 327

Court, District
Cases Pending 323
Filing Trends 342
Filings per Judge 338
Summary Report 346

Court, Juvenile Division
Activity Information 322
Caseload Information 321

Court, Municipal
Pending Cases 323
Summary Report 347

Court, Probate
Estate and Mental Health Division . . 334
Filings per Judge 331
Pending Cases 321
Summary Reports 337

Courts
Sentences 318

Credit Union 534
Criminal Offenses
Arrests 308
Index Offenses 307
Murder Statistics 312
Type of Offense 309
Crops 423

D

Deaths
Age and Sex 62
Cancer 76, 83
Cancers 76
Cause 62
County 68, 83
Death Rates 57
Deaths 57
Fetal 64
Firearm Injury 63
Infant 64, 65, 68
Injury 62
Leading Causes 60
Leading Causes by Race and Age . . . 61
Maternal 64
Michigan 57
Neonatal 64
Number 62
Perinatal 64
Postneonatal 64
Race 65
Rates 65, 68
Sex and Age 63
United States 57
Diseases
Communicable 87
Divorces and Annulments 88
Children Involved 88
Domestic Violence 264
Dwelling
see Housing

E

Earnings
Full Time or Part Time 169, 170
Major Occupational Group 169
Manufacturing 171

INDEX

Earnings - continued
Occupation 171
Sex 169, 170
Union Affiliation 171
Education, College and University
Attainment by MSA 630
Community College Enrollment
 Information 137
Community College Tuition 107
Earned Degrees 101
Earned Degrees Conferred 102
Educational Attainment 95
Private College and University Enrollment
 Information 138
Public University Enrollment Info . . 138
Student Expenses 106
Unemployment Rates 162
Education, Elementary and Secondary
Attainment by MSA 630
Dropout and Graduation Rates 108
Educational Assessment Program . . 117
Educational Attainment 95
Expenditures 99
Mathematics 100
Public School Statistics 96
Reading 100
Revenue and Enrollment 97
Revenues by Source 97, 98
SAT and ACT Scores 100
Science 100
Unemployment Rates 162
Electric Power
see Energy
Employment
Broad Industry Group 209
Earnings Category 171
Full Time and Part Time 164
Hours Worked 165
Incorporated Self Employed 611
Major Occupational Group . . . 158, 159
MSA 620
Occupational by Age Group 160
Scientific Workers 588
Unincorporated Self Employed 612
Upper Peninsula 620
Employment Status
County 145
Labor Market Area 145

Michigan 143
MSA 145
Race and Gender 150
United States 143
Energy
Expenditure Estimates by Source . . 503
Input at Electric Utilities 501
Price Estimates by Sector 502
Price Estimates by Source 503
Energy Consumption
Commercial 500
Industrial 500
Per Capita 498, 499
Residential 500
Total 498
Transportation 501
Type 499
Exports
see International Trade

F

Farm
Expenses 424
Income 424
Receipts 426
Fertility Rates
Michigan 58
United States 58
Finance
Companies 571
Finance, Insurance, and Real Estate
Average Weekly Wage 533, 535
Employment 533, 535
Units 533, 535
Wages 536
Forecast
see Projections
Foreign Trade
see International Trade
Forest Fires 418
Forests
see Timberland, Tree Volume

G

Gas
see Energy

INDEX

Government

Employment 350
Expenditures 358
General Fund Expenditures 360
Revenue 352, 354

Government, Local

Expenditures 359
Revenue 353, 357

Governors 364, 365

Gross State Product

Constant Dollar(1987) 247
Current Dollar 244

H

Home Help 261
Homicides

see Criminal Offenses

Hospital

Admission Statistics 91
Discharges 91
Patient Statistics 92
Surgeries 92

Hours and Earnings

see Manufacturing, Employment, Earnings

Housing

Built 47
County 47, 48
Mortgages 544
Owner, Renter, or Not Occupied . . . 48
Selling Prices 543

Hunting and Fishing 381

I

Illness

Average Lost Workdays 89
by Industry Group 89
Occupational 89

Imports

see International Trade

Income

Agriculture 425
County, Per-Capita Personal 239
County, Total Personal 237
Fishery 425
Forestry 425

Michigan, Total &
Per Capita Personal 235
MSA, Household/Family/Nonfamily   630
MSA, Per-capita 629
MSA, Total Personal 629
United States, Total and Per Capita
Personal 235

Income Maintenance Programs

AFDC 255, 256
Cases and Recipients 254
Emergency Assistance 255
Food Stamp Cases, Recipients, and
Payments 258
Food Stamps 255
General Assistance Payments and Recipient
Rates 262
Individuals Receiving Finance Pay . . 263
Medical Assistance Recipients and
Expenditures 254
Medical Assistance Recipients and
Payments 259
O.A.S.D.H.I. 253
State Assistance 255
State Assistance Cases, Recipients, and
Payments 257
State Emergency Relief 255
Supplemental Security Income 260

Injuries

Average Lost Workdays 89
Fatal Occupational 90
Fatality Rate 86
Industry Division 89
Major Industry 86
Occupational 86, 89

Insurance

Companies 570

International Trade

Employment 528
Exports from Michigan 529
Factory Shipments 528
Value of Export Shipments 527

J

Judicial System

see Court, Courts, Criminal Offenses,
Prison

INDEX

L

Labor Force
E.E.O. Category 203
Education Level 161
MSA 619-628
Participation Rates 152
School Enrollment 163
Upper Peninsula 619
Land and Water Areas 382
Life Expectancy
Michigan 72
Sex 72
Sex and Race 72
United States 72
Life Insurance
Amount 541
Household 541
Payments 542
Premium Receipts 542
Purchases 541
Life Insurance Companies
Mortgages Owned 542
Real Estate Owned 542
Life Table
Michigan 73
Sex and Race 73
Livestock
Inventory and Production 424

M

Magazines
see Periodicals
Manufacturing
Annual Hours 450
Average Weekly Earnings 448
Average Weekly Wage 445, 453
Capacity Utilization 473
Companies 568
Earnings 450
Employment 445, 453
Establishments 453
New Capital Expenditures 455
New Plant and Equipment 451
Payroll 449
Total Wages 454
Units 445

Value Added 449, 455
Value of Shipments 455
Manufacturing, Employment
Durable Goods 446
Employment Size Class 458
Foreign-Owned 457, 458
Nondurable Goods 447
Marriage 87
Metro Areas
Population, Subcounty Divisions . . . 615
Metropolitan Statistical Area
Educational Attainment 630
Household/Family/Nonfamily Income 630
Industry Employment 619
Labor Force 619
Per-capita Income 629
Personal Income 629
Population 617
Retail Trade, Sales/Selected Ratios . 632
Service Industry Receipts 631
Wholesale Trade, Sales 631
Michigan Employment Security Commission
Applicants 206
Openings 206
Placements 206
Mineral Production 429
Mining
Average Weekly Wage 430, 431
Employment 430, 431
Establishments 430, 431
Mortgages
see Life Insurance Companies, Housing
Motor Vehicles
Plant & Equipment Expenditures . . 472
Motor Vehicles, Employment
Automaker Employment 468
Employment 468
Related Employment 468
Motor Vehicles, Production
Domestic 463
Location in Michigan 469
Material Consumption 473
Transplant 467
World 461

INDEX

Motor Vehicles, Registrations 484
    New Passenger Car and Truck 471
Motor Vehicles, Sales
    Canada 464
    Passenger Cars 465
    Retail 470
    Trucks and Buses 466
    United States 464
MSA
    see Metropolitan Statistical Area
Multipliers: Output, Earnings, and Employment
    By Industry 590

N

Natural Resources
    see Mineral Production, Mining, Petroleum
      Rigs, Timberland
    Energy Consumption, Farm, Forest Fires,
      Land and Water Areas
    Tree Volumes, Wells
Newspapers 495-497
Nonmetro Areas
    Population, Subcounty Divisions . . . 615
Nonprofit
    Companies 572

P

Parks
    see State Parks
Patents
    By County 587
    By Industry 584
    Inventors 585
    Issued 584
Per-Capita Income
    see Income
Periodicals 497
Personal Income
    see Income
Petroleum Rigs
    also see Wells 432
Population
    Age, Ethnic, and Economic
      Characteristics 10

Age, Ethnic, Economic Characteristics 13
    Central City 617
    Change, by Subcounty Areas 614
    Components 7
    County 5
    Estimates and Projections 50, 52
    Michigan 3
    MSA 617
    Residence 36
    Subcounty Divisions, Metro, Nonmetro
      Areas 615
    United States 3
Poverty
    see Income Maintenance Programs,
      Population
Prices
    see Consumer Price Index, Purchasing
      Power
Prison
    Commitments 313
    Corrections Supervision Workloads . 318
    Descriptions 316
    Minimum Sentence 318
    Population 314
Projections
    Broad Occupational Group 209
    Detailed Industry 210
    Detailed Occupations 213
    Population by Age and Sex 52
    Population by County 50
Protective Services
    Abuse and Neglect Caseload 263
    Child Sexual Abuse Victims 263
    Neglected Children 264
    Referrals Studied 263
Purchasing Power 243

R

Railroad
    Carloads and Tonnage 492
    Ridership 492
Rapes
    see Criminal Offenses
Recreation
    see State Parks, Tourism, Sports, Hunting
      and Fishing

INDEX

Religion
 by Denomination 278
 County 281
Research and Development
 Auto Supplier 474, 475
 Expenditures 582
 Expenditures by Manufacturer 478
Retail Trade
 Average Weekly Wage 508, 526
 Companies 570
 Employment 508, 526
 Establishments 508, 526
 Sales 509, 519
 Sales by MSA 632
 Sales in Detroit MSA 524
 Selected Ratios 519
 Selected Ratios by MSA 632
 Selected Statistics 522
 Wages 518

S

Savings and Loan 534
Schools
 see Education
Service
 Average Weekly Wage . . . 547, 548, 551
 Companies 569
 Employment 547-549, 551
 Industry Receipts and Revenues . . . 553
 Receipts 548
 Receipts by County 562
 Receipts by MSA 631
 Receipts per Employee 557
 Receipts per Employee, County . . . 565
 Receipts per Establishment 557
 Receipts per Establishment, County . 565
 Total Wages 549, 552
 Units 547-549, 551
Sexual Abuse
 see Protective Services
Size of Firm
 Average Weekly Wage 592
 By County 596
 Employment 592
 Total Wages 592
 Units 592

Solid Waste
 Disposal 411
 Disposal Capacity 413
 Environmental Contamination 414
Sports 374
State Parks
 Location, Acreage, Number of Campsites,
 and Usage 377
 Use and Turnaway 376
Steel Production 452

T

Taxes
 Burden 351
 Collections 351
 Income 361
Teachers
 see Education, Elementary and Secondary
Timberland 429
Tobacco Abstinence 92
Tourism
 Expend, Payroll, and Employment . 373
 Impact of Travel 369
 Index and Component Indicators . . . 369
 Person-Trips 369
 Purpose of Trip 371
 Trips by State of Origin 371
Tourism, Domestic
 Employment and Expenditures 370
 Expenditures 370
Tourism, International
 Arrivals 372
 Employment 372
 Visitor Expenditures 372
Transportation
 Employment 483
 Fund 482
 Public 493
Tree Volumes 428
Trucks and Buses
 see Motor Vehicles, Factory Sales

U

Unemployment
 by MSA 619
 Duration 200

INDEX

Unemployment - continued
Reason 199
Sex, Age, Race 200
Unemployment Insurance
Average Weekly Wage to Average Benefit
Amount 274
Benefit Claims 270
Contribution Rates and Taxable Wage
Base 273
Federal Advances Received 269
Insured Unemployment and Rate . . . 277
Maximum Weekly Benefit 276
Payments Programs 271
Trust Fund 267
Unemployment Rates
by MSA 619
Education Level 162
Gender, Race, Teen, Adult 153
Major Occupational Group 159

Union
Affiliation 171
Earnings 171
Membership 198
Universities
see Education, College and Universities
Utility
Companies 570
Patents 584, 585, 587

V

Vital Statistics
County 66

W

Wage
Occupational 172
Wage and Salary Employment
Detailed Industry 156
Major Industry 154
Weather
Precipitation 383
Temperatures 396
Welfare
see Child Support, Income Maintenance
Programs

Wells
Cost of Drilling 433
Drilled 432
Oil and Gas 433
Producing 432
Revenues 433
Wholesale Trade
Average Weekly Wage 507, 525
Employment 507, 525
Establishments 507, 525
Operating Expenses 516
Sales 509-511
Sales per Employee 515
Sales per Establishment 514
Sales, MSA 631
Wages 517
Workers' Compensation
Injury 265
Paid 266
Policies, Premiums, and Payroll . . . 265